COLLINS

DICTIONARY OF

ART TERMS & TECHNIQUES

D1099558

COLLINS

DICTIONARY OF

ART TERMS & TECHNIQUES

SECOND EDITION

Ralph Mayer

*Revised and edited by Steven Sheehan
Director, Ralph Mayer Center
Yale University School of Art*

HarperCollins*Publishers*

HarperCollins Publishers
P.O. Box, Glasgow G4 0NB

First published 1993

Reprint 9 8 7 6 5 4 3 2 1 0

© Bena Mayer 1991

ISBN 0 00 470122 4

A catalogue record for this book is available from the British Library.

Printed in Great Britain by HarperCollins Manufacturing, Glasgow.

A

Aaron's Rod a rounded decorative moulding with a motif of an entwined serpent, vines, leaves and tendrils.

abaculus a little-used word for TESSERA.

abbozzo (*It.* sketch) **1.** *(painting)* the first outline or drawing on the canvas.

2. the first underpainting.

3. *(sculpture)* a block of stone, lump of clay or chunk of wood that has been reduced to a rough form of the ultimate work.

ABC art see MINIMAL ART.

abraum a red EARTH COLOUR used as a mahogany stain.

absolute alcohol or **anhydrous alcohol** ETHYL ALCOHOL freed of all traces of water by chemical processes – ordinary grain alcohol contains about 6% water. Anhydrous alcohol may be mixed with mineral spirits, turpentine, or a number of other solvents.

abstract art any art in which the depiction of real objects in nature has been subordinated or entirely discarded, and whose aesthetic content is expressed in a formal pattern or structure of shapes, lines and colours. Sometimes, the subject is real but so stylized, blurred, repeated, or broken down into basic forms as to be unrecognizable. Art that is partly broken down in this way is called *semiabstract*. When the representation of real objects is completely absent, such art may also be called *nonrepresentational* or NONOBJECTIVE, a term first used by Wassily Kandinsky (1866–1944), one of whose watercolours, done in 1910, is considered by some authorities to be the first completely abstract painting.

   An abstract element or intention appears in works of art and decoration throughout the history of art, from Neolithic stone carvings onwards. Abstraction as an aesthetic principle began in the early 20th century with the development of CUBISM by Pablo Picasso (1881–1973) and Georges Braque (1882–1963). Other important early stages in the development of abstract art were NEOPLASTICISM in Holland and SUPREMATISM in Russia. See also ABSTRACT EXPRESSIONISM; ACTION PAINTING; GEOMETRIC ABSTRACTION; OP ART.

abstract expressionism a style of nonrepresentational painting that combines abstract form and expressionist emotional value. Abstract expressionism, which developed in New York City during the 1940s, became fully established during the 1950s and was the predominant style associated with the NEW YORK SCHOOL. A variety of styles exist within the movement. The paintings are typically bold, forceful and large in size. The colours tend to be strident, and accidental effects are often present, such as the natural flow of oil colours without restraint. The movement's single most important figure is Jackson Pollock (1912–1956), a statement by whom gave rise to the term ACTION PAINTING, which is closely related to abstract expressionism. Pollock's fluid paints and enamels were poured, dripped and spattered on to the canvas; a single colour was often used to create a lacy mesh of opaque colour over the surface, much like the transparent VEIL in a conventional oil painting.

Abstract expressionism stems mainly from the European NEO-EXPRESSIONIST painting of Wassily Kandinsky (1866–1944) and others. It was stimulated by the presence in New York, during the Second World War, of a remarkable group of expatriate European painters, including Chagall, Duchamp, Léger, and Miró. A most important forerunner of the movement was Arshile Gorky (1904–1948), whose surrealist forms and discordant colour had great influence on the work of his contemporaries. Among the more prominent abstract expressionist painters are Willem de Kooning (1904–   ), Adolph Gottlieb (1903–74), Mark Rothko (1903–1970), Franz Kline (1910–1962), Philip Guston (1913–   ), and Robert Motherwell (1915–   ).

acacia see GUM ARABIC.

academic *(art)* conforming to traditional standards, or to a discipline based on the standards of an official ACADEMY, which are usually conservative. In the 20th century the term has come to be used mainly in a pejorative sense, to characterize a strictly representational type of art that still adheres to the canons of 19th-century taste and technique, although these have long since been challenged by modern developments from Impressionism onward. Modernists do not condemn all representational art. They usually admire its outstanding examples, while applying the epithet 'academic' to what they consider to be mediocre, repetitive and inconsequential.

academician 1. an elected member of an ACADEMY.

2. an adherent of ACADEMIC styles and principles.

academicism 1. conformity with ACADEMIC standards and precepts.

2. an element of academic influence in work that departs from traditional principles.

Académie des Beaux-Arts the academy of fine arts of the *Institut de France*. Its activities include sponsorship of the *Ecole des Beaux-Arts* (see BEAUX-ARTS, ECOLE DES) and the official salon, or art exhibition, held annually in Paris. Popularly known as 'the Academy,' it is not to be confused with the French Academy (*Académie Française*), a literary body. See also ACADEMY.

academy a body of artists organized for such purposes as promoting a national art, training artists, and enhancing the professional and economic status of its members through periodic exhibitions and through the conferral of membership as an honour. Academies were founded in Italy as early as the 16th century, in France in the 17th century, in Britain in the 18th, and in the United States in the 19th. Enjoying official or quasi-official status, the academies have consistently maintained conservative standards, excluding from recognition all artists whose works and ideas on art depart from the traditional academic criteria of excellence. Academies are notorious for embracing styles that had been rejected by a previous generation – at the same time rejecting the innovative work of their own times, which is left for a later generation to recognize and incorporate into a new standard, which too often turns out to be as inflexible as the old.

During the first quarter of the 20th century, the work of artists whose ideas had developed beyond 19th-century academic restrictions had little exposure apart from the one-man show. With the founding of museums of modern art and increasing public and commercial appreciation of abstract and other modern work, innovative artists lost their dependence on academic approval, and the traditional controversies between academician and heretic became far less virulent. The academies continue to flourish as centres for the work of traditionally or conservatively oriented artists. Among the important existing academies are the ACADÉMIE DES BEAUX-ARTS in Paris, the ROYAL ACADEMY OF ARTS in London and the NATIONAL ACADEMY OF DESIGN in New York.

academy blue *(US)* an unstandardized term for a blue COMPOSITE PIGMENT of a greenish shade, the best grades of which should be made of ultramarine blue and viridian.

academy board an inexpensive panel used for small oil paintings and sketches. It is made of heavy, smooth cardboard coated with a ground that has sufficient tooth, or surface roughness, for oil paint. Academy board has largely been replaced by CANVAS BOARD and various speciality boards, which may be embossed to imitate a canvas weave.

academy figure a drawing or painting of a human figure, half life-size, executed as a practice study or for purposes of instruction rather than as creative art. Hence, the term is used as a derogatory designation for any dull or lifeless rendition of the human form in a work of art.

acajou see MAHOGANY.

acanthus a semistylized leaf motif that occurs throughout the history of art, notably in capitals of the Corinthian order of Greek architecture and the Roman Composite order, and in carvings of the 12th century. The acanthus plant is widespread in the Mediterranean area. The acanthus

acanthus The motif carved on a Corinthian capital.

motif is sometimes used in a variant form showing a close resemblance to the leaves of the thistle, dandelion, celery, or parsley.

acaroid resin see ACCROIDES.

accelerated test a test of paints, pigments, or other materials used by painters. It is conducted in a laboratory with specialized equipment for subjecting such materials to forces that simulate the conditions that cause fading, cracking, or other failures to which paintings are liable on long ageing. Accelerated test conditions do not duplicate those of natural ageing exactly, but are far more severe and concentrated. However, they do give an accurate indication of the comparative resistance of various materials and combinations of ingredients, and make it possible to rate their relative resistance.

A typical accelerated test is one used to compare the relative resistance of various coating materials to PHOTOCHEMICAL EMBRITTLEMENT on ageing. Thin metal panels are coated with the material with a film applicator and then exposed to ultraviolet light for a predetermined number of hours under scientifically controlled conditions. One panel of each material is then bent over a standard steel rod, or mandrel, and examined for indications of cracking. The ultraviolet exposure is continued intermittently until sufficiently definite results are obtained. A few days of such exposure will cause embrittlement comparable to the effects seen after many years of exposure to daylight. See also FADE OMETER; WEATHER OMETER.

accelerator any substance that speeds up a reaction.
1. *(sculpture)* the alum used to hasten the setting of plaster of Paris or the material added to Portland cement to speed the development of strength.
2. the chemical added to a mixture of polyester resin and hardener to speed the hardening process and enable the hardening time to be controlled.
3. *(painting)* a chemical DRIER.

accroides, acaroid resin or **gum accroides** a strongly coloured RESIN occurring in two different forms, red and yellow, collected from Australian grass trees (genus *Xanthorrhoea*). The resin has fairly good film-forming properties and has long been used in the manufacture of yellow, red and orange VARNISHES. Despite the development of bright dyestuffs for this purpose, accroides is still employed for certain industrial purposes. Older names for the resin are *Botany Bay gum*, *black-boy gum* and *xanthorrhoea*. See COLOURED RESINS.

acetate see CELLULOSE ACETATE.

acetic ether see ETHYL ACETATE.

acetone or **demethyl ketone** one of the most powerful VOLATILE SOLVENTS of the lacquer-solvent or paint-remover type. It is one of the least toxic solvents when properly handled. Acetone is highly flammable: its vapours will flash or catch fire even below the freezing point. See also METHYL ACETATE.

acetylene a gaseous, colourless hydrocarbon. When used in a burner, it gives off nearly 15 times as much light as ordinary illuminating gas. It contains a triple bond and polymerizes readily. Acetylene is used for OXYACETYLENE WELDING in a torch or blowpipe that combines acetylene and oxygen.

acetylene black one of many varieties of CARBON BLACK; similar to BENZOL BLACK.

achromatic colours white, black, and the greys, as distinguished from the chromatic colours. See CHROMA.

acid bath the container or tray of MORDANT in which the object to be etched is immersed (see ETCHING). In etching metal plates for printing, the tray containing the mordant must be of an acid-resistant material, such as porcelain or glass. Sometimes WALLING WAX is used to build a containing wall around the edges of the plate, obviating the use of an acid bath.

acid number or **acid value** a laboratory measurement used to indicate the amount of free fatty acid contained in a vegetable DRYING OIL – an important consideration in selecting an oil for a given purpose. The acid number represents the milligrams of potassium hydroxide required to neutralize the free fatty acids in a gram of oil. Oils of higher acid number (5 to 10) are preferred for grinding paints, while those of lower denomination (1 to 3) are considered more suitable for use in varnishes and other clear coatings. In the production of artists' oil colours, however, the superior colour stability or nonyellowing properties of the lower-numbered varnish oils is a more significant factor than ease of grinding, so lower-numbered oils are frequently employed.

acid resist RESIST specifically used to block the corrosive action of a MORDANT on a surface.

acrolith a statue, especially of ancient Greece, with head and extremities of marble, supported by a trunk of wood or other material, covered with real or metal-plate draperies, and sometimes gilded.

acrylic brush see BRUSH, ACRYLIC.

acrylic canvas canvas especially prepared with polymer primer for use with POLYMER COLOURS. These paints have greater and longer-lasting flexibility than oil colours. Painting in oils on an acrylic canvas, however, is contrary to the FAT-OVER-LEAN rule. Because polymer primer does not expand and contract as much with changes in atmospheric moisture, adhesion of an oil film to an acrylic surface has so far not proven to be permanent.

acrylic colour artists' colour made by dispersing pigment in a vehicle made from a polymethyl methacrylate (see ACRYLIC RESIN) solution in white spirit. Acrylic colours are sometimes called *plastic paints* to distinguish them from POLYMER COLOURS, which contain acrylic and other resins dispersed in water. Acrylic colours do not yellow, they dry very rapidly, and they are easy to remove with mineral spirits or turpentine. Because of these qualities, they have been used for INPAINTING to restore damaged or obliterated areas in conservation work. Acrylic colours with a plasticizer added are sold in tubes as is a special VINYL-RESIN solution that is insoluble in turpentine and mineral spirits. This serves as an ISOL-

ATING VARNISH, since acrylic paint is so soluble that it cannot be overpainted. It may also be used in oil painting for the same purpose.

acrylic resin any of a group of synthetic resins made by polymerization of acrylic acid esters. Polymethyl methacrylate is the most important of the group. One form of it is readily soluble in turpentine and mineral spirits; it is available as a heavy solution in mineral spirits. Another type, insoluble in these solvents, is sold as a heavy solution in toluol. Methyl methacrylate or acrylic solutions are used in the manufacture of PICTURE VARNISH and ACRYLIC COLOURS, and in lacquers and many other industrial products. Another type of acrylic resin is produced in a water dispersion, polymerized by emulsification. It is used in the manufacture of POLYMER COLOURS. Polymethyl methacrylate in solid form, best known by the trade name *Perspex*, is a permanent, nonyellowing, glasslike PLASTIC that is frequently used in modern sculpture and constructions. It may be cast, extruded, machined, and welded or shaped by heating.

acrylic varnish see PICTURE VARNISH.

actinic light see ULTRAVIOLET LIGHT.

action painting a form of ABSTRACT EXPRESSIONISM associated with the NEW YORK SCHOOL, sometimes used as a synonym for abstract expressionism. Action painting is done by applying the paint with rapid, forceful, impulsive brush strokes, or by splashing or hurling it directly onto the surface, in order to create a work that records the force of the artist's feelings as well as the dynamism of the act of painting. The most celebrated action painter is Jackson Pollock (1912–1956). The French equivalent of action painting is TACHISME.

additive system see COLOUR, sense 1.

à deux crayons a chalk drawing done in two colours, almost always red chalk and black chalk or charcoal.

adhesion of oil paint the prevention of separation of paint from its ground, by using fresh colours that have not thickened on the palette and so lost some of their adhesiveness. The ground should have enough absorbency to grip the paint by penetration, although not enough for it to sink in completely. The ground should also have a certain amount of tooth, or surface roughness, to afford the paint mechanical anchorage.

adjustable curve ruler a ruler that can be bent and held in any curve desired. One type is made of a flat, thin strip of metal, which functions as the straightedge, welded to a flexible metal cable that can be bent into any curve desired and will retain that position. Another type consists of a lead rod encased in a flexible plastic body that has a smooth edge along which the artist traces with a pencil or ruling pen. Both types of adjustable

adjustable curve ruler

curve rulers are available in a number of lengths up to about 30 inches. The adjustable curve ruler is used as a ruler in general drafting, either in conjunction with or as a replacement for the FRENCH CURVE. See also SPLINE.

adjustable triangle a draughtsman's TRIANGLE, one side of which has an adjustable arm that can be clamped at various angles. A protractor between the adjustable arm and the side to which it is hinged measures the angle at which the triangle is clamped. The adjustable triangle was designed to obviate the draughtsman's need for many differently shaped triangles. See also DRAUGHTING MACHINE.

Adrianople red see TURKEY RED.

adsorption molecular cohesion in which a thin layer of one substance adheres strongly to another, as if it were glued on. (Adsorption is distinguished from the more common word 'absorption', which denotes the propensity of a solid to imbibe or soak up a liquid as a sponge soaks up water.) All matter – gases, liquids and solids – can be adsorbed by solid surfaces. The process may be considerably enhanced when a substance is transformed, either chemically or physically, into the colloidal state and when the receiving surface is absolutely clean. The resulting adsorbed layer becomes so firmly attached to the surface of the receiving substance that it can usually be removed only by strong abrasion. An example is seen in lithography, in which the entire process depends on the ability of the crayon or TUSCHE to produce on the stone or plate an adsorbed layer of fatty acid that will be receptive to the printing ink.

advancing and retreating colours the apparent tendency of the WARM COLOURS (the reds and oranges) to advance towards the viewer and the COOL COLOURS (the blues and violets) to recede. This concept is in part derived from the phenomenon observable in nature that moisture in the atmosphere affects not only the SATURATION, or intensity, of the colour of a distant object but also its HUE. That is, an object seen far away will seem bluer or greyer than it does when viewed up close. Accordingly, advancing and retreating colours have been considered an aspect of AER-IAL PERSPECTIVE and have been employed in landscapes that attempt to portray recession by using atmospheric perspective as well as geometric systems of perspective. The concept of advancing and retreating colours has for over a century been applied with reserve, however, by artists who realize that its strict application in landscape painting would result in such effects as blue sunsets. Because of the erratic behaviour of colour in nature, the advancing and retreating colour theory cannot be considered infallible in painting.

adze or *(US)* **adz** a cutting tool, used in sculpture to rough-shape wood. The simplest form of adze has an arched blade with a slightly curved chisel edge, set at right angles to the handle. Adzes are frequently double-ended tools with, for example, a gouge bit and a curved bit.

ae. or **aet.** abbreviations for the Latin word *aetatis* ('at the age of' or 'aged'). Inscribed with a number on the background or rear of a portrait, it indicates the age of the sitter at the time he or she was painted. Such

adze Two examples.

inscriptions were fairly common on portraits up to the middle of the 19th century, after which they were rarely used.

Aegean art art of the 26th-12th centuries BC in mainland Greece and the Greek islands. See MINOAN; CYCLADIC; HELLADIC; MYCENAEAN.

aerial perspective an illusion of recession obtained in landscape painting by the depiction of atmospheric effects. When seen through a volume of air, the colours of a distant object or scene appear progressively fainter and, depending on the amount of moisture in the air, progressively cooler or bluer (see ADVANCING AND RETREATING COLOURS). This phenomenon dictates that the background of a landscape should be less distinct in both outline and colour than its foreground. Chinese painters achieved atmospheric recession in landscapes by interposing mists or clouds, in progressively weaker tones, between middle distances (often hills) and the mountains of the background. Aerial perspective, insofar as it relates to gradation of colour and distinctness, is relevant to all conventional landscapes that employ spatial illusion; it is usually an adjunct to LINEAR PERSPECTIVE.

aerugo or **verdigris** corrosion or rust on metals, especially the green PATINA on copper or bronze.

aesthetics the philosophical study of the quality of beauty perceived in works of fine art.

aestheticism a largely 19th-century artistic philosophy that can be summed by the French philosopher Victor Cousin's phrase: 'Art for art's sake'. Essentially, the followers of aestheticism believed that art and its creation had its own intrinsic merit apart from any need for it to represent or display moral, social, or religious values. Well-known exponents of aestheticism include James MacNeill Whistler (1834–1903) and William Morris (1834–1896), the founder of the Arts and Crafts Movement.

aes ustum an ancient name for the copper oxide or corrosion that constitutes the PATINA on copper and bronze.

African blackwood, grenadilla or **Mozambique ebony** a hard, close-textured hardwood (from *Dalbergia melanoxylon*) of a dark purple or plum colour. It has good carving properties. Because it also has good resonance qualities, it is used for clarinets and other woodwind instruments. African blackwood is botanically related to ROSEWOOD.

African cherry see CHERRYWOOD.

African mahogany see MAHOGANY.

African rosewood see BUBINGA.

African walnut see TIGERWOOD.

African whitewood see AYOUS.

after word used in an artist's inscription to indicate that his or her picture or sculpture was modelled on the work of another artist. It generally signifies a faithful copy of the original, but may also be used for a work that differs somewhat from the earlier work, as in Van Gogh's drawing after Millet's *The Reapers*. A typical inscription on the back of a painting would read: 'Portrait of James Smith by Robert Jones, 1898, after Gilbert Stuart, 1793.'

afterimage the optical phenomenon whereby the human eye retains an image after the source of the image is removed. Most usually, the new image will appear in a colour that is complementary or opposite on the COLOUR CIRCLE to the colour of the original image.

after-yellowing see YELLOWING.

agalma *(Gk)* originally, any piece of sculpture in Ancient Greece, later, a statue of a god. Sometimes the term was also used for a painted portrait.

agalmatolite or **pagodite** a soft greyish, greenish, or yellowish stone. It was used by the Chinese for carving pagodas and images.

agate a very hard, semiprecious stone with a striped or variegated pattern. Polished grey agate is used to make the BURNISHERS used in gilding, which are sometimes called agates.

agglutinant any glue or adhesive, especially a BINDER used in aqueous paints, pastel crayons and drawing inks.

aggregate 1. the inert material or materials mixed with cement to make concrete. A fine material such as sand, a material with medium-sized particles such as marble dust, or a coarse material such as crushed rock may be used. Sometimes all three of these materials are used in a mix. **2.** similar inert materials used to create coarse textures in plaster, stucco and mortar.

airbrush an implement resembling an oversize fountain pen, with an attached container that holds an ounce or less of fluid paint and with a thin hose leading to a source of compressed air or carbonic gas. The airbrush is used to create smooth gradations of tones and colours. It is a delicate miniature version of the SPRAY GUN. Airbrush technique is usually distinguishable from brush painting and is used much more frequently by commercial artists than by fine-arts painters.

aircraft curve see FRENCH CURVE.

air drain see VENT.

air eraser an implement resembling an oversize fountain pen, with an attached container and with a thin hose leading to a source of compressed air or carbonic gas. The reservoir holds an ounce or less of a finely divided abrasive that removes ink or paint from paper.

air jet see VENT.

à jour or **ajouré** decorated with pierced or translucent shapes, letting in the daylight, as the French words imply. The terms apply to openwork designs in silversmithing and other metalwork (see PIERCING), in wood-work, and in lace and embroidery.

Alabama Cream *(US)* a type of American MARBLE, suitable for sculp-ture. Among the hard, fine-grained, creamy white varieties are *Madre Cream* and *Cream Blanc.*

alabaster a snow-white, translucent or semitranslucent variety of gypsum (calcium sulphate), so soft that it can be blocked with a handsaw and readily carved. It is so easily scratched that it is durable only indoors, under conditions of careful conservation. The alabaster referred to by the ancients is a different and more durable stone, onyx marble.

alabastron a form of ancient Greek pottery – a small, tear-shaped oil flask with a rounded bottom. It was used for many purposes, such as to carry the oil that athletes rubbed on their bodies. See VASE SHAPES for illustration.

à la Grecque in the Greek style. This term was long used to describe works of art done in imitation of, or strongly influenced by, the style of ancient Greek art, particularly of its more obvious characteristics.

Albani stone see PEPERINO.

Albany slip *(US)* a SLIP CLAY obtained near Albany, New York. It can produce a blackish-brown glaze. Albany slip and similar clays from other localities were used by early American potters in making STONEWARE.

Alberene stone *(US)* a tradename for a Virginia SOAPSTONE that ranges in colour from a medium grey to a fairly deep black.

alcohol see ETHYL ALCOHOL; METHANOL; ABSOLUTE ALCOHOL; DE-NATURED ALCOHOL.

alcohol colours brilliant liquid colours made from alcohol-soluble aniline dyes in a water-miscible vehicle. Alcohol colours are especially designed to be applied with an airbrush and to be used for work that is to be reproduced. They are particularly useful in cartography and can be used on many surfaces that will not take water paints. Alcohol colours are not sufficiently lightproof to be used for permanent fine-arts purposes.

alembic an obsolete term for a STILL. The invention of distillation is generally credited to the physicians of Alexandria in the 3rd century, and the term derives from the Arabic *alanbig,* meaning a still, which in turn comes from the Greek *ambix,* meaning a spouted cup.

Alexandria blue or **Alexandrian blue** see EGYPTIAN BLUE.

Alexandrian art see HELLENISTIC PERIOD.

alizarin brown a rather dull, reddish, transparent brown pigment. It is made by a variation of the ALIZARIN CRIMSON process and has the same pigment properties. It may also be the product of an occasional off-colour or unsuccessful batch of alizarin crimson.

alizarin carmine an obsolete term for ALIZARIN CRIMSON.

alizarin crimson a bright, transparent, red LAKE pigment with a maroon mass tone and a bluish undertone; made from the synthetic dyestuff alizarin (dihydroxy anthraquinone), a derivative of anthracene, a coal-tar product. Although it is not in the same class of absolute permanence as the furnace-made mineral pigments, alizarin crimson is acceptable for permanent easel painting under the normal conditions for preservation of works of art. The artist's principal deep-red pigment, alizarin crimson is a clear ruby-red when used transparently, and produces bright, rosy pinks when mixed with white. Careful painters will not attempt to use it at full strength for its mass tone in oil, since it tends to crack in a fine alligator-skin pattern when spread out in layers without the structural reinforcement of denser pigments. The superlative type of alizarin crimson available since the 1920s is more brilliant than the older types; it can be freely mixed with all other pigments on the approved list for artists, will not react with white lead, and will not turn brown when mixed with iron-bearing pigments.

Discovered in 1868 by two German chemists, C. Graebe and C. Liebermann, alizarin was the first of the natural dyestuffs to be synthesized. In the ensuing years, synthetic alizarin superseded natural alizarin both in pigment manufacture and in textile dyeing, while alizarin crimson soon replaced an older pigment, MADDER LAKE. Alizarin crimson has far greater tinting strength than madder lake, and since it is free from purpurin, which is impermanent, it also has greater colour stability. However, the artists' colour called *rose madder* is still available. Alizarin crimson or burnt sienna is sometimes mixed with SEPIA to make Roman sepia. *Alizarin carmine* is an obsolete term for alizarin crimson.

alizarin violet or **violet madder lake** a transparent violet pigment made from synthetic PURPURIN. Alizarin violet is similar to ALIZARIN CRIMSON in pigment properties but not sufficiently permanent for artists' use, since it turns dark or blackish on long exposure to light.

alizarin yellow a dull, rather brownish, transparent yellow pigment. Made by the same process as ALIZARIN CRIMSON, alizarin yellow has identical pigment properties but is not reliably permanent.

alkaline glaze a ceramic GLAZE whose FLUX is an alkali, such as borax or soda ash, rather than lead. The alkaline glazes are fired at low temperatures and are capable of producing spectacular effects, such as the Egyptian and Persian blues. Since alkalis are soluble and have a tendency to cake while in a glaze suspension, there are limitations on their use.

alkanet a red NATURAL DYESTUFF extracted from the root of a European plant, *Alkanna tinctoria* (false alkanet), and also from an Oriental plant, *Lawsonia alba* (true alkanet). Since alkanet fades with relative rapidity, it is no longer used for dyeing textiles or for making lake pigments.

alkyd resin any of a group of synthetic resins with excellent film-forming properties, used in fine-quality industrial house paints, enamels and varnishes since the 1930s. Some use has been made of the alkyds in artists' materials. The most successful varieties, which have good retention of colour and flexibility, are of considerable promise as ingredients of oil-painting mediums. The type in use is known as oil-modified alkyd; it contains a drying oil as part of its makeup. The varieties made with safflower, soya bean, or tobacco-seed oils have greater colour retention than those made with linseed oil, which in turn have greater resistance to weathering.

alla prima or **direct painting** a method of oil painting in which the final effects are achieved in the initial application of paint. *Alla prima* (*It.* at the first) is the alternative to the technique of covering the canvas layer by layer. The French term for *alla prima* is *au premier coup.*

alligatoring or **alligator cracks** a form of CRACKLE that appears on paintings in a pattern resembling the design of alligator hide.

all-over painting a method of painting first devised by the American abstract expressionist Jackson Pollock (1912–1956), in which the entire field of a canvas is covered in a fairly uniform manner, thus eschewing traditional notions of top, bottom and middle of a painting.

alloy a combination of two or more metals that have been melted or fused together. Brass is an alloy of copper and zinc; bronze is an alloy of copper and tin. Steel, which contains iron and carbon, may also be classed as an alloy, although carbon is a nonmetal. In general, alloys are harder and more fusible, though less malleable, than the substances of which they are made. They also tend to be more resistant to corrosion and to have a lower melting point than the parent metals. The colour or appearance of an alloy is different from that of the metals that compose it.

all-purpose ground see MULTIPURPOSE GROUND.

altarpiece a decorative screen, a painting, a set of painted or carved panels, or a structure incorporating painting, statuary or relief carving, set on or behind and above an altar. A typical Renaissance altarpiece consisted of a set of religious paintings on hinged panels (often a TRIPTYCH), the frames of which might be finely carved, gilded, or polychromed, even encrusted with jewels. A PREDELLA often appeared below the main panels. The Italian word *ancona*, the French *retable*, the English *reredos*, and the Spanish *retablo* are used more or less interchangeably as synonyms for altarpiece. Reredos sometimes refers more specifically to an ornamental stone or wooden screen or wall behind an altar. The term ancona is used of a panel painting elaborately framed or an ornate polyptych elaborately carved and gilded or polychromed. Some Renaissance Italian altarpieces were made of Della Robbia ware, with figures in high relief. The magnificent *Pala d'oro* altarpiece in the cathedral of St Mark, Venice, includes gold work, Byzantine enamel, and statuary. Some of the largest and most luxurious altarpieces are those of Spain and Latin America, in the baroque and churrigueresque styles. Carved in wood or stone, and often gilded and painted, these retablos sometimes reach from the floor into the vaulting. Others are made of elaborately worked silver.

alto-rilievo Italian for high RELIEF.

alumina hydrate aluminium hydroxide; it is manufactured in the form of a white, fluffy, lightweight powder, and used as an INERT PIGMENT. Alumina hydrate is valuable as a BASE for LAKE pigments, as it becomes virtually colourless when dispersed in oil. It tends to impart a desirable brushing consistency to oil colours and to assist in stabilizing pigment dispersion.

aluminium a very lightweight, bluish, silver-white metal. Because of a protective oxide that forms on its surface, it has a high resistance to corrosion. It melts at 1220° F and can be cast and welded. It is available in a wide variety of colours and is used when lightness combined with strength is desired. Although aluminium is the most abundant metal in the Earth's crust, it was not discovered until 1825 and was not used extensively until the 20th century.

aluminium leaf a thin leaf used in GILDING for a silvery effect. Because it has a relatively dull, leaden appearance, aluminium leaf is an inferior substitute for SILVER LEAF and PALLADIUM LEAF. It is used chiefly in the commercial arts for such purposes as sign writing and for stamping titles and designs on book covers.

aluminium paint an industrial paint or lacquer pigmented with powdered aluminium metal (see ALUMINIUM POWDER). It is used as a protective coating and to create a dullish silvery decorative effect. It should not be used in works of art, because its metallic lustre is coarse and dull and becomes more so with age, as does the lustre of paint made with BRONZE POWDERS.

aluminium powder a metallic pigment that is mixed with bronzing liquid to make so-called *silver paint*. Aluminium paint will not tarnish, but it lacks the lustre that real silver leaf has when first applied to a surface. Because of this leaden quality and a slightly grainy texture, aluminium paint is not suitable for gilding, but it has wide commercial and industrial applications.

aluminium stearate an INERT PIGMENT used by manufacturers of oil paints as a stabilizer to help prevent separation of pigment and oil in the tube.

Alundum *(US)* the tradename for a form of aluminium oxide used as an abrasive.

amalgam gilding see FIRE GILDING.

amaranth 1. (also called **purpleheart**) a hardwood of a rich, purplish colour, from trees (genus *Peltogyne*) native to the Guianas and sometimes used for carving. It has a close, even texture, and much of it has an interesting, variegated grain.
2. a natural purple dyestuff made from amaranth wood. Named after a mythical unfading flower, its permanence is equally mythical, for pigments made from it fade badly in sunlight.

amarna art a style of Egyptian art coinciding with the reign of the pharaoh Akenaten (1379–1361 BC), found in the ancient city of Amarna. Different in form from what went before it and, finally, what followed it, Amarna art exhibits a greater naturalism and fluidity of line. It is now believed to have been influenced to a certain degree by Akenaten's break from polytheism in favour of monotheism.

amasette the French term for a horn spatula formerly used to gather the colour while grinding paint. Its modern equivalent would be a stainless-steel SPATULA or slice.

amber a fossil RESIN dug from the ground, the most extensive deposits occurring in beds in East Prussia along the shores of the Baltic Sea. Amber is familiar through its use in beads and ornaments, and it has long been considered the varnish resin *par excellence* because it is the hardest of all resins, but it is also the least soluble. Only a small amount can be made to go into solution at high temperatures, even when mixed with oils and other resins, so amber varnishes actually contain little amber. Investigators feel that mediaeval writers, who constantly referred to it in their recipes, may have confused amber with some other resin, possibly sandarac, and that this may account for its widespread reputation.

American scene painting a style of naturalistic, representational art extant in the United States during the 1920s and 1930s, indicative of a movement by certain artists away from ABSTRACT ART and the AVANT-GARDE. Edward Hopper (1882–1967) and Charles Burchfield (1893–1967) are the best-known representatives of this style of painting.

American Society for Testing and Materials (ASTM) an independent organization th t tests, evaluates, and creates standards for indutrial materials. ASTM standard specifications for artists' paints have replaced the older CS 98–62 standards, which were established by the National Bureau of Standards. See PAINT STANDARD.

American vermilion, imitation vermilion or **vermilionette** a heavy LAKE pigment made on a base of red lead, orange mineral, or chrome red, with a brilliant synthetic dyestuff such as eosine. It is not permanent for use in artists' paints.

American walnut see WALNUT.

Amherst sandstone *(US)* a pale SANDSTONE from Lorrain County, Ohio. It is available in grey, buff and variegated colours.

ammonia a colourless alkaline gas, a combination of nitrogen and hydrogen, commonly used in various concentrations as a cleaner and emulsifier in a solution known as ammonia water. When a recipe used in permanent painting calls for an alkali, ammonia is preferred, because it is volatile and therefore leaves no remnant or alkaline by-product.

amorino see PUTTO.

amorphous (of a homogeneous solid material) lacking either a regular crystalline structure or a sharply defined melting point and that breaks with a conchoidal fracture, that is, with an undulating surface like that of a lump of broken glass or a lump of resin. Both glass and resin are amorphous materials.

amphora an ancient Greek vase form. The amphora is a large, tapering ceramic jar with two handles that was used for storage of such items as oil, wine, and grain. One type tapered to a foot, or base, while another had a point at the bottom and was stored in a rack rather than standing upright. A third type, the neck amphora, had an offset neck. See illustration at VASE SHAPES.

amyl acetate see BANANA OIL.

amyl alcohol see BANANA OIL

A.N.A. *(US)* an associate member of the NATIONAL ACADEMY OF DESIGN.

anaglyph a piece of sculpture or a decoration worked in RELIEF, as a CAMEO or a BOSS, as distinguished from a DIAGLYPH.

Analytical Cubism see CUBISM.

anamorphosis 1. a painting or drawing that is distorted or unrecognizable except when viewed from a particular angle and distance or with a correcting mirror or lens.

2. the technique by which such an image is drawn. Essentially an artistic stunt, anamorphosis was especially popular in the 18th century. It was usually achieved by SQUARING an original drawing done in proper perspective and then copying each square into the corresponding area of a distorted grid. The original might also be drawn deformed, by copying it with the aid of a distorting optical device or by perforating lines of the original, shining light through the perforated drawing to a curved surface (or at an angle through the perforations to a flat surface) and then drawing connecting lines between the points of light. Sometimes, anamorphosis was used in conjunction with normal perspective: a skilful artist could create what appeared to be an orthodox landscape or still life that, viewed from an extraordinary angle, became an entirely different subject or was discovered to contain a hitherto hidden element, such as a face.

anastatic printing a RELIEF PRINTING process in which all but the printing area of the plate is etched, leaving in relief only the lines and areas to be inked. Anastatic printing is distinguished from ETCHING, which is an INTAGLIO printing process. The best known anastatic printing procedure is sometimes called *zinc etching*. The design to be printed is painted directly on a zinc plate with asphalt varnish. When the varnish has dried, the plate is placed in a MORDANT bath of dilute nitric acid, so that all the nonprinting areas are bitten away (see BITING). William Blake (1757–1827) executed both the text and the illustrations of many of his books with this relief-etching process.

ancien French studio cant or argot for a monitor or senior student in an art class or atelier.

ancient dating from the ages before the mediaeval period; in general, before the 5th century.

Ancients a loose association of early 19th-century British Romantic artists whose name was indicative of their great love and admiration for all things mediaeval, despite the fact that their work itself was mostly pastoral in nature. The group's inspirational force was the English poet-artist William Blake (1757–1827).

ancona see ALTARPIECE.

androsphinx see SPHINX.

angular liner see LINERS AND STRIPERS.

angular perspective linear perspective in which a rectangular solid is oriented so that only the set of lines defining one dimension of the object is parallel to an axis of the PICTURE PLANE. Therefore, only two faces of the object will be shown, neither of which is parallel to the picture plane. Thus, both of the surfaces shown recede at angles from the picture plane. These angles may be the same for both surfaces, or they may differ, depending on the angle at which the object is inclined to the picture plane and the object's position relative to the HORIZON LINE. The defining lines of only two of the object's three dimensions will converge on the horizon line. They will have separate VANISHING POINTS. Because there will be two vanishing points in the depiction of an object in angular perspective, it may also be said to be shown in two-point perspective. See also OBLIQUE PERSPECTIVE, PARALLEL PERSPECTIVE. See illustration at LINEAR PERSPECTIVE.

anhydrous completely free from water.

anhydrous alcohol see ABSOLUTE ALCOHOL.

aniline one of the INTERMEDIATES derived from benzene, which in turn is derived from the distillation of coal tar. Because all the earliest synthetic dyes and many subsequently developed dyes were made from aniline, synthetic dyes and pigments in general were formerly called aniline colours. Aniline, however, does not enter into the production of many synthetic pigments; moreover, the impermanence of most colours that are made with aniline has given the word a derogatory connotation. The more precise term *synthetic organic pigment* is now used to designate colours produced from coal-tar derivatives.

aniline purple an obsolete name for MAUVE.

animal black an infrequently used name for BONE BLACK.

animé a generic term for any of a group of RESINS otherwise known as East African COPALS.

ankh, ansate cross, crux ansata or **Egyptian cross** a figure in the form of a Latin cross, but with a loop in place of the part of the shaft above the cross arm. This symbol of life is widely used in Egyptian art and, to a lesser degree, in Assyrian art. See CROSS for illustration.

annatto, orlean or **terra orellana** a yellow NATURAL DYESTUFF made from the fruit of the annatto tree (*Bixa orellana*); alcohol-soluble and oil-soluble. No longer considered permanent for pigment use, it has been widely used for colouring butter and cheese.

annealing the process of heating a material to make it less brittle, so that after it has cooled it will be more easily workable for various purposes. Annealing relieves internal strain on the molecular structure of the material, thereby enabling it to be subjected to increased force during shaping, and making it stronger in its final state. Glass is strengthened and toughened after it is blown by annealing it in a kiln and then slowly cooling it. Metal is made more malleable so that it may be fashioned by such treatments as hammering, twisting, and bending. Since these operations tend to strain-harden metal, repeated annealing is sometimes required to work it beyond a certain point. In some cases, as for glass or steel, the cooling after annealing must be gradual; in others it may be sudden, as for copper or brass.

anodizing an electrolytic process in which a metal, made the anode of a cell, is given a protective or decorative coating. The deposition of a uniform layer of aluminium oxide on aluminium by anodizing protects the metal from corrosion and greatly increases its ability to hold paints and other coating materials permanently.

ansate cross see ANKH.

anthemion or **honeysuckle ornament** a decorative group of simplified leaf and flower forms. It was used in ancient Greece in stone carving, bronze casting, engraving, and vase painting and has survived as a traditional motif. There are three or four principal types of anthemia, which may be used singly or in combination with each other. See PALMETTE.

anthemion

anthrapyrimidine yellow a very transparent SYNTHETIC ORGANIC PIGMENT with excellent lightfastness qualities. This pigment may exhibit solubility in strong organic solvents.

anti-art see DADA.

antic work 1. grotesque and fanciful art, especially in groupings of human, animal, and floral figures, sometimes in the form of arabesques. **2.** work that has a ludicrous character.

antimony orange and **antimony vermilion** obsolete permanent pigments made of antimony trisulphide in a limited range of reddish-orange and orangy-red hues. Invented and patented by Murdock in Scotland in 1847, they are quite dull and pale in the dry state but brilliant in oil. Since they have the undesirable trait of blackening in contact with flake white and other lead pigments, antimony orange and antimony vermilion were replaced in the 1920s by the CADMIUM REDS.

antimony sulphide a pigment made by pulverizing the grey-black mineral stibnite, the black form of antimony trisulphide; it may also be made by chemical means. The powder, which has little colour value, is used exclusively as a camouflage paint; on being photographed with infrared film, it has the same reflectance value as green foliage.

antimony white antimony oxide coprecipitated with about 70% barium sulphate. Although its properties are similar to those of titanium white, antimony white has been considered unnecessary on the artist's palette, since it is less inert than titanium and tends to turn yellow on exposure to sulphur fumes. The pigment was introduced in Britain in 1920 under the tradename Timonox; it has rarely, if ever, been used in the United States.

antimony yellow see NAPLES YELLOW.

antioxidant any material that when introduced into an oil paint will prevent or delay the oxidation or skinning over of the surface. See also RETARDANT.

antiquarianism interest in or devotion to art of the past, especially that of ancient times. The term implies admiration of a style or object simply because it is old. It is often employed in a derogatory sense.

antiqua see ROMAN.

antique 1. *adj.* pertaining to the art of ancient times.

2. *n.* a work of art or other object made in a bygone era.

Antwerp blue or **Haarlem blue** a pale variety of PRUSSIAN BLUE containing 75% INERT PIGMENT. It is not used for permanent painting. See also MINERAL BLUE.

Antwerp red see LIGHT RED.

Antwerp school those Flemish painters who worked in Antwerp in the early 16th century. Dominated by Quentin Massys (?1466–1530) and his followers, they introduced many elements of Italian Renaissance style into their works, without, however, relinquishing their identity as Flemish painters.

anvil a block on which metal is shaped by hand hammering or forging. It is usually made of steel-faced iron and is used especially for forming wrought metal, or metal that has been heated until it is red and malleable and then hammered into shape.

apple wood see FRUITWOOD.

applied art art that is employed in the design or decoration of useful objects and that remains subservient to the function of those objects. Examples are the design of manufactured items, illustrations, and lettering used in advertising. Commercial art may be considered a branch of applied art. Applied art is distinguished from FINE ART, whose chief function is aesthetic, but the line between the two is often difficult to draw.

appliqué decoration in which pieces of a material are fastened to a surface of the same or another material to form a design. It is most common in sewing, where cloth cutouts are stitched on a cloth background. Appliqué is also used in metalwork and in paper, where it is called *découpage*.

appuie-main French for MAHLSTICK.

apricot gum a clear, pale gum that exudes from apricot trees. See CHERRY GUM.

aqua fortis (*Lat.* nitric acid) a dilution of the acid, which is the principal MORDANT used in ETCHING. The term *aquafortist* designates an etcher in the same way that one who works with paint is known as a painter.

aquarelle 1. the technique of painting in transparent watercolour.

2. a work so executed.

aquatint an ETCHING technique characterized by the control of tonal areas to produce an unlimited series of gradations from pale grey to velvety black and a pleasing granular effect. The term *aquatint* is derived from the resemblance of prints made by this method to drawings done with watercolour washes. In aquatint, a copper or zinc plate is dusted in a DUST BOX with a fine layer of powdered rosin. The plate is carefully warmed to fuse the rosin to the metal, so that when the plate is placed in an acid bath, the mordant, usually SMILLIE'S BATH, eats around each minute spot of the acid-resistant dust. This produces in the plate a series of fine pits that, if inked, would print as a uniformly translucent, grainy tone. Varied tones are produced by STOPPING OUT some areas of the plate and biting others more deeply. Stopping out and rebiting are repeated until the desired results are achieved. Areas that are not to be toned, but are to print completely white, are covered with a resist before the plate is immersed in the mordant. Along with the rosin dust method, invented by Jean-Baptiste Le Prince in 1769, SAND-GRAIN GROUND and STAPART'S GROUND can be used to produce a pitted plate surface. Sublimed sulphur is also used to corrode and pit the plate to produce tones in the prints.

The technique of aquatint is seldom used alone except for colour prints, for which it is well suited. In black-and-white printmaking, the plate is usually first given a grained surface with aquatint; it may then be either incised by line ENGRAVING or DRYPOINT or covered again with an etching ground and etched in lines. Paul Sandby (1725–1809) was the first British artist to be widely known for the use of aquatint, and Francisco de Goya (1746–1828) was its greatest practitioner. The majority of the graphics of Goya are done in aquatint with etched and/or drypoint lines. Aquatint continues to be popular among graphic artists today, especially for colour prints.

aqueous paint any paint that may be diluted with water, as distinguished from oils and other paints that may be thinned only with VOLATILE SOLVENTS. See CASEIN COLOURS; DESIGNERS' COLOURS; GOUACHE; POLYMER COLOURS; POSTER COLOURS; SCENIC COLOUR; TEMPERA; WATERCOLOUR.

arabesque a style of linear ornament consisting of interlaced lines, sometimes with leaf, fruit, flower and animal motifs interspersed in the design. Most arabesques are curvilinear and flowing, although some have an angular character. The ancient Greeks and Romans used arabesques, taken perhaps from Oriental or Near East sources. During the Renaissance they were used extensively as decorative embellishments in drawing, painting, low relief, sgraffito and metalwork. The term should not be confused with Arab styles, which are known as *Moresque*.

arabesque

arabic, gum see GUM ARABIC.

arariba see BALAUSTRE.

archaic, *adj.* belonging to a relatively unsophisticated, but not primitive, period in the development of the art of a particular region. More specifically, the term is used for the art of a period immediately preceding one in which artists attained a high level of technical mastery over their media.

ARCHAIC PERIOD

architect's rendering brush

It may be applied to works of art that emulate styles and techniques of an earlier period, as well as to those that survive from the earlier period.

Archaic period the fourth phase of HELLENIC ART (600–500 BC), following the ORIENTALIZING PERIOD and preceding the CLASSICAL PERIOD. Vase painting reached its peak during the Archaic period. Scenes from mythology and everyday life were painted in animated and naturalistic detail, although the figures were essentially line drawings filled in with flat colour. No examples of mural and panel paintings of the time survive, but authorities assume that they displayed a similar technique. The first Hellenic monumental sculpture – probably the first freestanding statues in the history of art – was created during this period. At first the stiff, stylized figures betrayed their Egyptian origin. As the style evolved, however, statues became more graceful and lifelike. The later works were rendered with great attention to anatomy. Even in clothed figures, the drapery had an organic relation to the body. An invariable feature of the Archaic figure was the so-called *Archaic smile*, a formal sign of animation. The statues were originally painted, which must have added greatly to their beauty and realism. Since monumental architecture developed concurrently with monumental sculpture, this period saw the rise of relief and of pedimental sculpture, usually freestanding, in stone or terracotta.

archaistic, *adj.* characteristic of art that seeks to emulate art of the past. In Greek sculpture, it is applied specifically to a period of development, during the Hellenistic era (323–100 BC), when the Archaic style was admired and imitated throughout the Hellenistic world, although the imitation was modified by highly developed stone carving techniques that had evolved during the intervening centuries. Archaistic Greek sculpture, being imitative, is generally regarded as inferior to the work it was modelled on, the character of which was determined in part by less sophisticated carving techniques. See ARCHAIC PERIOD; HELLENISTIC PERIOD.

archiepiscopal cross or **archbishop's cross** see PATRIARCHAL CROSS.

archil see ORCHIL.

architectonic, *adj.* **1.** relating to architecture, especially to its basic structural principles.

2. (of a painting or other work of art) presenting an interrelation of parts showing a structural unity of the type associated with architectural design.

3. having monumental qualities suggestive of the massiveness of architecture.

architects' rendering brush a brush, made in several extra-large sizes, that resembles the round, pointed watercolour brush. Many watercolour painters use the brush for broad washes and for finer work with the point. The architects' rendering brush is sometimes made of red sable, but it is more commonly made of ox hair, which is much less expensive and which for most purposes performs better than red sable in a brush of this size.

architects' scales see SCALES, ARCHITECTS'.

architectural sculpture sculpture that is intended to form an integral part of a building, or is created especially to embellish it, as distinguished from works created for display as independent pieces. This distinction parallels that between easel painting and mural painting. See ATLANTES; CARYATID; TELAMON.

arc welding the technique of WELDING with electrical equipment, as opposed to oxyacetylene or gas welding. In arc welding, coalescence is produced by heating with an electric arc or arcs. Depending on the method used, pressure may or may not be applied, and a FILLER ROD may or may not be used.

arenato see SAND COAT.

argilla Latin for POTTER'S CLAY.

armature a skeleton construction on which the sculptor builds up his or her work in plaster, clay, or another plastic substance. The armatures of small figures are commonly made of stiff wire; those of larger works may be constructed of any rigid and durable material. See also BUST PEG; BUTTERFLY.

armature Hanging within the body cavity is a *butterfly*, crossed sticks that help support a heavy mass of clay or other plastic material.

ARMENIAN BLUE

Armenian blue an old name for native ULTRAMARINE BLUE, made from powdered lapis lazuli.

Armenian bole see BOLE.

Armenian stone see AZURITE.

Armory Show the art show held in the 69th Regiment Armory in New York City in 1913 that was the project of a group of American artists led by Arthur Davies (1862–1928) and Robert Henri (1865–1929) whose aim was to exhibit the work of contemporary American and European artists. Most of the work exhibited – approximately 1600 pieces in all – was avant-garde in nature, thus causing great controversy among art critics and a public totally unfamiliar with the ideas represented by ABSTRACT ART. Paintings such as *Nude Descending a Staircase*, by Marcel Duchamp (1887–1968) were greeted with derision and scorn by the undiscerning public. However, the very novelty of the Armory Show attracted huge audiences, and the show can therefore be viewed as a watershed in the history of American art and a spur to the growth of modern American painting and sculpture.

arm palette an extra-large palette with a flaring curve, designed so that the forearm bears most of its weight. Some artists are particular about its balance and feel, choosing it as a sensitive instrument; others reject it as a romantic affectation or a relic of former times. The arm palette was commonly used in the 19th century.

arm palette

Arnaudon's green a variety of hydrated CHROMIUM OXIDE GREEN very similar to VIRIDIAN. It is no longer produced.

Arretine ware see TERRA SIGILLATA.

arribida red a native red iron-oxide pigment.

arriccio see BROWN COAT.

arris a sharp, protruding edge or angle formed by the meeting of plane or curved surfaces, especially an edge of a moulding or a stria. See illustration at FLUTING.

arsenic orange see REALGAR.

arsenic yellow see ORPIMENT.

art autre see TACHISME.

art brut the name given by French artist Jean Dubuffet (1901–1985) to art that is created by people outside the art world. These individuals can include anyone from mental patients to prisoners, in short, anyone not producing art for profit or recognition. Dubuffet felt there was great power and honesty inherent in the work of such people, because they did not adhere to the cultural norms or fashions that influenced most artists.

art deco a style of design and decoration popular in North America and Europe in the 1920s and 1930s. While art deco was essentially an offshoot of ART NOUVEAU, the characteristic patterns or designs of art deco, unlike those of its predecessor, are geometric, not naturalistic in style, reflecting the influence of industry and mass production in the early 20th century.

arte povera the name given by Germano Celant, an Italian art critic, to a type of art that combines elements of CONCEPTUAL ART, MINIMAL ART, and PERFORMANCE ART. Conceived in reaction to what Celant perceived as the ever-increasing commercialism of the art world, arte povera embraces such ideas as the use of valueless materials, for instance, earth, gravel, or rocks, in the creation of works of art that are not saleable products.

art for art's sake or *(Fr.)* **l'art pour l'art** a phrase used since the 1870s to proclaim the independence of aesthetic values intrinsic in a work of art from storytelling, moral values, or any other purposes or motives. See also AESTHETICISM.

artificial porcelain see SOFT PASTE PORCELAIN.

artificial ultramarine a term used in the 19th century to distinguish the ULTRAMARINE BLUE in standard use from the original native variety obtained from lapis lazuli.

artist's proof one of the PROOFS in a LIMITED EDITION of ORIGINAL PRINTS. An artist's proof must bear the artist's signature or mark and, since the early 20th century, is usually numbered.

art mobilier 1. small portable works of art found in archaeological or prehistoric sites. Examples include figurines, carvings, and jewellery. **2.** the art objects of nomadic peoples.

art nouveau a style in art, manifested in painting, sculpture, printmaking, architecture and decorative design at the turn of the last century. It arose in Britain in the 1880s and held sway as the avant-garde movement of its day from about 1895 to about 1905. Among its principal characteristics were a cursive, expressive line with flowing, swelling reverse curves, entrelacs (interlaced patterns), and the whiplash curve. In decoration, plant and flower motifs abounded, used for the first time in naturalistic form. Art nouveau had a concurrent phase, prevailing towards the close of the movement, in which straight lines and rectangular motifs predominated.

The style derived from several sources prominent in British culture during the second half of the 19th century: the arts and crafts movement, Celtic art, rococo, Oriental calligraphy, Japanese art, and Japanese architecture. The last of these influences was the strongest in the style's rectilinear phase. From Britain, art nouveau spread rapidly over Europe and North America, where it had a great influence on design in all fields of applied arts and decoration. This influence can still be discerned in some modern work in these fields. Its expressive lines appear even in poured-concrete buildings, such as Frank Lloyd Wright's Guggenheim Museum and Eero Saarinen's TWA Terminal at Kennedy Airport, both in New York. Among the many examples of art nouveau in its heyday are the buildings of Antoni Gaudí and Victor Horta, the drawings of Aubrey Beardsley, the glassware of Louis Comfort Tiffany, the architectural ornament and interior decoration of Henri Van de Velde and Louis Sullivan, the furniture of Charles Rennie Mackintosh, and the posters of Alphonse Mucha. The style also has been known as the *yachting style* in France, JUGENDSTIL in Germany, *Sezession* in Austria, and STILE LIBERTY in Italy. See also DECADENCE; FIN DE SIÈCLE.

Some art historians have traced connections between art nouveau and the revolutionary movements that succeeded it. The curvilinear phase influenced the work of the Cubists, the rectilinear phase that of the followers of Neoplasticism. The style also left its mark on expressionist painting. Among the outstanding painters and sculptors who were influenced by it were Gauguin, Van Gogh, Toulouse-Lautrec, Rodin, Edvard Munch, and Gustav Klimt.

art rupestre the French term for the mural art of prehistoric cave dwellers.

arts and crafts 1. in modern usage, the art of forming handmade articles, usually decoratively designed and often useful or purposeful. The various handicraft skills employed include metalwork, woodwork, weaving, needlework, and manipulation of plastics, as well as techniques such as carving, printmaking, and painting. Arts and crafts is taught professionally in schools and other institutions, sometimes as a hobby or recreational activity and sometimes as therapy.
2. the name of a movement that began in England during the last third of the 19th century. Its founding is generally attributed to William Morris, but it was inspired by the doctrines of John Ruskin and Augustus Pugin. The movement was a conscious reaction against the results of the industrialization of design crafts. It fostered a return to handcrafted individuality. The new styles, which appeared in furniture, decoration and ornament, hand-blocked textiles, typography and book design, broke away from the prevailing Victorian fashions and laid the groundwork for acceptance of ART NOUVEAU in the late 19th and early 20th centuries.

arylide yellow a bright, pale, transparent yellow SYNTHETIC ORGANIC PIGMENT. One of the earliest azo pigments (see AZO COLOURS) to be adopted by the old CS 98–62 Paint Standard. This pigment creates brilliant effects quite different from the more golden tones that cobalt yellow produces. It greatly improved lightfastness, but may bleed in some organic solvents and mediums.

arzica see WELD.

asbestine *(US)* a species of TALC mined in northern New York State. Asbestine is used as an INERT PIGMENT in house paints to prevent rapid settling or caking because of the flat-plate shape of its particles.

Ashcan School see EIGHT, THE.

ash glaze a ceramic GLAZE utilizing wood or vegetable ashes as the fluxing ingredient. Ash has been used as a glaze material since the Han Dynasty in China. Waste materials such as leaves, vegetable hulls, sawdust or fireplace ashes may be employed. The principal disadvantage of ash glazes is the unreliability of their sources.

askos an ancient Greek ceramic oil flask. Its form was derived from ancient goatskin containers. See VASE SHAPES for illustration.

asphalt any of a fairly large group of black or blackish-brown bituminous substances, classed among the natural RESINS and taken from pits and lakes in many parts of the world. Their physical characteristics and performance vary little except for hardness and melting point; some are very soft, others quite hard. All are highly acid-resistant and so are useful for such purposes as RESISTS in etching. Although they have been used in durable, weather-resistant coatings since the earliest recorded times, and by the Egyptians in embalming mummies, they develop surface faults on ageing and therefore are not used in artists' paints. Among the soft varieties are *Trinidad asphalt*, *manjak* (from Barbados), and *California asphalt*. Uintaite, commonly known in the United States by its tradename, Gilsonite, is a very hard variety from Utah, brittle and lustrous. It is widely used to provide hardness in acid-resistant mixtures that contain softer ingredients.

asphaltum a dark brown, transparent, bituminous oil colour made by dissolving an ASPHALT in linseed oil; it is not a true pigment colour. Asphaltum is soluble in oils and VOLATILE SOLVENTS and melts at relatively low temperatures; areas of old paintings containing it have degenerated to masses of wide-open fissures. Especially popular in the 19th century, asphaltum was replaced by TRANSPARENT BROWN and UMBER after its bad effects became known. MUMMY is a variety of asphaltum. Asphaltum was also used in ACID RESIST for etching.

assemblage 1. the technique of creating three-dimensional works of art by combining various elements, especially found objects, into an integrated whole.
2. a composition so constructed. An assemblage may be either freestanding and therefore related to sculpture, or mounted on a panel, in which case it is more like a COLLAGE. It may include elements painted, carved or modelled by the artist. The first composition so called is Picasso's *Glass of Absinthe* (1914).

astragal 1. a small, plain, convex moulding, from half to three-quarters round.
2. a glazing bar.

asymmetry the absence of precise symmetry in a work of art. In painting and sculpture, asymmetry for purposes of realism, especially in representations of the human face and figure, is justified by the observation that no two sides of a living form are identical. Asymmetry is also used for aesthetic reasons, since balanced two-sidedness usually makes for a static and superficial composition. To keep a work of art from appearing lopsided, however, the principles of EQUILIBRIUM are often applied in the execution of an asymmetrical composition.

atelier 1. an artist's or craftsman's workshop. The term is often used to designate a studio in which an artist trains students or in which assistants or apprentices work under the artist's supervision. See BOTTEGA.

2. (atelier libre) a studio that provides a nude model during fixed sessions. There is no teacher and no tuition as such. The most famous of these studios was opened about 1825 in Paris by the model Suisse. It was used by Delacroix, Courbet, Manet, Monet and Cézanne. The Atelier Julian, which opened in Paris in 1860, was an extension of the atelier concept and provided instruction. Matisse and Léger studied there.

atlantes a plural of *atlas*, the term used by the ancient Greeks for a column carved in the shape of a man. It is the male counterpart of a caryatid. Named after the giant Atlas, this form of architectural sculpture was called a TELAMON by the Romans. See illustration at CARYATID.

atmosphere *(pictorial arts)* **1.** the feeling conveyed or the mood created. **2.** three-dimensional space in a composition, especially when achieved with AERIAL PERSPECTIVE.

atomizer a device used by artists for spraying coatings of thin fluids on a surface in the form of mist. The typical atomizer consists of a glass jar, brass- or chrome-plated tubes, and a rubber bulb. Atomizers are used for spraying water on freshly applied watercolour to delay its drying; for applying fixatives to pastels and charcoal drawings; and for sizing grounds and underpaintings to reduce their absorbency. The introduction of fixatives and varnishes sold in cans as pressurized aerosol sprays, and of modern SPRAYERS, diminished but not entirely eliminated the use of atomizers.

atramentum 1. a generic term in ancient Rome for various kinds of carbon black used in making paint and ink, and for the ink made from it.

2. an unknown substance employed by the Romans as a glaze or varnish in painting. Scholars believe this was a solution of asphalt compounded with resin or oil so as to lighten its dark colour sufficiently to impart a desirable tone to the underlying colours.

à trois crayons a chalk drawing done in three colours, almost always red and white chalk and black chalk or charcoal. Watteau executed a great number of fine drawings in this medium, using SANGUINE as his red crayon.

attapulgite a fibrous clay containing magnesium silicate; one of the components of MAYAN BLUE.

attribute any object or accessory used in a painting or sculpture to identify the character or profession of the person portrayed. For example, scales of justice might be used to signify a lawyer or judge.

attribution the process whereby a work of art is ascribed to a particular artist. This is by no means a certain business, as when several art experts undertake an attribution, they will often disagree.

Augsburg Renaissance developments in German painting and sculpture centred in Augsburg at the beginning of the 16th century. Led by the painter Hans Burgkmair the Elder, artists in this city introduced many characteristics of the art of the Italian Renaissance into Germany. They were particularly influenced by the artists of northern Italy and Venice.

au premier coup see ALLA PRIMA.

aureole or **glory 1.** a depiction of radiance surrounding or emanating from the figure of a holy personage, especially in mediaeval and Renaissance art.

2. the radiance surrounding the head of a holy personage (see NIMBUS). The almond-shaped aureole surrounding the figure of Christ or the Virgin Mary in mediaeval art is called a *mandorla* (Italian for almond) or *vesica piscis* (Latin for fish bladder).

aureolin or **cobalt yellow** cobalt-potassium nitrite, a permanent pigment with a brilliant golden-yellow transparency useful for glazes and for tinting. Aureolin is not used in opaque layers, where it has a dull tannish hue of no particular value. Discovered in Breslau, Germany, by N.W. Fischer (1848), aureolin was introduced as a paint pigment by Saint-Evre in Paris (1852) and was first sold in Britain and the United States about 1861. It was a welcome addition to the artist's palette, which had theretofore depended on unsatisfactory transparent yellow lakes of doubtful permanence.

auripigmentum see ORPIMENT.

aurora yellow a variety of CADMIUM YELLOW introduced into Britain by Winsor & Newton in 1889, at which time it represented a considerable improvement in clarity and performance over earlier cadmiums.

aurum musivum a Latin term for MOSAIC GOLD.

autolithography LITHOGRAPHY as a graphic art in which ORIGINAL PRINTS are made, as distinct from commercial or industrial lithography. As the term implies, autolithography is thought by some artists to be more autographic than the other graphic arts, that is, more immediate and truer both to the artist's concept and to the nature of the artist's materials. The artist draws directly on the stone and makes prints directly from that drawing. The intermediate steps of engraving or etching the design that are needed in the other graphic processes are not necessary in lithography. The texture of the stone, the graininess of the crayon, and the brushstrokes of the TUSCHE are all reproduced exactly in the proofs. It is not uncommon for a lithographer to use a pale tan or greyish-blue paper to duplicate in the proofs the colour of the stone on which the original drawing was made.

automatism the technique of creating a work of art without the exercise of thought or will, or any intervention on the part of the conscious mind. As a deliberate method, it has been employed by the Surrealists (see SURREALISM) and in some ACTION PAINTING. It is sometimes equated with doodling, but although automatism is rarely a deliberate action at the start, it usually becomes conscious and selective as the artist progresses.

avant-garde (*Fr.* vanguard) that which departs from the existing norm in an original or experimental way. The term is used of an artist's technique, style, or choice of subject matter. A group of practitioners or advocates of a new art form may also be called 'avant-garde'. Since avant-garde works may somewhat shock those who are used to traditional, established styles, the term is also sometimes extended to mean 'outlandish' or 'extremist'.

avellan cross a cross with each arm made in a conventionalized filbert shape. It looks rather like four long, trumpet-shaped blossoms joined at the stem ends to a small circle. The name comes from *avellano*, a filbert or hazelnut from Avella, Italy. See CROSS for illustration.

Avignon berries see BUCKTHORN BERRY.

Avignon school the school of painting consisting of mostly Italian artists who resided in and near Avignon, France, beginning when Avignon was home to the Papal Court in the 14th century and continuing through the 15th century, when Flemish art began to have an impact on the school's style.

avodire an African hardwood from the tree *Turraeanthus africana*. Avodire is pale yellow and has a fine, silky texture. It comes in planks and is widely used for decorative work.

axonometric projection see PROJECTION.

ayous, African whitewood or **samba** an African wood from the obeche (*Triplochiton scleroxylon*), whitish or light yellow, with a pronounced stripe. It is usually available in large logs. Ayous is lightweight but relatively strong, and is easy to work.

Ayr stone, snakestone or **water-of-Ayr** a very hard, fine-grained stone from Ayrshire used as a whetstone for sharpening sculptors' and engravers' tools and for polishing marble.

azo colour any of the bright SYNTHETIC ORGANIC PIGMENTS from which fairly permanent pigments are produced for industrial paints, printing inks, varnishes and other products. Most are not sufficiently permanent or reliably nonbleeding to be acceptable for artists' use, with a few exceptions.

azure blue 1. a hue designation for any sky-blue colour.
2. an 18th-century name for SMALT.

azure cobalt a special variety of COBALT BLUE, lighter in shade than the normal type.

azurite, blue malachite or **chessylite** a clear, deep-blue, crystalline mineral, basic copper carbonate. In powdered form, azurite was used at least as early as Roman times as a permanent paint pigment, and it remained as a prominent blue for tempera and watercolour use until superseded by more readily available and cheaper blues. SMALT replaced it in the 17th century. It does not work well enough in oil to be used as an oil colour. Azurite has some variation towards the green due to the presence of MALACHITE in some specimens. BREMEN BLUE is similar to azurite in chemical composition but has a different crystalline structure. The mineral was called *Armenian stone* by the Romans. The old Italian name for the pigment was *azzuro della magna*, and in the 17th or 18th century it shared the name *mountain blue* with Bremen blue. In the United States, the unstandardized term *mineral blue* has been applied to azurite.

azzurro oltremarino see ULTRAMARINE.

B

babul gum or **babool gum** an obsolete name for GUM ARABIC. Babul, or babool, is the popular name of an acacia tree that is a source of the gum.

background the part of the composition of a picture that appears to be farthest from the viewer. The background is one of the three ZONES OF RECESSION in LINEAR PERSPECTIVE. *Lointain* and *offscape* are little-used terms for the most distant parts of a landscape.

background paper another name for coloured SIGN PAPER in wide rolls.

back-painting 1. a method of transferring a print to a sheet of glass and colouring it from the rear so that the picture seems to have been done directly on the glass.

2. (also called **glass coloured print**) a work so produced.

Back-painting was popular in the late 17th and early 18th centuries. The print, usually a line engraving or a mezzotint, was given a long soaking in water to remove the sizing and soften the paper. When it had dried, it was laid face down on a sheet of glass to which a thin coating of a balsam such as Venice turpentine or Strasbourg turpentine had been applied. When the adhesive had set, the back of the print was sponged with water and the paper carefully rubbed away until only a thin, virtually transparent layer remained. The back of the print was then painted with watercolours and given a coat of pale varnish for protection. The process was revived for a time in the 19th century as a means of colouring photographs.

badger blender a BLENDER made of badger hair, which is grey with a black band. The hair of a badger blender is held by a plastic ferrule fastened with twisted wire, to minimize the breakage of hairs.

badger blender

badigeon a stiff paste used to STOP small defects in stone. The traditional ingredients are plaster and powdered limestone.

bag wall the wall in a down-draught KILN that separates the combustion area from the kiln proper. Baffles are constructed to channel the flame indirectly through the kiln in order to conserve heat and achieve higher temperatures. The circuitous flow of heat prevents its direct expulsion through the stack. Such heat loss is the principal drawback of the older up-draught kiln.

baked enamel see STOVE ENAMEL.

balance see EQUILIBRIUM.

balaustre, arariba or **canarywood** a South American wood (from trees of the genus *Centrolobium*), usually brilliant orange, although it may be yellow or red and is sometimes streaked with red or black. It is used in shipbuilding and as a veneer for cabinetwork. Balaustre logs run from 6 to 8 inches in diameter and 8 feet or more in length.

baldachin, baldacchino or **baldaquin** a canopy suspended over a throne or altar, or supported over an episcopal chair or throne carried in processions; also, a permanently constructed canopy over an altar. An example is the massive bronze baldachin by Bernini over the high altar in St Peter's in Rome. Its name derives from *baudekyn*, a rare textile fabric from Baghdad (Baldacca) that was used to make such canopies.

ball clay a special kind of ceramic clay of exceptionally small particle size and, consequently, very good plasticity. It is used to impart plasticity to other CLAY BODIES.

ball mill a revolving horizontal cylinder that contains steel balls, used to disperse pigments in a paint vehicle (see PAINT). Its inner surface is made of or lined with material hard enough to resist the wear from the balls. When the vehicle and pigment are put into a ball mill, the grinding action of the tumbling balls produces a satisfactory dispersion, but of a thinner, more fluid consistency than the stiff pastes that can be produced by the ROLLER MILL. An advantage of the ball mill is that it may be used when the vehicle evaporates too rapidly to be ground efficiently in an open mill. Pigmented lacquers and ethyl silicate colours must be dispersed in ball mills. Small-scale versions are sometimes improvised, using steel balls in glass or porcelain jars or tin cans riding on two revolving rollers. A mill that uses flint pebbles instead of balls is called a pebble mill. See also MULLER.

In ceramics, a ball mill is used to grind and blend glazes and the ingredients of clay bodies.

balsa one of the lightest of woods; obtained from the tree *Ochroma lagopus*, native to South America. Balsa is very soft and porous, and is easily carved. It is quite strong for its weight.

balsam any of various thick, viscous fluids, sometimes called *oleoresins*, exuded by cone-bearing evergreen trees and containing volatile and solid resinous ingredients. Chief among those that are specifically named balsams are CANADA BALSAM and COPAIBA BALSAM; others are VENICE TURPENTINE and STRASBOURG TURPENTINE. Balsams have been used as ingredients of varnishes and painting mediums since the earliest days of European easel painting. See also BURGUNDY TURPENTINE.

bamboo brush a widely used misnomer for any Oriental brush, which is more frequently set into a reed than a bamboo handle. However, there is a true bamboo brush, not in very wide use; the so-called bristles are the pointed end of a bamboo stalk, finely divided or shredded and shaped so that it resembles a conventional pointed brush with exceptionally long hairs.

bamboo pen a Japanese pen made from a bamboo stalk; it is cut to pen shape like a reed pen (see PEN) and used for drawing and calligraphy.

banana oil a popular term for amyl acetate, a commonly used LACQUER SOLVENT. It has a sharp, penetrating, banana-like odour. Amyl alcohol, a lacquer DILUENT, has a similar but less penetrating odour.

banderole a carved or painted decoration in the form of a ribbon or long scroll, sometimes bearing an inscription.

banding wheel or **liner's wheel** a small turntable used in decorating pottery with circular stripes or bands of colour or gold. The wheel, on which the piece is centred, is twirled while a brush loaded with glaze or underglaze colour is held steady against the piece.

banker a large, sturdy workbench, sometimes with a turntable top, used for stone, wood or clay sculpture.

banner paper see SIGN PAPER.

Barbizon school a group of French landscape painters active between about 1830 and 1880, who formed an informal school, or art colony, in the village of Barbizon, on the edge of the Forest of Fontainebleau. They were the first to paint from nature, rather than creating their landscapes in a studio. In this, and in their realistic portrayal of rural scenes and characters, they foreshadowed the Impressionists. Leaders of the Barbizon school were Théodore Rousseau (1812–1867) and Charles François Daubigny (1817–1878). Associated with them more by propinquity than by similarity of style were Camille Corot (1796–1875), whose landscapes were less realistic and more suffused with light, and François Millet (1814–1875), who was less interested in the countryside than in the peasants who inhabited it. See PLEIN AIR.

bardiglio an Italian MARBLE with dark veins on a bluish or dark-grey ground.

baren a smooth, flat, round or oval pad, furnished with a handle so that it may be used to take an impression from a wood block by rubbing the back of paper that has been placed on the inked face of the block. The original *baren*, a Japanese implement, is made of layers of glued cardboard, cushioned with a coil of tough cord and covered with a sheath of bamboo. The ridges of the bamboo help concentrate the pressure of the baren as it is drawn across the block. A modern model, sheathed with nylon instead of bamboo, is used by some printmakers. Also available are barens made of wood and of Teflon.

barite see BARYTES.

barium sulphate see BARYTES; BLANC FIXE.

barium yellow see LEMON YELLOW.

Baroque the style dominating European art and architecture throughout the 17th century and persisting in some places as late as 1750. It was a dynamic, theatrical style that used realism, illusionism, ornate forms, and a blending of the arts to achieve its effects.

The style is found in its purest form in the work of Gianlorenzo Bernini (1598–1680) and Francesco Borromini (1599–1667), who fused architecture and sculpture, creating an illusion of immediacy for the beholder by their use of light and space. Painting of the High Baroque in Italy often took the form of fresco, especially illusionistic ceiling decorations (see SOTTO IN SÙ) designed to merge with the elaborate mouldings and carved cornices surrounding them. Among its practitioners were Pietro da Cortona (1596–1669), Giovanni Lanfranco (1582–1647), and Guercino (1591–1666).

The painter Caravaggio (1573–1610) is usually considered the first Baroque artist. In his realistic, even earthy treatment of the traditional religious subject matter and his dramatic use of chiaroscuro, he paved the way for Peter Paul Rubens (1577–1640), Rembrandt van Rijn (1606–1669), and Jan Vermeer (1632–1675). Although Rubens' paintings were usually devoted to Christian or classical themes, Rembrandt and Vermeer, along with Franz Hals (1580–1666), often chose contemporary subjects, depicting peasants and burghers in realistically domestic surroundings. Other painters of the Baroque were Anthony van Dyck (1599–1641) and Diego Velásquez (1599–1660). See also ROCOCO.

barwood a red NATURAL DYESTUFF obtained from a tropical African hardwood of the genus *Pterocarpus*. *Camwood*, extracted from a very similar African dyewood, *Baphia nitida*, is generally held to be the same substance. Both have been used to dye textiles, but they resist fading poorly.

baryta an obsolete term for barium, which survives in the term BARYTA WATER.

baryta green an obsolete name for MANGANESE GREEN.

baryta water a saturated solution of barium hydroxide, sometimes used in place of limewater to saturate plaster before applying SECCO colours.

baryta white an obsolete name for BLANC FIXE.

barytes, barite, Bologna stone or **heavy spar** native barium sulphate. When ground to a fine, white powder it is used as an INERT PIGMENT and FILLER in industrial paints. The use of powdered barytes as a paint filler does not seem to antedate the late 18th century. Barytes is not used in artists' materials or the finer types of industrial paints, but precipitated barium sulphate, called BLANC FIXE, is widely used as an inert pigment. The name 'heavy spar' is an allusion to its high specific gravity or heaviness. Barite is a geological term. An archaic Latin name is *terra ponderosa*.

basalt a dense, hard volcanic rock used for carving and as a building stone by the ancient Egyptians. It is black or blackish green or brown, sometimes with glittering particles. Because of its hardness and fine grain, it was sometimes used for finely wrought vases and other delicate objects.

basalt ware or **basaltes ware** a decorative black ceramic stoneware, developed by Josiah Wedgwood in 1768. It resembles the natural mineral basalt and is usually decorated with Neoclassical motifs in white or in colour.

base 1. (also called **lake base**) the INERT PIGMENT or colourless powder on which a dye is precipitated to form a coloured pigment. Alumina hydrate is considered the best base for transparent results; BLANC FIXE is usually employed when body or opacity is sought.

2. the foundation or support on which a piece of sculpture rests. Besides giving physical stability to the work, it is chosen to enhance the appearance of the sculpture by means of its size, shape, colour, and texture. Nearly every material has been used for a base, although wood is most frequently employed. The bottom of a smoothly finished base is usually either left rough or glued to a piece of felt to prevent it from being slippery or insecure.

basin slant see SLANT.

bas-relief see RELIEF.

bassetaille a technique of applying porcelain ENAMEL to metal, employed principally on flat articles of jewellery, such as brooches. The metal is fashioned in low relief (the high points being about $\frac{1}{30}$ inch below the rim) either by carving or REPOUSSÉ, and charged with translucent or transparent coloured enamels. Since there are no dividers between the colours, each charge of enamel must be permitted to dry out before the next is applied. Two or three coats of colour, plus a final clear coat made flush with the rim of the piece, are applied before the piece is fired.

basso-rilievo Italian for low RELIEF.

basswood a common softwood obtained from trees of the genus *Tilia*, especially *T. americana* (the linden), native to the United States and Canada. Basswood has a plain, even texture and is easily worked.

bat *(ceramics)* a plaster or fireclay slab on which pottery is formed and dried. When made of fireclay, it may be placed in the KILN. A plaster bat may also be used to absorb excess water from the ware.

Batesville marble *(US)* a LIMESTONE from Arkansas. It may be grey or cream-coloured.

Bath stone a type of limestone, varying greatly in colour and texture, found in particular concentration around the city of Bath, in England, and used in the work of modern British sculptors such as Henry Moore (1898–1986).

batik an Indonesian method of printing textiles by coating part of the fabric with wax to resist dye, dipping the cloth in cold dye solution, and boiling off the wax so that the design stands out in the original colour of the fabric; the process may be repeated for several colours.

Bauhaus a German school of architecture and industrial arts (1919–1933). Founded by the architect Walter Gropius, the Bauhaus attempted to achieve a reconciliation between the aesthetics of design and the commercial demands of industrial mass production. The school did not subscribe to a particular style or aesthetic formula, but stood for a basic approach to the problem of art in an industrial world. Internationally renowned artists and architects, including Paul Klee, Lyonel Feininger and Gropius himself made the Bauhaus enormously influential. Opened in Weimar, it was moved to Dessau, then to Berlin. Hitler closed it in 1933.

bead and reel a convex moulding with a profile that is half round or more and in which bead-shaped elements alternate singly or in groups with discs. See illustration at BEAD MOULDING.

bead moulding a small convex moulding, either half round or half spherical, carved in a continuous row of bead-like protuberances.

bead moulding (top) Bead moulding; (bottom) bead and reel.

beak moulding a protruding moulding, the profile of which resembles the short, downward-curving hawk's beak.

beak moulding

beam compass see COMPASS.

Beaux-Arts, Ecole des the school of fine arts of the ACADÉMIE DES BEAUX-ARTS, located in Paris.

beaver board see WALLBOARD.

Bedford stone *(US)* a light-coloured oolitic LIMESTONE from Lawrence County, Indiana. It is one of the best American limestones for building purposes. See INDIANA LIMESTONE.

beeswax the WAX found in honeycombs. Two grades, white refined and virgin or yellow, are sold. Melted beeswax is added to pigments in the method of wax or encaustic painting, and is the basic ingredient of etching grounds and preservative coatings and it also serves as a plasticizer and stabilizer in oil colours, as well as an ingredient in tempera emulsions. Beeswax is sometimes used as a flatting agent to produce a mat varnish but cannot be recommended for this purpose because it tends to become glossy when rubbed. White refined beeswax is often referred to in recipes merely as 'wax.'

Belgian black a dense, hard MARBLE from Belgium, esteemed above all other black marbles for carving. Its fine, deep colour and freedom from veins or streaks make it most desirable.

Belgian marble see RANCE.

Belleek a ceramic ware made in Northern Ireland since 1857. It is famous for its thinness and high ring, and has a soft, iridescent glaze.

Bell's medium a 19th-century British proprietary oil-painting medium, originally made of blown linseed oil thinned with spike oil. It has been superseded by more modern mixtures.

belly 1. the widest place in the round red sable brush.

2. the bulge in a single red sable hair. See BRUSH, RED SABLE; FLAG.

Bengal cutch see CATECHU.

bent gouge and **bent chisel** a wood-carving GOUGE or CHISEL, the shank of which is either curved for its entire length (a long bent) or straight for most of its length with a sharp bend near the tip (short bent or spoon). It carves a deeper cut than the straight gouge or chisel. A bent gouge or chisel is often simply called a *bent*. See illustration at WOOD-CARVING TOOLS.

bentonite an extremely fine natural clay formed by the disintegration of volcanic ash, used mainly to increase the plasticity of a ceramic CLAY BODY. As a plasticizer, bentonite is about four times as effective as the most plastic ball clays. It may also be used to keep some glazes in suspension, and as an inert pigment or filler in various compounds.

benzene see COAL-TAR SOLVENT.

benzimidazolone orange a transparent SYNTHETIC ORGANIC PIGMENT with good lightfastness and solvent stability. However, this pigment is soluble in some organic solvents and exhibits a slight dullness in tints.

benzimidazolone yellow a SYNTHETIC ORGANIC PIGMENT with good lightfastness, as well as excellent heat and solvent stability for a monoazo pigment. However, this pigment may exhibit poor alkali resistance.

benzine a VOLATILE SOLVENT distilled from crude petroleum. Its volatility, flammability, and solvent action are about midway between those of mineral spirits and petroleum. Familiar as a dry cleaner and spot remover, it is not an ideal paint thinner. Its flash point, rapid rate of evaporation, and pungent odour make it less suitable than mineral spirits for artists' use.

benzol see COAL-TAR SOLVENT.

benzol black the most intense and bluish variant of CARBON BLACK. It is made by burning solvents.

Berlin blue a name for PRUSSIAN BLUE that is most frequently used in France.

Beva *acronym for* Burger ethylene vinyl acetate, a heat-sensitive adhesive used primarily by conservators for LINING canvases. Beva is less difficult to apply and remove and is more dimensionally stable than the older wax/resin method of lining, especially when used in conjunction with a SUCTION TABLE.

biacca Italian for flake white, artists'-quality WHITE LEAD.

bianco sangiovanni calcium hydroxide plus calcium carbonate; a white pigment recommended by Cennino Cennini (*Il Libro dell' Arte*) and still used for FRESCO painting. Bianco sangiovanni is made by moulding LIME

PUTTY into small pieces and exposing the pieces to air in a dust-free place for several months; the hydrated lime putty becomes partially carbonated by the air, and the result is an intimate mixture of calcium hydroxide and calcium carbonate.

Bible paper see INDIA PAPER.

bice blue bice and green bice are names formerly used for BREMEN BLUE and BREMEN GREEN. Green bice survived as a water pigment into the 20th century.

Biedermeier 1. *adj.* a satirical epithet applied to a phase of German art and furniture design prevalent from the 1820s until the 1850s. It was characterized in furniture by a simplified, uninspired adaptation of the French Empire style. A self-conscious simplicity was the keynote in painting, as well, with sentimentalized views of peasants and scenes of nature.

2. *n.* an object or work of art of philistine conventionality and dullness.
    One of the most successful centres of Biedermeier art was the DÜSSELDORF SCHOOL.

binder the agglutinant or cementing ingredient of a paint VEHICLE. Its functions are to hold the pigment particles to one another to form a cohesive coating and to attach it securely to the ground. The term is also used for the gum or other agglutinant used in pastel crayons, drawing inks, and ceramics glazes and bodies.

biomorphic form an abstract form whose contours are more related to plant and animal configurations than to geometric shapes. The term is particularly applicable to the works of the sculptor and painter Hans Arp (1887–1966), whose forms suggest vermicular or visceral relationships.

birch any of the common hardwoods obtained from trees of the genus *Betula*. Birch is strong, durable, and relatively inexpensive. Birch veneers may have a curly, wavy, or other figure, although the solid wood used for carving usually has a rather plain and uninteresting grain. It is used in plywood boards that are suitable for use in panels for painting.

bird's eye a natural figure, found in wood or stone, of many small nuclei or eyes surrounded by swirling and dappled patterns, as in bird's-eye maple.

bird's-eye view a scene depicted as if observed from a point sufficiently far above it in space to include the entire spread of the subject. Any correctly drawn bird's-eye view will be in OBLIQUE PERSPECTIVE (see illustration at LINEAR PERSPECTIVE). The HORIZON LINE is shown or imagined high in the picture or actually above it, so that most or all of the composition lies below the horizon line, causing a downward convergence of vertical lines. The raised horizon line corresponds to a high position of the POINT OF STATION. The bird's-eye view is especially suitable for panoramas, such as historical scenes in which the artist wants to show the full scope of an event. See also WORM'S-EYE VIEW.

biscuit 1. see BISQUE.
    2. the mass or body under the glaze in any glazed porcelain.

biscuit mould a MOULD made from bisque-fired clay, used in ceramics. Since the bisque is not glazed or fired to the point of vitrification, it is porous and yet is strong enough to withstand repeated use.

bishop's length see CANVAS SIZES, PORTRAIT.

bismuth white, Bougival white or **pearl white** bismuth nitrate, in limited use in the early 19th century as a less poisonous substitute for white lead. Bismuth white soon became obsolete as a result of technical and economic improvements in zinc white production.

bisque 1. (also called **biscuit**) fired ceramic ware that is to be glazed. **2.** hard-fired, vitreous ceramic ware that is not to be glazed. The term is most frequently applied to unglazed but finished figurines and other small objects of extreme delicacy.

bisque fire the first firing of a ceramic body, preliminary to its being glazed or fired again at a higher temperature (see GLOST FIRE).

bistre, brown lampblack or **soot brown** a brown pigment derived from the tarry soot made by burning beechwood. It was widely used in watercolours and wash drawings from the 14th to the 19th century. Though fairly permanent in diffused light, bistre fades in bright sunlight. It is now replaced by permanent, lightproof pigments. Bistre, like sepia, was especially liked for its pleasing tonal effects in wash drawings. Compared with sepia, bistre is cooler and less reddish. Their relationship is analogous to that between raw umber and the more reddish, or less greenish, burnt umber. Sepia was more popular because of its wider range of tones.

bit see BITSTONE.

biting the corrosive effect a MORDANT has on the metal plate when the plate is placed in a bath of the acid (see ETCHING). The composition, concentration and temperature of the mordant and its skilful application to the plate determine the control of the process (that is, the depth, width and evenness of the etched lines) and the durability of the plate (that is, its ability to stand up under the wear of printing a reasonably large edition). Etching mordants bite in all directions and therefore tend to produce a weakened, undercut structure at the face of the plate. FERRIC CHLORIDE, either used alone or added to nitric acid, promotes a more vertical bite, thus etching lines that will better withstand the wear of printing. When for some reason the mordant bites through or undercuts the ETCHING GROUND, an undesirable phenomenon known as FOUL BITING occurs. CREVÉ, another defect that can occur on an etching plate, results from overbiting.

The extent of biting is controlled not only by the nature of the mordant but also by the length of time the plate is left in the acid bath. After the plate has been in the mordant for a while, it may be removed, and the lines that are to be faintest may be stopped out (see STOPPING OUT) before the plate is replaced in the bath. The procedure is repeated, selectively producing successively deeper lines until the plate is etched to the artist's satisfaction.

bitstone or **bit** coarse, crushed quartz (silica) spread on the bottom of a

SAGGER to prevent delicate ware from sticking to it or being blemished by contact with it during firing.

bitumen native ASPHALT, tar, etc. ASPHALTUM was a bituminous material especially prepared for oil painting.

Bizen ware a utilitarian Japanese ceramic ware. It has been made at Imbre in the province of Bizen since the 14th century. The body is a grey or brown stoneware. What appears to be a reddish or tea-green glaze is the result of fireflash or accidental ash.

black-and-gold marble or **Porto marble** an Italian LIMESTONE, the best grade of which is jet-black, evenly patterned with dull golden veins. Inferior grades have a dark-greyish or brownish ground and irregular veins. It is quarried in Porto Venere and the island of Palmaria in the Gulf of Spezia.

black-boy gum see ACCROIDES.

black chalk a black or dark-grey native CHALK containing carbon or shale, sometimes used as a crayon. However, black pastels and chalk crayons are usually made with black pigments.

black cherry see CHERRYWOOD.

black ebony see EBONY.

black-figured pottery ancient Greek pottery decorated in black on a red or pinkish background. This style was the earlier of the two principal ways of decorating pottery. It was most prevalent in Athens during the Archaic period (6th century BC). RED-FIGURED POTTERY, produced by a more sophisticated technique, increasingly replaced it.

black iron oxide a native variety of magnetic black iron oxide, the artificial counterpart of which is Mars black (see MARS PIGMENTS). It is brownish in undertone, nongreasy, and wets easily, but is coarse and not suitable for artists' use.

black japan see JAPAN.

black lead an obsolete designation for GRAPHITE. The terms *black lead* and *plumbago* were used before the actual composition of graphite was known; they continued to be used until the first quarter of the 19th century.

black-letter hand see GOTHIC.

black-letter type see GOTHIC.

black metal see PEWTER.

black mirror see CLAUDE LORRAIN GLASS.

black oil linseed oil cooked at a high temperature with as much white lead or litharge as will combine with it. Formerly used in making MEGILP, it was called 'strong drying oil.' Its present name came into use in the 1940s in connection with the MAROGER MEDIUM.

black oxide of cobalt or **cobalt black** a rather coarse native black pigment, the properties of which are similar to those of BLACK IRON OXIDE; it is not in use as a paint pigment. Black oxide of cobalt is used in ceramics to impart a cobalt-blue colour to glazes.

black oxide of manganese native manganese dioxide, used principally as a raw material in the preparation of DRIERS and DRYING OILS. Used as a pigment in early civilizations, black oxide of manganese is now seldom produced in a finely ground form suitable for use in paints. An artificial variety is described under MANGANESE BLACK.

black pigments *(US)* those black pigments which are approved in the United States for use in oil paints by the ASTM and are generally acceptable in all other easel- and mural-painting techniques. They include LAMPBLACK, IVORY BLACK, and Mars black (see MARS PIGMENTS).

black walnut see WALNUT.

black watercolour another name for Japanese ink, or sumi. See INK.

blackwood, African see AFRICAN BLACKWOOD.

bladder a container for artists' oil colours, known as early as the mid-17th century, that became widely accepted with the rise of enterprising and well organized artists' supply firms in Britain, France and Germany towards the end of the 18th century and in the United States in the early 19th. The bladder was the first packaging for oil colours; prior to its introduction, the artist or artist's helper had to grind colours for each painting session. The bladder was a fairly tough animal membrane, such as a thick sausage casing, filled to a globular shape with paint and securely tied with twine. The painter would puncture the bladder with an ivory tack and, after squeezing out the colour, replace the tack as a seal. Colours kept this way did not remain fresh for more than a few months. About 1835 appeared a syringe-like container, consisting of a refillable brass tube with a plunger, but this can be classed as studio equipment rather than commercial packaging. The collapsible tin TUBE supplanted both about 1840.

bladder green a 19th-century name for SAP GREEN.

blanc d'argent *(Fr.)* flake white, artists'-quality WHITE LEAD.

blanc fixe, baryta white, enamel white or **permanent white** precipitated barium sulphate. One of the best of the INERT PIGMENTS, blanc fixe is used as a BASE for opaque LAKE pigments, and also used to reduce or let down their strength with a minimum effect on clarity. In water mediums, blanc fixe retains much of its whiteness, and it has been used as a GOUACHE pigment under the name of constant white. Blanc fixe should not be confused with BARYTES (native barium sulphate), a coarser crystalline material used only as an extender in the cheapest of house paints. The invention of blanc fixe has been credited to F. Kuhlmann of Lille, France (c. 1835).

blanket a piece of heavy white felt placed between the paper on the intaglio plate and the upper roller of an ETCHING PRESS. The blanket helps to hold the paper in place on the printing surface and to distribute the pressure of the press evenly over the surface. It also prevents the edge of the plate from tearing the paper under the great pressure of the rollers in the press.

Blaue Reiter, der *(Ger.* the Blue Rider) a group of German artists who created an abstract variety of EXPRESSIONISM. The group was founded in Munich in 1911 by Wassily Kandinsky (1866–1944) and Franz Marc (1880–1916), and included Paul Klee (1879–1940) and August Macke (1887–1914). The *Blaue Reiter* was the avant-garde art movement of its day and, together with the BRÜCKE movement that preceded it, exerted a profound influence on the development of modern art.

Blaue Vier (*Ger.* Blue Four) a group consisting of four highly individual-istic painters – Kandinsky, Klee, Lyonel Feininger (1871–1956), and Alexei von Jawlensky (1864–1941) – who exhibited their work together in Germany in 1922 and in the United States and Mexico in 1924.

bleed 1. *vb (oil colour)* to stain or migrate into an adjoining area of lighter colour. Many synthetic organic pigments, including some of the brilliant modern pigments with good lightproof qualities, may not be used in oil painting because they bleed. White paint brushed over or painted adjacent to a bleeding colour will become tinged with the colour, and the stain will increase as the painting ages.

2. *(graphic arts)* to be printed (as a picture or other illustration) so as to run up to one or more edges of the paper rather than being bounded by a margin.

3. *n.* an illustration so printed.

blender, softener or *(formerly)* **sweetener** a type of brush, usually of badger hair, whose hairs flare out like those of a shaving brush instead of coming to a point. Blenders are used clean and dry, in a perpendicular, staccato tapping motion, to blend together two adjacent colours or tints of wet paint. If skilfully used, they can produce an imperceptible, smooth gradation or fusion of one tone into another. The BADGER BLENDER is not held together by a metal ferrule, as are most brushes, including blenders of fitch hair, which is grey with a black band, and dark squirrel, known as camelhair. The badger blender is usually considered the best, the fitch blender second. The camelhair blender is also called a mop. The flat FAN BRUSH is also used as a blender.

blending the gradation of colour in painting so that two hues or values merge imperceptibly. Oil colours and pastels may be blended, but tempera, gouache, casein paints, and polymer colours do not blend easily. The flowing of watercolour washes may also be considered to be blend-ing. Although most oil and pastel techniques emphasize individual brush-strokes, soft edges and partially fused tones frequently accompany them. Most art students are trained in bold and definite brushwork, because the habitual use of blending can lead to weak and fussy work, and because its use as a major stylistic influence in paintings is outside the mainstream of art. However, blending has been an important technique ever since the beginning of oil painting. A general blend may be made by brushing two areas of wet paint into each other, but a flawless gradation is usually achieved by tapping the area of fusion with a dabber, or clean, dry brush. The BADGER BLENDER is especially made for this purpose. Pastel blends are made on finely grained paper by going over the colours with a STUMP or with the fingertips. Gradated effects in aqueous paints are achieved by HATCHING and crosshatching. In the silk-screen process, blending may be produced by working adjacent charges of colour with the squeegee before the printing surface is placed under the screen. In any relief printing technique, or in direct printing or painting with a brayer, smooth gradations of tone can be made by working two inks or paints together on a glass slab with the brayer.

bleu cendres see ULTRAMARINE ASH.

blind printing the technique of printing an uninked plate to produce a subtle embossed texture. This process, used for many Japanese prints, has been revived by contemporary artists to create a white-on-white image, highlighted by the shadow of the relief image on the uninked paper. Blind printing is effected by covering the uninked plate with damp paper and running the two through an etching press.

blister a raised area of a painting that indicates cleavage between the paint layer and the ground or between two layers of paint. Blistering is caused by external forces acting on a painting, such as fire, moisture, or more rarely, a spot of foreign matter on the ground. Blisters on an oil painting may be caused by water seeping through the canvas support from the rear; even a gummed label applied to the rear of the canvas may cause a blister. Since part of the paint surface is irretrievably lost when a blister breaks, conservators must perform painstakingly the delicate operation of flattening blisters when they appear.

blister glaze a ceramic GLAZE that produces a broken blister effect, sometimes used for decorative purposes on modern wares. It is made by combining an ordinary glaze with grains of a material that will become gaseous under the heat of firing. Calcium or magnesium carbonates, calcium sulphate, and manganese dioxide are some of the materials used to create this effect. Accidental blistering is called SPIT-OUT.

block book a book in which the text and illustrations are entirely printed by WOOD ENGRAVINGS or WOODCUTS, made to actual reproduction size, one block to a page. In addition to copying by hand, this was a method of duplicating manuscripts before the invention of printing with movable type. Block books were especially popular in the 15th century in northern Europe, when woodcuts were used to print illustrated prayerbooks.

block-out stencil method a technique by which the nonprinting areas of the screen, in SILKSCREEN and SERIGRAPHY, are stopped out by brushing them with water-soluble glue, leaving the design open to the passage of paint to the printing surface. This simple process is used for bold and simple freehand designs in serigraphy, but is not suitable for work of any great degree of delicacy or intricacy, nor can it be used to print watercolours, since these would dissolve the glue. In variations of the block-out method, the nonprinting areas are stopped out with either shellac or lacquer, and a somewhat more complicated process involves spreading a glue sizing over the entire screen with a squeegee, brushing the nonprinting areas with shellac or lacquer, and finally washing out the glue in areas that are to be open and pervious to paint. In any of these processes the translucent glue may be tinted with a water-soluble colour, to make it more visible on the screen. When glue is used as the stopping-out medium, the process is sometimes called the *glue-cutout method*.

block print 1. an original print made from a single carved wooden block, that is, a WOODCUT or a WOOD ENGRAVING. See also BLOCK BOOK.

2. a textile printed from blocks rather than from a cylinder. The term 'hand-blocked' designates a textile that was printed by an individual artisan, who may also have carved the block.

block scraper a sculptor's tool for reducing the surface of plaster blocks or moulds. The usual model is a rectangular piece of thin steel $2\frac{1}{2}$ by 6 or 9 inches. Sometimes one or both of its long edges are finely serrated.

blond painting painting done in a high key, or high values, as distinguished from that done in deep, dark, or full-toned colours. The paintings of Botticelli can be called blond, but those of Rembrandt cannot.

bloom or **chill** a whitish, cloudy or foggy effect on the surface of a varnished oil painting. It may be caused by moisture condensation in the fresh varnish, or it may be an inherent defect of the varnish itself.

Bloomsbury group a group of 20th-century British artists, writers and intellectuals that had a great impact on the cultural life of the country, especially in the 1920s and 1930s. The artists Vanessa Bell (1879–1961), who was the sister of fellow member Virginia Woolf, Duncan Grant (1885–1978), and the art critics Roger Fry and Clive Bell, Vanessa's husband, were especially influential in their espousal of the merits of contemporary art. Their efforts went a long way towards creating a climate favourable to modern art in Britain.

blot drawing a type of art devised in the 18th century by English landscapist Alexander Cozens (1717–1786) in which an accidental blot or stain on a piece of paper is used to inspire the drawing of a purely imaginary landscape.

blown oil linseed oil that has been bleached and thickened to the consistency of honey by blowing air through it while it is being heated in an open kettle. It is the least costly and least desirable kind of thickened, or bodied, oil. Because it is already partially oxidized, blown oil has poor durability and on exposure to light eventually darkens even beyond the colour of the original raw oil.

blow-up an enlarged photographic copy, as of a smaller photograph or a piece of original art work, particularly graphics.

blue ashes see BREMEN BLUE.

blue bice see BREMEN BLUE.

blue black see IVORY BLACK.

blue frit see EGYPTIAN BLUE.

blue lake a reduced or let-down variety of PRUSSIAN BLUE. See REDUCED PIGMENT.

blue malachite see AZURITE.

blue pigments those blue pigments that are approved for use in oil paints in the United States by the ASTM and are acceptable in all other easel- and mural-painting techniques. They are listed below in order of their UNDERTONES, from purplish to greenish: ULTRAMARINE BLUE; COBALT BLUE; CERULEAN BLUE; MANGANESE BLUE; PHTHALOCYANINE BLUE and indanthrone blue.

Blue Rider see BLAUE REITER, DER.

Blue Rose a group of painters in Russia, active just before the 1905 revolution. They took refuge from the current oppressive environment in symbolism and fantasy, creating blue-shadowed impressionistic landscapes haunted by grotesque forms. Mistiness and nostalgia characterized their art, which cultivated a spirit of Oriental mysticism and detachment. Among the Blue Rose painters were Lancères, N. Sapanov and Konstantin Somov.

blue verditer see BREMEN BLUE.

blunger a mixing machine used to prepare clay SLIPS and glazes. One type, called a slow blunger, has a paddle that moves slowly over a long period of time. This action is more efficient for dissipating lumps than the action of the fast blunger, which has high-speed propellers that may cause splattering when lumpy clay is used.

blush clouding or opacification of a clear lacquer; it is the equivalent of BLOOM on varnished surfaces.

board 1. one of the two basic categories of paper; the other is simply called paper. Board, further subdivided into cardboard and paperboard, is generally stiffer, thicker, and heavier than paper. Cardboard includes thinner boards than paperboard, although each of these terms is sometimes used as a synonym for board in general. Boards may be laminated or solid. Surfaced with paper, cloth, or a ground, they are sometimes used as supports for drawing and painting. See ACADEMY BOARD; CANVAS BOARD; CHIPBOARD; COQUILLE BOARD; ILLUSTRATION BOARD; BRISTOL BOARD; ROSS BOARD.
2. see PANEL.

bodied linseed oil linseed oil that has been thickened by heat (as in the case of LITHO VARNISH, STAND OIL and BOILED OIL), by exposure to sunlight (SUN-REFINED OIL), or by oxidation (BLOWN OIL). Each variety of bodied oil has distinctive properties.

body 1. the viscosity of oils and varnishes. There is an optimum relationship between the thickness or viscosity of a coating material and its weight or specific gravity. An oil or varnish with high viscosity accompanied by an abnormally low specific gravity is said to have false body.
2. see CLAY BODY.

body art a style of conceptual art in which the body of the artist is literally the artist's medium. Related to the so-called happenings of the 1960s and of performance art, body art can embrace anything from so-called living sculptures to the infamous *Rubbing Piece*, by Vito Acconci, in which the artist rubbed his arm until he produced a sore.

body colour 1. opaque COLOUR EFFECTS as distinguished from transparent or glaze painting.
2. gouache as distinguished from transparent watercolour.
  The colour effects of a pastel painting or of solidly applied oil paint are visually different from those of a transparent watercolour or of a thin, transparent layer of oil paint (glazing) over an underpainting. When the opaque properties of a specific pigment or paint are discussed, the more technical term MASS TONE is used.

body stain 1. *(ceramics)* any colourant mixed into the CLAY BODY, as distinguished from colours applied in glazes, slips, underglaze, and overglaze (see CERAMIC COLOURS).

2. the pigments used in integrally coloured cement.

Bohemian earth one of the best commercial grades of GREEN EARTH.

Bohemian School the name given to a group of mostly anonymous 14th-century artists who were active during the reign of Charles IV of Bohemia. Centred in what is now Prague, in Czechoslovakia, the group is recognized for the beauty of its panel painting and fresco work.

boiled oil linseed oil that has been heated, usually with a liquid drier added. It is a house painters' material, not intended for artists' use. Raw oil to which driers have been added without heating is sometimes derisively called bunghole-boiled oil, as distinguished from kettle-boiled oil. Its use with oil colours is likely to lead to yellowing and other defects in the finished painting.

boîte (*Fr.* box) a container for an assemblage of an artist's work to be shown to clients, a sort of artist's sample case.

bold resin designation for the best commercial grade of any tree resin, consisting of clean lumps of the largest size in which the particular resin is marketed. Grades that are made up of small pieces, fragments and dust are less desirable, since they are likely to contain impurities or adulterants.

bole, Armenian bole or **poliment** a fine red earth colour of velvety smoothness, composed of clay and iron oxide and resembling the native red iron oxide pigments. Bole is used in water gilding as a ground and a GOLD SIZE.

Bologna chalk SLAKED PLASTER OF PARIS, an INERT PIGMENT.

Bologna stone see BARYTES.

bolting cloth a fine silk fabric of even weave made in a number of mesh sizes. It is used for sifting powdered materials such as pigments. It is also the basic textile used in the SILKSCREEN process, especially for serigraphy. The high tensile strength of the mesh is due to knots at each cross-weave; these knots also act as miniature suction cups when paint is applied to the screen with a SQUEEGEE. The best double-weight (the so-called XX quality) Swiss bolting cloth comes in 2- to 18-gauge mesh; 12 XX is the gauge and weight of the silk most used by serigraphers.

bond paper a strong, durable paper widely used for documents, letterhead and plain stationery, and typewriter paper. It has an immense range of quality; the best bond papers, which do not turn yellow or brittle with age, are made entirely of rag and have excellent writing, printing and erasing qualities. Many artists prefer the smooth finish of bond paper for sketchbooks and for pen drawing.

bone ash the ash of calcined bones, used as a body FLUX in ceramics, especially in English and Irish BONE CHINA. Animal bones, usually obtained from slaughterhouses, are burned to obtain calcium phosphate.

bone black or **animal black** an industrial pigment made by charring bones; it is a very impure form of carbon. Ordinary bone black is not recommended for use in paints or plaster, but a fine grade made for artists' use under the name IVORY BLACK is satisfactory and widely used.

bone brown a blackish-brown carbon pigment made like BONE BLACK; it is less completely carbonized than bone black and therefore even less desirable for use in permanent painting.

bone china a hard, white, translucent chinaware, made with a large amount of bone ash. The formula for bone china was perfected in England by Josiah Spode about 1800, and most of this chinaware is still produced chiefly in England and Ireland.

bone folder a thin, opaque white or ivory-coloured strip of plastic shaped like a doctor's tongue depressor, with smoothly rounded ends and edges. Originally made of bone and sold by stationers for folding paper, it is often recommended for rubbing monotypes and block prints. Any flexible blade that will not mark paper, such as a stainless-steel spatula, will serve this purpose.

bone white an obsolete INERT PIGMENT, made by burning bones to a white ash; it was formerly used on panels as a ground for drawing. Writing in the 15th century in *Il Libro dell' Arte*, Cennino Cennini said that 'the best bones are from the second joints and wings of fowls or capons; the older they are, the better; put them into the fire just as you find them under the table.'

bonyon see LAUREL sense 3.

book of hours a mediaeval book containing prayers appointed to be said at specified hours of the day. Books of hours were made in monastic workshops both for churches and for the private devotions of nobles and wealthy merchants. These books were richly illuminated. Surviving ones contain some of the finest examples of miniature painting.

bordering wax see WALLING WAX.

boss a raised ornament, in metalwork, furniture, architecture, etc., carved or chiselled from a protuberance left for that purpose in wood or stone or hammered out in metal by the REPOUSSÉ technique. It most frequently takes the form of a rosette but may also be of geometric or foliate design. Bosses are used as ornamental studs on doors – usually of metal and applied to the surface rather than carved out of it – and as decoration for hollow ware and for shields and other armour. In architecture, they are often used on ceilings, placed at the intersection of ribs in a vault or in the centre of coffers. Protective and/or ornamental studs on book covers are also known as bosses.

Botany Bay gum see ACCROIDES.

bottega the studio-shop of an Italian artist where a master (*maestro*) trains students and where apprentices or assistants contribute jointly with the master to the execution of works that will bear the master's signature. During the height of the Renaissance, there were 20 or 30 *botteghe* in Florence. Leonardo and Rubens maintained famous *botteghe*. See ATELIER.

bouchard see BUSHHAMMER.

Bougival white see BISMUTH WHITE.

boulle-work, boulle or **buhl** ornamental furniture inlaid with brass, tortoiseshell, and other materials, named after a French cabinetmaker, André Charles Boulle (1642–1732).

BOW COMPASS

bow compass see COMPASS.

boxwood a dense, hard wood (from trees of genus *Buxus*) of a pale creamy colour, with a fine, uniform texture. It is extremely difficult to carve. It is used to make blocks for wood engraving, inlay, and articles that must resist wear, such as architects' scales, slide rules, modelling tools, and musical instruments. Turkish boxwood (*Buxus balearica*) is the most desirable variety for engraving blocks. West Indian boxwood is second choice.

bozzetto see MAQUETTE.

BP *abbrev. for* BRITISH PHARMACOPOEIA.

brass 1. an alloy of copper and zinc, usually having two parts of copper to one part zinc; sometimes, small amounts of other metals are added. Brass usually has a bright golden or yellow colour, and is stronger and harder than copper. It is malleable and ductile, although its properties vary widely with its composition.
2. an incised brass plate, especially one done during the mediaeval and Renaissance periods as a memorial to the dead, usually showing a stylized portrait of the deceased. Brasses are found in churches throughout Britain and Europe. See also RUBBING.

brass rubbing see RUBBING.

brass sand see FOUNDRY SAND.

brass shim see SHIM.

bravura a display of brilliant, spirited brushwork.

brayer a hand roller for inking relief blocks (see RELIEF PRINTING). The most common brayers are rollers faced with rubber of varying degrees of firmness. A soft gelatin roller is sometimes used in special processes and procedures. It will cover irregular surfaces, as in relief block printing, depositing ink on slightly depressed printing areas that the firmer rubber-faced brayer might ride over. In abstract and experimental art, brayers are sometimes used to lay paint and ink in large areas, both of solid colour and of gradated tones (see BLENDING). Paint works well with a rubber brayer, but ink used in direct printing is much more effectively spread to a smooth, uniform texture with a gelatin brayer. In printing colour woodcuts (see COLOUR PRINT), direct printing with the roller obviates cutting a separate colour block for an area that is to print an overall colour or a solid blended tone, such as a sky. Because a gelatin brayer is highly impressionable and its shape is easily distorted if it is left lying on a surface for any length of time, it must be hung on a hook

brayer

when not in use. A modern version of the soft brayer is made of synthetic material, but the original gelatin brayer is still preferred.

Brazilian mahogany see MAHOGANY.

Brazilian rosewood see ROSEWOOD.

Brazilian satinwood see SATINWOOD.

Brazilian walnut see IMBUYA.

Brazil wax see CARNAUBA WAX.

Brazilwood lake a LAKE pigment made from Brazilwood, a blood-red NATURAL DYESTUFF introduced into Europe from Central America in the 16th century. For centuries an article of commercial importance, Brazilwood has been used as a pigment, and it is still employed in some trades, for which its low cost makes it preferable to better colours, despite its lack of permanence. The lake called rose pink is made from Brazilwood.

brazing a type of WELDING using nonferrous metals that melt at lower temperatures than that of the base metal. It is usually done by applying a brass FILLER ROD made of 60% copper and 40% zinc to the joint. The brass melts and is deposited on the base metal, where it may hold two pieces of metal together. Sometimes a bronze rod is used. Brazing produces weaker joints than are produced by FUSION welding. The process may be used to cover a metal surface with metals of different colour and texture, and may be varied by using alloys of different metals.

breccia a marble or other stone in which angular fragments are embedded. The surrounding stone or matrix may or may not be of the same composition as the fragments. One kind of breccia marble is SARRANCOLIN MARBLE.

Bremen blue, blue ashes, blue bice, blue verditer or **copper blue** precipitated, hydrated copper carbonate; an azure-blue pigment. Probably originating in the 18th century, Bremen blue was widely used in the 19th century, becoming of less importance during the 20th century as the more satisfactory, nontoxic ultramarine blue became cheaper. The copper carbonate-hydroxide blues and greens are toxic and are not sufficiently permanent for use in creative painting. Copper blues comparable to Bremen blue were used extensively in mediaeval painting; in the early 19th century they began to be produced in standard grades by European manufacturers. LIME BLUE and *Neuwied blue* are varieties of Bremen blue. Variants of Bremen blue and lime blue were also sold in the 19th century under the name MOUNTAIN BLUE.

Bremen green, green bice or **green verditer** a pale green variant of BREMEN BLUE, produced in a range of hues of varying degrees of greenishness. VERNET GREEN (or Horace Vernet green) is a variety of Bremen green. Unstandardized terms for Bremen green in the United States include *mountain green, mineral green* and *oil green*.

brick liner see LINERS AND STRIPERS.

brick red see LIGHT RED.

bridge an elevated handrest used to keep the artist's hands from touching the surface of a drawing or painting being done on a drawing board or a lithograph stone; it also steadies the artist's hand. A type of bridge made of a narrow strip of wood with end-pieces raising it an inch or so above the surface is commercially available; artists frequently make their own version of this type.

bright a type of brush used in oil painting, named after an Englishman who is said to have invented it. The bright, in either bristle or red sable, is a flat, thin brush with a straight, sharp end; the length of the tip is $1\frac{1}{2}$ times its width. The bristle bright is popular for manipulating very SHORT paints. See BRUSH, BRISTLE.

bringing up *(etching and engraving)* a process in which excess ink is removed from the unetched surface of a plate in progressive amounts in order to bring greater definition to etched or engraved lines.

brilliant scarlet another name for IODINE SCARLET.

brilliant yellow another name for NAPLES YELLOW.

bristle brush see BRUSH, BRISTLE.

Bristol board a stiff, durable cardboard made in thicknesses of from one to four .006-inch plies, and in several smooth finishes, especially a high or plate finish. Suitable for drawing and for painting with any water paint, Bristol board may be used on both sides, and is especially popular for lettering and clear, sharp ink drawings and diagrams.

Bristol glaze a type of porcelain glaze containing feldspar and a rather large amount of zinc oxide. It is fired at high temperature and used for finishes that show another colour coming through in spots from below.

britannia metal a high-quality PEWTER developed during the last half of the 18th century in England. The best grade of britannia metal is an alloy of 90% tin with 10% antimony. More commonly, however, the proportions are 94% tin, 5% antimony, and 1% copper; the addition of the copper gives the alloy a yellowish tinge, and the higher percentage of tin makes the alloy somewhat softer. Britannia metal was the only kind of pewter used to any extent after 1825. It can be electroplated with silver and was used widely in this way from the mid-19th century on. Wares made of silver-plated britannia metal are often stamped *quadruple plate* in the United States.

British gum a grade of DEXTRIN used as a paper adhesive and in the manufacture of gouache, watercolour, and other aqueous paints.

British Pharmacopoeia (BP) the British standard for chemicals or drugs. The initials BP indicate that the material meets the standards of purity and potency of the British Pharmacopoeia and is suitable for pharmaceutical use. BP grades are not necessarily chemically pure (see CP). In the United States the initials USP, for United States Pharmacopoeia, are used in a similar fashion.

British pigment standard the popular name for the *British Standard Specification for Artists' Use*, B.S. 2876: 1957, a pamphlet issued by the British Standards Institution, listing standard terms for pigments. This standard is no longer current and a new one has not been issued. A few of the permanent pigment names in BS 2876 differ from those listed in the United States PAINT STANDARD. Because the British pigment standard deals only with pigments, without reference to qualitative paint standards, it includes the names of some two dozen pigments that do not appear in the more selective American list, which is confined to those approved there for fine-arts purposes.

broad manner and **fine manner** a classification devised in 15th-century Italy to distinguish between two widely diverse effects created in the newly invented art of line ENGRAVING. The term *fine manner* applies to engravings done with fine, close lines and light crosshatching, while *broad manner* describes prints in which the lines are broad, coarse and bold. The distinction is comparable to the differences between a pen-and-ink drawing done with a fine crow-quill pen and a sketch made with a blunt-nibbed pen. The same distinction naturally applies to the effects created in NIELLO work, since it was from techniques of niello and CHASING that 15th-century goldsmiths derived the process of line engraving.

broken colour 1. colours in painting applied as an OPTICAL MIXTURE instead of being thoroughly mixed on the palette.
2. (also called **broken tone**) a colour whose brilliance has been dulled or toned down by addition of its complementary colour. Broken tones tend to be muddy, but they are frequently used to fit a colour scheme or to remedy a raw or garish effect.

bronze an ALLOY of copper and tin, sometimes containing small proportions of other elements, such as zinc and phosphorus. It is stronger, harder and more durable than brass, and, since antiquity, has been the metal used most extensively in cast sculpture. Bronze alloys vary in colour from a silvery hue to a rich, coppery red.

bronze blue another name for PRUSSIAN BLUE, especially those varieties that have a pronounced bronzy sheen.

bronze disease a malignant corrosion of bronze that has a progressively destructive effect on the metal, as opposed to a normal PATINA, which has a protective effect. Bronze disease is generally attributed to the corrosive effect of chlorides on the metal; chlorides are therefore avoided in the chemical processes used to induce a patina on new bronze.

bronze doré gilded bronze (see ORMOLU).

bronze leaf see DUTCH METAL.

bronze powder powder made from various bronze or brass alloys and used principally in lacquer or varnish vehicles, or with BRONZING LIQUID as the so-called GOLD PAINT. This powder can be prepared to duplicate every shade of gold, from a pale or lemon colour to a deep coppery hue; sometimes, dyes are added to the paint mixture. Bronze powders darken or discolour after a relatively short time. Because they are not permanent and because the paint made from them has a lacklustre, grainy quality, bronze powders are seldom used in the fine arts.

bronzing 1. the painting of plaster casts to imitate the colour or PATINA of bronze. VERT ANTIQUE is the finish usually applied to achieve the effect of patinated bronze.
2. see BRAZING.

bronzing liquid a BANANA OIL vehicle in which ALUMINIUM POWDER or

BRONZE POWDER is mixed to make metallic paint. Although ready-mixed metallic paints are available, it is preferable to mix bronze powders with the bronzing liquid only as the paint is needed, since the vehicle has a tendency to oxidize and therefore discolour the metal.

brown coat or *(It.)* **arriccio** the second of the layers of plaster that make up the support for a FRESCO; it usually consists of two and a half parts of sand or marble dust to one part of LIME PUTTY. Before the brown coat is applied, the first (or SCRATCH COAT) must be completely set and dry, and then freshly soaked with water. Sometimes the brown coat is applied in two layers. The first, called a *skim coat*, is diluted with water and laid thinly. Over this, a standard brown coat can be applied more thickly; it will then hold its moisture longer and be less prone to develop mechanical faults as it sets. See also INTONACO; SAND COAT.

brown ebony see COFFEEWOOD.

brown lampblack an obscure name for BISTRE.

brown ochre a dark, dull variety of YELLOW OCHRE.

brown pigments *(US)* the brown pigments approved for use in oil paints in the United States by ASTM and generally acceptable in all other easel-painting techniques. They include RAW UMBER, BURNT UMBER, BURNT SIENNA and RAW SIENNA.

brown pink, buckthorn pink, Dutch pink or **stil-de-grain** a transparent, golden-yellow LAKE pigment made from dried, half-ripe BUCKTHORN BERRIES. Although not sufficiently lightfast for use as an artists' pigment, brown pink has been popular since the 16th century as a decorators' colour, and has survived to some small extent into the 20th century.

brown sauce a derisive term applied by early 20th-century painters to the recently passed academic trend of infusing painting with an all-pervading brownness; see GALLERY TONE.

brownstone *(US)* an American SANDSTONE that contains iron. It is available in several shades, from pinkish to deep chocolate-brown. Connecticut, New Jersey, and Pennsylvania brownstones are well known.

Brücke, die *(Ger.* The Bridge) a group of expressionist artists, founded in Dresden in 1905 by Erich Heckel (1883–1970), Ernst Ludwig Kirchner (1880–1938), and Karl Schmidt-Rottluff (1884–1976). Later adherents were Axel Gallén (1865–1931), Emil Nolde (1867–1956), Max Pechstein (1881–1955), and Otto Mueller (1873–1930). These artists practised a representational form of EXPRESSIONISM, and were strongly influenced by Van Gogh, Gauguin, Munch, and the FAUVES. A contemporary vogue for the primitive and the exotic also had its influence on them. Before the group disbanded in 1913, it had introduced modern art to Germany and contributed to a revival of interest in the graphic arts. Its representational tendencies ran counter to those of a later expressionist group, the BLAUE REITER.

Bruges school those Flemish painters working in Bruges during the 15th century. First and most outstanding of these painters were Jan and Hubert van Eyck, who have often been called the founders of the entire Flemish school. The Bruges group introduced into religious painting, partly from the art of the miniature, a loving attention to detail in the physical surroundings of their subjects. The painter Petrus Christus continued the aristocratic style of the van Eycks, while the work of Hans Memling and Gheeraert David appealed more to the bourgeois patrons of Bruges.

bruising see STUN.

Brunswick blue a variety of PRUSSIAN BLUE containing relatively large amounts of added barytes and sometimes small amounts of French ultramarine; it is not used in high-quality industrial paints or in artists' colours.

Brunswick green or **Prussian green** an inexpensive variety of CHROME GREEN made from Brunswick blue and a reduced grade of chrome yellow.

brush a tool used to apply paint to a surface. It consists of a gather of animal hairs or bristles set in a plastic compound, held in a metal ferrule to which a wooden handle is attached. The most highly prized variety of hair (see BRUSH, HAIR) is red sable (see BRUSH, RED SABLE); differently shaped brushes are used for oil and watercolour painting. The bristle brush (see BRUSH, BRISTLE) is used for oil painting. Acrylic and nylon fibres are used to make brushes for use with acrylic and polymer paints (see BRUSH, ACRYLIC).

Standards for the quality, design, and behaviour of artists' brushes have been established over centuries of experience. Although inferior grades are common, those of top quality reflect the age-old striving for perfection, through the selection of materials from sources throughout the world and attention to manufacturing details. Today brushes are among the few remaining mass-produced items that are the products of a handicraft industry, with all significant operations being carried on by skilled workers.

When an artist's brush is made, the natural tips of the hairs or bristles (see FLAG) are always preserved. The various shapes – pointed or blunt, flat or round – are produced by cutting, trimming, and fashioning the

brushes Bristle brushes for oil colour. Left to right, round, flat, bright, filbert.

root, or butt, ends of the hairs. A pointed brush, for example, is shaped by inserting a measured amount of hair or bristle, tips down, in a small, hollow, brass *cannon* of the size and shape desired, tapping the cannon so the hairs settle into it, and trimming them off at the root end. They are then tied and set into a metal ferrule with a thermoplastic cement, and attached to a handle of appropriate size and shape for the specialized purpose of the brush. Some fine brushes have a considerable hold of bristle or hair within the metal ferrule, in some cases to a depth equal to the length of the exposed tip; in others, the hold is very shallow. See also BLENDER; CAMEL HAIR; FITCH; LINERS AND STRIPERS; OX HAIR; SINGLE-STROKE BRUSH.

brush, acrylic any of variously shaped brushes made with nylon or acrylic fibres and designed especially for use with acrylic and polymer artists' paints. Because these colours dry very quickly, paint-laden brushes that are shortly to be reused are kept in water. Acrylic and nylon brushes, unlike those made with hair and natural bristle, are not affected by prolonged soaking. They hold a heavy charge of paint and are easily cleaned with cold water when the paint is fresh, and with hot water when the paint has hardened. Other types of brushes may, of course, be used with acrylic and polymer paints.

brush, bristle the standard brush for oil painting, made of selected hog bristles. The most common bristle brushes, categorized by shape, are rounds, flats, brights, and filberts or ovals. All come in sizes numbered from 0 to 12; a number of special extra-wide or extra-long brushes are usually available. The length of the bristles in a flat brush is $2\frac{1}{2}$ times the width. The bristles of the best brushes are curved, and in the flats they are set so that the outer bristles curve inward; the bristles therefore retain an even width when stroked on a surface, rather than splaying outward like a broom. Brights, which are also flat in shape, are stubbier, thinner and stiffer. Prior to about 1860, round brushes were used almost exclusively; flats and brights, which most present-day painters find more versatile, have been popular for about a century. Manufacturers recently have combined synthetic fibres with bristle brushes to reduce costs and to add to their versatility. Brushes such as these may be used either in oil or acrylic mediums, though they may not perform as well as a brush designed for a particular medium.

brush, hair any brush made of flexible animal hair rather than stiff bristle. The finest hair brushes are made of red sable (see BRUSH, RED SABLE). Second-quality brushes may either have less red sable gripped within the ferrule or be a mixture of red sable and some less expensive hair, such as ox hair. Russian sable, which is dark grey rather than reddish but otherwise resembles red sable, is also used in second-best hair brushes. Fitch and badger hair, as well as dark squirrel (known as camelhair), are also popular, although camelhair is rather soft and floppy, so that it may be used only for certain special effects. Ox hair, on the other hand, is a little more rigid and springy than red sable and most other hairs used for artists' brushes.

brush, quill any artists' sable or badger hair brush in which the hair is mounted in the tapered end of a quill, formerly from birds, now plastic, instead of the customary metal ferrule. A plain wooden handle that fits snugly into the open end of the quill is supplied, but quill brushes are sometimes used without handles. Quill brushes, which have been in use since mediaeval times, were supplanted for general use by those made with metal ferrules and permanently attached handles about the beginning of the 19th century. They are still made, however, particularly as lettering brushes, and are preferred by some artists because quill does not break the hairs, as the edge of a metal ferrule sometimes does, and because of their lower cost. A flat piece of split quill wrapped around the hairs and fastened with twisted wire replaces the metal ferrule in the BADGER BLENDER which, because of the pouncing motion with which it is used, would be particularly susceptible to having its hairs cut by a metal ferrule. A fine red sable watercolour brush in a quill is convenient for pocket-size watercolour boxes, in which the separated brush and handle can be carried. See also LETTERING QUILL; see illustration at LINERS AND STRIPERS.

brush, red sable the finest brush for watercolour, tempera and other aqueous paints, as well as for smooth oil painting. The hair is valued for its unsurpassed combination of firmness and resiliency, for its fine points, and for its shape. Each hair has a bulge, or belly, between its root end and its tapering point. The shape of the brush – and therefore, the effects that may be obtained with it – is determined by the point at which the ferrule grips the hair, that is, above, below, or at the belly. The best round watercolour brushes are convex and tapered, with a pronounced belly about midway between the ferrule and the sharply pointed tip. Any concavity is detrimental to proper control. The single-stroke brush, for lettering and watercolour painting, is also made of red sable. Red sable oil brushes are used to achieve smoother or more precise stroking than can be executed with the usual bristle brush. The round oil brush is tapered from ferrule to tip, without a belly. Long-handled red sable flats, brights and longs are also made for oil painting. The finest red sable brushes are graded as 'pure red sable' or 'finest quality red sable.' The second-quality brushes, known simply as 'red sable,' contain some ox hair.

brush cleaner or **brush washer** a receptacle for turpentine or other solvent used to clean paintbrushes. A typical modern washer for watercolour brushes, like that shown in the illustration, is a glass jar or metal cup with an overhead spiral holder in which the brush handles are clipped to keep the brushes suspended in the solvent. The standard oil-brush cleaner is a deep aluminium container into which is inserted a shallower container with a perforated bottom or a wire mesh on which brushes can be lightly scrubbed. The pigment settles through the bottom of the inner container, leaving the upper portion of the solvent clear. Soldered across the opening of the inner container is a wire or thin bar on which the brush may be scraped. Oil-brush cleaners for use with proprietary solvents are also

brush cleaners (left) A watercolour brush cleaner; (right) a two-part cleaner for oil brushes.

sold. The container is a covered glass jar with a heavy scraping coil near the bottom of the jar.

bubinga or **African rosewood** a hard, durable wood (from the tree *Guibourtia tessmanii*) from West Africa, known as African rosewood because it is striped with pink or red. It is not related to the woods of the genus *Dalbergia*, which are also known as rosewood. Bubinga is used chiefly for veneer.

bucchero ware a black pottery made by the Etruscans before they learned about black glaze from the Greeks. It was made with an iron-rich clay that was fired in a comparatively low reduction fire.

buckeye a term of disparagement for a type of oil painting, mostly landscapes, turned out for the American mass market and characterized by slipshod yet facile rendition, and stereotyped, flamboyant or sentimental treatment of subject matter. The heyday of the buckeye was the second half of the 19th century, but production of such paintings has never really ceased.

buckling 1. the appearance of waves or bulges in a canvas that has slackened on its stretcher, or in paper that is supposed to be flat.

2. the appearance of a raised wave, ridge or bulge in a paint surface, due to cleavage between the ground and the support. A buckled area is a kind of continuous BLISTER.

buckthorn berries, Avignon berries, French berries, Persian berries or **yellow berries** the dried, half-ripe, pea-sized, greenish-brown berries obtained from various species of *Rhamnus*, a shrub grown in Europe and in Asiatic Turkey. Buckthorn berries are boiled to make a dye that was once extensively used in making the yellow lake-pigment BROWN PINK. Completely unripe berries were similarly used in making sap green.

buckthorn lake see BROWN PINK.

bucranium the decorative sculptured ornament of an ox skull, usually adorned with flowers and found on classical architecture.

buhl see BOULLE-WORK.

building board see WALLBOARD.

bull point see POINT.

buon fresco true FRESCO, that is, painting in which colour is applied to freshly laid plaster, as distinguished from SECCO or other mural techniques that imitate the effects of fresco.

Burgundy pitch see BURGUNDY TURPENTINE.

Burgundy turpentine the oleoresin or BALSAM obtained from *Pinus maritinus*, the European pine tree that is the source of the French turpentine and rosin industry. A somewhat refined and partially solidified grade of Burgundy turpentine, known as Burgundy pitch, is frequently called for in antiquated recipes. In practical use, neither of these products has any advantage over the more easily available VENICE TURPENTINE.

Burgundy violet see MANGANESE VIOLET.

burin see GRAVER.

burl wood cut from the swellings or knobs that grow on some trees. Burl planks and veneers exhibit a swirling or irregularly mottled grain of attractive appearance.

burnisher an implement with a hard, smooth, rounded end or surface, used for smoothing and polishing. In GILDING, burnishers are usually small forms of polished agate mounted in wooden handles. They are available in a number of sizes and shapes and are quite expensive. The 15th-century artist-writer Cennino Cennini recommended burnishing with a dog's tooth or with haematite. A flat broad burnisher of haematite is still sometimes used for flat gilding, especially on book edges. The ceramic artist uses a burnisher of spun glass to give a bright tone to gilding on china or porcelain.

Because burnishing is a smoothing process, it can be used only for leaf that has been laid on a gesso or bole ground with WATER GILDING. Stroking the gilded surface with a burnisher smooths the gesso surface, and the malleable gold leaf, being pressed to this perfectly even surface, takes on a high, specular gloss. Gilding done with gold ink (see GOLD POWDER) in illuminated manuscripts can also be burnished if the paper or parchment has first been prepared with a thin gesso-like wash. Special techniques are required to burnish gilding. The ground must be thoroughly dry, or the burnisher will rip the surface. The practised gilder can determine when the work is sufficiently dry by listening to the sound made by tapping the gilded surface with the burnisher. Usually, the surface is first burnished with gentle circular strokes and then gone over with firmer strokes in a uniform direction. MORDANT GILDING on sized or shellacked gesso or other nonporous surfaces cannot be burnished.

In etching and other metal-plate printmaking techniques, a smooth,

burnisher (above) Two steel burnishers, used in etching and other metal-plate printmaking techniques. (below) An agate burnisher, used in gilding.

rounded, polished steel burnisher is used to remove scratches and unwanted marks and to take down over-heavy areas to reduce the darkness of their printing (see REPOUSSAGE). A steel burnisher was also sometimes used to burnish SHEFFIELD PLATE.

burnt carmine a deep brownish-purple or purplish-brown pigment made by carefully roasting or charring CARMINE.

burnt green earth see TRANSPARENT BROWN.

burnt gypsum GYPSUM from which all the water of crystallization has been driven off, as distinguished from PLASTER OF PARIS. It is used in KEENE CEMENT and other plasters where hardness and resistance to wear are required.

burnt ochre RED OCHRE made by calcining selected grades of yellow ochre.

burnt-oil varnish, plate oil or *(US)* **litho varnish** a heat-BODIED LINSEED OIL that is the vehicle in LITHOGRAPH INK and, usually, in other PRINTING INKS. Depending on the duration of heating, burnt-oil varnishes acquire varying degrees of viscosity and are sold in light, medium, and heavy grades. At the end of heating, the linseed oil is set afire and allowed to burn for a limited time. Like stand oils, which they resemble, burnt-oil varnishes are polymerized and, depending on their degree of polymerization, acquire distinctive properties. For this reason, more than one type of burnt-oil varnish is often called for in formulas for altering the degree of oiliness or tackiness of ready-made printing inks.

burnt sienna an EARTH COLOUR with an opaque, red-brown mass tone, displaying a bright, transparent, orangy undertone when viewed by transmitted light, and yielding salmon-coloured or peach-coloured tints when mixed with white. Made by calcining raw sienna, burnt sienna is one of the most versatile of the permanent pigments. It is employed in all painting techniques, and is especially useful in mixtures of dark colours because of its clarity and freedom from chalkiness. The most desirable grades of burnt sienna have a deep, mahogany mass tone; those of paler appearance are less highly esteemed. Both raw and burnt sienna are named after the Tuscan city of Siena, and the finest varieties are still imported from Italy. An old name for both raw and burnt sienna is *Italian earth*. Burnt sienna or alizarin crimson were formerly mixed with sepia to make Roman sepia.

burnt umber see UMBER.

burr or **ridge** the ragged edge of the furrows cut by the needle, or burin, in the surface of a metal plate in DRYPOINT and ENGRAVING. In drypoint, the burr is preserved to produce the soft, blurred line characteristic of that technique. In engraving, where a clean, sharp line is desired, any burrs are removed with a SCRAPER.

bushhammer or **bouchard** a stone-carving tool, usually with a chunky, brick-shaped head, that has two striking ends, each covered with rows of pyramidal metal teeth or points. It comes in several sizes, and may have a long, slender head rather than a chunky one. The bushhammer is used to dress the surface of a stone by pulverizing the rock and removing it little by little. It is also used for rough shaping of sculpture in hard stone.

bushhammer

bust 1. *(sculpture)* a portrait that includes the head, neck, and part of the shoulders and breast, usually mounted on a base or column.
2. *(painting)* a portrait that shows the same portion of the figure, including the upper arms.
bust peg a heavy, flat board with a vertical post in its centre, on which sculpture, especially a BUST, is modelled.
butterfly 1. *(sculpture)* a cross-shaped piece of wood hung within an open ARMATURE to prevent the slipping or sagging of a heavy plastic mass. Small wedges of wood may be wired to the armature at intervals to perform the same function.
2. the prop bar in the SILK-SCREEN apparatus.
butternut see WALNUT.
butt join a join made without any overlapping of the two parts. The several sections of a large mural canvas are laid with such a join. See MAROUFLAGE.
button see TREFLED CROSS.
button lac see LAC.
butyl lactate a VOLATILE SOLVENT or diluent used in lacquers and other industrial coating materials as a retardant, to delay setting or drying. It has an extremely low rate of evaporation, and artists have used it occasionally to delay the setting of paint for several days.
Byzantine pertaining to the art and civilization of the Christian empire that succeeded the Roman Empire in the East. The Byzantine period lasted from AD 330, when Constantinople (ancient Byzantium) became the capital of the empire, to the mid-15th century, when the Turks conquered Constantinople. Byzantine styles in art and architecture survived for some time in the Balkans and for another two centuries in Russia.

Byzantine art was predominantly religious. Churches were decorated with mosaic, fresco, and stone carvings. The churches of Ravenna, in Italy, seat of the Roman emperors from AD 404 and an appanage of the Byzantine Empire from 534 to 752, that were decorated with a monumental series of mosaics, may still be seen. During the Iconoclastic Controversy (726–824), a richly decorative art based on plant and geometric motifs developed. Subsequently, icons and other figurative work were based on a system of iconography that was strictly regulated by the Church. Human forms were stylized, subject matter was restricted to certain events in the history of Christianity, and even the positions of the various characters in a scene were prescribed. This uniformity applied not only to wall decoration but also to icons, which were painted on panels in a rudimentary tempera technique. Although relief was the only form of Byzantine monumental sculpture, carved ivory was common and attained a high degree of elaboration, as did metalwork, work in enamel, and illumination. The distinctive Byzantine style of architecture is an amalgam of Hellenistic and Oriental elements with the basic Roman styles; lavish surface enrichment takes the place of Classical boldness of form. This architecture attained a characteristic style about the middle of the 5th century in Constantinople and Italy, with later development in other lands.

Byzantium purple bluish shades of TYRIAN PURPLE.

C

cabinet picture a small easel painting, usually no wider than 30 inches, meant to be viewed at close range and which is therefore suitable for hanging in a small room.

cabochon 1. a convex or dome-shaped gem.

2. a convex or dome-shaped element in a design in wood or stone carving.

cachet a monogram or cipher of original design, used in lieu of a signature. A good cachet has simplicity, treats the letter forms inventively, and sometimes cleverly takes or suggests the shape of an object or animal.

cachou see CATECHU.

cadmium green or *(US)* **permanent green** an artists' colour made of a mixture of cadmium yellow and viridian.

cadmium red and **cadmium yellow** cadmium yellows are cadmium sulphide; cadmium reds are composed of cadmium sulphide and cadmium selenide in various proportions. All are dense, opaque, brilliant, and reliably permanent pigments. Cadmium yellows, the principal bright yellows of the artist, are available in pale and light (lemon) shades, medium and deep (golden) shades, and orange. The cadmium reds come in light (replacing the older, less reliable vermilion), medium, and deep (maroon) shades. Cadmium red was introduced in Germany by de Haen in 1907. Variations in hue between different brands of tube colours offer artists a choice of several nuances of the yellows and reds.

Both cadmium reds and cadmium yellows are available in either a pure grade or a cadmium-barium type, which contains barium sulphate as an integral component of the pigment. The cadmium-barium type is just as permanent, but is less powerful in tinting strength than the pure cadmium. The cadmium-barium type is used in most artists' colours; the more expensive pure cadmiums are used only in some of the top-grade lines.

Cadmium yellow was discovered in Germany by Friedrich Strohmeyer in 1817, but came into use slowly because of the initial scarcity of the metal. Made in England in 1846, it apparently did not appear there as an artists' colour until 1851. It begins to appear in artists' supply catalogues in New York as early as 1842. Artists are known to have used cadmium yellow in Germany in 1829 and in France about 1832, perhaps obtaining the pigment from experimental sources.

Caen stone a cream-coloured French LIMESTONE. It is soft, fine-grained, and easily carved.

caeruleum (*Lat.* sky-blue pigment) a pigment mainly used for EGYPTIAN BLUE. See also CERULEAN BLUE.

CALAMANDER EBONY

Calamander ebony see EBONY.

calcareous tufa see TUFA.

calcine to roast at high temperatures in a furnace. The end product of this process is usually a fine powder. Calcining is done to change the hue of an earth pigment, or to alter the properties of an inorganic or mineral substance by driving off some or all of its water of crystallization. In ceramics, clays and certain glaze ingredients are sometimes heated to red heat, to drive off volatile matter and to reduce subsequent shrinkage.

calcined magnesite one of the materials from which OXYCHLORIDE CEMENT is prepared. It is made by roasting magnesite (native magnesium carbonate) until about 90% of it is converted to magnesium oxide. Completely calcined or 'dead-burned' magnesite is all magnesia, and will not react to form oxychloride cement.

Caledonian brown a native earth somewhat similar in hue to burnt sienna, but vastly inferior as a paint pigment.

Caledonian white lead chlorosulphide, introduced in the 19th century, and now obsolete, as a paint pigment.

calendering the process of giving paper a smooth surface by running it between rollers under strong pressure. Supercalendering produces a polished surface.

calfskin glue a hide glue of high quality.

California asphalt a soft variety of ASPHALT.

California walnut see WALNUT.

calipers a measuring device with two moveable jaws. Sculptors' calipers were originally made of wood with brass fittings; the modern type is made of aluminium. They are regularly used to take the measurements of figures in the round during the course of work, and are also useful in making copies of an original. Several sizes are available for use according to the magnitude of the work. See PROPORTIONAL CALIPERS.

calipers (left) Proportional calipers;
(right) sculptors' calipers.

calking see TRACING.

calligraphic 1. pertaining to CALLIGRAPHY.

2. *(handwriting)* elaborate or ornate in design and execution.

3. *(painting and drawing)* free and rhythmic, with expressive brushstrokes or lines that have the variety and flexibility of beautiful handwriting.

4. *(pictorial arts)* design elements resembling or reminiscent of cursive letter forms.

calligraphy handwriting as art; elegant penmanship that has aesthetic value apart from its textual content. It may sacrifice legibility somewhat for the sake of decoration and design. Three important writing 'hands' or 'scripts,' as they are also called, were evolved between the 12th and 15th centuries. All three – the GOTHIC, the ROMAN, and the ITALIC – are to some extent still used today and have also been adopted as typefaces (see TYPOGRAPHY). The chief tool of calligraphy is the LETTERING PEN, although much of the beautiful lettering in mediaeval manuscripts was done with reed or quill pens or with a fine brush. See also ILLUMINATION.

Calvary cross a LATIN CROSS on a stepped platform. The three steps of the base, representing the hill of Calvary, and sometimes replaced by a conventionalized mountain, have occasionally been said to symbolize the Christian virtues of faith, hope and charity. See CROSS for illustration.

camaïeu 1. a painting or decoration executed in several shades of a single colour; a monochrome painting. When done in various shades of grey, it may also be called GRISAILLE; when in yellow, *cirage*. Friezes and wall decorations that imitate bas-relief are frequently done in camaïeu, in the manner of cameos.
2. a painting in two or three tints, in which the objects represented are not rendered in their natural hues.

Camden Town Group an early 20th-century group of British painters, of whom Walter Sickert (1878–1961) is perhaps best known. The paintings of the widely varied group, whose members shared a dislike for the formality of the Royal Academy, are characterized by realism, everyday subject matter and a tendency towards bold, flat colours. The Camden Town Group's work is considered a precursor of modern British art.

came or **calm** a strip of lead used in stained-glass windows. A came is thin and flat, with grooves in both sides, into which are fitted the pieces of glass to be joined. In well-designed windows the pattern formed by the cames is an integral part of the design of the entire window.

camelhair a fine hair used for brushes. Despite its name, it comes from the tail of a squirrel. The camelhair brush, used for watercolour and other aqueous paints, is relatively soft and floppy. See BRUSH, HAIR.

cameo a precious or semiprecious stone, a shell, paste, or glass carved so that there is a raised design on a background, which is usually of a different colour.

camera lucida (*Lat.* light chamber) an optical contrivance for projecting the virtual image of an object or a scene on a surface so that it can be traced. Because the device makes it possible to reproduce, enlarge or reduce the subject accurately, the camera lucida has been extensively used, especially by commercial artists. It consists essentially of a stand with an adjustable arm, at the end of which is a prism. Light from the object is deflected by the prism, and a virtual image is interposed between the eye and the drawing surface, allowing the object to be traced. By adjusting the distances between the subject, the prism, and the drawing surface, or by placing a convex or concave lens between the viewer and the prism, or between the prism and the surface, the user can vary the size of the projected image. The camera lucida was invented about 1674 by Richard Hooke but was not widely used until after 1807, when it was redesigned and patented by William Hyde Wollaston. It largely replaced the CAMERA OBSCURA and has in turn been supplanted by the OPAQUE PROJECTOR and more elaborate optical devices.

camera obscura (*Lat.* dark chamber) an optical contrivance for projecting the image of an object or scene on a surface, from which it is traced and thus is more accurately reproduced than by being drawn freehand. It is essentially a box with a small aperture in which a double convex lens is fitted. Light is transmitted through the lens, and the image is projected, usually by a mirror, onto a surface of ground glass or translucent paper, from which it is easily traced. The camera obscura was often a portable box – either homemade or, in the 17th and 18th centuries, bought from an instrument maker – or a closet-like chamber in which the artist sat. An entire room has also been used as a camera obscura, into which an outdoor scene is projected by a periscope-like apparatus. There is a notable camera obscura in Edinburgh.

The invention of the camera obscura is variously attributed to Leone Battista Alberti (1404–1472) and to Erasmus Reinhold of Wittenberg (1511–1553). It was in both principle and name the forerunner of the modern camera. For practical purposes, the portable camera obscura has long been supplanted by the CAMERA LUCIDA and by 20th-century large-screen developments (see OPAQUE PROJECTOR).

Campan marble see GRIOTTE.

campeachy lake a red LAKE pigment made from LOGWOOD.

campeachy wood see LOGWOOD.

camphorwood the wood of the camphor tree (*Cinnamomum camphora*), a scented hardwood imported from Formosa and Borneo. It may be used for carving.

camwood see BARWOOD.

Canada balsam the thick, resinous exudation from *Abies balsamea*, the balsam fir of the eastern United States and Canada. The tree is similar to some of the firs of middle Europe that produce BALSAMS or oleoresins, such as Strasbourg turpentine and Venice turpentine, used by artists for centuries as ingredients in oil painting mediums. Canada balsam has not been used as a substitute for these, perhaps because of the high cost involved, although it has been used as an adhesive in the optical, cigar, and other industries.

canalete or **canaletta** a hard, dense wood, suitable for carving, from the tree *Cordia gerascanthus*, native to the West Indies. It has black streaks with a metallic lustre, and its heartwood is purplish lilac.

canarywood see BALAUSTRE.

cancellation see ORIGINAL PRINT.

candelilla wax a brown vegetable wax obtained from a weed native to Texas and Mexico. It is next to CARNAUBA WAX in hardness, with a melting range of 67 to 71 °C. Like carnauba wax, it is used to impart hardness to mixtures of waxes and other compounds, but its hardening effect is definitely below that of carnauba wax.

candlenut oil see LUMBANG OIL.

cannon see BRUSH.

cantharus or **kantharos** **1.** an ancient Greek pottery vessel, a capacious, footed drinking cup with two handles that flare out gracefully in loops rising above the edge of the cup. See illustration at VASE SHAPES.

2. *(church architecture)* a stoup, or basin, that holds holy water.

Canton enamel a Chinese ware of the late 19th century, consisting of metal vases and other ornamental items decorated in bright colours on white or pale-coloured backgrounds of porcelain enamel.

canvas **1.** a heavy woven fabric used as a SUPPORT for oil or acrylic painting. Its surface is prepared for painting by priming with a white GROUND. The standard canvas, sold by the roll, is made of strong, specially woven LINEN, much of which is imported from Belgium and Ireland. A less expensive alternative to linen is heavy cotton duck, which is an unacceptable substitute. For use in painting, a cut piece of canvas is stretched tightly by tacking it to a chassis or STRETCHER frame. Sometimes a painting is done on canvas and then cemented to a wall or panel; this procedure is called MAROUFLAGE. See also ACRYLIC CANVAS; JUTE CANVAS; TWILL CANVAS; CANVAS BOARD.

2. a stretched canvas ready for painting.

3. a finished oil painting.

canvas board common grey cardboard or pasteboard to which a white cotton cloth, prepared for oil painting, has been glued or pasted. Canvas boards are sold in stock sizes and in large volume; their light weight and easy portability make them suitable for outdoor sketching, and, because of their low cost, they serve as canvas substitutes for the beginner and for the amateur painter to whom that virtue is of more importance than the quality or longevity of the finished paintings.

canvas carrier a wood or metal device for carrying two canvases face to face, consisting of a set of clamps and a handle. It is constructed so as to separate two wet canvases sufficiently for them to be transported without smudging.

canvas pin or **canvas tack** a small metal or wood pin about $\frac{1}{2}$ inch thick, with a sharp steel point protruding from each flat side. When canvas pins are pressed into the four corners of the face of a freshly painted canvas, another canvas of the same size can be pressed face down on them. The pins act as separators, making it possible to protect wet paintings from smudging when transported or stored in a rack. The CANVAS CARRIER serves the same purpose.

canvas sizes, French stretched canvases are available in France in three groups according to their proportions – *paysage* (landscape), *portrait*, and

canvas pins

CANVAS SIZES

marine. The dimensions (in centimetres) of the 19 standard sizes of each type of canvas are as follows:

No.	Portrait		Paysage		Marine	
1	22 × 16		22 × 14		22 × 12	
2	24 × 19		24 × 16		24 × 14	
3	27 × 22		27 × 19		27 × 16	
4	33 × 24		33 × 22		33 × 19	
5	35 × 27		35 × 24		35 × 22	
6	41 × 33		41 × 27		41 × 24	
8	46 × 38		46 × 33		46 × 27	
10	55 × 46		55 × 38		55 × 33	
12	61 × 50		61 × 46		61 × 38	
15	65 × 54		65 × 50		65 × 46	
20	73 × 60		73 × 54		73 × 50	
25	81 × 65		81 × 60		81 × 54	
30	92 × 73		92 × 65		92 × 60	
40	100 × 81		100 × 73		100 × 65	
50	116 × 89		116 × 81		116 × 73	
60	130 × 97		130 × 89		130 × 81	
80	146 × 114		146 × 97		146 × 89	
100	162 × 130		162 × 114		162 × 97	
120	195 × 130		195 × 114		195 × 97	

As their names indicate, the sizes and shapes of each series were traditionally considered suited to the type of painting to be done. For example, a *marine* canvas was supposed to be of the appropriate proportions for a seascape. Artists today do not feel at all limited by the arbitrary name of the canvas in their selection of its size and shape. The system of categorizing French canvas sizes is thought by some to have been founded on some such theory of proportion as the GOLDEN MEAN or DYNAMIC SYMMETRY. No matter why the system was devised, however, it gives painters a wide choice of canvas shapes and sizes while holding the dealer's stock to a minimum, and it also makes possible standardization of frame sizes. See also CANVAS SIZES, LANDSCAPE; CANVAS SIZES, PORTRAIT.

canvas sizes, landscape in Britain and the United States, three standard canvas sizes were traditionally used in LANDSCAPE painting. The three traditional landscape sizes are 30 × 50 inches, 36 × 54 inches, and 40 × 60 inches. For the conventional French landscape sizes, see the table at CANVAS SIZES, FRENCH. See also CANVAS SIZES, PORTRAIT.

canvas sizes, portrait the standard canvas sizes used by portrait painters in Britain and the United States have traditionally been designated as follows (measurements in inches):

Whole-length canvases are usually used for painting full-length figures. The kit-cat size, originally designed for hanging in a low-ceilinged room, took its name from the 18th-century Kit-cat Club in London, that met in an eating house kept by one Christopher Cat, for which a series of

bishop's whole length	70 × 106
whole length	58 × 94
small whole length	52 × 88
bishop's half length	44 × 56
half length	40 × 50
small half length	34 × 44
kit-cat	28 × 36
three-quarter	25 × 30

portraits of the members was painted by Sir Geoffrey Kneller. For the conventional French portrait sizes see the table at CANVAS SIZES, FRENCH. See also CANVAS SIZES, LANDSCAPE.

canvas tack see CANVAS PIN.

caposcuola *(It.)* founder or leader of a school of thought or art.

Cappagh brown a native Irish brown earth, similar in hue to UMBER, but inferior in colour and pigment properties.

capriccio 1. any fantastic adornment or decoration in sculpture.

2. a composition that contains bizarre, fantastic or grotesque subjects, such as *Los Caprichos*, a series of etchings by Goya (1746–1828).

3. an extravagantly conceived architectural scene, or VEDUTA, the elements of which are accurately depicted but anomalously combined, as in *St Paul's, London, with the Grand Canal, Venice*, by William Marlow (1740–1813). The 18th-century *vedutisti*, Francesco Guardi (1712–1793) and Antonio Canaletto (1697–1768), painted many such *capricci*. A veduta with purely imaginary elements is more properly called a *veduta ideata*.

caput mortuum an obsolete name for a fully burned, permanent red iron oxide, deeper and more bluish than Indian red.

Caravaggisti see TENEBROSI.

carbon bisulphide a VOLATILE SOLVENT with a strong, disagreeable odour and a toxic effect. It is used in the conservation of wooden art objects for destroying wood beetles.

carbon black, diamond black or **gas black** a pure carbon pigment made by collecting the soot from burning natural gas by impingement; that is, the flames impinge on metal surfaces, from which the soot is scraped. Very similar pigments are made by burning other substances, such as benzol to obtain benzol black, or acetylene to produce acetylene black. Lampblack, another carbon pigment, is made by burning oil by a different method – the soot is collected from flues. Many types and grades of carbon black are used in printing and lithograph inks, in industrial black coatings, and in rubber. Although the best carbon black is a more intense jet than the other black pigments, it is not in general use as an artists' pigment because it shows in streaks when used as a tinting or mixing colour.

carbon pencil a drawing pencil made with lampblack or another carbon pigment, instead of with graphite. It is available in various degrees of hardness, producing different intensities of line, from jet-black to charcoal grey. The carbon pencil has a fine tonal quality and a sensitivity of control and is usually used for final drawings, rather than for sketches and casual work.

carbon pigment a black pigment composed of pure or impure carbon, such as BONE BLACK; CARBON BLACK; CHARCOAL; IVORY BLACK; LAMP-BLACK and VINE BLACK. Graphite is also a form of carbon, but its properties are so different that it is not classed with the others.

carbon tetrachloride a VOLATILE SOLVENT with a rapid evaporation rate and excellent solvent properties, especially for waxes. Carbon tetrachloride, unlike most volatile solvents, is nonflammable and has even been used as a fire extinguisher. It is highly toxic and must be used only in freely ventilated surroundings.

Carborundum a trade name for one of the sharpest and hardest of the artificial abrasives, silicon carbide. It is available in grains of several degrees of coarseness. The finer grades are particularly useful for grinding glass.

cardboard see BOARD.

caricature pictorial ridicule or satire, effected by distortion of personal physical characteristics or through exaggerated depiction of the foibles and vices of individuals, social classes and human institutions. Caricature has been used to evoke the gamut of human emotional responses, from gentle laughter to fiery indignation. It has been effective as a general illustrative technique and as the vehicle for social, religious, and political commentaries. Practically all modern caricature has been executed in some form of engraving, often in a series of prints that deal with various aspects of a single subject. It has been at least a diversion for most artists throughout the history of art. Among the more notable practitioners of the form are William Hogarth (1697–1764), Francisco Goya (1746–1828), Thomas Rowlandson (1756–1834), James Gillray (1757–1815), George Cruikshank (1792–1878), Charles Philipon (1800–1862), Honoré Daumier (1808–1879), Thomas Nast (1840–1902), Max Beerbohm (1872–1956), and David Low (1891–1963).

carmine, Munich lake, Vienna lake or *(formerly)* **nacarat carmine** a fairly permanent red LAKE pigment made from cochineal, a dyestuff of insect origin imported from Mexico. It was an important artists' colour from the mid-16th to the 19th century. The first European recipes for the manufacture of carmine appeared about 1560 in Spain; the best 17th- and 18th-century grades were made in Venice and Antwerp and in France. During the 18th century its chief competitor was the older crimson lake, a less beautiful and less permanent colour. An 18th-century writer, bemoaning the scarcity of good domestic carmine in England, said that English ladies were responsible for the great consumption of French carmine, 'almost the only substance used . . . as a red paint for living faces.' During the latter part of the 19th century, carmine was superseded by more permanent reds, first NATURAL ROSE MADDER then ALIZARIN CRIMSON. BURNT CARMINE was a brown-purple pigment made by delicately roasting carmine.

carnation an outmoded term used in art criticism to denote the natural rosy skin colouring in a painting.

carnauba wax or **Brazil wax** the hardest of the vegetable waxes, obtained from the leaves of a Brazilian palm. Its melting range is 83 to 86 °C. The grades of carnauba wax vary in colour from a creamy, yellowish white to a deep tan. It is used in compounds of waxes and other materials to impart hardness and durability.

Carolingian art Frankish art from the mid-8th to the early 10th century. Under the impetus of Charlemagne's dream of reviving the civilization of Rome, the fine arts flowered both at the emperor's court at Aachen and in the monasteries. Manuscripts of, for example, the Gospels were richly illuminated in a style that revitalized Roman and Byzantine models with barbarian intensity. The Utrecht psalter and the Ebbo Gospels, turned out at the remarkable Reims scriptorium (manuscript workshop), and the Ada group of manuscripts, are especially fine examples. Elaborate and beautiful work was also done in the Carolingian workshops in gold, silver and gems, as in the cover of the so-called *Lindau Gospels* (*c.* 870).

carpenter's pencil see FLAT SKETCHING PENCIL.

Carrara marble the most famous of all MARBLES, quarried in the Carrara district of Apuania in Italy. It has a fine, compact grain, and ranges in colour from snow-white to creamy white. It is saccharoidal, or sugary, and has a translucent appearance in the finest grades. Carrara marble was used in ancient times and again during the mediaeval and Renaissance periods. Much of Michelangelo's work was done in this marble. Two of the best commercially available grades for sculpture are Italian Statuary and Bianco P.

carte-de-visite (*Fr.* calling card) a card measuring about $2\frac{1}{2} \times 3\frac{1}{2}$ inches, bearing a photographic portrait, popular in the 19th century. Mass-produced cartes-de-visite of celebrities and royalty are now collectors' pieces.

cartoccio see CARTOUCHE.

cartoon 1. a full-sized, detailed, and usually full-colour preparatory drawing or painting on heavy paper. The term is derived from *cartone*, the Italian word for the paper on which the drawing is done and, by extension, for the cartoon itself. When a cartoon is used for a mural painting, as was almost always the case with FRESCO, it is usually transferred to the wall by SQUARING or POUNCING. Frequently a SPOLVERO is pounced in order to keep the original cartoon intact. In mural painting the cartoon also serves as a reference, giving the artist a full-scale view of the project at any point during its execution; it may also be used as a guide for the artist's assistants. Cartoons are also used for tapestries, stained-glass windows, mosaics, or any other works of art the final execution of which is sufficiently divorced from the creative aspects to be entrusted to craftsmen, such as weavers in the case of tapestry. Outstanding examples of cartoons of this latter type are those executed by Raphael for the tapestries intended for the Sistine Chapel and now in the

CARTOUCHE

Vatican Museum. Seven of these cartoons are in the Victoria and Albert Museum in London.

2. an often humorous or satirical drawing or series of drawings, the main interest of which is the subject matter rather than the style of execution. Cartoons are generally rendered in a simple, linear manner. They are usually entertaining but may also serve the purposes of instruction and political or social commentary.

cartouche 1. a painted, engraved, or sculptured ornament of irregular or fantastic form, enclosing a plain central space, usually oval or lozenge-shaped, used as a field for inscriptions. Such ornaments were much used during the 16th and 17th centuries to decorate wainscotings and the title pages of books.
2. a lozenge-shaped outline within which an inscription can be made. The term is especially applied to Egyptian hieroglyphs on monuments, where the names of gods and royalty were enclosed in cartouches.
3. (also called *cartoccio*) a plate attached to a work of art and inscribed with such information as the title, artist's name, and date of execution

cartouche (left) An ornamental cartouche; (right) an Egyptian cartouche, the nameplate of the ancient king Cheops (Khufu).

cartridge paper the coarser, less expensive grades of drawing paper. The name is derived from the use of such papers for making gun cartridges and wrapping dynamite.
carver a knife with a short, angular blade and a cord-wrapped handle, used in woodcutting. See illustration at WOOD-CARVING TOOLS.
carving the art of cutting or incising wood, stone, or other material into the desired form. Among the tools used for this purpose are knives, chisels, gouges, points, adzes and hammers. In the most common method of carving, a chisel is held in one hand and driven into the wood or stone by a mallet held in the other. Carving and MODELLING are the two major sculptural techniques, although other metalworking techniques such as welding and assemblage have become increasingly important in the past century. A carved work may be called a carving, but the word *sculpture* is usually preferred for work of serious artistic and aesthetic intent. See DIRECT CARVING; POINTING.

caryatid *(architectural sculpture)* a female figure that serves as a column supporting an entablature. Caryatids are graceful figures dressed in long robes. The word is Greek and was originally used for the maidens of Caryae in Laconia who performed ritual dances at the festival of Artemis. The male counterparts of caryatids are ATLANTES or telamones (see TELAMON).

caryatid (left) Caryatid; (right) atlas or telemon.

Casali's green an early variety of VIRIDIAN.

casein a milk protein, used as a binder in casein colours and as an adhesive. It is produced by drying the curd of soured skim milk to form a yellowish powder. Casein is water-soluble only in the presence of an alkali such as ammonia; hence paints with a casein binder and casein adhesives are water-resistant on drying. Casein was first introduced commercially in the 19th century. Before then, a crude form of it, sometimes called by its Latin name, *caseum*, had been made from ordinary pot cheese. Some authorities believe that casein was the binder used in some of the paints of early civilizations. Curd glue was used by the ancient Egyptians, Greeks, Romans and Hebrews. Casein is mentioned as an adhesive in 11th-century manuscripts, but its use as a paint binder does not seem to be recorded earlier than the 18th century. It may also be used instead of glue as a binder for GESSO. Unlike glue, it can be used cold.

casein colour a paint made by mixing artists' pigments with a solution of CASEIN, a milk protein. Casein colours are usually applied with a brush on a wallboard panel coated with gesso, but can also be used on watercolour paper or board. Canvas cannot be used, because dry casein is the most inflexible of the permanent paint binders and becomes increasingly brittle as it ages. For the same reason, the palette knife should be used with restraint, as the paint will crack if laid on too thickly; a heavy impasto should be avoided. The colours dry rapidly to a pleasing and durable mat finish; some artists, however, varnish their pictures to obtain a glossy finish more characteristic of oil paints. Caseins may be used to produce effects ranging from smooth areas of flat colour to the robust textures of semi-impasto, for which a full bristle brush is used. Casein is also frequently used as an underpainting for oil paints and glazes.

Besides the mat quality of casein colours and their high drying speed, some artists prefer them to oils because they can be mixed with water. Although dried casein paint may be damaged if spattered with water, it is not readily water-soluble and will resist dampness. A casein painting may be sprayed with formalin to increase its resistance to moisture. It may be cleaned with acetone.

Before the Second World War, artists in the United States had built up a considerable tradition of painting with caseins, making their own colours by grinding pigments with fresh casein solution. In the late 1940s, American manufacturers of artists' materials brought out complete lines of improved casein colours in tubes, and the technique became quite popular.

cashew lake see MAHOGANY LAKE.

Cassel earth or **Cologne earth** a native brown earth containing organic matter, closely similar to VANDYKE BROWN.

Cassel green see MANGANESE GREEN.

Cassel yellow see TURNER'S YELLOW.

cassone painting a painting on Italian household chests (*cassone*) of the 15th century. Frequently elaborately carved, gilded, and painted in a variety of scenes and ornamental designs, these chests were made by master craftsmen and occasionally painted by renowned artists, such as Botticelli and Paolo Uccello.

cast 1. *vb* to reproduce an object, such as a piece of sculpture, by means of a MOULD; also, a copy so produced. The original piece is usually of a less durable material than the cast.

2. *n.* a minute difference in colour effect, too small to be called a TINGE; it is discernible only on close examination.

casting see CENTRIFUGAL CASTING; LOST-PATTERN CASTING; LOST-WAX PROCESS; MOULD; SAND CASTING.

casting plaster a type of PLASTER OF PARIS especially prepared to have the properties most desirable for casting and carving. It is very fine-grained, absorbent, brilliantly white, slow setting, and capable of taking fine detail.

casting stone see IMITATION STONE.

castor oil the only NONDRYING OIL that is completely miscible with alcohol. It has been used as a plasticizer, to add flexibility to a coating material such as shellac or lacquer, whose strong and rapid drying action is thereby retarded and its brittleness permanently decreased.

cast shadow the shadow of a figure or an object portrayed in a painting or drawing as it falls or is cast on another surface. The accurate representation of cast shadows is important in realistic depiction. The shadows as well as the objects that cast them must be drawn in perspective, and the shape, sharpness and intensity of the shadows must correspond to the position and intensity of the source or sources of illumination in the picture. The Impressionist painters frequently used interesting effects of colour in their depiction of cast shadows, but since the 1920s there has been a tendency among representational artists to eliminate or minimize cast shadows. See also CONTAINED SHADOW.

cast shadow Contained shadow and cast shadow. Woodcut from *Underweysung der Messung (Nuremberg, 1538)* by Albrecht Dürer. *(The Metropolitan Museum of Art, Gift of Felix M. Warburg, 1918.)*

Catabond see PHENOLIC RESIN.

catalyst a substance that triggers or hastens a chemical reaction without itself entering into the reaction. The action of a cobalt DRIER on linseed oil is one example of catalysis. If the oil is left to dry by oxidation and polymerization, it may take several days to become dry to the touch, but the presence of a moderate amount of cobalt drier will produce the same result overnight.

catechu, Bengal cutch, cachou or **cutch** a natural dyestuff obtained from the heartwood of various species of acacia and mimosa growing in the East Indies. It is one of the most nearly permanent vegetable colouring matters, used to produce shades of brown, black and olive. The colouring principle of catechu, a crystalline substance called *catechin*, can also be obtained from a few other vegetable sources. Catechu is also employed in tanning leather.

catenary curve a curve like that made by a flexible cord of uniform thickness suspended between two points on the same level. Catenary curves are common design elements.

cat's-eye dammar see MATA KUCHING DAMMAR.

cat's gold see MOSAIC GOLD.

caulking see TRACING.

caustic magnetite see CALCINED MAGNETITE.

cauteria the equipment and implements used to apply colours in Roman ENCAUSTIC painting. The more important of the *cauteria* were a copper or silver palette; a metal drum containing glowing charcoal on which the palette was placed; the portable heat source, a charcoal brazier; and the CESTRUM, or painting knife.

CARAVAGGISTI

Caravaggisti see TENEBROSI.

cavalier projection see OBLIQUE PROJECTION.

cavetto a concave moulding with a quarter-round profile. See illustration at OVOLO.

cavityless casting see LOST-PATTERN CASTING.

cavo–rilievo Italian for hollow RELIEF.

cedar, oil of one of the fragrant essential oils used in preference to sweet or flowery odorants to mask disagreeable odours in water–paint binders, polishes, and cleaners.

celadon a soft ceramic GLAZE containing iron. It is made in a reduction fire, in which red iron oxide (ferric) is reduced to black (ferroso–ferric). The reduced colour of the glaze may be olive green, grey-green, or grey. Celadon ware was developed and perfected during the Sung Dynasty. It was apparently valued by the Chinese for its resemblance to jade, and has always been highly esteemed in the West.

celadon green another name for GREEN EARTH, the colouring principle of which is celadonite, an iron silicate. Chinese celadon porcelain was so named from the resemblance of its colour to this willow-green shade. The name *celadon* comes from a character in Honoré d'Urfé's romance *L'Astrée* (1610).

celestial blue an inexpensive variety of PRUSSIAN BLUE containing up to 95% BARYTES. It is not used in permanent painting.

Celite *(US)* a tradename for several grades of DIATOMACEOUS EARTH used as INERT PIGMENTS, FILLERS, and flatting agents in prepared paints.

cellophane tape see PRESSURE-SENSITIVE TAPES.

Cellosolve *(US)* a tradename for ethylene glycol monethyl ether, a lacquer solvent.

celluloid a former tradename for a PLASTIC that was the first commercially produced synthetic plastic. In 1876 its inventor marketed billiard balls and other so-called imitation ivory products made from CELLULOSE NITRATE, plasticized with camphor. Much ingenuity was exercised in the manufacture of early plastic products. Thin sheets of opaque and translucent celluloid were stacked alternately, laminated, and fashioned into articles that appeared to have been made of elephant ivory. Imitation tortoise shell was also a favourite. It was many years before the natural properties of plastics were exploited for their own distinctive virtues, rather than for imitating the markings (or, as it has been said, the defects) of natural substances. Despite the tremendous rise of modern synthetic resins, nitrocellulose plastics are still in use, and camphor is still one of the best plasticizers used in their manufacture. None of the cellulose plastics, however, is sufficiently permanent for use in the fine arts.

cellulose acetate a cellulose derivative used in the manufacture of photographic film, plastics, textile fibres, and lacquers. It is superior to CELLULOSE NITRATE in film because it is far less dangerously flammable. In lacquers it does not yellow as much in daylight as cellulose nitrate, but is inferior in hardness, durability and other desirable lacquer properties. No cellulose products have sufficient stability to be used in permanent painting or constructions.

cellulose cement a viscous solution of PYROXYLIN or cellulose material in a LACQUER SOLVENT, sold in tubes for general adhesive and repair purposes. It is especially useful when a cement that dries rapidly is required.

cellulose nitrate or **nitrocellulose** an industrial raw material made by nitrating cellulose fibres. It is the principal ingredient of LACQUERS and is also used to make various plastics and films. Highly nitrated grades of cellulose nitrate are known as *guncotton*. None of the lacquers or solid plastics based on cellulose nitrate are used in permanent painting.

Celotex *(US)* a tradename for a loose-structured board of roughly webbed texture, made of sugarcane waste. The texture of Celotex sometimes appeals to painters, but this type of board is not recommended for use as a painting support, as it becomes brittle and friable upon relatively short ageing. See INSULATING BOARD.

Celtic cross a LATIN CROSS with a ring or halo about the intersection of the arms. The circle crosses the three short arms of the cross near their ends. See CROSS for illustration.

cement 1. any strong adhesive used to join or repair materials; examples are tile cement, rubber cement, and cellulose cement.

2. a building material made of lime, silica and alumina. See PORTLAND CEMENT.

central visual ray the line of sight at the exact centre of the CONE OF VISION. It is the line that makes an angle of exactly 90° with the PICTURE PLANE. The central visual ray is also known as the line of vision. See illustration at PERSPECTIVE.

centrifugal casting a method of casting by the LOST-WAX PROCESS, using a machine in which the mould revolves so that its cavity is filled with molten metal by centrifugal action and pressure. The resulting cast may be very thin and highly detailed. A high degree of finish may be obtained by this method of casting, thus reducing tedious surface treatment and finishing. It is used most commonly in the casting of small objects in precious metals such as gold, silver, and platinum, although other metals such as bronze, brass and aluminium may also be cast centrifugally.

cera colla a mediaeval term for an emulsion of glue solution and molten beeswax. A modern version would be composed of white, refined beeswax saponified with ammonia and mixed with various gum solutions and/or casein. It is called for in various old recipes as an ingredient of aqueous paint binders.

ceramic colours see PORCELAIN COLOURS.

ceramics the art of making objects of clay and FIRING them in a KILN. Wares of EARTHENWARE and PORCELAIN, as well as sculpture, are made by ceramicists. ENAMEL is also a ceramic technique. Ceramic wares may be decorated with SLIP, ENGOBE or GLAZE, applied by a number of techniques, including RESIST, MISHIMA and SANGGAM. Pots may be made by the COIL METHOD, the SLAB METHOD, or some other manual technique, or on a POTTER'S WHEEL. The making and decorating of pottery is among the most ancient of the arts. It reached a high degree of development in China and also in ancient Greece. Because ceramic practice involves the fashioning of a plastic mass, many technical terms relating to it also apply to sculpture.

ceresin a pure white or slightly yellowish mineral wax refined from OZO-KERITE. It resembles PARAFFIN but has a higher melting point in the range 60–80 °C, which makes it a suitable substitute for beeswax as an ingredient of polishes and protective coatings for sculpture, among other uses.

cerography 1. the art of making designs or inscriptions in wax, as on wax-coated tablets.

2. the art of ENCAUSTIC painting.

3. *(printing)* the process of making electrotype plates from engraved sheets of wax.

ceroplastic the art of modelling in wax; this method was developed in ancient times and was used extensively by both the Greeks and the Romans, especially in their portraiture.

cerulean blue cobalt, stannate, or cobalt chromium; a bright, deep sky-blue permanent pigment of very greenish undertone, made by roasting cobalt and tin or chromium oxides. After a few attempts by colourmakers late in the 18th century to produce a satisfactory cobalt tin blue, the process was perfected in Germany in 1805. Cerulean blue was introduced as an artists' pigment in Britain by G. Rowney in 1870 under the name *coeruleum* (from *caeruleum*, classical Latin for sky-blue pigment, such as Egyptian blue). Cerulean blue chromium is a pigment similar in hue and performance to the tin variety and is of later development.

ceruse an obsolete name for WHITE LEAD.

cestrum the principal tool used to apply the molten colours in Roman ENCAUSTIC painting. *Cestra* were spatulate bronze implements, often double-ended. Their modern counterparts are flexible stainless-steel PALETTE KNIVES and painting knives in assorted shapes.

Ceylon lacquer see LACQUER, ORIENTAL.

Ceylon satinwood see SATINWOOD.

chalk 1. see WHITING.

2. see PRECIPITATED CHALK.

3. a chalk crayon.

4. a drawing done with chalk crayons.

chalking the disintegration of the surface layer of a coat of paint through failure of the binding medium to hold the particles of pigment; the paint thus becomes powdery and is easily rubbed off. Chalking is more common in house paint, which is exposed to the weather, than in artists' colours.

chalk manner see CRAYON MANNER.

chalk roll a variant of the roulette, used in CRAYON MANNER. See illustration at ROULETTE.

chamois an obsolete name for the pigment YELLOW OCHRE.

champlevé or **en taille d'épargne 1.** a technique of enamelling. The design consists of a number of shallow depressions carved out from or ground into a metal surface, filled in with ceramic pastes, and fired. Champlevé can readily be distinguished from CLOISONNÉ by the irregular widths of the metal surrounding the coloured areas. Champlevé has been used for decorative purposes since Roman times. In mediaeval times it was employed for the enrichment of precious liturgical and secular objects.
2. an article of ENAMEL work produced by this technique.

charcoal a black crayon made of charred twigs of wood, usually willow, or pieces of vine. It is available in various degrees of hardness and thickness. Charcoal is a very old and universally used drawing material. When used for itself in drawing, it is usually applied on CHARCOAL PAPER, but it is also used for preliminary drawing on oil-painting grounds. Charcoal is also the usual black crayon used in chalk drawings. Like pastel, charcoal smudges easily and when applied may be manipulated by the artist with the finger or with a STUMP or other soft shading material or implement. The finished drawing must be sprayed with a FIXATIVE to be made resistant to smudging.

charcoal black and **charcoal grey** pigments made by pulverizing charcoal. They have poor pigment properties and are seldom used by artists. *Vegetable black* is an unstandardized term applied to various grades of charcoal black and vine black. See also PEACH BLACK.

charcoal paper a soft paper of moderately rough grain that takes and holds charcoal well and is also adaptable to other drawing and painting mediums. It is available in pure white and a variety of tints. The best grades have a high rag content and usually a laid or watermark finish.

charcoal pencil a slender stick of charcoal encased in wood, used extensively by artists for drawing and sketching. See PENCIL.

chasing the art of ornamenting a metal surface with indentations created by holding a blunt steel chasing tool or punch against the surface and striking it with a hammer.
2. the resulting engraved design.
3. *(sculpture)* the process of finishing the surface of a bronze cast by chiselling and polishing it, thus removing small imperfections and seams left by the casting mould and emphasizing incised details.
   In metalwork, chasing, or directly creating, intaglio designs on the obverse of an object, is distinguished from REPOUSSÉ work, in which relief designs are created on the obverse of a sheet of metal by hammering its reverse.

chasse French for a RELIQUARY.

chassis 1. *(painting)* the wooden framework on which an artists' canvas is mounted. See STRETCHER; STRAINER.
2. *(sculpture)* a calibrated wooden framework, used in making an enlarged or a reduced copy of a plaster model.

chatoyant a term used to describe the inner glow or lustre of certain gems, notably cat's-eye. By extension it is also applied to the reflection from SHELL MARBLE and similar stones.

chatter mark *(ceramics)* a series of shallow vertical grooves on a pot, created by a trimming tool. It may be a defect, occurring when the potter attempts to trim a pot after the clay has dried too much, or it may be done deliberately as a kind of decoration.

chay a red NATURAL DYESTUFF obtained from the root of an East Indian plant *(Oldenlandia umbellata)*. One of the slowest-fading of the natural colouring matters, chay is used to dye textiles. There is no record of its use in paint pigments, but this may have occurred locally.

checking 1. CRACKLE in a pattern of squares on a painting or any other surface.

2. cracking or partial splitting in wood, along the grain, caused by shrinkage due to loss of moisture when the wood dries. It can be prevented by proper seasoning.

chef d'œuvre see MASTERPIECE.

chemigraphy those printing processes in which a metal plate is incised by chemical means (that is, BITING, as in ETCHING and AQUATINT) rather than by mechanical means (as with a BURIN in engraving or with a needle in drypoint).

cherry gum a clear gum exuded by all species of wild and domestic cherry trees. When allowed to soak, the gum swells and absorbs water; it is then used as a binder for pigments, especially as a substitute for gum arabic in gum tempera colours. Although cherry gum is not widely used commercially, its history as a water-paint binder goes back to the 10th or 11th century in northern Europe. Peach, plum, apricot and almond trees also yield gum whose properties as paint binders are identical to those of cherry gum.

cherrywood the wood of the black cherry *(Prunus serotina)*, a strong, close-grained, lustrous brown or reddish wood that takes a high polish. It is used for fine carvings and is prized for cabinetwork. It has a straight, regular grain and may have dark red growth lines. *African cherry* or *makore* *(Mimusops heckelii)*, used chiefly for veneer, has similar growth lines.

cherub see PUTTO.

chê shih a Chinese earth pigment of a brownish terracotta colour. It is sold with a glue binder as a prepared Chinese watercolour.

chessylite see AZURITE.

chestnut brown a little-used name for UMBER.

chiaroscuro the rendering of forms in drawing, painting, and the graphic arts through a balanced contrast between pronounced light and dark areas. The technique, which was introduced in the Renaissance, is effective in creating an illusion of depth and space around the principal figures in a composition. Leonardo da Vinci and Rembrandt were painters who excelled in its use. See also TENEBRISM.

chiaroscuro woodcut 1. a WOODCUT technique for printing single-colour prints in which the effects of light and shadow (chiaroscuro) are produced by using a different wood block for each tone in the print. The blocks are designed and cut as if for multicolour printing (see COLOUR PRINT), carefully marked to print in REGISTER. A KEY BLOCK is printed in the darkest tone, usually black or dark brown. Sometimes the darkest tone, which is generally used for the outlines of the design areas, is printed with an etched or engraved copper plate, and only the tints are printed with wood blocks. After the darkest tone is printed, the tint blocks (usually one to three, although more can be used) are inked and printed with graduated shades of the same colour or tones of a different single colour. The most popular colours for chiaroscuro woodcuts are grey, brown, green, and sepia.

The chiaroscuro woodcut was devised in the early 16th century as an inexpensive imitation of or substitute for the chiaroscuro wash and watercolour drawings that were so popular during the Renaissance. Ugo da Carpi, who worked from drawings and copied paintings of Raphael and Parmigianino, is said by Vasari to have discovered the process in 1516. Lucas Cranach's woodcutter, Jost de Negker, is also credited with the invention of the chiaroscuro woodcut four years earlier. Although neither man was a creative artist in his own right, both cut blocks for some of the finest prints ever made in the medium. When, in the 17th century, the woodcut began to be replaced by metal-plate printmaking techniques, the popularity of the chiaroscuro woodcut in continental Europe began to wane, but the technique continued to be used in Britain throughout the 18th century.

2. a print made by this process.

chic anglais an admiring French expression of the 18th century for the brilliant colour effects of English painters, such as Sir Thomas Lawrence and later R.P. Bonington, who revived the use of transparent colour over brilliant white grounds.

chill see BLOOM.

China clay or **pipe clay** a native hydrated aluminium silicate, called China clay because it is used to make chinaware. As an INERT PIGMENT in paints and pigments, China clay serves chiefly as a low-cost EXTENDER or adulterant. Kaolin is the whitest and purest variety of China clay.

china-marking crayon see GREASE CRAYON.

china painting the decoration of chinaware with ceramic colours, a handicraft activity that was extremely popular during the late 19th and early 20th centuries. Special stocks of brushes, colours, and white porcelain articles were sold, and the work was sent to a professional kiln for firing and, frequently, the addition of gold decoration.

China stone see PETUNTSE.

China wood oil an obsolete name for TUNG OIL, little used after about 1930.

Chinese blue see PRUSSIAN BLUE.

Chinese green see LOKAO.

Chinese ink see INK.

Chinese insect wax a rather hard wax with a melting range of 79–83 °C, used for general purposes in China and Japan and encountered in various recipes in the arts. It is a fairly good substitute for beeswax. The insects that produce Chinese insect wax swarm on a species of tree that grows in Yunan province. When insect development reaches a certain stage, the insects are gathered and transported several hundred miles to Sichuan province, where they are placed on trees of a different species to complete their life cycle. The wax is finally gathered from the second type of tree.

Chinese lacquer see LACQUER, ORIENTAL.

Chinese red another name for chrome red (see CHROME YELLOW).

Chinese vermilion originally, the VERMILION made in China and called *chu sha*; today, commonly, the British or American product. Vermilion was invented in China independently of, and earlier than, its mediaeval European counterpart; for hundreds of years the Chinese product was mistakenly believed superior.

Chinese white a prepared ZINC WHITE watercolour introduced in 1834 by the English firm of Winsor & Newton.

Chinese yellow see ORPIMENT.

chinoiserie decorative work influenced by Chinese art. The vogue for chinoiserie, manifested in architecture, interior decoration, furniture, porcelain, tapestry, wallpaper and knick-knacks, as well as in the fine arts, reflected the romantic interest in China and reached its height during the 18th century. The vogue came to an end about 1795, although the Chinese style still provides standard motifs in the decorative arts. See also JAPONISME.

chipboard *(US)* an inexpensive grey or brownish cardboard made entirely from wastepaper; not recommended as a support or as a mounting or matting material for works of art.

chi-rho a Christian symbol formed of the Greek letters chi () and rho (Greek cross. The chi-rho, widely used in Christian art, surmounted the *labarum*, or standard, adopted by Constantine, the first Christian emperor of Rome.

chi-rho

chisel any of a number of steel tools with a cutting edge at the end of a rod or handle. The chisel is usually held in one hand at an angle to the surface to be carved and driven by a MALLET held in the other hand. Chisels are used by sculptors for carving or working stone, wood, metal and other materials and by graphic artists for making woodcut blocks. The chisel used in wood carving is often simply called a *straight*, to distinguish it from a bent chisel (see BENT GOUGE). See also COLD CHISEL;

FISHTAIL TOOL; PITCHING CHISEL; SKEW CHISEL; T-CHISEL. See illustrations here and at WOOD-CARVING TOOLS.

chisel Points (A), bull point (B), flat chisels (C), tooth chisels (D), cold chisel (E), pitching chisel (F), t-chisel (G), and star drill (H), used in stone carving.

chisel brush, chisel-edge brush or **chiselled brush** a brush with a straight, wide working edge whose bristles or hairs are set so that its flat sides are bevelled towards its tip. A chisel brush is desirable in some paint applications, especially for sign writing, in which the brush retains its original shape in use and deposits a uniform coating of paint. See FITCH; SIGN-WRITER'S CUTTER; SLICKER.

chondrin see GLUE.

chopped strand mat a mat of randomly distributed glass fibres, each about 2 inches long and consisting of many filaments, bound together with a sizing that is soluble in polyester resin. These glass fibres are the most commonly used reinforcement for polyester resin. The two materials, when combined in a laminate, form an extremely strong, durable casting material for sculpture. See FIBREGLASS.

Christogram a monogram or other symbol of Jesus Christ. The most common Christogram is the CHI-RHO.

chroma the hue and saturation, or degree of vividness, of a colour other than black, white, or grey. It is the dimension that distinguishes the so-called chromatic colours from those in the black–white scale. Chroma is one of the three coordinates of the MUNSELL SYSTEM of colour notation.

chromatic colour any colour except black, white and the simple greys, the achromatic colours.

chromaticity 1. the chromatic or colour property of a thing.
2. the dominant wavelength of a colour in scientific colour measurement, plus its purity. A chromaticity diagram (called also colour triangle and Maxwell triangle) is a triangular or tristimulus chart that indicates the ratio or percentage of each of the three primaries in the colour's makeup. These numerical elements are termed chromaticity coordinates. See also TRISTIMULUS VALUES.

chrome green, royal green or **zinnober green 1.** a COMPOSITE PIG-

CHROME OCHRE

MENT made with chrome yellow and Prussian blue, widely used in house paints and other industrial products. Chrome green is unsuitable for artists' colours because it has the defects of both its ingredients. Since there are many shades of chrome yellow and Prussian blue, a great variety of chrome greens can be produced. Among the many hue variants of chrome green are leaf green, leek green, moss green, and myrtle green. Varieties of chrome green include BRUNSWICK GREEN (also called Prussian green) and NITRATE GREEN.

2. **see** OIL GREEN.

chrome ochre see GOLDEN OCHRE.

chrome orange see CHROME YELLOW.

chrome red see CHROME YELLOW.

chrome yellow; also chrome orange and **chrome red** basic lead chromate. This is produced in a large range of shades, from palest primrose yellow to scarlet red, by altering the manufacturing conditions. Described in 1809 by L.N. Vauquelin, who had discovered chromium in 1797, the lead chromate pigments were first produced commercially in 1818 and have been widely used ever since for house paints and other industrial purposes. In spite of their brilliant colours and excellent pigment properties, the lead chromates are unsuitable for permanent painting as they turn brown on contact with sulphur in the atmosphere, they react with other pigments, they may turn green on exposure to sunlight, and they may cause lead poisoning.

The cadmium reds and yellows are perfectly suitable replacements for the lead chromates. There has really been no necessity for artists to use chrome yellow since the cadmium colours were introduced; nevertheless, some artists have used them, almost always with unfortunate results. J.M.W. Turner is said to have employed chrome yellow and chrome orange, and the discoloration that some of van Gogh's sunflowers have undergone is a rather well-known example of what happens when, because nothing else is to hand, an artist uses a material he knows is bad. Chrome yellow, for all its faults, was superior to a number of earlier pigments that it replaced and made obsolete, such as TURNER'S YELLOW, TURPETH MINERAL, and KING'S YELLOW. Chrome red is also known as *Chinese red* and *Derby red*, chrome yellow as *Leipzig yellow* and *Paris yellow*. *Persian red (US)* is an unstandardized name for a variety of chrome red. *Vienna red* is also a variety.

chromium oxide green a dense, completely opaque, pale-green pigment of medium saturation. A FURNACE PRODUCT, it is absolutely permanent for all pigment purposes and conditions, including the highest temperatures. Compared with viridian and phthalocyanine green, chromium oxide green has a rather dull colour effect, is quite low in tinting strength, and is much less versatile in mixtures; hence, despite its pleasing hue, it is less frequently used by artists. Discovered in France by Vauquelin in 1797, chromium oxide began to be used in the early 19th century as a ceramic colour. It was first used as an artists' pigment about 1840 and became widely available by 1862. Experiments during the 19th century aimed at developing chromium oxide green produced varieties called *Plessy's green*, *Dingler's green*, *Arnaudon's green* and *Schnitzer's green*. Chromium oxide used as a polishing ROUGE, particularly for platinum and stainless steel, is called *green rouge*.

chromo 1. *abbrev. for* CHROMOLITHOGRAPH.

2. a term of disparagement, by extension, for a cheap or gaudy picture.

chromolithograph an obsolete term for a colour lithograph, used particularly for the product of those processes from which modern COLOUR LITHOGRAPHY developed. The typical chromolithograph, or chromo, as such a print was commonly called, was poorly executed compared with colour lithographs produced by later techniques. Many chromolithographs had little or no merit. See also OLEOGRAPH.

chryselephantine made of, or adorned with, ivory and gold. Chryselephantine figure statues, usually with flesh of ivory and hair and garments of gold, were much prized by many ancient peoples of the Orient, the Near East and the Mediterranean. Greek sculptors of the 5th century BC made chryselephantine statues of the gods to adorn their greatest temples. Among the most famous were the Olympian Zeus and the Athena Parthenos, 40-foot colossal sculptures by Phidias.

chrysocolla a native green copper silicate. Like malachite, it was used as a green pigment in early civilizations, though it was replaced in some instances by greens made from Egyptian blue, notably in Crete.

chrysography the use of gold or silver ink for lettering. The ancient Greek and Roman practice of lettering with gold on purple and rose-coloured vellum was continued on natural and tinted parchment in the Middle Ages. Especially fine examples of chrysography occur in Hiberno-Saxon illuminated manuscripts of the 6th and 7th centuries. This style of lettering was widely used until the 10th century, after which chrysography declined, although it was somewhat revived during the Renaissance.

churrigueresque a lavishly ornate style of Spanish architecture and decoration popular in the late 1700s and early 1800s, which took its name from its chief exponents, the Churriguerra family of Seville. The term is nearly synonymous with ROCOCO.

chu sha see VERMILION.

CIE see COMMISSION INTERNATIONALE DE L'ECLAIRAGE.

ciment fondu (*Fr.* melted cement) aluminous cement, used in casting sculpture. It sets in about four hours and then hardens very rapidly. When mixed with sand, it forms a kind of concrete, whose surface and texture may be varied by the addition of different aggregates. It may be reinforced with glass fibres to make a strong, thin, light, hollow cast.

cinnabar native mercuric sulphide ore. It was used as a red pigment by ancient peoples prior to the invention of the much superior VERMILION (manufactured mercuric sulphide). According to Theophrastus, in the *History of Stones*, an outcropping of cinnabar on inaccessible cliffs on the Spanish coast was worked by shooting arrows to dislodge the ore. See also MINIUM.

cinquecento the 16th century. The term is commonly used to designate Italian art of that period.

cinquefoil see FOIL.

cipolin or **cipollino** any white MARBLE variegated with green and grey because it contains layers of mica or mica-like minerals. Its name, from the Italian word for 'onion,' comes from its fancied resemblance to the cross section of an onion. The stone originally named cipolin came from the Island of Euboea, in the Aegean Sea.

cirage see CAMAÏEU.

Circassian walnut see WALNUT.

circle cutter see COMPASS CUTTER.

cire perdue the French term for the LOST-WAX PROCESS of metal casting.

cissing see CRAWL.

citron yellow a hue designation for any pale yellow that tends towards the greenish, but not to the extent of being considered a greenish yellow. Examples are STRONTIUM YELLOW and ZINC YELLOW.

clam *(ceramics)* to seal a KILN by daubing the door with a mixture of fireclay and fine GROG. It is not necessary to clam an electric kiln or a portable gas kiln, since these usually have tight-fitting, hinged doors.

classical 1. pertaining to the art of the Greeks and the Romans. See HELLENIC ART; ROMAN ART.

2. pertaining to the period of highest achievement and purest form of a style or technique. See also CLASSICAL PERIOD; CLASSICISM.

classical abstraction see GEOMETRIC ABSTRACTION.

Classical period the period of highest achievement in HELLENIC ART, from 500 to 323 BC between the ARCHAIC PERIOD and the HELLENISTIC PERIOD. One of the early discoveries of the period was the principle of CONTRAPPOSTO, or counterpoise, whereby the weight of a standing figure was borne mainly by one leg, giving the figure a relaxed, harmonious pose. This development made possible the creation of balanced figures, and even interlocking groups of freestanding figures, in motion. While the harmonious proportions and over-perfect anatomy of the figures indicate that they were idealized portrayals of the human body rather than individual portraits, they conveyed emotion through facial expression as well as through the expressive, kinetic pose of the body. Relief sculpture, in the form of complex narrative friezes, displayed a high degree of compositional harmony and spatial subtlety. Classical painting was probably distinguished by the evolution of techniques for giving the illusion of space, such as modelling and foreshortening, although it survives today only in examples of vase decoration, an art that had passed its peak. In architecture, the serene balance and harmony that characterized classical art were exemplified in such buildings as the Parthenon.

classicism 1. any manifestation of the style of CLASSICAL Greek and Roman art.

2. adherence to standards of simplicity, restraint, and proportion considered to characterize classical art.

Since the Renaissance, classicism has had a powerful and recurrent influence on Western art and architecture, alternating in favour with periods of ROMANTICISM or impinging on romantic styles. In its second sense, classicism may also be considered the opposite of the elaborately ornamented BAROQUE style. NEOCLASSICISM, the Adam and Empire styles of decoration, and Georgian and Palladian architecture were all derived from classicism, as were most of the architectural styles from the mid-18th to the mid-19th century. Nineteenth-century ACADEMICISM, which influenced public taste for 150 years, was also based on Greek and Roman ideals.

Claude Lorrain glass a convex black glass used as a mirror to reflect a landscape in reduced size, muted colour, and merging detail. The glass is said to have been devised by the painter Claude Lorrain (Claude Gelée, 1600–1682) and to have also been used by Il Bamboccio (Pieter van Laar, 1592 or 1595–1642) and Gaspard Poussin (Gaspard Dughet, 1613–1675). It was popular among artists of the 17th and 18th centuries, and was still in common use in the 19th century.

clay a native earth consisting mainly of decomposed feldspathic rock containing kaolin and other hydrous aluminous minerals. Powdered clay is used in painting as an inert pigment (see CHINA CLAY). Moist clay is the material used in CERAMICS. Potters and ceramic sculptors choose clays that are suitable for firing (see POTTER'S CLAY). Clays containing a large proportion of kaolin harden at higher temperatures than other clays. Fine porcelain is composed of relatively pure kaolin, mixed with refractory and fluxing ingredients. A sculptor who plans to cast a work uses either WET CLAY or MODELLING CLAY for the original model. Sculptor's clay is selected for its moisture-holding and plastic properties. It is prepared by being mixed with water. The sculptor builds up the clay model over an ARMATURE, keeping it moist overnight or between working sessions by wetting it and covering it with an impermeable cloth. The finished clay model, when dry, is used in making a mould for casting the final sculpture in bronze or another durable material.

clay body the material used for making ceramic wares. The body is a mixture of clays and other earth materials combined to meet the performance requirements for its specific purpose. The physical properties of clays, such as plasticity, texture, colour, shrinkage and thermal resistance, vary greatly. Different methods of forming a piece, such as throwing, building, casting and pressing, require different formulas. Different body properties are also required for different methods of firing, that is, oxidizing or reduction firing at any of numerous possible temperatures. The ultimate body composition is therefore usually a compromise of many characteristics to achieve a certain purpose. The unadorned ceramic piece, as distinguished from the glaze or decoration that may be applied to it, is also known as the *body*.

cleavage any separation between paint layers, between paint film and ground, or between ground and support. Cleavage occurs where adhesion between layers has deteriorated; it is commonly due to faulty materials or improper methods of application. It causes BLISTERS, WRINKLES and flaking of paint.

cloison (*Fr.* cell) a cell or area in enamelling, enclosed by a metal border, into which coloured ceramic pastes are placed. See CLOISONNÉ; ENAMEL.

cloisonné a type of surface decoration in porcelain ENAMEL on metal and, rarely, on pottery, in which each colour area is surrounded by a thin line of metal that is flush with the enamel surface. Thin fillets of flattened wire are set on edge and attached to the base in the desired pattern. The cloisons, or cells, between the wires are filled in with ceramic colour pastes. The work is then fired in a furnace, ground smooth, and polished. Cloisonné can easily be distinguished from CHAMPLEVÉ enamel by the uniform thinness of its metal lines. Beautiful examples of cloisonné were created in the Byzantine era and throughout the mediaeval period in Western Europe. The art has been successfully practised in China and Japan in more modern times.

cloisonnism a type of painting that is similar to the creation of cloisonné enamels, in which bright colours are surrounded by darker shades that serve to highlight the bright colours. The French artist Paul Gauguin (1848–1903) worked in this style.

clove see OIL OF CLOVES.

clunch a soft limestone varying in colour from white to grey and found particularly around Cambridgeshire in England. It is highly suitable for interior carving and decoration and thus was often used by mediaeval English sculptors.

coach varnish a fine-quality glossy varnish of the type suitable for use on coaches and motor vehicles. The term went out of use after the 1920s, when spray lacquer finishes replaced the older compounds, which required laborious hand-finishing.

coal-tar colours those SYNTHETIC ORGANIC PIGMENTS that are derived from products of coal-tar distillation, a by-product of the coal and coke industry. Coal tar yields five basic raw materials: benzene, toluene, xylene, naphthalene, and anthracene, from which numerous compounds, called intermediates, are made by a number of different chemical reactions. These intermediates are combined in various ways to produce thousands of synthetic products, including a vast range of dyestuffs. A number of these are eligible for use in permanent painting, but the greater number are not sufficiently lightfast or nonbleeding in oil. Because of these shortcomings, the terms coal-tar colours and ANILINE colours have acquired a pejorative meaning. Consequently, these terms are no longer in wide use, especially in referring to the better synthetic colours.

coal-tar solvent a VOLATILE SOLVENT obtained by the distillation of coal tar; benzol, toluol and xylol are the principal solvents so obtained. Industrial grades of these substances are widely used as solvents for rubber and many resinous materials. While each has a distinctive odour and solvent properties, the three resemble one another in these respects. Benzol is the most powerful solvent, xylol the least. The vapours of benzol are rated as dangerously toxic; toluol and xylol are much safer and therefore are frequently used in coating materials that must be closely handled. The chemically pure grades of these solvents are known as benzene, toluene and xylene; they are so called in reference to chemical reactions. They are classed as aromatic hydrocarbons. In addition to their use as solvents, they are among the basic raw materials of synthetic organic chemistry and are used in the manufacture of dyes, resins and pharmaceuticals.

A fourth coal-tar derivative, called *solvent naphtha*, has a strong naphthalene or mothball odour, contains mixed hydrocarbons and is in general a weak solvent, useful for the superficial cleaning of coatings that would be damaged by stronger solvents.

coated paper paper whose surface has been coated with a thin layer of an inert pigment such as clay in an adhesive binder, for example glue or casein. Some coated papers have a dull or satin finish but most have a high gloss, which is produced by CALENDERING. Glossy coated paper is called *enamel paper*.

cobalt black see BLACK OXIDE OF COBALT.

cobalt blue, Leyden blue or **Thénard's blue** a bright, clear blue pigment, permanent for all techniques, including fresco; it is a FURNACE PRODUCT made by combining cobalt and aluminium oxides with phosphoric acid. The MASS TONE of cobalt blue is somewhat similar to that of ULTRAMARINE BLUE, but its undertone is more greenish than the comparatively purplish undertone of ultramarine. One of the painter's standard colours, cobalt blue was discovered by Baron L.J. Thénard in France in 1802, and was introduced to artists about twenty years later. It was manufactured in Vienna soon after its discovery in France. It replaced the unsatisfactory SMALT and superseded several other varieties of cobalt-aluminium pigments then being developed. These included *Gahn's blue*, *Leithner blue*, and NEW BLUE. Other early names for cobalt blue are *Olympia blue* and *Vienna blue* or *Vienna ultramarine*. Azure cobalt signifies a light shade of one variety of cobalt blue. See also HUNGARY BLUE; KING'S BLUE.

cobalt drier see DRIER.

cobalt green, Swedish green or **zinc green** a compound usually described as cobalt zincate, a FURNACE PRODUCT made by roasting cobalt and zinc oxides. The resulting cobalt green is a fairly bright, bluish-green pigment of medium saturation – fairly opaque but with rather low tinting strength. Despite its absolute permanence, cobalt green is not widely used, since its hue can easily be matched by mixing greens and blues that are more versatile and hence more useful to the painter. Invented in Sweden about 1780 by Sven Rinman (and called Rinman's green), cobalt green began to be used as an artists' pigment in 1835. An early name for cobalt green is *green smalt*; *Gellert green* was a variety made by a somewhat different process from that of Rinman.

cobalt ultramarine a name formerly given to GAHN'S BLUE and later appropriated by manufacturers of imitation cobalt blue, a special shade of ultramarine blue.

cobalt violet cobalt phosphate or cobalt arsenite; a clear, semiopaque, permanent pigment made in two general types, bluish and reddish violet. Although various pinkish and purplish cobalt compounds had been tried since the early 19th century, successful cobalt violets did not come into use until about 1860, after which they were the only permanent bright violets available to artists until the 1950s. The original cobalt violet was the poisonous cobalt arsenite. The present material is nontoxic cobalt phosphate, and is so labelled. Manganese violet is a satisfactory, less costly substitute for the bluish type of cobalt violet, but not for the reddish.

cobalt yellow see AUREOLIN.

cochineal a red NATURAL DYESTUFF of insect origin, imported into Europe from Mexico as early as 1560. An important article of commerce for four centuries, cochineal was used to make CARMINE and, to some extent, to make SCARLET LAKES, until the introduction of synthetic dyes in the 19th century. One of the few surviving natural dyestuffs, cochineal is still on the market and is used for purposes where low cost is a more significant factor than permanence.

cocking see CAULKING.

cocobolo or **cocobola** wood from any of several reddish South American trees of the genus *Dalbergia*, especially *D. retusa*. Cocobolo is dense, extremely hard, and difficult to carve. It may cause swelling or blisters on the skin of those allergic to its dust or splinters.

coefficient of expansion in matter, the ratio of increase or decrease in size to increase or decrease in temperature. This physical law, when applied to clays and glazes, explains such defects as CRAZING, which occurs when the glaze does not fit the clay body.

coelanaglyphic sculpture hollow RELIEF.

coelin or **coeruleum** names of Latin derivation used for CERULEAN BLUE.

coffeewood a South American hardwood obtained from the tree *Caesalpinia granadilla;* also called South American grenadilla and brown ebony.

cogging see TRACING.

coil method the technique of forming a pottery vessel by building up a series of clay ropes or sausages coiled on top of one another on a flat clay base. Lengths of rolled clay are added until the wall of the vessel reaches the desired height, after which the piece may be shaped and smoothed by hand. Much of the pottery of primitive cultures was made by the coil method. It is a good technique for beginning potters because it is simple, requires no complicated tools, and provides experience in handling clay.

colcothar an obsolete name for the artificial red oxides of iron, LIGHT RED and INDIAN RED.

cold chisel a hard steel rod with a straight, flat, bevelled edge at one end. It is so called because it may be used to cut cold metals when struck with a hammer or MALLET, and to distinguish it from a wood-carving chisel. It is used by sculptors in stone carving. See illustration at CHISEL.

cold cut see SIMPLE-SOLUTION VARNISH.

cold-pressed oil any vegetable oil that has been extracted from seeds or nuts by pressing them without the aid of heat and high pressure. Until the 1930s all the best oil colours were made with cold-pressed linseed oil. Since that time, specially refined, modern, hot-pressed oils have been in use, and cold-pressed linseed oil is no longer mass-produced. In the absence of conclusive data on the subject, there is some controversy as to the relative merits of artists' colours made with hot-pressed or cold-pressed oil, in regard to their durability, manipulative excellence, and control over the SUEDE EFFECT.

cold-pressed paper see WATERCOLOUR PAPER.

cold-rubber mould see RUBBER MOULD.

collage the technique of creating a pictorial composition in two dimensions or very low relief by gluing paper, fabrics, or any natural or manufactured material to a canvas or panel; also, a work of art so produced. An entire work may be executed in collage, but the technique is also used in combination with painting in oil or with other techniques. When heavy three-dimensional objects dominate the composition, the work is usually called an ASSEMBLAGE, a term used also for a freestanding construction more closely related to sculpture than to painting.

Collage evolved out of *papiers collés*, a 19th-century so-called art recreation in which decorative designs were made with pasted pieces of coloured paper. It was adapted to the fine arts about 1912–1913, when Picasso and Braque began to incorporate into their Cubist paintings a wide variety of prosaic materials (newspaper clippings, tickets, folded paper, pieces of wood and glass, wire, sand, etc.) selected primarily because they offered new mediums with which to represent planes and textures. Later, when the Dadaists and Surrealists began to combine such materials on the basis of their connotative and associative values, the technique was called *collage*. The Dadaist series of *Fatagaga* paintings (1919) by Max Ernst and Hans Arp may be the most notable early works in collage. Another outstanding figure in the development of collage as an art form is Kurt Schwitters (1887–1948).

Collages constructed with inappropriate glues or with pulp paper and materials with fugitive colours are susceptible to rapid deterioration, and the use of intricate and fragile elements sometimes precludes cleaning. Most present-day artists working in the form use the regular POLYMER MEDIUM as an adhesive and give their works a protective coating of mat polymer medium. See also COLLAGRAPH; FROTTAGE; MONTAGE.

collagraph or **intaglio print** a contemporary INTAGLIO printmaking process in which proofs are pulled from a block similar to that used in RELIEF BLOCK PRINTING, that is, a block on which the design or pattern is built up in the manner of a COLLAGE, whence the name *collagraph*. As in relief block printing, a great variety of objects may be adhered to the block, and if the objects are likely to be affected by the printing fluid, they are treated with a plastic spray. The surface of the collagraph block is inked, wiped to leave ink only in the depressions, and the block is then printed in an etching press. The technique has many variations for creating interesting effects of tone and texture. Sometimes, etched or photoengraved plates are made an element of the composition. When constructed to a relatively level surface, with firm materials, a collagraph block may also be used to make embossed prints. Paper that has been dampened is placed over the block, and the two are run through the press. Such a block may be wholly or partially inked; it creates embossed areas similar to the effects of BLIND PRINTING.

Cologne, School of see SCHOOL OF COLOGNE.

Cologne earth another name for CASSEL EARTH.

Cologne spirits see ETHYL ALCOHOL.

colonial spirits see ETHYL ALCOHOL.

colophony an old word for ROSIN, now obsolete in English but still encountered in French and German writings. Some say that the word is derived from the Greek for 'sound glue,' an allusion to its use on violin bows, but it was more likely taken from a place name, Colophon, in Ionia.

Colorado Yule Statuary a fine-grained American MARBLE, suitable for sculpture. It is pure white, although some grades of Colorado Yule are clouded with grey.

colorimeter a laboratory device for measuring or specifying colour by comparison with synthesized colours. The typical colorimeter has a built-in, standard light source, three coloured filters, photoelectric cells or phototubes, a standard reflecting surface and, in modern types, photoelectric cells and electronic circuits to replace the human eye as the receptor and thus speed up results. The results of a colorimeter examination are expressed as CHROMATICITY coordinates.

colorimetry the science of measuring colour. See COLORIMETER; SPECTROPHOTOMETER; COLOUR COMPARISON; CHROMATICITY; TRISTIMULUS VALUES.

colossal (of a figure sculpture) larger than twice life-size. See also HEROIC.

colour 1. a sensation aroused in the observer's mind as a response to the stimulus of the radiant energy of certain wavelengths acting on the eye's mechanism. White light contains all the colour wavelengths, and when white light passes through a prism, it separates into its component parts in the familiar rainbow SPECTRUM. A surface hit by light will reflect certain wavelengths determined by the nature of the surface – what we call its colour – and absorb the rest. For example, a surface of the pigment cadmium red reflects only the portion of the light that produces a red sensation and absorbs all the rest. An alizarin pigment reflects some blue along with the red, causing the observer to see a more bluish red. White reflects all the light and absorbs none, while black absorbs all and reflects none. All pigments and dyes reflect a certain amount of white light along with the part of the spectrum corresponding to their ostensible colour.

Pigments, as well as paints, dyes and inks, are mixed with one another to create new HUES according to the subtractive system, so called because each element of such a mixture subtracts another segment from the light absorbed. Theoretically, any chromatic hue can be obtained by a mixture of the three primaries – red, blue and yellow. In practice, however, many hues can only be approximately achieved by mixing primaries, so the painter requires a multiplicity of pigments, especially when bright colours and clear tones are desired. A mixture of two or more pigments is apt to be muddy and dull in comparison with a single pigment of the same hue.

The secondary colours are made up of pairs of primaries. The secondary colours are green (blue and yellow), violet (blue and red), and orange (red and yellow). Tertiary colours are mixtures of three colours. Each colour has its complementary colour, which lies opposite to it on the COLOUR CIRCLE. Red and green, blue and orange, and yellow and violet are pairs of complementary colours. A given colour reflects exactly those wavelengths that its complement absorbs. A red substance, for example, reflects exactly those wavelengths that a green one absorbs. In addition, a colour gives a greater degree of colour contrast to its complement than to any other colour.

Coloured lights, as opposed to pigments and dyes, conform to the system of additive colour mixture. In coloured light behaviour, the primary colours are red, green and blue. Beams of these three colours projected together will produce white light. The *additive system* is of more interest to colour photographers than to painters. See also CHROMA; CHROMATICITY; CHROMATIC COLOUR; COLOUR COMPARISON; COLOUR NOTATION.

2. a paint prepared expressly for artists' use. Artists' colours are customarily put into tubes, jars or cakes and sold in a useful assortment of hues. The types of artists' colours available include OIL COLOURS; WATERCOLOURS; TEMPERA COLOURS; GOUACHE; CASEIN COLOURS; POLYMER COLOURS; DESIGNERS' COLOURS and POSTER COLOURS.

colour chart a group of chromatic samples assembled to illustrate a scheme of colour nomenclature or classification, demonstrate a colour theory, or show the colours available in a manufacturer's line of goods.

colour circle a circular arrangement of the hues of the SPECTRUM in the order in which they appear in nature. See diagram overleaf.

The WARM COLOURS lie within the half circle that contains red and yellow, the cool colours within the half that contains green and violet. COMPLEMENTARY COLOURS appear opposite each other. See also COLOUR WHEEL.

colour comparison the three methods in use for evaluating colour differences: visual examination, use of the SPECTROPHOTOMETER, and use of the COLORIMETER. An experienced person can evaluate colour properties by observation alone with sufficient accuracy to serve many practical purposes (see RUB-OUT). The use of colour charts, cards and swatches is widespread, but because colour is a subjective phenomenon, total accuracy and precise results can be obtained only by wavelength in a laboratory. In recent years electronic circuits have been used instead of the human eye to observe the results of such measurement.

coloured cement white Portland cement or concrete to which

COLOURED PENCIL

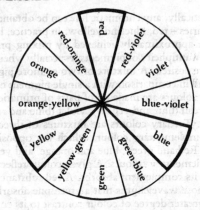

colour circle Primary colours are those within the heaviest lines. Pairs of hues opposite each other are complementary colours. The three complementaries of the primary colours are called secondary colours. The remaining three pairs are intermediate colours.

LIMEPROOF PIGMENTS have been added. In one technique of outdoor mural decoration, such cements are trowelled flat or modelled in relief. Durable cement coloured with permanent pigments is a practically indestructible art and decorative medium for outdoor use.

coloured pencil a drawing pencil made with chromatic pigments instead of graphite. The pigments are mixed with a clay binder, and the pencils are manufactured in the same way as LEAD PENCILS. A number of brands of coloured pencils are sold, so a wide spectrum of hues is available. But because few brands are labelled with the names of the pigments they contain, and since the majority of these pigments are not approved for artists, coloured pencils are not generally recommended for fine-arts purposes. (Some manufacturers use lightfast pigments and promote their pencils as lightfast.) Special varieties, such as those made with water-soluble dyes, are also available. They are used like ordinary coloured pencils, and the marks are then gone over with a wet watercolour brush to blend tones and create the effect of washes. Because they contain soluble dyes, they are never suitable for permanent work.

coloured print a print made by a single impression, with the colour added by a separate process (by hand, POCHOIR, roller, or solid, uncarved wood blocks). Compare COLOUR PRINT.

coloured resin a highly coloured resin sometimes used as an ingredient in red, yellow, and orange coloured VARNISHES. The yellow resins used for colouring varnishes are GAMBOGE and yellow ACCROIDES; for red, DRAGON'S BLOOD and red accroides are used. Transparent coloured varnishes are not used in fine-arts painting, because the colours are not sufficiently permanent and cannot be manipulated to give uniform or

controlled effects. However, they are sufficiently permanent for lacquering or toning gilded frames and for other decorative purposes. In
recent times, oil- or lacquer-soluble dyes have largely supplanted
coloured resins. When the effects of a transparent coating are needed in
a painting, the artist uses a GLAZE of such permanent transparent pigments
as COBALT VIOLET; COBALT YELLOW and HANSA YELLOW.

coloured sculpture see POLYCHROME.

colour effect the total appearance of a colour, including all its colour
properties and physical properties, such as vividness, opacity and value.
The term is frequently used in reference to the suitability of a particular
colour for a specific use.

colour field painting a style of 20th-century abstract art, associated
mostly with the American painters Mark Rothko (1903–1970) and
Barnett Newman (1905–1970), in whose works large areas are covered
with unmodulated colour.

colouring power, **staining power** or *(US)* **tinting strength** or **tinctorial power** the power of a pigment to tint paints, as measured by its
relative strength in colouring a standard white pigment in oil. In the test
for colouring power, one part of the pigment is mixed with ten parts of
zinc white and ground (as in RUB-OUTS) with a measured amount of
linseed oil. The results are evaluated by laboratory instruments or by
skilled visual comparison with a standard colour. This test also reveals
the nuances of a pigment's undertone. In general, the high colouring
power of a pigment is an indication of its economy, purity, and superiority over materials of lower strength. However, pigments with excessively
high colouring powers, such as pure Prussian and phthalocyanine blues,
tend to create imbalances with other colours unless reduced by adding
an inert pigment.

colourist a painter whose most outstanding quality is successful use of
colour; one who has mastered colour as a major means of expression.

colour lithography the technique of producing a multicolour lithograph
from a series of lithograph stones, one for each basic colour to be printed
(see COLOUR PRINT). These so-called colour stones are made from a
keystone the artist first prepares and processes as though the colour sketch
were to be a black-and-white print (see LITHOGRAPHY). The drawing on
the keystone may be complete or it may be entirely linear, with the
shading to be reproduced in the proofs done later on the separate colour
stones. The colour stones are made by pulling several proofs from the
keystone on a special transfer paper. To transfer the master drawing to
the colour stones, the backs of these proofs are dusted with powdered
red chalk or sanguine CONTÉ CRAYON, which enables them to be traced
on to the stone surfaces, producing nonprinting red-chalk drawings. The
respective colour area of each stone is then drawn in with LITHOGRAPHIC
CRAYON, TUSCHE, or both, and processed as if for black-and-white lithography, except that the final printing is done with a coloured printing
ink. The successive impressions of the colour stones are kept in REGISTER
with the aid of REGISTER MARKS that were placed in the margin of the

COLOUR NOTATION

keystone and transferred to each colour stone. The first major artist to exhibit a colour lithograph – the only work he did in this medium – was Edouard Manet. He used seven stones for *Punchinello* (1874). Slightly more than a decade later, Henri de Toulouse-Lautrec discovered the medium, and it became 'the passion of his brief life.' Colour lithography remains a very popular graphic-arts technique today. See also CHROMO-LITHOGRAPH; OLEOGRAPH.

colour notation any numerical system of classification and identification of colours according to their optical properties, as HUE, VALUE and SATURATION. Such notation, expressed in precise, scientific terms, is invaluable for technical and scientific use, although *hue designation* is a more appropriate system of nomenclature for everyday use, as in reference to the products of commerce or fashion. The two most widely used systems of colour notation are the MUNSELL SYSTEM and the OSTWALD SYSTEM.

colour oxides *(ceramics)* colouring ingredients, most of which are metallic oxides. See CERAMIC COLOURS.

colour print a print made by a process in which a separate block, stone, plate, or silk-screen stencil is inked and printed for each basic colour that appears in the multicolour proofs. A colour print may also contain additional colours made by overprinting the basic colours used.

Lithography (see COLOUR LITHOGRAPHY) and woodcut are well suited to multicolour printing, and silkscreen is seldom used for anything but colour work. Intaglio plates are almost always printed in black and white, although single-colour intaglio prints (that is, a coloured ink, especially blue or brown, is used instead of black) are sometimes made. Multicolour etchings are infrequently seen. The only metal-plate techniques widely used for colour printing are aquatint and mezzotint, both of which emphasize tonal masses rather than line. Although there is no limit to the number of colours that may be used in lithographs and woodcuts, artists generally limit them to two, three, or four colour impressions plus secondary colour effects from overprinting. The aesthetic criteria and practical considerations that impose these limitations on lithography and woodcut do not apply, however, to silkscreen, whose colour and textural effects are closely related to those of painting and whose range of colour effects is unlimited.

In all multicolour graphic-arts processes except serigraphy (silkscreen), the separate colour blocks, stones, or plates from which each colour impression is pulled are made from the KEY BLOCK, keystone or key plate that the artist prepares first from a colour sketch. The artist processes the printing surface of this key and pulls several black-and-white proofs from it. These proofs, which show the REGISTER MARKS that the artist has indicated on the key, are used to transfer the master drawing to the individual colour blocks, stones or plates in such a way that all the impressions of these separate colour printing surfaces will be in REGISTER. The key is sometimes also used itself in printing. Although no such key is used in silkscreen, the artist's original drawing serves the same function in the production of separate stencils for each colour to be printed. The drawing is placed in the register guides on the bed of the silkscreen apparatus; the screen is lowered on it; and the parts of the drawing to be printed in any one colour are traced onto the screen, which is then treated to make that particular colour-run stencil. Serigraph stencils are also registered in this way for alignment in printing. See also CHIAROSCURO WOODCUT; PROGRESSIVE PROOFS. Compare COLOURED PRINT.

colour properties the colour characteristics of a pigment, as distinguished from the rest of its physical, chemical, or structural qualities, which are known as PIGMENT PROPERTIES.

colour scheme the dominant colours used in a limited area, such as a picture or a decorated room, conceived as imposing a discipline on the whole. For example, the colour scheme of an autumn scene might be red and gold, that of a misty scene blue and grey.

colour sketch a sketch done in colour with pastel, watercolour or oils. Colour sketches are often made as preparation for a landscape painting. Such factors as changing weather and shifting light make it difficult for a landscape artist to paint from a particular scene for more than a few hours, an insufficient period of time for most painters to execute a carefully worked-out, full-sized painting. Unless, therefore, the painter can return to the same site at the same time on successive days when the weather is the same, a sketch is needed if the artist wants to capture the setting's actual effects of colour, light and movement in order to incorporate those effects in the final work. Many landscape painters, however, do not use such colour sketches but employ pencil drawings and written notes (see NOTE). Other painters can keep on painting through changes in light and weather but adhere closely to their original perceptions. See also POCHADE.

colour solid see OSTWALD SYSTEM.

colour stability the property of resistance to change of colour (fading, darkening, or hue variation).

colour triangle see CHROMATICITY.

colour wheel a rapidly spinning vertical wheel on which coloured paper discs are mounted. It is used for various experiments in the optical mixture of colours. If the entire colour spectrum is put on a disc and spun rapidly, it will appear white in accordance with the additive behaviour of spectral colours. See COLOUR CIRCLE.

Columbian spirits see METHANOL.

combed decoration a method of decorating clay forms. A rakelike tool is used to draw parallel lines through glaze or plastic clay.

combine painting a term coined by the American artist Robert Rauschenberg (1925–) to describe a type of painting in which objects or photographs are combined with the painted surface of the canvas.

commercial artist an artist whose work is commissioned for such uses as advertising, illustration, and the design, embellishment, or decoration of industrial products. Such art must meet the standards and requirements of its user and generally is subject to the user's refusal. The term is used principally to distinguish the commercial artist from the fine-art or creative artist, whose work is primarily done as an independent aesthetic, emotional, or intellectual expression. The distinction is professional or vocational rather than pejorative, for a useful art can be of high aesthetic content and accomplishment, and the line between the two in such ventures as illustration and portrait painting cannot always be sharply defined.

Commercial Standard for Artists' Oil Paints see PAINT STANDARD.

Commission Internationale de l'Eclairage (CIE) the International Commission on Illumination. This is the authority that in 1931 established the present system for specifying colour by mathematically defining each colour sensation with TRISTIMULUS VALUES obtained by spectrophotometry. It has also been known, particularly in the United States, by the initials *ICI*.

compass a mechanical drawing instrument for describing circles and arcs, usually consisting of two hinged legs or a rod with sliding points that adjust for different diameters. A *bow compass*, the most common type, has two legs hinged at the top. One leg ends in a sharp steel point, the other in a holder for a ruling pen or a pencil. Both holder and point ends are replaceable. The *beam compass*, also frequently used by draughtsmen, consists of a rod with a point fixed perpendicularly at one end as a pivot and a drawing point, ending with a pen nib so attached that it slides along the rod and can be fixed at any point. Both types can be used as DIVIDERS. There also are several kinds of compasses for special purposes, among them the COMPASS CUTTER.

compass cutter a device for cutting circles from paper, cardboard, etc. It is constructed like a draughtsman's COMPASS, but a razor-sharp cutting edge replaces the pen or pencil.

compensating planimeter see PLANIMETER.

complementary colour one of a pair of colours usually considered to be in extreme contrast to each other, as it reflects exactly those wavelengths that the other absorbs. Red and green, yellow and violet, and blue and orange are pairs of complementary colours. The complement of a PRIMARY COLOUR is made by mixing the other two primaries: for example, green (yellow and blue) is the complement of red. The complements of intermediate colours are shown on the COLOUR CIRCLE.

composite pigment 1. any PIGMENT that contains more than one basic ingredient, as cadmium-barium yellow, which contains both cadmium sulphide and barium sulphate coprecipitated.
2. any mixture of pigments, such as PERMANENT GREEN (phthalocyanine green plus cadmium yellow), used by manufacturers of artists' materials to supply a pigment with properties or advantages that cannot be obtained from a single pigment.

composite white an artists' colour containing a mixture of white pigments, usually TITANIUM WHITE and ZINC WHITE, in proportions of 40 to 60 % of either. Since the 1920s, experience with white house paints has shown this combination to be superior in durability of paint film to either of its ingredients used alone.

composition leaf see DUTCH METAL.

concave relief hollow RELIEF.

conceptual art a type of art in which the idea or concept expressed and executed by the artist is considered more important than the final product. Mostly a phenomenon of the 1960s, the term embraces a wide variety of styles, forms, and ideas, including happenings, PERFORMANCE ART, ARTE POVERA, autodestructive art, and the like. The common strain in all these manifestations of conceptual art is the notion that the act of artistic creation, in and of itself, is of greater value than what, finally, is created.

conceptual colour colour used by a painter for reasons other than reproducing the colour the artist sees, for example, to express a meaning, depict the effects of reflections or shadows, or conform to a theory or doctrine.

concours (*Fr.* competition, meet, match or tournament) an exhibition of the selected work of art students at the end of a session, or, in some schools, an exhibition of the results of a competitive examination. See HORS CONCOURS.

concrete a mixture of Portland cement, sand and crushed stone, used as a building material. Cast concrete has also been used by sculptors.

concrete art a type of abstract art that eschews all naturalistic or figurative references in favour of purely geometric form. The name was coined by the Dutch artist Theo van Doesburg (1883–1931).

cone, ceramic see PYROMETRIC CONE.

cone of vision the field of vision of the observer of a work of art. The cone of vision may be thought of as an infinite number of sight lines radiating from the eye, or POINT OF STATION, in a conical pattern, although in reality the rays of light come to the eye from the subject. See illustration at PERSPECTIVE.

confluent colours areas of colour that merge or gradate into one another.

Congo copal see COPAL.

conservation the reconditioning and preservation of works of art. The practitioner is called a *conservator*. Formerly, such work was known as restoration and its technicians as restorers, but now the term restoration properly refers to only one aspect of the field, the replacement of missing parts and the filling in of missing areas in a damaged work of art. It is still correct, however, to say that a work treated by a conservator has been restored. Modern conservation is performed on a high scientific and ethical plane. Museum technicians and many private conservators enjoy the benefits of modern equipment and techniques, new advances in knowledge through research, and international cooperation. See also CRADLING; INPAINTING; LINING; PARQUETAGE; RESTRAINER; STOP; STRIP; TRANSFER.

consistency the condition or state of a substance defined by its qualities of firmness, softness, and resistance to movement either by deformation

(PLASTICITY) or by flow (VISCOSITY, MOBILITY, or fluidity). The branch of physics that pertains to these properties of materials is called *rheology*. In modern artists' OIL COLOURS, the standard consistency is described as *short* or buttery. Although painters always desired this quality, the current practice of using very short, paste-like paints began about 1860, when the more emphatic preference of painters (especially the Impressionists), coupled with the introduction of improved paint-grinding machinery, made this consistency standard. To employ the techniques and manipulations that require more fluid colours, a painting MEDIUM must be added to this type of tube colour. The painter can thus choose between a short colour to be pushed about with stiff bristle brushes or a more flowing colour to use with soft ones. The more flowing colour must retain enough of the short quality for the brushstrokes not to run or drip. Each pigment has its own effect on the consistency of an oil colour. Some, such as raw sienna, yield smooth, buttery pastes; others, like ultramarine, tend to produce a sticky or stringy consistency. The older painter was familiar with these differences and adjusted painting manipulations accordingly, but the modern painter has become accustomed to having all colours squeeze out of their tubes with a uniform consistency. The manufacturer accomplishes this result by scientific control of grinding procedures (see PAINT) and the use of STABILIZERS, PLASTICIZERS, and sometimes excess oil. Only the finest quality oil colours, which do not rely on these additives, will exhibit the short, paste-like consistency of paint that has the optimum pigment-to-oil ratio.

constant white BLANC FIXE used as a pigment in GOUACHE and designers' colours.

construction 1. the art of building or erecting.

2. an object that is built or erected; a structure.

In sculpture, a construction is a work that is put together out of different pieces, rather than cast, modelled, or carved. An ASSEMBLAGE is one type of construction.

construction paper an inexpensive coloured paper available in a large assortment of hues, used for innumerable cutout and design purposes. Its colours are not sufficiently permanent nor is the paper itself durable enough for use as a permanent fine-arts material.

Constructivism a nonobjective art movement that began in Russia and had far-reaching effects on modern art. It first appeared in the work of Vladimir Tatlin (1885–1953) about 1913, as a development of Cubist relief constructions, and was first called *Tatlinism*. Its theorists did not name it Constructivism or fully establish its principles until 1921. Constructivist work utilized materials such as iron, tin, wood, glass and plaster in its attempt to bridge the gap between everyday life and art. An early name for it was *production art*, and one of its aims was to revolutionize industrial design by creating a body of artist-engineers. Tatlin came to believe that art itself was outmoded, although the brothers Antoine Pevsner (1886–1962) and Naum Gabo (1890–1977), who were to bring Constructivism to the West, felt that it still had a place in society.

Among the principles of Constructivist art in its nonfunctional form were dynamism and an integral use of space. Gabo started making kinetic models, (see KINETIC ART) and Alexander Rodchenko (1891–1956) made Constructivist mobiles in 1920; Tatlin's model for a proposed monument to the Third International was also created in 1920. Another important figure in the movement was El Lissitzky (1890–1941). Constructivism and SUPREMATISM were very closely related, and most of their early adherents belonged to both groups. During the four years following the Revolution of 1917, the Constructivists and other progressive, experimental artists were at first encouraged by the Soviet government to reorganize the artistic life of the country, and they set up art schools and museums. When experimental and abstract art were proscribed in 1922 (see PROLETCULT), they left Russia for France and Germany to continue the movement and contribute its principles to the mainstream of abstract art.

contained shadow the shaded area on a depicted three-dimensional figure or object on the side that is away from the supposed light source. A contained shadow is depicted as lying within the object, as distinguished from a cast shadow, which is thrown by an object onto another surface. See illustration at CAST SHADOW.

Conté crayons a widely known, long-established tradename of a brand of French crayons in the form of square sticks and wood-encased pencils. Conté crayons are made of a unique compressed compound of pigments and a binder. Their composition and properties sufficiently resemble those of chalk and hard pastels for them to be frequently used in chalk and hard-pastel drawings. Conté crayons are completely grease-free, which makes them useful in lithography for drawing lines on the stone that will not appear in the proofs (as for squaring, ruling guide lines, etc.). These crayons are available in sanguine, the most popular shade, and in sepia, white, and three grades of black – soft, medium, and hard. They are named after Nicolas Jacques Conté (1755–1805), inventor of the modern graphite pencil.

content the subject matter or MOTIF of a work of art and its intellectual, aesthetic, spiritual or narrative values considered apart from the artist's formal accomplishment or the excellence of the artist's technique. A work of art can be viewed as consisting of two elements, FORM and content.

continuous representation the mediaeval pictorial device in which two or more episodes from a narrative or story are combined in a single image.

contour the outline or periphery of a figure or object; the line that bounds or delimits a form or an area. See also CONTOUR DRAWING.

contour drawing a method of drawing popularized by Kimon Nicolaïdes in his book *The Natural Way to Draw* (1941), which presents contour drawing as an effective training aid or discipline. The student, fixing his or her eyes on the outline of the model or object, draws the contour very slowly in a steady, continuous line without lifting pencil or looking at the paper; the student's eyes slowly follow the outline of the object being drawn in unison with the pencil. The student may look at the paper to place an internal feature, but once beginning to draw, does not glance down, but follows the same procedure as for the outline. A well-done contour drawing frequently has sufficient quality and character to be preserved as a work of art. An OUTLINE DRAWING, according to Nicolaïdes, is 'a diagram or silhouette, flat and two dimensional,' while a contour 'has a three-dimensional quality; that is, it indicates thickness as well as the length and width of the form it surrounds. We do not think of a line as a contour unless it follows the sense of touch, whereas an outline may follow the eye alone.'

contour drawing Still life rendered by contour drawing (left) and in outline (right).

contrapposto or **counterpoise** (*figure sculpture*) a balanced but asymmetrical attitude in which the figure stands poised with most of its weight on one leg, the so-called *engaged leg*, and with the vertical axis of the body in a slight S-curve. This attitude first appeared in statues of the CLASSICAL PERIOD in Greece. It was copied and much admired by Italian sculptors of the Renaissance, who gave it its name and considered it the epitome of harmony and balance in a standing figure.

conversation piece a painting of a group, especially a family, in its familiar surroundings, indoors or out.

cool colours those colours in which blue is dominant, including greens and violets. Bluish greys are called cool greys. The term may be used in a relative sense, so that raw umber is said to be cooler than burnt umber, although both are warm colours. All cool colours lie in the green-violet half of the COLOUR CIRCLE. See also WARM COLOURS.

copaiba balsam a viscous, fluid oleoresin obtained from several species of tropical trees of the genus *Copaifera*. There are two general types of copaiba balsam: *Maracaibo balsam*, from Venezuela; and *Pará balsam*, with more volatile ingredients and fewer solids, from Brazil. Copaiba balsam, a very slow-drying material, is no longer used as an ingredient of painting vehicles and mediums because of its instability. It was once employed in the conservation of oil paintings as a RESTRAINER for cleaning solvents and as a conditioner or *regenerator* of aged paint films, especially in the now-discredited PETTENKOFFER PROCESS. Most authorities doubt its effectiveness in treating the surface of paintings, but it is still encountered in proprietary liquids sold for that purpose. See BALSAM.

copal tree RESIN, whether fossil or recent; unless preceded by a designation of the place of origin or the species of tree, it is not a specific term. The hard fossil copals melt at high temperatures and when cooked with oil produce strong, durable SPAR VARNISHES and vehicles for deck and machinery enamels, but since the late 1930s they have been replaced for such purposes by synthetic products with superior properties, notably the PHENOLIC RESINS. Hardest among the copals is *Congo copal*, a clear, almost colourless fossil resin dug from the ground and the beds of streams. Next are the East African copals, known collectively as *animé*. *Sierra Leone copal* and *kauri copal* are of medium hardness. A distinct and separate variety, *Manila copal*, is a softer resin, soluble in alcohol.

During the 19th century artists used copal varnishes both as ingredients in painting mediums and as picture varnishes. Much of the cracking and darkening of 19th-century paintings has been attributed to their use. Copal does not meet one important requirement for a PICTURE VARNISH – easy removal from paintings with mild solvents. Although it still has its proponents and is available in some art supply shops, hard copal varnish has been rather generally discredited by paint technologists and museum workers. The hard fossil copals require expert treatments by experienced varnish makers in order to dissolve properly in oils. These include a thermal treatment known as GUM RUNNING. The 19th-century varnish makers developed this difficult trade to a high degree.

copolymer a polymer (see POLYMERIZATION) that contains two or more different types of monomer molecules, as, for example, a synthetic resin that contains both acrylic and vinyl groups within its chemical formula. Such a material is used in some POLYMER colourS in place of the usual straight acrylic type.

copper a metallic element that is malleable and ductile and has a characteristic reddish-brown colour. It is used in the manufacture of such alloys as BRASS and BRONZE, which are harder than copper and do not corrode as easily. When exposed to or combined with oxygen, copper takes on a greenish PATINA.

copper blue see BREMEN BLUE.

copperplate engraving see ENGRAVING.

Coptic art art of the early Christians of Egypt, especially during the 4th–7th centuries, when Egypt was part of the late Roman and, later, the Byzantine Empire. Like BYZANTINE art in general, Coptic wall painting was flat and highly stylized; the Coptic work, however, also had roots in the realistic Fayoum portraits of the 1st–4th centuries. The Copts also produced woven tapestries employing decorative patterns of plant and bird forms in wool and linen, as well as stone and ivory carvings, illuminations and pottery.

copy 1. any reproduction or facsimile of an original work of art, done in the same art form although not necessarily in the same size or with the same materials. See also FORGERY; ORIGINAL; REPLICA; REPRODUCTION.
2. any one of a series of reproductions, especially printed reproductions, of the same original work.
3. *(printing)* any written or typed text or illustrative material (as a picture, photograph, or drawing) that is to be reproduced.

4. (rare) a model, a subject, or an original work of art considered as a PROTOTYPE.

copying press a heavy cast-iron press that was widely used in offices before the day of typewriter carbons to make copies of letters and documents that were written in a special copying ink and, of course, long before the invention of xerographic equipment. It is now almost exclusively used by artists, who find many uses for this device. It may be used to press and flatten objects with a large surface area, to exert pressure on paper and boards in pasting and gluing operations, and to flatten wrinkled or buckled paper after dampening it. In the graphic arts it can function as a press on which proofs can be pulled. The copying press is made in several sizes, the largest having a bed of 20 by 24 inches. It is operated by turning a horizontal wheel at the top, which by means of a screw applies downward pressure on a broad, flat plate that in turn applies pressure to whatever is placed on the bed of the press.

copying press

coquille board an ILLUSTRATION BOARD whose working surface has a dotted, stippled, or otherwise embossed texture. When it is drawn on with pencil or crayon, it produces a HALFTONE effect that makes it a useful, less expensive substitute for the half-tone process plate. See also SHADING FILM.

corail see PADOUK.

cordate heart-shaped.

core *(sculpture)* the solid internal portion of a MOULD for casting a hollow piece of sculpture. The amount of space left between the core and the mould determines the thickness of the cast. The core is made of FOUNDRY SAND in SAND CASTING and in the LOST-WAX PROCESS.

Corinthian order one of the three Grecian architectural orders (see DORIC ORDER, IONIC ORDER), of which it is the lightest and most ornate, having a bell-shaped capital adorned with ACANTHUS leaf foliage. The style, developed by the Greeks, was even more prevalent later in Roman architecture.

cork black see VINE BLACK.

Cornish stone or **Cornwall stone** a decomposed feldspathic rock found in southwest England and used as a FLUX in clay bodies and glazes. It is very similar to PETUNTSE.

Coromandel see EBONY.

coroplast *(Gk* doll maker) a sculptor, in ancient Greece, who created figurines of clay or terracotta.

corporation piece a portrait of a member or a group portrait of members of the organization that commissioned it. Perhaps the most famous is Rembrandt's *The Company of Captain Franz Banning Cocq* (1642), better known as *The Night Watch*.

correction white a quick-drying, fluid white paint of high HIDING POWER, used in drawing to obliterate areas of ink that require alteration. It contains either a lacquer or a synthetic binder and is commonly sold with a special volatile thinner. Correction white is designed to supplant the water-medium whites used by illustrators, designers, and others who work on paper for reproduction. It is not intended for use in permanent works of art.

corrosion a gradual disintegration or transformation by a chemical process. The oxidation of iron, producing rust, and of bronze, producing PATINA, are forms of corrosion.

Cosmati a school of marble workers, mosaicists and sculptors active in Rome from the 12th to the 14th centuries. They enriched many existing churches and other buildings with their glass and marble mosaic pavements, altars, and other church furniture and decoration. The Cosmas and Cosmatus families, two of several families working in the same style, gave the group its name. The Cosmati's practice of signing their work represented a departure from the anonymity of the mediaeval craftsman. The term *Cosmati work* is often used to designate the decorative art of 13th-century Rome in general, especially mosaic work in marble with inlays of glass or coloured stones.

cosmorama *(US)* any of several 18th- and 19th-century techniques for exhibiting characteristic scenes or views of various countries. The paintings were reflected from mirrors and viewed through lenses. See also DIORAMA; PANORAMA.

costruzione legittima see LEGITIMATE CONSTRUCTION.

cotton canvas CANVAS made of cotton and widely used as a less expensive substitute for linen canvas. It does not have the boldness of weave found on linen canvas. Homemade canvas of extra-heavy cotton duck, carefully prepared, is believed by some to be adequately durable; others hold that the hygroscopic nature of cotton and its lower receptivity to grounds and sizings make it less desirable than linen. The appearance of the duck weave is quite different from the traditional textural effect of linen.

couch a layer, underlayer, or substratum. Grounds for painting are no longer called couches in technical usage.

counterchange a method in drawing and painting in which the artist deliberately juxtaposes smaller light forms against larger dark masses and vice versa in order to achieve forceful value contrasts.

counterpoise see CONTRAPPOSTO.

counterproof a reverse impression taken from a print or drawing by passing it through an etching press with a sheet of damp paper. Some of the ink of the print or drawing is drawn off by and transferred to the damp paper, duplicating the original in mirror image. A graphic artist may make a counterproof of an engraving or etching as an aid in correcting a plate, since it allows the artist to see a printed duplicate of the plate, on which the drawing or design is also in reverse. The process has been used to make forgeries of valuable prints and drawings, but the weakness of the ink and the left-handed composition tend to expose such copies. A counterproof may also be made of a MONOTYPE impression by pressing a sheet of paper against the monotype print while the paint is still wet.

coupling agent see MUTUAL SOLVENT.

covering power the surface area that a defined volume of paint or varnish will cover acceptably in one coat. In industrial coatings, covering power is expressed in square feet per gallon. The term is sometimes confused with HIDING POWER.

Cox paper a type of rough, tinted paper introduced in the 1800s by the English artist David Cox (1783–1859). Cox paper found great favour among the watercolourists of the East Anglican School, who prized it for its highly absorbent nature.

CP 1. chemically pure. A chemical so labelled has been made as free as possible from impurities, and is suitable for laboratory use.

2. cold-pressed. See WATERCOLOUR PAPER.

crack any separation in the paint layer, the ground, or the support, perpendicular to the surface of a painting; it should not be confused with CLEAVAGE. A crack may be hairline or wide, straight, radial, or spiral, individual or part of a network of reticulations. Cracks may be caused by accidental blows, long storage at low temperatures, sudden changes in temperature or defects in the materials.

crackle or *(Fr.)* **craquelure 1.** a network of cracks in a fine, overall pattern on the surface of a painting, usually resulting from the embrittlement of the paint film as it ages.

2. any of several reticulated patterns of cracks in ceramic glazes; they are deliberate effects, intended to enhance the appearance of the glazed surface.

cradle 1. a brace of hardwood ribs and crosspieces attached to the back of a painted wooden panel to reinforce it and to prevent warping and cracking. See CRADLING.

2. see ROCKER.

cradling 1. *(conservation)* a traditional technique for reinforcement of wooden panels. After the thickness of a damaged panel has been reduced with various tools, rigid strips of hardwood are glued vertically to the rear of the panel at intervals along the grain of the wood. There are rectangular slots of regular intervals on the undersides of these strips, through which flat strips of the same hardwood are run to form horizontal bracing. These horizontal strips are not glued, but move freely to allow for expansion and contraction of the panel and to preclude future cracking. Cradling was practised for over 200 years but is no longer recommended. Conservators have replaced cradling with other methods of reinforcement.

2. the simple reinforcement of a wallboard panel by cementing or gluing it to a completely rigid framework of wooden strips.

craft 1. technique or skill, considered apart from the aesthetic aspect of a creation.

2. a constructive manual activity performed by artisans or craftspersons, as distinguished from the specific group of techniques known as FINE ARTS that are practised by creative artists as aesthetic expressions or as APPLIED ARTS. See ARTS AND CRAFTS.

craquelure see CRACKLE.

crater see KRATER.

crawl, cissing or **creep 1.** the behaviour of a water paint that is repelled by a surface or does not wet it properly (see WETTING AGENT). See also TRACTION FISSURE.

2. *(ceramics)* the behaviour of a faulty glaze that migrates or creeps, leaving unglazed spots.

crayon any drawing material made in stick form; especially, in the fine arts, a stick of CHALK or material with a chalk base, including CONTÉ CRAYONS, blackboard chalk, and hard PASTELS, and other drawing sticks such as CHARCOAL, GREASE CRAYONS, and LITHOGRAPHIC CRAYONS; it also commonly indicates the paraffin wax crayons used by children. Crayons may be made or purchased in round or square sticks. Some are wrapped with paper or encased in wood.

crayon manner or **chalk manner** an ETCHING or ENGRAVING technique in which an effect that approximates to the texture of crayon strokes is created by manipulating various multipoint tools in the etching ground or directly on the plate. The roulette, the MACE-HEAD, and two wider variants of the roulette, the chalk roll and the matting wheel (see ROULETTE), can all be used to create closely dotted lines and areas having the grainy effect of chalk lines, similar to the effect characteristic of lithography. The crayon manner can be used by itself or in conjunction with etched, engraved or drypoint lines. In contrast to the relief plate in STIPPLE ENGRAVING, which is essentially a white-on-black technique, the plate in crayon manner is inked and printed as an INTAGLIO plate.

The crayon manner was in particular vogue in 18th-century France, where it was used chiefly to reproduce drawings. Extensive crayon-manner reproductions were made, for example, of Boucher's chalk drawings. Sometimes ink of a red-chalk or bistre tone was used in printing the plates for crayon manner to give the proofs a more autographic quality.

crayon sauce, sauce or **stumping chalk** pastel in soft cake form, to be applied with a STUMP. A prominent item in art material catalogues during the 19th century, crayon sauce is no longer in use.

crazing an undesirable network of small cracks in a ceramic glaze or a lacquer film. In ceramics, this defect occurs when the glaze and the clay body contract at different rates as they cool after firing. Lacquer crazing is due to the inherent defects of a poorly formulated lacquer. Compare CRACKLE.

creep see CRAWL.

Cremnitz white, Kremnitz white or **Krems white** a high-quality variety of WHITE LEAD, made by a 19th-century process differing from the Dutch process used in making FLAKE WHITE in that its basic raw material is litharge instead of metallic lead. Although the differences between Cremnitz and flake whites are not great, individual artists have preferred one or the other for slight variations in handling qualities.

crenellation a continuous angular line pattern, as of a battlement or parapet, that is alternately and evenly depressed and raised. The design has been commonly used since the earliest times to decorate mouldings, pottery, textile borders, etc.

creta laevis a tradename for coloured chalk pencils made in an extensive range of colours. They were especially popular in the late 19th and early 20th centuries.

crevé a defect in ETCHING caused by overbiting of the plate (see BITING). A crevé may either be lines that are too deeply bitten or a fusing of adjacent lines between which there were to have been spaces. Such defects can be repaired only by resurfacing the affected part of the plate (that is, by rubbing the area with a SCRAPER, smoothing it with a BURNISHER, and relevelling the surface by REPOUSSAGE) before etching it again.

cribbled or **criblé** 1. covered with dots or small punctures; a technique of decorating wood and metal surfaces.

2. (of an engraving) flecked with white dots produced by a plate pocked with holes, in the technique called *manière criblée* (see DOTTED MANNER).

crimson a hue designation for a deep-red colour rather than a pigment name. The word crimson is derived from kermes, a dyestuff of insect origin from which the obsolete pigment crimson lake was made.

crimson lake or **Florentine lake** a deep, transparent ruby-red LAKE pigment with a bluish undertone, made from kermes, a natural dyestuff of insect origin. Crimson lake was used by the ancient Egyptians, Greeks, and Romans; carmine, a better pigment, introduced in the 16th century, became its chief competitor. Until it was superseded in the 19th century by madder and alizarin lakes, crimson lake continued to be used by artists for transparent ruby-red and rose-pink effects.

criosphinx see SPHINX.

crocus martis or **crocus martius** 1. a dark-red ferric oxide, used as a colorant for ceramic glazes and, industrially, as a metal polish.

2. an obsolete term for red iron oxide pigments of the most bluish shades, such as Indian red, caput mortuum, and Mars violet.

croquis 1. a French term, little used in English, for a preliminary SKETCH done in pen, pencil or crayon to get down on paper the concept of a projected work of architecture, sculpture, or painting. Because it serves to fix the impression of a scene, object, or figure that the artist has seen or to indicate the building or the subject that the artist imagines, the croquis has been called the shorthand of painting and drawing. It uses broad energetic lines and strokes to capture the characteristic feeling of the thing drawn.

2. a sketch class without instruction, in academies and art schools.

cross a figure composed essentially of two or more intersecting bars. The cross in its simpler forms has been used in art from prehistoric times, usually with a symbolic, and often a sacred, significance. The ANKH, or crux ansata, was widely used in Egyptian and Assyrian art. The LATIN CROSS is the form usually depicted in scenes of the crucifixion of Jesus, although the TAU CROSS has an older tradition of being shown for that purpose. Certain variations of the cross came to have special religious and liturgical associations. Others lent themselves to architectural use in mediaeval churches. The greatest proliferation of forms, however, developed in the art of heraldry at a time when noble families were eager to have crosses appear in their escutcheons, originally to indicate that their ancestors had taken part in the Crusades. For forms of individual crosses, see illustration overleaf and separate entries: AVELLAN CROSS; CALVARY CROSS; CELTIC CROSS; CROSS CLECHÉE; CROSS-CROSSLET; CROSS FITCHÉ; CROSS FLEURY; CROSS FORMÉE; CROSS FOURCHÉE; CROSS GRING-OLÉE; CROSS MOLINE; CROSS POMMÉE; GREEK CROSS; MALTESE CROSS; PAPAL CROSS; PATRIARCHAL CROSS; POTENT CROSS; QUADRATE CROSS; ST. ANDREW'S CROSS; TREFLED CROSS. See also CHI-RHO.

cross ancrée see CROSS MOLINE.

cross botonée see TREFLED CROSS.

cross bourdonée see CROSS POMMÉE

cross clechée a cross with pointed arms that is *voided*, that is, drawn in outline with the interior hollowed out and the background showing through. The three points of the triangle formed by the end of each arm are often ornamented with small circles, or *pearls*. The form received its name from the resemblance of the decorated arms to the handles of mediaeval keys. See CROSS for illustration.

cross-crosslet a cross with short crossbars intersecting the arms near the ends. It is occasionally called the *holly cross* or *German cross*. It should not be confused with the *potent cross*, which has crossbars at the ends of the arms. Both forms are common in heraldry. See CROSS for illustration.

cross fitché a cross with the upright shaft pointed at the bottom. This form of cross, so shaped to enable it to be driven easily into the ground, found its way into heraldry. The other arms of the cross may have any of the standard forms. See CROSS for illustration.

cross fleuretté a cross with the arms ending in conventionalized fleurs-de-lis which appear to be applied decoration. Compare CROSS FLEURY.

cross fleuronée see TREFLED CROSS.

cross fleury or **cross flory** a cross with the arms ending in conventionalized fleurs-de-lis, which is represented as a part of the arm. See CROSS for illustration.

cross formée, cross formy, cross pattée or **cross patty** a cross with wedge-shaped arms of equal length meeting at their points. The sides of the wedges may form concave curves. This cross is often confused with the MALTESE CROSS, which properly has V-shaped indentations at its ends. See CROSS for illustration.

cross fourchée a cross of which the four arms are divided in half at the ends and the halves angled outward to form squat V-shapes. It differs

ankh

avellan

Calvary

Celtic

cross clechée

cross-crosslet

cross fitché

cross fleury

cross formée

cross fourchée

cross gringolée

cross moline

cross pommée

Greek

Latin

Maltese

papal

patriarchal

potent

quadrate

cross Examples.

St. Andrew's

tau

trefled

106

from the CROSS MOLINE and CROSS ANCRÉE in that the divided ends are not curved. See CROSS for illustration.

cross gringolée a cross similar to the CROSS MOLINE, but with the recurving tongues in the form of serpents' heads. See CROSS for illustration.

crosshatching see HATCHING.

cross-link the tendency for long-chain molecules in synthetic or natural resins to form more complex bonds with one another or with the molecules of other resins or paint films. A dammar varnish, for example, might not yet have formed cross-links with the underlying dried linseed oil film and could therefore be easily removed with turpentine. However, after cross-linking has occurred, a stronger solvent is required to break the bonds formed between the molecules in the dammar varnish resin with the linseed oil film. The solvent needed to perform this function will also dissolve the oil film, jeopardizing the paint surface.

cross moline a cross of which each of the four arms is divided at the ends into two pointed tongues curving outward. The CROSS ANCRÉE is very similar, but the tongues may be longer and more sharply curved. In the *cross recercelée* they are curved back in the form of ram's horns. These forms are most usually found in heraldry. See CROSS for illustration. See also CROSS GRINGOLÉE.

cross pattée or **cross patty** see CROSS FORMÉE.

cross pommée a cross with balls or circles (*Fr. pomme*, apple) at the ends of the four arms. Another term for this form is *cross bourdonée*, referring to a pilgrim's staff. See CROSS for illustration.

cross recercelée see CROSS MOLINE.

cross section a drawing of the inside of an object or structure, seen as though it had been cut through and the face of the cut were visible. A horizontal cross section of an orange, for example, would show the lines of its segments radiating from a central point; a vertical cross section would show its halves equally divided into segments. A cross section is conventionally indicated with SECTION LINES.

cross section (left) Horizontal cross section of an orange; (right) vertical cross section.

cross-section paper a type of bond or ledger paper that is ruled into small squares; each square inch, consisting of from 16 to 100 squares, may be outlined with a heavier line. It is intended for use in making charts and graphs. Quadrille paper is a type of cross-section paper that lacks the heavier inch lines. Both may be ruled in either blue or green.

crow quill the finest of steel drawing pens. The nib of the crow quill is extremely slender and firm, allowing delicate and precise lines to be drawn. Prior to production of steel nibs in the early 19th century, the crow-quill pen was actually made from the wing feather of a crow.

crucible a ceramic pot used for melting metals for casting.

cruciform in the shape of a cross. Gothic churches characteristically have a cruciform floor plan.

crushed relief see RELIEF.

crux ansata see ANKH.

crux commissa see TAU CROSS.

crux decussata see ST. ANDREW'S CROSS.

crux immissa see LATIN CROSS.

cryolite sodium aluminium fluoride, a native crystalline mineral used as a flux and opacifier in porcelain ENAMEL.

crystalline glaze a ceramic GLAZE in which well-defined patterns of crystals are formed on firing. The most successful crystalline glaze is made of zinc silicate, but other substances are also used. The creation of such a glaze is complex and exacting.

Cubism a revolutionary art movement (1907–1914), of which the leading figures were Georges Braque (1882–1963) and Pablo Picasso (1881–1973). The Cubist style had three stages of development: *Facet Cubism*, in which the artist began to separate objects or figures into definite geometrical elements, or facets, while placing them in a composition that still showed the influence of Cézanne; *Analytical Cubism*, in which objects were increasingly broken down and analysed through such means as simultaneous rendition, the presentation of several aspects of an object at once; and *Synthetic Cubism*, in which the artist was further liberated from traditional reality, appearance and illusion. Cubism in its early phase was encouraged by the Parisian interest in Cézanne, Seurat, and African sculpture. The collage or paste-up technique and the use of such materials as sand and cloth on canvas were Cubist innovations. Despite the enormous hostility with which it was greeted by the world, the Cubist movement was epoch-making. It was the inspiration or point of departure for many artists in the next few decades (see ABSTRACT ART). Its innate vigour and productiveness were the result of the intensive collaboration between Picasso and Braque, who were later joined by Juan Gris (1887–1927) and Fernand Léger (1881–1955).

cudbear another name for ARCHIL.

cupid see PUTTO.

curcuma another name for TURMERIC.

cure to retard the setting of concrete with wet coverings, a procedure that ensures development of maximum strength throughout its mass.

Currier and Ives prints *(US)* a series of 19th-century hand-coloured lithographs published by the New York firm of Currier and Ives, depicting sentimental and patriotic scenes of American life, as well as public events and natural disasters. The widely popular lithographs, which were inexpensive in their day, are now considered to be collectors' items.

cursive 1. a style of printing type imitative of running handwriting but in which the letters are not actually joined.
2. of design, free-flowing and curvilinear, in the manner of running handwriting.

curtains one of several terms for the irregular waves and drips that may form in varnish or thin paint that has been applied to a painting while it was in a vertical position. The descriptive names for this and similar defects also include FRILLING or sagging, TEARDROPS, and STREAMLINES.

curve see FRENCH CURVE.

cushion, gilder's see GILDER'S CUSHION.

cusp *(architecture and design)* the intersection of two arcs, as the point made by two adjacent FOILS in TRACERY and other Gothic ornament.

cut 1. *vb (varnish making)* to dissolve resin in a solvent.
2. *n.* the solution so produced. When preceded by a weight designation, it refers to the concentration of the solution in terms of pounds of resin to each gallon of solvent. For example, the standard dammar varnish is a five-pound cut.
3. *(commercial printing)* the block or plate with which an illustration is printed or a photograph is reproduced.
4. the print made from such a block or plate.

cut-card work a decorative technique in metalwork in which a design cut out of a sheet of metal is superimposed on the surface of an object of the same metal, usually around a protuberance such as a handle or a FINIAL. Cut-card work is used almost exclusively for silver. It was especially popular during the 18th century and is found on French, English, and American silverware of that period.

cutch see CATECHU.

cutter see SIGN-WRITER'S CUTTER.

cutter, compass see COMPASS CUTTER.

cuttlefish ink the principal ink of the ancient Romans, made from the ink sacs of cuttlefish and other cephalopods. Sepia comes from the same source.

cyan a hue designation derived from a Greek word meaning 'dark blue'. It is applied to deep, saturated blues of greenish undertone (like Prussian and phthalocyanine blues), as distinguished from the relatively purplish ultramarine, and the paler, or azure, blues. Cyan is the primary blue of the additive system (see COLOUR). The term is more frequently used in colour photography than in painting.

cyanine blue 1. a COMPOSITE PIGMENT made of Prussian and cobalt blues.
2. a synthetic dyestuff.

Cycladic pertaining to the art and civilization of the Cyclades islands in the Aegean Sea, between 2600 and 1100 BC. Their art survives in numerous decorated objects, particularly pottery, and in marble figures found in graves, especially female cult figures and statuettes of musicians. The cult figures, which include the first examples of the life-size female nude, represented the female figure in a spare, elegant form that marked a departure from the heavy-bodied fertility goddesses of earlier times. Because the maritime activity of the Cyclades was far-flung, Cycladic art circulated throughout the Mediterranean and influenced the art of other Aegean cultures, particularly that of Crete (see MINOAN).

cylix see KYLIX.

cyma 1. (also called **ogee**) a moulding, the profile of which is formed by a continuous line in a double curve. The moulding is *cyma recta* when the concave portion is at the top or, in a picture frame, closest to the picture; it is *cyma reversa* when the concave portion is at the bottom or, in a frame, farthest from the picture.

2. *(design)* an S curve or inverted S curve.

cyma (left) Cyma recta moulding; (right) cyma reversa.

Cyprian green earth a somewhat yellowish variety of GREEN EARTH of high quality. It is mined in Cyprus.

Cyprus umber, Turkey brown or **Turkey umber** the best quality of UMBER, mined on the island of Cyprus.

D

dabber 1. *(graphic arts)* a pad of wadded material, usually leather or flannel, with which ink is applied to a block or plate. Dabbers were used in relief printing until the 19th century, when they were replaced by BRAYERS. In the intaglio processes of etching and line engraving, a dabber is still used to force ink into the etched or incised lines and area. It is also used in etching to spread the etching ground on the face of the plate.
2. *(painting)* a wad of cotton-wool wrapped in cotton cloth, tied and shaped to form a flat-bottomed bag, that is used with a tapping or pouncing motion for spreading and BLENDING oil colours. The dabber can produce smooth, flawless fields of colour, perfect gradation, and glazes.
3. a bulky, moplike camel-hair brush used for blending watercolour.

dabber Leather dabber used in the graphic arts.

Dada an art movement that began in Zurich during the First World War. The name was chosen at random from a dictionary, in 1916, and the movement spread throughout Europe and America. Its founders were the artist Hans Arp and the writers Tristan Tzara, Hugo Ball, and Richard Hülsenbeck. Its credo, 'Everything the artist spits is art,' provoked much controversy and outrage, as did such unusual methods of producing art as doodling and automatic writing. Practitioners of Dada also ascribed artistic qualities to the FOUND OBJECT, the READY-MADE, the COLLAGE and other historically unacceptable materials and techniques. The movement was antipathetic to traditional styles and materials, an attitude that led some critics to term it *anti-art*.

Among the important artists who participated in the Dada movement were Marcel Duchamp (1887–1968), Max Ernst (1891–1976), Hans Arp (1887–1966), Francis Picabia (1878–1953), Man Ray (1890–1977), and Kurt Schwitters (1887–1948). Among the remarkable Dada works were *The Fountain* by Marcel Duchamp, a porcelain urinal, illustrative of the Dada aim to exalt the commonplace by taking it out of its usual context; and the same artist's photograph of the Mona Lisa with a moustache, typifying the Dadaists' gleefully iconoclastic attitude toward tradition.

111

dagger striper a soft brush with a short thumb-and-finger handle and long hairs that taper from a thick belly to a sharp, scimitar-shaped point. Designed for accurate straight-line striping in decorative work, it has been occasionally used by artists. See illustration at LINERS AND STRIPERS.

daguerreotype the process invented in 1839 by a Frenchman, J.M. Daguerre, in which a photograph is produced on a silver or silver-coated copper plate made sensitive by the action of iodine. The daguerreotype, which was non-reproducible, was replaced by the negative/positive process, which allowed unlimited prints of the image to be made.

damar see DAMMAR.

damascene 1. to inlay one metal with a more precious metal, creating ornamental patterns and sometimes even representational designs. Fine wire or thin strips of gold, silver, electrum or copper are hammered into depressions that have been engraved in the steel, bronze or iron ground; the inlaid metal is then smoothed and polished. This type of ornamentation is very old – it decorates daggers of the 16th century BC that have been found at Mycenae. Damascening was much used by the early goldsmiths of Damascus, whence its name, and is still characteristic of metalwork in the Middle East.
2. to decorate fabrics or metal surfaces with a wavy or watery pattern, like that of objects made with Damascus steel. Damascus steel was specially forged with iron until the two metals were thoroughly mixed, each, however, retaining its identity. Objects made from this hard but elastic composite metal, such as the famous mediaeval sword blades crafted in Damascus, were lightly etched to bring out the watered pattern. The effect is comparable to the appearance of damask, a damascened fabric that also takes its name from Damascus, the original city of its manufacture.

dammar or *(US)* **damar** a pale, straw-coloured resin gathered from forest trees of the family *Diptero-carpaceae* in Malaysia and Indonesia. Varieties are named according to their shipping points – Batavia, Singapore, Padang, etc. Number One SINGAPORE DAMMAR is considered the best for use in artists' materials. Dammar is one of the few tree resins still approved for use in PICTURE VARNISH and RETOUCH VARNISH and as an ingredient in painting mediums, emulsions, and encaustic colours. It dissolves in pure turpentine but not in petroleum solvents. See also MATA KUCHING DAMMAR.

Danube school painters working in various cities of the Danube valley about the beginning of the 16th century. These painters, including Lucas Cranach the Elder, Albrecht Altdorfer and Wolf Huber, were particularly notable for their imaginative and often romantic use of landscape. A fine example is Altdorfer's *Forest with St George*.

Davy's grey a grey pigment made of finely powdered slate. It is no longer in general use.

daylight fluorescent colours see FLUORESCENT PAINT.

dead colouring an obsolete term for UNDERPAINTING.

de-air *(ceramics)* to remove the air from plastic clay preparatory to use.

Clay may be de-aired in a PUG mill equipped with a vacuum pump or by wedging. See WEDGE.

death mask a facial impression or cast made after the subject's death. Since the Renaissance such masks have been made by oiling the skin of the deceased and taking a plaster cast. The ancient Egyptians made death masks of thin plates of gold. See also LIFE MASK.

decadence or **decadent period** a period of decline in creative excellence, vitality, and originality in the history of an art movement or style. Although the artists of such a period are usually regarded as lesser figures than those who represented the movement at its height, the so-called decadence of one style may be, in reality, the period of transition to another, as well as being inherently valuable. The period of Italian art beginning in the last quarter of the 16th century, sometimes known as the Italian Decadence, included such figures as the Carracci, Caravaggio, Guido Reni, Domenichino, Pietro da Cortona, and Luca Giordano, whose Baroque realism influenced the French painters of the 17th century.

decadent art a derogatory term for the works of the so-called Aesthetic Movement in England in the last two decades of the 19th century, when artists and writers showed a concern for form and beauty rather than content and morality, and were sometimes preoccupied with morbid, neurotic, and occult themes. The drawings of Aubrey Beardsley (1872–1898) are representative of this period. See also FIN DE SIÈCLE.

decadent period see DECADENCE.

decal paper on which a design has been printed in a way that permits it to be transferred to another surface. The paper is usually wetted and applied face down. The printing attaches itself to the second surface, and the backing is then stripped away. Industrial or mass-produced ceramic wares are commonly decorated with transfers of this type.

decalcomania 1. the process of making a DECAL.
2. a technique practised by certain Surrealists (see SURREALISM) in which the artist spreads gouache on a sheet of paper, lays another sheet on top of it, presses the second sheet in various places, and then strips it off (see LIFTING). This technique produces effects suggesting exotic flowers, mineral deposits or spongy growths. Max Ernst (1891–1976) developed this technique to a high degree in oil media, beginning a painting with a decalcomania base and then achieving greater definition of form through brush effects. In recent years, particularly in PSYCHEDELIC ART, decals have been used as adjuncts to an overall artistic effect. See also MONOTYPE.

deckle the rough, uncut or unfinished edge of a sheet of paper; fine watercolour and printmaking paper is often deckle-edged.

decorative art art that is used to ornament or embellish an object that has a practical purpose, as distinguished from FINE ART, which exists as an end in itself. Decorative art is a class of APPLIED ART.

découpage 1. decoration of a surface by covering it completely with cutout paper figures or designs.

2. an object so decorated.

deep colour any colour with a high degree of SATURATION and low VALUE. Full-strength phthalocyanine blue is a dark, deep colour, and strong, intense cerise or mauve hues are deeper than pink. A painting in which very little white is mixed with the colours may be called *deep-toned*.

deep relief see RELIEF.

deesis a depiction of Christ (usually enthroned), with the Virgin Mary and John the Baptist, either in a single painting or in separate, joined paintings. In the many-tiered iconostases that were introduced in the 14th century in Russian churches, the deesis occupied the most prominent place, above the door leading into the sanctuary.

deflocculate 1. to dissipate lumps or clusters in a mixture, creating a smooth, homogeneous dispersion or fluid suspension.
2. *(ceramics)* to convert clay into SLIP by adding electrolytes such as sodium silicate and soda ash to produce a suspension of the particles.

degame or **lemonwood** a Cuban hardwood obtained from the tree *Calycophyllum candidissimum*. Degame is yellowish to creamy white in colour and is sometimes used for carving. It is one of the lancewoods of commerce.

degenerate art the name given by Adolf Hitler and his followers to all art that did not reflect their own notions of so-called Aryan supremacy and racial superiority. As this applied to almost all modern art, much of that to be found in German museums, galleries, and private collections of the time – including works by Picasso, van Gogh, and Kandinsky – was either confiscated and destroyed or sold out of the country.

degraded colour a paint mixed with dulling or greying colours, producing a colour below its normal degree of saturation or brightness.

del. an abbreviation of the Latin word *delineavit*, meaning 'he (or she) drew it'. *Del.*, EXC., IMP., INC., INV., PINX., and SCULP., preceded by the names of persons or firms, are sometimes inscribed in a lower corner of the margin of a print, particularly an engraving, to indicate who did what in preparing the plate and pulling the proofs. *Del.* follows the name of the artist from whose original drawing the plate was engraved or etched. *Pinx.* may appear on a print copied from an original painting. *Inv.* is more general, referring merely to the original artist, either draughtsman or painter. *Inc.* and *sculp.* both refer to the person who actually engraved the plate. Thus, 'Brown *del.*, Smith *sculp.*' on a print means that Smith made the engraving from an original drawing by Brown. If the inscription on an engraving reads 'Brown *del.* and *sculp.*,' the engraving is an ORIGINAL PRINT by Brown. 'Brown *pinx.*, Smith and Jones *sculp.*' means that the engraving was copied by the firm of Smith and Jones from Brown's original painting. When a printer's name is not indicated, the engraver is assumed to have also printed the plate. When the plate is engraved by one person or firm and printed by another, the printer's name may be followed by *imp.* or *exc.* 'Brown *del.* and *sculp.*, Carter *imp.* (or *exc.*)' indicates that Carter printed a plate the design of which was drawn and engraved by Brown. *Lith.* or *litho.* mean 'lithographed by.'

delft or **delftware** an earthenware covered with an opaque tin enamel and decorated with cobalt blue. It was originally produced in Delft, in the Netherlands, in the mid-17th century.

demirelief see RELIEF.

dentil one of a series of rectangular, projecting blocks that form a moulding. Dentil mouldings are common in cornices of the Doric, Ionic, Corinthian, and Composite orders.

dentils

Derby red another name for chrome red (see CHROME YELLOW).

desco da parto a mediaeval Italian basin or tray in which gifts were brought to a woman after childbirth. These were usually painted with the Nativity, and sometimes with other appropriate subjects.

design the selection and arrangement of the formal elements in a work of art, expressing the artist's conception in terms of a composition of these elements. Factors such as the direction, size, and shape of lines, angles, and forms and such considerations of composition and organization as spatial relationships, symmetry or asymmetry, rhythm and dynamics are all elements of design. Among the features of visual art that are not specifically design elements are colour, texture, the artist's handling of his or her materials, and the subject matter or emotional content. Giorgio Vasari entitled the technical treatise that was incorporated in the 1568 edition of *The Lives of the Painters, Sculptors, and Architects*, 'The Three Arts of Design: Architecture, Painting, and Sculpture.' Accordingly, these three arts have continued to be classified as the arts of design. See also DISEGNO.

designers' colours good quality GOUACHE tube colours with a DEXTRIN binder. Designers' colours are widely used by illustrators whose original work is infrequently preserved after being reproduced. Manufacturers' lines of designers' colours therefore include some brilliant, nonpermanent colours in addition to the standard artists' pigments.

dessus de cheminée see OVERMANTEL.

dessus de porte *(Fr.)* or *(It.)* **supra porta** a horizontal painting designed to hang over a doorway. The use of paintings in this position was popular in the 18th century.

De Stijl see NEO-PLASTICISM.

détrempe see DISTEMPER.

Devonshire clay a variety of CHINA CLAY found in England.

dextrin a gummy material made from wheat starch and used as an adhesive, as a paint binder, in coated paper, and in textile manufacture.

DIABLERIE

Designers' colours have a dextrin binder, and sometimes it is added to gum arabic in the manufacture of watercolours. Dextrin is available as a pure, white powder and also in a yellow form (canary dextrin), which is unsuitable for use in artists' materials. It has a characteristic mild odour and taste familiar from its use on envelopes and postage stamps.

diablerie the satanic as represented or symbolized in art.

diacetone alcohol one of the most powerful solvents used by professional conservators, especially to soften or dissolve dried linseed oil films. It has toxic effects when its vapours are breathed in large-scale operations, but can be safely handled, like most solvents used by conservators, over relatively small areas.

diaglyph a piece of sculpture or a decoration in which all the forms lie below the level of the plane surface; an INTAGLIO. The opposite of a diaglyph is an ANAGLYPH.

diamond black see CARBON BLACK.

diaper an all-over, repeat pattern or design on a flat surface, usually composed of clearly defined geometrical elements. The term is most frequently applied to wall decoration.

diaper

diarylide yellow a SYNTHETIC ORGANIC PIGMENT whose tinting strength is much greater than that of any of the inorganic yellows. It is very transparent and, at full strength, exhibits good solvent and light resistance. However, it is slightly soluble in some organic solvents and may fade in tints with white.

diatomaceous earth or **Kieselguhr** a light, fluffy, absorbent clay or silica that contains the inorganic remains or skeletons of plant life, the lacy forms of which are visible under a microscope. Diatomaceous earth is used as an INERT PIGMENT or FILLER in paints and other industrial products. *Fuller's earth*, a variety of diatomaceous earth, is also used in the refining of oils.

dichroism the property whereby a substance exhibits two different hues or colour effects when viewed under different circumstances. Cobalt yellow and alizarin crimson, for instance, are examples of oil colours whose hues show a marked difference when seen by reflected light and when spread out in a thin layer and viewed by transmitted light. Another example is the property of some oil colours of displaying a different visual or colour effect when brushed vertically from when brushed horizontally on the same area of a canvas. This has been called the *suede effect*.

die board see MAPLE DIE BOARD.

diethyl ether see ETHER.

diffraction the apparent deflection of light rays as they pass through very close parallel lines incised on a transparent piece of glass or plastic, or through a monomolecular or very thin layer between two different media. This passage produces the brilliant spectrum colours known as DIFFRACTION COLOURS and the colour effect of IRIDESCENCE.

diffraction colour or **prismatic colour** any brilliant rainbow or spectrum colour produced by the diffraction of light rather than by pigmentation. An ever-changing play of diffraction colours is called iridescence. The iridescence of oil layers on water, or of soap bubbles, demonstrates the general rule that a thin layer surrounded by two media of different refractive index (in these cases, air and water) will usually diffract light. Diffraction colours may also be produced by use of a prism or of a diffraction grating, a piece of glass or plastic on which microscopically small, closely parallel lines have been engraved. Diffraction colours appear in nature when light passes through a surface that is either structured so that it acts as a selective diffraction grating or, like the plumage of certain birds, is equivalent to myriads of tiny lenses or prisms. Diffraction colours differ from pigment colours in their almost metallic intensity and in the fact that they are produced by the additive or light-ray process rather than the subtractive process (see COLOUR).

diluent any liquid that is miscible with a given solution and can be used to thin or dilute it. A diluent may be, but is not necessarily, a good solvent for the material in solution. However, some inert diluents, particularly those used in lacquers, have latent solvent power, contributing to the effect of solvents already in the lacquer. See also THINNER.

demethyl ketone see ACETONE.

dimetric projection a projection used in mechanical drawing in which two axes or dimensions have the same degree of foreshortening in relation to their length and are therefore drawn to the same scale. The foreshortening in the third axis is different, causing the scale of that dimension to be different. In a dimetric projection of a rectangular solid, two of the three angles made where the axes meet will be equal. See illustration at PROJECTION.

diminishing glass or *(US)* **reducing glass** a small hand glass with a double concave lens (the reverse of a magnifying glass). It is used for viewing work that is intended to be reproduced smaller than the original, so that the artist can get an idea of how effective the work will be in the smaller size.

dinitraniline orange an inexpensive bright reddish orange of clean colour, good chemical resistance and full to medium tone lightfastness. However, this SYNTHETIC ORGANIC PIGMENT may tend to bleed in some organic solvents and plasticizers with relatively poor lightfastness in the lighter tints.

DINGLER'S GREEN

Dingler's green one of the early varieties of CHROMIUM OXIDE GREEN.

diorama 1. a three-dimensional representation of a scene, either full-size or scaled, and sometimes with a painted background that merges imperceptibly with features and objects nearest it by means of aerial and linear perspective. A diorama may be constructed on a platform with or without a glass case, set in an illuminated niche, and viewed from a darkened room, or, in miniature form, boxed and viewed through a peephole. It has been used for realistic wildlife exhibits in natural history museums, exhibits of engineering and industrial projects, and advertising displays. **2.** a popular form of instructive entertainment, in the 18th and 19th centuries, consisting of a painted transparency illuminated from the front or the rear and giving the illusion of a real scene. See also COSMORAMA; PANORAMA.

diorite a hard, granular, crystalline igneous rock, most commonly black or grey in colour, used by the ancient Egyptians for sculpture.

dipper, dipper cup or *(US)* **palette cup** a small cylindrical vessel, usually tin, soldered singly or in pairs to a bent strip. The strip is clamped to the edge of a PALETTE so the painter has a handy supply of turpentine or medium in which to dip his or her brush while working.

dipper Double dipper.

diptych 1. a painting or bas relief done on two panels, hinged so it can be opened and closed like a book.
2. any painting consisting of two individual panels or canvases. See also TRIPTYCH.

direct carving or **en taille directe** the carving of a piece of sculpture directly in its final form, as distinguished from casting a piece from a modelled original. Many sculptors do make clay or wax models of a projected sculpture before cutting into a stone block. Sculpture may also be executed by the artist who designed it, rather than be copied from a model by artisans, by POINTING, or by another method.

direct metal sculpture the fine-arts technique of shaping a piece of metal or putting together a metal construction, as opposed to casting. It employs such techniques as welding, hammering and soldering to produce a unique work of art. The work of Alexander Calder, John Chamberlain, and George Rickey consists mostly of direct metal sculpture.

direct painting see ALLA PRIMA.

disegno 1. design.
2. drawing.

This Italian term was applied to all the visual arts, as well as to the specific elements that the word denotes. Some theorists of MANNERISM include in it the *disegno interno*, the artist's ideal visualization of an object or scene as opposed to the actual appearance of the model. This concept was later involved in the arguments of the proponents of design over colour in the conflict between *Poussinisme* and *Rubénisme*. See RUBÉNISME.

dispersion see PAINT.

display face see TYPOGRAPHY.

disposable palette a pad of white oil-proof paper in the shape of a rectangular thumbhole palette; it is available in several sizes. After a painting session the used sheet is pulled off, exposing the next clean sheet. The advantages of a disposable palette are obvious: cleaning of the palette is eliminated, and colours remain uncontaminated and can be transferred to a new sheet as the top one becomes fouled.

disposable palette

distemper any of several aqueous paints made with simple glue or casein binders and used for flat wall decoration and stage scenery. The term is usually used for bulk or wall paints rather than artists' colours. It is sometimes confused with tempera because the French word *détrempe* has both meanings.

distillation one of the basic processes of refining, purifying and producing liquid materials. The original substance is placed in a STILL, and heat is applied and increased until the substance vaporizes. The vapour is then passed through the condenser of the still, becoming a liquid that is free of impurities. A primitive sort of distillation was known to the ancient Greeks and Romans (see TURPENTINE), but distillation in a still was first practised by physicians and experimenters in the 3rd century in Alexandria. It did not come into established, practical use in Europe until the 15th century, when volatile solvents such as alcohol, turpentine, spike oil (and later the petroleum distillates) came into widespread use and furthered the development of oil paints and varnishes. See also ALEMBIC.

distortion any departure from what is generally accepted as the normal depiction of an object, figure or scene, usually effected by a deviation from the canons of PERSPECTIVE and FORESHORTENING or from the rules of proportions for a figure (see SCHEMA). An exaggeration of size, shape, or a distortion of spatial ordering subordinates order and precision to emotion, giving emphasis to the artist's feelings about his or her subject matter and, perhaps, evoking the same feelings in the viewer. Furthermore, some objects and scenes appear purer in design when distorted than when realistically depicted. Thus, in Mannerist art, which widely employed distortion, human anatomical proportions might be stretched not only to evoke an emotional response in the viewer but also to express what the artist conceives of as an intrinsic harmony of size and shape. Even academic realism often distorts details to produce an overall effect of correct proportions. When, as in some Chinese paintings, the viewer is informed about a side of an object that would not be seen in normal perspective, another type of distortion results; this may be called 'informative distortion'.

Distortion has been consciously used by artists throughout history, notably in Gothic sculpture, in Mannerist painting (most obviously by El Greco), and in the work of many Cubist, Surrealist and expressionist painters, for example, Picasso, Dali and Modigliani. Distortion is also found, however, in works from more classical, reserved periods of art. Some 15th- and 16th-century sculptures of, for example, Donatello and Michelangelo, display distortions not unlike those characteristic of certain Hellenistic Greek sculptures.

dividers a draughtsman's instrument used to transfer measurements and to divide lines. It has the same design as a bow COMPASS, but both legs terminate in steel points. Most compasses, both bow and beam types, can be converted to dividers by substituting a steel point for the pencil or pen fitting.

dividing brass see SHIM.

divisionism the principle of OPTICAL MIXTURE applied to painting; POINTILLISM. Seurat and the other practitioners of the technique preferred this term to *pointillism*.

doctor or **doctor blade** a straightedge used for scraping off fresh paint or other pasty materials. It may be made of metal, rubber or plastic. An example is the steel bar that removes the oil colours from the roller of a mill.

dolomite any LIMESTONE that contains 45% or more of magnesium carbonate, as well as calcium carbonate. Many varieties of marble are metamorphic forms of dolomite.

dolomitic limestone limestone containing as little as 10% of magnesium carbonate

dominant colour the prevailing colour or tonal character of a painting or other multicoloured object.

Doric order one of the three Grecian architectural orders, of which Doric is the first or oldest, the strongest and the simplest. It is distinguished by fluted columns and plain capitals. Compare CORINTHIAN ORDER; IONIC ORDER.

dossal a painted or decorative cloth hung behind an altar.

dotted manner a 15th-century method for creating a CRIBBLED, or dotted, area on a print – chiefly for backgrounds and textural details – by stamping dots in a metal plate with a PUNCH. The dotted-manner process, which was not widely used after the early Renaissance, was to some extent revived toward the end of the 18th century. The French term *manière criblée* was used in the 15th century to describe the effects created by this process.

dotted print a combination of dotted-manner engraving (see DOTTED MANNER) and line ENGRAVING, is printed as a relief plate; the stamped dots and engraved lines show as whites in the proof (see RELIEF PRINTING).

double-end tool see MODELLING TOOLS.

double image a figure or object that can be identified as two separate images, for example, a cloud that is also a human head, or a series of hills that is also a reclining figure. Many examples of the double image may be found in the work of Pavel Tchelitchew (1898–1957).

double-primed see PRIMER.

Dowicide *(US)* the trade name for a synthetic organic preservative and fungicide used as a component of water paints. Dowicide A, chemically, sodium orthophenylphenate, is used with casein and other glue binders. Dowicide B, sodium trichlorphenate, is used with gums. See also PRE-SERVATIVE.

drafting see MECHANICAL DRAWING.

drafting machine a device that combines all the functions of a STRAIGH-TEDGE, a T SQUARE, and an ADJUSTABLE TRIANGLE with a protractor and SCALES for precise calibration. One arm of the machine is attached to the drawing board, anchoring the apparatus so that it can be entirely controlled with one hand by the draughtsman, leaving the other hand free for drawing. Used by draughtsmen, designers, architects, and engineers, the drafting machine is available in several precision-engineered professional models and in a compact, portable model of lightweight aluminium.

drafting paper a high-quality DRAWING PAPER with a relatively high finish, hard surface, and excellent water resistance and erasing qualities. It may be used for both ink and pencil work.

drafting tape see PRESSURE-SENSITIVE TAPES.

dragging another name for *retroussage* (see WIPING).

dragging stroke or **scruffing** a technique of stroking oil colour lightly over a rough surface so that it covers the high spots and leaves the depressions untouched, thus creating a broken area of colour with irregular spots of the undercolour showing through. See DRY-BRUSH PAINTING.

dragon's blood a transparent, ruby-red, resinous exudation of the fruits of several rattan palms of genera *Daemonorops* and the genus *Calamus*, native to Asia. Dragon's blood was traded into Italy as early as the Roman period. Although it is not a true pigment, it was used as a colour by mediaeval manuscript illuminators. It has long since been replaced by more permanent pigments. It has been most commonly used to colour varnishes, especially ormolu varnish, and has also been used as a resist in a special etching technique. It is readily soluble in alcohol, benzol, and a few other solvents, but practically insoluble in white spirit and turpentine.

Pliny the Elder (1st century AD) propagated the myth that dragon's blood is actually the commingled blood of those legendary enemies, the dragon and the elephant, spilled during their mortal combat. For his remark about the use of dragon's blood in Roman painting, see INDIGO.

draperie mouillée (*Fr.* wet drapery) thin, clinging drapery in figure sculpture, that reveals the form beneath.

draughtsman 1. in art, one who is adept at DRAWING; traditionally, draughtsmanship is one of the criteria of excellence in a work of art.
2. one who renders an architect's or an engineer's drawings proficiently and in accordance with professional standards. See MECHANICAL DRAWING.

drawing 1. the delineation on a surface of shapes and forms. It may be further elaborated with applications of colour, highlights and shading with HATCHING or washes to produce the effect of light and shadow. Drawing is a major fine-art technique in itself, but it also serves as the basis of all pictorial representation and as a preliminary step in most painting, sculpture, and architecture. Although it is an integral part of most painting, drawing *per se* is distinguished from painting (in which mass, defined in areas of colour, dominates line) by the predominance of the linear element.

The techniques of drawing vary widely according to the effect desired by the artist and the purpose that the drawing will serve, that is, whether it is an end in itself or a preliminary to some other medium or form. A sharp PENCIL line or PEN stroke on a smooth ground will produce a more LINEAR drawing with relatively clear contours. A more PAINTERLY effect is created, especially on rough paper, with thicker or more pliant media such as soft pencil, CRAYON (wax, chalk, pastel or charcoal), and ink or watercolour washes. In WASH DRAWINGS, as works executed in the last two named media are called, gradated areas replace hatching.

Drawings may be separated into two categories according to their function as art. Some drawings are independent and finished works of art. Others, although distinct from the final product, also have intrinsic artistic value. This category includes general stylistic exercises (for example, CONTOUR DRAWING; LIFE DRAWING; DRAWING FROM THE ANTIQUE and DRAWING FROM CAST; DRAWING FROM THE FLAT), as well as separate SKETCHES (for example, CROQUIS; ESQUISSE; NOTE) and STUDIES. CARTOONS, which are worked out in greater detail than sketches and are more immediately related to the finished work than studies are, also fall into this category. A third category could also be defined: drawings preliminary to other works of art that are actually incorporated into those works and thus deprived of independent artistic value. An example is the underdrawing in fresco and panel painting (such as SINOPIA and ABBOZZO).

Because drawing implies spontaneity, it has been highly appreciated since the Italian Renaissance, when it was revered as the embodiment of the artist's ideas. This spontaneous quality has always been used to particular advantage in CARICATURE and ILLUSTRATION. The invention of

DRAWING FROM THE FLAT

printmaking techniques in the 15th century made possible the duplication and dissemination of drawings, further establishing drawing as a definitive art form. See also MECHANICAL DRAWING.

2. *(ceramics)* removing ware from a kiln after firing.

drawing board 1. an ILLUSTRATION BOARD.

2. a squared panel used as a base for drawing paper. A typical drawing board is a rectangle of softwood about $\frac{3}{4}$ inch thick, with a perfectly plane, smooth surface. To give the board perfectly parallel and smooth edges and to prevent warping, it is reinforced on each of its shorter sides either with a strip of wood mortised to it or with a metal cleat running the length of the edge. An accurate horizontal base against which triangles may be placed is made by holding the head of a T square against the true mortised wood or metal edges of the board. For outdoor sketching and watercolour painting, artists often improvise readily portable boards from such materials as wallboard and corrugated board. In the studio, a DRAWING TABLE may be used either to support a drawing board or to replace it.

drawing curve see FRENCH CURVE.

drawing frame a device used to frame the subject that an artist intends to draw or paint. Rectangular and usually made from wood, drawing frames have been used since at least the 15th century by artists as varied as Leonardo da Vinci and van Gogh.

drawing from nature the drawing of a landscape or an object or element from nature. Sketched outdoors, such a drawing may be finished in the studio, but it differs from a STILL LIFE in that even an inanimate object is shown in its natural setting. Drawing from nature and other stylistic exercises, such as LIFE DRAWING, DRAWING FROM THE ANTIQUE and DRAWING FROM CAST, and DRAWING FROM THE FLAT, are often part of an artist's academic training. In addition to being a finished work of art, a drawing from nature can serve as a note or a study for further work in the studio.

drawing from the antique and **drawing from cast** drawing classical sculptures or their parts or fragments precisely and accurately, showing every nuance of shading. The sculpture drawn may be either in the round or in relief, either an original work (the antique) or a white plaster copy (a cast). Although the term *drawing from the antique* denotes the copying of classical sculpture, more recent works are sometimes used, notably the sculpture of Michelangelo, Donatello, Bernini and Rodin. *Drawing from cast* was a traditional academic art course, the satisfactory completion of which was requisite for entry into a class in LIFE DRAWING. Nowadays very few art schools include drawing from the antique or from cast in the required curriculum. See also DRAWING FROM NATURE; DRAWING FROM THE FLAT.

drawing from the flat the drawing of a copy of a painting, a print, or another drawing. The artist may use this technique, along with LIFE DRAWING, DRAWING FROM NATURE, and DRAWING FROM THE ANTIQUE OR FROM CAST, as a tool in the development of his or her own style.

DRAWING PAPER

Rubens' copy of Leonardo da Vinci's cartoon for *The Battle of Anghiari* is one of the most brilliant works of this kind.

drawing paper a close-textured, hard-surfaced paper with a dull finish, good erasability, and good water resistance. There are many specialized varieties of drawing paper, such as CHARCOAL PAPER and DRAFTING PAPER.

drawing pen see RULING PEN.

drawing pin a short steel tack with a broad, flat or slightly domed head, used in drawing and painting to fasten paper to a DRAWING BOARD.

drawing table a table whose top may be adjusted to any degree of slant to suit the artist's or draughtsman's needs or preferences. Some drawing tables are also adjustable in height. Many styles are available for general use, in a number of drawing-surface sizes, from about 20 by 30 inches to about 40 by 60 inches.

draw-out a sample of two transparent pigments on a pad of paper, made for purposes of comparison and quality testing. It is made by placing two dabs of oil colour close to one another on the edge of a sharp, clean wallscraper, spreading them thickly on the paper over an area of an inch or so to show their mass tones, then bearing down heavily so as to bend the scraper's flexible blade and scrape the colour down so that it makes a wide, transparent stain on the paper. Minute differences in colour, undertone, and tinting strength can be discerned by holding the transparent draw-out to the light. This technique is especially useful in comparing printing inks; since they are a form of oil colour usually applied as a thin stain on paper rather than as a massive paint layer, evaluations of their transparent colour are usually more significant than comparisons of mass tone.

Dresden liner see LINERS AND STRIPERS.

dress to impart a smooth or other desirable texture, when finishing stone, with chisels, hammers, or other tools.

drier a compound of any of several metals, notably lead, iron, manganese, and cobalt, that has a siccative (drying) effect when cooked at a high temperature with linseed oil. When a small amount of such a linoleate is added to an oil paint or oil varnish, it will greatly accelerate the speed (called the speed of dry) with which the coating becomes dry to the touch. Modern liquid driers are more apt to be napthenates than linoleates. Cobalt drier is by far the best of the driers; it is the only kind now used in artists' materials and is also preferred in industry. The action of driers is generally held to be catalytic: that is, it triggers the polymerization and accelerates the oxidation of the oil. A substance producing a reverse, or antioxidant, effect on oil, slowing its speed of dry, is called a retardant. In modern practice, adding a liquid drier to varnish or paint is generally preferred to the older procedure of cooking the metallic oxide directly in the oil. A prepared liquid drier is sometimes called a *siccative*. Pigments also affect the rate of drying of oil colours, some accelerating and some retarding it.

drollery or *(Fr.)* **drôlerie** a comic picture or one characterized by humour, especially one depicting animals dressed as humans or engaged in human pursuits.

drop black, Frankfort black or **German black** an industrial grade of VINE BLACK originally sold in the form of small, moulded lumps or drops. Many DROP PIGMENTS were sold during the 19th century.

dropout 1. a HALFTONE area in PHOTOENGRAVING, in which the dots are in part painted out on the film with opaquing fluid or etched away on the plate in order to create a highlight. Halftones with dropped-out areas are also known as highlight halftones.

2. a print or area of a print containing such a highlight.

drop pigment a pigment marketed formerly, and especially in Germany, in the shape of moulded drops or cones an inch or less in length. Of a soft consistency, these drops could be crushed or ground into paint as easily as powder. Cleaner and more dust-free than powdered pigments, drop pigments were a boon to the user of simple open equipment because they greatly reduced the health hazard of breathing in dust during handling. Pigments were also made in cylindrical and in flat, corrugated shapes, to suit the preferences of various trades. At the end of the 19th century, the expansion of the paint industry, along with improvements in mills, mixers and paint-factory techniques in general, made drops obsolete.

dry-brush painting the technique of creating a broken or mottled effect, revealing traces of the paper or underpainting, with water paint or ink. It is done by holding the brush at such an angle that its side lies almost flat against the paper, or by drawing it rapidly across the surface. In oil painting, a similar broken effect is usually called a DRAGGING STROKE or scruffing.

dry colour powdered pigment for industrial paint.

dryfoot 1. *vb* to clean the bottom rim of a piece of glaze-coated pottery before firing so that it remains unglazed.

2. Such a cleaned rim.

drying oil any vegetable oil that will solidify to a tough, leathery film when spread out in thin layers, either alone or with the assistance of a metallic salt known as a DRIER. This property makes drying oils valuable for use in paints and varnishes. They do not dry by evaporation, as do other liquids, but react with the oxygen in the air to become converted into a new compound, a solid with different properties from those of the original oil, to which it cannot be reconverted by any means. Among the drying oils, LINSEED OIL, WALNUT OIL, POPPYSEED OIL and SAFFLOWER OIL have been used in artists' colours. Others include HEMPSEED OIL, LUMBANG OIL, PERILLA OIL and TOBACCO-SEED OIL. See also NONDRYING OIL; SEMIDRYING OIL.

drying time or **speed of dry** the measured interval between the application of a paint or other coating material and the point at which the entire film, or the surface of the film, may be considered dry. A film of oil paint or varnish is completely dry when it has reached its ultimate state of solidity and strength, but according to the requirements of the user, the film may have a functional degree of dryness at any of several intermediate states, as: dry dust-free; dry to the touch; dry resistant to the application of overpainting; and dry resistant to the imprint of a heavy, grinding pressure of the thumb. Among the factors that influence drying time are the thickness of the film, the inherent accelerating or retarding action of its various constituents (as the presence of a DRIER or a DRYING OIL), and temperature and humidity.

In the United States, an acceptable drying rate is one of the general requirements an artists' oil colour must meet in order to be approved by ASTM.

dry mounting a method of attaching a drawing, print, photograph or other work of art done on paper to a cardboard backing. Instead of paste or another moist adhesive, a thin sheet of DRY-MOUNTING TISSUE is sandwiched between the paper and the mount, and a smooth, secure bond is obtained by first tacking the three layers together with a TACKING IRON and then applying heat and pressure in a special dry-mounting press or with a HAND-MOUNTING IRON. Some dry-mounting tissues are designed to adhere permanently; others are removable. Dry mounting is extensively used in commercial work but not generally approved for use in the fine arts.

dry-mounting tissue a thin sheet of rubberlike, thermosetting resin used as the adhesive in DRY MOUNTING.

dry painting see LINEAR.

drypoint 1. an INTAGLIO printing process in which a copper or zinc plate is inscribed directly with a pointed needle of steel or, more rarely, with a JEWEL POINT.

2. a print made by this process.

The incising process leaves an almost imperceptibly ragged edge, or BURR, which when printed produces the softness of line that is a distinguishing characteristic of the drypoint. The first proofs pulled will be of the highest quality. Because the burr soon gets worn down, broken, or pressed into the furrows in the etching press (where a drypoint is printed like a regular etching or copperplate engraving), few good proofs – thirty at most – can be made from a drypoint plate. The proof number (see PROOF) is therefore much more significant in drypoint than in other printing techniques. A drypoint edition may be enlarged by giving the plate a STEEL FACING.

A good drypoint is esteemed not only for its subtlety and pleasing tonalities but for the effect of spontaneity produced by the direct nature of the process. Etching is a comparatively indirect process, requiring many steps to translate the artist's conception into the finished etched drawing on the plate. Even line engraving, in which the plate is incised directly with a graver, is a necessarily deliberate process that results in a rather strict linear quality. On the other hand, the drypoint needle can be used on a metal plate with almost as much ease and flexibility as a pencil on paper; the artist's execution of the design on the plate can keep pace with his or her inspiration. Since the time of Rembrandt, artists

DUTCH CARAVAGGISM

have used drypoint not only by itself but also in combination with other printing techniques to enhance etchings and engravings.

dry rot a fungal decay to which wood is subject; it occurs in the absence of moisture. The wood becomes very weak and powdery. Dry rot in picture frames can be prevented by avoiding a hermetic seal at the rear of pictures, so that air has access to panels and stretchers.

ductile *(of metals)* having the property of being pliant, easily shaped, and capable of being drawn out into wire. Gold and silver, for example, are ductile metals. They may be drawn out or hammered permanently yet remain malleable.

duecento the 13th century. The term is commonly used to designate Italian art of that period.

Dumont blue see SMALT.

dunt *(ceramics)* to crack because of over-rapid cooling in the kiln after firing.

Dunville stone or **Dunn County stone** *(US)* an easily worked, fine-grained, buff to cream-coloured SANDSTONE from Wisconsin. Like much sandstone, it is soft when first quarried, but gradually hardens on exposure as its moisture (see QUARRY WATER) evaporates.

Düsseldorf school an academy of art founded in Düsseldorf in Germany, in 1767. The school is best known for the works it produced in the 1830s and 1840s, which infused genre landscapes with emotion in a manner derived from the Romantic painters of the Nazarene school. These works may be classed as BIEDERMEIER art, but the painters received rigorous training. Their influence spread even as far as the United States, as seen in the work of the romantic landscape painter Albert Bierstadt and others.

dust box a wooden box in which an AQUATINT plate is coated with finely powdered rosin. (Lump rosin is easily powdered by wrapping it in strong cloth and pounding it with a hammer.) A number of contrivances have been designed for this purpose. The simplest is an airtight plywood box about 3 feet high and 18 to 20 inches square. A 2-inch slit near the bottom of one side is covered with a hinged flap. The box, containing about 4 ounces of powdered rosin, is shaken vigorously and set down with a light thump. After about two minutes, when all but the most minute particles of rosin have settled, the metal plate is inserted into the slit, faceup on a plywood tray that sits on runners along two inside walls of the box. The finest particles of rosin gradually cover the plate with a uniform coat. The length of dusting time and the amount of powder used are determined by trials made to establish the desired graining of the plate, and are also related to the strength of the mordant that is to be used and to the duration of biting.

dusting brush a flat brush with long, coarse bristles set in a wooden or plastic handle. The dusting brush is used by artists and draughtsmen to sweep away eraser crumbs from work being done on a drawing board.

Dutch Caravaggism a movement in Dutch painting in the first half of the 17th century. The Caravaggists, fervent imitators of the Italian painter Caravaggio's highly dramatic lighting effects, gathered in Utrecht. Their most gifted painter, Hendrik Terbrugghen, assimilated Caravaggio's distinctive style successfully, but most of his fellow artists imitated only its most striking effects of lighting. Rembrandt, who did not belong to this group, was the one Dutch painter to use Caravaggio's techniques to evoke profound emotional responses.

Dutch metal, bronze leaf, composition leaf or **metal leaf** brass with a low zinc content that is made into leaf for use in gilding as an imitation of GOLD LEAF. Dutch metal must be lacquered, shellacked or varnished to prevent it from tarnishing rapidly. It is used primarily to gild inexpensive frames and to decorate furniture. Because the colour of Dutch metal is inferior to that of gold and because its natural metallic lustre is impaired when it is coated to prevent tarnish, it is not a satisfactory substitute for gold in a fine work of art.

Dutch mordant a carefully compounded solution of potassium chlorate and hydrochloric acid that is used as a MORDANT in ETCHING, particularly when very fine lines are to be produced. Dutch mordant, which was not used for etching until the 19th century, acts efficiently on copper plates but is less violent than nitric acid and thus less likely to make the sharp lines in the ground ragged. *Smillie's bath*, a mordant used in aquatint, has essentially the same composition as Dutch mordant but is much more concentrated.

Dutch pink see BROWN PINK.

Dutch-process white lead another name for WHITE LEAD made by corroding metallic lead with vinegar or acetic acid, a process that goes back at least to the ancient Greeks. The method described by Theophrastus (*History of Stones*) and Pliny (*Natural History*) is substantially the same as that used today.

Dutch white an unstandardized term that has been applied variously to a species of clay, to pure WHITE LEAD, and to a special white lead cheapened by reduction with blanc fixe or barytes.

dyes and **dyestuffs** soluble colouring matters that impart their colours to textiles, INERT PIGMENTS or other substances by staining or being imbibed by them. Dyes differ from pigments, which are insoluble materials that impart colour by being spread over a surface, as in painting, or by being mixed in as an ingredient, as in colouring plastics, rubber or paper. The painter has little concern with soluble dyes as such, though some of the colours he or she uses (LAKE pigments) are made from them. NATURAL DYESTUFFS are colouring matters extracted from plant and animal sources, as distinguished from the synthetic dyestuffs manufactured from coal-tar derivatives and other raw materials by modern chemical processes. The latter have largely replaced natural dyestuffs in modern times.

dynamic symmetry a theory of proportion believed to have been practised in ancient art and architecture, especially in Egyptian art and in Greek art of the 5th century BC. The existence of such a system, which is not now widely credited, was first postulated by the artist-writer Jay Hambidge (1867–1924), who, in his treatise *Dynamic Symmetry* (1917) and in his extensive subsequent writings on the subject, became its most articulate exponent. The concept proposes that the determining factor in imposing a sense of symmetry on a particular form is the relationship between various areas around its centre of balance rather than the relative length of its lines. Thus, although there might be a measurable inequality in corresponding lines on opposite sides of an object, an overall sense of symmetry around the centre of mass might still be felt as the result of the relationship of mathematically symmetrical subareas within the complete structural pattern. Dynamic symmetry is so called because it is said to correspond closely to the organic, kinetic symmetry of living things, as opposed to the *static* symmetry of inanimate forms. Hambidge related dynamic symmetry to the mathematical ratios he observed in plant life, especially in the spiral forms of sunflower heads and pine cones and in the orderly distribution of leaves in plants. See also GOLDEN MEAN.

E

early Christian art Christian art produced from the 4th to the 8th centuries both in Italy and in what was left of the Western Roman Empire, that is, art that was distinct from what can be termed Byzantine.

earth colours 1. paint pigments made by refining naturally coloured clays, rocks, and earths.
2. the pure iron-oxide reds (Indian red, light red, and Mars red), which, although artificial counterparts, are still classified with the native red earths. Earth colours are also classified as MINERAL PIGMENTS, along with manufactured inorganic pigments.

earthenware any opaque ceramic ware fired under 2000° F, as distinguished from porcelain, which is fired at higher temperatures. Earthenware has a relatively coarse, highly absorbent body and is commonly of a reddish colour. When it is glazed, soft or semihard glazes are used.

earthwork a large-scale alteration of an area of land, using rocks, soil, or other such elemental materials, designed by the artist to create a specific artistic effect. The earthwork, one of many manifestations of CONCEPTUAL ART, made its first appearance in the late 1960s. See also ARTE POVERA.

easel a freestanding structure designed to hold an artist's CANVAS or PANEL during painting. The studio easel usually has a square or rectangular base made of four sturdy wooden bars mounted on casters, and two sturdy uprights with crossbars at the top and middle braced by a diagonal strut at the rear. A vertically adjustable sliding tray, held at intervals by a spring catch that grips the notches in a vertical metal strip, holds the painting; a sliding clamp secures it at the top. The sketching easel, made of wood or aluminium, is small, lightweight and portable, the parts folding to a compact bundle; its design is a compromise between rigidity and portability. The most common type has three legs, of which two stand forward, holding a rest for the paintings, and the third may be slanted back to adjust the angle of the board or canvas. The school or art-class easel is sturdier than a sketching easel and lighter than a studio easel. Most easels may be folded for easy storage. See also TABLE EASEL.

easel painting a creative or fine-arts PAINTING done on a portable support in one of the standard techniques, such as oils, watercolour, or tempera, as distinguished from other kinds of painting, such as mural painting, decorative work, illustration, and commercial art.

East African copal see COPAL.

East Indian rosewood see ROSEWOOD.

East Indian satinwood see SATINWOOD.

eau de Javelle see JAVELLE WATER.

eau de Labarraque see JAVELLE WATER.

ébauche *(oil painting)* **1.** the first underpainting.

2. a rough sketch in oils, particularly for a proposed portrait.

ebony any of various black, dense, smooth-grained hardwoods obtained from trees of the genus *Diospyros*. Ebony is extremely durable, but difficult to carve because of its toughness. Among the finest and most intensely black ebonies are black or Gaboon ebony (*D. dendo*) from Africa and *D. ebenum* from Ceylon and India. Other ebonies are usually considered inferior, as they have golden-brown or purple streaks rather than being a uniform jet-black, and are coarser in texture. However, they are fine woods in their own right and are highly valued for their decorative effects. Other Asian ebonies include Calamander ebony (*D. quaesita*) and Macassar ebony (*D. melanoxylon*), also called Coromandel. Several black or deep-hued woods from trees not related to *Diospyros* are also popularly known as ebony; these include green ebony, brown ebony (see COFFEEWOOD), blue ebony and Mozambique ebony (see AFRICAN BLACKWOOD).

échoppe a NEEDLE whose point is bevelled to an oval facet, and which is used in ETCHING and line ENGRAVING. It is used in etching to draw lines of varying widths in the ground. In engraving, the échoppe is used to enlarge or slightly widen lines that have already been engraved with a burin. It is especially useful for varying part of a line, for example, making a line that has been cut in the plate swell or taper at some point along its length.

eclecticism the practice of borrowing and combining stylistic features from other art movements or from the works of other artists. In theory, by taking what is best from various schools or masters, the eclectic artist produces a work that surpasses any of them. In practice, the reverse is more likely to be the case. Elements of eclecticism have existed in all phases of the world's art, although the term is rarely used when the borrowed elements are harmoniously fused into a creative new style. This is not to say that the eclectic point of view may not result in works of some artistic value. The most notable historical example of eclecticism is the Academy of the Carracci in late 16th-century Bologna, although some authorities deny that their work is any more influenced by previous art than is the work of most artists, or that they worked according to deliberately eclectic principles. Elements of eclecticism are also found in Etruscan, Hellenistic, late Roman, Byzantine, Romanesque and Mannerist works, among others.

écorché a drawing or statue of a flayed human or animal figure, used in the study of musculature.

ectype 1. a replica of an original, such as a lithograph proof from the artist's drawing on stone.

2. any copy of an original, such as a reproduction of an artist's picture or a painting that is copied from another. See also PROTOTYPE.

efflorescence a white, powdery crust formed from the salt residue of moisture that seeps through concrete walls, mortar and cement, and evaporates, adhering to their outer surfaces. Some pigments used to colour cement or the mortar joints in a wall are subject to efflorescence, for example, lampblack or ivory black. Others, such as Mars black, are free from efflorescence.

egg, use in painting egg yolk is the traditional medium for TEMPERA colours. When mixed with water and pigments, and exposed to air and sunlight, it forms a tough, leathery adherent layer that has been proven over the centuries to be the most durable of all paint films. Although Cennino Cennini, writing in the 15th century, advised using only pale-coloured yolks, the colouring matter in egg yolk, carotin, is extremely fugitive and thus does not affect the colours in the dried painting. Egg white is carefully excluded from egg tempera, although egg-and-oil tempera is made with whole egg. The white of egg was probably used as a binder in manuscript illumination and has been employed as a size in gilding (see GLAIR); but in comparison with the yolk, it has little use in painting.

egg and dart a continuous banded design of alternate, engaged ovoids and arrowheads carved in high relief. This motif was a familiar feature of capitals and entablatures of the Ionic order of ancient Greek architecture, and has been adopted as a conventional moulding in decorative woodwork.

egg and dart An example of egg-and-dart moulding.

eggshell finish see MAT.

egg tempera the traditional form of TEMPERA paint consisting of pigments ground with pure egg yolk.

Egyptian art the art of ancient Egypt, from about 3200 BC to the conquest of Egypt by Alexander the Great in 332 BC. Funerary statues and decorated tombs were the primary forms of Egyptian art. The pyramids of the Pharaohs and smaller tombs of the lesser nobility were found in extensive funerary districts. Every tomb housed sculpture, wall paintings and household implements intended for the use of the spirit of the deceased. The paintings, narrative scenes of everyday activity or ritual, were done in aqueous paints on various grounds. Many that have survived for millenniums in the perfectly dry air could be removed with the wipe of a damp cloth. The pigments the Egyptians used are well known. The exact nature of the binders, however, has never been determined, although it is certain that milk, plant juices and gums were all used. Resin colour was sometimes used to fill in incised lines. Reliefs sculptured on the tomb walls were also painted.

Massive portrait statues of the dead were the chief form of sculptural expression. Carved in stone, usually in a standard erect or seated position, they were painted for realistic effect; the faces, unlike the bodies, were usually individual likenesses. The Egyptians also attained a high level of craftsmanship in working with gold, ivory, glazed terracotta, and semiprecious stones.

Egyptian blue, Alexandria blue, blue frit, Pozzuoli blue, Vestorian blue or **Venetian blue** a mixture of copper silicates; it is the celebrated ancient Egyptian frit, or pottery glaze, processed into pigment form. One of the earliest known artifical pigments, Egyptian blue was used as a water-paint pigment for blues and greens in ancient Egyptian wall paintings. It was imported into Mesopotamia, Crete, and other Mediterranean lands, and later manufactured in Italy under the name POMPEIAN BLUE. According to Vitruvius (1st century BC) the process for Egyptian blue was brought from Alexandria to Pozzuoli (Puteoli), Italy, where its production was established by Vestorian (Pozzuoli blue). Genuine Egyptian blue is extremely difficult to make in soft pigment form, though it was available in the early 20th century from a Parisian firm; in recent years, there has been little demand for it. Since so many mixtures of modern pigments can substitute for real Egyptian blue, interest in it is mainly antiquarian. Unless specifically identified as genuine, any modern pigment offered as Egyptian or Pompeian blue would be a synthetic lake colour of doubtful permanence. Greenish shades are called Egyptian green, but most of the Egyptian and Mediterranean greens used in ancient painting were palette mixtures of the blue with yellow ochre. See also ITALIAN BLUE.

Egyptian brown see MUMMY.

Egyptian cross see ANKH.

Egyptian green see EGYPTIAN BLUE.

Egyptian paste a self-glazing ceramic ware, first produced in ancient Egypt. The earliest glazed ware, it is sometimes anachronistically called Egyptian Faience. It probably consisted of clays, some soda ash or other sodium salts, and pulverized copper ore. Egyptian paste tiles and figures, as well as simple pottery, were produced by the First Dynasty (3200–2980 BC). Egyptian paste is easy to reproduce and is therefore popular with modern hobbyists.

Eight, The a group of American painters and illustrators of the early 20th century, led by Robert Henri (1865–1929) and John Sloan (1871–1951), and including George Luks (1867–1933), William Glackens (1870–1938), Everett Shinn (1867–1953), Maurice Prendergast (1859–1924), Arthur B. Davies (1862–1928), and Ernest Lawson (1873–1939). These artists were also called, derisively, the *Ashcan School*, because their work depicted such prosaic subjects as the streets and inhabitants of big cities (chiefly New York) with a vigorous realism that many of their contemporaries found offensive. The epithet was subsequently extended to other artists of the first two decades of the century, notably George Bellows (1882–1925), another champion of the commonplace in art.

electroplating an electrochemical process for coating a surface or object with a layer of metal. In its simplest terms, an electrical current set up in a bath of salt solution decomposes a metal and deposits it either on another metal or on a nonmetal that has previously been mechanically coated with a metal or graphite. In metalworking and sculpture, gold and silver are often electroplated on to a base metal, frequently brass, copper, or britannia metal. The process, which was discovered in the 19th century, has also been used by sculptors to metallize objects of wax, plaster and wood (provided that they have first been given a metal or graphite coating) to make them resemble metal sculpture.

electrum a natural alloy of gold and silver, pale gold in colour. It is used for jewellery and other precious metalwork.

elementarism a style of painting that was essentially a reaction to the work of De Stijl. The name was coined by the 20th-century Dutch artist Theo van Doesburg (1883–1931). Eschewing the strict verticals and horizontals insisted upon by Piet Mondrian (1872–1944), van Doesburg introduced diagonal lines and forms into his painting, purposely creating a feeling of instability in his work.

elemi a soft RESIN obtained from several tropical trees of the family *Burseraceae*. Elemi was much used during the 19th century to impart flexibility and toughness to varnishes made from hard, brittle resins. It is soluble in alcohol, benzol, and the strong lacquer solvents but does not dissolve satisfactorily in turpentine or white spirit. The best grade, called *Manila elemi*, is obtained from trees on the island of Luzon. Less valuable grades come from Mexico and Brazil. Manila elemi is white, opaque, soft and granular, and tends to darken and harden as it ages. It was formerly employed in industrial finishes and in some artists' varnishes and mediums, but its use diminished during the early 20th century with the introduction of resins such as dammar and the synthetic resins that do not require its softening effect. Modern opinion does not rate its durability and colour stability sufficiently highly to qualify it for use in materials for permanent painting.

elephant's ear a soft, naturally flat sponge found in the eastern Mediterranean; it is used by potters for finishing clay.

Eleusinian marble a fine black MARBLE from Attica, prized in ancient Greece especially for friezes and interior decoration.

elevation a geometric drawing of a building or other object made in projection on a vertical plane, as distinguished from a ground plan. Such drawings ignore perspective, showing the plan in two dimensions only.

ellipse guide a TEMPLATE with elliptical cutouts, used in drafting and the commercial arts for drawing ovals and for ruling curves. Ellipse guides are available in two varieties. Some templates have cutout ellipses of the same projection degree (for example, 45°) but with major axes of different lengths. Other templates have a number of ellipses in a range of projection degrees, usually 10 projections, in 5-degree increments, from 15° to 60°. See also FRENCH CURVE.

Elsner green a COMPOSITE PIGMENT made with Bremen blue and a fustic lake. It is not used for permanent painting.

emblem a picture with a motto or a set of verses intended as a moral lesson or a subject of meditation. Tomes filled with these pictures, known as *emblem books*, were common in the 17th century.

embossing the technique of creating raised figures or designs in relief on a surface. Embossing on leather, paper, metal or cloth, for book covers and various kinds of ornamental work, is usually accomplished by stamping the surface in a press with a pair of matched dies, a relief die striking from the underside into an intaglio die on the obverse. The process of creating relief designs on coins is known as *striking* rather than embossing. An old method of embossing on wood is to drive a blunt tool such as a chisel into the wood along the lines of the desired pattern, then plane the surface down to the level of the sunken design, and wet the entire surface. The moisture causes the compressed areas forming the design to rise to their original height and thus to project from the planed surface. In sheet-metal work, the process of executing designs in relief by hand, rather than by mechanical means, is called REPOUSSÉ.

embrittlement the loss of flexibility or elasticity. In a paint film, ground or support, it is a common cause or contributory element in the deterioration of pictures over a long period of time. Of all types of paint, oil and polymer colours retain their elasticity best, making it possible to use them on flexible supports. Of all natural textiles that might be used as supports for painting, linen canvas has the greatest and most lasting degree of resistance to embrittlement. See also PHOTOCHEMICAL EMBRITTLEMENT.

embu *(Fr.)* a sunken area in an oil painting. See SINKING IN.

embuya see IMBUYA.

emerald chromium oxide an obsolete and confusing name for VIRIDIAN; it does not denote emerald green.

emerald green or **Schweinfurt green** copper aceto-arsenite, an extremely brilliant pigment unequalled in clarity and vividness by any green in the artist's permanent palette. Although emerald green was used by painters during the 19th century, it has since been rejected because it is dangerously poisonous and it reacts with other pigments, causing some mixtures to become dark or brownish and some varieties to fade. The closest approximations of emerald green are mixtures of phthalocyanine green and Hansa yellow. Emerald green is known in Europe as Schweinfurt green, after the German town where it was invented by F.W. Russ and Wilhelm Sattler in 1814 and marketed in 1816. Before the adoption of the American standardized system of nomenclature, VIRIDIAN was sold in the United States under its French name, *vert émeraude*, and confused with emerald green; this confusion was kept alive in the 1960s by translators of French and Italian books who were not conversant with English usage. Early varieties of emerald green include MITTIS GREEN (also known as Vienna green) and IMPERIAL GREEN; other names are English green, *vert cendre* (French) and *verde ceniza* (Spanish). Emerald green used as an insecticide is known as Paris green.

ÉMERAUDE GREEN

émeraude green an incorrect and confusing name for VIRIDIAN; it does not denote emerald green.

emery an abrasive used in finely powdered form for polishing, in coarser form for smoothing rough surfaces. Emery is natural black corundum or aluminium oxide, the hardest mineral after the diamond.

empathy the emotional identification of the viewer with a work of art. The term, a translation of the German *Einfühlung*, became widely known through its use by Wilhelm Worringer in his *Abstraktion und Einfühlung* (*Abstraction and Empathy*, 1908).

empyrematic having the odour of an oil, wood tar, or other organic substance that has been burned or smoked.

emulsion a suspension of one liquid in another with which it is immiscible, as a dispersal in water of microscopic droplets of oil. To form a stable emulsion, a third ingredient must be present, a substance (called an *emulsifier* or *emulsifying agent*) that forms adsorbed films about the tiny globules of the dispersed fluid and keeps them from coalescing. The droplets of the dispersed fluid are known as the inner phase of the emulsion, the surrounding liquid as the external phase. An emulsion is usually made by dripping or slowly pouring one of the ingredients into the other while stirring vigorously.

A familiar emulsion that occurs naturally is whole milk, the inner phase of which consists of globules of butterfat; the external phase is a watery solution of casein, sugar and other substances. Another natural emulsion is egg yolk, the vehicle used in the classic tempera process, which consists of egg oil in an aqueous solution that contains albumen and lecithin, among other substances. Lecithin is a lipoid (fatlike) substance that is one of nature's most efficient emulsifying agents. Albumen, too, is a good emulsifier.

Milk and egg yolk are oil-in-water emulsions. There is also a second type, the water-in-oil emulsion, in which the phases are reversed. An example is butter, which has aqueous constituents dispersed in tiny globules throughout the butterfat. Water-in-oil emulsions are not frequently encountered among artists' materials, although an oil tempera has been used experimentally. Most manufactured emulsions are made by combining the OILY INGREDIENT with colloidal solutions, as of casein or albumen, which are not only good emulsifiers but also confer desirable properties when the emulsion is used as a paint binder. Like all emulsions, those used in painting are milky or opaque because of the refraction and dispersion of light by the minute droplets, but when dry they become transparent or nearly so.

emulsion ground a GROUND made by combining, or emulsifying, GESSO and oil. Emulsion grounds tend to be soft and spongy when fresh, unlike pure gesso grounds, but become brittle when they age. They lack the complete absorbency of gesso grounds and the flexibility of oil grounds, and combine to some extent the disadvantages of each. Emulsion grounds are sensitive to moisture and are generally considered less durable than oil grounds on canvas or gesso on panel.

enamel 1. a vitreous porcelain or ceramic glaze applied as a surface decoration to pottery or metal and fused in a furnace or kiln to produce a hard, durable finish, usually smooth and lustrous.
2. an object so decorated. The opacity of enamels and their use on metal distinguish them from other glazes used on ceramics. Enamelling techniques include CLOISONNÉ; CHAMPLEVÉ; BASSETAILLE; and PLIQUE-À-JOUR. These are delicate techniques, appropriate for jewellery and *objets d'art*. Ceramic or porcelain glaze applied to metal panels on a larger scale is known as VITREOUS ENAMEL. Genuine porcelain enamels are inorganic and are fired at temperatures of 1500° F or more.
3. a fluid paint that dries to a hard, glossy, smooth finish suggesting that of vitreous enamel. The vehicle of enamel is a resinous varnish. The two types are air-drying enamel and stove enamel. The latter achieves a tough, resistant character after it has been baked in an oven at 250 to 450° F.
4. a translucent glaze made of ground glass and coloured with metallic oxides for use in painting on glass. The development of this form of vitreous enamel in the 16th century revolutionized the art of STAINED GLASS by enormously increasing the range of colours that could be used on a single piece of glass. Until then, only a limited number of colour effects had been possible with GRISAILLE, SILVER STAIN, and JEAN COUSIN. The wide use of enamels finally converted the art of stained glass from a form of mosaic to a form of painting.

enamel paper a glossy COATED PAPER.

enamel white see BLANC FIXE.

encarnado a Spanish term for the painting of the exposed body parts of a wooden sculpture in naturalistic or flesh-toned paint.

encaustic or **encaustic painting 1.** the art or technique of painting with hot wax colours that are fused after application into a homogeneous layer and fixed to a support with heat.
2. a painting so executed. The technique, invented by the ancient Greeks, takes its name from the Greek *enkaustikos* (burning-in), the term now used for the last step in the process. Any wax technique that omits this final thermal treatment is not encaustic.

Encaustic colours are made by mixing pigments with molten beeswax and a little resin; they are kept fluid on a hot palette, and painting is done on any permanent support with brushes or spatulate instruments. When all the colours have been laid, the panel or canvas is set face up on a table, and the heat element is passed above it at a fixed distance until the colours are hot enough to fuse into a uniform film, but not so hot that they flow or run into one another. As the paint cools, the resin helps harden the film. In the encaustic technique the heaviest impastos may be used with safety; the paintings are permanent, and when polished with a soft cloth they have a pleasing dull sheen.

The burning-in (or *inustion* as it was formerly called) is done with any radiant heat source, such as a therapeutic heat lamp or a reflector light bulb. While the painter is at work he or she may hold a heating device in the free hand, warming the colours to a plastic consistency so they can be manipulated and blended. Without such surface heating, the colours will congeal quickly into crisp, separate brushstrokes.

Encaustic palettes with built-in heating elements and depressions for the paints are on the market, but equipment may easily be improvised by setting a metallic tray on a box heated with light bulbs or on a stand over an electric hot plate. The best working temperature for most purposes is about 200° F.

The ancient Greeks heated their wax colours on a copper or silver palette set over a metal drum filled with glowing charcoal, and for burning-in they used a brazier filled with charcoal. They applied colours to the painting with a bronze spatulate instrument. The Romans called this tool a *cestrum,* and all of the instruments used in encaustic, collectively, *cauteria.* The wax used in ancient times was called *Punic wax* by Pliny the Elder, but because of differing interpretations of his description of its preparation, the exact nature of this material was long in dispute. It is now generally held to have been the equivalent of modern white refined beeswax.

No Hellenic encaustic painting has survived, but the use of the technique by both the Greeks and the Romans is quite thoroughly documented in Roman writings and in relics. It was employed not only in artistic works but also, in some cruder form, as a protective coating, as on ships. Of the extant ancient encaustics, the most notable are mummy portraits from the Fayoum district of Upper Egypt, which date from the 2nd to the 4th centuries.

As is true of fresco and other techniques that originated in antiquity, encaustic is basically a simple process, but the modus operandi made its execution a cumbersome task. It was abandoned at some time during the Roman era, and the evidence concerning easel and mural painting from that time to the Renaissance indicates the use only of aqueous media and the early use of oils. During the 17th century alla prima oil painting began to come into use, and for the first time since the age of the encaustic painters, artists again had the means of creating direct, impasto, painterly works.

During the 18th century and again in the mid-19th, a number of experimenters studied the old methods with the aim of reviving encaustic for murals that could withstand harsh climatic conditions. They had little success, however, because like other surface coatings, encaustic is susceptible to damage from moisture seeping in from behind, and because no substantial improvements had yet been made in the awkward heating arrangements.

The technique was successfully revived for easel painting during the first quarter of the 20th century, when the availability of electric heating appliances made the process easy to manage. It has maintained its appeal for many artists even after the introduction of polymer colours, which can, to some extent, reproduce the effects of wax colours and their full, rich impasto.

engaged *(sculpture)* attached, embedded in, or otherwise connected to another element; not freestanding. A figure that is carved with no open space between the arms and torso or between the legs has engaged limbs. Much ARCHITECTURAL SCULPTURE is engaged rather than freestanding.

English green see EMERALD GREEN.

English pink see BROWN PINK.

English red *(US)* an obsolete term for LIGHT RED.

engobe a variety of SLIP used for decorating pottery. Engobe contains COLOUR OXIDES as well as clay, feldspar and silica. Usually of heavier consistency than the typical slip, it is applied to leather-hard or dry bodies.

English white see WHITING.

engraving 1. the process of incising a design, inscription, etc. on a hard surface, usually metal or wood, with a sharp tool, especially a GRAVER, either as ornamentation or as preparation of a printing surface.
2. the incised design.
3. the print made from an engraved plate.

In metalwork and sculpture, engraving is used for the surface decoration of objects in silver, gold or other materials; sometimes it is a step in another decorative technique, such as NIELLO. In the graphic arts, engraving is the process whereby the graver or other sharp tool is used to create an INTAGLIO or RELIEF PRINTING surface on a metal plate or a wood block, as in line, or copperplate, engraving (see below), STIPPLE ENGRAVING, and WOOD ENGRAVING. Plates for prints done in the CRAYON MANNER can be either engraved or etched. Although the WOOD-CUT and the LINOCUT employ the principles of engraving, they are really knife-and-chisel carving processes and are not classified as engraving. The plates made for PHOTOENGRAVING are not engraved but etched (see ETCHING).

Until quite late in the 19th century, engraving was used as a generic term for all graphic-arts processes; the terms *line engraving* and *copperplate engraving* were adopted to designate both the specific intaglio printmaking process of incising a metal plate in lines, rather than tonal areas, and an ORIGINAL PRINT made by this process. Today, the term *engraving* is almost always used as a shorter designation for line engraving. In this process, the engraver first transfers the design in reverse to the plate, which is usually copper but may be steel, and then incises the polished metal with a graver, or burin. The thickness of the furrows cut by the burin can be varied either by carefully manipulating the tool (the graver should not be used at too great an angle, however, or the resulting cut will be too slanted to one side to hold ink); by changing tools to get cutting surfaces of different sizes; or by using an ÉCHOPPE. The depth of the furrow is increased not by forcing the tool but rather by retracing shallow lines with the burin until the desired depth is achieved (as in etching, the deeper the incised line, the darker it will print). Hatching and crosshatching are used to indicate form and space, light and shadow. As the burin digs into the plate, it throws up small shavings of the metal, leaving behind a minute ridge, or BURR, on each side of the furrow. This must be removed with a SCRAPER in order that the printed lines should not be blurred. TRIAL PROOFS are repeatedly pulled throughout the execution of any metal-plate engraving so that the engraver may see as the work progresses which furrows need deepening or widening, whether hatching needs to be denser, etc. Each set of trial proofs is called a STATE. The artist prints the regular editions of the plate in an ETCHING PRESS.

Line engraving, like etching, developed from metalworking techniques. The earliest engravers were goldsmiths. The early link between metalworking and printing is shown by the application of the terms BROAD MANNER and *fine manner* to both the art of engraving and the art of niello, from which decorative technique engraving may have been derived. It is not known who executed the first line engraving. The technique developed simultaneously in Germany, the Netherlands, and Italy during the 15th century. The foremost early German engraver was Martin Schongauer (c.1450–1491), the son of a goldsmith, whose 115 copper engravings influenced artists throughout Europe – not the least of whom were Albrecht Dürer (1471–1528) and Lucas Cranach the Elder (1472–1553). In Italy during this period, both Sandro Botticelli (c.1445–1510) and Andrea Mantegna (c.1431–1506) were influential in the development of the art of line engraving. The 16th century, which produced such masters as Dürer, Cranach, Lucas van Leyden (c.1494–1533), and Marcantonio Raimondi (c.1480–c.1534), was the heyday of engraving. During the 17th century graphic artists began to be lured away from engraving by the freer and more expressive technique of etching, and engraving declined to the status of a reproductive technique. Nevertheless, the 17th-century produced some very fine engraved portraits and copies of drawings.

enlarging the process of increasing the size of a work of art without changing the scale of the elements contained. The various methods of enlarging – both by hand, such as by SQUARING, and by use of such devices as the PANTOGRAPH and the slide projector – are employed especially for increasing the size of an artist's preparatory sketch or a photograph to fit the larger surface on which the finished work of art is to be executed. A small preliminary drawing for a mural, for example, may first be enlarged by one of these methods to a CARTOON, which is then transferred to the wall surface by POUNCING, or it may be directly enlarged on the wall itself. The same principles, many of the same techniques, and much of the same equipment are used to reduce the size of an original work of art, although this is less frequently required.

en taille d'epargne see CHAMPLEVÉ.

entrelac a linear motif of intertwined lines and whiplash curves, often found in Art Nouveau designs.

environment an art form related to assemblage and usually employing large elements designed to be walked among or through, rather than merely viewed. These elements often include found objects, as well as painted or sculptured pieces. The environment is regarded as an extension of collage to the point that the work no longer has the illusory space of a two-dimensional painting but occupies real space, which it shares with the viewer. Forerunners of the environment, in the form of paintings with the dimensions of rooms, were produced in Munich in the late 1930s. A group of young New York painters in 1952 and the Gutai group in Japan in 1955 gave a new impetus to the concept of environmental art, which, now widespread, has been further extended by the use of action to include the so-called happening. Among the leading creators of environments are Walter Gaudnek, Allan Kaprow, James Dine, Claes Oldenburg and Salvador Dali.

epigone or **epigon** an inferior imitator or follower of a great artist, school or art period; from the Greek *epigonos*, 'one born after'.

epigraphy 1. the deciphering and interpretation of ancient inscriptions incised on stone, clay, metal or some other hard surface. In this study everything from noble sentiments chiselled on the marble of a temple to random scratchings on a wall (see GRAFFITO) is of interest and value. Much of the archaeologist's knowledge of the past comes from it.
2. the study of more recent inscriptions.
3. the practice of carving inscriptions.
4. a collection of incised inscriptions.

epoxy resins a group of synthetic thermosetting resins, developed during the late 1940s and early 1950s, widely used in industrial moulded products and in stove enamels, and popular with sculptors. The epoxies require a catalyst or hardening agent that is added at the time of use. They are well adapted to moulding because of the accuracy of the reproduction, there being practically no shrinkage or loss of volatile ingredients. All sorts of fillers – chopped fibreglass, fibreglass mats or fabrics – and pigments are used with the resins. Baked coatings made of epoxy resins have excellent resistance to chemical attack and protect surfaces from corrosion. The resins are perhaps best known as adhesives, for which purpose they are sold in sets of two tubes, the resin and the hardener, to be mixed in equal volumes just prior to use. Epoxy cement has the advantages of forming a secure join without the necessity of using clamps or pressure while it sets, and of creating a permanent bond of very great strength.

Epoxies must be handled with careful safeguards against the highly toxic effects of their solvents and the skin irritation caused by their hardeners.

equilibrium a balance of elements in a composition. A work that lacks equilibrium may be one-sided or without coherence. A composition in which most of the prominent shapes and masses are on one side, for example, would seem to be lopsided unless the other side had interest – spatial, linear, or colour – to balance it. Directional lines at different angles, balanced distribution and intensity of colour, and proportionate areas allotted to the significant and the secondary parts of the composition all contribute to balance.

eschel a mixture of smalt and ZAFFER, considered a grade of SMALT.

esparto a coarse grass that may be used in the production of paper. It is grown in Spain and North Africa.

esquisse *(Fr.)* or **schizzo** *(It.)* a preliminary sketch for a drawing, paint-ing or sculpture. The artist uses the esquisse to experiment with and work out the composition, the proportions, and the schemes of perspective and colour that he or she will want to incorporate in the ultimate work of art. The *esquisse en sculpture* is a small model in clay or wax that roughly indicates the thoughts and forms that the sculptor will later articulate explicitly in the final work. The French term *esquisse* and the Italian word *schizzo* are derived from the same root and may be used interchangeably, but both words are considered somewhat of an affectation when used in English.

essential oil or **essence** a fragrant liquid that is extracted or distilled from any of numerous flowers, leaves, woods and other vegetable sources as well as from some animal sources. An essential oil is not an oil in the same sense as linseed or petroleum oil. OIL OF CLOVES, OIL OF LAVENDER, SPIKE OIL and oil of ROSEMARY have some uses in oil painting, and certain other essences are used as odorants in such products as water paints, polishes, and cleaners (see CEDAR, OIL OF).

ester the chemical designation of any of a wide group of organic com-pounds that are made up of an acid and an alcohol (or a phenol) and that during HYDROLYSIS break down to these component parts; it can also be more simply regarded as a salt of an organic acid. An ester may be specified by either constituent: for example, ethyl silicate can be called the silicon ester of ethyl alcohol or the ethyl ester of silicic acid.

ester gum a ROSIN that has been hardened, bleached, and had its acid neutralized by chemical and mechanical treatments. Its properties are improved so greatly as to make it suitable for use in good-quality indus-trial products but it is not used in artists' paints or varnishes. It has found some use in the wax-resin adhesives formerly used in LINING. Its name is an instance of the varnish maker's use of the term *gum* interchangeably for *resin*.

etch, lithographic see LITHOGRAPHIC ETCH.

etching 1. BITING; the process whereby a surface is partially eaten away by a MORDANT in order to create a design, either as decoration, as on glass, or as an INTAGLIO or RELIEF PRINTING surface on a metal plate. In the latter capacity, etching is the process used to prepare the printing surface of the metal plates used in ANASTATIC PRINTING, PHOTOENGRAV-ING (both line and HALFTONE), and PHOTOGRAVURE, as well as the plates made for the specific fine-arts print-making technique that is known as *etching* (see below). Etching is a chemical process and differs, therefore, from the mechanical methods of creating a raised or lowered design on a surface, as in ENGRAVING.

2. an intaglio printmaking process.

3. an original print made by this process.

Etching is, traditionally, the pre-eminent graphic-arts technique. The drawing is made with a steel-etching NEEDLE through a thin coat of an acid-resistant ETCHING GROUND, blackened, if necessary, by SMOKING, on a highly polished metal plate, usually copper. The actual engraving agent in etching is the mordant; the lines drawn with the etching needle merely expose areas of the metal plate – the point touching but not digging into the surface of the metal. When the design has been drawn on the plate, the back and the edges of the plate are protected with an asphalt-varnish RESIST, and the plate is subjected to biting by immersion in a mordant bath. After a measured period of time, the plate is removed, rinsed and dried, and the lines the etcher wants to be faintest are protected with STOPPING-OUT varnish (the deeper a line is etched, the darker it will print). The plate is then placed for a second time in the ACID BATH to deepen the etch of those lines not stopped out. This procedure of stopping-out and rebiting may be repeated several times to create progressively deeper lines on the plate. When the plate is bitten to the etcher's satisfaction, it is cleaned and polished and then inked with a dabber and wiped to leave the ink in the etched lines only (see WIPING). The PROOFS are printed, or pulled, by running the inked plate and sheets of damp paper through an ETCHING PRESS. The print is a reversed copy of the drawing on the plate. Most etchers make LIMITED EDITIONS of 20 to 50 proofs; collectors generally seek low-numbered proofs, pulled before the plate begins to show signs of wear. When a large edition of an intaglio point is needed, as for a book illustration, the plate is given a STEEL FACING, a process that prolongs its printing life.

There are wide variations in materials and procedures in almost every step of the etching process. Sometimes the less expensive but less sensitive zinc plate is used instead of a copper plate. Because of the variety of techniques and materials available to the etcher, and because etching can be very successfully used in combination with other techniques such as DRYPOINT and AQUATINT, etching affords a multiplicity of effects and a completely individual artistic expression.

The etching of metal plates as a printmaking process developed from the common mediaeval practice of etching designs on armour with acid. It was, in fact, an etcher of armour, Daniel Hopfer (1493–1536), who is thought to have first inked and printed an etched iron plate. The first dated etching, however, was executed by Urs Graf, a Swiss artist, in 1513. Although copper plates were always used for etching in the Netherlands and in Italy, iron plates were used elsewhere until the 17th century. Iron plates required the most skilful handling in order to obtain acceptable results from that coarse-grained metal. Perhaps the fact that Albrecht Dürer used iron for the five etchings he executed between 1515 and 1518 explains the small success he had with the medium. During the 17th century, particularly in the hands of two virtuoso etchers, Hercules Seghers (1589 or 90–?1638) and Rembrandt (1606–1669), etching so progressed in versatility of technique and subtlety of effect that it surpassed engraving as the most popular graphic art. Seghers was the first graphic artist to use the process of *vernis mou* or SOFT-GROUND ETCHING, and Rembrandt used drypoint extensively in his etchings to achieve the directness that is characteristic of his work. With simple line etching and drypoint, Rembrandt achieved effects that have never been surpassed, even by artists using more modern methods and exploiting more sophisticated variations in technique. Anton van Dyck, a contemporary of Rembrandt, was also a master etcher and is especially well known as a graphic artist for his *Iconography,* a superb series of more than 100 etched portraits of contemporary artists and writers, only about 18 plates of which were completely prepared by van Dyck himself. Etching innovations in the 18th century, such as CRAYON MANNER and aquatint, were taken up in Spain by Goya (1746–1828), who was certainly one of the greatest masters of the technique of etching, as his *Los Caprichos, The Disasters of War,* and *Los Proverbios* series well demonstrate. The great 19th-century painter-etchers, among them James McNeill Whistler and Joseph Pennell, obtained new effects with etching. Picasso, Rouault and Chagall are among the significant 20th-century painter-etchers.

etching ground the thin resist, or acid-resistant coating, that is applied, in ETCHING and AQUATINT, to the face of the copper plate and through which the drawing is incised with a needle in etching, and the plate is grained in aquatint. A good etching ground must resist the MORDANT for the duration of BITING. It must be of the proper consistency – soft enough and not too adhesive – to be penetrated easily by the needle, but it must also be hard enough to withstand a certain amount of handling. Various combinations and proportions of beeswax and resins are used, but the wax is usually slightly less than double the amount of the other ingredients. Many etching grounds contain a highly acid-resistant, soft asphalt such as manjak or Trinidad. A few basic types of ground may be either made up by the etcher (see REMBRANDT'S GROUND) or bought ready-made. The ground is applied by rubbing a lump of it on a heated plate and spreading it with a DABBER. Since most grounds are transparent (even those containing asphalt have only a light-brown tinge when spread thinly and evenly on the plate), etchers usually blacken the surface of the plate by SMOKING the applied ground. The addition of an equal quantity of tallow to a regular etching ground produces a suitable resist for SOFT-GROUND ETCHING. This soft ground, or *vernis mou,* does not require blackening by smoking. See also STOPPING OUT.

etching press a printing press used in INTAGLIO printing (etching, engraving, drypoint, aquatint, etc.), consisting of a large upper roller, a lower roller about half the diameter of the upper one, and a flat steel bed or iron plate that moves on gears through the rollers as the SPIDER WHEEL is turned. The inked and wiped (see WIPING) intaglio plate is printed by placing it, printing surface uppermost, on the bed plate of the press; covering it with a piece of damp paper, which is in turn covered with a felt etching BLANKET; and running the entire sandwich of bed, plate, paper and blanket through the rollers. Sensitive proofs can be printed only if the artist has complete control of the press. An etching press can also be used for printing a metal-plate MONOTYPE and for creating a SAND-GRAIN GROUND on an aquatint plate.

ethanol see ETHYL ALCOHOL.

ether, diethyl ether or **ethyl ether** a colourless, volatile, highly inflammable liquid made principally by the distillation of alcohol and sulphuric acid and used chiefly as a solvent and anaesthetic. Ethyl ether is called for in some antiquated recipes for etching grounds, but because it is dangerously explosive and toxic, it has long been replaced by less hazardous solvents such as acetone.

ethiop amorphous black mercuric sulphide; it is an intermediate stage in one method of making VERMILION.

ethyl acetate or **acetic ether** a VOLATILE SOLVENT that has a mild, fruity odour and is not dangerously toxic if properly handled. It is extensively used as a LACQUER SOLVENT.

ethyl alcohol, Cologne spirits, ethanol or **grain alcohol** a VOLATILE SOLVENT widely used in industry but of relatively minor importance to artists. It is the solvent for shellac and a few other resins, a diluent for some of the fixatives, and a mildly active wetting agent. Pure ethyl alcohol is the basis for alcoholic drinks and is therefore subject to a heavy tax. For this reason, METHYLATED SPIRITS are far more readily available for artists' use. Those who require pure alcohol for technical purposes can usually get a permit to obtain it in small quantities. ABSOLUTE ALCOHOL, which is free of water, is also available from chemical supply sources. The vapour of pure ethyl alcohol is less harmful to the health than that of most solvents.

ethyl ether see ETHER.

ethyl silicate a LIQUID SILICATE used as a vehicle in mural painting. It is a clear, thin liquid that superficially resembles a volatile solvent. When carefully formulated with alcohol and a small amount of water, it will hydrolyse into a pure silica binder, after going through a viscous, adhesive intermediate stage while drying. Painted on any absorbent or porous surface, ethyl silicate colours produce effects comparable to those of fresco; in their durability and resistance to adverse conditions and the brilliance of their colours, they surpass fresco. The colours must be freshly prepared each day, because once water has been added, HYDROLYSIS cannot be halted. Ethyl silicate is the best and most readily available of several SILICON ESTERS. It was first introduced as a paint vehicle by George King in England in 1931.

Etruscan art the art of the people of ancient Etruria, now Tuscany, in western central Italy, who ruled in Rome itself during the 6th century BC but were under Roman political domination by the end of the 3rd century BC. The Etruscans may have come from Asia Minor or the Middle East, or may have been at least partly indigenous to Italy. They were thoroughly established in Etruria by 700 BC, and their civilization reached its peak in the 7th and 6th centuries BC. Their art shows MINOAN, MYCENAEAN, HELLENIC and EGYPTIAN influences, but also contains some original elements, which in turn affected the development of Roman art. See EGYPTIAN ART; HELLENIC ART.

The elaborate stone tombs of the Etruscans, in a huge necropolis, or city of the dead, at their ancient capital of Tarquinii (near modern Tarquinia), were decorated with lively wall paintings depicting scenes of activity and pleasure from daily life. Some of these murals were done in true fresco, others in a sort of tempera – both on white plaster grounds. Terra-cotta statues, of life size or larger, on the sarcophagi of the dead, differed from their Egyptian counterparts in that the deceased were shown happy and vigorous, as in life, rather than solemn, as in death. In the 6th century BC such figures had the so-called Archaic smile of Hellenic sculpture of the period (see ARCHAIC PERIOD), although later statues were more solemn, possibly in response to a similar change in Hellenic work. Pottery, painted vases, ivory objects, gold jewellery, and bronze statuettes were also made by Etruscan artisans. In the 3rd century BC, superb bronze portrait heads of living individuals began to appear. Roman writers tell us that the Etruscans were also master architects and city planners, but of their temples and homes, built in wood on stone foundations, almost nothing remains.

étude French for STUDY.

euchrome an archaic name for burnt UMBER.

Euston Road School the name given to a group of mid-20th century British artists, who rebelled against abstraction (see ABSTRACT ART) in favour of a return to a more naturalistic, representational style of painting. Most of the artists were either students or teachers at an art school in the Euston Road, London.

Euville stone see LIMESTONE.

evangeliar see GOSPEL.

evangelistary see GOSPEL.

even-sided (of paper or board) having the same surface on both sides and thus capable of being used for drawing, painting, or printing on either side.

exc. an abbreviation for the Latin word *excudit,* meaning 'he (or she) executed it'. A synonym for *imp. (impressit,* 'he (or she) printed it'), *exc.* is sometimes inscribed in a lower corner of the margin of a print following the name of the printer and identifying the printer as such. For an explanation of other terms used for marking prints, see DEL.

exploded view *(mechanical drawing and commercial illustration)* a rendering of a complex object in which each of its components is shown separately but in the same scale as the other parts. The parts are in correct relative position (except for the distance between them), as if they were ready to be pushed into reassembly.

expressionism a concept of painting in which traditional adherence to canons of realism and proportion is overridden by the intensity of the artist's emotions, resulting in distortions of line, shape and colour. Whereas the Impressionists were concerned with rendering nature in a new and more valid way, such painters as the Fauves and Van Gogh, by considering their emotions as important as their subject matter, became the forerunners of expressionism. It was brought to the status of a full and vigorous movement by artists in Germany during the first quarter of the 20th century, especially by the BRÜCKE, BLAUE REITER and NEUE SACHLICHKEIT groups. Among the prominent early expressionists were

Edvard Munch (1863–1944), Max Beckmann (1884–1950), James Ensor (1860–1949), Oskar Kokoschka (1886–1980), Emil Nolde (1867–1956), Georges Rouault (1871–1958) and Chaim Soutine (1894–1943). Like much of modern art, expressionism owes a great deal to the impact of African sculpture on Europe in the decade preceding World War I.

The artistic tendency to distort forms for emotional emphasis and impact can be traced back to such individual masters of fantasy and feeling as Hieronymus Bosch (active 1488–1516) and Matthias Grünewald (c.1475–1528) in the late Gothic period. See also NEO-EXPRESSIONIST; ABSTRACT EXPRESSIONISM.

extender any substance, such as an INERT PIGMENT, that is added to a material in order to increase its bulk. It is classified as a FILLER if its function is to cheapen or downgrade the material. Extenders may serve necessary or desirable functions, such as controlling the excessive tinting strength of a pigment like phthalocyanine blue. A printing-ink extender of semipaste consistency enhances the working qualities of the ink and improves its transparency. The transparent base used in silkscreen paints is also known as extender.

ex-voto an object presented at a shrine as a votive offering. Pictures and other art objects have often been commissioned for this purpose.

F

f. or **fec.** *abbrev. for* FECIT.

fabric *(ceramics)* the whole nature of a body of work done in a given period, including its workmanship, materials, technique and general style.

Fade Ometer *(US)* the tradename for a laboratory accelerated testing device in which samples of coloured materials or coatings are exposed to a xenon arc to determine their degree of resistance to fading. The arc emits an intense actinic light which has, in a few hours, the destructive effect of many days of ordinary daylight. Although it does not duplicate exactly the effect of long exposure to sunlight, it serves as a very efficient indicator of what degree of lightfastness can be expected of a material, and of the comparative resistance to fading of a number of samples. See also ACCELERATED TEST.

fading of colours the gradual loss of colour of pigments and dyes that are chemically unstable. Entering into chemical reactions on exposure to the ultraviolet rays in daylight, and to the oxygen and moisture of the atmosphere, they form colourless or less highly coloured compounds. Dyes and pigments subject to such reactions are called FUGITIVE COLOURS. The technologists' term for the property of colour permanence is colour stability or fade resistance. There is no way of preventing the fading of unstable colours. A protective coating such as polymer medium will preserve fragile materials from damage but will not block out light; the acrylic and vinyl resins have the highest transmission of ultraviolet light of all materials.

faïence earthenware with a colourful, opaque glaze, such as MAJOLICA. Faïence is the French name for the Italian town of Faenza, famous for such pottery since the 16th century.

fake see FALSIFICATION; FORGERY.

falciform having the shape of a scythe or sickle.

false biting see FOUL BITING.

false body see BODY.

falsification any form of misrepresentation about the authenticity of a work. FORGERY, the creation of a fake, is a form of falsification, but falsification is specifically used for the circulation of a copy or an imitation (that is, a work not originally made as a deliberate deception) as something genuine. Four examples of falsification were bas-relief heads in Pentelic marble that were declared spurious in 1954. They were apparently made without dishonest intention in the mid-19th century as facsimiles of carvings from the Parthenon, but subsequently were sold and traded as true antique works.

famille rose a class of Chinese porcelain decorated with multicoloured flower patterns in which reds and pinks dominate.

fan brush a sparsely bristled fan-shaped brush set in a flat metal ferrule at the end of a long handle; it is also available in red sable and badger hair. It is used dry for subtle or delicate blending of wet paint and for special manipulations in representing hair, foliage, and other fine, soft details. See also BLENDER.

fan brush

fancy picture an 18th-century genre picture, in which depiction of the life of rural people is sentimentalized beyond any connection with reality.

fantastic realism a school of Austrian painters after the Second World War who were greatly influenced by the great Dutch artist Pieter Breughel (*c.*1525–1569), who combined the diverse elements of fantasy and imagination with a strict attention to realistic detail.

fast colours or **lightfast colours 1.** *(in textile dyeing and other industrial processes)* colours that will satisfactorily resist fading for the effective life of the product in which they are used.

   2. *(in artists' paint pigments)* nonfading over long exposures to daylight.

fat *(ceramics)* denoting a clay that has great plasticity. A fat clay such as BALL CLAY or BENTONITE may be added to a SHORT clay to make it more workable. Sometimes GROG or a less plastic clay must be added to an extremely fat clay to make the body more porous and enable it to dry uniformly.

fat over lean the practice of applying layers of colour rich in oil over an underpainting that contains less oil and is therefore less flexible. It is the recommended way to apply oil colours, as painting the lean over the fat would make the resulting work likely to crack after ageing: the more brittle overpainting would be unable to adjust to the underpainting's expansions and contractions due to temperature and atmospheric changes.

fatty acid any of the organic acids combined with glycerin to produce fats and oils. Fatty acids are sometimes separated from and used instead of the whole oil in alkyd resins and varnishes.

Fauves, les a group of revolutionary painters whose work, especially during the first decade of the 20th century, was influenced by such Postimpressionist masters as Van Gogh, Gauguin and Cézanne, while it rejected the formal aspects of earlier Impressionism. The term *fauves*, meaning 'wild beasts' and first used by a contemporary critic, referred to the violent liberties the artists took with colour and, to a lesser degree, with form. Rejecting the Impressionist technique of breaking colour up, they painted an object in the colours – often brilliant and explosive – that they thought best expressed its inner qualities, rather than as it appeared in nature. Although they were never a coherent group, the Fauve artists were linked by their intense use of colour and their liberation from the restrictions of earlier art, as well as by personal friendship. Among them were Henri Matisse (1869–1954), André Derain (1880–1954), Maurice de Vlaminck (1876–1958), Albert Marquet (1875–1947), Raoul Dufy (1877–1953), and Georges Rouault (1871–1958).

fawn brown see VELVET BROWN.

fecit a Latin word meaning 'he (or she) made it' that is sometimes inscribed on a painting, print, sculpture, or building after the artist's name or initials. It is sometimes abbreviated to *fec.* or *f.*

Federal Art Project *(US)* one of President Franklin Roosevelt's New Deal programmes. It sought to employ American artists who were out of work during the Great Depression. These artists were set to work at tasks varying from decorating public buildings and designing posters and prints, to teaching art in their own communities. While it may be said that little of value survives from the period in which the Federal Art Project was active, the programme's overall significance cannot be discounted. It was the first time that the federal government officially recognized the important contribution that artists make to cultural life in the United States.

feldspar a crystalline mineral used as a FLUX in porcelain and glazes or frits. It contains aluminium silicates together with other compounds in varying compositions.

felt-tip pens pens with felt or nylon tips. They are widely available in great variety, whether pointed or blunt. Because they make possible a great flexibility of line and an ease of control in drawing, felt-tip pens are especially popular for sketching. The ink reservoir is in the shaft of the marker. These pens come in a wide range of colours, none of which is sufficiently permanent for use in the fine arts, since the inks contain soluble dyes. A special refillable pen is available that has interchangeable felt tips and may be filled with a special ink made with a carbon-black pigment.

fence *(in casting)* a thin wall of either clay or sheet metal (usually brass) set on or into a model to create a separation in a waste mould or piece mould made of plaster.

Ferrarese school a group of 15th-century Italian and Flemish artists, in and around Ferrara, in Italy, of whom Jacopo Bellini (1400–1471) is the most widely known and who painted in both the Gothic and Renaissance styles.

ferric chloride an iron salt used in ETCHING as a MORDANT or as an additive to another mordant in order to obtain more vertical biting and to lessen undercutting at the edges of lines. It tends to deposit salts rapidly on the walls of the etch, thus protecting them from further corrosive action, while the bottom of the etched furrow, where the mordant collects, clogs up less rapidly.

Ferrite or **Ferrox** *(US)* tradenames for Mars yellow, one of the MARS PIGMENTS.

ferrule the metal, plastic, or sometimes quill cylindrical device designed to align and hold paintbrush hairs together in a resinous adhesive. The ferrule is attached to the brush handle by crimping.

festoon or **swag** any decorative design of gracefully curved lines caught up in loops, as of cords or fabrics; specifically, a decorative carving or painting of a garland of leaves, flowers, and fruit arranged in a hanging loop between two points from which depend wavy ribbons or vine-like extensions of the foliage and flowers.

festoon

fête champêtre a certain type of idealized outdoor party scene, most commonly depicting 18th-century French aristocrats, costumed as shepherds and shepherdesses, flirting and making merry in a rural setting.

fettle *(ceramics and sculpture)* to trim away unwanted material, such as mould marks and coarse edges, from cast and plastic substances with a knife or other implement. A *fettling knife*, also called a POTTER'S KNIFE, is often used.

fibreboard see WALLBOARD.

fibreglass glass that has been drawn into filaments of very fine, hairlike particles. It is nonflammable, light and strong. In sculpture, it is used to reinforce polymer and polyester resins, since its tensile strength is very great. Fibreglass is available as CHOPPED STRAND MAT, glass fibre scrim, fibre cloth, tissue and surface mat. Glass cloth is sold under the tradename Fibreglas.

field painting see COLOUR FIELD PAINTING.

fig milk the tradename for a German ready-made tempera EMULSION (*Feigenmilch*) of undisclosed composition.

fig-tree juice the milky juice of the fig tree, recommended in the 15th century by Cennino Cennini as an additive to egg TEMPERA. Cennini suggested beating or whipping the egg yolk with fresh, young fig-tree shoots. There have been various explanations for this practice. It may have been used as a preservative, or to give additional toughness and flexibility to the paint film, or as a plasticizer to improve brushability. Since fig-tree juice closely resembles LATEX, the latter has been proposed as a modern substitute for it. However, practically no tempera painters of succeeding periods have followed Cennino's advice, feeling either that the twigs provided too small an amount of juice to be effective, or that Cennino meant to recommend them merely as conveniently available whisks to beat the egg to a light consistency.

figurative *(in painting, drawing, and sculpture)* representing the human form by means of a figure, symbol, or likeness.

figure 1. a representation of the human body in the pictorial and sculptural arts.

2. *(design)* any given pattern or repeated decorative motif, as in a figured textile.

figurine a small statue, especially one a few inches in height and not over 10 inches.

filbert brush or **oval brush** a bristle brush, used in oil painting, that is flat and oval in shape. While the flat and the bright brushes have straight edges, the filbert tapers to a blunt point, resembling a flat whose edges have been rounded by wear. See BRUSH, BRISTLE.

filigree fine wire, usually gold, silver or SILVER-GILT, worked into delicate, intricate designs, either as open-work or as surface decoration for a gold or silver ground to which it is soldered. The wire, which may be curled, twisted or braided, is often varied with beads or grains of the metal. If the filigree is to stand alone, it is usually set within a framework of either heavier wire or strips of the metal, or bands may actually be intermixed with the wrought wire. The use of filigree for jewellery and other ornamental work is both old and extensive. Ancient Greek tombs have yielded fine examples, as have Anglo-Saxon and Celtic treasures. The art of making filigree reached its peak in 17th-century Italy, where some of the finest filigree is still produced today.

filler an INERT PIGMENT added to a paint or pigment to cheapen or adulterate it. An inert pigment used to impart desirable properties to, or to enhance the performance of, a pigment is classified as an EXTENDER.

filler rod a thin stick of bronze, brass or another metallic alloy, used for BRAZING or welding a metal with a higher melting point. An acetylene torch is used to melt the rod, which is then deposited on the base metal as a means of joining pieces together or of covering the surface.

fillet 1. (also called **reglet** or **quadra**) a very narrow, flat, plain moulding, which may be used as a border or as the raised part of a design in any of a number of patterns.

2. a narrow, flat band that separates two mouldings or other elements of a decorative design.

film *(painting)* a continuous layer of paint. A dried paint coating is referred to as a paint film in discussions of its composition, structure and behaviour.

film-former 1. the fluid ingredient in a paint, varnish, or other coating material that enables it, on application to a surface, to form a continuous adherent layer.

2. the nonvolatile components of a vehicle or medium, as distinguished from its volatile thinners. Various drying oils and solutions of resins, gums, waxes and casein are the more common film-formers used in artists' materials. The effectiveness of an oil as a film-former is indicated by its IODINE VALUE.

film integrity the flawless continuity – without breaks or pinholes – of a paint or varnish film.

film-stencil method a SILKSCREEN technique in which the stencils are cut from a paper-backed stopping-out film. This transparent sheet is composed of a thin film of coloured lacquer (the colour makes the design visible on the screen) laminated to a sheet of glassine backing paper. The design to be printed is traced onto the film and then cut out with a stencil cutter, through the lacquer layer only. These cut-out printing areas are then stripped from the backing paper, and the film is attached to the underside of the screen with an adhering thinner. Before the stencil is printed, the paper backing is removed from the film, leaving the design areas open and pervious to the paint or ink that is applied with a SQUEE-GEE. Nonprinting areas of the screen outside the stencil are also blocked out, either with paper (for short runs) or lacquer (for larger editions). The film-stencil method of silk screening is especially suited to commercial work requiring precision in printing and is also used in SERIGRAPHY for geometrical designs and simple drawings.

film-thickness gauge a laboratory device especially designed to measure the thickness of wet or dry films of paint or other coating materials. Several different types of mechanical and electronic instruments are used in the preparation of test samples.

filter press a machine for filtering solids from liquids. It consists of a series of square frames held in position between solid plates, with a square of filter cloth attached to each frame. The fluid is pumped into the press under strong pressure until the areas between the plates are filled with solid cakes of paste or pulp material. This may be given a final rinse by pumping water through the press. The filter press is essential equipment in pigment manufacture, where the filter cake is dried and pulverized, and in ceramics, where it is used to concentrate, or remove water from, clay SLIP.

fin-de-siècle (*Fr.* end of the century) characteristic of the arts and mores of the last two decades of the 19th century. The period was notable for its artistic and literary spirit of jaded sophistication and world-weary aestheticism. See also ART NOUVEAU; DECADENT ART.

fine art art created primarily as an aesthetic expression, to be contemplated or enjoyed for its own sake. Unlike APPLIED ART, it is not used as an instrument for some other activity. Examples of fine art include painting, drawing, sculpture, print making and architecture. The distinctions between fine and applied art are, however, arbitrary at best. For instance, a Greek vase or a mediaeval manuscript illumination that may have been functional at the time of its creation is enjoyed today as a purely aesthetic object. See also MINOR ARTS.

fine manner see BROAD MANNER.

FINGER PAINTING

finger painting the application of colours to a surface with the fingertips. With the expansion of organized art activities for children in the 1930s, special materials were developed for their use. Finger paints, available in jars, are nontoxic, easily worked and easily washed away. Some serious artists have experimented with finger painting, using both water-miscible and oil paints. Chinese artists of various periods have also practised finger painting, both alone and in conjunction with brushwork.

finial an ornament in architecture, furniture, metalwork, and ceramics that serves as the crowning detail, as at the apex of a roof or gable, or on the lid of a tankard or covered bowl. The finial serves chiefly as decoration. It may also be functional when it is used as a knob to grasp or when it locks elements together, as on a lampshade. In ceramics and metalware this protuberance usually takes the shape of a flower bud, a bunch of foliage, an acorn, etc. A flame, steeple, or urn – the traditional finials in a broken pediment – are more common in furniture and architecture.

finish 1. the surface appearance of a work of art, such as a painting or sculpture, or another object, such as a sheet of paper or a piece of furniture: for example, a glossy finish, rough finish, smooth finish, or mat finish. Industrial coating materials are sometimes called *finishes*. See also PATINA.

2. *(in art criticism)* careful attention to perfection of line, form, and detail, as distinguished from a rough, spontaneous, or casual treatment.

finishing trowel a flat-faced tool used to produce a smooth, level surface on plaster or concrete work.

finishing trowel

firebrick a brick made from infusible material such as FIRECLAY, used for constructing or lining furnaces, kilns, and chimneys, which are to be subjected to extreme heat.

fireclay a highly refractory clay, that is, one that fuses at higher temperatures than those used in firing pottery, glazes and enamels. It may thus be used for making a MUFFLE, FIREBRICK, and KILN linings. Fire clay commonly contains a considerable proportion of alumina.

fire gilding a chemical process for applying a coat of gold to another metal by coating the surface with an amalgam of gold and mercury and vaporizing the mercury with heat. The thin coat of gold that remains is then treated with GILDER'S WAX and a paste of salts in water or weak ammonia to heighten its colour. This process is also called *amalgam gilding* and, rarely, *wash gilding*. It should not be confused with the mechanical process known as WATER GILDING, in which leaf is laid on a gesso or bole surface that has been moistened with water. Fire gilding, which is probably the oldest technique for gilding metals, was used particularly to decorate arms and armour. The process is seldom used today and is, in fact, forbidden by law in most places, since the fumes of the volatilized mercury are toxic. It has largely been replaced by METALLIZING processes.

fire marble see SHELL MARBLE.

fire red *(US)* an industrial or printing-ink pigment of a hue associated with fire-engines; usually made from TOLUIDINE RED. Fire red is not sufficiently permanent or nonbleeding for artists' use.

firing *(ceramics)* the process of exposing a clay body, glaze or enamel to intense heat, usually in a KILN. Firing hardens clay permanently by changing it physically and chemically. Glazes and enamels are vitrified during firing. See MATURATION; REDUCTION FIRE; GLOST FIRE; BISQUE FIRE.

first coat see UNDERPAINTING.

fish glue a glue made from fish bones or skin. It is sold in liquid form for use as an adhesive on wood and other materials. Although it is a much weaker adhesive than hide glue, it is adequate for many purposes.

fishtail tool a woodcarving chisel or gouge that flares out widely at its cutting end. See illustration at WOODCARVING TOOLS.

fissure a crack in the paint film that leaves visible the ground or underpainting. Such a crack is called a TRACTION FISSURE when caused by contraction of the paint.

fit *(ceramics)* the mechanical suitability of a glaze to a clay body. If the glaze and the body have similar coefficients of expansion, certain glaze defects, such as CRAZING, will be minimized.

fitch 1. the hair of the fitch or polecat, used in making brushes.
2. a brush made of fitch hair.
3. a CHISEL BRUSH made of bristle or camelhair, with a ferrule that tapers toward the handle and straight bristles that flare out slightly. Fitches are employed primarily for sign writing and decoration, using the side edges of the brush, but a good fitch can also be used on its flat sides like a SINGLE-STROKE BRUSH.

fitch A fitch brush.

fixative a thin liquid consisting of a resinous or glutinous binder and a volatile solvent, sprayed over pastels and drawings, especially CHARCOAL drawings, to protect them from smudging. Fixatives for charcoal and pencil drawings usually contain a small proportion of resin dissolved in a large amount of alcohol or other rapidly evaporating solvent. Their action binds the particles securely so that the work will not rub or smudge when given careful handling. To remain invisible, a fixative cannot be used excessively or it will build up to a continuous layer, like a varnish film. The artist applies fixative with a spray, mouth blower or atomizer, and it has also been available in a pressure spray can. *Workable fixative* is one that allows the drawing to be worked on even after the fixative has been applied. (The resinous deposit of some fixatives repels water and so precludes further work.)

Fixatives for pastels differ from the common variety in that they are not intended to supply full protection, but only to render the surface less fragile so that the particles will not dust away of their own accord; the work is then framed under glass with a mat sufficiently thick to prevent contact with the glass. During the two centuries in which pastel has been popular as a fine-arts medium, much effort has been directed toward the invention of a protective fixative that would neither alter the colours nor destroy the characteristic soft pastel quality. Unfortunately, this is optically impossible, for when a pigment is surrounded by a medium, both its colour effect and its opacity are altered so that its appearance differs from what is displayed when it is surrounded by air. Some binders produce less colour change in relation to their binding power than others. An alcoholic solution of casein is one of the best in this respect.

fixed oil a rather outmoded term for the nonvolatile component or film-forming oil in a paint vehicle or varnish, as distinguished from the volatile solvents formerly called *volatile oils*.

flag or **split end** the end opposite the root, or butt, end of a bristle used to make a brush. Flag ends are always set as the free end of a brush. See also BELLY; HEEL.

flake white an artists'-quality WHITE LEAD oil colour. The same precautions should be taken in using this colour as in using other lead-based pigments.

Flamboyant style see GOTHIC.

flame black an inferior carbon pigment made by burning waste coal tar and mineral oils. It tends to be brownish and to contain oily impurities. Flame black can be considered an impure LAMPBLACK.

flashing a method of colouring glass by dipping clear glass, while still pliant, into a bath of molten glass of a deep colour, or by fusing a thin sheet of dark glass to a thicker one of clear glass. Flashing has been practised at least since the 12th century in making STAINED GLASS and in other glassmaking techniques. It is necessary because the darker shades of glass, in the thickness required for use in windows, would be nearly opaque. See SGRAFFITO.

Flashe see VINYL RESIN.

flask see SAND CASTING.

flat denoting a mat, or lustreless, surface finish.

flat colour a uniform, unbroken, unshaded area of colour.

flat sketching pencil a broad, flatpointed LEAD PENCIL, useful for sketching and lettering, especially for drawing in wide lines and shading large areas. It is available in several degrees of softness, from 2B to 6B. The common carpenters' pencil is comparable in composition, size and use. Although it is sold in one degree only (approximately 4B) and is not made to the same standard of quality as a flat sketching pencil, artists nevertheless use carpenters' pencils for many of the same purposes.

flatware *(US)* utensils or receptacles that are relatively flat. Although the term can be applied to ceramic, glass and metal objects, in common usage flatware refers almost exclusively to pieces made of metal, especially silver. See also HOLLOW WARE.

flavine lake a fugitive LAKE pigment formerly prepared from the natural dyestuff quercitron (see QUERCITRON LAKE). It was made in a number of shades, including greenish yellow, dull yellow, bright orange, olive and greenish black. The name *flavine* is also associated with a series of synthetic dyes.

flax a plant (genus *Linum*) that grows in all temperate and cold countries. The linen for artists' canvas is made from flax fibre, and linseed oil is pressed from its seeds.

Flemish white an obsolete name for WHITE LEAD.

flesh colour the paint used to depict the skin colour of so-called White people. Typically, it is a mixture of white and yellow ochre or raw sienna tinted with very small amounts of red or a trace of black, green, or another colour for subtle variations. Oil colours and pastels labelled *flesh colour* are ready-made mixtures of no standard composition, but they can usually be depended on to be permanent.

flesh ochre a special YELLOW OCHRE modified by admixture of other pigments; it is useful in creating FLESH-COLOUR effects.

flint a form of quartz used as a source of silica in ceramic glazes and in clay bodies. The terms *flint, silica*, and *quartz* are frequently used interchangeably in ceramic terminology.

flitch a log or section of a log that has been specially selected and prepared for cutting veneer. Some woods used extensively for veneer and not available in blocks for carving may be obtained in this form.

float a flat-faced tool for finishing plaster, cement and similar materials. In plastering for fresco painting a float with a roughish wooden surface is usually preferred; it may be made by fastening an angled handle to a cedar shingle. In other kinds of plastering, floats covered with cork, carpet, felt or glass may be used.

floating signature an artist's signature applied to a painting on top of the coating of varnish. A floating signature is obviously not an integral part of the painting, since if the painting were cleaned and the varnish removed, the signature would come away with it. Although an artist might conceivably sign his work after varnishing it, the discovery by test that a signature is floating is usually accepted as evidence that the signature is fraudulent.

flocking the strewing of pulverized cloth over a surface coated with PASTE or other adhesive to create a felt or velour effect. One kind of PASTEL PAPER is made in this way. There are a great many industrial uses of the process, especially in the decoration of surfaces such as wallpaper by stencilling or printing the designs with adhesive. The process is not sufficiently durable to be used in works of art. In commercial flocking, a flock gun, similar to the SPRAY GUN used for liquids, is employed to apply the flock.

flong a material made of layers of tissue paper held together with wet paste, used in PAPIER MÂCHÉ and other moulded paper techniques.

Florence zinc oxide *(US)* a tradename for FRENCH-PROCESS ZINC OXIDES.

Florentine brown the brown shades of VANDYKE RED.

Florentine lake see CRIMSON LAKE.

floriated decorated with realistic or stylized representations of flowers.

fluidity see MOBILITY.

fluorescence 1. the property whereby certain substances become luminous, or emit light, when viewed under ultraviolet light or another source of electromagnetic radiation.

2. the property whereby a number of synthetic organic dyestuffs and some transparent solids exhibit a two-toned colour effect. Examples are fluorescein (uranine), solutions of which are transparent yellow with a strong green fluorescence, and rhodamine, which is pink with a greenish-yellow fluorescence. See FLUORESCENT PAINT; URANIUM YELLOW.

fluorescent paint or **daylight fluorescent colours** any of a group of paints derived from a series of SYNTHETIC ORGANIC PIGMENTS, the colours of which have great intensity and which, in daylight, create a glowing or luminescent effect. They can also be activated by ultraviolet (black) light to glow in the dark. A familiar tradename of fluorescent paints is Day-Glo Colours, available in brilliant red, orange, yellow, blue and green. Although nontoxic and sufficiently permanent to serve the decorative and industrial purposes for which they are intended, fluorescent paints do not have sufficient lightfastness for use in fine-arts painting. Originally, the term *fluorescent paint* applied only to paints containing materials that even in daylight require excitation by ultraviolet light; now, however, the term applies almost exclusively to paints that are luminescent in daylight. See also LUMINOUS PAINT.

fluorite or **fluorspar** native calcium fluoride, used in ceramic or porcelain glazes as a FLUX.

fluting closely spaced parallel or nearly parallel grooves, used to embellish mouldings and other surfaces. Fluting is commonly used in architecture for the decoration of columns and pilasters. The raised area between two adjacent flutes, as the grooves are called, is known as a *stria* or an *arris*. See also REEDING.

fluting (left) Fluting. (right) Reeding.

flux or **fluxing ingredient** a substance that promotes fusion or vitrification by lowering the melting point of a substance or compound to which it is added. In ceramics, the fluxes used in various glazes and enamels include feldspar, white lead, red lead and borax. Clay bodies usually contain sufficient fluxing ingredients to complete their vitrification at the temperature used, but sometimes they require an added flux, such as feldspar or a clay that functions at a lower heat. A REFRACTORY substance may also be present to balance the effect of the flux. In metalwork, fluxes are used in soldering, welding and brazing to promote fusion by removing impurities on the surface of the metals to be joined.

foam plastic plastic material throughout which air- or gas-filled cells, or bubbles, have been distributed during manufacture. These expanded plastics are strong, lightweight, and usually buoyant and water-resistant. They may be hard or soft, rigid or flexible. In sculpture, they are used for solid forms and in making moulds for casting, especially in the recently developed method called LOST PATTERN casting. The plastic foam most commonly used by sculptors is polystyrene, although foamed urethanes, methanes, and vinyls are also used.

foil 1. one of several small arcs, which when joined together make points, or CUSPS, and create a decorative effect that was especially popular in Gothic architecture and design. Thus, *trefoil* refers to a three-lobed decoration in a stylized trifoliolate leaf pattern (tre: three; foil: leaf), most often clover-shaped. By extension, the terms *quatrefoil* and *cinquefoil* apply to four-lobed and five-lobed designs, respectively. Trefoil, quatrefoil and cinquefoil designs are the most common shapes used in TRACERY.

foil Typical Gothic tracery. The centre circle encloses a quatrefoil, and various forms of the trefoil occur in pairs around it. The point formed where arcs meet is called a cusp.

2. a very thin sheet of metal, the thinnest variety of which is nevertheless heavier than LEAF.

3. a sheet of paper to which foil has been laminated.

foliated 1. *(design)* decorated with foliage designs or leaf shapes. **2.** ornamented with FOILS, as in TRACERY.

3. *(of a material)* built up of or separable into thin layers, as mica.

folium a mediaeval term for mulberry-coloured pigments made from various vegetable dyestuffs.

folk art the art, handicrafts, and decorative ornament produced by people who have had no formal art training but have an established tradition of styles and craftsmanship. A country or region may have a characteristic folk art.

fondo d'oro see GILDING.

Fontainebleau school a group of Italian and French painters working at Fontainebleau, near Paris, in the mid-16th century. The flowering of this group of painters began with the arrival of Il Rosso (Giovanni Battista de'Rossi) in 1530. He was followed to Fontainebleau in the next few years by other Italian Mannerist painters, including Niccolo dell'Abate and Primaticcio, and by Benvenuto Cellini. Somewhat later in the century the group, dominated by French artists, developed MANNERISM into an almost international style.

foots mucilaginous sediment that falls out of some vegetable oils on storage.

fore-edge painting a watercolour painting on the surface formed by the long edges of the pages of a closed book. Fore-edge painting is found in conjunction with fine bindings of the 18th and 19th centuries. It is scarcely ever practised today, but constitutes a recognized specialty for book collectors.

foreground that part of a composition that appears to be closest to the viewer. The foreground is one of the three ZONES OF RECESSION in LINEAR PERSPECTIVE.

foreshortening the diminishing of certain dimensions of an object or figure in order to depict it in a correct spatial relationship. In realistic depiction, foreshortening is necessary because although lines and planes that are perpendicular to the observer's line of vision (CENTRAL VISUAL RAY), and the extremities of which are equidistant from the eye, will be seen at their full size, when they are revolved away from the observer they will seem increasingly shorter. Thus, for example, a figure's arm outstretched toward the observer must be foreshortened – the dimensions of lines, contours and angles adjusted – in order for the arm not to appear hugely out of proportion. The term *foreshortening* is applied to the depiction of a single object, figure, or part of an object or figure, whereas the term *perspective* refers to the depiction of an entire scene.

forest marble or **landscape marble** *(US)* a pale-coloured MARBLE whose surface, when polished, displays dark markings that suggest the profile of woodlands or fields and streams. See also FORTIFICATION MARBLE; GRAPHIC GRANITE; PAGODA STONE; RIVER MARBLE.

forgery 1. *(fine arts)* the creation of a spurious work with the intention of deceiving or defrauding.
2. the spurious work itself. A forgery is rarely a copy of an original. Sometimes it is created as an anonymous work of a previous age or of an artist otherwise unknown; more commonly, it is offered as a newly discovered work of a renowned artist. Since it is almost impossible to

avoid some anachronistic element of style, technical method, material, or subject matter, the fraud is usually ascribed to an obscure period, a period of great experimentation, or to a little-documented so-called transitional period of an artist's life. The forger may use materials (for example, obsolete pigments or a support stripped from a painting of little value) contemporary with the purported date of the forgery, or the forger may use old or new materials and age the work artificially. If convincing documentation cannot safely be forged, the work is represented as having been dug up – literally or figuratively.

To detect or confirm such frauds, the modern art expert has at his or her command, in addition to the aesthetic and critical criteria first brought to bear, a wide array of scientific aids. These include standard chemical analyses; dating (of organic materials) by measuring the residual radio-activity of carbon 14; and examinations made with the use of optical instruments, X-rays, and infrared and ultraviolet light. In 1967 a gamma-ray shadowgraph confirmed suspicions about a bronze horse in the Metropolitan Museum of Art in New York – a figure that until then was acclaimed as a magnificent 2400-year-old example of Greek art. The museum's test proved that the piece had not been made by the ancient *cire perdue*, or lost wax, process, but was a fake, made by a sand-core technique not used before the 14th century. See also FALSIFICATION.

form 1. the manner in which the artist presents his or her subject matter or CONTENT in creating a work of art. Form is the product of organiz-ation, design, composition and manipulation of materials.
2. the individual masses, shapes, or groupings in an art work are its forms. This is the more common meaning of the word.

Formalin a tradename for a 40% solution of formaldehyde with a small amount of methanol. A dilute solution, made by adding 9 parts of water, is sprayed on coatings of glue or casein in order to toughen them and render them more resistant to moisture.

formalism 1. rigid observance of established rules, methods, or tra-ditions.
2. emphasis on form rather than content. In the Soviet Union, art critics attached the term to work that departed from ACADEMIC depiction of subject matter and so was not in accordance with SOCIALIST REALISM.

Formica a tradename for sheets of laminated PHENOLIC RESIN, sold in many opaque colours.

fortification marble *(US)* any stone whose markings suggest towers and battlements. See also FOREST MARBLE.

fossil resin see RESIN.

foul biting or **false biting** a plate defect in ETCHING that produces unin-tended spots of ink in the prints. Foul biting is usually caused either by a faulty RESIST or by too violent action of the MORDANT, causing BITING in areas that are supposed to be blank.

foundation hue see OSTWALD SYSTEM.

found object or **objet trouvé** an object that is found, selected, and exhibited by an artist, usually without being altered in any way. The display of such objects is a 20th-century art form, practised by the Dadaists and Surrealists. The found object may be natural, for example, a shell, stone or piece of driftwood, or it may be manufactured, for example, a household item, piece of clothing or piece of machinery; a manufactured object is also called a READY-MADE. It may be given new aesthetic qualities by inventive methods of mounting and display. The artist's role in its presentation is creative only in that it points out aesthetic values that the object already possesses but that were not deliberately considered in its construction. When a found object is altered in any way it is sometimes called a *found object interpreted*. The concept of the found object is in accordance with a Surrealist doctrine holding that anything with aesthetic value, even inadvertently so, is a work of art and worthy of being exhibited as such.

foundry sand, brass sand or **French sand** a special kind of sand used in SAND CASTING. It is composed of silica, alumina and clay that is refractory, that is, capable of resisting great heat. It may be used as a CORE in other methods of casting.

fountain brush a brush used for painting or drawing that has a reservoir in its handle for paint or ink.

foxing the yellowish or brown spots and splotches that appear on paper in a scattered pattern, that are caused by a species of MOULD that is encouraged by dampness. Skilled conservators can use bleaching processes to remove these stains from paintings, drawings, and other works of art on paper.

fractional rendering *(pictorial arts)* the practice of rendering the elements of a composition individually rather than as an organized and unified whole. Since the individual elements of a fractional rendering are more significant than the work as an integrated whole, isolated forms are often meticulously depicted. Fractional rendering is characteristic of the art of primitive cultures and early civilizations, notably Egyptian painting, and is also apparent in much of the work of modern primitive and naive painters. Unity has always been a precept of composition in all sophisticated schools of art, and the absence of this quality is one of the reasons for the low esteem in which primitive art was held prior to the 20th century, when it came to be appreciated for its virtues.

fraktur or **fractur** 1. *(US)* (also called **fraktur painting**) an illuminated style of writing used by the Pennsylvania Dutch. It is a form of German Gothic calligraphy ornamented in colour with flowers, birds, and other motifs. It is employed in framed household mottoes and especially in documents such as wedding and baptismal certificates, outstanding examples of which are valued as folk art.
2. German black-letter text type (see GOTHIC).

frame sizes see PICTURE FRAMES.

Frankfort black see DROP BLACK.

free-form shape any amorphous, curvilinear, asymmetrical shape, not bounded by geometric lines, but shaped in accordance with biomorphic or visceral conformations. Such forms are widely employed in contemporary interior decoration. Free-form shapes are characteristic of the work of the sculptor and painter Hans Arp (1887–1966) and are also to be found in the Chinese oil spot technique of the Sung Dynasty. See also BIOMORPHIC FORM.

freehand drawing drawing executed without the aid of mechanical devices.

freestone any stone that can be carved freely in any direction without fear of its splitting or flaking. Limestones and most sandstones are freestones.

French berry see BUCKTHORN BERRY.

French blue a name for ULTRAMARINE BLUE originating in the first half of the 19th century, when the pigment was first imported from France.

French chalk see TALC.

French curve, drawing curve or **irregular curve** a thin, rigid piece of clear plastic or other material cut in a continuously curved or scroll shape so that it can be used as a guide for ruling curves through a series of points that are not on the arc of a circle. French curves are available in a great many shapes and sizes; some have names that relate to the special function for which they were designed, such as the *aircraft curve* used extensively for designing aerofoils and the *ship curve* used in nautical design. French curves, which are sold individually and in sets, are widely used by commercial artists and draughtsmen. See also ADJUSTABLE CURVE RULER; ELLIPSE GUIDE; SPLINE.

French curve Two designs.

French polish the traditional finish for fine furniture, achieved by applying oil and a very dilute solution of shellac. It was formerly used in preference to varnishing because of its flawless depth and lustre, but has been superseded by modern synthetic finishes of superior resistance to wear and less tendency to spotting. The application of French polish demands much skill and patience, as it includes multiple wet-into-wet rubbings with oil and dilute shellac.

French-process zinc oxide pure ZINC OXIDE made by burning the zinc vapour from molten metallic zinc and collecting the fumes. The artists' term for zinc oxide made by the French process is ZINC WHITE. Chemically pure 100% zinc oxide is distinctly inferior in pigment properties to the French-process pigments. Because the latter are produced by the fume process, they have been called *white lampblack*.

French purple or **pourpre français** a lake made from ORCHIL.

French red see GRIOTTE; LANGUEDOC MARBLE.

French sand see FOUNDRY SAND.

French ultramarine a name for ULTRAMARINE BLUE surviving from the late 1820s and 1830s, when the pigment was first imported from France.

French Veronese green an obsolete name for VIRIDIAN. Colours labelled simply Veronese green in the United States are likely to contain almost anything, as the name is unstandardized.

French walnut see WALNUT.

French white *(US)* an unstandardized term that has been used for both FLAKE WHITE and ZINC WHITE.

fresco *(It.* fresh) **1.** the pre-eminent mural-painting technique, in which permanent limeproof pigments, dispersed in water, are painted on freshly laid LIME PLASTER.

2. a mural so painted.

Fresco is sometimes referred to as *buon fresco* or *true fresco* to distinguish it from techniques such as SECCO or MEZZO FRESCO that approximate to its effects.

In fresco, the pigments are absorbed into the wet wall by capillary action and become an integral part of the wall's surface. Indoors, on a properly prepared support, fresco is one of the most permanent painting techniques. Its colours are stable not because they are protected by a calcareous film or *limeskin*, as formerly believed, but because they are made with chemically inert pigments. Fresco is not adaptable to exterior murals; its chief enemies are polluted air and abrasion by windborne particles.

Fresco meets all the requirements for an ideal mural painting: it has a perfectly mat surface; its colour effect is brilliant; it lends itself especially to monumental styles; and it ages nobly.

The fresco wall must be constructed according to an exacting procedure, in several layers of lime plaster. Typically – there are many variations – the support consists of a rough layer called the SCRATCH COAT (*trullisatio* in Italian), a BROWN COAT (*arriccio*), a SAND COAT (*arenato*), and finally the painting coat, or *intonaco*. Usually, when the penultimate coat is dry, a CARTOON of the entire composition is pounced on it (see POUNCING), and its lines are strengthened with dark watercolour. (During the Renaissance the preliminary sketch was often executed directly on the *arenato* with paint pigmented with SINOPIA, and the term sinopia came to be applied to the underdrawing itself.) The intonaco is laid over the drawing in sections as large as the artist expects to finish painting in one day (hence the name *giornata* for such a section) and the appropriate portion of the cartoon is then repounced on the wet plaster. The artist paints on the intonaco to the end of the day or until the wall becomes too dry to imbibe the colours. Areas of the plaster that remain unpainted must be cut away and relaid just before the next session of painting. The plaster joins are carefully planned to follow the contour lines of the composition and to avoid crossing an area of flat colour except in murals on high walls, where a newly plastered area, called a *pontata*, must be a horizontal strip determined by the height of the scaffolding, which is gradually lowered.

Fresco was used in most of the early Mediterranean civilizations, notably the Minoan in Crete, and throughout the entire history of art in Europe. A remarkable series of frescoes painted between 200 BC and AD 600 in cave temples at Ajanta, India, have puzzled scholars because they were executed without the plaster joins normal to the process.

The Renaissance Italian masters brought fresco painting to its highest stage of development. Among the most magnificent of the celebrated Italian frescoes are those by Giotto (?1267–1337) in the Arena Chapel at Padua and the church of San Francesco at Assisi; Piero della Francesca (c.1420–1492) in the church of San Francesco at Arezzo and the Palazzo Communale at San Sepolcro; Michelangelo (1475–1564) in the Vatican's Sistine Chapel; and Raphael (1483–1520) in the Stanza della Segnatura and the Logge of the Vatican.

After the 17th century the use of true fresco declined considerably. It had its greatest modern revival in Mexico, in the works of José Clemente Orozco (1883–1949) and Diego Rivera (1886–1957). In the United States, the FEDERAL ART PROJECT commissioned frescoes for many public buildings.

The painting of a large-scale fresco, an expensive and time-consuming undertaking, has in modern times become an event and an adventure. Because the artist requires the help of a crew of plasterers and other assistants, and because their work would interfere with the use of a room or delay the opening of a new building, fresco is often passed over in favour of more expeditious techniques. Indoor murals are now done primarily in oil colours, but also in casein colours, polymer colours, secco, and tempera. Most contemporary fresco work in confined to single panels in small rooms.

For methods of transferring frescoes see STACCO and STRAPPO.

fresco liner see LINERS AND STRIPERS.

fresco secco see SECCO.

fret 1. a piece of interlaced or perforated ornamental work, as in pierced woodwork.

2. see GREEK KEY PATTERN.

fretwork openwork patterns cut in wood with a fretsaw; commonly used in interior decoration of the late 19th and early 20th centuries.

frilling or **sagging** the appearance of irregularly scalloped horizontal waves in picture varnish or thin paint that has been applied while the painting was in a vertical position. Other defects similar to frilling include CURTAINS, STREAMLINES and TEARDROPS.

frisket a stencil cut from tracing paper and attached to a drawing or painting with rubber cement to protect part of the work or to maintain blank areas while further application of colour is made; it is subsequently peeled away. Friskets are primarily employed by commercial artists for AIRBRUSH work, but watercolour painters have also used them, especially to protect areas from overall washes. Ready-made frisket paper, coated on one side with a pressure-sensitive adhesive, is available and in common use, as is a liquid frisket, which is more easily controlled than paper coated with ordinary rubber cement, the protective covering being easily removed when the work has been completed.

frit 1. *n.* a ceramic glaze material containing a FLUX, silica or another refractory, and colouring ingredients, melted together and pulverized.

2. *vb* to melt and pulverize these ingredients to produce a frit.

Many materials must be fritted for specific reasons. For example, lead glazes must be fritted because lead is extremely toxic but the lead silicate produced by fritting is not. Borax and soda ash are fluxes that are fritted to make them insoluble in water. A glaze that has not been fritted and contains no fritted ingredients is called a *raw glaze*. Some paint pigments are identified as frits, notably Egyptian blue, cobalt blue and smalt.

frontal depiction the head-on representation of a figure, object or scene. The so-called convention of frontality is the strict use of frontal alignment (that is, PARALLEL PERSPECTIVE) in representation. Frontality was a guiding principle of composition in Egyptian art. Portrait statues of standing and seated dignitaries were conceived front-on and often have nearly perfect bilateral symmetry.

frottage 1. the technique of making an impression of the texture of wood, stone, fabric, etc. or of the configurations of a subject such as a twisted mat of string, by placing paper over the object and rubbing the paper with a crayon or pencil.

2. the impression itself.

Frottage is an adaptation by the Surrealists of the traditional method of making a RUBBING. Painters in that movement, especially Max Ernst (1891–1976), who first introduced them in his works, often used such rubbings as part of a collage, or combined frottage with painting techniques.

frottis *(Fr.)* **1.** a thin wash of paint, especially a transparent or translucent one.

2. a GLAZE.

3. a SCUMBLE.

4. the thin colour left after wet oil paint has been rubbed away.

fruitwood *(US commercial)* the woods of various fruit trees, especially apple, pear, and plum. Imported apple and pear woods are often used for carving, while plum wood is used more rarely. All these woods are rather soft, but have great stability and permanence, and are smooth and uniform in grain and texture. They range in colour from golden yellow to yellowish red.

fuchsine see MAGENTA.

fugitive colour a pigment or dye that fades, especially one that loses colour rapidly on exposure to daylight. Although still in general use, the term is rather old-fashioned, wrongly implying that FADING is an evanescence or flying away of the colour rather than the result of an actual chemical change.

fuller's earth see DIATOMACEOUS EARTH.

full length designating a portrait in which the entire figure of the subject is shown.

full mould casting see LOST-PATTERN CASTING.

fumigation *(conservation)* the process of exposing a work of art, especially a print, to the vapour of a volatile crystalline substance within a closed cabinet in order to destroy mould. Thymol is the substance most commonly used, although paradichlorobenzene has the same effect. A few crystals of the fumigant are sometimes placed inside a closed exhibition case or glass frame to prevent further infestation.

fundamental colours the basic hues of the spectrum: red, orange, yellow, green, blue, and violet.

funk art the name given to a style of art in which repellent subject matter is treated in a purposely repugnant manner, often pornographically. The style emerged in California in the 1960s.

furnace product an inorganic pigment whose manufacturing process includes roasting in furnaces at various temperatures from dull-red to bright-white heat. Pigments that have undergone this treatment are of the highest degree of permanence. Among them, only ultramarine blue has a limitation: although completely permanent in easel painting techniques, it cannot be used in fresco. Viridian, which is roasted to a dull-red heat, would convert to chromium oxide green if it were subjected to white heat. The various iron-oxide pigments – Indian red, light red, and Mars colours – vary in hue according to the temperature and duration of their roasting and their chemical treatment in the intermediate or wet stage.

furring 1. the creation of an insulating space of a few inches between an exterior wall of a building and the lath of the plaster wall.
2. the material (thin strips of wood or metal) used in this process.
   Such insulation is necessary for mural paintings on the plaster of exterior walls in order to protect the plaster and its paint from moisture and rapid changes in temperature.

fusion the melting together under heat of two objects or substances, and especially, the joining of metals in this way. The technique of WELDING employs fusion.

fustet see YOUNG FUSTIC.

fustic a yellow NATURAL DYESTUFF made from the wood of *Morus tinctoria*, a tree native to the Americas; a rather weak dye of poor lightfastness. Fustic is also known as old fustic; another yellow dyestuff called YOUNG FUSTIC (or fustet) is a different substance.

Futurism a revolutionary movement in the arts, beginning in Italy in 1909 with the publication of a manifesto by the poet Marinetti, and followed a year later by the Manifesto of Futuristic Painters, signed by Carlo Carrà (b. 1881), Umberto Boccioni (1882–1916), Luigi Rossolo (1885–1947), Giacomo Balla (1871–1958), and Gino Severini (1883–   ). The futurist movement abandoned most of the traditional concepts of art. All previous art, including the Cubism of the day, was held to be static and outmoded, although Futurist paintings actually had much in common with Cubist work. Futurism was aggressively dynamic, expressing movement and encompassing time as well as space; it was particularly concerned with mechanization and speed. Objects were reassembled in terms of so-called lines of force; animals in motion were given a multiplicity of legs; and colours were rich and vibrant. Although the organized movement did not survive the First World War, it was an important force in the development of 20th-century art: Dada, Surrealism, Vorticism and Cubism itself owed something to its influence.

fylfot see GAMMADION.

G

Gaboon ebony see EBONY.

gadroon 1. *(metalwork)* a decorative edging or border of vertical, slanted or spiralled REEDING, usually done by REPOUSSÉ. Gadrooning was commonly used on 17th- and 18th-century silverware and is still widely found in traditionally styled wares. It is used chiefly on the edges of trays and the rims and bases of hollow ware.
2. *(woodworking)* any carved or notched design on a rounded moulding.

Gahn's blue a forerunner or inferior earlier version of COBALT BLUE, made by a process invented in Germany in 1777. Gahn's blue has also been known as *cobalt ultramarine*, a name later appropriated by manufacturers of imitation cobalt blue, a special shade of ultramarine blue.

gaine *(sculpture)* the quadrangular, tapered pillar of a TERM or HERM. **2.** the lower part of any figure sculpture in which the head or bust alone is detailed or realistic, the remainder being either rough-hewn or carved in the general form of a tight sheath tapering downward, as in many Egyptian and Archaic Greek examples.

galipot or **gallipot** the thick, resinous exudation from a pine (*Pinus pinaster*) of southern Europe, especially France.

gallery tone a 19th-century euphemism for the lowering of tone in old oil paintings caused by darkening of the varnish and accumulation of dirt and grime. During the 19th century and the early part of the 20th, such golden-brown discoloration was admired and even imitated (see BROWN SAUCE); today's taste, however, requires that the colours in a painting appear as the artist first created them, and modern conservation standards demand removal and replacement of discoloured varnish.

gallery varnish the coating devised by early curators of the National Gallery in London, in order to protect their paintings from the elements. While highly complimentary to the paintings at first – imparting a golden hue to the Old Masters – the varnish darkened as decades passed, and many of the paintings were barely discernible until the 1940s, when a solution to dissolve it was formulated.

galliolino a little used term for NAPLES YELLOW.

gallipot 1. a miniature porcelain container used in laboratories and by painters to hold their oils and mediums.
2. a variant spelling of GALIPOT.

gall nut see OAK GALL.

gallstone an obsolete yellow LAKE pigment, similar to BROWN PINK. It was said to have been made from oxgall, although it came more often from vegetable sources such as quercitron (see QUERCITRON LAKE).

galvanized metal a metal, usually iron or steel, that has an electroplated

169

zinc coating that makes it resistant to weather and rust. It is used in welded sculpture.

gambier or **Bengal cutch** a variety of CATECHU made from a species of *Uncaria*, a Malayan vine.

Gambier-Parry spirit fresco see SPIRIT FRESCO.

gamboge or *(Ger.)* **Gummigut** a bright, transparent, golden-yellow gum resin produced by trees of the genus *Garcinia*, native to southeast Asia, especially Thailand. It has been used in the arts since the mediaeval era. Formerly it was used in powdered form as a paint pigment, because it was one of the most satisfactory available transparent yellows for glaze and watercolour techniques, but it has long since been replaced for these purposes by cobalt yellow. It fades slowly in oil paints; in watercolour it fades rapidly in sunlight, less rapidly in diffused light. Since it is a resin, it does not meet all the requirements for a desirable paint pigment; nevertheless, it finds a few uses in the arts, such as for the colouring of varnishes. It is soluble in alcohol, and is poisonous.

gammadion a design or device formed by the junction of four gammas (of the Greek alphabet). Examples are the swastika and the voided Greek cross. A swastika is also called a *fylfot*, from the old English word for the pattern used to fill the foot, or lower part, of a painted window.

gammadion (left) A swastika or fylfot;
(right) a voided Greek cross.

ganosis the process, employed by the ancient Greeks, of applying a non-glare wax polish on plain or painted marble sculpture. The surface of the marble was warmed, rubbed with sticks of wax, and then polished with cloths. The same treatment was used on plaster walls, to protect the vermilion or other colours with which they were frequently decorated, and to create a finish with a uniform sheen.

garance *(Fr.)* the madder plant (*Rubia tinctorum*), source of madder lake (see NATURAL ROSE MADDER).

garnet lac see LAC.

garnet paper an abrasive paper. Apart from its pink colour, it resembles sandpaper, but is coated with fine fragments of garnet, which are much sharper than sand. The finest grades, 4/0, 5/0 and 6/0, are excellent for smoothing gesso and for other artists' purposes.

garzone *(It.)* a studio boy, or artist's apprentice.

gas black another name for CARBON BLACK.

gate or **runner** *(casting)* **1.** any of several small channels or ducts through which molten metal is carried from the main channel, or SPRUE, to the hollow part of the MOULD.
2. the waste piece of material formed by such a duct.

gaude yellow another name for WELD.

gauffrage see GOFFER.

gauge to mix plaster, plaster of Paris or casting plaster with the exact amount of water necessary to obtain the desired consistency. When the usual medium consistency is desired, the water is placed in a mixing bowl, and plaster is lightly scattered over its surface in small handfuls until the plaster settles just below the surface of the water; when there is no longer any movement in the water, the mixture is stirred to a uniform smoothness. For a thicker consistency, plaster is added until it lies somewhat above the water level.

gelatin a protein material, made by prolonged boiling of animal tissues; it is a highly refined GLUE. The best grades of gelatin are colourless, odourless, and tasteless. When dry, gelatin is hard and flexible. It is used in various photocopying processes, in dyeing, and in the preparation of sizes and cements. Because of its purity, gelatin is sometimes recommended as a binder for gesso, but its extremely high glutin content makes it a weaker adhesive and a more poorly balanced binder than hide glue. In sculpture, the negative containing MOULD for casting may be made of flexible gelatin.

gel-coat the first application of resin to the mould, in casting with polymer resins. The gel-coat is the outer layer of the finished sculpture. It may be coloured with pigments, or may contain fillers for economy as well as visual effect.

Gellert green see COBALT GREEN.

gel medium a prepared painting medium of gelatinous consistency. It is added to oil colours and aqueous paints to impart a smooth, fluid, facile quality without reducing viscosity so that brushstrokes stay in place, and also to add transparency to the paint. The first gel medium, MEGILP, was abandoned by painters during the 19th century. Gel mediums were reintroduced by manufacturers of artists' materials in the United States and Britain in the mid-20th century. The handling properties of gel mediums are attractive, and, unlike megilp, they are made of nonyellowing, permanent ingredients. A modern gel medium for oil painting is made either by dispersing a colloidal inert pigment in an oil or synthetic resin solution, or by mixing an oil or synthetic resin with another synthetic resin that is not entirely compatible with it, thus forming a gel instead of a clear solution. So far, no data based on either experience or scientific tests indicate that gel mediums are not permanent. It is nonetheless suggested that use of any gel medium, however excellent the properties of its components may be, will produce a weak and underpigmented paint film, likely to wrinkle and eventually to crack. This may happen only in the case of oil colours, since gel mediums for watercolour and polymer colours are usually made of materials whose properties are identical with, or closely resemble, those of their vehicles, and whose films need not be reinforced by closely packed pigment particles.

genre painting painting representing some phase of everyday life, such as a domestic interior or a rural or village scene.

geometric abstraction abstract painting whose shapes are those of simple geometry, for example, the straight line, the circle, the square, the rectangle. This style includes neither free-form elements nor the blended areas, freehand brushstrokes, and textural qualities that characterize most representational paintings. Sometimes referred to as *classical abstraction*, geometric abstraction is frequently contrasted with ABSTRACT EXPRESSIONISM. The pioneers in geometric abstraction were Malevich, who propounded the theory of SUPREMATISM in 1915, and Mondrian, whose work during the early 1920s was incorporated in the doctrine of NEOPLASTICISM.

Geometric period the second phase of HELLENIC ART (900–700 BC). Surviving examples are mainly of painted vases decorated with coloured circles, parallel lines, frets, spirals, and other basic linear and geometric elements. Towards the end of the period, human and animal figures were included or even formed elaborate scenes within the design, which was still dominated by abstract shapes. Geometric sculpture consisted of small ceramic and bronze figures of birds, animals and occasionally human beings.

Georgia white *(US)* a fine American MARBLE, excellent for sculpture. It is saccharoidal, or sugary, in texture and is capable of taking a high polish.

geranium red or **geranium lake** one of the most intense and brilliant of the red synthetic organic pigments; a bright red geranium petal hue. It is used only by illustrators and others whose work is done for reproduction, as it fades after relatively short exposure to daylight.

German black see DROP BLACK.

German cross see CROSS-CROSSLET.

gesso a white fluid or plastic coating material made by mixing chalk or whiting with a glue solution or, occasionally, casein. It is used as a GROUND on wood or hardboard supports in painting, gilding and other decorative processes. The concentration of the glue solution must be carefully controlled to obtain the desired degree of hardness. When applied to flat panels or to carved mouldings, frames or furniture, gesso is normally sandpapered to a flawlessly smooth, ivory-like surface. It is fully absorbent and is thus an ideal ground for tempera painting and water gilding. For oil and casein painting and oil gilding, a gesso surface requires sizing. A gesso ground is too brittle to be used on canvas.

Gesso has been used in Europe since mediaeval times. The early gesso was made from parchment glue and slaked plaster of Paris; modern gesso uses rabbitskin glue and precipitated chalk or whiting. In Renaissance practice, two grades of gesso were applied to wood panels for painting: an undercoat of *gesso grosso* (coarse gesso) and several coats of *gesso sotile* (fine gesso). Modern workers almost universally omit the coarse layer, presumably plain plaster of Paris, which our presmoothed panels and mouldings seem to render unnecessary.

The Italian word *gesso* comes from gypsum, from which plaster of Paris is made, and has been used for the specific substance described above for centuries. However, in the United States, manufacturers in recent years have applied the term to polymer primers, which are entirely different from gesso in composition and cannot be used as a substitute for it.

gesso duro plaster of Paris hardened by the addition of glue solution. This mixture is much more durable than plain plaster and is therefore suitable for decorative moulding or modelling.

gestural painting the name given to a variation of the style known as ACTION PAINTING, differing only in that a gestural painting is viewed not only as a visual document of the artist's actions, but as a record of the artist's thoughts and feelings during the act of painting.

giallolino or **giallorino** obsolete and obscure Italian terms for an opaque yellow containing lead. The one mentioned by Cennino Cennini in his 15th-century treatise was probably Naples yellow; other writers refer to MASSICOT as giallolino, giallorino and giallolino di Fiandra (Flemish yellow).

gilded or **gilt** covered with gold or a golden finish, whether by gilding with gold leaf, by electroplating or metal spraying, or by applying gold paint. See also PARCEL-GILT; SILVER-GILT.

gilder's cushion a pad used in GILDING, on which the leaf is flattened and cut. The cushion consists of a thin wooden board about 6 × 12 inches in surface, covered with a thin layer of cotton batting over which a piece of suede is stretched and tacked. Two loops of soft leather are attached to the underside of the board, one in an appropriate spot to act as a thumb grip for holding the board as a palette, and another tacked flat at one edge of the board to serve as a sheath for the GILDER'S KNIFE. A stiff piece of kraft paper about 8 inches long is sometimes fastened to the rear edges, running around three sides to enclose about a third of the board; it acts

gilder's cushion (left) The underside of the cushion, showing the leather thumb grip and the sheath with knife in place. (centre) A top view of the cushion, showing the stiff paper that prevents draughts from disturbing the fragile leaf. (right) The gilder's tip.

as a windshield to protect the fragile leaves from air currents. In gilding with Dutch metal, a gilder's cushion is not used; the leaf is simply pressed from the book. See also GILDER'S TIP.

gilder's knife a knife used in GILDING to cut metal leaf into the size and shape desired for application to the ground. About the size of a table knife, the gilder's knife has a slightly flexible blade of steel with an oblique end. It must be sharp enough to cut the leaf with a single back-and-forth stroke, but not so sharp that it will cut the leather of the GILDER'S CUSHION. See also GILDER'S TIP.

gilder's tip an implement used in GILDING to pick up the sensitive and fragile leaves of metal and transfer them to the area to be gilded. The tip is a sort of brush, a row of camelhair mounted between and protruding from two cards about four inches wide; the density of the hold of hairs varies. Tips may be bought in varying hair lengths: a tip of long hairs is used to pick up whole leaves; a short-hair tip is used to pick up cut pieces of leaf. The gilder holds the GILDER'S CUSHION in the left hand and makes the tip slightly oily by running it over the gilder's hair. This causes the leaf to cling to the tip until the leaf is touched to the wet size on or in the ground, which holds it securely. A tip is not usually needed for metal leaves that are heavier and easier to handle than gold, but a tip may be necessary for silver leaf, in which case a special tip with a double thickness of hairs is used. Considering the antiquity of gilding, the tip, which apparently dates from the 18th century, can be called a modern improvement. The old methods of lifting and handling leaf, such as those described in the 15th century by Cennino Cennini in his treatise *Il libro dell'arte*, would be too crude for modern thin gold leaf. See also GILDER'S KNIFE.

gilder's wax a preparation used to heighten the colour of gold that has been applied to another metal by FIRE GILDING. Gilder's wax is a combination of beeswax with verdigris or some other copper salt and an acidic substance, such as alum, borax or vitriol. The wax is applied to the surface to be treated, which is then exposed to fire until the wax has been burned off. The gilded surface is cleaned both by the acid in the preparation and by the firing process, which serves to drive off any mercury that may remain in the gold after fire gilding. The pigment in the wax imparts a warm tone to the gold surface.

gilding the art of adhering thin metal LEAF to a surface to simulate the effect of solid or inlaid metal. The laying of leaf is the traditional method for creating a metallic effect in a work of art, and the use of such other materials as metallic powders dispersed in a liquid medium produces a vastly inferior effect. Although the term gilding is derived from a word for gold, it also designates the application of other metal leaf to a surface. GOLD LEAF, SILVER LEAF, and PALLADIUM LEAF may be used in painting, sculpture, and fine decorative work. DUTCH METAL and ALUMINIUM LEAF are cheap imitations of precious-metal leaf. They yield inferior results and are not sufficiently permanent for fine-arts use. On the other hand, they are definitely superior in both effect and permanency to the so-called

GOLD PAINT made with BRONZE POWDER and to the silvery paints made with ALUMINIUM POWDER.

There are two currently used techniques for the application of leaf to a surface. MORDANT GILDING, the simpler of the two, may be used with any kind of leaf on any properly treated surface. In WATER GILDING, the older method, the leaf is laid on a gesso or bole ground, producing a bright metallic sheen which may then be brought to a brilliant specular finish, if desired, by rubbing the gilded surface with a BURNISHER. Leaf laid with mordant gilding cannot be burnished. Mordant gilding and unburnished water gilding are known as *mat gilding*. A third method, FIRE GILDING, is a chemical process. It is the oldest method for gilding metals, and is no longer practised, having been replaced by ELECTROPLAT-ING and METAL SPRAYING. Precious-metal leaf is beaten so thin that it is economically feasible to use in works of art; GOLD POWDER is a great deal more expensive to use and is practical only when it is made into watercolour or ink and used with a pointed brush or a pen to apply fine lines to a surface.

Gilding is a very old practice. It was used by the ancient Egyptians and Chinese, and it is mentioned in the Old Testament and by Homer. Gilding developed to a high degree of craftsmanship during the Middle Ages, when it was used in manuscript illumination and in panel painting, not only for figures and lettering but also for the frequently used solid gold background (*fondo d'oro*) that is especially notable in Sienese tempera panels. The craft reached a high point during the 19th century and the first quarter of the 20th century, when gilded objects and ornaments were the Victorian fashion (see ORMOLU) and when gold-leaf frames were almost compulsory for artists exhibiting their work. Although fine gold-leaf work is still produced by professional gilders, there are few gilders' workshops today.

Gilsonite *(US)* a tradename for UINTATE, a hard ASPHALT.

gilt see GILDED.

giornata (*It.* a day's work) the area of new plaster, in FRESCO painting, that could be painted in one day. Since the paint had to be applied to wet plaster, only as much of the INTONACO, or final plaster coat, could be laid as the artist could paint before the coat dried. The seams between adjacent *giornate* are clearly visible in some old frescoes. On high walls requiring scaffolding, the plaster was laid in horizontal sections, called *pontate*, corresponding to the level of the scaffold, which was gradually lowered.

Giotteschi a group of painters of the mid-14th century whose work appears to have been strongly influenced by that of Giotto di Bondone (?1267–1337). Few of their names are known.

gisant a sculptured, recumbent, effigy of a deceased person, usually part of a monumental tomb. Late Gothic sepulchral monuments often included both a lifelike statue of the deceased and a gisant that was a decaying corpse; the transient nature of the flesh was occasionally emphasized even more gruesomely by showing the corpse crawling with vermin. Renaissance monuments characteristically reflect the classical attitude towards death: the gisant may be an idealized portrait, and the entire monument is conceived as a poignant commemoration of the dead person rather than as a memento mori.

glair 1. a GOLD SIZE used in GILDING, made of beaten egg white mixed with a little water and left to stand overnight. It may be used to lay leaf the morning after it is prepared, but if left longer, it becomes stickier and even better for sizing. Glair has long been used as a size, but most modern gilders prefer a weak solution of hide glue or gelatin because unless a fresh batch of glair is made fairly frequently, the egg white develops a putrid odour that is unpleasant in the draught-free conditions preferred by gilders.

2. *(painting)* a little-used medium, with relatively weak binding and film-forming qualities. Glair was sometimes used in manuscript illumination to bind very pale or reactive colours for which an egg-yolk medium was unsuitable. The chief use of egg white today is in the whole-egg composition used in egg-oil TEMPERA emulsions. See also EGG, USE IN PAINTING.

glance an outmoded word for GLOSS.

Glasgow school 1. a group of Scottish artists, active in the late 1880s, who rebelled against what they felt were the stifling strictures of the Royal Academy and advocated outdoor painting. They had a somewhat limited influence on the second Glasgow school.

2. a loose association of early 20th-century painters in Glasgow, who developed an interesting variation of ART NOUVEAU style, for which they are best known.

glass coloured print see BACK PAINTING.

glassine paper *(US)* a smooth, glossy, transparent or translucent paper, familiar through its use in packaging and envelope windows. It is used by art conservators as a facing when mounting a work on paper with Japanese paper hinges.

glass painting 1. painting with ceramic colours on pieces of glass, which are fired in a kiln and used as segments of a stained-glass window or transparency.

2. painting with oil or gouache colours on sheets of clear glass, to be viewed from the unpainted side of the glass.

glaze 1. *(oil painting)* a thin film of transparent colour laid over a dried underpainting. The technique of applying such a film is called glazing. The total colour effect of glaze painting has a luminous quality which differs from that of solid, opaque painting. Light impinging on an opaque surface is reflected back directly; on a glazed surface it penetrates or is transmitted through a darker layer and reflected from a lighter underlayer back through the glaze, so that the colour effect is a mixture of the colours used in the two layers. Glazing is best done by mixing oil colour with an oil-resin glaze medium, applying it evenly with a brush, and stippling or pouncing the wet surface with clean, dry brushes or dabbers until the colour coat is sufficiently thin for the desired effect.

2. *(ceramics)* a thin, vitreous coating that is fused to a ceramic body by firing in a kiln. A glaze may be applied by dipping, pouring, spraying, or brushing before the ware is fired; or glazing may be accomplished in a firing atmosphere containing alkali vapour, as in salt glazing. The function of glaze on a ware may be to waterproof the body, change its colour or texture, or generally enhance the appearance of the ware. See ALKALINE GLAZE; ASH GLAZE; CELADON; MAT GLAZE; PEACH BLOOM; SANG DE BŒUF; SALT GLAZE; BLISTER GLAZE; BRISTOL GLAZE; CRYSTALLINE GLAZE.

glory see AUREOLE.

gloss a specular, or mirrorlike, reflection from a surface. Gloss is measured by the sharpness or definiteness of the image it reflects. Any brilliant, highly reflective surface is said to have high gloss or to be glossy. The average oil paint or waxed surface has a dull gloss. A low sheen or satiny finish is called *semigloss*. In the 19th century, paintings that had a high-gloss finish were admired; today, a low or dull gloss is preferred. A finish without gloss or lustre is called a MAT finish.

glost glazed ceramic ware.

glost fire the second firing of ceramic ware, done to vitrify a glaze applied to biscuit ware, that is, ware that has already been bisque fired (fired once to harden the clay body). See BISQUE FIRE.

glue 1. any viscous material used as an adhesive to join surfaces or, in weak dilution with water, as a size.
2. any adhesive made from the bones or hides of animals; the best glues are made from hides. Glue contains two groups of proteins: chondrins, which account for its adhesive strength; and glutin, which contributes jelling strength. The best hide glues are well balanced between the two. The standard top-quality glue, with the best balance of adhesive strength and jelling strength, is rabbitskin glue. Made in the United States and in France, it is sold in solid form in sheets or granules, and is dissolved by soaking overnight in water. For full-strength adhesive use, the water is drained off and the glue melted in a glue pot or double boiler. For use as a size or binder, the water is carefully measured and allowed to remain in the pot while the glue is heated. If glue is boiled, its properties alter and the strength of the solution changes erratically.

The finest glue used in mediaeval times was made from parchment clippings; the modern, commercially produced rabbitskin and calfskin glues give comparable results with the advantage of greater uniformity. Glues made from animal hides are used to make gesso and to manufacture inexpensive water paints, such as scenic colours and show-card colours. GELATIN may be considered a highly refined glue.

glue–cutout method see BLOCK-CUT STENCIL METHOD.

glutin see GLUE.

glycerin or **glycerol** a clean, pure nontoxic heavy liquid. It has some oily properties, but is miscible with water and alcohol. Glycerin is an ingredient in watercolour and gouache paints, where it serves to delay initial drying so that brush manipulations can be carried on before drying begins.

glyph 1. a carved channel or vertical groove, such as is found on a Doric frieze.

2. certain symbolic or conventionalized forms in Mayan sculpture.

glyptic art 1. the art of incising or carving designs and ornaments on gems and semiprecious stones.

2. carved sculpture as distinguished from modelled sculpture.

Gmelin's blue a name given to ULTRAMARINE BLUE after Christian Gmelin, who published his process for its manufacture in Germany in 1828.

goffer or **gauffer 1.** *vb* to decorate a surface by indenting or embossing it, as in the stamping of linen book bindings or gold leaf surfaces.

2. *n.* the tool used in this work.

Goffered work is also known as *gauffrage*.

golden mean or **golden section** a canon of proportion in painting, sculpture and architecture. It is based on the ratio between two unequal parts of a whole when the proportion of the smaller to the larger is equal to that of the larger to the whole. As applied to a SCHEMA of figure drawing, the golden mean would dictate that the distance from the foot to the knee be half the length of the whole leg and, correspondingly, that the length of the leg be half the height of the whole body. The so-called ideal proportions of a rectangle are determined by the golden section; in such a figure, the longer side is equal in length to the diagonal of a square whose side is equal to the shorter side of the rectangle. This ratio works out numerically to .618 to 1, or approximately 5 to 8. In a rectangle drawn or constructed according to the golden section, therefore, the width should be .618 of the length. Based on a Euclidean theory, the golden mean was worked out in the 1st century BC by Vitruvius, who used it in his treatise *De architectura* to establish architectural standards for the proportions of columns, rooms and entire buildings, with the understanding that individual variations were expected of the architect. During the Renaissance, *De divina proportione* (1509), written by Luca Pacioli and illustrated by Leonardo da Vinci, defined the golden section as the *divine proportion*, which is the subject of the treatise, and thus perpetuated the canon. The French term *Section d'Or* was adopted by a group of Cubists, without reference to the principle, as a name for both an exhibition they held and the magazine they published. Perhaps the most familiar geometrical proportion system to be advanced in recent years is DYNAMIC SYMMETRY.

golden ochre *(US)* or **cadmium ochre** a house paint or industrial pigment made in the United States by brightening yellow ochre with chrome yellow; not to be confused with the permanent artists' pigment TRANSPARENT GOLD OCHRE.

golden section see GOLDEN MEAN.

gold leaf gold that has been beaten into leaf for use in GILDING. Gold is the most malleable of metals. It may be drawn out to a cobweb filament and beaten so thin that the resulting gold leaf will transmit light and display a characteristic greenish colour when held up to a light source. Since gold is also one of the most inert metals, it does not tarnish or become dull. Because of these properties, its occurrence in pure form in nature, and its intrinsic value, early civilizations learned how to use gold decoratively as leaf, an art that developed over the centuries into a highly refined craft.

Gold leaf is sold in books of 25 three-inch-square leaves, packed between tissue papers dusted with bole to keep the leaves from sticking. It is also sold in ribbon form in tissue paper rolls of various widths and lengths. The standard leaf is $23\frac{1}{2}$ carat; leaf of this so-called rich gold is about $\frac{1}{300,000}$ of an inch thick, and about 2,000 leaves weigh an ounce. Two other types of leaf also available are lemon gold ($18\frac{1}{2}$ carat) and pale gold (16 carat). Since these are alloyed with the less malleable silver, they are somewhat thicker and thus easier to handle than pure gold. Rich gold is also available as *transferred gold*, for *gilding in the wind*, with each leaf pressed onto a piece of tissue paper. Transferred gold is applied like a transfer, making its handling easier for outdoor MORDANT GILDING, but creating a finish of inferior quality in work that is seen closely. Available on special order is a double-thick leaf that is believed to be the equivalent of a pre-19th-century leaf, judging by old writings and handling instructions, which indicate a less fragile and more easily manipulated material than the modern product.

Gold leaf has been used at various times and in various ways to gild sculpture, domes and doors of buildings, household furnishings and decorations (see ORMOLU), frames, etc. Before the advent of oil painting, gold leaf played an important part in tempera painting, fresco and manuscript illumination, where it was used for large initial letters, backgrounds, halos and other details. It is still used for some of these purposes but not nearly as much as formerly.

gold paint chiefly, a misnomer for BRONZE POWDER mixed with BRONZING LIQUID to make metallic paint. (Similarly, paint made with ALUMINIUM POWDER is sold commercially under the misnomer *silver paint*.) This so-called gold paint, which is sold in paint, hardware and art-supply shops, produces a relatively coarse and lacklustre coating and is not sufficiently permanent for use on fine works of art. Much bronze-powder gold paint is used for commercial decoration and industrial products. Real GOLD POWDER mixed in a watercolour vehicle to make gold ink was used in the Middle Ages for the writing and illumination of manuscripts, and in the Renaissance, by such artists as Andrea Mantegna and Giovanni Bellini, for details and highlights in panel paintings. It is used occasionally today for gilding details in fine works of art but to a much smaller extent than gold leaf. See also SHELL GOLD.

gold powder pulverized gold. Gold powder dispersed in an aqueous binder has been used to highlight tempera paintings and was used to illuminate mediaeval manuscripts. As gold powder is more difficult to obtain and considerably more expensive to use than gold leaf, gilding with leaf has always been much more common in works of art. Probably the chief use of gold powder today is in the preparation known as Liquid Bright Gold used to decorate ceramics. This solution (pulverized gold mixed with a small amount of oxide of bismuth, gum water, and a flux, usually borax) is applied with a brush to the ceramic surface, which has previously been fired and glazed. The piece is then refired in a kiln, and the applied gold is cleaned and burnished.

Tiny cakes of imported gold watercolour, not unlike 19th-century SHELL GOLD, can be obtained from an art-supplier. Artists can obtain actual gold powder by the mediaeval method of grinding gold leaf with honey and water in a glass mortar and then rinsing out the honey by repeated washings and settlings with hot water, but electrolytic and reduction methods for powdering gold commercially have chiefly replaced the older mechanical means. Gold cannot be powdered dry because of its ductility; friction would cause the particles to lump together.

gold size the adhesive used in GILDING to hold the metal leaf to the ground. In WATER GILDING, the glue or gelatin already contained in the gesso or bole supplies the adhesive; it is activated by brushing the ground with water containing a small amount of glue just prior to laying the leaf. GLAIR was formerly used instead of glue. The commercial red *gold size* sold in glass jars is simply bole made up to paste consistency with water, which the gilder prepares for use by thinning with a solution of glue in water. In MORDANT GILDING, the size must be applied to a nonabsorbent ground; a porous surface must first be shellacked and sanded to a smooth finish. Two types of mordant size, oil and varnish, may be used. Oil, or slow-drying, size is a cooked-oil varnish that takes 48 hours to become completely dry; applied in the evening, this varnish retains the tackiness necessary to hold the leaf throughout the following day. This size usually contains golden chrome-yellow pigment so that when applied it clearly marks the areas that are to receive the leaf. Varnish, or quick-drying, size is usually based on synthetic resins. Thinly applied, it reaches the correct stage of tackiness in 30 to 45 minutes but remains in this state for only 20 to 30 minutes, although the period can be lengthened somewhat by adding oil colour or oil size to the varnish size. POLYMER MEDIUM serves as an easy-to-use gold size of this type; the leaf may be pressed on the wet size immediately after its application without waiting for it to reach a critical stage of tackiness.

gospel book, evangelistary or **evangeliary** a mediaeval book containing the four gospels (*Lat.* evangelarium) or the passages or portions of the Gospels forming part of the liturgy. Gospels were often richly ornamented, especially with an imaginary portrait of the author at the beginning of each Gospel, and are among the finest examples of the art of illumination. Among the best-known of the surviving gospels is the famous 8th-century *Book of Kells*, produced in Ireland, but a number of other Irish examples, as well as various German, Frankish, and English manuscripts also show a high degree of artistry.

Gothic 1. pertaining to European art between the mid-12th and mid-15th centuries. The first Gothic cathedral was begun in France in 1137, and the style spread to other countries from about 1200. The High Gothic period spanned the 13th and 14th centuries, although the Late Style was not fully developed until the early 15th century. In painting and sculpture, a fairly homogeneous International Style existed about 1400–1420, after which the Renaissance style gradually replaced it, beginning in Italy.

Gothic architecture, especially in the great cathedrals, was characterized by pointed arches, cross-ribbed vaults and flying buttresses, which made possible relatively thin stone walls and an airy interior space. The vertical orientation of the space was symbolic of a striving toward heaven. In the 14th century, carved ornamentation became extremely lacy and profuse.

In England the early, middle, and late styles of Gothic architecture are known as Early English, Decorated, and Perpendicular, respectively.

In France, the late Gothic style is known as Flamboyant, characterized by flamelike curvilinear tracery. It influenced Scottish architecture of the period.

Monumental sculpture in the round was revived for the first time since antiquity during the Gothic period. It had a graceful, sinuous elegance and great emotional appeal, although the International Style showed a renewed concern for weight and volume, as well as for realistic observation.

In painting, manuscript illumination reached its peak during the Gothic era, although panel painting and fresco became increasingly important, especially in 14th-century Italy with the Sienese school and Giotto. The International Style was notable for subtle modelling, acutely observed realistic details, and the beginnings of the use of light as an independent element. During the first half of the 13th century, the great age of cathedral construction, stained-glass work also reached its high point.

2. *(calligraphy)* (also called **black letter hand**) a hand that was developed during the 12th century, when this art was practised chiefly in monasteries, which were the literary and artistic enclaves of the Middle Ages, and in the universities, which were the legal centres. Gothic is a highly stylized hand, with thick downstrokes and thin upstrokes bent back at the ends. It has a decidedly vertical character and is a very compact hand, giving the impression of almost covering the page with ink, whence its other name, black-letter hand. As well as regional variations, it took three main forms during the Middle Ages according to its use. The formal Gothic book hand was used for liturgical texts, inscriptions and seals. More graceful, cursive forms were used for legal documents, the most notable of which were the Italian chancery hand and the French bastard (*bâtarde*) hand. An informal Gothic cursive was developed for personal use.

The Humanist movement of the 15th century brought about a reform in handwriting, and the Gothic was largely replaced by the ROMAN and ITALIC hands. It continued to be used for some time in England and Germany, however, and is still employed to a certain extent in Germany. Although the Gothic hand was copied in type by such early printers as

Gutenberg and William Caxton, it did not have the good fortune – as did the roman and italic hands – to be extensively used for printing and thereby standardized. It survives only in several so-called black-letter typefaces that are used for display purposes and special effects. In the United States, the modern sans-serif typefaces, such as Futura, Vogue, and Franklin Gothic, are known also as gothic type, usually written with a lower-case 'g'. They bear no resemblance, however, to the calligraphic hand from which they take their name. Indeed, gothic fonts tend to be almost starkly simple, characterized by the absence of SERIFS and by a relative uniformity in the thickness of the strokes or lines. See illustration at TYPOGRAPHY.

gouache 1. the technique of applying opaque watercolour to paper. **2.** a work of art so produced. The usual gouache painting displays a light-reflecting brilliance quite different from the luminosity of transparent watercolours.

Gouache colours, sold in tubes, contain the same ingredients as transparent watercolours, but chalk is added to the pigments to make them more opaque. Other opaque, water-miscible paints, such as designers' colours, Chinese white watercolour, and casein colours, may be used as well as the special gouache colours in what is called a gouache painting. Gouache, watercolour, pastel, and India ink are frequently combined in the same painting.

Gouache was occasionally used in mediaeval manuscript illumination, and for miniature painting in the 16th through 18th centuries, although toward the end of this period its use was confined to emphasizing highlights. In the 18th century, it was popular with Italian, French, and Swiss watercolourists. Nineteenth-century painters, like the later miniaturists, used it for special effects in transparent watercolour paintings. But because of its potentially dulling effect, it is more difficult to add gouache touches to watercolour successfully than it is to add transparent watercolour to a painting done predominantly in gouache.

gouge a curved chisel with a keen cutting edge, used in wood carving. When the blade is a deep, pronounced scoop shape, the tool is known as a *U-gouge*; when the blade is V-shaped, the tool is called a *V-gouge*, *V-tool* or PARTING TOOL. Very small gouges, both U-shaped and V-shaped, are used in making woodcuts. See also BENT GOUGE; see illustration at WOODCARVING TOOLS.

gradation 1. a series or progression of shades, tints, or values, as a sequence of greys from light to dark. **2.** the smooth, imperceptible fusion of adjacent colours or tones (see BLENDING).

Graecian purple see TYRIAN PURPLE.

Graeco-Roman pertaining to the period (late 2nd and 1st centuries BC) when HELLENIC ART was assimilated and imitated by ROMAN ART. The major types of Greek sculpture were reproduced, as were individual works by such renowned Greek sculptors as Polyclitus and Praxiteles; it is to these copies that we owe most of our knowledge of the most famous

Hellenic works. Although we have no surviving examples of Hellenic painting on which to base an idea of its style, the Fayoum mummy-case portraits of the 1st to the 4th century AD, naturalistic paintings done in a province of Egypt governed by Rome and settled largely by Greeks, are generally known as Graeco-Roman work.

graffito (*It*. scratch) **1.** *(archaeology)* a casual scribble or pictograph on an ancient wall, stone, or other surface. In recent years the term (almost always in the plural, graffiti) has been applied to humorous, satiric, or obscene writings and drawings executed anonymously on walls, especially in public lavatories.
2. *(formerly)* the technique of decoration now commonly referred to as SGRAFFITO.

grain see KERMES.

grain alcohol see ETHYL ALCOHOL.

graining 1. the art of imitating the characteristic markings of attractive and popular hardwoods by the skilful application of colours with special brushes, sponges, or combs.
2. the preparation of a LITHOGRAPH STONE for use in making prints.
3. the granulation of metals. For example, aluminium in noticeably coarse particles is called grained aluminium rather than aluminium powder.

grain lac see LAC.

grand manner a style of HISTORY PAINTING, in which subjects of great significance are treated in a manner that elevates them above the realm of the commonplace. All detail in background, costume or physiognomy is either eliminated or greatly simplified, thus transcending the ordinary and achieving the ideal. Well-known practitioners of this style included Raphael and Poussin.

granite a hard, compact igneous rock, composed mostly of silica and silicates. Granite is more difficult to carve than marble and is esteemed for its durability and permanence of polish. There are many greyish, reddish and variegated kinds of granite. See GRAPHIC GRANITE.

grape black see VINE BLACK.

graphic arts or **graphics 1.** *(fine arts)* the various multiple-replica processes by which ORIGINAL PRINTS are created. The principal graphic-arts processes are AQUATINT; CRAYON MANNER; DRYPOINT; ETCHING; line ENGRAVING; LITHOGRAPHY; MEZZOTINT; MONOTYPE; SERIGRAPHY; SOFT-GROUND ETCHING; STIPPLE ENGRAVING; WOODCUT; WOOD ENGRAVING and mixed-media methods in which several of the above techniques are combined. A number of simplified printmaking methods, among them linoleum cutting (see LINOCUT), potato printing, and the making and printing of simple cardboard relief prints, are less accepted for serious creative work and are more accurately classified as arts and crafts.
2. *(graphics)* the individual prints, or proofs.
3. *(commercial arts)* all the processes, including the noncommercial processes, used in the entire field of commercial printing and lithography for reproducing both text and art work.

graphic granite or **Hebrew granite** a GRANITE whose polished face displays markings that give the effect of being inscribed with Hebrew or cuneiform writings. See also FOREST MARBLE.

graphics see GRAPHIC ARTS.

graphite an allotrope of carbon that is greyish-black, semicrystalline, flaky, and greasy. These qualities limit its usefulness as an artist's pigment, but favour its use for PENCILS, special industrial paints, and lubricants. Graphite was first mined in Borrowdale, in the Lake District, in 1664 and used for writing purposes in small lumps mounted on a stick. It was not until the 18th century, however, that its true composition was determined and the material was given the name graphite. It had previously been called *plumbago* or *black lead*. The latter misnomer has persisted in the designation of the modern graphite pencil as a LEAD PENCIL. The mixture of graphite and clay now used to make lead pencils was discovered simultaneously in 1795 by Nicolas Jacques Conté in France and Joseph Hardmuth in Austria. Graphite, also made artificially by passing an electric current through granular anthracite, is also used to make the stirring rods and crucibles used in sculpture for casting molten metal. Because graphite is extremely stable at high temperatures, it does not contaminate the molten metal or conduct its heat.

graphite paper a thin transfer paper coated on one side with graphite. The lines transferred are as erasable as ordinary pencil lines, making graphite paper superior to carbon paper for artists' use.

grater see RASP.

graticulation see SQUARING.

graver or **burin** any of a class of rod-shaped steel ENGRAVING tools with variously shaped points and a wooden handle that is generally rounded to fit against the palm. The graver is either an elliptical lozenge-shape in section, ending in an oblique point, or rectangular in section, with an oblique face that comes to a blunt, rounded or sharp point. The point and width of the cutting face vary according to the depth and width of the lines to be engraved. Gravers are sold in a wide range of sizes and shapes and with either bent or straight shanks. See also TINT TOOL.

gravure 1. a generic term for any or all INTAGLIO printing processes.
2. PHOTOGRAVURE.

grease crayon or **grease pencil** a black or coloured crayon, usually in the form of a pencil with a peel-off paper casing. It is used to write on glass, china and other surfaces to which other pencils and crayons will not adhere and is, therefore, often called a *china-marking crayon*. Artists frequently use black grease pencils for drawing on paper, but the pigments suspended in the greasy base of coloured grease pencils are not always permanent. LITHOGRAPHIC CRAYONS, which are considered a type of grease pencil because of their comparable composition and their use on stone and metal, are often preferred by artists for use on paper as well. Their range of hardness (five degrees in pencil form and seven degrees in stick form) and their more uniform quality make them superior to other grease pencils for drawing.

graver (above) Typical straight-shanked and
bent-shanked gravers. (below) Common cutting points:
lozenge (A); flat (B); round (C); point for multiple lines
(D); elliptical (E).

Greek art see HELLENIC ART.

Greek cross a cross with four arms of equal length that intersect at their middles, as in the plus sign. This symbol is found widely among pre-Christian cultures. It is often inscribed with a circle. See CROSS for illustration.

Greek key pattern or **fret** an angular, continuous band design, which in several variations was much employed in ancient Greek and Roman decoration and is still a traditional motif for mouldings and borders.

Greek key pattern

Greek pitch an obsolete name for ROSIN.

Greek pottery the ceramic ware of the ancient Greeks, painted with decorative motifs, figures, mythological scenes and the events of daily life – highly valued by museums and collectors not only as works of art but also as documents of the times and as indications of what Hellenic painting was like, in the absence of any surviving mural or easel paintings. The most outstanding examples of painted vases are from Athens; it is believed that the major successive developments of the art (see ARCHAIC PERIOD; GEOMETRIC PERIOD; ORIENTALIZING PERIOD) began there. Corinth was the second most important site. See VASE SHAPES.

green bice another name for BREMEN GREEN. It has also been used for GREEN EARTH. See BICE.

green earth a native clay containing iron silicate; it is a permanent pigment occurring in a limited range of clean, medium-pale willow or celadon shades. Green earth comes from various parts of the world; the best commercial grades, found in small deposits in central Europe and Cyprus, are called Tyrolean and Verona (relatively bluish), Bohemian (clear middle-green) and Cyprian (relatively yellowish). Green earth has been a favourite pigment for watercolour and other aqueous media since the time of Byzantine and early Italian tempera painting. Although green earth is available as an oil colour, its chief attraction is its low cost, since it becomes dark and muddy in oil, with very little hiding power or tinting strength. Other names for green earth are CELADON GREEN, green bice, holly green, stone green, verdeterra (Italian), and the old Italian term, *verdetta*.

green gold a modern synthetic organic pigment, one of the few azo yellow pigments with lightfastness and bleeding properties that are considered acceptable for artists' use.

green marble see SERPENTINE.

green pigments any of the following pigments that are approved in the United States for use in oil paints by ASTM and are generally acceptable in all other easel- and mural-painting techniques: VIRIDIAN, PHTHALOCYANINE GREEN; CHROMIUM OXIDE GREEN; GREEN EARTH; COBALT GREEN; LIGHT GREEN OXIDE and GREEN GOLD. See PIGMENTS.

green rouge see CHROMIUM OXIDE GREEN.

green smalt see COBALT GREEN.

greenstone 1. any of various compact green rocks suitable for building or carving.

   2. an alternative name for nephrite (see JADE).

green verditer an alternative name for BREMEN GREEN.

greenware pottery that has been formed and allowed to dry, but has not yet been fired.

grenadilla see AFRICAN BLACKWOOD.

grenadilla, South American see COFFEEWOOD.

griotte, Campan marble or **French red** a purplish red MARBLE, occasionally spotted with white, from the Pyrenees. It is esteemed as one of the finest red marbles.

grisaille 1. a monochrome painting executed in shades of grey, as its French name implies; a camaïeu done in greys. Grisaille is often used as an imitation of bas-relief and as such is especially suited to architectural subjects. Not having the techniques of chiaroscuro at their disposal for the representation of relief, the ancient Greek painters relied heavily on grisaille for gradation and modelling. Some Gothic miniatures were illuminated in grisaille. It was also used later as underpainting, especially by Northern Renaissance artists. Thus, some extant paintings in grisaille are merely unfinished works, although the medium has been used also for separate sketches and studies, such as Ingres' study *en grisaille* for his famous full-colour *Odalisque*.

2. a mixture of crushed glass with iron or copper oxides, cobalt or other mineral pigments in a liquid medium such as wine. Resins were often added to increase the adhesive properties of the mixture. Grisaille was used, beginning in the 9th century, to alter the colours of single pieces of STAINED GLASS, to which it was fused by firing. Prior to its invention, forms could be shown in stained glass only through the juxtaposition of separate pieces of glass. The use of grisaille, made in tones of black, brown and green, made it possible to shade and delineate detail in figures, such as facial features and drapery; to achieve a three-dimensional effect through modelling of figures; to darken areas bordering the leaden strips (see CAME) in order to enhance their structural function in the picture; and to tone down the brightness of pieces of glass that contrasted too strongly with adjacent pieces. Detail was often drawn by scratching through areas of grisaille with stiff brushes or pointed tools to reveal lines of clear glass. Modelling and shading were often achieved through the use of hatching.

3. a decorative glazing or enamelling technique used on pottery, glass, or metal in which an opaque or semiopaque colour is applied to the surface in varying degrees of thickness, the design or decorative effect being created by the dark undercolour showing through the thinner areas of enamel.

grog ground, previously-fired ceramic material, such as pulverized pottery, brick or fired earth clay. It is mixed with plaster to impart strength to a casting formula and with fresh, unfired clay to thicken its consistency while wet; to reduce shrinkage and increase its hardness when fired; and to create interesting surface textures. Grog is also used in the manufacture of crucibles and other products that must resist extreme heat.

grotesco (*pl.* groteschi) *(It.)* a work of art in the GROTESQUE style.

grotesque 1. a style of decorative painting, engraving, sculpture, and ornamental work in which fantastic human and animal figures are combined with leaf and flower forms interlaced in ornate curvilinear ARABESQUES.

2. a work of art done in this style.

3. one of the figures or designs in a work of art of this style.

The word comes from the Italian *grotte* (grottoes), the name given to underground chambers created by the excavation of ancient Roman buildings, in which much decoration of this kind was found. Raphael is generally credited with the revival of grotesque forms, which have continued to be important motifs to the present day.

ground 1. a surface to which paint is applied.

2. a coating material used to prepare a surface for painting. An oil ground, consisting of oil and white pigment, is used on canvas; either an oil ground or GESSO is used on boards or panels. The SUPPORT is coated with one or more layers to provide uniform texture and absorbency for painting. Special grounds are used for certain types of painting: polymer colours, for example, are used on supports prepared with a special POLYMER PRIMER. Some painting surfaces, such as watercolour paper and parchment, serve as ground and support in one. See EMULSION GROUND; MULTIPURPOSE GROUND.

3. *(relief sculpture)* the flat surface from which figures project.

4. see ETCHING GROUND.

group the historical classification of a number of artists, not always implying a closely knit association of artists working under a programme of aesthetic doctrines. Different groups have banded together for different reasons: for example, for economic or political advantage, for companionship with artists of similar aesthetic philosophies, to foster art locally, or to unite artists of divergent tendencies in opposing established authority.

grout 1. wet mortar or any soft cement used to fill joints between the tesserae in mosaic; it is also used for setting tiles, decorative stones, or other small objects in a wall.

2. *(building construction)* a wet cement or concrete that can be poured into cavities or around the bases of steel columns.

guide, printmaker's see REGISTER MARK.

Guignet's green one of the various older names for VIRIDIAN. It distinguishes the standard product from products made by other processes.

guild an association of artisans or craftsmen specializing in a specific craft or skill, for example, woodworking or metalworking. Guilds, originally formed to promote and protect the highly prized skills of their members, reached their zenith during the Middle Ages, although some guilds exist in various forms even today.

guilloche an ornamental design or a band moulding formed of interlaced curved lines.

guilloche

gum a hardened sap or exudation from any of various trees and shrubs. Some gums are soluble in water; the rest absorb water and swell enormously when soaked in it. Gums are used in vehicles or binders for aqueous colours, in tempera emulsions, and as adhesives, sizes, and stiffeners. Typical examples are GUM ARABIC and GUM TRAGACANTH. In the varnish industry RESINS are invariably called gums (*gum dammar, gum copal*, etc.), but this confusing usage does not extend to artistic or scientific discussion, where the precise terms are always used. Gums are insoluble in the volatile solvents (alcohol, turpentine, etc.) in which resins may be dissolved. Starches and similar water-miscible adhesives are generally classed with the gums because of their similar behaviour and uses. For example, a particular grade of dextrin can be used as an adhesive backing for so-called gummed paper.

gum accroides see ACCROIDES.

gum arabic a GUM obtained from various trees of the genus *Acacia*, growing in Africa, Asia and Australia. The best varieties have always come from North Africa. Gum arabic is soluble in hot water. It is used in solution as the medium in watercolours and gum tempera, and as a binder in ceramics to help the glaze adhere to the clay body. It is widely used in pharmaceuticals, confectionery and various industrial products. When a solution of gum arabic is heated to the boiling point its character changes. It becomes dark, acquires a pronounced odour, and will not function properly in the recipes calling for a hot water solution; however, it may be used as a paper adhesive. Common mucilage is cooked gum arabic. The best grades of gum arabic come from the *Acacia senegal*; they are sometimes identified as *Senegal gum* or *Kordofan gum*. Gum arabic may be obtained in lump or powder form. Its pharmaceutical name is *acacia*.

gum eraser a firm yet soft and crumbly rubber eraser made in tan blocks. It is used on paper to eradicate pencil lines and smudges without tearing the paper or harming its surface.

gum karaya a vegetable gum that swells enormously in water, used as an inexpensive substitute for GUM TRAGACANTH. It is usually preferred to gum tragacanth for use as the gel base in marbling paper.

gummigut see GAMBOGE.

gumming up the brushing of a solution of gum arabic and water over the stone in LITHOGRAPHY, to seal off and desensitize the nonprinting areas and margins of the surface so that when wet with water they will repel ink. This process is the final treatment given to the stone after the lithographic etch and before ROLLING UP. After the gum-arabic solution has been applied, the stone is dried with a fan or an electric blower, and then the excess gum is washed away. The gum is dried in order to have the highest possible concentration of gum in contact with the stone; this occurs just before the gum is completely dry, creating the greatest adsorption of gum onto the stone.

gum resin a small class of gums with resinous ingredients obtained from various shrubs and trees. The typical gum resin has the appearance of a resin and is insoluble or incompletely soluble in water but dissolves freely in alcohol. Little or no use is made of gum resins in artists' materials.

gum running a preliminary thermal treatment that some RESINS, notably the COPALS, require when they are used in the manufacture of cooked oil-and-resin VARNISHES. During the process, the resin is improved by the loss of some of its constituents through distillation. Gum running is one of the skills of the experienced varnish maker. The use of the term GUM for what should properly be called resin is one of the peculiarities of the varnish industry and the resin trade.

gum spirits of turpentine see TURPENTINE.

gum tempera 1. artists' colours consisting of pigments ground in an EMULSION medium in which the oily ingredient is linseed oil, STAND OIL, or, most often, a mixture of stand oil and DAMMAR varnish, emulsified by shaking it together with a gum arabic solution plus a small amount of glycerin.

2. the technique of painting with such colours.

Gum tempera colours are brilliant and have working qualities that appeal to many painters. Their resistance to accidental damage by water is low, so works of art in which they are used are usually framed under glass. Gum tempera is one of the accepted permanent painting techniques. See also TEMPERA.

gum thus *(US)* the oleoresin or balsam from pine trees of the southern United States. It is the exudation from which TURPENTINE and ROSIN are obtained.

gum tragacanth a GUM obtained from various species of a shrub (genus *Astragalus*) native to Asia Minor. It is commercially available in hard, thick flakes of a dull greyish-white to yellowish colour, and in powder form. When soaked in water overnight, it swells to a translucent, gelatinous mass, which is used in various dilutions as a binder for pastel crayons and industrially as a thickener and stiffener in many substances, including foods and pharmaceutical products. In ceramics, it is sometimes used to help a glaze adhere to a clay body.

gun cotton see CELLULOSE NITRATE.

gypsum, mineral white, terra alba or *(formerly)* **land plaster** native calcium sulphate; it is used in the manufacture of PLASTER OF PARIS, wall plasters, and to some extent as a FILLER. It has been argued that the SLAKED PLASTER OF PARIS recommended by Cennino Cennini (*Il libro dell'arte*) for use in GESSO is an ideal material because of the felting property of the long, needle-shaped crystals contained in precipitated or chemically manufactured calcium sulfate; however, few, if any, of the varieties of native gypsum have this monoclinic structure. Other names for gypsum are mineral white and terra alba. The type of alabaster in most common use is a variety of gypsum. See BURNT GYPSUM.

gypsum plaster any of the common wall plasters in general use, all of which contain various amounts of gypsum, as distinguished from the pure lime plaster used in fresco. It is inferior to lime plaster in that it tends to effloresce (see EFFLORESCENCE) because of its slight solubility in water.

H

Haarlem blue see ANTWERP BLUE.

Haarlem school a group of late 15th-century Dutch painters, working mainly in Haarlem. This was the earliest Dutch school to produce paintings quite distinct in style from the already established Flemish tradition. Geertgen tot Sint Jan was the most distinguished of the Haarlem painters, many of whom are unknown by name. About 1600, the city became the site of the earliest Dutch art school, which trained students in the classical style, as opposed to the Mannerism that had prevailed in the Low Countries throughout the 1500s.

hachure HATCHING, especially in cartography as a system for indicating relief.

hafner ware a well-known German salt-glazed stoneware. The term was first applied to ceramics made in 14th-century Germany by the Rhineland stovemakers, who became famous for their lead-glazed tiles; later they made container forms.

Hague school a group of late 19th-century Dutch painters centred in The Hague, who are best known today for their use of light, as illustrated in their outdoor paintings, scenes of Dutch life, and church interiors.

happening see PERFORMANCE ART.

half-chalk ground a misnomer for EMULSION GROUND, which is called *Halbkreide*, literally 'half-chalk' in German but is better translated as 'semi-gesso'.

half length see CANVAS SIZES, PORTRAIT.

half-relief see RELIEF.

halftone 1. a shade of grey or a chromatic colour whose value is intermediate between the darkest and the lightest tone of that colour.
2. in printing, an area of ink either black or coloured that has been broken up into dots. The dots vary in size and density according to the value of the halftone. The more white space between black ink dots, for example, the lighter grey the area will appear (see also DROPOUT). There is a procedure for making halftones in all three categories of printmaking techniques – intaglio, planographic and relief. Halftones are also produced by commercial printing methods. The terms *halftone cut* and *halftone engraving* usually refer to the products of photoengraving and photogravure, made by photographing the original through a screen.

half uncial a smaller, more cursive adaptation of the UNCIAL hand. It was used as a book hand in Latin codices from the 5th to the 9th centuries. A modified half-uncial hand with both minuscule and majuscule forms was developed in England and Ireland from the sacred texts brought there from the Continent. This Insular half uncial was used in Hiberno–Saxon manuscripts until the 11th century.

hallmark an identifying series of marks stamped on a British silver or gold object in some inconspicuous place, usually on the REVERSE of the object. The term is derived from Goldsmith's Hall, in London, home of the Worshipful Company of Goldsmiths; gold and silver articles assayed there were stamped to indicate their purity and quality.

British silver wares generally have five marks: the maker's initials or registry; a mark representing the town in which the article was made, an assay mark indicating quality, a tax-paid or official mark, and the year of manufacture, which is indicated by a letter of the alphabet from *a* to *u*, the font being changed every twenty years. Other European silverware usually has two marks, the maker's initials and the town mark; the latter sometimes indicates quality as well and usually incorporates the date. American silver was generally stamped with one mark only, the maker's name or initials, until the mid-19th century; later the word STERLING was added as a statement of the metal's purity. No official standards or regulations for marking metal wares were ever established in the United States. Town names and other marks were used occasionally as trademarks, and some silversmiths used pseudo-marks that resemble English hallmarks but have little or no significance. 17th-century pewterers and 18th-century makers of SHEFFIELD PLATE sometimes also used imitations of silver hallmarks on their wares. More commonly, however, a special mark known as a TOUCH appears on PEWTER.

halo see NIMBUS.

hand-blocked see BLOCK PRINT.

hand colouring see POCHOIR.

hand illustration see POCHOIR.

hand-mounting iron an electrically heated iron used in DRY MOUNTING. It is lightweight, flat and rectangular and is used when a dry-mounting press is not available.

handrest see BRIDGE.

hand vice a clamp with a handle used by the artist to hold a small object in one hand while working on it with the other. The hand vice is often used for holding an object against a grinding or buffing wheel or over a flame. The illustration shows the type of hand vice used to hold an ETCHING plate while blackening, or SMOKING, its surface.

hand-wiped see WIPING.

Hansa yellow a brilliant, transparent, light-yellow pigment made from a series of synthetic dyestuffs called *pigment yellow*, which were developed

hand vice

in Germany in the 20th century. Hansa yellow is one of the modern organic pigments qualified by colour stability and pigment properties for use in permanent painting. The name 'Hansa yellow', which was originally a German tradename, has been accepted as a designation for the pigment itself. This pigment, mixed with phthalocyanine blue, produces greens that may substitute for emerald green and other fugitive greens. Used alone, it gives brilliant effects, but it does not replace the golden tone of cobalt yellow in glazes.

hardboard any firm, dense, rigid WALLBOARD.

hard-edge painting a painting technique in which shapes are clearly and sharply defined, often in a simple, austere design. The term is of 20th century origin and is more frequently applied to GEOMETRIC ABSTRACTION than to representational work.

hardening on a process by which ceramic ware is heated to 600° F. in order to burn off organic material that may be present in the colours used in underglaze decorations. Hardening on is necessary to prevent such defects as crawling and blistering.

hard paste 1. (also called **hard-paste porcelain**) a hard, high-fired PORCELAIN. It is a so-called true porcelain, as distinct from the somewhat softer and lower-fired porcelains called SOFT PASTE.
2. the clay mixture used to make a high-fired porcelain. It usually contains feldspar as a flux, and flint as a refractory ingredient, and is fired at or below 2420° F.

hard solder a SOLDER that requires red heat for fusion. See also SOFT SOLDER.

hardwood the wood of most deciduous trees, including walnut, maple and birch. It is dense and rather hard, unlike the wood of conifers such as the pines and firs and of a few deciduous trees such as poplar. The latter, called *softwoods*, are less resistant to mechanical forces.

hare's fur see TEMMOKU.

harewood see SYCAMORE.

Harrison red a bright cherry-red of the PARA RED or LITHOL RED type. In the early 20th century this pigment was such a great improvement over the earlier synthetic organic reds that it was prematurely adopted for artists' use. Its shortcomings soon became evident, as it began to show signs of bleeding and fading after ageing for a year or two.

Hatchett's brown see VANDYKE RED.

hatching shading or modelling with fine, closely set parallel lines. When a second series of lines crisscrosses the first set, the technique is called *crosshatching*. By varying the size and closeness of the lines, an artist is able to indicate tones and suggest light and shadow in drawing, linear painting, engraving and etching. Hatching is also used for shading and modelling in tempera and other aqueous media where tones cannot be made to fuse by blending as they do in oil painting. A similar technique is used for highlighting and shading in tapestry, where hatched lines are produced by weaving in contrasting threads.

hawk or **mortarboard** a plasterer's implement formed of a sheet of aluminium with a wooden handle, usually cushioned with a large circle of sponge rubber on the underside of the board about the handle. A hawk may be a foot square or larger in size. The plasterer's working supply of mortar is placed on the hawk, from which the plasterer takes it up with a trowel much as a painter takes a load of colour from a palette.

hawk

HC *abbrev. for* HORS CONCOURS.

heartwood the wood at the centre of a tree. It consists of dead cells, unlike the SAPWOOD that surrounds it, and is harder and more resistant to decay. It is often a darker or more vivid colour than the sapwood, and is usually the part of a tree that is commonly known and commercially valuable as wood.

heavy spar see BARYTES.

Hebrew granite see GRAPHIC GRANITE.

heel the point at which the bristles of a flat or round brush bend when its point is applied to the painting surface. A high-grade bristle brush is both supple and resilient. Its heel occurs about a quarter of its length from the ferrule. A brush whose bristles are too limp or too firm will not possess this desirable feature.

heelball a prepared mixture of beeswax and lampblack or chromatic pigments, used to make a RUBBING. Cobbler's wax may be used in place of heelball.

heighten *(painting)* to complete the rendition of forms by raising the VALUE of appropriate areas with white or pale colour.

Helladic pertaining to the Bronze Age on the Greek mainland. Helladic civilization is divided into early (2600–2000 BC), middle (2000–1580 BC) and late (1580–1100 BC) periods. See MYCENAEAN.

Hellenic art the art of Greece and the lands under Greek influence, from about 1100 BC to 100 BC. Hellenic art may be divided chronologically into six stylistic periods: PROTOGEOMETRIC PERIOD, 1100–900 BC; GEOMETRIC PERIOD, 900–700 BC; ORIENTALIZING PERIOD, 700–600 BC; ARCHAIC PERIOD, 600–500 BC; CLASSICAL PERIOD, 500–323 BC and HELLENISTIC PERIOD, 323–100 BC. During the second and first centuries BC, as Roman political influence grew, Rome absorbed Hellenic art and so modified it as to make it her own. See GRAECO-ROMAN; ROMAN ART.

Hellenistic period the final phase of HELLENIC ART (323–100 BC), considered to have begun with the death of Alexander the Great. Thanks to his conquests, Hellenic art in this period was produced far beyond the borders of Greece and was therefore subject to cosmopolitan influence.

The harmony resulting from the concept of ideal beauty gave way to a dynamism and individuality verging at times on melodrama. Realistic portraits of the aged and suffering, as well as of the young and vigorous, were produced. Private emotions and psychological states were portrayed for the first time. Great rulers were depicted with a stature previously reserved for the gods. Draperies acquired a sensuous life of their own. Architectural and landscape backgrounds were introduced in figure compositions. In addition to monumental sculpture, artists produced small statuettes, in bronze for example, whose subject matter was even more mundane and whose treatment was even more realistic and personal than was common in the larger works.

haematite a native red iron oxide; it is the chief ore used for smelting iron. Used in powder form as a red pigment, haematite is mentioned by Cennino Cennini (*Il libro dell'arte*) and other Italian writers of the 14th to the 16th century. In the arts, however, the term *haematite* usually refers to a type found in dense stones of extreme hardness, which is used to make the broad, flat burnishers used in some kinds of gilding.

hemp a strong fibre used for making ropes and textiles. Hemp fabric has been used as a support for paintings, especially in India, and is believed to be as satisfactory as linen for that purpose.

hempseed oil a vegetable drying oil expressed from the seeds of the hemp plant (*Cannabis sativa*) that has been used as a substitute for linseed oil, especially in India. Its properties, which resemble those of POPPYSEED OIL, are less suitable than those of linseed oil for use in oil colours.

herm or **herma** a statue or monument in which the head is fully carved and the rest of the figure, in proportion, is a plain quadrangular column tapering downward. Herms are named after the Greek god Hermes, the subject of many such statues that were placed along thoroughfares in ancient Athens. Compare TERM.

heroic (*of figure sculpture*) larger than life-size without being COLOSSAL; it usually means a foot or two higher than lifesize.

hide glue see GLUE.

hiding power the degree of opacity of a coating material; its ability to obliterate anything over which it is spread. Hiding power is a direct function of the refractive index (see REFRACTION) of the coating and is also influenced by fluidity. See also COVERING POWER.

hieracosphinx see SPHINX.

hieratic (*of a style*) adhering to earlier types or methods, as in ancient Egypt or Greece, that have been fixed by religion.

highlight 1. the spot or one of the spots of highest VALUE in a picture (see LIGHT).
2. a depiction of the high point of a form to give final emphasis to a convexity.

highlight halftone see DROPOUT.

High Renaissance see RENAISSANCE.

Hispano-Moresque ware a lustreware originally made by Moorish craftsmen at Manises, a potters' community near Valencia, in Spain. It

HISTORY PAINTING

was later made by Spanish potters, who adapted the Islamic inscriptions to purely decorative purposes.

history painting a type of painting that depicts scenes from recorded history, the Bible, and great literature. See GRAND MANNER.

Hogarth's line the so-called *line of beauty*, a term introduced by the English painter William Hogarth (1697–1764) in his book *The Analysis of Beauty* (1753). It is a graceful S curve, which he presented as the basis of all successful artistic design.

Hogarth's line

hold-down a home-made clamp that holds objects on a workbench while they are being tooled, but enables them to be readily turned. The object to be sawed, or carved, is placed under one end of a plank. A long loop of rope or leather is passed through a hole drilled beyond the midpoint of the plank and through a corresponding hole in the workbench so that the lower end of the loop forms a stirrup dangling near the floor. The rope is held at the top by a knot too large to slip through the hole. The user's foot in the stirrup pulls down the plank firmly on the object, but can release it readily to turn it.

hollow ware *(US) (metalwork, ceramics, glassware)* vessels or bowls; technically, any such pieces that are either hollow or deeply concave, as opposed to FLATWARE.

hold-down

holly an almost white wood with an unobtrusive grain. A well-made, sturdy plywood faced with a holly veneer and a colourless sizing makes an attractive ground for mural panels.

holly cross see CROSS-CROSSLET.

holly green another name for GREEN EARTH.

Honduras rosewood see ROSEWOOD.

hone to finish the sharpening process on an edged tool, usually by rubbing it on an OILSTONE or SLIP, after preliminary sharpening on a whetstone or grindstone. Knives, chisels and gouges used for wood carving should be honed.

honeysuckle ornament see ANTHEMION.

Hooker's green a SYNTHETIC ORGANIC PIGMENT that is almost unique in hue and in such demand that, like alizarin crimson, it is included in the ASTM approved pigment list in the United States even though it is considered a borderline pigment. It exhibits poor stability in acid vehicles, is slightly soluble in organic solvents and has poor tint lightfastness. At one time, Hooker's green was a mixture of Prussian blue and gamboge. It was sold in yellow and blue shades, both of which were olive in tone. This colour was not permanent, but a replacement made of phthalocyanine blue and cadmium yellow was in use before the development of modern Hooker's green.

Horace Vernet green see VERNET GREEN.

horizon line a line, either shown (as in a landscape) or theoretical (as when the horizon in a landscape is concealed by objects, when the line exists outside the PICTURE PLANE, or when, as in interior scenes, there is no actual horizon), on which are located all the VANISHING POINTS of all sets of horizontal lines. (The vanishing point of any set of receding parallel *vertical* lines in a drawing of an object in OBLIQUE PERSPECTIVE is not on the horizon line.) Since nature's horizon always appears at the observer's eye level, in any picture in which the CENTRAL VISUAL RAY intersects the picture plane at its centre, the horizon line will divide that plane horizontally in its centre. In a conventional view, then, the horizon line usually crosses the picture plane near its centre. In a view from above, however, the horizon line is high in the picture plane or may even be above it; in a view from below, it is low in the composition or even below the picture plane. Depending on the angles of the axes in a given composition and the corresponding angles of receding lines, the horizon line may extend beyond the sides of the picture. See illustrations at LINEAR PERSPECTIVE; PERSPECTIVE.

hors concours (HC) (*Fr.* out of competition) ineligible to compete for prizes in an exhibition. This is usually the case because an artist has won a prize at a previous exhibition of the same organization or because the artist is a member of the jury.

hot-pressed paper see WATERCOLOUR PAPER.

Hudson River school a group of American romantic painters in the 19th century who drew their inspiration from the American landscape. Although they ranged the continent, many of them painted scenes of the

Hudson River valley and Catskill Mountains. This area was accessible to artists from New York City, where the group frequently gathered. Among the early Hudson River painters were Thomas Cole (1801–1848), Asher B Durand (1796–1886), and Thomas Doughty (1793–1856); later artists included Frederick Edwin Church (1826–1900), John Kensett (1818–1872), and Albert Bierstadt (1830–1902).

hue the actual colour of anything, identified by a common name such as red or greenish yellow. In describing the direction towards which a hue tends, as in colour comparison, the standard procedure is to use the following terms: for blue, either greenish or purplish; for red, either bluish or yellowish; for green, bluish or yellowish; for yellow, greenish or reddish; for violet or purple, bluish or reddish; for orange, yellowish or reddish. A grey would be described as cool (bluish) or warm (toward the red or yellow); a brown as cool (greenish) or warm (reddish). Greys and browns can also be described as neutral, that is, neither markedly cool nor markedly warm, but a neutral hue is cooler than a warm one. Oils, varnishes and similar transparent liquids are said to range in hue from pale yellowish to dark brown, in degrees that include straw, amber, golden, golden amber, brown and blackish brown. An artists' colour is often designated according to its resemblance to some hue in nature, without reference to its chemical composition or origin. Examples are primrose yellow, sea green, sky blue and rose pink. Hue designations may also be made by reference to a familiar object, for example brick red and battleship grey. A paint that is given such a designation rather than a standard pigment name often contains impermanent ingredients.

hue designation see COLOUR NOTATION.

huile de térébenthine see TURPENTINE.

Hungarian green see MALACHITE.

Hungary blue 1. a rarely used term for COBALT BLUE.

2. a name used in the 16th and 17th centuries for SMALT.

hydrated lime or **slaked lime** calcium hydroxide. See LIME.

hydraulic 1. pertaining to any action or movement effected by means of water.

2. (of cements or concrete mixtures) having the property of setting while submerged in water.

hydria an ancient Greek water jug. It usually had rounded shoulders, with horizontally attached handles, and a vertical handle at the neck for use in pouring. See VASE SHAPES for illustration.

hydrofuge 1. a means of removing moisture from a substance.

2. a material (such as SILICA GEL or calcium chloride) or an apparatus (such as a FILTER PRESS) so used.

hydrolysis any chemical reaction that is caused by the action between water and a salt, resulting in chemical decomposition of the salt and formation of a new substance. An example is the conversion of silicon ester to silica in ETHYL SILICATE painting.

hydromel a mixture of honey and water, usually of equal proportions.

It is used as a PLASTICIZER in watercolour paints. The term is no longer in common use.

hydrophile a material that attracts or has an affinity for water. Ordinary, clean watercolour paper is a hydrophile, as is the adsorbed coating of gum arabic on the nonprinting portion of a lithograph stone.

hydrophobe a water-repellent material or surface. The crayon and tusche used in drawing on a lithograph stone are hydrophobes.

hypha see MOULD.

I

ICI see COMMISSION INTERNATIONALE D'ECLAIRAGE.

icon in churches of the Eastern rites, a venerated representation of Christ, the Virgin Mary, or another religious subject, done in the Byzantine manner in painting, mosaic, niello or other art form in two dimensions or very low relief. The typical icon is a small tempera painting on a wooden panel, sometimes embellished with an elaborate repoussé cover of silver or other metal, cut out to reveal the central part of the picture.

iconography 1. a set of images or symbols conventionally associated with a subject, for example, the iconography of Christianity.
2. the imagery used in a work of art, by a painter or artistic school, or in the art devoted to a particular subject; one could speak of, for example, the iconography of western religious art.
3. the meaning assigned to a set of images or symbols according to a particular convention.
4. a collection of pictures constituting a complete visual record of a specific subject, such as a person, a locality, or an activity. It especially denotes a collection of portraits.

iconostasis the screen or partition in a Greek Orthodox church that separates the sanctuary from the nave and to which icons are attached.

ideal a philosophy born out of the revival of the works of Plato and the rise of Classicism during the Italian Renaissance, and espoused most notably by the 17th-century Italian biographer Giovanni Bellori, holding that an artist should strive to attain a standard of perfection in art – a perfection often absent in nature. In short, the artist should actually seek to improve on the vagaries of nature by creating the ideal.

ideal landscape a painting in which the elements of nature are depicted in a strictly formalized manner. The great French painter Nicolas Poussin (1593–1665) is the best-known exponent of this kind of painting.

idiom the style or techniques peculiar to an individual artist or characteristic of a period, movement or medium. One might say that an architect's buildings were designed in the idiom of Palladio or that a painter works in the surrealistic idiom.

igneous rock see ROCK.

IIC the standard abbreviation for the INTERNATIONAL INSTITUTE FOR THE CONSERVATION OF HISTORIC AND ARTISTIC WORKS.

illumination the art of decorating manuscripts with gold, or less often, silver. The term has come to apply in general to the decoration of early manuscripts with designs and pictures in colour and the use of elaborate calligraphy. The oldest-known decorations are on Egyptian papyrus rolls, including the *Book of the Dead*. The art was practised in classical

Greece and Rome, but only a few Roman specimens of the 3rd to the 6th century survive. Byzantine religious manuscripts contain many dramatic illuminations, and 14th-century Persian editions of the Koran have marvellously delicate designs and calligraphy. In Europe throughout the Middle Ages, almost all manuscripts were produced in monasteries and consisted of Bibles and EVANGELISTARIES, antiphonaries and devotional works such as the type of prayer book called a BOOK OF HOURS. Most were decorated, with or without gold or silver. During the Renaissance a great variety of secular works, notably chronicles and romances, were also illuminated.

Early mediaeval manuscripts were executed in red lead and cinnabar (vermilion). One of the principal functions of ornamentation was to mark sections of text, since pages were not numbered. Ornamentation at first consisted of enlarged, intricately drawn initial letters and decoration also essentially calligraphic. Gradually the decorative elements became more important. Elaborate initial letters sometimes framed very small pictures; the letters and paintings often filled entire pages. Pictures were painted on gold grounds or were surrounded by Gothic architectural tracery, in imitation of stained glass; and pages were given elegant borders of linear elements combined with plant and animal motifs. The illuminations were done almost entirely with aqueous paints: grey monochrome (GRISAILLE), outline drawings tinted with pale water washes, and brilliant tempera colours, often with burnished gold. Some mediaeval manuscripts were partly or wholly lettered in gold or, less commonly, in silver, often on tinted parchment or vellum. This technique is known as CHRYSOGRAPHY.

The art of illumination began a slow decline in the 15th century, with the advent of printing. Many of the earliest printed books, however, resemble illuminated manuscripts, for initial letters and other coloured embellishments were often added by hand to texts set with movable type.

illusionism the use of pictorial and perspective techniques to create in a work of art the illusion of reality. Illusionism was the guiding principle of Roman wall painting and relief sculpture. In the wall paintings at Pompeii, for example, light and shadow were manipulated to create an illusion of realism and depth. Since no geometric system of perspective had yet been formulated, Roman artists used what are essentially the techniques of AERIAL PERSPECTIVE to achieve an illusion of recession in their paintings. Later, Renaissance and Baroque artists utilized detailed and accurate systems of perspective and colour to create in painting an illusion of reality. This technique was known as TROMPE L'OEIL.

illustration a picture especially executed to accompany a printed text, such as a book or an advertisement, in order to reinforce the meaning or enhance the effect of the text. A work of art originally created for another purpose may also be used as an illustration if it is appropriate to the content of a text. Art that appears in conjunction with a text but is not specifically related to it is decoration rather than illustration.

illustration board a sheet of cardboard to which paper has been pasted on one or both sides. The paper may be anything from an inexpensive drawing paper to the finest pure rag watercolour paper, in a limited variety of surface textures. Boards with paper on both sides are more resistant to warping than those mounted on one side only. Illustration boards are used by illustrators, draughtsmen, and others whose work is to be reproduced and is therefore much handled. They are not suitable for permanent fine-arts use because of the undesirable properties of wood-pulp cardboard. See COQUILLE BOARD.

ilmenite a black, lustrous titanium ore containing iron, from which titanium white pigments are made. It has also become popular with studio potters, who use it in milled form as a colouring agent for glazes and in granular form as an agent for producing speckled effects in glazes and ceramic bodies. See also RUTILE.

imagier a stone carver or sculptor who carved the figures and decorations of Gothic churches and cathedrals under the supervision of the clergy. The work of the imagiers is admired for its vigour, imagination and humour.

imagines à vestir the doll-like, clothed effigies of saints, displayed in Italian churches. The heads and extremities of such figures are delicately carved and tinted; the bodies are usually roughly constructed and covered with lavish garments, sometimes bearing precious jewels.

imbrication any decorative pattern composed of overlapping elements arranged like shingles or roof tiles.

imbrication

imbuyam, embuya or **Brazilian walnut** any of several brown woods with figured grain from Central and South American trees of the genera *Nectandra* and *Phoebe*. Excellent for carving, imbuya is also known as Brazilian walnut because of its colour.

imitation stone any of various mixtures of cements or plasters, aggregates and pigments that, when made up to a plastic consistency with water or a chemical solution, harden to a rocklike cohesiveness, appearance and durability. One such material is OXYCHLORIDE CEMENT mixed with aggregate and pigments; others are sold ready-mixed in supply shops as casting stone or under various trade names. Some of the latter use epoxy resin as a substitute for cement. Imitation stone is used for casting by sculptors, who may try to duplicate the colour and texture of various carving stones, or use the imitation stone to achieve new effects.

imitation vermilion see AMERICAN VERMILION.

imp. an abbreviation of the Latin word *impressit*, meaning 'he (or she) printed it'. Sometimes it follows the printer's name in engraving proofs that have been printed by someone other than the engraver. *Imp.* is synonymous with *exc.*, an abbreviation for the Latin *excudit* ('he (or she) executed it'). In lithography, the name of the printer is followed by the word *lith.* or *litho.* For an explanation of other terms used in marking proofs, see DEL.

impasto 1. paint applied in outstandingly heavy layers or strokes.
2. any thickness or roughness of paint or deep brushmarks, as distinct from a flat, smooth paint surface.

imperial green a reduced or let-down grade of EMERALD GREEN.

Impressionism the first great modern art movement. The Impressionists broke away from the traditional technique of continuous brush strokes, from the representation of clearly outlined objects, and from preconceived notions of the colour that things have in nature. They sought instead to break light up into its component parts and to render its ephemeral play on various surfaces. To achieve their effects, they worked in a succession of discontinuous strokes of colour, which were to be combined by the eye (see OPTICAL MIXTURE). Although Impressionist paintings did not conform to traditional ideas of how things should be depicted, they were in fact attempts to observe nature as it really is and transmit it to canvas. Bright colours in a high key were characteristic of Impressionist work.

The first Impressionist exhibition was held in Paris in 1874; seven more were held between 1876 and 1886. They were received with hostility and contempt. It was not until the group had disbanded, with the artists continuing their own artistic development, that the Impressionists achieved solid recognition. The leader of the movement was Claude Monet (1840–1926), whose paintings of haystacks and other subjects at different times of day perfectly exemplify the Impressionists' concern with the effects of light. Although the group was not formally bound together by doctrines or principles, Camille Pissarro (1831–1903) and Alfred Sisley (1839–1899) were close to Monet both artistically and personally. Other important painters who accepted Impressionist concepts were Pierre Auguste Renoir (1841–1919), Edgar Degas (1834–1917), and Paul Cézanne (1839–1906), who was to have a great influence on succeeding generations of artists. Younger men associated with the movement, such as Gauguin and Van Gogh, were rather practitioners of POSTIMPRESSIONIST PAINTING. See also POINTILLISM.

The term *impressionism* has been used in the 20th century to characterize discontinuous brushwork or an analytical approach to light in many works of the past. It has been applied to the work of ancient Roman mural painters and to the work of Hals, Velásquez, Turner and Constable, among others. The Impressionism of Monet and his group, however, is generally held to have been almost entirely free of such historical influences.

imprimatura see VEIL.

inc. an abbreviation of the Latin word *incidit*, meaning 'he (or she) cut it'. It sometimes follows the engraver's name in a lower corner of the margin of a print, where it has the same meaning as *sculp.*, an abbreviation for the Latin *sculpsit*, 'he (or she) carved it'. For an explanation of other terms used for marking proofs, see DEL.

incised relief hollow RELIEF.

incunabulum (*pl.* **incunabula**) (*Lat.* cradle, birthplace, or beginning) works created during the earliest stages in the development of an art form or technique or at the beginning of any new period of artistic productivity. The word is most frequently used as a specific term for books printed before 1501.

Indiana limestone *(US)* the limestone most widely used by American sculptors. It is oolitic, relatively soft, and easy to carve, especially when it is freshly quarried. Indiana Buff Statuary is especially fine-grained and attractive. BEDFORD STONE is another Indiana limestone.

Indian blue an old name for INDIGO.

Indian ink black liquid drawing INK.

Indian lake an obsolete red lake colour made from lac dye (see LAC).

Indian madder or **munjeet** an orange-red NATURAL DYESTUFF made from the East Indian plant *Rubia cordifolia*. It is one of the slowest-fading of the natural colouring matters, and is used extensively for dyeing textiles in the Orient.

Indian purple various mixtures of blue and red pigments. The most satisfactory of these MIXED PIGMENTS is composed of ultramarine blue and alizarin crimson.

Indian red pure iron (ferric) oxide, a furnace product, usually made from steel-mill wastes. One of the artist's basic pigments, Indian red is dense, opaque, permanent and of a relatively deep brick hue with a bluish undertone, as compared with the bright, scarlet top tone of light red, the other pure iron oxide pigment. Originally a native earth imported from the East, Indian red was first manufactured in the early 18th century. For a time afterwards, the native earth pigment was called true, or real, Indian red to distinguish it from the furnace product; since the 19th century, Indian red has been applied specifically to the latter. The term's usage antedates its reported introduction to Britain by the American painter Benjamin West (1738–1820), who used it in reference to the red earth-colour employed by the American Indians. Both Indian and light reds are called *red oxide* (see RED IRON OXIDES), and have also been known by the obsolete name *colcothar*. See also POMPEIAN RED.

Indian yellow an obsolete yellow LAKE formerly made in India from the urine of cows fed on mango leaves. It is less fugitive than most other yellow lakes. From the early 19th century, Indian yellow was widely used by Europeans, but its process of manufacture was kept hidden from them until the 1880s. Indian yellow was exported in a crude lump form called *piuri* (variously spelled pioury, puree, and pwree), which had to be purified and powdered for pigment use. In 1908 its production was prohibited on humane grounds, since mango leaves were harmful to the cattle. A modern colour labelled Indian yellow might contain any one of a number of yellow synthetic dyestuff or lake pigments.

India paper the thinnest paper that is sufficiently strong and opaque for book and print use. It is made from flax and hemp and is popular with pen-and-ink artists.

India rubber a rubber or rubber eraser.

indigo a deep-blue pigment originally made from a NATURAL DYESTUFF obtained from plants of the genus *Indigofera*, cultivated in India, but now made synthetically from coal tar. Exported to Europe since Roman times, indigo is not a very lightfast colour. Writing in the 1st century AD, Pliny says that the Greeks, with their simple mineral palettes, produced works superior to those of his own day, even though the Romans possessed such new resources as 'the slime of India's rivers (indigo) and the blood of her dragons and elephants (dragon's blood).' *Indian blue* is an old name for indigo; *intense blue* is a deep variety of indigo lake.

industrial art the design of those products produced by industry, that is, anything from shampoo bottles to submarines.

inert pigments a class of white or nearly white inorganic powders that become colourless or nearly colourless when ground in oil. Inert pigments can be used as FILLERS or weakeners of paint pigments, but their presence does not always indicate adulteration. Certain inert pigments, especially ALUMINA HYDRATE and BLANC FIXE, are necessary ingredients of LAKES and certain other coloured pigments; some are used as EXTENDERS to control various attributes of oil colours, such as CONSISTENCY, COLOURING POWER and bulk; others are added to create textures and to reinforce the paint layer. CHALK (or WHITING) is used to make GESSO and PASTEL CRAYONS. Other common inert pigments are clay, precipitated chalk, and gypsum.

infrared see SPECTRUM.

infusorial earth see DIATOMACEOUS EARTH.

inherent vice *(art conservation)* any condition in the materials of a work of art that may cause defects to develop, as opposed to extraneous causes of decay or damage. The term is used in scientific and technical discussion as well as in questions of insurance.

ink a fluid, semifluid, or paste material containing colouring matter and used for pen and brush drawing, writing and printing. Inks for these purposes differ from one another in their composition and physical properties. Black *writing ink* is a thin fluid consisting of a solution of tannic and gallic acids extracted from oak galls, combined with ferrous sulphate (copperas) or another iron salt, dilute hydrochloric acid, a preservative such as phenol, and a black or blue dye. On exposure to atmospheric oxygen, the tannin in the oak gall extract reacts with the iron to form an intense black stain on the paper. The added dye is needed to make the writing visible at once, since the chemical reaction involved takes a day or two for completion. Iron-gallotannate inks have been used since mediaeval days, but the fact that a surface treated with ferrous sulphate could be blackened by an infusion of oak galls was known in the first century. Writing ink will remain legible for centuries, especially when kept away from light, but the fading and colour changes that occur would be disastrous in a drawing, so writing ink is not used for permanent works of art. Coloured writing inks, as well as special writing fluids for ballpoint and felt-tipped pens, are made of soluble dyes and so are never sufficiently lightfast to be used in works of art. *Drawing ink,* or *Indian ink,* is especially made for use in permanent works of art, such as pen drawings and wash drawings, and in mechanical drawing. It consists of particles of a carbon pigment, usually lampblack, finely dispersed in an aqueous binder, with a wetting agent and a preservative added. Ordinary drawing ink dries water-resistant so that it may be gone over with a wash or watercolour; its traditional binder is a solution of shellac and borax. A soluble drawing ink, the dried layer of which may be washed away with water, is also available; it is sometimes preferred to water-resistant ink for fine lines and delicate manipulations. The Romans used *atramentum,* an ink comparable to Indian ink, which they made with lampblack obtained by burning rosin in a special furnace, for both writing and artistic purposes; their principal ink, however, was CUTTLEFISH INK. *Chinese ink* is similar to Indian ink, although various minor ingredients are added to enhance its brilliancy, working qualities, and range of tone. After the ink is made, it is dried and moulded into little sticks or cakes, which the artist puts into solution by rubbing their ends on an inkstone with a little water. *Japanese ink,* also called *sumi* or *black watercolour,* is made in sticks that resemble their Chinese counterparts. Distinguished by numerous subtleties of quality and grade, the sticks are made and used according to ancient traditions and, in Japan, with a connoisseurship that virtually amounts to a cult. Most coloured drawing inks make few claims to permanence; those that are made with permanent pigments are labelled with pigment names rather than hue designations. PRINTING INK is more closely related to oil colours than to the pen and brush inks.

inlay 1. *vb* to create a design or picture on a surface by inserting thin pieces of a material such as wood, metal, tile, stone, shell or ivory precisely in a series of shallow depressions or on a depressed ground.

2. *n.* a piece of work so produced.

See DAMASCENE; INTARSIA; MARQUETRY; MOSAIC; PIETRA DURA.

inpainting *(conservation)* colouring or painting an area that has been damaged or obliterated so that it blends with the surrounding colours, without covering any of the original paint that still remains. Although these restored areas are called *repaints,* repainting is not an accurate term for the procedure.

insect wax see CHINESE INSECT WAX.

in situ (*Lat.* in place) in the position for which it is intended. A work of art may be created or an edifice constructed *in situ.* A painting may be repaired or otherwise treated *in situ,* i.e. while it is hanging on the wall, or an artifact examined without it being removed from the site where it was found.

inspissated oil an obsolete term for oil that has been thickened or rendered viscous by any means.

installation see ASSEMBLAGE.

insulating board a weak, porous variety of WALLBOARD made for insulation and soundproofing. Since insulating boards are necessarily of loose, cellular construction, they have neither the durability nor the structural strength of the denser hardboards and so are unsuitable for use as supports for permanent painting.

intaglio 1. a sculpture in which the areas or lines that form the design, inscription, etc. are incised and lie below the surface, as distinguished from RELIEF sculpture.

2. *(graphic arts)* one of the three major categories of printmaking techniques (the others being RELIEF PRINTING and PLANOGRAPHIC PRINTING). It includes all metal-plate engraving and etching processes in which the printing areas are recessed, that is, line ENGRAVING; ETCHING; DRYPOINT; SOFT-GROUND ETCHING; AQUATINT; CRAYON MANNER and PHOTO-GRAVURE. COLLAGRAPH blocks are also printed as intaglio surfaces. Intaglio plates are printed by inking the plate and then WIPING the plane surface clean, leaving the ink only in the etched or engraved depressions. The ink is then transferred to damp paper by running the plate and the paper through an ETCHING PRESS. Gravure processes are an exception: the proofs are pulled on dry paper, and in rotogravure the plate is wrapped around a cylinder which forms part of the gravure press. Intaglio prints are distinguished from those made by a relief printing process, in which the areas of the block or plate left standing in relief are inked with a roller. Although the plate used to make a line or halftone PHOTO-ENGRAVING resembles the plates used in intaglio processes, the photoengraving plate is printed as a relief block, the etched areas producing the whites in the proof.

intaglio print see COLLAGRAPH.

intaglio rilevato *(It.)* hollow RELIEF.

intarsia or *(It.)* **tarsia** a decorative technique in which small pieces of wood veneer are inlaid in a wood surface. Woods of contrasting colours and grains are used to obtain striking effects. The art of intarsia, a form of MARQUETRY, reached a peak of development during the Renaissance in Italy, when it was used to depict figures and elaborate scenes in deep perspective on panelled walls. See INLAY.

intense blue see INDIGO.

intense white see OPAQUE WHITE.

intense black see OPAQUE WHITE.

interlace a pattern, found in art, architecture, design and the crafts, in which elements such as strips, bands, lines, branches, threads, etc., are designed to intercross with one another, passing alternately over and under, and thus intertwining.

intermediate compound a compound derived from the raw materials of coal-tar distillation and used in various combinations to produce a vast number of synthetic materials for various fields, including pigments, resins, and drugs.

intermediate colour any of the six colours that are located between the primary and secondary colours in the spectrum as shown on the COLOUR CIRCLE.

intermediate varnish any varnish or sizing that is applied between two layers of paint. It has been used to denote retouch varnish, ISOLATING VARNISH, and the thin sizing varnishes used between a tempera or casein underpainting and an oil glaze or overpainting to prevent the glaze from being absorbed.

International Institute for the Conservation of Historic and Artistic Works a society whose members include museum technicians and conservators. It fosters scientific methods of conservation and publishes research data on all areas of its field.

International Style see GOTHIC.

intimisme a branch of Postimpressionism, characteristically dealing with small domestic subjects such as interiors and garden scenes, treated in such a self-contained way as almost to deny the existence of an outside world. The term is associated with a group of artists called the Nabis, and its principal practitioners were Edouard Vuillard (1868–1940) and Pierre Bonnard (1867–1947).

intonaco the final or painting coat of plaster in FRESCO. Typically, the intonaco is composed of five parts of lime putty and seven of sand or MARBLE DUST; it is vigorously trowelled, and finished with a float. Of the four traditional Italian terms for coats of plaster, *intonaco* is the only one commonly used in English. The intonaco is laid in sections, called *giornate*, that are small enough to be painted before they dry. See also BROWN COAT; SAND COAT; SCRATCH COAT.

inustion obsolete term for the 'burning-in' operation in ENCAUSTIC PAINTING.

inv. or **invent.** abbreviations of the Latin word *invenit*, meaning 'he (or she) designed it.' They are sometimes inscribed in a lower corner of the margin of a print following the name of the artist who did the original drawing or painting from which the print was made. When used in this way, *inv.* and *invent.* are synonymous with either *del.*, the abbreviation of *delineavit* ('he (or she) drew it'), or *pinx.*, the abbreviation of *pinxit* ('he (or she) painted it'). For an explanation of other terms used in marking proofs, see DEL.

invest *(metal casting)* to coat or surround with refractory material, as in the LOST-WAX PROCESS, which is sometimes called *investment casting*.

investment a containing negative MOULD, used in sculpture for casting metals. In the LOST-WAX PROCESS it consists either of earth clay and sand or of plaster of Paris mixed with such materials as clay, calcined clay, pulverized calcined plaster, pulverized quartz or silex, asbestos fibres and glue size.

iodine scarlet, brilliant scarlet or **royal scarlet** mercuric iodide, a dangerously poisonous inorganic pigment of the most brilliant scarlet hue. It is useless as a paint pigment, because it fades to a pale yellow after short exposure to light.

iodine value or **iodine number** a laboratory measurement of the unsaturated state of an oil or fat based on the amount of iodine it can absorb. A proportion is set up of the number of centigrams of iodine absorbed by one gram of the substance being measured. The magnitude of the resultant iodine number, in the case of an oil, is an indication of the oil's excellence as a FILM-FORMER, that is, of its ability to form a tough, durable coating. A list of all the vegetable DRYING OILS arranged according to their iodine values shows that linseed oil leads poppyseed, safflower and walnut oils by a definite margin and is second only to perilla oil, which is unsuitable for permanent painting because of its tendency to darken.

Ionic order the second of the three Grecian architectural orders (see DORIC ORDER and CORINTHIAN ORDER). The Ionic order is characterized by the two lateral volutes of its columns and by the use of dentils in its cornices.

iridescence a play of variegated, brilliant, rainbow or spectrum colours, called DIFFRACTION COLOURS, which is caused by the DIFFRACTION of light rather than by pigmentation. Iridescence occurs when light is diffracted from a thin layer that lies between two media of different refractive index (for example, air and water), as in a soap bubble or a thin film of oil on water.

iris green 1. see SAP GREEN.
2. an obsolete colour made from the juice of iris flowers.

Irish cross see CELTIC CROSS.

iron a metallic element, silver-white in colour, which is readily oxidized, or rusted, in damp air. Iron is malleable and ductile, and may be cast or wrought for sculptural purposes. It has a high melting point, as well as low fluidity when in a molten state. Because of this, and because it contracts as it cools, it is more often wrought by sculptors rather than cast.

iron black precipitated metallic antimony, no longer in use as a pigment.

iron blue see PRUSSIAN BLUE.

iron brown see PRUSSIAN BROWN.

iron pigments the pigments that contain iron. Those in approved use in the United States are the iron oxides: Indian red and light red, raw and burnt sienna, ochre, and the Mars colours. Prussian blue, which contains iron, is called iron blue in the pigment trade.

irons *(sculpture)* mild steel reinforcements for moulds or casts. They are usually wrapped in strips of hessian or jute and saturated with plaster. They are frequently embedded in the final coating of plaster in a negative MOULD in order to strengthen the mould mass and prevent it from breaking as the clay model is removed.

iron yellow another name for Mars yellow, one of the MARS PIGMENTS.

irregular curve see FRENCH CURVE.

isabella *(US)* a hue designation for a light brown or drab colour. The term is sometimes used disparagingly of any dull or depressing colour or colour scheme. It is not a specific pigment name.

isinglass 1. a clean, colourless kind of fish glue made from the sounds (swimming bladders) of fish. The best grade, Russian isinglass, comes from the sturgeon. Isinglass is no longer used to any great extent, having been superseded by gelatin and synthetic materials.
    2. thin, translucent sheets of MICA.

isocephaly in reliefs, friezes, and other decorative works, the practice of modifying natural proportions in the interest of symmetry, and having the heads of the principal figures (whether mounted or on foot, standing or seated) carved at the same, or nearly the same, level. This practice, universal in Hellenic friezes, is illustrated in the frieze of the Panathenaic procession, from the Parthenon.

isoindolinone yellow a modern SYNTHETIC ORGANIC PIGMENT with excellent brightness and tinting strength properties.

isolating varnish a dilute varnish for spray application in a very thin layer over dry oil paintings in order to prevent the paint from being disturbed or picked up by the solvent action of another coat of paint. A recently dried painting protected by a coat of isolating varnish can be worked over freely, and false strokes can be rubbed away continually, because the varnish is made of resins that are insoluble in the oil, turpentine or white spirit used in the overpainting. An isolating varnish containing a vinyl resin that is soluble in alcohol and lacquer solvents is sold with straight acrylic colours.

isomeric colours colours that appear identical but have different chemical or physical properties. For example, a mixture of burnt sienna, black, and a touch of green create an exact imitation of the mass tone of burnt umber. See also METAMERISM.

isomers two or more chemical compounds with molecules identical in kind and number, but which differ in molecular structure and, consequently, in properties.

isometric projection a projection used in mechanical drawing that avoids the use of foreshortening, since foreshortening necessarily varies the scale of the dimensions of the object drawn. The height, width and depth of the object are drawn on the same scale at equal angles of 120° with one another. This projection produces an appearance of distortion that is increased as the scale of the drawing is increased, but it is useful to the craftsperson or engineer who needs to see things in their proper proportions. See illustration at PROJECTION.

Istrian marble a large-grained, buff MARBLE quarried in Istria on the Adriatic Sea, and on some of the Dalmatian islands.

Italian blue see EGYPTIAN BLUE. Since the term *Italian blue* is unstandardized in the United States, a modern pigment so labelled is likely to be a blue lake or Bremen blue.

Italian earth see BURNT SIENNA, RAW SIENNA.

Italianizers see ROMANISTS.

Italian ochre or **Roman ochre** yellow ochre produced in Italy.

Italian pink a name given to various shades of BROWN PINK.

italic *(calligraphy)* a hand that, like the *antiqua* or ROMAN hand, was developed in the 15th century as a result of the Humanist reaction against the mediaeval GOTHIC hand. It was a cursive script that was adopted at the end of that century as a style of type and was thus standardized. Most type fonts have an italic alphabet in addition to a roman alphabet. Italics slant to the right and are often used in conjunction with a roman alphabet to give emphasis to a word or group of words. See also OBLIQUE. See illustration at TYPOGRAPHY.

ivory a hard, calcareous substance of which teeth, including the tusks of the elephant and certain other large mammals, are composed. Ivory is fine-grained, opaque, and a striated creamy white in colour. When aged, it may become yellow or brown. Used as a medium for carving since ancient times, ivory is less brittle than bone and takes a high polish. It is easily sawed or filed, but must be carved with very sharp steel tools because of its grain. Its disadvantages are its high cost, scarcity, unavailability in large pieces, and a tendency to warp. Since the elephant ivory trade has resulted in great cruelty to the animals and a serious reduction in herds, it is now banned by international agreement, although, regrettably, poaching continues. Elephant ivory has been especially valued by sculptors for its beauty and homogeneity, and for the size of the tusks, although they have occasionally used the tusks of the walrus, hippopotamus and narwhal. Modern substitutes are inexpensive, easily worked plastics made to resemble ivory. See CHRYSELEPHANTINE; SCRIMSHAW.

ivory black, bone black or **blue black** a carbon pigment made originally by burning ivory but which is nowadays high-grade BONE BLACK. Ivory black, which has good properties for use in oil, is perhaps the most widely used black pigment in the artist's palette. *Paris black* is an inferior grade.

J

jacaranda the wood of trees of genus *Jacaranda*, including Brazilian ROSE-WOOD and so-called blue ebony.

jacaranta brown a little-used name for UMBER.

Jacobean relating to works of art – mostly architecture and furniture – produced in England during the reign of James I, from 1603 to 1625, and for a short time thereafter.

jade an extremely hard stone, ranging in colour from white to deep green. There are two distinct mineral forms of jade – nephrite (or greenstone) and jadeite. It is difficult to carve, but it is used, especially in the Orient, for intricate and delicate work.

japan 1. a type of clear varnish that is mixed with paints and oil colours to impart gloss and hasten drying. Such varnishes are used in decorative work, as on painted tinware, but they are too brittle for use in creative painting.
2. (also called **black japan** or **japan black**) an inexpensive decorative enamel, which almost always contains asphalt and therefore is usually black or transparent, brownish black. Both air-drying and baked forms of this enamel were once widely used for black japanned tinware and ironware.
3. (also called **japan colour**) a type of paint, composed of pigment ground in an oil-free resin varnish, which dries quickly to a mat or lustreless finish. Japan colours are used in sign painting and decorative work and are usually protected with a coat of durable varnish.
4. (**japan drier**) a liquid solution of a strong drier, usually with resin, used in sign painting and industrial coatings. None of these products are intended to be used in permanent painting.

Japanese lacquer see LACQUER, ORIENTAL.

Japanese paper any of several soft, tissue-thin artists' papers made in the Far East from the pith of fibres of various trees.

Japanese prints woodblock colour prints that were produced in Japan by the Yedo school, whose artists were active from the middle of the 17th century until the middle of the 19th century. Using various methods of printing and many different kinds of materials, the Yedo school produced prints of extreme subtlety and quiet beauty. Both the IMPRESSIONISTS and the POST-IMPRESSIONISTS were influenced by Japanese prints. Yedo is a former name of Tokyo.

Japan wax, Japan tallow, sumac wax or **vegetable wax** a wax obtained from a species of sumac tree as a by-product of lacquer manufacture in India and China. It is a soft, yellowish wax with adhesive properties. It has a melting range of 50–52 °C. but, when recently solidified, is likely to have an erratically lower melting point for some time. It is used in the manufacture of pharmaceuticals and cosmetics such as lipstick, among other industrial purposes, and is used in the arts as an ingredient in wax compounds to impart adhesive properties to the mixture.

Japonaiserie work done in the Japanese manner. Japonaiserie superseded CHINOISERIE as a motif in furniture and the decorative arts.

Japonisme the influence of Japanese art on Western art and decoration following the opening of Japan to the western world by Commodore Perry in 1854, and extending into the early 20th century. In the major arts of painting and graphics, the Impressionists and Postimpressionists owed something to its influence. See JAPONAISERIE.

jasper a compact, opaque type of impure quartz. It may be yellow, brown or dark green, and occasionally black or blue.

jasperware a ceramic ware developed in England in 1774 by Josiah Wedgwood that became popular for bas reliefs and cameos. Most jasperware is ornamented in the Neoclassical style in white relief on a coloured ground, especially blue and sage green, but also olive green, black, yellow, pink and lilac. It is also made in pure white. Wedgwood's masterpiece in jasperware is his reproduction of the Portland Vase, a cameo glass vase with figures from classical myths in white on a blue ground. The original was Roman, and is believed to date from about the 1st century AD.

jaune brillant an unstandardized French term for several pigments, including NAPLES YELLOW and cadmium yellow (see CADMIUM RED).

Javelle water a dilute bleaching solution that was once widely used. It was made from either sodium hypochlorite or potassium hypochlorite. The solution of sodium hypochlorite was also known as *eau de Labarraque*, while Javelle water was often called by its French name, *eau de Javelle*. Nowadays, ordinary bleaching powder (calcium hypochlorite) is universally used by conservators for bleaching prints.

Jean Cousin a red ceramic colour (trioxide of iron) used in the 15th and early 16th centuries to colour STAINED GLASS in local areas. Together with the older GRISAILLE and SILVER STAIN, it was the only material used to alter the colour of parts of single pieces of glass until the invention of vitreous ENAMELS for this purpose in the 16th century.

jequitiba see MAHOGANY.

Jerusalem cross see POTENT CROSS.

jet a hue designation, in painting, for an intense black, named after the highly polished mineral of that name.

jewel point a diamond or ruby point mounted in a handle, used in DRYPOINT to incise the plate. Curved lines can be drawn with greater facility with a jewel point than with a steel NEEDLE. A jewel point also functions as a glass cutter.

jomon ware the earliest Japanese pottery, dating from 7000 BC. The wares were formed by the COIL METHOD and baked in open fires.

journeyman a skilled worker who has served an apprenticeship in an art or manual craft and is qualified to work under a master artist or master craftsperson.

Judas hair bright-coloured or pronounced red hair in paintings, so called because early painters conventionally gave this colour hair to representations of Judas.

Jugendstil German term for ART NOUVEAU, from the magazine *Die Jugend*, meaning 'youth.'

junk art the name given to a type of 20th-century art, including painting and sculpture, in which the artist uses refuse, scrap material, and urban waste, in short anything viewed as useless because it is cast off from modern society, to create a work of art. The American artist Robert Rauschenberg (b. 1925) used junk to create his famous *combine paintings*. See ARTE POVERA.

Jura turpentine An oleoresin or BALSAM obtained from the red pine of the Vosges mountains in France.

jute canvas A canvas or hessian with a coarse, square weave that makes it attractive to painters. Jute, an East Indian fibre, turns dark and becomes weak and extremely brittle with age, and is therefore unsuitable for use as a support for permanent painting.

juxtaposition of colours see OPTICAL MIXTURE.

K

kalsomine see CALCIMINE.

kantharos see CANTHARUS.

kaolin the whitest and purest variety of CHINA CLAY, originally found in Kao-ling, Kiangsi (now Jiangxi) province, China.

karaya see GUM KARAYA.

Kassler yellow another name for TURNER'S YELLOW.

kauri a resin, either fossil or recent, produced by Australian trees of the genus *Agathis*, especially *A. australis*. Kauri is dark brown and has a pleasant odour. It was widely used in the early 20th century to make hardwearing floor and furniture varnishes of top quality and brilliant finish, but it has been replaced by the synthetic resins. The fossil deposits were depleted, and the growing trees became scarce before 1930, so that the resin is no longer readily available in large amounts. It has also been known as *kauri copal*, but this is a misnomer, for its properties are distinctly different from those of the copals.

Keene cement or **Keene's cement** a very hard plaster used for patching walls and other surfaces that are exposed to much wear. It consists of dead-burnt gypsum with additives of alum and other salts, and was invented by Richard W. Keene in England during the 19th century. It is used in fresco and by sculptors for modelling and repair.

kelebe see KRATER.

kermes a red NATURAL DYESTUFF obtained from an insect found on the kermes oak (*Quercus coccifera*), which grows in the Mediterranean area. Generally held to be the first natural colouring matter for which a standard production technique was developed, kermes was in ancient times the most important red for dyeing fabrics and for making lakes. In the mediaeval period, kermes was surpassed in Europe by lac from India, in the 16th century by materials from the New World like cochineal and Brazil wood, and in later times by madder. Although kermes and cochineal have the same chemical components, CRIMSON LAKE made from kermes is much inferior to carmine, the lake made from cochineal. The name *kermes* is Persian, and the English word *crimson* derives from it; the old English name for kermes is grain, from the Latin *grana*.

kernel black a variety of VINE BLACK made by burning peach kernels or similar material.

kerosene see PARAFFIN.

kettle-boiled oil see BOILED OIL.

key 1. *(painting)* the prevailing range of colour VALUES and tonal quality. A painting in a high key is dominated by light, bright or pale colours, while one in a low key is dark or subdued.

2. a thin, triangular wooden wedge hammered into the slot at an inner corner of a STRETCHER in order to tighten the canvas by expanding the stretcher.

3. *(casting)* one of the protuberances that act as registers on some moulds, by fitting into corresponding holes in the other half of the mould.

4. *(carpentry)* a similar projection on wood joints. See also NATCH.

5. *(of materials)* roughness or interstices in a surface, whose function is to strengthen the bond or anchorage of a material laid over it. Brick and stone walls may be hacked or scored before plaster is applied to them; the spaces between laths serve the same purpose; and in some jewellery techniques, metal is scored with a graver to receive enamel.

key block; key plate; keystone the template block, plate or stone from which is made each separate printing surface for each colour run (see COLOUR PRINT). In multicolour woodcuts this is the *key block*, in aquatints and mezzotints the *key plate*, and in lithographs the *keystone*. The key block, plate or stone contains the complete drawing, incised, etched or drawn with tusche or lithocrayon as though made for a final black-and-white print but sometimes done in outline rather than complete detail. From this key drawing, each partial drawing for each basic colour to be printed is copied on a separate plate, block or stone. REGISTER MARKS on the master block, plate or stone are duplicated on the separate-colour printing surfaces so that when all the blocks, plates or stones are printed on a single sheet, their impressions will be in REGISTER.

kiathos a teacup-shaped ancient Greek vessel for pouring. See VASE SHAPES for illustration.

kickwheel a POTTER'S WHEEL operated by a pedal or by simply kicking at a weighted wheel at the bottom of a vertical shaft.

kidney *(ceramics)* a rubber tool shaped like the profile of a kidney. It is used for smoothing plastic clay surfaces. It is sometimes made of spring steel and can be used for scraping clay.

kieselguhr see DIATOMACEOUS EARTH.

killed plaster CASTING PLASTERused to STOP holes and to smooth irregularities on fresh plaster casts. It is made by stirring the gauged mix until it is on the verge of setting, and is then applied with the fingers. It dries to the same hardness, absorbency and white colour as the plaster body.

kiln a furnace used for FIRING ceramic wares and sculpture and for fusing enamels onto metal surfaces. Kilns are lined with brick or stone, come in a large variety of sizes depending on the use for which they are intended, and may run on gas, oil or electricity. It is easier to regulate the temperature of an electric kiln than the temperature of a gas or oil kiln, but some potters and sculptors feel that an electric kiln heats up too quickly. Heat inside a kiln is measured by means of a PYROMETER or by PYROMETRIC CONES observed through a peephole. See MUFFLE; SAGGER.

kiln-dried wood wood that has been artificially seasoned by being heated in a kiln or oven. Wood for carving should be well dried and seasoned if it is not to split and crack as it dries and shrinks. Since natural seasoning is extremely time-consuming, hot-air or kiln seasoning is used commercially and by sculptors to dry and stabilize the wood. Kiln-dried wood is inferior to naturally seasoned wood in that it tends to reabsorb moisture from the atmosphere.

kinetic art all artistic constructions that include moving elements, whether activated by motor, by hand crank or by natural forces, as in MOBILES.

king's blue a name formerly given to the obsolete pigment SMALT; now sometimes applied to COBALT BLUE.

king's yellow a fine grade of ORPIMENT formerly prepared for artists' use.

kingwood (US) a hardwood (from a South American tree, *Dalbergia cearensis*), of a dark violet-brown colour, sometimes almost black, streaked with golden and light-yellow markings. It may be polished to a bright lustre. It is used principally for veneer. Kingwood is related to the rosewoods, which are also of the genus *Dalbergia*.

kit cat see CANVAS SIZES, PORTRAIT.

kitchen sink school a group of British painters who worked after the Second World War and are best known for the realism of their style and the commonplace nature of their subject matter.

kitsch a blatantly sentimental, slick or pretentious artistic production or design. Kitsch, usually of low quality and sometimes mass produced, is intended to appeal to popular tastes.

knife, gilder's see GILDER'S KNIFE.

knife-file a thin, tapered file, wedge-shaped in cross section, whose thin side resembles a knife edge.

knop 1. *(metalware, glassware, ceramics)* a small decorative knob or protuberance that may also aid in grasping a utensil, as a knob in the stem of a goblet or chalice or on the shaft of a candlestick.
2. a FINIAL.

koa a very light but durable hardwood suitable for carving, obtained from the Hawaiian tree *Acacia koa*. It may be red or brown in colour, depending on the age of the tree.

kolinsky the red marten native to the Kola Peninsula in northern Russia. The tail hairs from this animal produce the finest red sable brushes with optimum spring and performance for oil and watercolour painting. Due to the great rarity of this protected animal, true kolinsky hairs are no longer available. Today, brushes made from hairs from similar animals found in Siberia and China, though of lesser spring, are now called *kolinsky*.

Kordofan gum see GUM ARABIC.

krater or **crater** a rather large, wide-mouthed ancient Greek jug in which wine was mixed with water. Kraters were made in a great variety of shapes. The calyx and bell kraters are named for the respective shapes of their bowls; other types vary from a simple bowl to a rather tall jug with a single tubular foot. A usually ovoid krater with handles joining the shoulders to extensions of the lip is known as a *kelebe*. Kraters of several shapes often have columnar or volute handles; on others the handles are

KREMNITZ WHITE

horizontal. See VASE SHAPES for illustrations of some characteristic forms.

Kremnitz white or **Krems white** see CREMNITZ WHITE.

kufic script a type of Arabic script used to write the Koran in the time of Mohammed, and later used, because of the peculiar angularity of its shape, to decorate architecture from the 11th century to the end of the 16th century.

kylix or **cylix** *(ancient Greek pottery)* a drinking cup with a broad shallow bowl and two short handles affixed horizontally near the edge of the cup. Early examples have a low, round foot or base, while the later ones have a high, stemlike foot. To modern eyes the kylix seems a footed bowl rather than a cup; it has long been a popular model for such pieces as footed fruit bowls and shallow compote dishes. See illustration at VASE SHAPES.

L

labarum see CHI-RHO.

lac a resin of insect origin, collected in India from twigs of several species of tree of the acacia family. Lac is secreted as a kind of protective scale about the bodies of the insects (*Coccus lacca*), which attach themselves to the twigs to feed on sap and complete their life cycle. The crude resin, called stick lac, consists of twigs encrusted with the excretion and the insects' remains; it is processed in several steps to produce SHELLAC. The first step produces a granulated substance called *seed lac* or *grain lac*. This is melted to form thin sheets of *garnet lac*, which are broken into pieces. Further refinement produces button-shaped pieces known as *button lac* and an elongated form called *tongue lac*. The most refined form, shellac or orange shellac, is in flakes; it is free of impurities and has lost the greater part of its original ruby colour. Orange shellac may be refined further by a chemical bleaching process to produce the grade called bleached white shellac. Alcohol solutions of both orange shellac and bleached white shellac are widely used as varnishes.

The blood-red dye obtained from lac was formerly the most valuable product of the refining process. It has been used as a dyestuff since ancient times and was the dye used in the pigment Indian lake. The word *lac* (as well as the colour term *lake*) is derived from the Sanskrit *lāksā* (Hindi *lakh*), 'a hundred thousand'; one of the host trees is referred to in Sanskrit writings as 'Lakshatarn, the tree that nourishes a hundred thousand insects'.

lacewood or **silky oak** a wood with a distinctive lacy figure, from the Australian and European tree *Cardwellia sublimis*. Lacewood is pink with a silver sheen, and is used for veneer.

lacquer 1. a natural resin, the exudation of trees grown in several countries of the Far East; see LACQUER, ORIENTAL.
2. any of various clear or pigmented industrial coatings that are constituted principally of a cellulose derivative (such as CELLULOSE NITRATE) and dry quickly through evaporation of their volatile solvents. Lacquer films are glossy, hard, and resistant to wear and weathering. Pigmented lacquers are sometimes called *lacquer enamels*. Because of their ease of application (most are designed for use in sprays), their rapid rate of drying and their tough films, lacquers are used as finishes for a great number of mass-produced products, especially motor vehicles. In the 1930s, after the introduction of modern lacquers, made more durable by the use of alkyd resins (and, later, acrylics), several prominent and many lesser artists began painting with car lacquers. Their use in the fine arts, however, is condemned by all specialists in artists' materials.

LACQUER

All lacquers are diluted with powerful LACQUER SOLVENTS, which emit toxic fumes, and their films start to disintegrate after 12 to 15 years' exposure to the ultraviolet in daylight.

lacquer, Oriental lacquer providing hard, tough, permanent films. The term *lacquer*, now applied to modern cellulosic coating materials, originally referred to a resinous product obtained from a tree (*Rhus vernicifera*) native to China, cultivated in Japan as far back as the 6th century, and used throughout Southeast Asia. The Oriental lacquers are not exported, but are used locally to make clear and pigmented coatings for use on furniture, bowls, dishes and other small articles. Lacquer is also built up into solidified forms through the application of a series of thick coatings around a base material, then carved into artistic works known simply as *lacquers*. The fluid material of Oriental lacquers has toxic and irritant properties similar to those of poison ivy.

lacquer solvent any volatile solvent that can be used to dissolve or dilute cellulose lacquer. Most solvents or acrylic lacquers have a very high rate of evaporation and many have toxic or obnoxious fumes or residual odours. The milder ones, however, are occasionally used by artists as paint removers and for other special purposes. A liquid commercially labelled lacquer solvent is a blend of several of these fluids and may include ACETONE, ETHYL ACETATE, or BANANA OIL.

lacuna (*Lat.* gap; *pl.* **lacunae**) an area of a painting, manuscript, or other work of art that is missing completely as a result of any form of damage to the work.

lagynos a type of ancient Greek jar that is wide in its lower half, narrow in its upper half. See VASE SHAPES for illustration.

laid paper any paper that has a type of WATERMARK that covers the whole sheet and consists of closely spaced parallel lines in one direction and heavier, more widely spaced lines perpendicular to them; these are the wire marks of the screen from the roll or mould on which the paper is made. Paper that is not laid is called *wove*; a wove finish is produced on a screen so tightly meshed that the wire marks are not visible.

laitance a gelatinous material that sometimes exudes from a Portland cement wall; it must be removed by scraping or treating with a wire brush in preparing the wall for painting or plastering.

lake a pigment made by precipitating or developing a dyestuff on an inert pigment with the assistance of chemicals and other manufacturing aids, by a process comparable to the dyeing of textiles. All the older pigments made by this method are still called lakes, but few of the SYNTHETIC ORGANIC PIGMENTS developed in the Twentieth century use the name, even though some fit the above definition. The inert pigment in a lake is called its *base*; alumina hydrate is the standard base for transparent lakes, blanc fixe for those in which opacity is desired. Clay, chalk, gypsum, white earth, green earth and various chromatic pigments have all been used as lake bases at one time or another. The permanence or colour stability of a lake is a function of the permanence of the dye used. All lakes made from natural dyestuffs (except madder lake) are insufficiently permanent for artists' paints. Similarly, most of the early lakes made from synthetic organic dyes are not sufficiently nonbleeding for use in oil colours, even though the lightfastness of some of them has been increased in recent decades by the molybdic and phosphotungstic processing methods. Most modern synthetic organic pigments of good permanence – such as alizarin crimson, Hansa yellow, phthalocyanine blue, phthalocyanine green, and quinacridone red – are not lakes; they are insoluble compounds usable directly as pigments.

The word 'lake' may come from the Italian *lacca*, a term used by mediaeval Italian dyers for the scum that they removed from their dye vats and sold to painters, frequently with the addition of a little inert powder to increase the yield. The Italian term is related to *lac*, which derives through Persian from the Sanskrit *lāksā*. Lake making goes back to the ancient Egyptians and Greeks; Roman recipes still survive for making paint pigments from such natural dyestuffs as kermes and Tyrian purple. Writers of the 17th and 18th centuries frequently used the term 'lake' to mean transparent red lake, without specifying whether CRIMSON LAKE, CARMINE lake, or LAC lake was meant.

lake base the BASE, or inert pigment, used in making lakes.

lamination the process of building up a material in layers, usually for increased thickness and strength. Laminated materials in general are much sturdier for their weight than solid pieces of the same material. Plywood is a commonly used laminate. In sculpture, polymer resins are used in lamination; a layer of resin is followed by two or more layers of FIBRE GLASS impregnated with more resin.

lampblack a pure CARBON PIGMENT made by burning oils and collecting the soot from flues. It is an extremely light, fluffy powder, which is used in all techniques of permanent painting. One of the oldest manufactured pigments, lampblack was used in the earliest civilizations. *Oil black* is a seldom-used name. FLAME BLACK is an impure variety.

lancewood any of several elastic woods used in making bows, fishing rods, tool handles, and other objects of similar shape and function, and sometimes used for carving. Among the woods known by this name are the wood of *Oxandra lanceolata*, DEGAME and beefwood (from trees of the genus *Mimusops*), which is also known as *red lancewood*.

land plaster an old name for GYPSUM.

landscape a painting, drawing, or other depiction of natural scenery. Although figures and manmade objects may be included in a landscape, they are of secondary importance to the composition and incidental to the content. Prior to the 17th century, few artists painted or drew a landscape for its own sake; natural scenes were depicted merely as adjuncts to or backgrounds for figures and events. Landscape's first full flowering as a separate genre occurs in the works of such 17th-century Dutch painters as Ruysdael and Hobbema. England in the 18th and 19th centuries enjoyed another heyday of landscape under such painters as Gainsborough, Turner and Constable. It continues to be a popular genre today. The French word for landscape, *paysage*, also designates a series of French canvas sizes (see CANVAS SIZES, FRENCH). See also CANVAS SIZES, LANDSCAPE.

landscape marble see FOREST MARBLE.

Languedoc marble or **French red** a bright-red MARBLE with white blotches, quarried in the French Pyrenees. It resembles GRIOTTE.

lapis lazuli a semiprecious blue stone used for jewellery and small carvings; it is the raw material from which the original ULTRAMARINE BLUE pigment was prepared. Lapis occurs in Chile and various other parts of the world; a very fine quality has been imported to Europe from Afghanistan since mediaeval times.

lard stone see STEATITE.

latex 1. a viscous, milky-white fluid composed of RESINS or waxes in the form of tiny globules in aqueous suspension, and occurring in rubber trees, milkweed and other plants.
2. specifically, rubber latex.
3. any milk–white water dispersion or emulsion of a synthetic resin obtained by polymerization, such as polymer medium, so called for its resemblance to rubber latex. The term is used to designate house paints made with such vehicles.

Latin cross a cross in which the arms intersect the upright shaft above the middle. This cross, the *crux immissa* of the Romans, is traditionally shown in art as the cross used in the crucifixion of Jesus, although the *tau cross* occasionally appears in crucifixion scenes. The Romans also used the St Andrew's and tau crosses in executions. The Latin cross on a three-stepped platform is known as the *Calvary cross*. See CROSS for illustration.

laurel 1. a dark reddish–brown East Indian wood with a wavy grain, strong and elastic.
2. the California laurel or baytree (*Umbellularia californica*), from the west coast of the United States, which produces a hard, strong wood used for veneer; it is golden brown and yellowish green, sometimes with dark purple blotches.
3. (also called **tepesuchil, palmwood,** or **bonyon**) a tropical American wood from the tree *Cordia alliodora*. Used in cabinetwork, it resembles American walnut in colour and density, and has a uniform texture.

lavender, oil of see OIL OF LAVENDER.

lawn 1. a fine sieve used for screening ceramic glazes. Originally made of fine cloth, the lawn may also be of brass or copper mesh. Lawns are made in several degrees of coarseness.
2. to strain through such a sieve.

law of frontality a specific emphasis on the front view of figures or objects in a work of art. This manner of composition reached its zenith during the Classical period from the 5th century BC to the 4th century AD.

lay figure a manikin of average human proportions, jointed so that it can be made to assume any desired pose, and serving as a substitute for a live model. The best lay figures are carefully made of wood with all joints

lay figure

articulated, even the knuckles, although cheaper and simpler models are more generally available. They range from life size to less than a foot in height; animal figures, especially horses, have also been made. The artist may drape a lay figure by dipping a piece of muslin or other thin cloth in a glue or weak shellac solution and moulding it into the desired shape while wet; such drapery will hold its folds through any number of sittings.

lazuline blue an old name for genuine ULTRAMARINE BLUE made from lapis lazuli.

lead a very heavy, soft metallic element. It is bluish in colour, but tarnishes to a dull grey. Lead is malleable, ductile and easily fused; it melts at 620° F. In the fine arts, it is used for making pigments, for example, WHITE LEAD, LITHARGE, and ORANGE MINERAL; as a valuable constituent of alloys; and as a component of pottery glazes. It has been used as a casting material – Greek statuettes were occasionally made from lead – but its use has declined over the centuries, although it is still common in architectural and garden sculpture. Cast lead tends to shrink as it cools, a characteristic less noticeable in small casts, which cool and solidify quickly. Lead may also be wrought or hammered into form.

lead, white see WHITE LEAD.

lead pencil a writing or drawing tool of GRAPHITE, China clay and a binder, moulded or extruded into thin rods and encased either in lacquered red cedar or in a mechanical pencil holder. The lead pencil was given its name because the prevalent 19th-century name for graphite was *black lead*. Drawing with rods of real lead would be called *lead point* (see SILVER POINT). Since the introduction of the modern lead pencil in 1795, methods of production and the quality and uniformity of the materials used, not the least important of which is the wood, have been refined to produce a superior product.

Drawing pencils are normally available in 17 grades of hardness, depending on the proportions of pure graphite, clay and binder used. 9H contains the most clay and is the hardest, and 6B, which contains practically no clay, is the softest; between H and B are two medium grades, HB and the slightly softer F. Some manufacturers are now making drawing pencils in an even wider range of degrees of hardness. Standard writing pencils are usually graded numerically, from soft to hard, by the degrees 1, 2, 2½, 3 and 4. The diameter of harder leads is comparatively smaller than that of the softer leads, since hard leads are stronger and require less bulk. The diameter of the leads in the softer degrees (usually HB to 6B) increases progressively. The very soft, fat leads are particularly suitable for sketching. The size of leads made for mechanical pencil holders usually varies somewhat less throughout the range of degrees, so all the degrees may be used in the same adjustable holder. Both adjustable (or adaptable) lead holders and holders specialized for certain diameters of lead are available.

leaf metal beaten or rolled out to extreme thinness for use in GILDING. The kinds of leaf commercially available are GOLD LEAF, SILVER LEAF, and PALLADIUM LEAF; ALUMINIUM LEAF and DUTCH METAL are also used, but for less exacting purposes. Gilding with precious-metal leaf usually requires three special pieces of equipment – a GILDER'S CUSHION, a GILDER'S KNIFE, and a GILDER'S TIP.

leaf green applied to various shades, usually middle shades, of CHROME GREEN.

lean 1. *(oil paint)* having a relatively low oil content.
2. a ground such as GESSO that contains little or no oil. See FAT OVER LEAN.

leather-hard *(clay)* no longer in the plastic state, having dried to the limit of its shrinkage but still having enough moisture to retain its original wet colour. At this stage the clay body can be handled, trimmed and carved without becoming misshapen.

lecithin a lipoid, or fatlike, substance that is found in egg yolk and other animal and vegetable matter. It has been called 'nature's emulsifier', as it is one of the most effective materials assisting in the formation and stabilization of emulsions.

lecythus or **lekythos** *(ancient Greek pottery)* a slender, cylindrical jug, tapering to a disc foot. It has a narrow, rather long neck with a flaring spout; its handle springs from its shoulder and curves in to the neck. Later forms were squatter. The lecythus was used for oils and perfumes and often included among grave offerings. See illustration at VASE SHAPES.

ledger paper a strong, durable, smooth, and rather heavy writing and drawing paper, now made in many grades. It was originally used for handwritten records and documents. Provided it is of rag composition, it is suitable for pen-and-wash drawings and other work where a pronounced texture is not desired.

leek green 1. a hue designation for a rather yellowish medium-green. **2.** a CHROME-GREEN pigment of that shade.

legitimate construction the strict application of the rules of LINEAR

PERSPECTIVE. The composition is arranged as far as possible so that objects depicted will appear parallel to the PICTURE PLANE (see PARALLEL PERSPECTIVE) and the apportionment of the picture's area among the three ZONES OF RECESSION is determined mathematically rather than by free choice. This strict delineation of the zones of recession and the predominantly parallel ordering of the composition tend to break it up into planes. Thus, although the system of legitimate construction was devised to portray recession accurately and naturally, the end effect of this system, when rigidly adhered to, is more stilted than the freer schemes of recession subsequently practised. This can be readily seen in the work of Rembrandt, a so-called borderline artist between the Renaissance and Baroque styles. His earlier paintings, which adhere fairly closely to the conventions of legitimate construction, are more stilted in their representation of perspective than his later works, which depart somewhat from the rules. Perhaps the most frequent liberty taken by an artist whose work otherwise closely follows linear perspective is a shortening of the foreground.

The term *legitimate construction* is a translation of the Italian *costruzione legittima*, used by Renaissance writers for the rigid system of geometrical perspective developed notably in the writings of Filippo Brunelleschi (1377–1446) and in Leone Battista Alberti's treatise *Della Pittura* (1432). The Italian word *legittima* carries with it some of the meaning of the Latin root *lex, legis* that is lost in the English word *legitimate*; the original term implies construction according to the laws or rules.

Leipzig yellow see CHROME YELLOW.

Leithner blue an early variety of COBALT BLUE. First made by Joseph Leithner in Vienna (1795), it was superseded by Thénard's blue.

lekythos see LECYTHUS.

Lemnian ruddle a variety of RUDDLE mined on the Aegean island of Lemnos.

lemonwood see DEGAME.

lemon yellow or **barium yellow 1.** (also called *(US)* by the unstandardized term **permanent yellow** and the obsolete name **yellow ultramarine**) barium chromate, a permanent pigment of a fairly opaque, pale banana-yellow with a greenish cast. Since lemon yellow is much weaker or lower in saturation than cadmium yellow, which has identical colour properties, cadmium yellow is preferable as an artists' colour. Lemon yellow was first produced commercially in the first quarter of the 19th century, but was not widely used until the middle of the century, when chromium compounds became more available. **2.** a general hue designation for any pale lemon-yellow pigment, as distinguished from medium or deep (golden) yellows. Like primrose yellow, lemon yellow is an elegant name that contributed to confusion in pigment nomenclature but has now been controlled in the United States by ASTM, which permits it to accompany the pigment's standardized name.

Lepanto marble *(US)* a tradename for a SHELL MARBLE, grey with white and pink markings caused by embedded fossils. It is quarried near Platts-burgh, New York.

let-down undertone. See ILLUSTRATION.

let-down pigments REDUCED PIGMENTS.

lettering brush or **show card brush** a long, flat brush with a wide, straight-cut edge and made either of red sable or camelhair set in a metal ferrule or in a quill (see LETTERING QUILL). Such a brush is used to make clean, precise lines and for lettering. A lettering brush half the width of any of the standard sizes is called a RIGGER. Other brushes that may serve the same purposes as lettering brushes are CHISEL BRUSHES; LINERS AND STRIPERS; SINGLE-STROKE BRUSHES and SIGN WRITER'S CUTTERS.

lettering brush

lettering pen a penholder, usually made of a lightweight wood, into which specially shaped metal points can be fitted. These interchangeable nibs are available in a great number of styles, from extremely broad and flat to very narrow and pointed. Some are shaped particularly for facility in writing special calligraphic hands or for making serifs and flourishes on letters. All lettering pens must be dipped, and most are constructed to take up and hold a small supply of ink either between the two layers of those pen points that have a kind of double-blade construction or in the well that is made by an S-shaped piece of metal fitted into the nib.

lettering pens An assortment of Speedball nibs.

lettering quill a brush of CAMELHAIR, long, with a straight, square edge and bound with wire in a natural or plastic quill. Lettering quills are made in many sizes and are used for lettering and decorating on glass, metal, and other smooth surfaces with oils, japans, enamels, and gold size.

letterpress 1. commercial RELIEF PRINTING with movable type and with line and halftone cuts made by PHOTOENGRAVING.

2. text, as opposed to illustrations.

letterwood see SNAKEWOOD.

levelling the property whereby fluid coating materials flow out to form a smooth surface and dry free from brushmarks. STAND OIL is notable for its levelling property, which it imparts to oil paints, mediums and varnishes made with it. A smooth surface is desirable in some oil painting styles, but the textural effects of brushstrokes are more frequently preferred.

levigation 1. the process of grinding a material in a wet state, as in the preparation of paint pigments or the processing of clay for use in ceramics.

2. the separation by sedimentation of fine particles from a coarse material suspended in a liquid. In purifying and grading bulk materials such as clay or whiting, the wet material is run or pumped with added water into settling tanks, where the heavier, coarser particles settle much more rapidly than the finer particles and are separated out.

3. the entire process of grinding, settling, and separation into grades of fineness, as in the production of WHITING and SLIP CLAY.

4. the wet grinding of a surface to make it smooth or to produce on it a desired texture, as in the graining of a LITHOGRAPH STONE.

levigator a hand tool for grinding a flat surface with powdered abrasive and water, such as the heavy steel disc used in graining a LITHOGRAPH STONE.

This disc has an off-centre handle by means of which it can be revolved on the stone, grinding the surface with an abrasive (such as Carborundum) and water. It may also have wells, with openings at the bottom, by means of which the abrasive and water are fed onto the surface of the stone.

Leyden blue an early name for COBALT BLUE.

library paste a ready-for-use white paste, usually made from dextrin sold in jars. It does not stain paper and is generally accepted as a product of good quality for permanent application.

life cast see LIFE MASK.

life drawing the drawing of the human figure from a living model. Life drawing and other stylistic exercises such as DRAWING FROM NATURE and DRAWING FROM THE ANTIQUE OR DRAWING FROM CAST were in the past always part of an artist's academic training. See also ACADEMY FIGURE.

life mask or **life cast** an impression of the face of a living person. The technique for making a life mask was probably developed during mediaeval times and was practised during the Renaissance. Cennino Cennini, writing in the 15th century, gives detailed directions for greasing the subject's face, inserting a double-stemmed breathing tube in the subject's nostrils and applying plaster to form a mould from which a cast may be made. He also gives directions for casting the whole nude body by building a wooden form around the subject. See also DEATH MASK.

life-size *(figure sculpture)* of the same size as the actual model. Life-size statues are smaller than HEROIC and COLOSSAL figures.

lifting *(painting)* the technique of creating a special textural effect resembling that of the DRAGGING STROKE. A sheet of cloth or paper is laid on the surface of wet paint, rubbed lightly and lifted away, taking splotches of paint with it and thus altering the surface. The MONOTYPE necessarily has much of this lifted quality. See also DECALCOMANIA.

light an area or point of high VALUE in a picture as distinguished from the low and middle values that ordinarily occupy most of its area. See HIGHLIGHT.

lightfastness COLOUR STABILITY or the ability of a substance to withstand exposure to daylight without fading or changing colour. Truly lightfast pigments are not affected by daylight under the indoor conditions in which a work of art is normally exposed.

light green oxide a bright green pigment containing oxides of cobalt, nickel, and titanium. It is lightfast and permanent, and has medium tinting strength.

lightness see VALUE.

light red or **Antwerp red** a permanent pigment composed of 99% iron (ferric) oxide, a FURNACE PRODUCT made from steel-mill wastes. Light red has a bright, scarlet top tone, and when mixed with whites yields salmon pinks, as distinguished from the bluish mass tone and rose pinks of Indian red, the other type of pure iron oxide pigment. However, compared with brilliant red pigments like the cadmium reds and alizarin crimson, all the iron oxides would be referred to as *brick reds*. Light red and Indian red, which are solidly opaque and have great tinting strength and hiding power, have entirely replaced their native-earth counterparts on the artist's palette. In the United States, light red was formerly called *English red*. Other names no longer in use are *Prussian red*, *colcothar*, *morelle salt*, and *Persian red*. Both light red and Indian red are also called red oxides.

lignum vitae the heaviest, hardest and most dense of the commercially available woods. Although it is difficult to carve, some sculptors value it for the rugged, stone-like effects that can be created with it. Its colour varies from a light olive-green to a blackish brown. Its grain is uniform and fine, and it rubs up to a high natural polish. The tree (*Guaiacum officinale*) is native to the West Indies, Central America and northern South America.

lime calcium oxide, made by calcining or roasting native calcium carbonate with wood in a simple brick kiln. Calcium carbonate occurs plentifully in the form of limestone, marble, chalk, oyster shells, etc. Lime is an active, caustic alkali; when it is mixed with water, there is a violent reaction that generates much heat and forms calcium hydroxide, or slaked lime. Slaked lime, mixed with just enough water to make a soft paste (lime putty), is mixed with sand to form MORTAR. When the mortar dries, the particles of lime adhere very strongly to one another; the sand in the mortar stabilizes it by creating a constant volume below which the drying lime cannot shrink. When all the water has evaporated, the calcium hydroxide begins to be converted to calcium carbonate by reacting with carbon dioxide in the atmosphere. Eventually it becomes solid calcium carbonate, chemically the same as the original limestone or marble.

Carbonation below the surface may take years to be complete. A solution of lime is called LIMEWATER. Lime in lump or powder form is sometimes called *quicklime*, to distinguish it from slaked lime.

lime blue a variety of BREMEN BLUE in which slaked lime replaces salt in the manufacturing process. Used as a limeproof colour during the 19th century, lime blue has since been replaced by synthetic organic pigments. Neuwied blue is lime blue sold in DROP PIGMENT form. Variants of lime blue were also sold in the 19th century under the name MOUNTAIN BLUE.

limeproof pigment a pigment that maintains its colour stability in contact with alkaline substances. Limeproof pigments are suitable for use in FRESCO painting and in coloured-cement work.

lime putty lime that has been slaked with water and aged; it is a soft, plastic paste that is mixed with sand or marble dust to make the several types of mortar used in the plaster support of a painting in FRESCO. The lime used in fresco plastering must be pure or RICH LIME, and the putty must be aged for at least six months. There seems to be no limit to the improvement in plasticity and freedom from defects (such as POPPING) that is afforded by prolonged ageing. Since the Renaissance, Italian painters have aged their slaked lime in casks stored in pits dug below the frost line; such hoards are said to have been handed down through several generations. Aged lime putty used to be carried in stock by some building-supply firms, chiefly for use in ornamental plasters, but it has become increasingly scarce as the call for plastering of high craftsmanship has decreased.

limeskin see FRESCO.

limestone a crystalline stone of sedimentary origin, usually granular in appearance, composed chiefly of calcium carbonate. MARBLE is a metamorphic form of limestone. Limestone is softer, more easily worked and less compact than marble. When polished, it takes on a mat finish rather than the glossy surface that is characteristic of marble. In the United States, some of the more closely grained, highly coloured or intricately patterned varieties of limestone are sometimes called marble; examples are BATESVILLE MARBLE and BLACK-AND-GOLD MARBLE. Most of the limestones used in sculpture are buff-coloured or grey. Certain so-called oolitic limestones, such as CAEN STONE, are composed of tiny, rounded granules of calcium carbonate bound together compactly and resembling miniature fish roe.

French limestones enjoy a high reputation among sculptors for their excellent working and aesthetic qualities. Some of the more celebrated of these buff-coloured stones are Caen stone, Euville, Lotharinga, Normandeaux, and Peuron. Another limestone is TUFA, occasionally used by the ancients for sculpture. Solnhofen stone and other grey Bavarian limestones are the preferred stones for lithography (see LITHOGRAPH STONE).

limewash painting see SECCO.

limewater a solution of lime, used to saturate plaster before applying secco colours. Since lime is only partially soluble in cold water and still less soluble in hot water, limewater is always quite weak.

LIMITED EDITION

limited edition a set number of replicas of a work of art, of which the plate, mould, or die is destroyed or mutilated after the desired number of copies has been made. The practice of limiting editions and numbering PROOFS originated with ETCHING and DRYPOINT, in which the quality of the proofs declines as the copper plate begins to show evidence of wear. By thus limiting an edition to first-rate examples of the artist's work, the artist protects both his or her artistic integrity and the value of the work to the collector. There is no technical reason for limiting or numbering editions of works of art that are made by processes capable of producing an indefinite number of uniformly good copies, such as lithography, serigraphy, and casting methods that employ durable moulds. Editions are frequently limited, however, for financial reasons; by ensuring the relative rarity of the artist's work, he or she increases its value. See also ORIGINAL PRINT; RESTRIKE.

limited palette see RESTRICTED PALETTE.

limner 1. a painter of MINIATURES or, sometimes, watercolours, during the 17th to the 19th century.

2. (US) an itinerant and often self-taught painter, especially of portraits, up to the early 19th century.

3. (US) any painter.

4. a decorator of mediaeval manuscripts.

Limoges enamel a type of fine ENAMEL in which the design, frequently a realistic picture, is painted with ceramic colours on porcelain or on metal that has already been given a smooth coat of white enamel and fired. It is distinguished from other kinds of decorative enamelling by the absence of metal separators, or *cloisons*. It takes its name from the town of Limoges, France, where an excellent grade of kaolin, or fine porcelain clay, is found, and where fine porcelain has been made since the 18th century.

linear relating to the dominance of line rather than mass as a means of defining form in painting, sculpture and architecture. It was first used in this sense by Heinrich Wölfflin in his *Principles of Art History* (1915), along with its opposite, PAINTERLY (*Ger. malerisch*). Linear drawing or painting, for example, is draughtsmanlike, with modelling depicted primarily in terms of line and the forms clearly delimited. This sharp outlining of forms restricts the movements of the viewer's eye or directs the eye along a definite course; and tends to make the work appear more static. Painterly work, by contrast, de-emphasizes the edges of forms, leaving the eye able to wander more freely.

Italian painters from Giotto to Botticelli used a linear style, as did Dürer and most of the early Flemish painters. Tempera, their medium, is essentially a linear technique. In the work of later painters, oil painting was adopted to meet the preference for techniques that permit softer edges for forms, and the *malerisch* style of painting became dominant. *Dry painting* is a pejorative term sometimes used for linear painting. See also RUBÉNISME.

linear perspective the standard system of geometric PERSPECTIVE. It is based on the actual or imagined construction on the PICTURE PLANE of a perpendicular grille of parallel lines that converge on the HORIZON LINE at VANISHING POINTS. The picture plane is divided horizontally into ZONES OF RECESSION. There are three systems with which a rectangular solid may be depicted in linear perspective: PARALLEL PERSPECTIVE, ANGULAR PERSPECTIVE and OBLIQUE PERSPECTIVE. Linear perspective, which was clearly formulated and competently practised during the Renaissance, is distinguished from the colour-based system of AERIAL PERSPECTIVE and from special systems, like SOTTO IN SÙ, which is used to solve special perspective problems. When the rules of linear perspective are strictly applied, the system is known as LEGITIMATE CONSTRUCTION. However, most treatises and instructional handbooks written since the 18th century on the use of perspective admonish the artist not to apply the rules of perspective too mechanically.

linear quinacridone see QUINACRIDONE RED.

line drawing 1. a drawing in which forms are depicted exclusively by lines, as in OUTLINE DRAWING and CONTOUR DRAWING.

2. a drawing done in lines or masses with pen, pencil, crayon or drybrush that is used as an original for ENGRAVING, especially a drawing that can be reproduced with a linecut, that is, without the use of HALFTONES.

line engraving see ENGRAVING.

linen the fabric of which artists' canvas is made. Linen is made of fibres

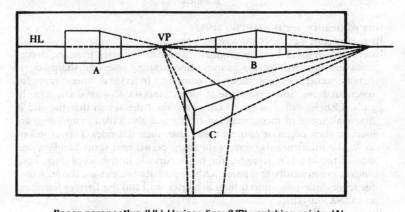

linear perspective (HL) Horizon line; (VP) vanishing points; (A) rectangular solid shown in parallel, or one-point, perspective; (B) solid in angular, or two-point, perspective; (C) solid in oblique, or three-point, perspective. Note in oblique perspective the convergence of a third set of lines to a third vanishing point not on the horizon line. Here, in a bird's-eye view, the convergence is downward. If the page is viewed upside down, figure C is seen in a worm's-eye view, with an upward convergence of its vertical lines.

of the flax plant. Although virtually every textile fabric has been used to prepare canvas for oil painting at some time or place, linen remains the first choice because it excels in durability, strength, stability, receptiveness to grounds, and ability to retain the bold texture of its weave, fine or coarse, after application of a ground. Most of the strong, unbleached linen woven especially for artists' canvas comes from Belgium and Ireland. Close-woven fabrics are most desirable; heavy linen is preferable to lightweight; and a square weave, with warp and weft of equal threads, is considered best. Twill weaves were popular in the 18th and early 19th centuries.

linenfold, linen pattern or **linen scroll** a decorative relief design or motif, representing a flatly folded cloth. This traditional relief pattern first came into use in Gothic woodwork of the late 16th century.

linenfold

line of beauty see HOGARTH'S LINE.

line of vision see CENTRAL VISUAL RAY.

liners and stripers brushes originally designed for coach painters, decorators and sign writers, for painting fine, straight lines and sharp edges. Artists sometimes use them in painting. Individual liners vary for specialized use. Some are made of long CAMELHAIR, with wide, straight ends. Others, called *angular liners*, have the hairs set so that the end is diagonal; some of these, made of bristle and also called *fresco liners*, are used on their edges or corners rather than their flat sides. *Dagger stripers* look like miniature daggers, with sharp points and short handles; one side of the brush is straight, the other curved. In the *sword liner*, both sides curve inwardly to a point. Other specialty brushes are the *brick liner* for representing the mortar lines in a brick wall and the *Dresden liner* used in CHINA PAINTING.

liner's wheel see BANDING WHEEL.

lining *(conservation of oil paintings)* the process of cementing a piece of fresh linen to the back of an old canvas that has become too weak to withstand further ageing or whose deterioration is too severe or extensive to be rectified by local treatments such as patching. Most paintings are now lined with the use of a thermoplastic adhesive compound; the support of the painting is impregnated with the adhesive, thus preserving the picture from further decay. The technique is carried out under vacuum on a HOT TABLE. Formerly, lining was done with animal glue, hot, heavy

liners and stripers (top to bottom) Angular liner, dagger striper, long-haired liner, sword liner.

irons and powerful clamps, all of which were potentially hazardous to the painting. The term *relining* is a common misnomer for the first application of the lining process to a painting.

linocut or **linoleum cut** a popular type of relief print (see RELIEF PRINTING), made by a process similar to woodcutting (see WOODCUT), that employs a block constructed of a layer of thick linoleum glued to a block of wood, the whole made TYPE-HIGH so that it may be used in a printing press. The soft linoleum surface is easily carved in relief with the same tools used in woodcutting (see WOODCUT TOOLS); special linoleum-cutting tools with lightweight, replaceable blades are also available. The block is inked with a brayer and printed like a woodcut, either by hand or in a press. It is durable and holds up well through many printings. Linoleum cuts are less expressive than woodcuts but are admirably suited to broad work and simple posterlike designs. The process can be mastered easily. Although the challenge of overcoming the resistance of an intractable material is virtually absent, some artists, such as Matisse and Picasso, have liked the medium and used it to good advantage.

linoxyn the tough, solid material formed when linseed oil is converted to a solid, as in the drying of oil paint or the manufacture of linoleum. See DRYING OIL.

linseed oil the principal DRYING OIL used in paints. It is expressed from the seeds of the flax plant, which is grown in all cold and temperate countries of the world. Quality is governed by the variety of seed, the absence of impurities (mostly foreign or weed seeds) and the degree to which the oil has been chemically or physically refined. Linseed oil of the best quality is superior to all other drying oils in resistance to embrittlement combined with colour retention or resistance to yellowing.

lipoid a substance whose superficial properties resemble those of a fat or oil.

lipophile a substance that is attracted to or easily combined with a fatty or oily material.

liquid drier a DRIER prepared in liquid form for use as an additive to paint, as distinguished from a solid or powdered material that is cooked into an oil or varnish.

liquid silicate any of various fluid silicon compounds, including sodium silicate or waterglass, a thick, viscous fluid with alkaline properties, and potassium silicate, as well as the SILICON ESTERS. Silica, which occurs in nature in the form of sand or quartz and as the sinter in several types of rock, is one of the most inert and durable of materials, as are some of the rocks composed of various silicates. A paint with a silica binder could therefore be expected to survive the most severe atmospheric conditions. From the early 19th century, when waterglass became available, artists and chemists made innumerable efforts to employ it as a vehicle in paints for mural painting, but their efforts were unsuccessful. The most nearly successful was a complex and impractical process called MINERAL PAINT-ING. The problem was solved in the 1930s, when the silicon esters became available. Paints with an ETHYL SILICATE vehicle have a pure silica binder and may be expected to withstand many of the adverse conditions that would destroy fresco and other traditional paints.

literary depicting a story. The word is applied to storytelling painting, sculpture, drawing or graphic works. Used pejoratively, it implies that the aesthetic value of the work has been sacrificed to some degree. The adjective *narrative* may be applied to storytelling elements that do not diminish a work as art.

lith. or **litho.** see IMP.

litharge lead monoxide; a heavy, yellowish powder which, when cooked with linseed oil, acts as a powerful DRIER. It is also used (chiefly in Britain and Europe) as a low-fired flux in ceramics. In the past it was occasionally used as a base for lake pigments. Litharge was known to the Greeks as *lithargyron* and to the Romans as *plumbum ustum*. MASSICOT is a lead oxide similar to litharge, but somewhat deeper or reddish in hue.

lithochromy the technique of painting on stone.

lithographic crayon or **litho crayon** an oily crayon with which the drawing is applied to the stone, plate or transfer paper (see TRANSFER LITHOGRAPHY) in LITHOGRAPHY. It is made of varying proportions of wax, soap, and lampblack – to which may be added spermaceti, shellac, tallow, or a combination of these – and it is sold commercially in a peel-off paper casing, like an ordinary grease pencil, or in square crayon-stick form. Lithographic crayons in stick form are available in seven degrees, from 00 (extra soft) to 5 (containing copal for extra hardness), while the pencil form is sold in five degrees. When printing ink is applied to the lithograph stone or plate, it adheres to only those areas that have been drawn on with the crayon but not to the unmarked, dampened areas. TUSCHE, a black liquid that contains the same ingredients as the litho crayon, is applied to the stone or plate with a pen or brush. Lithographic crayons are also often used for drawing on paper.

lithographic etch 1. the first step in creating the nonprinting areas on the stone in LITHOGRAPHY, that is, desensitizing the stone so that areas not drawn upon will, when wet, repel lithographic ink.

2. a solution used in this process.

After the drawing has been completed with LITHOGRAPHIC CRAYON or TUSCHE, the stone is sponged or brushed with a solution of gum arabic, water and a small amount of nitric acid. The solution is absorbed on all exposed areas of the stone, however minuscule, but the greasy printing areas are not affected by it. The etch is fanned dry to get its full, concentrated effect, and then the surface gum is sponged away with water. The adsorbed layer that remains is strengthened and made more durable in the subsequent process, GUMMING UP. Although there is no actual etching, or biting below the plane surface, in a lithographic etch, the process has always been so called.

lithographic points steel points or needles of various degrees of sharpness, used in a screw-grip holder for scratching crayon areas on a LITHOGRAPH STONE to create white-line effects.

lithograph ink the ink used in printing lithographs, similar in composition to other PRINTING INKS but somewhat less tacky than the ink used in letterpress printing. Lithograph ink, which is available in all colours in tubes and tins, is strongly pigmented and fairly opaque; a prepared extender is used to reduce a colour or make it more transparent. The consistency and behaviour of ready-made lithograph ink can be altered by the addition of a LITHO VARNISH. Lithographic TUSCHE, the black, greasy fluid used for brush drawing on the lithograph stone in place of or in addition to lithographic crayon, should never be referred to as *ink*. Lithograph ink and tusche differ in composition, purpose and performance.

lithograph plate a thin metal plate that has been treated so as to attract oil and repel water. It is lighter and less cumbersome than a traditional LITHOGRAPH STONE.

lithograph stone a thick, heavy, flat slab of limestone used in LITHOGRAPHY. The face of the stone is ground to a lightly grained surface to prepare it for being drawn on with LITHOGRAPHIC CRAYON or TUSCHE. The blue-grey Bavarian limestone that is mined at Solnhofen, Germany – on which the technique of lithography was discovered and perfected – is still preferred by most artists, though similar limestones are also used. A somewhat softer yellowish-tan variety can also be used for lithography, but it does not take as satisfactory a grain or hold up as well when a large edition is printed. Some lithographers, sticklers for maintaining the last degree of the autographic quality of the technique, pull their proofs on paper that matches the blue-grey or tan colour of the stone used.

Lithograph stones are too cumbersome to be handled freely, for they are hard but brittle and must be relatively thick to survive the stress of printing. The greater their surface area, the thicker they must be: a stone measuring 10 × 12 inches is more than 2 inches thick and weighs about 30 pounds; one 18 × 22 inches is about three inches thick and weighs about 100 pounds. The stone must be grained each time it is used. (A stone may be cleaned, refinished, and reused as soon as the complete edition of the previous drawing has been pulled.) Graining, which serves to make the surface of the stone perfectly level and free from tool marks, gives the surface a fine texture that, reproduced in the proofs, is characteristic of the lithograph. This texture on the stone permits better adhesion of the litho crayon or tusche to its surface. Graining is achieved by placing two stones face-to-face, with water and a fine abrasive such as carborundum or sand between them, and rotating the top stone by hand. This process gives a grain to both stones simultaneously. A single stone may be ground with a LEVIGATOR or with an abrasive block made commercially for such purposes.

lithography a PLANOGRAPHIC PRINTING process in which proofs are pulled on a special LITHO-PRESS from a flat surface that has been sensitized by chemical means so that the ink takes on the design areas only and is repelled by the blank areas. Lithography was invented in 1798 by Alois Senefelder of Solnhofen in Germany, who discovered that when a smooth-grained local limestone was drawn upon with a greasy crayon, and then wetted with water and inked with a ROLLER (see ROLLING UP), the oily printing ink would adhere only to the greasy drawing, making it possible to pull prints from the inked stone. The actual lithographic process, although based on the simple principle of the attraction of an oily ink by an oily surface and its repulsion by water, is somewhat more complicated. Several operations are necessary to create an absorbed water-attractive, grease-repellent condition on the blank parts of the stone (see GUMMING UP) and to give the areas that have been drawn on with the crayon an adsorbed fatty-acid layer that will take the ink with precision (see LITHOGRAPHIC ETCH). After its discovery, lithography rapidly became an important commercial reproduction process and a popular artists' medium. It has been refined and improved through the years, so that in both black-on-white and colour printmaking, it has held its own with intaglio and relief processes. It is a versatile printmaking technique. In addition to LITHOGRAPHIC CRAYON, TUSCHE – a water-miscible black liquid that contains the greasy ingredients of the crayon – can also be applied to the stone with a pen or brush. Crayon areas may be scratched with LITHOGRAPHIC POINTS. Although the LITHOGRAPH STONE gives softer and usually more expressive prints with finer nuances of line, an aluminium plate with an oxidized surface layer, or a zinc plate grained to imitate a stone surface, are also used in lithography; these have the advantage of being lightweight and portable. In TRANSFER LITHOGRAPHY the drawing is first done with litho crayon on paper and then transferred to the stone. When a lithograph is printed by the OFFSET method, it is not reversed. The process is known as *offset lithography*. The most important commercial application of lithography is photo-offset printing, in which the type and artwork to be printed are transferred to the plate by a special photographic process. Lithography is very well adapted to colour printing (see COLOUR LITHOGRAPHY). In the relatively short time since the invention of the process, artists have been continually attracted to lithography by the variety of effects it permits and by its autographic qualities (see AUTOLITHOGRAPHY).

The early history of lithography is dominated by such great French artists as Daumier, Géricault and Delacroix, although the process was always popular in its native Germany and was also taken up in Spain by Goya. Although lithography suffered a slight decline in popularity during the last four decades of the 19th century, it underwent a great fin-de-siècle revival in the hands of Degas, Bonnard, Munch and especially Toulouse-Lautrec, who executed 370 lithographs in the last ten years of his life. Throughout the 20th century lithography has been extensively used by many great artists, including Picasso, Bracque, and Miró.

lithol red a bright, cherry-red, synthetic organic pigment of fair permanence. Lithol red is used in printing inks and industrial paints, but it has been rejected for artists' use, since it is not sufficiently lightproof and most varieties bleed in oil.

lithopone zinc sulphide coprecipitated with barium sulphate; it is a dense white pigment used in house paints and industrial coatings. Because it is inferior to the widely accepted FLAKE WHITE, ZINC WHITE and TITANIUM WHITE, lithopone is not recommended for artists' colours; it is, however, suitable for use in GROUNDS. The first English patent (Orr's white) for the manufacture of lithopone was issued in 1874 to John Orr, presumably also its inventor. An early name for lithopone is *oleum white*.

litho-press the printing press on which proofs are pulled from a LITHO-GRAPH STONE or plate (see LITHOGRAPHY). The stone is placed drawing-side up on the bed of the press, inked, and covered with a sheet of damp paper, which is in turn covered with a piece of dry paper and a *tympan*. The tympan, a sheet of strong fibreboard, protects the paper as the stone is run through the press and evenly distributes the pressure of the scraper. The scraper, a leather-covered wooden bar under which the stone passes as the bed is cranked through the press, presses on the tympan, the top side of which is greased to facilitate its passage under the scraper. The pressure of the scraper effects a transfer of ink from the stone to the damp paper that covers it. An OFFSET press, employed for most commercial lithography, may also be used by artists.

litho varnish see BURNT-OIL VARNISH.

litmus a NATURAL DYESTUFF obtained from several lichens. Used by chemists as an indicator, litmus that is red turns blue on contact with alkali; when blue, it turns red on contact with acid. Two other natural colouring matters, orchil and turnsole, behave similarly. Litmus is not sufficiently stable for use as an artists' colour.

little masters the name given to a group of 16th-century German engravers, whose work comprised exceedingly small plates depicting scenes from the Bible, classical mythology and daily life – each a tiny masterpiece of its kind.

livering the solidification of tubed oil colour into a firm, rubbery mass, rendering it useless. Livering is caused by the reaction of impurities in the pigments, especially free sulphur, with the oil. It does not occur in colours made of high-quality, well-washed artists' pigments that have been skilfully ground in the best oils.

liver of sulphur a common name for potassium sulphide, used in recipes for staining or colouring bronze and other metals.

loaded *(painting)* fully charged. Loaded lights are the palest areas painted thickly, accompanied by darks of average or less than average thickness. A loaded brush is one that is charged with paint to its full capacity.

local colour 1. the true colour of an object in ordinary daylight, as distinguished from its apparent colour when influenced by unusual lighting, abnormal atmospheric conditions, reflected colour, and the like.

2. the normal colour of a thing, as distinguished from its rendition in an anomalous coloration that is merely the predilection of the artist.

logwood or **campeachy wood** a blood-red NATURAL DYESTUFF obtained from *Haematoxylon campechianum*, a tree indigenous to Central America, Mexico, and the West Indies. It produces blue, black, and violet colours by chemical treatment. Brought to Europe soon after the discovery of America, logwood was one of the most important of the natural colouring matters until the 19th century, when it was superseded by synthetic dyestuffs of superior brilliance. Logwood was formerly used to make a black ink; it is still in use for dyeing textiles black. Lake pigments made from logwood are *campeachy lake*, a dark reddish-purple, and *vegetable violet*.

lointain *(Fr.* background) the most distant part of a landscape. The term, little used in English, refers especially to those elements on or near the HORIZON LINE.

lokao or **Chinese green** a green NATURAL DYESTUFF of Chinese origin, prepared from the leaves, roots, bark, and twigs of *Rhamnus utilis, R. chlorophorus* and other buckthorns by treating an aqueous extract with lime. Among the more permanent of the natural dyestuffs, lokao is also one of the few green ones.

London white an obsolete, 19th century, name for WHITE LEAD.

long-oil varnish see OIL LENGTH.

lost-pattern casting, full mould casting, cavityless casting or **vaporization casting** a relatively new method of casting metals. The original is made of FOAM PLASTIC, usually expanded polystyrene. This positive is packed in FOUNDRY SAND, which forms the MOULD or negative. When molten metal is poured into the mould (that is, over the polystyrene), the plastic is vaporized, or lost, leaving the sand negative filled with metal. This method of casting, developed for sculptural use, is currently being adapted to industrial purposes.

lost-wax process, investment casting or *(Fr.)* **cire perdue** a method of casting metal in a mould, the cavity of which is formed with wax that is then heated and drained. The process is used especially for hollow bronze statues, but has also been adapted to the multiple production of small, solid objects such as statuettes and jewellery (see CENTRIFUGAL CASTING). A plaster cast is first made of the original. Then a negative (hollow) gelatin PIECE MOULD is made of the plaster cast. The piece mould is assembled, and the inside is coated with molten wax, to form a hollow wax model. This in turn is packed with a CORE of FOUNDRY SAND, at which point it may be corrected and reworked by the sculptor. Rods of wax are attached to the wax model, and the entire figure is encased, or invested, in heat-resistant plaster or clay. Metal PINS are inserted to keep the core in place. Next, the whole structure is placed in an oven and baked until the plaster mould has become dry and the hot wax has run away through vents created by the melting of the wax rods. The mould is then packed in sand, well supported by bricks, and molten bronze is poured through the vents into the space vacated by the melted, or lost, wax. After cooling, the inner sand is shaken out and the cast is cleaned and finished. Most cast metal sculpture is made by the lost-wax process; SAND CASTING, the other principal method of casting metal, is more commonly used in industry.

Lost-wax casting is a time-honoured technique. Greek craftsmen were using the method expertly by the fifth century AD, and it was known also by the ancient Egyptians, who cast over a core of ash.

Lotharinga stone see LIMESTONE.

loutrophoros a tall ancient Greek ceremonial vase with double handles. It was used to carry holy water for a bride's ritual bath and became a customary symbol on grave markers for girls who had died unwed. See VASE SHAPES for illustration.

Louvain school a group of 15th-century Flemish artists. Louvain became a leading centre of humanistic culture after the founding of the university there in 1425. The most influential of the Louvain painters was Dirk Bouts the Elder, whose strong realism was kept within the bounds of a refined style.

low colour colour of low intensity; weak or faint colour.

low key see KEY.

low relief see RELIEF.

luce di sotto see LUMINOUS.

Lucite see ACRYLIC RESIN.

Lukasbruder see NAZARENES.

lumachelle see SHELL MARBLE.

lumbang oil or **candlenut oil** a DRYING OIL from the Philippines that has been used in industry as a substitute for linseed oil, to which it is inferior. There is no record of its use in artists' materials.

lumbayao Philippine MAHOGANY.

luminism 1. the depiction of the play of light, of clear, brilliant lighting effects, or of glowing light, as a major characteristic of a painter's work. **2.** any school or method of painting, especially those of the latter half of the 19th century in France (such as IMPRESSIONISM and POINTILLISM), the principal concern of which is the technique of expressing the effects of light.

luminous appearing to give off a diffuse glow from within. For example, a clear oil or varnish GLAZE over a tempera painting on a brilliant white gesso ground has a luminous quality that an opaque gouache painting lacks. The Italian term *luce di sotto* (light from beneath) refers to this quality.

luminous paint paint that glows in the dark; a coating that contains a pigment called a phosphor (usually a form of zinc or calcium sulphide), which stores light when exposed to it for a length of time, emitting it as a greenish or bluish glow when the light source is removed. Luminous paint differs from fluorescent (daylight fluorescent) paint, which glows normally in daylight but must be specially activated with ultraviolet light to glow in the dark. Because luminous paint glows for a relatively short time, signs and other markings made with it serve best in situations where the light is renewed after a few hours or where its period of use is not prolonged, as in theatrical effects. Sometimes a trace of radioactive material is added, producing a continuous excitation rather than a gradually decaying one. This process is used in marking watch, clock and instrument dials with luminous paint. It cannot be employed in general painting because of the dangerously toxic nature of the radioactivity. See also FLUORESCENT PAINT.

lunette a semicircular panel, often over a window or doorway.

lustre surface GLOSS. Types of lustre include satiny or dull, vitreous (a hard, porcelain effect), nacreous (pearly) and metallic. See also SHEEN.

lustreware porcelain or earthenware decorated with a metallic, iridescent glaze.

lute 1. to seal an opening or leak in any vessel or tube with a compound of putty-like or semipaste consistency.

 2. *(ceramics)* to stop an opening or crevice in a wet clay body, or to join sections of a piece of pottery, especially using SLIP as an adhesive.

luteolin the yellow colouring principle of WELD.

Lutschism the Russian word for a native 20th-century movement in painting known in the West as RAYONNISM.

lye a powerfully active or caustic alkaline substance. Its corrosive or destructive action is effective in such processes as the removal of incrustations from metals. Ordinary lye is sodium hydroxide (caustic soda).

Lysippian proportions a canon of proportions for the human figure developed by Lysippus, a sculptor who worked at the court of Alexander the Great in the 4th century BC. Lysippus's ideal of the human figure differed radically from that of his predecessor, Polyclitus (see POLYCLITAN SCHOOL), who had also laid down laws of proportion, and even from the more graceful figures of Praxiteles. Lysippus's bodies were more slender and had rather small heads. He made great advances in conceiving the figure in three-dimensional terms, which made it possible to view sculptures with equal pleasure from several viewpoints.

lyrical abstraction the name given to a 20th-century style of painting that is virtually synonymous with ABSTRACT EXPRESSIONISM, but characterized by special attention to the use of colour, colour that is often rather luxurious in nature.

M

Macassar ebony see EBONY.

macchia (*It.* spot, stain, sketch, outline) **1.** (*pl.* **macchie**) the landscapes of a group of late 19th-century Florentine realist painters, that were painted in patches, or spots, of colour in order to emphasize the effects of chiaroscuro. These painters were consequently given the name *Macchiaioli*, a term that was later extended to all late 19th- and early 20th-century Tuscan painters whose tendencies toward realism had a strong foundation in the colour theories of Impressionism. Hence, *macchia* is sometimes used to mean an impressionistic painting or sketch.
2. the first underpainting in an oil painting, in which masses of light and shade are blocked out.

mace-head, matter or **mattoir** a tool used in CRAYON MANNER and MEZZOTINT, consisting of an irregularly spiked, rounded knob at the end of a handle of wood or metal. The wood-handled tool is most often used in crayon manner; in this technique, it is manipulated on the plate to create lines and areas that will print with a chalklike graininess. The metal-handled mace-head is used in mezzotint to go over those areas of the plate where the engraver wants a heavier burr than that produced by the rocker.

mace-head

McGuilp see MEGILP.

madder brown a brown alizarin lake, formerly made from madder. See RUBENS MADDER.

madder lake see NATURAL ROSE MADDER.

maestà (*It.* majesty) **1.** a mediaeval and Renaissance religious painting of the Virgin and Child enthroned, surrounded by angels and other symbols of glory. The most famous example is Duccio's altarpiece for Siena Cathedral, completed in 1311.
2. a painting of Christ enthroned in majesty.

Magen David see SOLOMON'S SEAL.

magenta or **fuchsine** a brilliant synthetic dye of poor stability. Magenta is widely used as a hue designation for a deep, dark, purplish red or bluish maroon.

magic realism a type of 20th century painting in which objects are painted with a precise kind of REALISM, but which paradoxically projects an effect of the fantastic resulting from the disparate juxtaposition of time-space elements, for example, an illuminated street light at high noon. Chirico and other painters of the *scuola metafisca* in Rome (see METAPHYSICAL PAINTING), French and Dutch painters of the 1920s, and some American social painters of the 1930s all practised magic realism. In the 1950s and 1960s, magic realism consisted of infusing ordinary subject matter with an air of mystery or strangeness by the use of flat colour without cast shadows in a kind of simplified or selective *trompe l' œil* technique.

magilp see MEGILP.

Magna *(US)* the tradename for a manufacturer's line of artists' ACRYLIC COLOURS and their isolating varnish.

magnesia white 1. see MAGNESIUM CARBONATE.

2. see MAGNESIUM OXIDE.

3. see MAGNESITE.

magnesite or **magnesia white** native magnesium carbonate, calcined for use in OXYCHLORIDE CEMENT, and occasionally used in powdered form as a FILLER or INERT PIGMENT.

magnesium carbonate or **magnesia white** a white pigment, probably the whitest of all pigments. It has the same general properties as PRECIPI-TATED CHALK. Magnesium carbonate is manufactured in two forms: a very fluffy, lightweight powder, not recommended for artists' use; and a heavy or dense variety suitable for use as an INERT PIGMENT. It is sometimes substituted for chalk in gesso by enthusiasts who want to use the whitest material in existence, but the practical advantage is nil.

magnesium oxychloride cement see OXYCHLORIDE CEMENT.

magnetic black iron oxide 1. native BLACK IRON OXIDE, which is strongly magnetic.

2. the synthetic counterpart, MARS black (see MARS PIGMENTS), also strongly magnetic.

mahlstick, maulstick or *(Fr.)* **appuie-main** a light, inflexible wooden rod, three or four feet long, which the painter uses as a support or rest to steady brush or hand while executing particularly detailed and exacting work. The typical mahlstick is ball-shaped at one end; the ball is sometimes covered with a piece of soft leather to minimize possible damage to the canvas. Some mahlsticks are joined in sections like fishing rods for portability; some are made of aluminium with screw joints and rubber-ball ends. The conventional mahlstick is frequently replaced by a yard-stick or other improvised prop. See also BRIDGE.

mahogany any of several species of close-grained hardwood from trees of the genus *Swietenia;* sometimes called *acajou.* Although it is strong and hard enough to be extremely durable, it is still easy to saw, plane,

mahlstick

and carve. It has less tendency than many other hardwoods to shrink, swell, or warp. Its only disadvantage as a wood for construction or cabinetwork is its weakness under lateral strain. In colour, it may be anywhere from light brown to dark or reddish brown.

Varieties of true mahogany grow in Mexico, the West Indies, and Central and South America. The most desirable varieties come from Mexico, Cuba, and the Dominican Republic. The latter, called San Domingo mahogany, is particularly esteemed.

Jequitiba (genus *Cariniana*) is also known as *Brazilian mahogany* or *Colombian mahogany*. *Philippine mahogany* is the popular name for two distinct woods: *lumbayao* (*Tarrietia javanica*), which has a purplish colour lacking in true mahogany, and *seraya* (genus *Shorea*), a wood from the Malay Peninsula that ranges from pink to purple-brown in colour. *African mahogany* or *red khaya* (*Khaya senegalensis*) may be anywhere from pink to red. Both Philippine and African mahogany have splintery and softwood characteristics that make them difficult to carve; they are commonly used for veneer and panelling.

Mahogany was first used for building in the Cathedral of Santo Domingo, completed in 1540. Sir Walter Raleigh is said to have repaired his ships with it in the West Indies in 1595. In the late 1700s, it became popular as a cabinet wood for such great furniture makers as Chippendale, Hepplewhite and the Adam brothers. Mahogany panels for painting were first used in 17th-century Holland and England, and remained universally popular throughout the 19th century.

mahogany lake or **cashew lake** a red or brown LAKE made with various dyes on a burnt sienna base. It is not a permanent pigment.

mahogany stain a wood STAIN made of linseed oil and thinners mixed with a lake colour or – for permanent results – with burnt sienna.

majesty see MAESTÀ.

majolica or **maiolica** an EARTHENWARE or FAIENCE of brownish-red body, decorated with heavily embossed, richly coloured, glossy, opaque glazes. The high reputation of majolica as a ware of outstanding design and quality was gained in Renaissance Italy from the 15th to the 17th century. Nineteenth-century examples of the ware made in English, French, German and American potteries are sought after as collectors' items. Its name comes from the Spanish island of Majorca, where pottery of this type has been made since the 12th century.

makore the African cherry; see CHERRYWOOD.

malachite, Hungarian green, mineral green or **mountain green** native green crystalline copper carbonate, pulverized and used as a pigment from Roman times until the introduction early in the 19th century of more powerful, permanent greens. The greenish shades of Bremen blue have the same chemical composition as malachite, but not the same crystalline structure. Malachite has the same general pigment properties and history as AZURITE, the blue variety of native crystalline copper carbonate.

Malay dammar see SINGAPORE DAMMAR.

malerisch see PAINTERLY.

malleable *(of a metal)* capable of being beaten or rolled in all directions without breaking or cracking under the stress. A malleable metal must have a certain structural plasticity, since the molecules adhere to each other when the metal is hammered. The most malleable of all metals is gold, which can be beaten to a foil $\frac{1}{300,000}$ inch thick. Other metals used by sculptors are, in descending order of malleability, silver, aluminium, copper, tin, platinum, lead, zinc (when hot), and soft steel. Cast iron and hard steel are not malleable. Alloys, such as brass and bronze, are usually less malleable than the metals of which they are made.

mallet a wooden hammer. A sculptor's mallet is shaped something like a milkchurn, with a truncated conical head and a handle that extends from the centre of the smaller end. It is made of hardwood, usually boxwood or lignum vitae, in one piece, and may weigh from three-quarters of a pound to two and a quarter pounds. It is used for striking chisels and gouges in wood carving. A one-pound mallet of similar shape, made of zinc, is used in stone carving, as are BUSHHAMMERS and soft-iron hammers with brick-shaped heads and inserted wooden handles, weighing from one to two and a quarter pounds.

mallet

Maltese cross 1. a cross with wedge-shaped arms meeting at the points and with V-shaped indentations at the outer ends. These indentations make it a cross of eight points, as it is sometimes called, especially in heraldry. The cross derives its name from its adoption during the Middle Ages as the emblem of the Knights of the Order of Malta.
2. the *cross pattée* or *cross formée*, similar in shape to the Maltese cross but with unindented ends. See CROSS for illustration.

mandala or **mandara** *(Hindu and Buddhist art)* a pictorial schema of mystical symbols of the universe, usually in the form of a circle surrounding a square, frequently shown with a symmetrical representation of a PANTHEON.

mandorla see AUREOLE.

manganese black or **manganese brown** artificially made manganese dioxide. A powerful drier in oil, it has also been used as a permanent brownish-black pigment. Manganese black (brown), which was patented in England by Rowan in 1871, is not in common use. The native variety is described under BLACK OXIDE OF MANGANESE.

manganese blue barium manganate, a brilliant, clear, transparent, azure or sky-blue permanent pigment with a very greenish undertone. It was introduced to artists about 1935. Due to a lack of demand in industry for this pigment, manganese blue is no longer produced and will become unavailable unless small-scale production is introduced for artists' pigments. MANGANESE GREEN is a green variety of manganese blue.

manganese green, Baryta green, Cassel green or **Rosenstiehl's green** a green form of barium manganate (MANGANESE BLUE). Manganese green has been known as a permanent pigment since the 19th century, though little used; it has not been available in the 20th century.

manganese violet, Burgundy violet, mineral violet, Nuernberg violet or **permanent violet** manganese ammonium phosphate, a permanent bluish-violet pigment with the same general colour properties as the bluish shade of cobalt violet. Manganese violet was introduced in Germany in 1868 by E. Leykauf, who gave it the name Nuernberg violet.

manière criblée see DOTTED MANNER.

manifestation see PERFORMANCE ART.

manifesto a public declaration or exposition in print of the theories and directions of a movement. The manifestoes issued by various individual artists, or groups, in the first half of the 20th century served to reveal their motivations and raisons d'être, and stimulated support for or reactions against them.

manikin see LAY FIGURE; ÉCORCHÉ.

Manila copal an alcohol-soluble resin tapped in the Philippines from trees of the genus *Agathis*. It has few properties in common with the other resins properly called COPALS. Manila copal occurs in many old recipes, especially for fixatives. It is, on the whole, a rather inferior resin; some of the synthetic polyvinyl and acrylic resins are improved substitutes for it.

Manila elemi see ELEMI.

manjak a medium-soft asphalt from Barbados. It is used in some recipes for ETCHING GROUNDS and as a constituent of various acid-proof and other protective coatings.

Mannerism an artistic style prevalent, especially in Italy, between 1525 and 1600. It developed in reaction to the classical balance and austere harmony of the High Renaissance and was characterized by a subjective, sometimes highly emotional, portrayal of its subject matter through elongated or otherwise distorted forms, exaggerated perspective, and relatively harsh, vivid colours. Its major exponents were El Greco (1541–1614) and Tintoretto (1518–1594); some of the late work of Michelangelo is also considered by some authorities to fall into the Mannerist category. Others working in this style included the painters Rosso Fiorentino (1494–1540), Parmigianino (1503–1540), Pontormo (1494–1557), and Agnolo Bronzino (1503–1572), and the sculptor and goldsmith Benvenuto Cellini (1500–1571). See also DISTORTION.

Mapico pigments (US) the tradename for a series of MARS PIGMENTS developed by Fireman in Alexandria, Virginia, about 1900.

maple one of the most widely used hardwoods (from trees of the genus *Acer*). About two dozen different species are found in the United States

alone. They are subdivided into hard and soft maple. The most important
hard variety is sugar maple (from *Acer saccharum*), used for dance floors
and bowling alleys, among other things. Soft maple is less expensive and
has a less interesting figure; it is used for carving rather than for veneers.
The red maple *(Acer rubrum)* is a common species of soft maple. It is
often used for wood-engraving blocks. See also HAREWOOD.

maple die board an all-maple, 5-ply plywood board, sold in several
thicknesses from 0.5 to 0.75 inches and in sizes of from 2 × 3 feet to 3
× 4 feet. It is intended for use in machine work, as the backing against
which dies are used. Since it is stronger and sturdier than other plywoods,
being made of plies of equal thickness, it is popular with painters for use
as a support.

maquette *(sculpture)* a small model in wax or clay, made as a preliminary
sketch, presented to a client for approval of the proposed work, or
entered in competition for a prize or a scholarship. The Italian equivalent
of the term is *bozzetto*, meaning 'small sketch.'

Maracaibo balsam see COPAIBA BALSAM.

marble a hard, crystalline form of calcium carbonate, fine-grained, dense,
and capable of taking a smooth, high polish. It is the traditional stone
used by sculptors. Marble is a metamorphic form of LIMESTONE, which is
similar in chemical composition although not in structure or appearance.
Some varieties of marble are metamorphic dolomites, containing magnesium carbonate as well as calcium carbonate. Because calcium carbonate is susceptible to the destructive action of acids or acidic impurities in
the atmosphere, marble is not the most durable stone for outdoor use in
sculpture.

Numerous varieties of marble, differing greatly in colouring and sur-
face appearance, are or have been quarried in all parts of the world. From
Greece come PARIAN MARBLE, PENTELIC MARBLE, ROSSO ANTICO, and
ELEUSINIAN MARBLE – all used by the sculptors and architects of antiquity.
The ancients also used PAVONAZZETTO NERO ANTICO. Italy's most
famous stone, CARRARA MARBLE, was used for many great works of the
Renaissance. Other Italian marbles are BARDIGLIO, CIPOLIN, and
PARMAZO MARBLE. Belgium produces RANCE, BELGIAN BLACK, and
SAINT ANNE MARBLE. Among the many French varieties are LANGUEDOC
MARBLE, GRIOTTE, and SARRANCOLIN MARBLE. SUSSEX MARBLE is an
English variety. In the United States, the three most highly rated marbles
for carving are VERMONT WHITE STATUARY, GEORGIA WHITE, and COL-
ORADO YULE STATUARY; additional marbles prized by sculptors are ALA-
BAMA CREAM, TENNESSEE PINK, and ROCKINGHAM ROYAL BLACK.
Marbles of unusual appearance or composition include SHELL MARBLE,
BRECCIA, and FOREST MARBLE.

marble dust crushed marble, the finest grade of which is used as an inert
pigment, the coarser form as an aggregate. Marble dust mixed into
plaster used as the support for a fresco is in the form of small cubical or
pyramidal grits. When the painting surface, the INTONACO, is trowelled,
some of the flat facets of the marble dust are exposed. The fresco colours

are not absorbed at these spots, which remain bright and add sparkle and brilliance to the work.

marbling 1. the imitation of marble patterns on wood or other solid surfaces.

2. the art of producing variegated and usually multicolour designs on paper in free, swirling patterns. It is used on endpapers for books, on book edges, and for other decorative purposes. The process consists of filling a shallow pan or trough with a gum solution of soft gel consistency, on which are floated fluid colours made by grinding pigments in a special gum vehicle. The colours are dispersed by adding a wetting agent. The flowing, curved patterns are controlled by dragging the surface with a steel comb that has widely spaced teeth. The design is then transferred to the paper surface by laying the paper against the fluid surface. Marbling was popular in Europe during the 17th and 18th centuries and in the United States as well in the 19th century, but its commercial use has declined during the present century. There has been some revival of marbling as a craft activity.

marc black see VINE BLACK.

marine 1. a pictorial representation of a nautical scene; a seascape.

2. a series of canvas sizes sold in France that were at one time considered appropriate to marine painting. See table at CANVAS SIZES, FRENCH.

Marinite *(US)* a tradename for an ASBESTOS BOARD.

marmolite a thin, laminated SERPENTINE, usually pale green.

Maroger medium a MEGILP or GEL MEDIUM for oil painting. It was introduced in the 1940s by Jacques Maroger, a painter and conservator, who presented it as a recreation of the highly effective medium of the Renaissance painters, supposed to have been lost to the world since the 17th century. Although the theory has followers among artists, it has been disputed by most technical specialists in the fine arts, on the grounds that Maroger's evidence is not historically valid and that the materials he recommends are not technically sound. The best consensus is that megilp and heavily leaded oils were more probably derived from the practices of 18th-century trade painters and decorators. Maroger's book, *The Secret Mediums and Techniques of the Masters* (1948), also attributes several other mediums to various schools and masters. These attributions also have been adversely regarded by specialists. Maroger's book contains few technical points that are not to be found in the *Art of Oil Painting* by J.F.L. Mérimée, published at the beginning of the 19th century and typical of the technology of the late 18th century, considered the dark age of painting techniques.

marouflage the process of cementing a painted canvas to a wall. Traditionally, the adhesive used in marouflage was commercial WHITE LEAD in oil, spread evenly on both the plaster and the back of the canvas with a wide brush, a spatula, or a wall scraper. The canvas is flattened wrinkle-free with the palm of the hand; a rubber-surfaced roller, used cautiously, can assist. Aqueous adhesives and some of the newer synthetics also have been used satisfactorily. Some architects recommend a delay of two years before painting a mural or attaching it to the wall in a new building, since the plaster may develop cracks as the structure settles.

When a large mural is to be laid in several sections, the separate pieces are cemented with a butt join, that is, without overlapping edges. Usually, one or both of the canvases to be joined are painted an inch or so beyond what is needed, with duplicate detail on the edges that are to meet. The canvases are then laid with an overlap, the matching detail in perfect alignment. While the adhesive is still fresh, the surplus canvas is cut away in a straight line with a razor-sharp blade held vertically to the wall surface.

marquetry 1. a method of decoration in which small pieces of wood veneer, mother of pearl, metal or ivory are inlaid in a floral or other ornamental pattern in a wood veneer or other surface, for use on furniture and panelling.

2. a decorative surface so produced.

Marquetry was an important art form during the Renaissance. See INTARSIA.

Mars pigments *(US)* originally a tradename, now the accepted artists' name for a group of iron oxide pigments made by a special furnace process. They include Mars yellow, Mars brown, Mars red, Mars violet and Mars black. The Mars pigments are ferric oxides except for the yellow, which contains ferric hydroxide, and the black, which is ferroso-ferric oxide. While Mars yellow closely approximates to the hue of yellow ochre, it is clearer, more brilliant, and has greater tinting strength. Mars brown is produced in a medium chocolate shade, and Mars red in shades ranging from scarlet to maroon, but these are less frequently used in artists' colours, perhaps because of the satisfactory performances of light red, Indian red, and the umbers. Mars violet, which may appear dull compared with the brilliant cobalt and manganese violets, is quite useful for producing lavender and orchid tints in paintings of low key. Mars black, which is dense and heavy, is widely used as an alternative to ivory black and lampblack, which are lightweight, fluffy pigments of high oil absorbency. Mars black produces oil films of greater stability and also works well in water media. Unlike the carbon blacks, Mars black does not effloresce when used to colour mortar or cement. Like its native counterpart, black iron oxide, Mars black is attracted by a magnet. One trade name for Mars colours is *Mapico pigments*. Other names for Mars yellow are *iron yellow*, *yellow oxide of iron* and the trade names *Ferrite* and *Ferrox*. Mars red has also been known as *totem*; Mars black, as *magnetic black iron oxide*.

mascaron a face or mask, often grotesque, used as a decorative device in carving, metalwork, and ceramics. It is derived from the Italian word *mascherone*. Familiar examples are the tragic and comic masks.

mascherone see MASCARON.

masking tape see PRESSURE-SENSITIVE TAPE.

Masonite *(US)* the tradename for a line of hard WALLBOARD, made by exploding wood fibres with steam, and reuniting them under great pressure. In this type of dense board, which is the most widely used support for panel painting, the fibres are bound by the natural components of the wood, without adding other binders. The variety most recommended for use by artists is called Standard Masonite Presdwood, a dark brown board that is perfectly smooth on one side, and bears the impression of wire screening on the other. Another type, called Tempered Presdwood, contains additional ingredients to strengthen it and increase its durability. But Standard Masonite Presdwood surpasses it in the ability to hold a ground (especially gesso) permanently – a property far more essential to its success as a permanent support.

mass *(painting and design)* any area of sufficient size or importance to be a significant element in the design – for example, a building or a group of trees against the sky.

mass colour see MASS TONE.

massicot or **plumbic ochre** an oxide of lead similar to LITHARGE, but deeper or more reddish in hue. It is occasionally referred to as GIALLOLINO, *giallorino* and *giallolino di Fiandra* (Flemish yellow). Massicot was used as an artists' pigment from the 15th century to the end of the 18th or the early 19th century.

massier a French term for the monitor or student in charge of an art class.

mass tone, mass colour or **top tone** the surface colour effect of a pigment when viewed by reflected light, as distinguished from its UNDERTONE.

master 1. an artist of high achievement, especially one of the leaders of a school or period.
2. one who was an artist or craftsman qualified to execute commissions alone or with a JOURNEYMAN.

masterpiece 1. one of an artist's works that represents his or her top level of accomplishment.
2. any work of art that ranks among the best of its kind.
A frequently encountered French equivalent is *chef d'oeuvre*.

mastic 1. RESIN obtained from a tree (*Pistachia lentiscus*) that grows in the countries bordering the Mediterranean. It comes on the market in pale amber-coloured drops or tears the size of small peas. Mastic is soluble in both alcohol and turpentine; a turpentine solution was popular as a PICTURE VARNISH during the 19th century, when a smooth, high-gloss finish for oil paintings was admired. It was superseded in the first half of the 20th century by DAMMAR, which does not have the defects of yellowing, clouding (bloom), or cracking with age that are characteristic of mastic, and which does not produce such a glassy finish. Nevertheless, mastic, the best grade of which is known as Chios mastic, makes a better picture varnish than any of the other tree resins. Mastic was also used as an ingredient of MEGILP. Its name derives from the local use of the resin as a chewing gum.
2. any of several adhesive, resinous cements of plastic consistency used in building construction to fill gaps in masonry, to insulate or waterproof,

and also to set tiles and the tesserae of mosaics. The term includes cements of various compositions, most of them black in colour and resistant to weathering. An oil-based mastic was in use as early as the 16th century as an improvement on plaster for setting mosaics. During the recent past, ASPHALT and coal tar were largely used, but the most successful present mastics for mosaic setting and other uses are trade products made with synthetic resins.

mat, matt or **matte 1.** lustreless; having a dead, flat surface appearance. Mat effects are due to a microscopic roughness or irregularity of surface, which causes light to be reflected in a diffused manner, in contrast to the specular or mirrorlike reflection of a glossy surface. Water paints usually dry to a mat finish, although sometimes they have a satiny sheen called *semimat finish* or *eggshell finish*. Oil colours are naturally glossy when dry and may receive added lustre if a glossy picture varnish is applied to them. Polymer colours dry with a gloss unless the mat medium is mixed with them to create a mat or semimat finish. See also GLOSS.

2. (mat) a stiff material, such as cardboard, cut out in the centre so that it forms a border between the outer edges of picture and the inner edge of its frame. Its thickness prevents the drawing or print from coming in contact with the glass. MAT BOARD is specifically designed for this purpose, but other types of paperboard have been used. A mat is occasionally used as the sole frame of a picture and, with glass and a backing, in the method of framing called PASSE-PARTOUT.

Mata Kuching dammar or **cat's eye dammar** traditionally, a DAMMAR resin of superlative quality – a selected grade of Singapore dammar that has been absent from the market for decades. *Mata Kuching* means 'cat's eye'.

mat board a stiff cardboard with a thin facing of paper on one side, used to make mats for pictures, especially those done on paper. Mat board, unlike illustration board, which has a base layer of grey cardboard, has a white or whitish base, to make a pleasing bevelled edge. Its surface may be smooth or pebbled, dull or glossy; the typical mat board has a fine, pebbled texture and a dull finish. Mat board comes in a wide variety of colours, although the most common are various shades of white, cream and grey; special finishes and textures, including linen, metallic, and wood-grain effects are available. Mat board is usually made of wood pulp. A pure rag board is best used for matting permanent works of art, since paper may become discoloured from prolonged contact with a wood-pulp board.

mat cutter a device used to make neat, accurate cuts, either straight or bevelled, in MAT BOARD. Of the several types made, one is built like a T-square, with a blade holder that slides along the long arm. Another is a heavy steel implement, its back shaped to fit the hand and with a perfectly smooth face meant to slide along the edge of a ruler. The face has a recess in which the blade is held. (See figure.) On all types, the blade may be adjusted for both the angle and the depth of the cut.

mat cutter Dexter mat cutter.

mat gilding MORDANT GILDING or unburnished WATER GILDING, producing an unpolished surface. Gilding on glass automatically has a specular finish, as though it were burnished. In order to obtain a mat finish on glass, therefore, the areas to be mat must be coated with dammar or mastic varnish before the leaf is laid. Burnished metal appears darker than an unburnished surface, and mat and burnished gilding may be used in combination to give a striking effect of reflected light and contrasting tones; lettering and designs on glass frequently have mat centres.

mat glaze *(ceramics)* an opaque glaze with a dull, nonreflective surface. A mat effect can be induced by adding barium or alumina (clay) to raise the maturation point of the glaze.

mat knife a knife with a short, thick handle and a razor-sharp blade. Two types are in use, one designed to hold a short, replaceable blade, the other with a long blade, most of which fits into the handle and which may be repeatedly sharpened and reset to the proper length as it wears away.

mat medium or **mat polymer medium** see POLYMER MEDIUM.

matrix 1. a natural mineral substance in which another material, such as a metal, crystal or fossil, is embedded.

2. by extension, any concave form that surrounds or encases a solid form, such as a mould used in casting, a recessed die used to strike or stamp a relief pattern, or a foundation for inlaid damascene work.

mat knife (above) A heavy-duty knife with a short, replaceable blade. (below) A knife with a long, adjustable blade that is lengthened as it is worn through sharpening.

3. the binder used to cement the particles in a composition or conglomerate material such as concrete or imitation stone.

matter see MACE-HEAD.

matting wheel see ROULETTE.

mattoir see MACE-HEAD.

matt surface see MAT.

maturation *(ceramics)* the hardening of a ware as a result of firing. The clay matures only when given sufficient time and heat. Overfiring causes deformation of the ware.

mat varnish any varnish intended to give a flat, nonglossy effect when applied. There are no completely successful nonyellowing mat varnishes for permanent, fine-art paintings. One mat varnish made by adding white refined beeswax to dammar varnish gives fairly good semimat or satin finish results but, like all wax coatings, polishes when it is rubbed, so that the mat effect is not reliably permanent. Special proprietary mat varnishes are used in MAT GILDING. Industrial mat varnishes are available and can be used by decorators and others to whom eventual yellowing and darkening are not as critical as they are to the artist.

maulstick see MAHLSTICK.

mauve, Perkin's violet or **aniline purple** a SYNTHETIC ORGANIC PIGMENT of medium saturation and a pale violet-purple hue, more intense than lavender. It resists fading poorly. Discovered by W.H. Perkin in 1856, mauve or PERKIN'S VIOLET was the first synthetic dyestuff produced from coal tar. Pink mauve is a reddish variety of mauve.

Maxwell triangle see CHROMATICITY.

Mayan blue a greenish-blue pigment found in Mayan artifacts and, to a lesser extent, in those of other pre-Columbian civilizations. The chemical identity of Mayan blue was unknown and searched for over three decades. According to extensive studies made in Belgium and published in 1967, it is now considered to consist of INDIGO and ATTAPULGITE.

meander see FRET.

mechanical drawing or **drafting** a type of drawing used by architects and engineers to convey specific information in graphic form. Its chief objective is to make it possible for someone to construct what someone else has designed. Mechanical drawing takes its name from the fact that the draughtsman uses mechanical devices to achieve the desired end. SCALES and detailed, accurate systems of PROJECTION and proportion, as well as such tools as the FRENCH CURVE, the T SQUARE and the COMPASS, are used to indicate the exact size and shape of the thing drawn and the relationship of the parts to each other and to the whole. The RULING PEN is a common drawing implement. Whereas in freehand drawing, the creative artist defines his or her ideas, in mechanical drawing the draughtsman communicates those ideas in a universal, unequivocal language. When the draughtsman sketches without the use of instruments but still adheres to the conventions of mechanical drawing, the practice is known as *technical sketching*. Nowadays, much of the draughtsman's work is done with the aid of a computer. See also ELEVATION; EXPLODED VIEW; RENDERING.

mediaeval art art of the Middle Ages in Europe, from the decline of Roman civilization about AD 500 to the 14th century, when it was supplanted by the Renaissance style and spirit. See BYZANTINE; GOTHIC; ROMANESQUE.

medium 1. (*pl.* mediums) a liquid that may be added to a paint to increase its manipulability without decreasing its adhesive, binding or film-forming properties. A highly recommended oil painting medium contains a small percentage of a nonyellowing resin such as dammar, an equal or somewhat larger amount of a nonyellowing, heavy-bodied drying oil such as stand oil or sun-refined oil, a rather large percentage of turpentine, and usually a small amount of cobalt drier. A nonyellowing, oil-modified alkyd resin is also recommended. The use of acrylic resin solution as an oil painting medium or ingredient is not recommended because of its imperfect miscibility with oils. The liquid in which pigments are dispersed or ground to make a paint is called a VEHICLE rather than a medium.

2. (*pl.* media) the specific tool and material used by an artist, for example, brush and oil paint, chisel and stone.

3. (*pl.* media) the mode of expression employed by an artist, for example, painting, sculpture, the graphic arts.

megilp, McGuilp or **Magilp** a gel painting medium. Megilp is made by mixing mastic varnish and linseed oil supersaturated with white lead. It was popular during the 18th and 19th centuries because of the facile and versatile manipulative qualities it gives to oil colours. As early as 1826, however, chemists advised against its use by artists, and by 1900 it had been completely discredited as a medium on the grounds that it was a major cause of embrittlement, cracking, and yellowing of oil paintings. It is generally believed that megilp was originated by decorators and trade painters of the 18th century, although it has been attributed, without much substantial proof, to artists of the Renaissance. See also MAROGER MEDIUM.

MEK see METHYL ETHYL KETONE.

memento mori (*Lat.* remember you must die) a motif used in art and elsewhere as a reminder of death. A skull is a common memento mori. During the Renaissance a small ornament in the shape of a skull was often carried; it was usually of fine craftsmanship and might be set with gems. In art, a typical memento mori is the skull in Dürer's *St Jerome in his Study* (1514). An entire painting may also be called a memento mori.

mending tape see PRESSURE-SENSITIVE TAPES.

mercury yellow see TURPETH MINERAL.

metal leaf see DUTCH METAL.

merz an artistic invention that is a variation of DADA. Created by the 20th-century German artist Kurt Schwitters (1887–1948), merz originally took the form of a series of collages made from discarded waste material, including used bus tickets and old sweetpapers. Schwitters later constructed a series of sculptures utilizing the same kind of materials.

metal cut the print that results from a metal plate that has been cut in relief. See DOTTED MANNER.

metallizing the coating of a surface with a metal by ELECTROPLATING, METAL SPRAYING or a modern vacuum process.

metal point see SILVER POINT.

metal spraying the depositing of a thin layer of metal on a surface or object with a spray gun. The spray gun is loaded with a coil of thin wire (gold, silver, bronze, etc.) and contains a heating element to liquefy the wire. The gun can deposit liquid metal on any surface, however flammable, in a smooth, even coating. This process is used by metal sculptors for gilding works executed in base metals.

metamerism the undesirable tendency of two coloured surfaces that appear alike when viewed under one kind of light (daylight, fluorescent tube, tungsten bulb, etc.) to appear different from one another when viewed under a different form of light. Such colours are called metamers or metameric pairs. Gloss, surface texture, transparency, and ratio of pigment to binder may contribute to metamerism in colours. But its main cause is difference in the composition of the two colours used. Painters may avoid its occurrence when repainting or adding new touches to a picture by using identical pigments instead of a mixture of other materials to match a colour.

metamorphic rock see ROCK.

metaphysical painting a style of painting that was a forerunner of SURREALISM. Developed by the 20th-century Italian painter Giorgio de Chirico (1888–1978), metaphysical painting is characterized by a strange, dreamlike quality, unreal perspectives, strange lighting, and oddly contrasted objects painted in realistic detail. See also MAGIC REALISM.

methacrylate resin see ACRYLIC RESIN.

methanol, methyl alcohol or **wood alcohol** a VOLATILE SOLVENT with solvent properties at least as good as those of ethyl alcohol. Both the liquid and its vapours are dangerously toxic and have a notably destructive effect on the optic nerve. Methanol was formerly called *Columbian spirits*. The chemical name *methanol* has long been preferred because of the dangerous confusion between methyl alcohol and ethyl alcohol.

methyl acetone an impure ACETONE, containing varying amounts of methanol and methyl acetate. Its solvent action is weaker and its vapours more toxic than those of pure acetone.

methyl alcohol see METHANOL.

methylated spirit ETHYL ALCOHOL that has been rendered unfit for drinking by the addition of various ingredients according to government-approved standards. The best varieties of methylated spirit for general use as diluents and cleaners are sold in cans under various tradenames. A typical recipe in wide use is for 5 gallons of methanol, 5 gallons of ethyl acetate, and 1 gallon of petroleum to each 100 gallons of ethyl alcohol.

METHYL CELLULOSE

An anhydrous variety is also available from specialized dealers. Methylated spirit is exempt from the heavy tax to which potable ethyl alcohol is subject.

methyl cellulose a cellulose product that resembles cottonwool. Methyl cellulose is related to the cellulosic compounds used in LACQUER, but it is soluble in cold water rather than in volatile solvents. It has found a few uses as an artists' material, principally as a binder in pastels and other crayons.

methyl ethyl ketone (MEK) a LACQUER SOLVENT used in industrial processes. Its properties are similar to those of acetone except that it is a more efficient solvent for some resins and is dangerously toxic. Its presence in epoxy and polyester resin materials makes those materials hazardous to use except under carefully controlled conditions.

methyl silicate see SILICON ESTER.

métier the specialty that an artist is best qualified in, most successful at, or most at home in.

Mexican onyx see ONYX MARBLE.

mezzo fresco a term used to distinguish a FRESCO technique of the latter half of the 16th century from that of *buon fresco*. In mezzo fresco, painting was done on partially dry intonaco. Because the colours sank only slightly into the firm plaster, lime was added to them to enhance their adherence. The drawing was incised on the half-firm intonaco by tracing on a cartoon with a stylus.

mezzo-rilievo *(It.)* middle or half-RELIEF.

mezzotint a RELIEF PRINTING process, that is, a kind of reverse ENGRAVING procedure, in which the entire surface of a copper or steel plate is heavily abraded with a special tool called a ROCKER or cradle. The overall burr thus created prints as a dark, velvety black. The areas to be white in the print are painstakingly rubbed with a BURNISHER and an engraver's SCRAPER, which smooth and depress those areas so that they do not take the ink in relief printing. Thus, the whites are extracted from the blacks, whereas the usual procedure in line engraving is to engrave the blacks and print the plate as an intaglio surface. For HALF-TONES (from which the process gets its Italian name, *mezzo* meaning half and *tinta* meaning tone), the burr is only partially removed with the scraper or burnisher, leaving areas of variously concentrated dots. A GRAVER, MACE-HEAD, ROULETTE or drypoint NEEDLE may be used to increase the burr of the printing areas, making them even darker in the proofs. Other abrasives and methods (for example, sand, pumice, and nitric acid) have been used to roughen the surface of a mezzotint plate, but none is as effective as the rocker.

Because mezzotint produces form in tonal areas rather than in line, it is particularly suited to colour printmaking. It was widely used in the 18th and 19th centuries to reproduce portraits and other paintings, but became obsolete for this purpose with the introduction of photoengraving and photogravure. Although some artists still use the mezzotint technique to achieve an extra textural effect on a plate done primarily in another medium, the laborious preparation of the mezzotint plate is a deterrent to its wide use in the fine arts.

mica a native complex silicate that occurs in laminated, colourless, plate form. Pulverized, it is used as an INERT PIGMENT in industrial products, such as white CASEIN wall paint, to which it adds sparkle and brilliance, and in which its plate structure retards settling of the heavier pigments. Mica is not highly rated as an ingredient of permanent paints because it is apt to split up into additional laminations. Micronized mica, an extremely fine variety used in ETHYL SILICATE paints, is considered more suitable for permanent uses than the ordinary pulverized grades.

Micarta *(US)* a tradename for laminated plastic sheets of a PHENOLIC RESIN, sold in many opaque colours.

microcrystalline wax a white wax produced in the refining of petroleum oils. Like other paraffin waxes, it is chemically inert. It came into wide use in the arts in the mid-20th century as an additive to, or replacement for, white refined beeswax in a number of operations, notably for modelling and lost-wax casting in sculpture and as an ingredient of lining adhesive in the conservation of paintings. It is available in various degrees of hardness and melting ranges to suit specific preferences. The harder varieties can be softened by adding up to 20% of mineral oil or petroleum jelly, or by adding softer waxes.

middle distance *(pictorial arts)* the part of the composition between the foreground and the background. The middle distance is one of the three ZONES OF RECESSION in LINEAR PERSPECTIVE.

migration period art the art objects created by the Teutonic tribes that precipitated the decline and fall of the Roman Empire from the 4th to the 9th century AD. Migration period art consists mostly of ART MOBILIER and objects carried about for personal use by the highly mobile tribes, including gold jewellery of great beauty.

mildew see MOULD.

mild steel or **soft steel** malleable steel with a low carbon content. Hard steel is not malleable and therefore cannot be worked. Mild steel will work well when heated to redness, although it is more difficult to shape than wrought iron.

milk of lime water containing a small amount of slaked lime (calcium hydroxide) in suspension, and used in SECCO painting.

Milori blue see PRUSSIAN BLUE.

mineral blue an unstandardized name for ANTWERP BLUE and AZURITE.

mineral green an unstandardized term applied both to MALACHITE and BREMEN GREEN.

mineral grey see ULTRAMARINE ASH.

mineral lake 1. tin (stannic) chromate, an obsolete yellow pigment. 2. POTTER'S PINK.

mineral oil any of several grades of oil refined from crude petroleum. These products have similar viscous qualities and the same lubricity or unctuousness as the vegetable oils. They are chemically inert, and are seldom used in artists' materials. A refined, white, medicinal grade of mineral oil has been recommended for removing or preventing BLOOM in varnished oil paintings. A drop or two on a paper tissue is rubbed sparingly over the surface of a painting that has aged for some time; it is not used on fresh varnish, which it might injure.

mineral painting, stereochromy or **water-glass painting** a method of mural painting with pigments ground in potassium silicate (potash water glass). The technique, known since about 1825, was perfected and standardized by Adolf Keim of Munich in the 1880s. It was so complicated that artists had small success with it, and it was abandoned before the end of the century. See also LIQUID SILICATES.

mineral pigments inorganic pigments of mineral origin and those made from inorganic chemicals or raw materials not in themselves colouring matters.

mineral spirits see WHITE SPIRIT.

mineral turbith see TURPETH MINERAL.

mineral violet 1. see ULTRAMARINE VIOLET.

2. see MANGANESE VIOLET.

mineral white see GYPSUM.

mineral yellow see TURNER'S YELLOW.

minette see YELLOW OCHRE.

Ming Dynasty a period in Chinese art taking its name from the Ming emperors, who ruled from the 14th until the mid-17th century, during which time new techniques for making fine porcelain were developed, including blue underglaze painting. The carving of jade and ivory reached new peaks of technical precision during this period, and the making of cloisonné enamelware was perfected.

miniature 1. (from *Lat.* miniare, to draw or colour with minium) a picture in a mediaeval manuscript. MINIUM (cinnabar) was the principal pigment used in early mediaeval miniatures.

2. a very small portrait, painted on ivory, card, or occasionally another surface such as chicken skin. Such portrait miniatures of the 16th–19th centuries developed out of mediaeval miniatures. Miniatures were done in water paints; transparent watercolours were used almost exclusively from the 18th century onwards, although before that time tempera and other mediums were commonly used. The round, oval, or occasionally rectangular miniatures were often framed in narrow gold or gilt frames and protected by flat or convex glass. They had their greatest vogue in the 17th and 18th centuries and were still popular in the 19th. The invention of photography caused the popularity of miniature portrait painting to wane. Nicholas Hillyard (*c.*1547–1619), Samuel Cooper (1609–1672) and Richard Cosway (1742–1821) are considered among the greatest of many English miniaturists. Among American miniaturists, Robert Field (1749–1819) and Edward Green Malbone (1777–1807) are outstanding. Well-known painters who occasionally worked in miniature include Holbein, Fragonard, Goya, and Rosalba Carriera. A miniaturist was often called a *limner*.

3. any very small picture in any medium.

minimal art, primary structure or **ABC art** the art of a movement in the late 1960s, in which three-dimensional structures of basic or simplified form and flat colour are created, suggesting the lines, planes, and solids of geometry. The individuality traditionally associated with creativity is minimized to such an extent that the artist is frequently able to have a work executed by a process of craftsmanship, such as cabinetmaking or tinsmithing, or of modern technology, such as the forming of plastics or fluorescent tubes. The artist's own role in its creation is that of originator, designer, and technical supervisor. Perhaps the major source of this development has been the rise of basic design courses in art schools, where pure geometric forms are studied intensively both for their own sake and for their application to industrial design. Most of the activities of the minimal art movement have centred on New York and Los Angeles.

minium 1. CINNABAR (native mercuric sulphide) in writings of the Classical period.

2. RED LEAD. This meaning developed some time during the Middle Ages. The use of the word continued into the 19th century. Through the verb *miniare*, meaning to draw or paint with minium, it gave rise to the word MINIATURE.

Minoan pertaining to the art and civilization of ancient Crete, which achieved a high level of artistic and technical development. Minoan civilization has been divided by scholars into early (3400–2400 BC), middle (2400–1580 BC), and late (1580–1100 BC) periods. It reached its peak about 1500 BC. Minoan pottery, fresco painting, and architecture are all noteworthy. Pottery was decorated with simple linear and abstract designs during the early and early-middle periods, and with a variety of plant, human, animal, and other naturalistic forms in the later phases. Frescoes on the walls of the great palace of Minos at Knossos, discovered in 1912 and restored partially since then, give some idea of Minoan social and religious life. While these frescoes are similar to the stylized wall paintings of ancient Egypt, with which the Minoans traded, they are far more naturalistic, sensuous and individualistic. Minoan architecture is best represented by the palaces of the middle to late periods, at Knossos, Phaistos, and Malia – each of which was built on the site of an earlier palace. Besides having elaborate wall decoration, these later palaces were remarkable for their sophisticated drainage systems.

minor arts all art forms other than architecture, painting, sculpture, drawing, and printmaking (which are ordinarily called FINE ARTS). Although the term is a standard classification, it tends to be misleading. Daniel F. Thompson, in his *Materials of mediaeval Painting* (1936), points out that artistic creations that touched the lives of other ages most closely – such as Greek pottery making, mediaeval book painting, Far Eastern ceramics, and Persian rug making – fall into the arbitrary category of so-called minor art. However, like APPLIED ART, the term is useful for making pragmatic distinctions, even if it will not bear intense philosophical scrutiny.

Mir Iskusstva see WORLD OF ART.

MISCHENTECHNIK

Mischentechnik see MIXED TECHNIQUE.

mishima a method of decorating ceramic ware that originated in Korea. Depressions are pressed or stamped into plastic clay and filled with an ENGOBE of a contrasting colour. Sometimes added glazes are brushed on the surface of the ware.

Mittis green or **Vienna green** a somewhat less clear and deep variety of EMERALD GREEN. Some believe that its invention by Baron Ignatz Von Mitis in Vienna antedated the discovery of emerald green in Schweinfurt (1814).

Mittler's green VIRIDIAN made by a method that was abandoned in favour of Guignet's process.

mixed media the use of two or more media in a single work of art, for example, the combining of watercolour and gouache.

mixed technique or *(Ger.)* **Mischentechnik** in painting, the technique of combining tempera colours with paints in an oleoresinous medium to produce various effects that cannot readily be duplicated by other means. The application of tempera colours with a fine, pointed sable brush on the wet glaze of an oil painting produces fine, crisp lines and touches; loose, free areas or opaque dragging strokes in tempera on darker areas of transparent glazes can yield a glowing effect. Some investigators have held that such techniques were used by painters of the transitional period between the era of tempera painting and the development of oils. Use of a stand oil–dammar glaze and an egg-and-oil tempera is believed to increase the permanence of the technique. Mixed technique first became known in Britain and the United States in 1934 with the publication in English of Max Doerner's *The Materials of the Artist and Their Use in Painting*. See WET-INTO-WET.

Mixed white a tradename for a COMPOSITE WHITE artists' oil colour.

mixing bowl *(sculpture)* a round bowl of rubber or thin, flexible brass used for mixing and containing wet plaster. Hardened remnants of plaster adhering to the bowl after use are easily turned out because of the bowl's flexibility.

mixing varnish any VARNISH that may be mixed with oil paints and other coating materials. For example, dammar varnish, when used as an ingredient of an artist's painting medium, confers such properties as hardness, quick setting and desirable manipulative qualities.

mizu-e the Japanese term for watercolour painting.

mobile *(sculpture)* a delicately balanced arrangement of thin rods or stiff wires and objects suspended from them. The entire construction hangs from a thin filament and is moved by slight air currents. The mobile was so named by its inventor, the American sculptor Alexander Calder (1898–1976), who made use of flat plates in bold colours and abstract, curvilinear shapes, usually hanging in rows like leaves on a branch. The form has been widely adopted by artists and decorators, who include in their mobiles a great variety of natural and abstract objects, materials and shapes. The *stabile*, also invented and named by Calder, resembles the mobile but is rigid and stationary rather than flexible and suspended.

mobility the ease with which a material flows – the opposite of VISCOS-
ITY. The word *fluidity* has the same meaning as mobility except that it
is generally applied to thin, free-flowing liquids, while mobility refers
to the flow of thicker or slow-moving oils, varnishes, and paints. See
CONSISTENCY.

mock gold see MOSAIC GOLD.

modelling 1. *(sculpture)* the technique of manipulating a plastic substance
such as clay.
2. *(sculpture)* the technique of building up a form in clay by an additive
process of shaping and enlarging, as distinguished from CARVING, or
cutting away.
3. the depiction of solid or three-dimensional form in drawing, painting,
and other two-dimensional media. It is usually achieved through the
representation of light and shadow.
4. posing for an artist.

modelling board a sturdy board that the sculptor may place on the work
table or MODELLING STAND as a base for the clay or other modelling
material on which the sculptor is working.

modelling clay 1.(also called **modelling wax**) a composite plastic substance used for MODELLING. It is nonhardening and cannot be used for
permanent work, but is useful for making models for casting, or for use
by students, as it can be reused many times if kept clean. The original
material, made in Italy, consists of tallow, sulphur, and a high-quality
clay. Inferior imitations are made of clay, an inert filler, and various
petroleum greases and oils; colouring matter is added, usually to produce
a grey-green colour. Modelling clay is sold under various tradenames,
such as Plasticine.
2. (also called **wet clay**) any natural CLAY used for modelling by
sculptors.

modelling paste a stiff white paste sold with the various brands of POLY-
MER COLOURS as a modelling material. It has many uses, such as making
textured effects in polymer painting, sculpture and collagraphs. It is
essentially a stiffer, less fluid form of POLYMER PRIMER.

modelling stand or **turntable** a 3- or 4-legged revolving stand on which
sculptor's CLAY is modelled. Made of wood or steel, a typical modelling
stand is about 3 feet high with a 16-inch-square revolving top that can
be elevated to about 20 inches higher. Another type of stand has a smaller
circular top, and some heavy models have a central supporting column
and a circular base. See figure overleaf.

modelling tools implements used in modelling or shaping clay and plaster. There are three basic types: the wooden tool, usually of boxwood,
in a great variety of pointed, spatulate, serrated, and rounded shapes; the
wire-end tool, with one end flaring out to form a wooden tool and the
other consisting of a loop of strong steel wire set in a brass ferrule, on a
rounded wooden handle; and the double-end wire tool, which has a loop
on each end of a wooden handle. The loops, used to carve or shave away
the clay, come in a wide variety of rounded and angular shapes. Boxwood

modelling stand

tools, shaped differently at each end, are usually 6 to 8 inches long. Wire-end and double-end tools of similar lengths are available, although very small, thin-line versions of these tools exist for modelling on faces and other delicate work, as do large, so-called professional tools up to 13 inches long with maple handles and brass wire loops.

modelling tools (a) Boxwood tools; (b) wire-end tools; (c) double-end tool.

modelling wax see MODELLING CLAY.

modello (*It.* model) a smaller version of a proposed work of art, sometimes sketchy, sometimes highly finished (see SKETCH). A modello of a projected work is often executed for discussion with a patron or teacher or for the approval of a client. A small model for a work of sculpture is also called a MAQUETTE.

model stand a low platform on which the model poses in an art class or a portrait-painter's studio. It is sometimes made in the form of a wooden box on rollers, which, when not in use, may be upended to save studio space. Its hollow interior may be used for storage.

Moderne Kunstkring *(Dutch* modern art circle) a distinguished group of painters – including Picasso, Cézanne, Mondrian, and Braque – who first exhibited together on 11 October 1910.

Mogen David see SOLOMON'S SEAL.

moiré effect the optical illusion observed when curved parallel or periodic lines are superimposed, forming a pattern that does not in fact exist. Watered silk exhibits the moiré effect, which has been used by such 20th-century practitioners of OP ART as J.R. Soto and Gerald Oster.

moisture trap a device attached to the air compressor of a SPRAY GUN or AIRBRUSH to prevent condensed moisture from entering the spray line.

Monastral blue and **Monastral green 1.** tradenames for PHTHALOCYAN-INE BLUE and PHTHALOCYANINE GREEN respectively.

2. several dyestuff pigments of entirely different composition made by the same firm.

monochrome painted or decorated in light and dark shades of a single colour, that is, one pigment plus white. See CAMAÏEU; GRISAILLE.

Monolite yellow *(US)* a tradename for HANSA YELLOW.

monolith (from *Gk* single stone) a massive bulk of uniform composition, a sculpture (usually huge) carved from or cast in one solid piece.

monomer see POLYMER.

monotype a one-of-a-kind print made by painting on a sheet or slab of glass and transferring the painting, while still wet, to a sheet of paper held firmly on the glass by rubbing the back of the paper with a smooth implement, such as a large hardwood spoon. The painting may also be done on a polished metal plate, in which case it may be either printed by hand or transferred to paper by running the plate and paper through an etching press. Any paint that does not dry too quickly can be used. Enough of the original paint remains on the glass or plate after the transfer that the same or different colours may be reapplied if subsequent prints of the same design are to be made. No two prints will be exactly alike, however, since variations in the repainting and transferring processes are unavoidable. Since each print is unique and executed separately by hand, monotype printing is not strictly a multiple-replica process. Because monotypes are prints on paper, however, they are generally classed and exhibited as graphics.

montage a picture made up of portions of various existing pictures, such as photographs or prints, and arranged so that they join, overlap, or blend with one another. See also ASSEMBLAGE; COLLAGE; DÉCOUPAGE.

montan wax a mineral wax refined from lignite coal. It is used in industrial paints, waterproofing, adhesives and leather finishes, and sometimes as a substitute for beeswax and carnauba wax. It is rather hard and brittle. The average grade of montan wax melts at about 80 °C.

Monthier blue see PRUSSIAN BLUE.

Montpellier green see VERDIGRIS.

Montpellier yellow see TURNER'S YELLOW.

monumental on a grand scale. In art criticism the term is often applied to a work of art that is usually, though not necessarily, large in size and elevated in idea, and that gives an impression of grandeur of form, nobility or simplicity of conception, enduring significance or ARCHITECTONIC quality. This effect is, for example, striven for in many murals of Puvis de Chavannes (1824–1898) and in the monument to Balzac (1897) by Auguste Rodin.

mop a very large, round camelhair brush used in watercolour for blending and other manipulations.

morbidezza (*It.* softness, mellowness) the soft blending of tones and the rounding off or hazing of edges in pictorial and sculptural representations. *Morbidezza* was a much-used term in 18th-century art criticism and often applied to the painting of Correggio.

mordant 1. the acid or acid mixture (in all printing processes in which a plate is produced by ETCHING and in the decorative etching of glass, steel, etc.) in a bath of which the object to be etched is immersed. The acid etches, or eats away, the lines, dots, or areas of design that are unprotected by a resist or ETCHING GROUND.

The mordants most commonly used in printing are dilute solutions of nitric acid (aquafortis) and hydrochloric acid (see DUTCH MORDANT; SMILLIE'S BATH). FERRIC CHLORIDE, which is also sometimes used, hydrolyses to form hydrochloric acid. A mordant must be of the correct concentration to act efficiently without also eating away the resist that protects the nonprinting areas. The term comes from the French *mordant* meaning 'biting' (from Latin, *mordere*, to bite); BITING is the term used in the graphic arts for the etching or eating-away effect that the mordant has on the metal plate.

Glass is usually etched with a mordant solution of hydrofluoric acid. When a mat or frosted etch is desired on glass, ammonium fluoride is added to the hydrofluoric-acid mordant. Sulphuric acid is sometimes also used as a mordant for etching glass.

2. *(dyeing)* a chemical additive that sets or precipitates the dye and assists in attaching the dye permanently to the textile fibres or other substance being dyed.

3. an oil or varnish GOLD SIZE used in MORDANT GILDING.

mordant gilding metal leaf laid with an oil or varnish GOLD SIZE rather than with water, as in WATER GILDING. As the technique of mordant gilding does not permit burnishing, a mat finish is produced. The size must dry to the correct degree of tackiness in order to perform properly and must maintain that consistency for the duration of the work being done. The surface of the ground must be sufficiently nonabsorbent to prevent the size from sinking in; if the surface is porous, like gesso, it must first be shellacked. (The shellacking of a gesso ground prevents it from being smoothed by a burnisher, so that even on gesso, mordant gilding must be mat.) Mordant gilding is used to lay leaf in oil painting.

morelle salt 1. artificial red iron oxide.

2. an old name for LIGHT RED.

moresque see ARABESQUE.

morinda a yellow NATURAL DYESTUFF obtained from several East Indian mulberry trees and shrubs of the genus *Morinda*. Unlike most natural colouring matters, morinda has rather good resistance to fading.

mortar 1. a mixture of aged LIME PUTTY and sand or marble dust used in fresco plastering.

2. the common cement used in bricklaying, stone setting, and masonry repair. It is made by mixing lime plaster or gypsum plaster, sand and Portland cement with enough water to obtain the desired plasticity.

3. see also MORTAR AND PESTLE.

mortar and pestle the mortar is a sturdy bowl made of metal, stoneware, or heavy glass, in which dry materials are crushed or pulverized with the pestle, a short rod with a bulbous working end, made of the same material as the mortar. Sometimes, the mortar is used for wet grinding, but for paints, the MULLER is more efficient.

mortarboard see HAWK.

mosaic 1. the art or technique of creating pictures or designs with TESSERAE set in a MASTIC or a plaster GROUT.

2. a work so made.

Mosaic is one of the oldest decorative and pictorial arts and certainly one of the most durable. It has been executed on walls, ceilings, floors, pavements, portable icons, and occasionally on furniture and (with exceedingly tiny units) on jewellery. The tesserae may be small pieces of coloured glass, stones, marble, wood, pottery, or any other hard, imperishable material. Mural mosaics are commonly made of opaque glass broken into small cubes. They are set with their fractured sides exposed, to reflect light and give the entire surface a sparkling brilliance. The same sparkle may be achieved by setting flat-surfaced glass tesserae at slight angles or at varying depths. Floor and pavement mosaics are usually laid with flat tesserae or tiles in a perfectly even surface.

Up to and throughout the Middle Ages, mural mosaics were almost always set piece by piece directly into a bed of plaster. Since that time they have usually been assembled in sections in a studio or a shop. In the most commonly used method, known to the Italians as *mosaico a rivoltura*, a small portion of the mosaic is set into dry sand on a tray. Paper or cloth is pasted over the face of the assembly to hold it together, and it is then set as a unit into a surface prepared with grout or mastic. The paper is scrubbed away after the work has set. Sometimes the tesserae are glued facedown on a paper cartoon, then transferred to the wall.

Mosaic was extensively used in Greek, Roman and other ancient civilizations. The earliest known works that may be classified as mosaic are Sumerian surface decorations, clay cones with plain or coloured heads driven into wet walls, which date from the 3rd millennium BC. Greek and Roman pictorial mosaic appears to have evolved out of nonfigural decoration with stones and shells set in cement, a technique in use in the 5th century BC in Greece, and several centuries earlier in Crete and Asia Minor. Polychrome pebble mosaics were being made by the 4th century BC. Two notable groups of this age, discovered at Olynthos and Pella in Macedonia, are elaborate works that typically contain a central mythological scene, a pictorial frieze and an intricate border. Stone tesserae with bevelled edges came into use during the 1st century BC, at first merely to delineate fine detail (such as facial features) in pebble mosaics, then as the sole element of composition.

One of the most notable extant pictorial mosaics of the Hellenistic period is that from the floor of the House of the Faun in Pompeii (c.100 BC), now in the National Museum at Naples, which depicts a battle between Alexander and Darius. Perhaps the finest mosaics of Imperial Rome are those decorating Hadrian's Villa near Tivoli, including a battle scene of centaurs and wild animals that was probably copied in the first half of the 2nd century from a Greek painting. Until about the 1st century AD, pictorial mosaic was done almost exclusively on floors and pavements; mural mosaic did not become common until the early Christian era.

The potentialities of pictorial mosaic using opaque glass tesserae were most fully realized in Byzantium and in the West in mediaeval works influenced by the Byzantine style, as evidenced by the sumptuous examples in churches at Constantinople, Ravenna, Venice and Rome. In Byzantium, mosaic was the predominant representational art form and was usually integrated with the architectural composition of a church. This integration is well exemplified in the mural mosaics of the 11th-century Catholicon at Daphne, in Greece. The mosaics include hierarchical arrangements of the figures of Christ, the Virgin, saints, and prophets – a common feature of Byzantine art. Dominating all is the resplendent *Christ Pantocrator* in the cupola, one of the glories of Byzantine mosaic.

During the Renaissance skilled mosaicists, or families of mosaicists, began to execute works designed by painters. Raphael, for example, supplied cartoons for mosaics done about 1516 in the dome of the Chigi Chapel of Santa Maria del Popolo in Rome, and several mosaics for the Basilica of St Mark in Venice were done between 1535 and 1545 from cartoons by Titian.

The attempt to duplicate in mosaic the effects of the paintbrush, and the delegation of its execution to craftsmen – concomitant developments of the 15th century – mark the beginning of the decline of mosaic art. Although it has been in eclipse for several centuries, it has never been completely abandoned. A taste for colour and decoration in architecture and the need for a durable medium that can withstand outdoor exposure brought about a considerable revival of the technique in the mid-20th century. One of the more striking modern mosaic works is that executed on the walls of the library of the University of Mexico in the 1950s from designs by Juan O'Gorman.

mosaic gold, aurum musivum, cat's gold, mock gold, porporino or **purpurino** tin bisulphide, a fairly permanent pigment with a strong metallic lustre. Mosaic gold was used as a cheap substitute for gold leaf and powdered gold as early as the 13th century, but was replaced by BRONZE POWDERS by the mid-19th century.

moss green one of the many hue variants of CHROME GREEN.

mother mould an outer case or container for a negative MOULD made of gelatin, rubber, or another weak, flexible substance. The mother mould is made of a rigid material.

motif 1. a distinctive recurring design, pattern, figure, shape, or form. **2.** a dominant theme or idea in a painting or piece of sculpture.

moulage the technique of taking an impression or making a cast from a ready-made or natural object. Plaster of Paris is often used for this purpose, but a specially prepared moulage plaster, available in sculptors' supply shops, may be used on delicate or valuable materials, such as art objects in museums and human skin and hair. See LIFE MASK; DEATH MASK.

mould 1. a hollow, or negative, container that is used in the process of casting to give its form to a substance placed within it and allowed to harden. A typical mould is made by coating an original piece of sculpture with plaster of Paris and removing it when the plaster sets. A plaster cast that is a duplicate of the original may then be made by pouring liquid plaster into the cavity of the plaster mould and allowing it in turn to harden. A one-piece mould that must be destroyed to get the cast out is called a *waste mould*. A mould consisting of two or more separable pieces is called a *piece mould*. Removal of the mould without damage to the cast is aided by shellacking the inside surface and using a PARTING COMPOUND. The rubber mould, a 20th-century development, is also in wide use for casting plaster; other materials used for moulds are glue, gelatin and latex. Metal casting is done by SAND CASTING, in which both the negative, containing mould and a positive CORE, allowing the final cast to be hollow, are made of foundry sand; or by the LOST-WAX PROCESS, in which a complex mould is made of gelatin, plaster, sand and wax. **2.** a kind of fungus that grows on various surfaces. It is implanted by spores, microscopic seeds that float in the air. Mould growth begins as a white downy mass, known as *hypha* and popularly called *mildew*. Later on, it becomes green, black, grey or yellow, depending on its species. The more common types, some of which have several variants, are *Penicillium* (green), *Aspergillus niger* (black), *Rhizopus nigrocans* (brown or black), and *Aspergillus flavus* (yellow and orange).

Mould on oil paintings is usually best removed by professional CONSERVATION methods such as fumigation and bleaching. Mould commonly occurs on prints in the form of FOXING, that is, brown spots and splotches; if the infestation is not too severe, it can usually be removed entirely by a hypochlorite bleach process. On the more fragile watercolour and pastel, the removal of mould is very difficult, if not impossible. Mould growth on works of art is encouraged by confined storage in a dark, warm, moist atmosphere – for example, the hold of a ship. Water paints and pastel crayons can easily be protected from it by including a tiny amount of a modern fungicide or mould preventative in their composition. Mould should not be confused with bacteria, which are invisible microorganisms. Whitish areas on an oil painting cannot always be identified as mould without a microscopic examination. Opacified or whitened varnish or an incrustation of foreign material can be mistaken for mould. See also PRESERVATIVE, SILICA GEL.

moulding a narrow strip used for framing pictures and for finishing or decorating walls, furniture, and other structures. It may be applied, as an ornamental strip of wood or metal edging, or it may be actually carved or shaped from the material of the structure it decorates. Picture-frame moulding is distinguished by the fact that it has a rabbet cut along one edge. Moulding may be flat or round, simple or highly ornamented in contour. Part of its decorative value lies in the shadows cast by its forms, which contribute an element of contrasting light and shade.

mountain blue; mountain green mediaeval and Renaissance names for AZURITE and MALACHITE respectively, that were, in modern times, applied to BREMEN BLUE and its greenish variant, BREMEN GREEN. In the 19th century several variants of Bremen blue and LIME BLUE were sold under the name *mountain blue* in an unsuccessful effort to produce a substitute for scarce and costly azurite.

mountain soap or **rock soap** saponite, a soft, blackish mineral with a soapy or greasy feel. It is used as a FILLER OR INERT PIGMENT in crayons.

mouth blower see SPRAYER.

moyen-âge of, pertaining to, or reminiscent of the Middle Ages.

Mozambique ebony see AFRICAN BLACKWOOD.

mucilage 1. a liquid adhesive made by boiling gum arabic solution with a small amount of a preservative and odorant. It is used principally as a paper adhesive.
2. a gummy or gluey water-miscible substance.

muddy colour the term applied to colours in a painting – usually one done in oils – that have lost their luminosity due to an overmixing of colours or by mixing too many colours together.

Mudéjar the name given to a type of architecture and decoration that synthesizes the Gothic and Islamic styles. It developed during and after the Spanish reconquest of the Moors, from the 12th to the end of the 15th century. The name derives from an Arabic word meaning 'permitted to stay.'

muffle; muffle furnace; muffle kiln a furnace or kiln with a compartment or a separate fireclay container, called a *muffle*, sometimes used in firing ceramic wares, and in the calcination of inorganic pigments. The material or objects to be fired are placed in the muffle to protect them from the direct flames of the fire.

muller an implement used for grinding paints by hand. It has a flat bottom and glides across a hard slab or tabletop. From ancient Egyptian times until the 18th century, both the muller and the slab were made of porphyry or other hard stone, and the muller was an irregular cone large enough to be held with two hands. Almost every old woodcut of an artist's studio shows a boy grinding away in a corner. Since the 19th century, the muller has been formed of solid glass, and the slab has been a sheet of plate glass or a marble tabletop. A large early 19th-century American muller was 11 inches high, weighed 22 pounds, and had a

muller

6-inch grinding face. Such mullers were used in commercial production of artists' colours until about 1860, when mechanical paint mills were introduced. A modern muller of conveniently efficient size has a 4-inch face and weighs 3 pounds, but many are smaller. The curved edge at its base is an important part of its design, as it furnishes a wedgelike entrance for stiff paste colours. Mechanical devices for grinding paints include the BALL MILL and the ROLLER MILL.

multiliner tool a wooden-handled metal SCRAPERBOARD tool with a broad, flat end that is serrated into several sharp points so that it can be used to scratch several lines with one stroke. This lightweight version of the MULTIPLE GRAVER is used not only for drawing closely parallel lines on scraperboard but also for scratching the ground on an etching plate, and the crayon on a lithograph stone. The multiliner tool is available in six widths having three to ten points.

multiliner tool

multiple graver see MULTIPLE-TINT TOOL.

multiple a work of art produced by any of the printing processes, usually in large numbers and replaceable at any time, whose value lies in its potential for reaching a vast audience.

multiple-tint tool, threading tool or (US) **multiple graver** a graver whose cutting end is divided into two or more evenly spaced points, making it possible to incise several closely parallel lines with a single stroke. The multiple-tint tool is used in line ENGRAVING and WOOD ENGRAVING, where it serves the same purpose that the MULTILINER TOOL does in etching and scraperboard. See illustration at GRAVER.

multipurpose ground a prepared canvas or panel designed for use with many media, such as oil, polymer and watercolour. Since each painting medium has its own ideal requirements for a ground, and since many of them are mutually exclusive, no multipurpose canvas or panel can equal the excellence of one prepared for a specific purpose, with the exception of the traditional gesso panel, which may be used or adapted for use with all artists' paints.

mummy or **Egyptian brown** ASPHALTUM recovered from ancient Egyptian tombs, where it was used for embalming. Supposedly superior to ordinary asphalt, mummy was extensively used in the 19th century despite its grisly origin.

Munich lake CARMINE.

munjeet see INDIAN MADDER.

Munsell system *(US)* a system of colour notation based on three responses of the human eye to colour: the perception of HUE, VALUE and CHROMA. Each colour is identified with reference to these three characteristics. The system has been widely used since its introduction by Albert F. Munsell in 1915. Since then certain faults in the spacing of colours have been observed and work has been done towards correcting them and improving the system. This method of colour notation is explained in *The Munsell Book of color* (1929) and in *A Practical Description of the Munsell System* (1937) by T.M. Cleland. Compare OSTWALD SYSTEM.

mural 1. a painting executed directly on a wall or ceiling.
2. a painting done on canvas and cemented to a wall (see MAROUFLAGE).
3. a painting done on a panel that is made an integral part of a wall.

Mural painting has, in addition to the technical requirements it shares with easel painting, a set of its own requirements, which make it a distinct branch of painting. A successful mural is not merely superimposed embellishment: it must be appropriate to and partake of its architectural setting. Unlike easel paintings, most of which are intended for viewing at or near eye level, the elevation of all or part of a mural, as well as its great expanse, often present rather formidable problems of perspective. Ideally, a mural painting's surface should be mat and textureless, so that it may be viewed without glare from any point. It must also be permanent for the expected life of the building and must be able to withstand periodic cleanings.

Fresco, the traditional and ideal technique for interior murals, is a complex, laborious and expensive process that is not widely employed nowadays.

Most modern indoor murals are done in OIL COLOURS and, to a lesser extent, in SECCO, TEMPERA, CASEIN COLOURS and POLYMER COLOURS.

Murals on exterior walls must resist conditions much more adverse than those under which paintings are preserved indoors. Hence, they are best executed with imperishable materials such as mosaic tesserae of stone, glass or ceramics; glazed terracotta tiles; coloured cement; porcelain enamel on iron; or relief stone carving painted with flat colour that can be replaced periodically. No surface paints for exteriors have yet been devised that meet the fine-arts definition of permanence, for none can long withstand the continual bombardment of ultraviolet rays, airborne dust particles, chemical pollutants, rain and snow, and precipitate changes in temperature and humidity. Although fresco has been used out of doors in the drier climates of southern Europe, on walls protected from direct exposure (such as those of porticos and cloisters), it has always failed on exteriors in moist climates. The SILICON ESTER paints offer good possibilities for a longlasting surface paint for partially sheltered outdoor murals.

murex purple see TYRIAN PURPLE.

murrey an old name for a mulberry hue, not used after the 18th century.

mutual solvent or **coupling agent** a VOLATILE SOLVENT that is miscible with more than one class of liquids. ACETONE, for example, mixes with water as well as with oil, alcohol or ethereal fluids. It is also known as a coupling agent because it can cause two ordinarily immiscible liquids to combine with each other to form a clear solution.

Mycenaean pertaining to the art and civilization of Mycenae and other cities on the Greek mainland during the late HELLADIC period (*c.*1600–1100 BC). In elaborate tombs comparable to those of ancient Egypt, the Mycenaeans buried their dead, wrapping and sometimes preserving them, and covering their faces with golden masks. Jewellery, decorative cups and weapons, often in gold, show Minoan as well as Near Eastern influence. Ornamental stone carving and ivory sculpture have also been found. The Homeric account of the Trojan War was first confirmed by excavations at Mycenae, Tiryns and Troy, discovered by Heinrich Schliemann beginning in 1870.

Mylar the tradename of a polyester plastic available in the form of sheeting and used as a facing to prevent materials from sticking to a surface in operations that require any degree of pressure. The sheeting, which does not adhere permanently to waxes and many plastics in the unhardened state, is readily peeled away after the operation has been completed. It is used in the LINING of paintings and in laminating with polyester and other plastics.

myrtle green one of the many hue variants of CHROME GREEN.

N

NA *(US) abbrev. for* National Academician. A member of the NATIONAL ACADEMY OF DESIGN is entitled to put these letters after his or her name.

Nabis a group of painters formed in France in the late 19th century, of whom perhaps Pierre Bonnard (1867–1947) and Edouard Vuillard (1860–1940) are the best known. They were greatly inspired by, and thus worked in the style created by, Paul Gauguin (1848–1903), particularly imitating his patterning and use of colour. The name *nabis* comes from the Hebrew word for prophet.

nacarat carmine an obsolete term for the highest grade of CARMINE.

naïve art a style of painting characterized by a deliberate lack of sophisticated artistic technique. The use of colour is uncomplicated by unnecessary fidelity to reality, perspective is often askew, and subject matter is usually childlike or naïve. Artists as diverse as Henri Rousseau (1844–1910) and Grandma Moses (1860–1961) have employed this style to capture their unique and refreshingly simple visions.

naphtha a term applied to several VOLATILE SOLVENTS, including solvent naphtha, a COAL-TAR SOLVENT; VM & P naphtha, a petroleum solvent similar to WHITE SPIRIT; and petroleum naphtha, a general term for petroleum solvents of various degrees of volatility. From ancient times to the 19th century, naphtha meant any highly volatile and flammable liquid. In the late 19th and the early years of the 20th century it was most commonly applied to all volatile petroleum solvents of greater volatility than paraffin, including petrol and benzine.

naphthol red a SYNTHETIC ORGANIC PIGMENT exhibiting superior chemical resistance. Its solubility is reduced because of its molecular size and complexity. Although this characteristic improves its lightfastness in the mass tone, it continues to exhibit poor lightfastness in tints.

Naples yellow, antimony yellow, brilliant yellow or *(Fr.)* **jaune brillant** a permanent but rather pale yellow pigment made by calcining lead and antimony oxides. It has long been a favourite among painters because of its agreeable manipulative qualities in oil. Said to have been found in Babylonian tiles, it was used by European artists as early as the 14th century. Naples yellow was supposed by older writers, including Cennino Cennini, to be a native earth from Vesuvius. The dry pigment is manufactured on a small scale, since it is used only for artists' oil colours. Naples yellow is also used in ceramics as a stain to impart a yellow or ivory colour. Because of its lead content, the same precautions recommended for WHITE LEAD apply to it.

Napoleon grey a dark American LIMESTONE.

narrative *(of art)* depicting a story or idea. The word can be used as a nonpejorative synonym for LITERARY.

natch *(ceramic casting)* a protuberance on one of the halves of a mould that fits into a depression in the other half to prevent the halves from getting out of alignment.

National Academy of Design *(US)* the principal ACADEMY of art in the United States, founded in New York in 1826. The Academy and its school for the training of artists served as a powerful influence on the American art world until the rise of modern or revolutionary movements in the 20th century. It is now the leading institution for conservative or traditional painters, sculptors, and architects. A member is entitled to place the letters NA (National Academician) after his or her name. The standard procedure is to admit a new member as an Associate (ANA), who may be elected to full membership after a period of time.

natural dyestuffs colouring matters extracted and processed from plant and animal sources, as distinguished from the dyestuffs manufactured from coal-tar derivatives by modern chemical processes (see SYNTHETIC ORGANIC PIGMENTS). The use of natural dyes for making paint pigments and dyeing textiles has been traced back to the earliest peoples. Other dyestuffs were developed in the ancient civilizations of Greece, Rome, and the Orient; still others, in mediaeval and Renaissance times. Insofar as their use in creative painting is concerned, all the natural dyestuffs can be considered obsolete. However, some are still used for specialized purposes or for reasons of economy; despite their lack of permanence and relative dullness, their low cost makes them preferable to more durable materials in colouring cheap products, such as wrapping papers, scribbling pads and handbills.

The LAKE pigments made from natural dyestuffs were superseded during the 19th century by synthetic pigments of greater brilliance, which have been followed in turn by newer products of superior colour stability. All the natural-dyestuff pigments fade, at varying rates, on exposure to light. On fading, most of them also undergo a change in hue: for example, all the yellows except weld become reddish or brownish; some of the reds become more bluish, and a few will darken before fading. Many of the natural dyestuffs are still employed for colouring foods and cosmetics.

Some traditional natural dyestuffs are:

Synonyms or alternative names for these dyestuffs are listed and cross-referred to the above main headings.

naturalism see REALISM.

natural rose madder a transparent ruby-red LAKE pigment made from the natural dyestuff madder, obtained from the root of the madder plant, *Rubia tinctorum* (Fr. garance); it is known to artists as *rose madder*. Madder was used in ancient Egypt, Greece and Rome for dyeing textiles and, to some extent, for making pigments. It was said to have been introduced into Italy by the Crusaders. By the 13th century, madder was being cultivated on a fairly large scale in Europe, but there is no evidence of its

alkanet	flavine	quercitron
annato	fustio	safflower
archil	Indian madder	saffron
barwood	indigo	turmeric
brazilwood	kerme	turnsole
buckthorn berries	litmus	Tyrian purple
chay	logwood	ventilago
cochineal	lokao	weld
cutch	madder	woad
dragon's blood	morinda	

use in mediaeval or Renaissance painting. Madder lake was most widely used in the 18th and 19th centuries, though never as extensively as the ruby-red lakes made from kermes, cochineal, Brazilwood, and lac.

In 1826 two French chemists, Robiquet and Colin, isolated the colouring principles of madder – alizarin and purpurin – by treating the root with sulphuric acid. The resulting extract, known as garancine, was used to make madder lakes, rose madder, and madder carmine. Prior to this improvement, madder lake had been so costly that its use was confined to miniature painting. For fifty years afterwards, no other ruby-red or rose-pink colouring matter gave better or more permanent results.

Synthetic alizarin was first made in 1868. In the following years, madder lake was superseded by ALIZARIN CRIMSON, a pigment superior to it in every respect. Synthetic alizarin did not replace natural madder immediately. The French government attempted to protect its madder-growing industry by making it mandatory to use madder in dyeing trousers for the army. Since many 19th-century painters believed that alizarin did not have the delicacy or subtlety of rose madder, the latter continued to be available into the 20th century. Today, most painters prefer alizarin, but a few artists' colours made from rose madder can still be found among the European brands. The dry pigment, which is difficult to obtain, is still available in small quantities from Holland. In typical pigment form, rose madder is a very pale pink powder; in oil and watercolour, it seems like alizarin crimson enormously reduced with alumina hydrate. When viewed by transmitted light, paint films of rose madder have a pronounced bluish undertone.

nature morte *(Fr.)* a still life painting or drawing.

naval stores the U.S. Government's designation for supplies of TURPENTINE and ROSIN, products of the distillation of pine BALSAMS. This usage was established by the Naval Stores Act of 1924 and is now in general use in the United States.

naviform boat-shaped.

Nazarenes the derisive name given to the *Lukasbrüder* (Order of St Luke), the German-Austrian equivalent of what was called in England the PRE-RAPHAELITE BROTHERHOOD. This group of artists, founded in Vienna in 1809 by Johann Friedrich Overbeck (1789–1869), for the elevation of German art, aimed to revive the spirit of the Middle Ages and to encourage the concept of art as servant of religion. The movement sought to emulate the works of Raphael and Perugino, and its works displayed a heroic, or at least romantic, quality regarded as suitable to inspirational subject matter. Among its members were Peter von Cornelius (1783–1867), Karl Begas (1794–1854), Franz Pforr (1788–1812), and Julius Schnorr (1795–1872). Although the group was short-lived, it influenced certain painters of similar ideas in England and France, notably the Pre-Raphaelites and Ingres. Some of its characteristics were carried into the works of the DÜSSELDORF SCHOOL by its director, Wilhelm von Schadow.

needle or **point** a fine-pointed instrument used in ETCHING and DRYPOINT for drawing on the plate. In drypoint, the needle is used to incise the metal surface; in etching, it merely cuts through the ETCHING GROUND. Etching needles are available in a wide variety of styles but can also be homemade. The traditional kind, made in one piece, is a well-balanced, double-pointed steel rod about 4 inches long; sometimes the centre of its shaft is twisted, corrugated or squared for a good grip. A type of needle more widely used in etching is a pencil-sized holder of wood or cork into which is inserted a single point; some handles have a screw end that accepts points of different sizes and shapes and enables replacement of worn or broken points. A sharp point is adapted to certain kinds of drawing, but a needle with a slightly rounded point is the standard, preferred needle for general use; it is more easily manipulated and is less likely than a sharp point to dig in to a sudden stop. Lines that have already been inscribed with a graver can be made to taper or swell by using an oval-faceted needle called an ÉCHOPPE; in etching, the échoppe can widen these lines without necessarily causing deeper biting into the plate. The sharpness of a point can be increased by whetting it on an OILSTONE, or the point can be dulled slightly, to prevent it from digging into the plate, by drawing it across glass or cardboard. A blunted point creates coarser or somewhat wider lines. In drypoint, JEWEL POINTS are also sometimes used, facilitating the drawing of curved lines.

needle Etching needles.

needle-point pen see STYLOGRAPH.

negative mould see MOULD.

neoclassical art any art that revives, or is influenced by, the art of ancient Greece or Rome.

Neoclassicism a style of the late 18th and early 19th centuries, particularly in France. The painter Jacques Louis David (1748–1825) was not only influenced stylistically by classical art, but took classical themes for his subject matter. Other artists working in this style were Joseph Vien (1716–1809), J.A.D. Ingres (1780–1867), Anton Raphael Mengs (1728–1779), and the sculptor Antonio Canova (1757–1822).

NEO-DADA

Neo-Dada see POP ART.

neoexpressionist a term sometimes used to characterize all schools of abstract art whose forms are determined by emotional, impulsive or accidental forces, as distinguished from geometric abstraction or any other meticulously planned work. ABSTRACT EXPRESSIONISM can be classified as a neoexpressionist movement. Neoexpressionist art stems from Kandinsky, geometric abstraction from Mondrian.

neoimpressionism the name given to a late-19th century movement in French art, best characterized by the paintings of Georges Seurat (1859–1891), Paul Signac (1863–1935) and Camille Pissarro (1830–1903), which was, in effect, a synthesis of IMPRESSIONISM, with its emphasis on light and colour, and POINTILLISM, the methodical, nearly scientific application of dots of paint to create a very specific, highly formalized effect.

Neoplasticism or **de Stijl** an art movement adhering to principles of abstraction and simplicity. Form was reduced to the rectangle, and colour to the primary colours red, blue and yellow, in Neoplasticist paintings. The group of Dutch artists working in this style published an influential magazine called *De Stijl* between 1917 and 1928; *Neo-Plasticism* was the title of a manifesto published in 1920, and the term preferred for the principles of the movement by its leading figure, Piet Mondrian (1872–1944). Others active in the group were the painter Theo van Doesburg (1883–1931) and the architects J.J.P. Oud (1890–1963) and Gerrit Thomas Rietveld (1888–1964). Their interest in minimal elements greatly influenced graphics, industrial design and motion pictures, as well as painting and architecture.

neoromanticism a mid-20th century British movement in which certain landscape painters, as well as others in the creative arts, sought inspiration in the Romanticism of the 19th century – especially in the work of the poet and artist William Blake (1757–1827). The landscapes of, for example, Graham Sutherland (1903–1980), exhibit a marked romanticism that has been viewed as a singular reaction to the threat of Nazi Germany.

nepheline syenite a feldspathic rock used as a FLUX in ceramics. It fuses at a lower temperature than most potash feldspars, making possible a significant saving of fuel.

nephrite see JADE.

nero antico a black MARBLE with occasional white spots or lines. Used by ancient Greek and Roman sculptors, it is said to have been quarried on the promontory of Taenarum in Greece.

nesting saucers a set of small, flat porcelain dishes used for diluting and mixing inks, watercolours, or other aqueous paints, so called because their flanged bottoms allow them to be stacked up to occupy a small space, while preserving the washes and keeping them clean.

Neue Künstlervereinigung (NKU) a small group of early 20th-century artists, of whom the best known is Wassily Kandinsky (1866–1944). They were formed in reaction to the strictures of the German art academies, which were still too greatly influenced by *Jugendstil*, the German

Art Nouveau. The NKU artists, who were inspired by the new style developed by the FAUVES, eventually went on to exhibit their own work as well as the work of Picasso, Rouault and Vlaminck, among others. The NKU eventually gave birth to the BLAUE REITER.

Neue Sachlichkeit or New Objectivity a form of expressionist art practiced in Germany just after the First World War by such artists as Otto Dix (1891–1969) and George Grosz (1893–1959). It insisted on using representational detail in a clear and precise technique carried beyond the point of normal observation. A phrase often used to describe it is *clinically exact*. Unlike other forms of EXPRESSIONISM, it was often concerned with social and political criticism and satire as well as with the artist's emotions.

neutral colour a colour that is neither warm nor cool, that is to say, not dominated by red or blue. Medium greys and browns are usually considered to be neutral.

neutral orange a prepared artists' colour made of mixed pigments. The best grades contain cadmium orange or deep cadmium yellow and light red.

neutral tint a prepared watercolour of a greyish-violet hue; it is a COMPOSITE PIGMENT usually composed of Indian ink, phthalocyanine blue, and a small amount of alizarin crimson.

Neuwied blue LIME BLUE sold in DROP PIGMENT form.

new blue *(US)* **1.** an unstandardized name originally given to a variety of COBALT BLUE containing chromium.
2. special shades of ULTRAMARINE BLUE.

New English Art Club a society of artists founded principally by the English artist Walter Sickert (1860–1942) in reaction to the restrictions and formality of the Royal Academy. The group, which included at various times James MacNeill Whistler (1834–1903) and Augustus John (1878–1961), was a precursor of the Camden Town group and similar groups.

Newlyn school a loose association of British artists active late in the 19th century in the Cornish fishing village of Newlyn. They were leading exponents of PLEIN AIR painting in Britain.

New Objectivity see NEUE SACHLICHKEIT.

new realism a style of mid-20th century painting that was essentially a rebellion against ABSTRACTION. It embraced movements and styles as diverse as JUNK ART, SUPERREALISM, Rauschenberg's COMBINE PAINTINGS, and Andy Warhol's soup cans.

newsprint the type of paper on which newspapers are usually printed. It is a very cheap paper, made of wood pulp. Newsprint is available for artists' use in pads up to 18 × 24 inches in size, in single sheets up to 24 × 36 inches, and in rolls 42 inches wide. It takes charcoal, soft lead pencil and litho crayon well, and is therefore a popular sketching support in art school classes and for preliminary drawings. Since it turns brown and becomes brittle on relatively short aging, it cannot be used for permanent work.

NEW YORK SCHOOL

New York school the group of painters, working principally in New York City, who gained worldwide prominence in the decade after the end of the Second World War as the creators of ABSTRACT EXPRESSIONISM.

nickel dioxine yellow a new generation SYNTHETIC ORGANIC PIGMENT with excellent lightfastness. However, this pigment exhibits dull tints, having a colouring power less than that of DIARYLIDE YELLOW, and may be soluble in some organic solvents.

nickel titanite yellow a pigment of rather low colouring power, developed in the 1960s and exhibiting exceptional chemical, light, weather and heat stability. It has excellent exterior durability and is one of the cleanest and brightest pigments among the inorganic pigments.

niello 1. a black metallic compound of sulphur alloyed with an amalgam of silver, lead, and copper and used to decorate gold, silver and other metals by filling in incised designs.

2. the decorative metalwork so created. The incised metal surface is covered with pulverized niello mixed with borax, which acts as a flux, and is then heated until the niello becomes a solid mass. After cooling, the surface is scraped, leaving the black, enamel-like metal in the incised lines, and then burnished. The metal surface is then sometimes gilded. This technique, which is particularly adapted to very small, delicate work, dates from antiquity. Good accounts of the process were given by Theophilus Presbyter in the 11th century and by Benvenuto Cellini (1500–1571), who claimed in his writings to have revived it from a forgotten art. Niello is used to decorate both jewellery and larger surfaces – Russian TULA work is a notable example. See also BROAD MANNER; FINE MANNER.

nigged (*stone carving*) dressed, or finished, with a pick rather than with a chisel.

nimbus or **halo 1.** a radiance depicted about the head of a sacred personage as a symbol of glory or veneration.

2. a representation or stylization of such a radiance in a work of art.

The nimbus appears on representations of Christian saints, Old Testament figures, angels, imperial personages, ancient Greek and Roman deities, and venerated figures in Buddhist and other Asian art. The nimbus is usually circular, although it is sometimes hexagonal or lozenge-shaped, and may be rayed. A living person is sometimes shown with a coloured square nimbus, as a sign of reverence. After the 5th century, Christ was commonly depicted with a nimbus containing a cross.

The nimbus is occasionally called an *aureole*, although this term is usually reserved for the radiance surrounding the entire body, rather than the head, of the venerated figure.

nitrate green a variety of CHROME GREEN, usually of cool or bluish undertone.

nitric acid the MORDANT which, because of its powerful oxidizing properties, is most commonly used to bite the design on an etching plate (see BITING).

nitrocellulose see CELLULOSE NITRATE.

NKU see NEUEKUNSTVEREINIGUNG.

noir belge see BELGIAN BLACK.

noncrawl solution see WETTING AGENT.

noncreep solution see WETTING AGENT.

nondrying oil a vegetable oil that does not form a solid film on exposure to air, even over a long period of time, and does not dry even when a drier is added to it. CASTOR OIL is a nondrying oil.

nonobjective not representing any object, figure, or element in nature in any way; nonrepresentational.

nonobjectivism see SUPREMATISM.

normal butanol a volatile organic liquid used as a diluent or thinner for lacquers.

Normandeaux stone see LIMESTONE.

north light light that enters the studio through a window facing in a northerly direction, considered by many to be the ideal lighting for an artist's studio in the northern hemisphere, since north light is least apt to change throughout the day.

Norwich school a group of early 19th-century English regional landscape artists and watercolourists based in the city of Norwich, where they held regular exhibitions of their work. Its two most notable members were John Sell Cotman (1782–1842) and John Crome (1768–1821).

not pressed see WATERCOLOUR PAPER.

note a SKETCH, either in black and white or in colour, from life or nature, subsequently used as a reference for a work to be done in the studio. A note is frequently of a detail and is sometimes done to capture an ephemeral effect. It may be accompanied by written descriptions of colours, shapes, lighting, and atmospheric effects, which serve to refresh the artist's memory when he or she refers to the note for the final work.

not-pressed paper see WATERCOLOUR PAPER.

Nottingham white an obsolete name for WHITE LEAD, used during the 19th century.

nouveau *(Fr.)* a beginner or inexperienced student in an art class.

NP see WATERCOLOUR PAPER.

Nuernberg violet see MANGANESE VIOLET.

nutgall see OAK GALL.

nylon brush see BRUSH, ACRYLIC.

O

oak gall, gall nut or **nutgall** a small, round, nutlike swelling formed on an oak tree by the action of an insect, and used in the preparation of writing INK.

oak tag a strong, tough cardboard capable of standing much wear and tear. It is used for such purposes as making stencils and lightweight mounts, but is not durable enough for use in permanent works of art.

obeche see AYOUS.

obelisk a tapering four-sided shaft of stone, usually monolithic in nature, and having a pyramidal apex. The best-known examples are found among the monuments of ancient Egypt.

objective art art whose subject matter consists of recognizable objects. The term came into use with the introduction of NONOBJECTIVE or ABSTRACT ART and is used to designate REPRESENTATIONAL ART of all schools and periods, from cave paintings to the works of the Expressionists.

objet d'art *(Fr.)* a work of art that has intrinsic material worth over and above its aesthetic qualities. It is applied to all sorts of decorative and precious articles but ordinarily denotes relatively small objects, such as porcelains, metalwork, bibelots, and curios owned privately, rather than displayed in museums.

objet trouvé see FOUND OBJECT.

oblique a style of type that slants to the left, as opposed to ITALIC type, which slants to the right. Obliques are seldom used in printing except for special effects. Sometimes the term is erroneously used as a synonym for italic.

oblique perspective linear perspective in which a rectangular solid is oriented so that three of its faces are shown, none parallel with the PICTURE PLANE. Thus, all three of the sides shown recede from the picture plane at angles (the same or different for each surface, depending on the angle at which the object is inclined to the picture plane and the object's position relative to the HORIZON LINE). The defining lines of all three surface dimensions converge at a separate VANISHING POINT for each set of parallel lines. Because there will be three vanishing points in the depiction of an object in oblique perspective, such a depiction is also said to be in three-point perspective. See also ANGULAR PERSPECTIVE; PARALLEL PERSPECTIVE. See illustration at LINEAR PERSPECTIVE.

oblique projection a projection used in mechanical drawing in which an object is represented with two of its axes parallel to the picture plane, causing the face of a rectangular solid, for example, to be shown unaltered, that is, with four 90° angles. The third axis is drawn at an arbitrary angle and foreshortened by an arbitrary amount. When the third axis is inclined to the plane of projection at an angle of 45° and shown in the same scale as the other dimensions, the projection is called *cavalier*. See illustration at PROJECTION.

obverse 1. *n.* the face of a two-sided object, such as a coin, a medal, a seal, or a panel with a painting on each side, that carries the principal design. The other side is known as the *reverse*.
2. *adj.* *(of an object or figure)* having the top or apex broader than the base or point of attachment. A lightbulb is an obverse object. Any piece of flaring hollow ware, such as a goblet, might be described as obverse, but the word is more often applied to the shape and orientation of a design element, as in an abstract painting.

oceanic art the art produced by the indigenous inhabitants of the island chains of Melanesia, Micronesia, and Polynesia in the South Pacific. This art includes such varied works as the monolithic stone carvings on Easter Island, intricate tortoiseshell carvings, and elaborate skin tattooing.

ochre any clay used to make the earth colours YELLOW OCHRE and RED OCHRE. These clays may also be used as colorants in ceramic slips and glazes. In pigment terminology, the word ochre is often used as a synonym for yellow ochre.

odalisque a female slave in the harems of the East, especially that of the Sultan of Turkey. A favourite subject of 19th-century artists, the odalisque was depicted as a reclining nude or seminude in typically Turkish surroundings. Ingres and Matisse each painted several odalisques.

odorant a fragrant ESSENTIAL OIL added to a water paint or other compound to mask the unpleasant odours of some materials, or to maintain uniformity of odour in a mass-produced product. Traditionally, a so-called clean or simple odorant such as cedar or lemon is deemed more appropriate for this purpose than a sweet, flowery perfume.

oenochoe see OINOCHOE.

offscape; offskip obsolete terms for the distant part of a landscape. See LOINTAIN.

offset *(printing)* the transfer of the inked impression on a block, plate, or stone to another surface from which the actual proofs are pulled. In offset LITHOGRAPHY, for example, a rubber roller of large diameter passes over the inked stone, picks up the impression, and deposits it on the paper. The offset printing process obviates drawing on the stone or plate in reverse. The *positive* original drawing is reversed on the offset cylinder and righted again when it is transferred to the paper. The offset method is most widely used in commercial lithography. When an offset press is available to an artist, however, it may be used to pull proofs from the original stone without affecting their status as ORIGINAL PRINTS.

ogee a CYMA moulding.

oil see BODIED LINSEED OIL; COLD-PRESSED OIL; DRYING OIL; ESSENTIAL OIL; MINERAL OIL; NONDRYING OIL; SEMIDRYING OIL; VEGETABLE OIL.

oil black a rarely used name for LAMPBLACK.

oil colours artists' colours made by dispersing pigments in LINSEED OIL or another vegetable DRYING OIL to a smooth paste consistency. Other ingredients include a DRIER, when the pigment used has a naturally retarding effect on the drying rate of the oil, and a STABILIZER and PLASTICIZER such as wax or a waxy material like aluminium stearate, to give each colour the same buttery CONSISTENCY. A painter in oils may increase the manipulative control of the colours by adding a MEDIUM, and almost invariably uses a THINNER such as turpentine. Oil colours may be applied with a BRUSH or a PALETTE KNIFE, most frequently on a CANVAS support.

Oil colours are no longer made with the highly effective cold-pressed linseed oil, with the possible exception of those manufactured by one or two companies. Artists may still grind their own oil colours with a MULLER and SLAB, as artists did before the end of the 18th century, but the modern power mill can do a consistently better job. Oil colours are universally available in collapsible TUBES.

For five centuries, oil painting has been the standard, principal easel painting technique. Oils remain the most popular painting medium for many reasons: the great versatility of the technique; absence of colour change when the paint dries (there is a great difference in colour between wet and dry aqueous paints); ease of manipulation within a wide range of colour and tonal effects; freedom to combine opacity and transparency or linear and tonal areas in the same painting; light weight of canvas, permitting large-scale work; and universal availability of supplies. The defects of oil colours, such as cracking, yellowing and darkening, can be eliminated by correct handling and proper choice of materials. See OIL PAINTING, DEVELOPMENT OF; see also PROCESS OIL COLOURS.

oil green an unstandardized term for certain industrial, rather than artists', pigments. It has been applied to CHROME GREEN and to BREMEN GREEN.

oiling out the practice of rubbing an oil painting with a coat of linseed oil to obtain a pleasing dull sheen, as an alternative to the glossy finish produced by varnishing. After the oil is brushed on, the surplus is removed and the surface polished with a soft, absorbent cloth. Oiling out is now condemned as a substitute for varnishing, because it has been found to cause yellowish-brown streaks to appear over the paler portions of the painting after a moderate ageing period, through darkening or YELLOWING of the oil.

oil length the proportion of oil to resin in an OIL VARNISH. Long-oil industrial varnishes, such as spar varnish, contain 25 or more gallons of oil to each 100 pounds of resin; medium-oil varnishes, such as the typical varnish used on interiors, contain 10 to 29 gallons per 100 pounds; short-oil varnishes, such as furniture finishes, contain 10 gallons or less per 100 pounds. If an oil-modified ALKYD RESIN is used in the formulation of a painting medium, its oil length must be known so that the formula may be balanced as to the proportion of total oils to total resins.

oil of cloves an ESSENTIAL OIL, the standard RETARDANT recommended for delaying the drying of oil paints. It has also been used as a combination preservative and odorant in water paints. While not as efficient as more modern concentrated preservatives, it is a mild disinfectant, and it masks the unpleasant odours characteristic of some water binders.

oil of lavender an ESSENTIAL OIL (*Oleum lavandulae*) used in perfumery and sometimes recommended as a RETARDANT in oil painting. This fragrant oil is sometimes confused with the product of another species of lavender, SPIKE OIL or oil of spike lavender, formerly used as a thinner for oil colours.

oil of turpentine see TURPENTINE.

oil painting the use of OIL COLOURS on a canvas support. Oil painting was not an invention or sudden discovery, but was gradually developed over a period of 100 years during the 15th and 16th centuries by artists who strove to cope with the problems created by changing times and styles. The technical and stylistic requirements for 14th-century European easel painting were eminently served by the egg-tempera technique, but its dry and linear quality was ill suited to meet the new demands imposed by the development of new ideas and aspirations, the broadening of art forms, and the inclusion of other motifs than the devotional. Fifteenth-century painters turned to materials more amenable to the fluent depiction of flowing and billowing shapes and blended tones, utilizing oils and resins that had been employed for more than two centuries in strictly functional rather than creative painting. Oily ingredients were incorporated into tempera paints to create the intermediate tempera technique seen in some works of Piero della Francesca (*c*.1420–1492), Filippo Lippi (*c*.1406–1469), and Vittore Carpaccio (*c*.1470–1523). In these paintings there were effects that could not be obtained with the pure egg technique. Other painters, such as Antonello da Messina (1430–1479), and the 15th-century Flemish masters, such as Jan van Eyck (1385–1441), applied oil and varnish glazes over tempera underpaintings. Although these works lean definitely toward oil-painting effects, they are really tempera paintings in the modern sense of the term. Thanks to an anecdote by Vasari, however, van Eyck was credited for centuries with the single-handed invention of oil painting, although this claim was disproved as early as 1781. The Venetian painters used more and more oily ingredients, until by the time of Titian and Tintoretto oils were used throughout the painting, although the guiding principles of tempera were still in evidence. Velásquez is generally cited as the first of the great masters who used oils exclusively on a canvas or who could have painted his pictures out of a modern paint box. The whole development of the medium can be traced in the long life of one painter, Giovanni Bellini (1430–1516). His early work was pure or so-called primitive egg tempera (*Madonna Adoring the Sleeping Child*, Metropolitan Museum, New York); later, he used a meticulous, jewel-like glazed tempera (*Madonna and Child in a Landscape*, National Gallery, Washington); and finally he began to use oil colours in strokes rather than glazes. His later portraits and allegorical pictures have always been classed as oil paintings. It is not possible to chart the transition from tempera to oil chronologically, because different painters evolved their techniques at different times; some returned to former methods; some, such as Sandro Botticelli (*c*.1445–1510), never abandoned egg tempera, or if they tried the newer materials, did not alter their styles to utilize the new effects.

oil size see GOLD SIZE.

oil-soluble dyes a group of synthetic organic dyes that are soluble in oil and insoluble in water. They are used for colouring varnishes, lacquers, and such oily materials as petroleum products, candles, etc. The modern ones are unsulphonated azo dyestuffs, which are more permanent than the older resinate type made by precipitating brilliant water-soluble dyes with a rosin or resin soap. Available in quite a full range of colours, none of the oil-soluble dyes is sufficiently permanent for fine-arts use.

oilstone a fine-grained, hard WHETSTONE on which a very small amount of machine oil is placed. The oil reduces friction and carries away the tiny particles of metal that are ground off the edge or point of the tool being sharpened, thus keeping the grinding surface clean and always in contact with the metal. Oilstones are available in many shapes and sizes to suit various purposes. See also SLIP.

oil tempera a paint in which the vehicle is made with a water-in-oil EMULSION instead of the more usual oil-in-water emulsion. Such a vehicle is thinned with turpentine rather than water and is therefore not really TEMPERA as the term is generally understood. It has been experimented with, but is not a usual type of artist's colour.

oil varnish a VARNISH made by cooking together linseed oil or some other drying oil, resins, and driers, as distinguished from SIMPLE-SOLUTION VARNISH, which contains only resin and a volatile solvent. See OIL LENGTH.

oily ingredient the ingredient that, with water, forms an EMULSION in TEMPERA paint, it may be oil, wax or resin. In lithography, the ingredient of the LITHOGRAPHIC CRAYON or TUSCHE creates in the surface of the stone the greasy areas that will accept ink; the areas untouched by a crayon containing this ingredient remain blank when ink is applied to the entire surface of the stone.

oinochoe or **oenochoe** an ancient Greek wine jug with a handle at the neck. Another type of jug, the *olpe*, is similar in shape, but is less tapered at the bottom. Both were used for pouring wine into kraters for mixing. See VASE SHAPES for illustration.

oiticica oil a Brazilian DRYING OIL that has been used in industrial coatings as a substitute for TUNG OIL; it is not suitable for use in artists' materials.

old fustic see FUSTIC.

old master 1. a popular epithet for any of the great artists of the Renaissance period, especially those of Italy, Holland, and Belgium. **2.** any of their works.

oleograph a CHROMOLITHOGRAPH printed with a kind of oil-colour ink on cloth or textured board so as to be an inexpensive imitation of an oil painting. The oleograph was extremely widespread and popular during the second half of the 19th century.

oleoresin a BALSAM or exudation from trees, especially the conifers. Since the term implies that the material contains a resinous substance plus an oil, it is a misnomer, for few if any of the balsams contain an oil in the modern sense. Their fluid constituents are essences (ESSENTIAL OILS) and other volatile materials.

oleum white an early name for LITHOPONE.

olio d'Abezzo see STRASBOURG TURPENTINE.

olive green a hue designation for any of several dull, warm greens; it is not a specific pigment name.

olpe in ancient Greek pottery, a short-necked jug tapering to a foot (see illustration at VASE SHAPES). The word also denoted a leather flask used for carrying liquids. See also OINOCHOE.

oltremontani (*It.* those who dwell beyond the mountains) a Venetian Renaissance epithet for the Flemish painters of the time.

Olympia blue an early name for COBALT BLUE.

oneiric pertaining to a dreamlike quality. Much surrealist work contains oneiric forms or scenes.

one-point perspective see PARALLEL PERSPECTIVE.

one-stroke brush see SINGLE-STROKE BRUSH.

on-glaze or *(US)* **overglaze** *(ceramics)* colour that is applied on top of the GLAZE. In addition to the colorant, an on-glaze contains a flux and a fluid binder to control brushwork. Most on-glazes are fired at relatively low temperatures, thereby allowing the use of certain colours that a porcelain firing would destroy.

onyx a fibrous type of quartz with parallel striped markings, usually black and white or brown and white. It is used especially for cameos.

onyx marble or **oriental alabaster** the *alabaster* of the ancients, a pure white calcite, a precipitated form of calcium carbonate. It is often found in caves in the form of stalactites and stalagmites. Onyx marble from Mexico, called *Mexican onyx* and *tecali*, has been successfully used for sculpture.

oolitic rock rock consisting of small rounded granules that are bound together by a lime or silicate SINTER. Sandstone and certain limestones are oolitic in structure.

opacifier *(ceramics)* an additive used to render glazes opaque. The best and most expensive is tin oxide. Lower priced opacifiers are made from zirconium oxides.

opaque *(of a pigment)* incapable of transmitting light. An opaque paint is one that transmits no light and can readily be made to cover or hide what is under it. A *semiopaque* paint transmits very little light, but is incapable of concealing dark colours and strong markings under it unless an unusually heavy coat is applied. See also TRANSLUCENT; TRANSPARENT.

In painting techniques, opaque and transparent pigments produce colour effects in two different ways. Watercolour employs transparent colour, relying on the brilliant white paper to create white and pale colours; casein, gouache, and pastel are completely opaque, using white pigment to obtain whites and pale colours. Tempera is semiopaque, combining the effects of both systems, and oil painting is capable of utilizing opaque, translucent, and transparent effects, sometimes all in the same painting.

opalescence a cloudy IRIDESCENCE that resembles the play of colours in an opal; a translucent milkiness with a fiery red undertone.

opaline paper a glossy variety of PARCHMENT PAPER.

opaque projector a lantern that throws an enlarged image of a small drawing, painting, print or photograph on a blank surface, where it can be traced. Artists have used this device to enlarge a small work of art and to transfer a drawing to a canvas, panel or wall. Some of the more elaborate models can be mounted on a wall so that the image is projected down on to a drawing table; others, used in commercial art studios, have a built-in drawing board and a hood or curtains to screen the working area from room lighting.

opaque white; opaque black aqueous colours with great hiding power, especially prepared for use in retouching, correcting or heightening photographs, illustrations and drawings that are to be reproduced. These colours have excellent hiding power. Opaque white must be distinguished from CORRECTION WHITE, which does not have a water medium.

op art or **optical art** an abstract style of art that emerged in the early 1960s and culminated in 1965 with a major exhibition at the Museum of Modern Art in New York City entitled 'The Responsive Eye'. The movement differed from other styles primarily by its radical use of space and colour. Using hard-edged, flatly painted shapes in black and white, or complementary colours of full intensity, the artists made their viewers experience light, movement, transparency and illusion in a nontraditional way.

The early pioneers of this international style were Kasimir Malevitch, Joseph Balla, Piet Mondrian, Marcel Duchamp, Berlewi, Joseph Albers, Cunningham and Victor Vasarely. The younger generation was best exemplified by the American Richard Anuszkiewicz and in black and white by the British artist Bridget Riley.

open *(ceramics)* to render a CLAY BODY more porous by adding GROG. Opening the body expedites drying, thus permitting thicker cross sections for heavy pottery and sculptural pieces.

opening a private showing of an exhibition of works of art, usually held on the day prior to its opening to the public. It was formerly called VARNISHING DAY.

ophite any of several mottled rocks, usually green, whose surface appearance resembles the skin of a snake; SERPENTINE is an example. The name is derived from the Greek word for serpent.

optical mixture *(painting)* the close placement of small strokes or dots of separate colours on a painting surface, so that when the picture is viewed from beyond a certain distance they create the effect of mixed colours of considerable brilliance. For example, numerous dots of blue and red appear as violet to the observer when viewed from a distance, according to the principle of optical mixture. This painting technique was fully explored by the practitioners of IMPRESSIONISM and POINTILLISM.

opus sectile stone inlay or tiling pieces cut to follow the outline of the design.

orange mineral a lead oxide similar to RED LEAD, but more yellowish and less intense. It is not sufficiently permanent for artists' use. Orange mineral has better pigment properties than red lead and is more desirable as a pigment in some industrial coatings.

orange-peel effect a surface texture that some coating materials exhibit when they dry, resembling in miniature the irregular surface of an orange. Although this is a normal, acceptable condition of some coatings, notably shellac, it is considered an aberration or defect in coatings such as varnishes, that are intended to dry to a perfectly smooth surface.

orange pigments pigments of an orange hue, the following of which are approved for use in oil paints in the United States by ASTM and are generally acceptable in all other easel-painting techniques: DINITRANILINE ORANGE, CADMIUM ORANGE, BENZIMIDAZOLINE ORANGE, PERINONE ORANGE and QUINACRIDONE GOLD. Obsolete orange pigments no longer used by artists include ANTIMONY ORANGE, REALGAR, ORANGE MINERAL, and ORANGE VERMILION.

orange shellac see LAC.

orange vermilion a term sometimes applied to the more yellowish kinds of VERMILION.

orant 1. *(ancient Greek art)* a figure in a praying posture.
2. *(Christian art)* a standing figure with arms raised in prayer.

orchil, archil, endbear or **red indigo** an obsolete ruby-red NATURAL DYESTUFF prepared from various species of lichens. Bluish-violet shades were produced by treatment with alkalis, as in the case of LITMUS and TURNSOLE. Since orchil is only moderately lightfast, it was used for dyeing wool and silk and for colouring foods and pharmaceuticals rather than for making paint pigments. FRENCH PURPLE, or *pourpre français*, was a lake pigment made from orchil.

order *(architecture)* any arrangement of columns. There are five orders in classical architecture. These include the DORIC ORDER, the IONIC ORDER and the CORINTHIAN ORDER, which were developed by the Greeks and later adopted by the Romans; and the Tuscan and Composite orders, introduced by the Romans.

organic pigments 1. *(formerly)* pigments of vegetable or animal origin, as distinguished from the inorganic pigments of mineral origin.
2. pigments containing the element *carbon* in their composition. The modern organic pigments are those made synthetically from coal-tar derivatives, such as phthalocyanine blue, quinacridone red, and hansa yellow, to name a few, along with the LAKES made from synthetic dyes. Those that are included on the ASTM list of approved pigments are generally bright, clean pigments of high colouring power and acceptable lightfastness.

Oriental alabaster see ONYX MARBLE.

Orientalizing period the transitional period in HELLENIC ART (700–600 BC) between the GEOMETRIC PERIOD and the ARCHAIC PERIOD, during which the influence of such Eastern civilizations as Syria, Egypt, and Phoenicia enlarged the scope and transformed the goals of art in Greece. Vase decoration, which was the most important form of art during the Orientalizing period, took on a narrative form; human and animal figures became more important and were portrayed with descriptive rather than geometric precision; and new motifs, such as battle scenes, fighting animals, and winged monsters, were introduced. Perhaps the most significant innovation of the period was the idea of using stone for permanent architecture and sculpture, a concept to which we owe a large part of our knowledge of Hellenic art, as well as the full measure of its greatness.

orient yellow a variety of deep cadmium yellow. See CADMIUM RED.

original 1. an artist's independent creation.

2. a work of art considered as a PROTOTYPE, such as that from which copies and reproductions have been made. See also COPY; ORIGINAL PRINT; REPLICA; REPRODUCTION.

3. the person or an object that is represented in an artist's work.

original print any print made by a recognized graphic-arts process in which the artist has created the master image on the plate, block, stone, screen, or transfer paper and has printed it himself or herself. In the case of a technically involved process such as lithography, a professional printer may assist the artist in pulling the proofs. Since the early 20th century, original prints have been signed in pencil on the lower right-hand margin of the print, close to the bottom of the impression. In limited editions, the artist also records in the margin the size of the edition and the number of the PROOF.

Nowadays, the artist is expected to identify clearly a second edition, both by altering it in some way (as by a change in colour) and by marking it '2nd Ed.' If the artist makes any significant change in the printing surface while pulling an edition, proofs of the reworked surface should be marked '2nd st.' (second state).

When the artist decides that he or she will make no additional prints from a plate, stone or stencil, the artist either obliterates the image (as, for example, by cleaning the lithographic stone), or cancels the printing surface. A *cancellation* is any form of alteration (such as by rounding off square corners) or defacement (such as by incising a line through a printing area) that ensures that further proofs cannot be confused with those of the limited edition.

orlean see ANNATTO.

ormolu 1. gilded bronze or brass used as pure or functional decoration. Although the word is of French derivation (from *or moulu*, ground gold), it is not used in that language but is instead considered the English equivalent of the French *bronze doré*. Ormolu is used chiefly for mounts and ornaments on furniture, clockcases, candlesticks, chandeliers and jewelry. Authentic ormolu is cast and chiselled by hand, and its finish is gold leaf or, formerly, FIRE GILDING. Ornaments made this way should be distinguished from those that, although often cast from the same moulds, are not gilded but merely coated with a golden lacquer. The art of making ormolu reached its peak in France at the beginning of the 19th century, when it figured strongly in the Empire style of furniture, and the finest ormolu cost almost as much as similar objects in precious metal. It continues to be produced today, mostly in France.

2. a transparent reddish-orange varnish used to give lustre and a warm tone to surfaces gilded with gold leaf or Dutch metal and to make silvered surfaces look like gold.

Orphism a style of painting that employed overlapping planes of brilliant, contrasting colours. Related to Cubism, it was more abstract, as well as more concerned with colour. The term was first used by the French poet Apollinaire in 1913. The chief exponent of the style, Robert Delaunay (1885–1941), preferred the name *Simultaneism*. In America it was known as *Synchronism*. The Czech artist Frank Kupka (1871–1957) was also associated with this style.

orpiment, arsenic yellow, auripigmentum or **Chinese yellow** native arsenic trisulphide, a pigment ranging from bright golden-yellow to orange that was used in many early civilizations. It occurs in early Egyptian, Syrian, and Persian art. It has appeared in Chinese cave paintings and is found extensively in illuminated manuscripts, but it has seldom been used in the West by oil painters. Originally, it was made by coarsely grinding arsenic trisulphide into a pigment that worked well in oil but was not reliably permanent, especially in mixtures with other pigments. In the 18th century, arsenic trisulphide began to be produced artificially by precipitating or sublimating the native mineral. The artificial product was both purer and cheaper than the native variety it replaced, but because it was extremely poisonous it was later abandoned for large-scale use. However, a fine grade known as *king's yellow* continued to be prepared for and used by artists until it was replaced by cadmium yellow (see CADMIUM RED). *Sunflower yellow* is a variety of orpiment found in Chinese painting. See also REALGAR.

Orr's white a name given to LITHOPONE after John Orr, the holder of the first English patent (1874) for its manufacture.

ostrum a Latin name for TYRIAN PURPLE.

Ostwald system a system of COLOUR NOTATION introduced by the German scientist Wilhelm Ostwald in 1931. The system covers a comprehensive range of chromaticity variations, arranged in the form of a so-called *colour solid* and gradates its 24 *foundation hues* with both white and black. Compare the MUNSELL SYSTEM.

Ottonian art German art between the early 10th and early 11th centuries. In this period, which takes its name from Otto the Great of Saxony, elements of Carolingian, Roman, and Byzantine styles developed quite quickly into an unmistakably German style notable for an intense expressiveness. Outstanding work was done in sculpture in wood, ivory, gold and silver, especially at Reichenau. The art of manuscript illumination also reached a high point at Hildesheim, Regensburg, and Cologne, as well as at Reichenau.

outline drawing a drawing in which an object or model is depicted by its outline alone. The lines are of equal width and strength throughout. No shading is employed, and no internal features are drawn (as distinguished from contour drawing, in which some internal details may be included). See also SILHOUETTE and the illustration at CONTOUR DRAWING.

oval brush see FILBERT BRUSH.

overglaze see ON-GLAZE.

overmantel or *(Fr.)* **dessus de cheminée 1.** a painting or carving of relatively elongated horizontal shape, suitable for hanging over a mantelpiece.

2. any decoration so located.

overpainting the finishing coat of colour applied to a painting after the preliminary layer, or UNDERPAINTING, has dried. This method of applying colour in two stages is practised in many types of painting, including oil and tempera. The underpainting may be used to establish the forms and design, so that in applying the overpainting the artist can concentrate on the details of technique. The multiple applications of colour may create a desirable colour or textural effect that cannot be achieved with one coat of paint. Overpainting is also useful when many touches or brushstrokes are required for a complex effect, and when a thick layer of paint is desired. Thin, transparent or translucent overpainting is called either GLAZE or SCUMBLE, depending on its nature. Broken overpainting, through which the underpainting is revealed in spots, is called DRAGGING STROKE or scruffing.

overpigmentation the condition of a tube colour that has insufficient oil to impart the proper soft consistency for normal manipulation. This condition may be the result of the manufacturer's overzealousness in avoiding an excessive amount of oil. Some well-made oil colours may be considered to contain too great a proportion of pigment to oil by painters who have become accustomed to very oily colours. The defect of becoming a rubbery, insoluble mass is called LIVERING.

ovolo a convex, quarter-round moulding with narrow horizontal bands top and bottom. The lower part of its curve and the lower band recede deeply. A concave quarter-round moulding is called a *cavetto*.

Oxford ochre, stone ochre or **stone yellow** a fine grade of English YELLOW OCHRE used in artists' colours.

oxgall a powdered material prepared from bile taken from the gall-bladders of cattle. It has been used as a WETTING AGENT in water paints, but modern synthetic products have largely replaced it.

ox hair a fine hair obtained from the ears of cattle, and used in artists' brushes. It is firmer and more resilient than red sable, and is therefore

ovolo (left) Ovolo moulding. (right) Cavetto moulding.

not as suitable for use in the best watercolour brushes. Second-grade watercolour brushes are usually blends of red sable with ox hair. However, the properties of ox hair make it desirable for use in larger brushes, such as the architect's rendering brush, and some painters also prefer a large second-grade SINGLE-STROKE BRUSH, containing some ox hair, to the pure red sable variety.

oxide 1. any compound of oxygen and another element, either artificial or natural. Rust, PATINA and other corrosive surface effects are sometimes oxides.

2. *(ceramics)* the colour ingredients, almost always regardless of their composition.

oxidizing fire *(ceramics)* the normal kiln firing, during which an ample supply of oxygen is maintained in the atmosphere of the kiln. Firing in an atmosphere deficient in oxygen, called REDUCTION FIRING, produces colour changes in the colour oxides of the glaze and clay body.

oxyacetylene welding the process of WELDING with a torch in which the fuel is acetylene mixed with oxygen. Separate tanks of each gas under pressure are connected with a nozzle through which a mixture of the two is emitted, when ignited, as a concentrated jet of blue flame. Oxyacetylene welding is done at 6300° F, a temperature sufficient to melt most metallic substances. It is used in direct metal sculpture.

oxychloride cement or **Sorel cement** a hard, durable, stonelike composition made of CALCINED MAGNESITE mixed with a strong solution of magnesium chloride to a plastic consistency. Like Portland cement, it is used to bind together a mass of inert material, as in stucco or imitation stone.

oyster white a hue designation for any grey-tinted off-white of a neutral shade, that is, neither bluish nor brownish, obtained by tinting a white paint with controlled small amounts of raw umber and black.

ozokerite a mineral wax occurring in the vicinity of petroleum deposits. It is the crude, dark-coloured wax from which CERESIN is refined.

P

paddle *(ceramics)* to form a hollow cylindrical shape from a slab of moist clay by pressing or beating it against a round wooden form with a flat paddle.

padouk, vermilion or **corail** a deep-red or bright-red hardwood from trees of the genus *Pterocarpus*, found principally on the west coast of Africa and in the Andaman Islands.

pagoda stone *(US)* a Chinese marble whose markings, when the stone is cut sectionally, resemble the shape of a pagoda. The markings are due to fossil content. See also FOREST MARBLE.

pagodite see AGALMATOLITE.

paint a fluid or pasty coating material made by grinding a PIGMENT in a liquid VEHICLE to form a dispersion. It is used for colouring and for protecting surfaces by close adhesion. The process of grinding the pigment with strong friction is necessary to disperse the particles, that is, to distribute them evenly throughout the liquid vehicle so that no dry or lumpy portions remain. The mill does not reduce the size of the pigment particles; its action is one of squeezing, not pulverizing. Pasty paints, such as artists' oil colours, are made in a steel ROLLER MILL, while paints of a more fluid consistency may be made in a BALL MILL. Small batches of colour may be handmade with a MULLER and slab.

painted tinware, tole or **toleware** tin flatware, boxes, trays, and other domestic wares that have been decorated with gay painted or japanned (see JAPAN) designs as a means of giving charm to this otherwise rather prosaic metal. Designs are painted freehand or are stencilled on a usually solid-colour background; black, red and yellow are, in that order, the most popular background colours. Details, highlights and borders are sometimes gilded. Painted tinware was particularly popular in the 18th and early 19th centuries, when it provided inexpensive, practical (it did not need polishing) and decorative utensils. It was widely made in Europe from *c.*1760 to *c.*1820. In the United States, the wares of the itinerant tin pedlar were at first unpainted but by the early 19th century they were usually painted. They were produced and distributed chiefly in New England and Pennsylvania. Toleware is still widely used, and although it is not produced commercially as much as in the past, the decoration of tinware has become a popular handicraft.

painterly 1. having the quality of expertly brushed workmanship; technically excellent in terms of control of the brush and the medium of painting.

2. pleasing in terms of the handling of colour effect. The term may be used of painting in which every element, including content, is handled in accordance with high technical and aesthetic standards.

3. relating to the dominance of tonal masses over line as a means of defining form in painting, sculpture and architecture. It was first used in this sense by Heinrich Wölfflin in his *Principles of Art History* (1915), along with its opposite, LINEAR. Because the word *painterly* has other senses, Wölfflin's original German term, *malerisch*, is more precise. *Malerisch* painting, for example, relies less on draughtsmanship to depict modelling than on the juxtaposition of areas of colour, or of dark and light. Because the outlines of forms are relatively indistinct, the viewer's eye wanders quite freely over the whole painting, which gives it a greater illusion of movement. Wölfflin regarded Rembrandt's paintings as the epitome of this approach. The oil-painting medium, developed in the 15th and 16th centuries, lent itself to the *malerisch* style, since soft-edged forms could be more easily depicted than they could be in the tempera medium. See also RUBÉNISME.

painter's etching an obsolete term for an ORIGINAL PRINT.

painting *(art)* the creation of a work of aesthetic import by the skilled application of paint to a surface or ground. The principal accepted fine-arts techniques for permanent easel and mural painting are oil, tempera, watercolour, gouache, pastel, polymer, encaustic and fresco painting. The artist chooses his or her technique, materials, and working methods from among these, according to the effects the artist wishes to obtain, their appropriateness to the work in hand, and personal preference. The artist needs to acquire a thorough knowledge of the craft in order to ensure control of effects and the permanence and appropriateness of the artist's work. The artist paints to express himself or herself aesthetically, to depict persons, objects or scenes, or to commemorate an event. Painting may be used in association with other arts, as in mural painting and decoration (architecture) and illustration (literature). It may also be used in applied art, in such areas as industrial design and advertising. Applied or commercial artwork is almost always done for reproduction and, because the original is seldom preserved, the designer or commercial artist can disregard the technical rules for permanence and employ any means whatsoever to secure desired effects, including the use of super-brilliant, fugitive colours.

painting knife a very thin and flexible blade of tempered steel, sometimes with a rounded end but more generally elongated and triangular, and usually with a long offset or angular tang, used for so-called palette-knife painting – the ordinary PALETTE KNIFE is less suited to accurate deposition of colour. The painting knife is a delicate implement made especially for this work. Artists who specialize in palette-knife painting are most particular about their equipment and soon become collectors of well balanced, finely tempered knives of various sizes and shapes. Although various spatulas, palette knives and slices have been in use since primitive days, the delicate painting knife did not appear before the latter half of the 19th century. See figure overleaf.

painting knife Two examples.

painting medium see MEDIUM.

paint knife see PALETTE KNIFE.

paint mill see BALL MILL; ROLLER MILL; PAINT.

paint quality *(of a painting)* beauty of surface. The term implies the skilful handling and fully realized use of the medium. Although it can be used for any type of painting, it is usually applied to oil painting. It is related to such PAINTERLY effects as a full, substantial paint layer and a pleasing combination of colour and brush-stroking. The term *paint quality* refers solely to the artist's proficiency, and not to the quality of the materials used.

paint remover a fluid or paste compound sold in ironmongers' and DIY shops and used for removing old, hardened paint from furniture, walls and other surfaces. A coat of remover is brushed on the surface and allowed to remain until its active ingredients soften or dissolve the old coating. It is then scraped away with a broad, flat blade such as a putty knife or wall scraper. Paint removers are compounded of several powerfully active solvents and a wax or other ingredient of pasty consistency, which keeps the active solvents in contact with the old coating and reduces flowing on vertical surfaces. Since most paint removers contain ingredients that may attack the skin, they should be handled with care; since all of them contain solvents that emit toxic fumes, they must be used in a ventilated place, preferably out of doors. The uncontrolled strength of paint removers and the fact that they deposit waxy materials that are difficult to remove make them unsuitable for use on artists' paintings.

Paint Standard *(US)* a popular name for the Commercial Standard for Artists' Oil Paints CS 98–62. This is a set of standard specifications defining the minimum quality required for top-grade artists' oil colours. The Standard was established and was maintained by voluntary agreement among manufacturers, representatives of artists' organizations, and the National Bureau of Standards. It was first promulgated in 1942. The Paint Standard established a rational system of pigment nomenclature in the United States. Before the Standard was established, pigment nomenclature was in a chaotic state: some pigments had as many as six names, sometimes as many as three different pigments went by the same name, and new proprietary names were brought out every year. The Paint Standard has been replaced by similar ASTM Standards. Some American names differ from the British ones – for example, French ultramarine is known as ultramarine blue.

palette 1. a thin oval or oblong board or tablet with a thumb hole and finger grip at one end, on which the painter arranges his or her colours. Palettes are traditionally of lightweight wood, although some are now made of aluminium or plastic. Some painters use a palette of a dark wood colour, others prefer a lacquered white or pale neutral colour. Sometimes a glass or marble-topped table is preferred to a hand-held palette. See also ARM PALETTE; DISPOSABLE PALETTE.

2. the complete set of colours suitable or available for use in a technique, method, or medium of painting.

3. the selected group of colours an artist has chosen to use in a particular picture.

4. see POTTER'S PALETTE.

palette, limited see RESTRICTED PALETTE.

palette cup see DIPPER.

palette knife a flexible, spatulate blade of tempered steel with a rounded end, securely set in a strong hardwood handle. Straight and tapered palette knives are made in numerous sizes. Those commonly used by artists have blades from 3 to 4 inches long. Some are set straight in their handles; others have angular tangs that help keep the artist's knuckles from touching the paint. Palette knives serve a number of purposes: they are used for handling paint on the palette, for scraping, for mixing pigments with oil or other vehicles, and for spreading paint on the canvas. This last operation, however, is better served by the PAINTING KNIFE. Larger knives or spatulas (6- to 8-inch blades) for heavy-duty mixing of pigment and vehicle are called *paint knives*. After considerable use, the edges of a palette knife are apt to become dangerously sharp and it should then be discarded.

palette knife Two examples.

palette-knife painting a painting technique in which oil colours are applied with spatulate blades instead of with brushes. The most useful implement for palette-knife painting is the PAINTING KNIFE, especially made for this purpose. The ordinary PALETTE KNIFE, designed for heavy-duty use in mixing colours on the palette, is not as well adapted for use in painting. A blade was occasionally used to spread on or smooth out oil paint on canvas at least as far back as the 17th century, but palette-knife painting appeared as a technique after the standardization of the plastic consistency of commercial tube colours in the mid-19th century.

palette, restricted see RESTRICTED PALETTE.

palimpsest 1. *(originally)* a PARCHMENT that had been used more than once. The original writing on a piece of parchment could be eradicated by washing, bleaching, abrasion or a combination of methods, so that the parchment might be reused for another manuscript. The use of palimpsests for letters, documents, and literature was common in ancient Greece and Rome and increased throughout the Middle Ages as parchment became scarcer. Although the practice of reusing parchment was forbidden during the Renaissance, it was only with the advent of printing that it ceased altogether.

2. *(modern usage)* any canvas, panel, or paper that has been reused. Thus, a second painting done over an earlier one or on the back of a canvas, one side of which has already been used, may be called a palimpsest. The term is also applied to a memorial brass that has inscriptions on both sides, the side not exposed being the older and often, though not necessarily, the more important.

palisander see ROSEWOOD.

Palissy ware a glazed ceramic ware made in France in the 16th century and named after the potter Bernard Palissy (*c.*1510–1589). It is decorated with coloured natural shapes, such as flowers and seashells, in high relief.

palladium leaf a thin, beaten leaf used in gilding for a silvery effect. Palladium is a precious metal belonging to the platinum group of elements. Although it is somewhat duller than silver and has a slightly leaden quality, it does not tarnish at normal temperatures and is therefore frequently preferred to silver when a permanent result is desired.

palmette the conventionalized palm leaf ornament; a radiating cluster of petals. The palmette was widely used in classical architecture and occurs often as an element of an ANTHEMION.

palmette

palmwood see LAUREL sense 3.

panel any rigid, flat support for painting, such as wood or wallboard, prepared with a ground. GESSO panels, made primarily for tempera painting, can also be used for oil; more often, an oil ground is used for oil painting. Although panels may be textured, most artists who prefer them to canvas do so for their flat smoothness, as well as their rigidity. A wooden panel is sturdier than a canvas and so would be expected to be more durable, but museum conservators observe that both show the effects of time to about the same degree.

Pannetier's green an obsolete name for VIRIDIAN, after its inventor.

panorama 1. a broad, all-inclusive view of a wide landscape.

2. an 18th- and 19th-century display or exhibition technique, popular for its entertainment and educational value, consisting of a continuous landscape, sometimes depicting a long journey, painted on a long roll of canvas that could be stretched around the walls of a room. In the mid-19th century the panorama became a travelling entertainment, especially in America: the long roll was wound on two cylinders to be slowly unrolled behind a frame, accompanied by a lecture and sometimes by music. It may be considered a crude forerunner of the stereopticon slide and the motion picture. Generally painted in a broad, simple style with few aesthetic pretensions, the panorama had the great advantage of portability over such displays as the COSMORAMA and the DIORAMA.

pantheon *(classical architecture)* **1.** a temple dedicated to all the gods. **2.** a representation of all or several of the gods of a given religion. See also MANDALA.

pantograph a device used to copy, enlarge, or reduce a work of art. It operates on essentially the same principle as lazy tongs. Four strips of wood or some other material are hinged together in a square so that they overlap and can be adjusted according to the scale of the copy to be made; the end of one of the strips is anchored to the drawing board. The four sides move in unison so that as the lines of the original are followed by a tracing point, they are repeated in the same or a different scale by a pencil point on the surface on which the original is to be copied. The pantograph is available in a number of grades, from professional models of great precision to inexpensive, rather inaccurate toys.

pantograph

papal cross a Latin cross with two additional crossbars above the main crossbar, each shorter than the bar below it. It is carried before the Pope in processions. See CROSS for illustration.

paper a felted or weblike mass of interlaced plant fibres in sheet form, used as a combination ground and support in drawing, watercolour and pastel painting, and the various graphic art techniques. Fine-arts papers are made of pulped linen and cotton rags; lower quality, impermanent papers are made of wood pulp or of a combination of wood pulp and rag. See DRAWING PAPER; PASTEL PAPER; WATERCOLOUR PAPER. The best watercolour paper is handmade and comes in a number of standard sizes; see PAPER DIMENSIONS.

The forerunners of European paper were papyrus in ancient Egypt, and PARCHMENT from Roman times to the end of the Middle Ages. Paper mills were widely established, and paper was often used as a support for works of art by the 15th century, when the printed book and the artist's engraving came into being.

paperboard see BOARD.

PAPER DIMENSIONS

paper dimensions the standard sizes of watercolour and drawing papers, which have distinctive names. Because the best of these papers are hand-made, the dimensions in inches, given below, are only approximate. Some traditional paper sizes are Demy, 15 × 20; Medium, 17 × 22; Royal, 19 × 24; Super-Royal, 19 × 27; Imperial, 22 × 30; Elephant, 23 × 28; Double Elephant, 27 × 40; and Antiquarian, 31 × 53. See also WATERCOLOUR PAPER.

paper-stencil method a SILKSCREEN technique in which the stencil design is made from cutouts in paper. The original design is covered with a special transparent stencil paper, and the printing areas of the design are trace-cut with a STENCIL CUTTER. The screen is then lowered on the stencil and squeegeed with thick paint, which causes the stencil, with its design areas still intact, to adhere to the bottom of the screen. The design areas are then stripped from the stencil, leaving them open to the passage of paint. If multicolour prints are to be made, a separate stencil must be cut for each colour.

The paper used may be either a special transparent stencil paper or any thin, white bond paper that lies perfectly flat and is somewhat absorbent, so it will soak up enough paint to adhere to the screen. Ordinary tracing paper is not absorbent enough to be used in silkscreen. If need be, the stencil paper or the bond paper can be made more transparent by rubbing it with turpentine or paraffin.

The paper-stencil method is used to make large silkscreen prints of simple designs, such as posters. The method is particularly suited to a kind of impasto work, since paint can be applied more thickly with a paper stencil than with any other kind. Paper cutouts cannot be used, however, with water-based paints, since these would quickly wrinkle the paper and make it impossible to print clean-cut impressions.

papier mâché (*Fr.* chewed paper) a moulding material made of paper torn into strips or pulped and soaked in a binder of starch or flour paste or dextrin. It is easily made and is widely used to make decorative and functional objects, which are usually painted and varnished. See also FLONG.

papiers collés see COLLAGE.

papyrus a material for writing on, prepared from thin strips of the pith of the papyrus plant laid together, soaked and pressed, and then dried. It was used by the ancient Egyptians, Greeks and Romans.

Pará balsam see COPAIBA BALSAM.

paraffin the least volatile and expensive of the solvents distilled from petroleum. It is intended primarily as a fuel and makes an ineffective paint thinner, drying very slowly and leaving a lingering odour and an oily residue.

paraffin wax a semitransparent white wax, one of the products of refining petroleum. It is quite inert chemically and has the characteristics of petroleum or MINERAL OIL rather than of the vegetable and animal waxes. It is sold in several grades, whose melting points range from 50 to 60 °C. Ordinary paraffin wax has few uses in the fine arts, but special refined grades, such as MICROCRYSTALLINE WAX and CERESIN, are employed in wax compounds and adhesives.

parallel perspective linear perspective in which a rectangular solid is oriented so that one of its surfaces is parallel with the PICTURE PLANE, that is, seen full face. Thus, the lines defining two of the dimensions of the object will be parallel with the picture plane and therefore parallel or at right angles to each other. These lines do not recede to a VANISHING POINT, but the lines defining the other visible face or faces of the object do recede away from the picture plane at an angle (depending on the position of the object relative to the HORIZON LINE), converging on the horizon line at a single vanishing point. Because there will be only one vanishing point in the depiction of an object in parallel perspective, such a depiction is also said to be in one-point perspective. See also ANGULAR PERSPECTIVE; OBLIQUE PERSPECTIVE. See illustration at LINEAR PERSPECTIVE.

parallel rule a device used in mechanical drawing to facilitate the drawing of many parallel lines. It consists of two flat rulers hinged together near both ends by two metal strips, on which the rulers swing parallel to each other. Another model consists of a single ruler that slides in a frame.

para red a lake or toner of a bright, opaque, cherry-red colour with a bluish undertone. It is made from paranitraniline, a coal-tar derivative. Para red is fairly permanent for many industrial uses, but not sufficiently so for artists' colours, since it not only fades but also bleeds badly in oil. SIGNAL RED is a variety of para red.

parcel-gilt partially gilt; it describes an object, usually silver, that is gilded on only one surface, such as the inside of goblets and bowls, or that is decorated with gilded designs.

parchment the skin of an animal, often a sheep or goat, processed so that it has a smooth, pale surface suitable for writing on with ink or for painting on with aqueous colours. VELLUM is parchment made from calfskin, although the term is also used today for any fine-grained parchment.

Parchment was first used in the 2nd century BC in Rome and the Near East. The word comes from Latin *pergamena*, meaning from Pergamum, in Western Turkey. Pliny attributes its introduction to Eumenes II (197–158 BC), king of Pergamum, of whose fine library the Ptolemies were so envious that they prohibited the export of papyrus on which writing had previously been done (see PALIMPSEST). Because of its excellent surface and durability, parchment immediately became popular for significant writings and records. During mediaeval times it was widely employed in sheets, books and scrolls for religious and secular writings and music, often lavishly decorated with ILLUMINATION and painting. It continued to be used to a limited extent by artists, especially in portrait painting, up to the 17th century.

parchment glue see GLUE.

parchment paper any of several types of paper that resemble PARCHMENT. Vegetable parchment is paper that has been treated with sulphuric acid to make it resistant to oil and grease. Parchment deed is a tough, durable bond with a parchment-like finish. Imitation parchment is a wrapping paper with some of the characteristics of vegetable parchment.

parergon 1. a work of art created as an activity apart from or subsidiary to one's profession or principal employment. A doctor's painting, for example, is a parergon. The term is derived from the Greek *para*, meaning 'beside,' and *ergon*, 'work.'
2. an accessory or subordinate part of a work of art, as a background scene in a portrait or room details in a painted scene, such as the still lifes in the foreground of many of Vermeer's paintings.

Parian marble a pure white saccharoidal MARBLE of coarse, sparkling texture, used by the ancient Greeks for fine sculpture as well as for building. It is quarried on the island of Paros in the Cyclades.

Parian ware a fine, unglazed white porcelain or biscuit ware whose surface appearance resembles that of Parian marble. It was first made in England about 1840 and was popular during the rest of the 19th century. Decorative pieces are valued as Victorian antiques.

Paris, School of see SCHOOL OF PARIS.

Paris black an inferior grade of IVORY BLACK.

Paris blue another name for PRUSSIAN BLUE.

Paris green see EMERALD GREEN.

Paris white a superfine grade of WHITING.

Paris yellow see CHROME YELLOW.

parmazo marble an Italian MARBLE with a white or greyish ground and black or blue veins. It comes from the Miseglia, Pescina and Bocca del Probli quarries in the Italian Alps.

parquetage the gluing of thin strips of wood to the back of a wooden panel, formerly practised in the conservation of panel paintings to repair cracks, correct warping and safeguard against deterioration. Strips laid flat against the panel are called *parquetage à plat*, while other thin strips, glued on edge, are called *parquetage de champ*. Both of these methods of reinforcement have been abandoned, as has CRADLING, because they frequently lead to further damage to the panel.

parting agent, release agent or *(US)* **parting compound** a paste or liquid material used in casting to coat the interior of a mould in order to prevent the plaster cast from adhering to it. Soft soap or tincture of green soap is frequently used as a parting agent.

parting tool, V-gouge or **V-tool** a GOUGE used in woodcarving, with a steel blade that is a sharply angled V-shape rather than curved or scoop-shaped. Smaller versions are used for woodcut. See illustration at WOODCARVING TOOLS.

passe-partout a method of framing, in which a picture on paper, a MAT and a cardboard backing are bound together by means of adhesive paper, cloth, or plastic tape glued all around the edges.

paste 1. an adhesive substance with a starch base. Common paste, made by cooking wheat flour or cornflour with water, is the standard adhesive used by conservators for mounting and joining paper. Prepared, ready-to-use pastes sold in containers are made of various ingredients such as dextrin and synthetic agglutinants. They also contain a mould preventive and an odorant.

2. *(ceramics)* clay prepared for potters' use. The word is used in such terms as SOFT PASTE and HARD PASTE.

paste blue another name for PRUSSIAN BLUE.

pastel 1. a coloured crayon that consists of pigment mixed with just enough of an aqueous binder such as GUM TRAGACANTH to hold it together.

2. a work of art produced with pastel crayons.

3. the technique itself.

Pastels vary according to the volume of chalk they contain; the deepest in tone are pure pigment. Pastel is the simplest and purest method of painting, since pure colour is used without a fluid medium, and the crayons are applied directly to the PASTEL PAPER.

Pastels are called paintings rather than drawings, for although no paint is used the colours are applied in masses rather than in lines. Soft pastels are used for this purpose; the artist may build up his or her colours without touching them once they are applied, or may blend them by rubbing them in with the fingers or with a STUMP. Although soft pastels are the basic tools of the medium, some artists have used the harder grades of crayon, sharply pointed, to obtain effects similar to those achieved by drawing.

Pastel paintings are among the most fragile works of art, as the colour remains on the surface in a powdery form. When properly cared for, however, they can survive indefinitely. They must be framed and sealed under glass with a thick mat to keep the glass from touching the surface of the painting. A thin spray of fixative is applied to the surface to reduce its fragility, but if used heavily it will alter colour effects, colour relationships and the characteristic soft quality of the pastel.

Artists have used soft chalks and other dry lumps of coloured material since the earliest days of art. One could even claim the method goes back to the prehistoric cave painters. But pastel painting as it is known today was first made popular in Paris in the 1720s by the Venetian painter Rosalba Carriera (1675–1757). Among the great 18th-century pastel artists were Maurice Quentin de La Tour (1704–1788), J.B.S. Chardin (1699–1779), and Jean Etienne Liotard (1702–1789); in the 19th century, Edgar Degas (1834–1917) produced outstanding pastel work.

pastel paper 1. any paper with a fibrous structure that will take and hold pastel colours. Pastels will adhere to a variety of ordinary rag drawing papers, which may be hard or soft, rough or smooth, for various effects. Many pastel papers are grey, blue, or another permanent colour that may contribute to the total effect of the painting, although white is also used.

2. a paper made especially for use in pastel painting. One variety has a surface coated with an abrasive such as finely ground pumice; it is generally preferred for precise, realistic work and for smooth blends. Marble paper, coated with marble dust, also has a granular texture. Another type of coated pastel paper has a flock or velour finish. Muslin pasted on rigid boards has also been used for pastel painting when an especially large surface area was desired. In general, fibrous drawing paper and coarse-grained pastel paper are best for broad, free work, and fine-grained pastel paper for smoothly blended effects.

pastel shades any pale, delicate colour of high KEY, but pastel paintings can be, and often are, done with full-toned, deep colours.

pastiche or **pasticcio** a work of art done in diverse styles borrowed from other works.

pastiglia the technique of duplicating the effects of carving, low relief, or repoussé on a surface by building up a fairly thick layer of GESSO, which is then modelled or tooled and enriched with paint or gilt. In the Middle Ages and the Renaissance, craftsmen used the process to embellish chests, mouldings, and other wood surfaces, and painters built up elements such as jewels and halos with gesso before applying tempera colours or gilt. Occasionally, entire compositions were executed in painted relief. Modern artists have sometimes used gesso under a paint film of normal thickness to achieve very heavy textures. The process is durable only on rigid supports, such as panels; any gesso layer is too inflexible for use on canvas.

pastose thickly painted. See IMPASTO.

pâte or **patte** *(ceramics)* the paste or clay mixture of which pottery is formed.

patent-gold leaf see GOLD LEAF.

patent yellow see TURNER'S YELLOW.

patera a circular or oval ornament with a rayed geometric or leaf pattern, used in furniture or wall decoration. A patera was a Roman saucer or shallow bowl used as a drinking vessel.

pâte sur pâte *(ceramics)* surface decoration in low relief, created by brushing thin layers of SLIP on the body.

patina, aerugo or **verdigris 1.** a film or incrustation, usually green, that forms on copper and bronze after a certain amount of weathering and as the result of the oxidation of the copper; an ancient name for it was *aes ustum*. A fine patina enhances the aesthetic value of antique bronze sculpture and is sometimes induced on new bronze casts by special treatments that duplicate the green copper carbonates and hydrated oxides of natural bronze patinas. The rarer bluish and reddish patinas that are sometimes found on bronze may also be duplicated. A patina is normally a kind of protection, tending to retard further corrosion considerably. Occasion-

patera

ally, however, a malignant kind of corrosion known as BRONZE DISEASE occurs. The process whereby a patina is either naturally acquired or artificially induced is known as *patination*. In a quite different practice known as *bronzing*, a VERT ANTIQUE or other finish is applied to casts of plaster and materials other than bronze to imitate the patina of real bronze.

2. by extension, a mellowing of tone or texture in paintings, prints, stone sculpture, furniture and other woodwork, as the result of age and use.

patriarchal cross, archbishop's cross or **archiepiscopal cross** a Latin cross with a second and shorter crossbar intersecting the upright shaft above the main crossbar. The effect is often that of a Greek cross standing on a tau cross. This cross, especially when the lower crossbar intersects the shaft well below the middle, is also known as the *cross of Lorraine*, because of its use as the emblem of the dukes of the French province of Lorraine. See CROSS for illustration.

pattern 1. the overall composition or layout of a work of art.

2. a decorative design, usually of a repeated figure or motif.

3. a model or MOULD from which something is copied or made; especially the final positive model, usually of plaster, from which a negative mould of foundry sand (see SAND CASTING) or gelatin (see LOST-WAX PROCESS) is made in the casting of BRONZE. When the piece being cast is of so complex a shape that removal of the pattern in one piece would break the mould, the pattern may be made in two or more pieces and dowelled together.

pavonazzetto or **pavonazzo** (*It.* peacock blue) **1.** a white to drab yellow MARBLE with purplish veins.

2. a similarly coloured marble found on ancient Roman buildings and said to have been much favoured by the Emperor Hadrian. This ancient marble has also been known as *Phrygian marble*, because it is believed to have come from Phrygia in Asia Minor.

Payne's grey a COMPOSITE PIGMENT composed of blue, red, black, and white permanent pigments. It is especially useful for watercolours. Although ready-mixed pigments are generally considered undesirable additions to the artist's palette, the continuing popularity of Payne's grey has proved it to be an exception.

paysage 1. (*Fr.*) landscape.

2. a series of French canvases in sizes at one time considered appropriate for landscape painting. See table at CANVAS SIZES, FRENCH.

peach black a variety of CHARCOAL BLACK made from peach stones. It is deeper and more intense than ordinary charcoal. Peach black is no longer in general use.

peach bloom or **peachblow** (*ceramics*) a peach-blossom-pink Chinese glaze with a mat finish. It is obtained by firing an alkaline glaze with copper as the colorant and cooling it slowly to achieve a devitrification of the surface.

peach gum see CHERRY GUM.

peacock blue a rich greenish-blue LAKE pigment made from any of several synthetic organic dyes. Unless labelled with the name of a permanent blue pigment, it can be taken to be a nonpermanent synthetic lake pigment.

pearl see CROSS CLECHÉE.

pearl white a name given to two obsolete pigments, BISMUTH WHITE and pulverized mother-of-pearl waste. The latter was used in the 19th century as a delicate watercolour white, but has since been abandoned as overly precious and superfluous.

pear wood see FRUITWOOD.

pebble mill see BALL MILL.

peep-show a cabinet containing an exhibition of objects and/or pictures that are viewed through a small aperture or with a magnifying glass. The invention is usually attributed to the 15th-century artist Leon Alberti (1404–1472).

pellicular denoting the binding action of a paint vehicle in which the particles of pigment are completely contained in a film, as in oil paint and polymer colours. In watercolour, on the other hand, the binding action is a simple gluing together of particles without an enveloping film, and is described as *cementitious*.

Peloponnesian school one of the more significant schools of sculpture during the classic age in Greek art. The school's style is characterized by simplicity and strength of form. The Peloponnese is the southern peninsula of Greece.

pen an instrument for drawing and writing with ink or a similar fluid. Until the 19th century, most writing and drawing with ink on papyrus, parchment and paper were done with pens made from the stalks of marsh reeds or, more commonly in the Western world, with the shafts of the wing feathers, or quills, of various birds. The metal pen is also a very old instrument, dating from ancient Roman times if not earlier, but it was never widely used until practical methods for mass production of steel nibs were developed in England in the 19th century, after which metal pens soon supplanted quill and reed pens. Bamboo pens are still frequently used, however, by Chinese and Japanese artists, and reeds and goose quills are occasionally employed in calligraphy. The name CROW QUILL still survives to designate the smallest steel drawing pen.

Most pens have a similar construction. The tubular material, whether metal, quill or reed, is cut to a point, which may be sharp or blunt, fine or wide, according to the artist's needs. The nib is usually split a short distance up the middle to give the point greater flexibility, and an S-shaped piece of metal is fitted into the hollow of the point to act as an ink reservoir. The nib may be permanently fitted into a holder or may be removable so that a single holder can be used with a variety of interchangeable points, as is the case with a LETTERING PEN. Certain specialized drawing pens such as the STYLOGRAPH, the FELT-TIP PEN and the RULING PEN used by draftsmen do not have a nib.

pen and ink a sketch or drawing executed with a steel-nibbed pen dipped in ink. Indian ink is usually the ink of choice. The nibs of these pens are made in various sizes, enabling the artist to make wide or narrow marks.

pen-and-wash drawing see WASH DRAWING.

pencil until the advent of the so-called LEAD PENCIL at the turn of the 19th century, the word referred exclusively to a small, pointed brush, such as any of the brushes used for watercolour, which were usually made of squirrel or sable hair. Pencilling was the painter's draughtsmanship. The name 'pencil' is now more commonly applied to a writing or drawing utensil made of a hard, pigmented stick or rod in a case or holder. Most pencils can, if desired, be brought to a fine point. The lead pencil (actually containing graphite) is the most extensively used of all the implements that are called pencils, but there are many other types for drawing and writing, such as COLOURED PENCILS, CARBON PENCILS, FLAT SKETCHING PENCILS, charcoal pencils, and graphite pencils with extra-soft, extra-thick leads. Wood-encased pencil forms of virtually all the chalks, coloured crayons and litho crayons that are usually made in stick form are also available.

penetrant a fluid that, when added to a coating material, will increase its penetration into the surface. This is a useful property in, for example, a wood stain. All the volatile solvents have this property to some degree.

pentacle a five-pointed star, usually including the pentagon formed by extending the sides inward. This figure has had a long history as a magical symbol and amulet. Some of its magical attributes may have arisen from the fact that so complex a figure can easily be drawn with a continuous line, as can SOLOMON'S SEAL.

Pentelic marble a famed Greek MARBLE quarried at Mt Pentelicon, near Athens; it ranges from white to greyish in colour. It was used as early as the 6th century BC and remained the favourite Athenian stone for building and sculpture. The Parthenon is made of Pentelic marble.

pentimento (*It.* repentence) the reappearance on the surface of an oil painting of paint or drawing that the artist had covered by overpainting, as a result of the increasing transparency of the overpainting on ageing. Examples of pentimento can be found in most museums, especially among the thinly painted panels of 17th-century Dutch artists such as De Hooch, in which checkerboard marble floors were painted before the figures were put in, so that the black tiles eventually showed through women's dresses and furniture. Sometimes, there is the ghost of one of the children or small dogs that so often inhabit these scenes. More modern paintings may also exhibit such unintentional effects after some years of aging, and they are sometimes blemished by evidence of brushstrokes running in a different direction from those of the overpainting. A modern painter who has profited from the example of older painters will take steps to preclude the eventual disclosure of these 'repentances'. The painter may, for example, remove lines or colours that are darker than the new paint with a knife or scraper, and smooth out any thick impasto in the first layer of paint before overpainting.

peperino or **Albani stone** a volcanic rock found near Rome. Its name is due to its black specks, which resemble peppercorns. Peperino has been used extensively in architecture since classical times and was occasionally employed in the 16th century as a support for painting in oils.

perforating wheel or **tracing wheel** a finely spiked or serrated wheel mounted at the end of a handle, used to perforate paper along the lines of a drawing in order to transfer it to another surface by POUNCING. This implement is available both in a straight model, with the wheel fixed in one position so that it turns essentially on a straight line, and in a swivel model, in which the wheel swings freely on a rotating axle. Although the swivel wheel was designed to follow the curves in a drawing more easily, the straight model can also be used to trace curved lines.

perforating wheel

performance art, manifestation or **realization** an extension of the art form called ENVIRONMENT to include action. The term 'performance art' has largely replaced *happening* in recent years. Performances are often brief dramas juxtaposing symbolic, often vaguely disturbing, bits of action. The viewers may be seated like audiences at a play, but the art elements and even the action itself often invade the viewing areas.

Pergamene school one of the Hellenistic schools of sculpture of the 3rd century BC, in the ancient city of Pergamum (Pergamon) in Asia Minor. The works of this school were remarkable for their extraordinary vigour and power. The human body was usually shown in positions of extreme muscular tension. One of the best-known major works of the Pergamene school was the elaborate altarpiece of the great altar of the temple of Zeus at Pergamum.

perilla oil a DRYING OIL obtained from the seeds of the plant *Perilla ocimoides*, grown in southeast Asia. It has excellent film-forming properties and is highly recommended for use in house paints and other industrial coatings, but cannot be used in artists' colours because of its strong tendency to turn yellow and spotted with age.

perinone orange a clean, strong SYNTHETIC ORGANIC PIGMENT that exhibits excellent lightfastness in full strength as well as in tints. This pigment may, however, tend to exhibit solubility in some organic solvents.

Perkin's violet or **mauve** see MAUVE. **Permalba** *(US)* a tradename for a COMPOSITE WHITE artists' oil colour, introduced in 1920 by F. Weber of Philadelphia.

permanent blue a name given in the mid-19th century to ULTRAMARINE

BLUE. Since that time the term has been applied to so many products, including synthetic organic pigments, that it is not a reliable pigment designation, unless the name of its colour ingredient is also printed on the maker's label.

permanent green or **cadmium green** a bright, opaque, yellowish-green artists' tube colour. It is a COMPOSITE PIGMENT usually composed of cadmium yellow and phthalocyanine green. Before the invention of the latter, viridian was used. Permanent green is not a standard pigment name, so its reliability is ensured only if its ingredients are stated on the label. Although it is not one of the artist's essential pigments, many painters like the convenience of its ready-mixed hue.

permanent violet see MANGANESE VIOLET.

permanent white 1. see BLANC FIXE.

2. the tradename for a COMPOSITE WHITE artists' oil colour.

permanent yellow an unstandardized term applied variously to BARIUM YELLOW and to some of the permanent yellow synthetic organic pigments.

peroba a pink hardwood obtained from the Brazilian tree *Aspidosperma peroba* and used for furniture and flooring. Peroba is also useful for carving, as it has a firm, close grain and an even texture.

Perpendicular style see GOTHIC.

Persian berries see BUCKTHORN BERRIES.

Persian Gulf oxide a native RED IRON OXIDE. It is the brightest and best of the native red earth-colours, but has been superseded for artists' use by LIGHT RED.

Persian orange an opaque lake made from various dyestuffs precipitated on a base of barytes or blanc fixe; it is not used in permanent painting.

Persian red an unstandardized name applied to LIGHT RED, PERSIAN GULF OXIDE and a variety of chrome red (see CHROME YELLOW).

Perspex see ACRYLIC RESIN.

perylene red a SYNTHETIC ORGANIC PIGMENT of excellent brightness and colouring power. It is soluble in strong organic solvents, however, and its lightfastness is not adequate for exterior use.

perspective a system of representing three-dimensional objects on a two-dimensional surface so that the effect is the same as if the actual scene were viewed from a given point, the objects appearing three-dimensional and receding in depth with the same space relationships. Perspective is a basic element in representational art of the Western world and, traditionally, one of the criteria of its excellence. The use of perspective in depicting an individual form is ordinarily called FORESHORTENING, the term *perspective* usually being reserved for the depiction of entire scenes and structures.

There are a number of different methods, both geometric and illusionary, for indicating perspective. An artist often uses several of them in conjunction to achieve the effect of spatial ordering and depth that the artist desires. The principal geometric system used by artists is called LINEAR PERSPECTIVE. Objects are made to recede in space by being drawn

PÉTARD

progressively smaller and closer together toward the horizon, and are projected on the PICTURE PLANE by means of a system of guidelines ruled to a point or points on the HORIZON LINE called VANISHING POINTS. Structures, roads, and areas of terrain are placed in perspective, for example, by having their parallel vertical lines, when theoretically extended, converge on one or more points. Depending on the orientation of an object, its depiction will involve one or more vanishing points, and depending on their number, the object is said to be drawn in PARALLEL PERSPECTIVE (one-point perspective), ANGULAR PERSPECTIVE (two-point perspective), or OBLIQUE PERSPECTIVE (three-point perspective).

There is a procedure to cover any problem in perspective, but in creative work it is seldom desirable to adhere rigidly to the last degree of LEGITIMATE CONSTRUCTION, as geometrically correct linear perspective is called. Departures within small tolerances have always been made in spirited work to avoid a mechanical or stilted effect. In 20th-century representational work, some of the rules of legitimate construction have been greatly relaxed, particularly those that govern the proportions of the three ZONES OF RECESSION in a composition. In addition to linear perspective, AERIAL PERSPECTIVE, which makes use of such illusionary devices as ADVANCING AND RETREATING COLOURS, may be employed to depict recession and space.

The earliest writer on perspective, according to Vitruvius (1st century BC), was the painter Agatharchus of Athens. His description in the 5th century BC of his stage setting for a new tragedy by Aeschylus led Anaxagoras and Democritus to write further about the depiction of receding and advancing objects on a flat surface and about the CONE OF VISION, the pattern of sight lines from the 'observer's eye' at the POINT OF STATION to the picture plane. Roman wall paintings reveal an understanding of such principles and show a well-organized parallel perspective. The rules of linear perspective were developed and codified by painters and architects of the 15th century. Notable studies were made by Leone Battista Alberti (1404–1472), Piero della Francesca (c.1420–1492), Paolo Uccello (1396 or 1397–1475), Albrecht Dürer (1471–1528), Leonardo da Vinci (1452–1519) and others. See also PROJECTION; SOTTO IN SÙ.

pétard (*Fr.* firework) an outrageously wild or extravagantly coloured painting designed to attract attention. Twentieth-century developments in painting have made this term obsolete.

petite nature a painting in which the figures are between life-size and half-size.

petroleum jelly a grease sold under the tradename *Vaseline*. It occurs in the arts as an ingredient in lubricating and moisture-protective substances.

petroleum ether the most highly volatile liquid obtained from distillation of petroleum oil. It evaporates instantaneously and is dangerously flammable and explosive.

petroleum solvent see WHITE SPIRIT.

petroleum spirits see WHITE SPIRIT.

Pettenkofer process a method of giving a new gloss to dull or whitened varnish on an old oil painting by treating the surface with copaiba balsam and exposing it to alcohol fumes. The process, introduced by Max von Pettenkofer in Germany about the middle of the 19th century, has been discarded as unsound.

petuntse, **petuntze** or *(US)* **China stone** a partially decomposed feldspathic granite found in China and used with clay to make oriental porcelain. Petuntse has a finer grain and a more complicated formula than the feldspars of Europe and the United States. China's supply of this mineral accounts in part for the very early development of porcelain in that country. CORNISH STONE is sufficiently similar in composition to petuntse to be considered its equivalent.

Petworth marble see SUSSEX MARBLE.

Peuron stone see LIMESTONE.

pewter an alloy of tin with some other metal or metals in varying proportions. Pewter is used for tableware, for hollow ware, both domestic and liturgical, and for applied decorations, usually functional, such as door latches. The additional metal, usually copper, antimony, or both, is added to harden the malleable tin and to give it strength, but even with these additives, pewter is easily bent and melted. The quality of the pewter depends on the amount of tin it contains and the metals with which the tin is alloyed. The highest grade of pewter contains a large proportion of tin and a small amount of copper; the low-grade pewter that is sometimes called *black metal* is almost half lead.

Until the 19th century, pewter was made by casting the molten metal in a brass mould, turning it on a lathe to smooth it, and sometimes hammering it to give it strength. Many old pieces of pewter have faint hammer marks left by this last process. During the 19th century, SPINNING replaced the older methods of shaping metal wares. This process eliminated the need for hammering, so that most later pieces have no hammer marks. About the time that the spinning technique was invented, an especially high quality pewter known as BRITANNIA METAL began to be extensively used.

Pewter wares that date from the Roman period have been found in England, but the alloy may have been used even earlier. Although it has been thought of as poor man's silver, pewter has aesthetic qualities of its own and is now highly prized for itself. Most pewter wares are similar in design to simply designed silver. Some continental pewter is engraved, but the soft alloy is not suited to such decorative techniques as repoussé and chasing. Fine pieces produced during the 18th and 19th centuries were marked by the artisans who crafted them with a TOUCH.

phenol carbolic acid, a disinfectant and mould preventive. The full-strength acid is a dangerously toxic material to handle. A 0.1% solution may be added to water paints as a PRESERVATIVE. Since phenol is volatile and does not remain fully effective after the paint has dried, it has been replaced in some products by the more modern permanent preservatives. An ODORANT is sometimes added to a paint containing phenol to mask its aroma.

phenolic resin a class or family of thermosetting resins, the most prominent of which, sold under the tradename Bakelite, is used for making hard, tough, and durable varnishes. The phenolics have replaced the older spar varnishes and copal varnishes but are not employed in permanent artists' materials because of their tendency to darken with age. Flat sheets of laminated phenolic resin, sold under a tradename such as Formica, have great durability and can withstand severe abuse. Artists have employed them in various constructions, such as murals executed by shaping and inlaying pieces of various colours. Catabond, a member of the Catalin group of phenolic resins used in industrial casting, is available in opaquely coloured, heavy solutions that can be used in the studio for slush moulding and solid casting through an easily mastered series of manipulations.

Philippine mahogany see MAHOGANY.

phosphor see LUMINOUS PAINT.

phosphotungstic pigments brilliant, powerful pigments of many hues made from some earlier synthetic dyes by a process that gives them greater colour stability than such colours produced by older methods. Phosphotungstic pigments were developed in Germany during the first quarter of the 20th century. Apart from their brilliance and improved lightfastness, they are not as good as the newer SYNTHETIC ORGANIC PIGMENTS in approved use, and they may show the fault of bleeding. None of the phosphotungstic pigments has been adopted by impartial authorities as suitable for permanent painting.

photochemical embrittlement the loss of flexibility or elasticity of a paint or varnish film through long exposure to the ultraviolet content of daylight. See EMBRITTLEMENT.

photoengraving a commercial RELIEF PRINTING process in which a photographic negative of the original to be reproduced, either linecut or halftone, is printed on a metal plate sensitized with a coating containing a bichromate. After the plate is processed, it is coated with powdered DRAGON'S BLOOD, which adheres to the photographic image only. When the plate is heated, the dragon's-blood dust fuses, forming an acid RESIST on the design areas of the plate. The plate is then etched (see ETCHING) as in an INTAGLIO process, but because the design areas remain in relief, the plate is inked and printed as a relief plate, differing in this way from photogravure, which is entirely an intaglio technique.

photographic realism see SUPERREALISM.

photographic stencil method a SILKSCREEN technique in which the stencil is prepared from a specially sensitized photo film. This method, which is rather more complicated than the other methods by which silkscreen stencils can be made, is essentially a reproductive technique, since no creation is actually done on the screen. Any original work of art done in any medium on any surface can be photographically transferred to the film from which the stencil is made. Every detail of the original is reproduced, including delicate halftones. This process is used chiefly for commercial work. An artist who is so inclined may make photographic-film stencils with only a few supplies in addition to those of standard silk screening, but for such work the artist usually is assisted by a commercial silkscreen specialist.

photogravure the most important commercial INTAGLIO printing process, noted for its high-quality reproduction of HALFTONES and colour artwork. The printing surface is either a flat copper plate (sheet-fed gravure) or a copper-covered cylinder (rotogravure). The original to be reproduced is photographed through a finely cross-ruled screen onto a sensitized copper plate, breaking up the photographic image into cells of even size. The margins and nonprinting areas of the plate are then covered with an acid RESIST, and the plate is etched (see ETCHING), producing wells in the surface. All these *ink cups* are of uniform size, varying only in depth, so that when the plate is inked, the small amount of ink contained in the shallowest cups barely stains the surface of the paper, printing pale areas, whereas the deeper cups take proportionately larger charges of ink and print deeper gradations of tone. The process differs from PHOTOENGRAVING, which is a RELIEF PRINTING process in which halftones are produced by raised dots that vary in size and density. In both sheet-fed gravure and rotogravure, the inking and printing processes are essentially those employed for printing an etching.

photomontage 1. the art of arranging photographs or parts of photographs into one pictorial composition, so that elements are both distinct and blended into a whole that expresses a single idea or theme. **2.** the picture arranged in this way.

photo mural a photographic blow-up enlarged to the dimensions of a wall space and attached to it with wallpaper paste or other adhesive – an art form of the mid-20th century.

photorealism see SUPERREALISM.

Phrygian marble see PAVONAZZETTO.

phthalocyanine blue copper phthalocyanine, a deep, intense, CYAN-blue pigment, with a very greenish undertone and very high tinting strength. It is permanent for all paint uses, and replaces the older and less reliable Prussian blue, which is identical in physical and colour properties. Both pigments, in dry powder form, exhibit a coppery bronze sheen when rubbed. Phthalocyanine blue was discovered accidentally in a British dyestuff plant, when a dark colour was observed in a kettle in which an intermediate (phthalamide) was being made. Curiously, Prussian blue and ultramarine blue were discovered through similar accidental observations. In the United States, the ASTM permits the labelling of phthalocyanine blue and phthalocyanine green with proprietary names, provided the pigments are identified in small print. This exception to the rule was condoned because of the wide acceptance of such names during the period prior to 1942, when the new pigments were being developed. Phthalocyanine blue was put on the market in Britain in 1935 and in America in 1936.

phthalocyanine green chlorinated copper phthalocyanine, a brilliant, cool, transparent emerald-green pigment, with the same pigment properties and permanence as PHTHALOCYANINE BLUE. Phthalocyanine green can be used in place of viridian, although many painters still prefer viridian's less vivid effects.

phyllomorphic resembling a leaf. The term is applied to painting, drawing, engraving or carving that has leaflike details.

physionotrace a device for tracing the profile of a sitter, used in the late 18th and early 19th centuries, the heyday of the SILHOUETTE.

picture frame a structure, usually of wood, in which an easel painting, print or drawing is enclosed to improve or enhance its appearance, to isolate it from a wall, or to link it to a decor, as well as to support and protect it. Prints, watercolours and pastels should be matted and framed under glass with a dustproof seal at the back. To prevent warping, a canvas on the usual lightweight stretcher should be braced in a frame of substantial construction before it is hung on a wall. The mid-20th-century vogue for hanging unframed canvases calls for a more solid and substantial stretcher than the ordinary lightweight variety. Stripping (see STRIP) also fails to support and protect a canvas and should not be considered a permanent means of framing a painting on an ordinary lightweight stretcher. The floating frame, in which there is a space between the canvas and the wood, will not give a painting the necessary reinforcement either, unless it is strengthened at the rear. Traditionally, an unframed painting was considered incomplete. Until the second quarter of the 20th century, the great majority of picture frames were gilded; since then, painted and raw wood frames have also come into wide use.

picture frames (American stock sizes) the ready-made picture frames in various styles and widths that are made in the United States in the following sizes (measurements in inches):

(a) relatively broad, sometimes ornate frames for paintings:

(b) simple, narrow frames with glass for prints and drawings:

picture plane the plane occupied by the surface of the picture. It is conceived of theoretically as a transparent plane through which pass all the lines of sight between the eye of the viewer and the apparent positions of the subjects depicted in the picture. The painter draws these subjects on the canvas as if it were a pane of glass held up in front of a scene. The

8 × 10	18 × 24
11 × 14	20 × 24
12 × 16	24 × 30
16 × 20	24 × 36
5 × 7	11 × 14
8 × 10	12 × 16
8½× 11	14 × 18
9 × 12	16 × 20

painter indicates their supposed distance beyond the picture plane by variations in size and by other means, with attention to laws of perspective. The picture plane is conceived of as perpendicular to the CENTRAL VISUAL RAY, the viewer's most direct line of sight. See illustration at PERSPECTIVE.

picture putty a cement used by conservators for stopping or filling in holes in paintings. It is made with stand oil and chalk or another inert pigment, plus cobalt drier and, if desired, tinting pigments. Ordinary window putty, a mixture of linseed oil and whiting, is not stiff enough to be used as picture putty.

picturesque a style of landscape painting that represented, in effect, a transitional phase between the NEOCLASSICISM of the 18th century and the ROMANTICISM of the 19th. Picturesque paintings are characterized by an emphasis on the interesting and unusual in a scene. The formality of Neoclassicism was rejected in favour of the fanciful, with ruins, follies and natural phenomena illustrative of the subject matter sought by painters of the picturesque.

picture varnish a VARNISH used as a final coating over a thoroughly dried oil painting to protect and preserve it and to create a uniform gloss. Casein paintings are sometimes varnished to imitate the depth of colour in oil painting. The two modern varnishes that come closest to meeting an ideal set of requirements are DAMAR, which dries to a bright gloss finish, and clear acrylic (methacrylate) varnish, which dries quickly to a dull or satiny gloss. An oil painting accumulates adhesive grime and must be cleaned periodically. A good picture varnish must be readily soluble in mineral spirits or other mild solvent so that dirty varnish can be removed by safe, routine conservation methods. MASTIC varnish was popular in the 19th century, when a smooth, glassy finish was admired; damar has replaced it because it has a duller gloss, may be used in thinner coats, as yellow, and is not as susceptible to BLOOM. Copal varnish does not qualify for this use because such powerful solvents are needed for its removal that the colours of the painting would be damaged.

piece mould a rigid mould made in sections, for casting forms that are too complex to be handled in one piece and for making multiple replicas of a model. The face of each piece has two or more small protuberances that fit closely into corresponding depressions on the other piece, keeping them aligned during use. Since a piece mould can be taken apart without breaking it to remove the cast inside, it is reusable, unlike a WASTE MOULD.

piercing a decorative technique in metalwork in which areas of the metal are cut out, leaving pierced designs. It is used chiefly on handles of trays, porringers, etc. A fretsaw is usually used for piercing silver, but a special tool is needed to pierce SHEFFIELD PLATE so that the copper does not show in the cut-out edges. See also À JOUR.

pietà, *(Ger.)* **Vesperbild,** *(Fr.)* **Vierge de Pitié** a painting or sculpture showing the Virgin Mary holding the body of the dead Christ. It is a prominent motif in devotional art.

pietra dura *(It.* hard stone) **1.** inlaid work in which pieces of hard, polished stone are set into marble or another hard surface.
2. stone suitable for such work.

pigment a finely powdered colouring material used in making paint, printing ink and a number of industrial products. A pigment is insoluble in the liquid vehicle with which it is mixed, imparting its colour effect by being spread over a surface. Soluble colours that impart their hues to substances by staining or being absorbed by them are called DYES. A pigment made by precipitating a dye on a colourless, or inert, BASE (see INERT PIGMENTS), thus rendering the dye insoluble, is called a LAKE. A synthetic organic compound that is insoluble and can be used directly as a pigment is called a TONER. In general, toners require reduction with inert pigments to be used in artists' colours.

A pigment is usually classified according to its origin. Those made by processing coloured earths are called EARTH COLOURS; those made by chemical means from inorganic raw materials that are not in themselves colouring matters are known as synthetic inorganic pigments. Earth colours are mined and processed the world over, but the finest grades occur in specific localities: For example, French yellow ochre, Italian raw and burnt sienna, and Cyprian umber are traditionally preferred. Among the earliest pigments used in the arts were native earths such as the RED IRON OXIDES and yellow ochre, and manufactured pigments such as crimson lake, lampblack, and white lead. While a very few of the permanent, artificial inorganic pigments are produced in small amounts almost exclusively for artists' use, the great majority are mass-produced for industrial purposes.

To be acceptable for use in artists' materials, a pigment must be fine enough to pass through a screen of 325 meshes to the square inch; must meet very exacting standards of brilliance, clarity, and COLOURING POWER; and must possess the degree of opacity or transparency and the general colour properties characteristic of its type. In addition, a pigment must be chemically inert, so that it will not react harmfully with other pigments or liquids with which it may be mixed, and it must be lightfast, so that it will not fade or darken on exposure to normal indoor conditions (that is, indirect sunlight, artificial light of average intensity, and controlled temperature and humidity variations). All pigments approved for artists' use will survive indefinitely under the aforementioned conditions, although some may undergo loss of colour if exposed to direct sunlight. In painting outdoor murals, the artist must limit his or her palette to pigments that are absolutely permanent under all conditions of exposure, such as cobalt blue, cerulean blue, manganese blue, Indian red, light red, Mars red, viridian, chromium oxide green and yellow ochre. In fresco painting, the palette is even more restricted, since a fresco pigment must also be limeproof and resistant to acid impurities in the atmosphere. Many brilliant colours used in house paints, printing inks, etc., are labelled permanent, but the industrial connotation of permanence is limited – a pigment that lasts long enough to serve its purpose is called *permanent*, and fading during the required period is called *premature failure*.

See BLACK PIGMENTS; WHITE PIGMENTS; BROWN PIGMENTS; YELLOW PIGMENTS; RED PIGMENTS; BLUE PIGMENTS; GREEN PIGMENTS; ORANGE PIGMENTS; and VIOLET PIGMENTS. See also SYNTHETIC ORGANIC PIGMENTS.

pigment nomenclature the naming of pigments. For centuries the nomenclature of artists' pigments was in a chaotic state. A BRITISH PIGMENT STANDARD was established in 1957 to standardize the names of all permanent pigments. With minor exceptions, the makers of the best British, American and European artists' colours now adhere to correct nomenclature.

pigment properties all characteristics of a pigment other than its COLOUR PROPERTIES, such as fineness of grain, behaviour in paints and chemical stability.

pigment yellow an azo dyestuff used to make a number of yellow pigments of fair to excellent permanence, including HANSA YELLOW, one of the SYNTHETIC ORGANIC PIGMENTS accepted for permanent painting.

pine oil one of the products of the steam distillation of pine wood in the manufacture of WOOD TURPENTINE. Although not a common or standard ingredient of artists' materials, it has been used because of its very slow rate of evaporation as a retardant for oil paints that dry too rapidly during the painting process, and as a preservative. It has an agreeable terpene odour resembling that of some of the perfume oils.

pine-soot black LAMPBLACK made by burning pitch pine. The name is a translation of the Chinese term.

pink 1. a pale red.

2. *(formerly)* any of several yellow lakes of vegetable origin, such as brown pink.

pink colour a pale reddish pigment made by roasting chromium and zinc oxides in a furnace. It is similar to POTTER'S PINK. Although pink colour is useful as a ceramic colour, its low saturation and high cost preclude its use as a paint pigment. Pink colour was made as early as 1836 in Germany, where it was known by its English name.

pink mauve a reddish variety of MAUVE.

pins nails used in the casting of metals to maintain the space between the MOULD and the CORE. They are often made of iron, although bronze pins are used in casting bronze, so that no spots of alien matter will appear on the finished piece.

pinx. an abbreviation of the Latin word *pinxit*, meaning 'he (or she) painted it', formerly inscribed on a painting after the artist's signature but rarely used this way today. *Pinxit* or *pinx.* is still sometimes inscribed, however, in a lower corner of the margin of a print, where it may have the same meaning as *inv.* or *invent.*, abbreviations of the Latin *invenit*, 'he (or she) designed it'. For an explanation of other terms used in marking prints, see DEL.

pipe clay see CHINA CLAY.

pisciform fish-shaped.

pitchers *(ceramics)* pulverized shards of unglazed pottery used as GROG. Faulty glazed ware cannot be used for this purpose since the glaze would change the chemistry and reduce the porosity of any clay body in which it is used.

pitching chisel a short, sturdy, one-piece steel chisel with a relatively broad tip, used to create an edge on the flat surface of a stone. See illustration at CHISEL.

pithos an ancient Greek storage urn. Pithoi, some of which were very large, were often half buried in the earth. They were used for storing both grains and liquids such as wines and olive oil. See VASE SHAPES for illustration.

piuri, pioury, puree or **pwree** INDIAN YELLOW in crude lump form.

plafond painting a painting on a ceiling, usually of ornate or elaborate design.

planimeter or **compensating planimeter** a draftsman's instrument that determines the area of a surface on maps, plans, and diagrams drawn to scale by tracing the perimeter of the area to be calculated. The planimeter automatically compensates for the irregularities in nongeometric forms, enabling the area of any shape to be measured in this way.

planographic printing one of the three major categories of printmaking techniques (the others are INTAGLIO and RELIEF PRINTING). The term was devised to categorize LITHOGRAPHY, in which proofs are pulled from a flat surface (hence the name planography, 'flat writing') rather than from indented or relief areas of a plate. In lithography, both the printing and the nonprinting areas lie in the surface of the lithographic stone or metal plate. The two areas are differentiated only by their respective attraction and repulsion of printing ink when it is applied to the dampened surface of the stone or plate.

plaster a fine, white powder which, when mixed with water to paste or cream consistency, sets to a hard, cohesive mass. Three kinds in common use are lime plaster, used in mortar for fresco, wall plastering, ornamental plastering and fine stucco; GYPSUM PLASTER, used in ordinary wall plastering and made either from gypsum or gypsum and lime; and PLASTER OF PARIS, used by sculptors.

plasterboard see WALLBOARD.

plaster of Paris a soft white powder consisting of gypsum that has been calcined or roasted until three-fourths of its water of crystallization is driven off. When mixed with water to a cream or paste consistency, the plaster soon sets to a firm, hard mass without shrinkage or loss of volume, because it sets before all the water can evaporate. Its speed of setting may be retarded by the addition of a glue solution, or accelerated with a small amount of alum. Plaster of Paris is widely used as a CASTING PLASTER, for modelling and carving, for moulds used in sculpture and ceramics, and as an ingredient of other cements and plasters for special purposes. See also SLAKED PLASTER OF PARIS.

plaster primer or **wall primer** an industrial white paint made specifically to be applied as a first coat to a plaster surface. Its vehicle is oil or oil and resin; it penetrates well and dries to a mat finish. If made by one of the manufacturers of the highest quality house paint, it is a good base or PRIMER for mural painting in oil.

plaster print the end result of a process in which a plaster cast is made of an intaglio plate, thus creating a relief print whose lines stand out above the surface of the plate.

plaster tool a sculptors' implement made of forged and tempered steel, used for cutting, shaping, and incising hardened plaster. Plaster tools may be pointed, square, rounded or hooked, with straight or tapered ends and smooth-edged or serrated blades.

plaster tool Examples.

plastic 1. *adj.* capable of being readily moulded. Common putty and moist clay are plastic materials.

2. *n.* any of a large group of synthetic organic POLYMERS that can be moulded to any desired shape and are capable of retaining the new shape. The industrial plastics, made from synthetic RESINS, are formed (shaped) by moulding, casting, or extruding. Several of the synthetic resins have been used in plastic sculpture for work that cannot be accomplished by using traditional sculptors' materials, and some of them have been adapted to printmaking techniques. See ACRYLIC RESIN; POLYESTER RESIN; VINYL RESIN.

plastic art 1. three-dimensional art, such as sculpture, as distinguished from drawing and painting.

2. art in which three-dimensional effects are created, such as realistic painting.

3. (plastic arts) the creative visual arts, including sculpture, architecture, painting, drawing, and the graphic arts, as distinguished from poetry, music, drama, and literature.

plastic gesso a stiff GESSO, used for modelling and filling in. To minimize shrinkage, it is made with only as much water as will make it plastic.

plasticity the property of a solid material that permits it to be moulded and to retain its new shape. Modelling clay, for example, has good plasticity, as have artists' oil colours, which can readily be brushed on to a surface but then stay put instead of flowing. This latter quality is the opposite of fluidity and the LEVELLING tendency of some paints. The plasticity of a material is measured by the degree to which it resists deformation when a finite force (the stroke of a brush, a palette knife, a modelling tool) is applied to overcome its internal friction and make it assume another shape. Various materials become plastic only when heated, and set rigidly after cooling. Some familiar examples are glass and the synthetic resin products of the thermoplastic type, which permanently retain new shapes after being subjected to heat and moulded.

plasticizer an ingredient that is added to a paint, lacquer or varnish to impart a necessary property or overcome an undesirable one. Ordinarily, a plasticizer is used to impart flexibility and overcome a tendency to brittleness, or to improve brushing qualities and bring about the smooth compatibility of pigment and vehicle. Beeswax has been used as a plasticizer for oil colours, sugar for watercolours, and castor oil for shellacs and lacquers.

plastic magnesia see CALCINED MAGNESITE.

plastic paints see ACRYLIC COLOURS.

plate any thin sheet of metal that is engraved or etched so as to be printed from. The metals most commonly used for plates are steel, copper and zinc.

plate-finished paper a flawlessly smooth, stiff paper or card, widely used for drawing with Indian ink.

plate mark a rectangular impression made on the paper in all intaglio PROOFS except photoengravings, by the embossing action of the ETCHING PRESS along the bevelled edges of the plate. (The edges of the plate are usually bevelled to keep them from cutting the paper in the press.) The plate mark, which forms a kind of frame around the print, is a distinctive characteristic of an original INTAGLIO print, although artificial plate marks are sometimes embossed on photographic reproductions of prints. An ETCHING or ENGRAVING that does not have a plate mark has had its margin trimmed and is not considered a choice collector's item.

plate oil see BURNT OIL VARNISH.

plein air out of doors. The French expression *en plein air* (in the open air) was used during the second half of the 19th century to describe painting done out of doors. Prior to that time even landscape painting was done wholly in the studio. The *plein air* painters, by working directly in the ambience of light and atmosphere, were able to develop new techniques to achieve new effects in their paintings. The new practice led to a realist philosophy that challenged the prevailing Romantic doctrine and strongly influenced the development of later art movements. The mid-19th-century BARBIZON SCHOOL comprised the first painters to work outside almost exclusively, but the artists specifically called *pleinairistes* were a group of Impressionists of the 1880s and 1890s, notably Camille Pissaro (1830–1903), Claude Monet (1840–1926), Alfred Sisley (1839–1899), and Pierre Auguste Renoir (1841–1919). See also IMPRESSIONISM.

Plessy's green an early variety of CHROMIUM OXIDE GREEN made by a special process. It was named after its inventor.

plexiform resembling plaiting, braiding or weaving.

plinth 1. a block that is sometimes placed between a statue and its pedestal.

    2. *(architecture)* the block on which a column rests.

plique-à-jour an ENAMEL technique in which the spaces in a delicate wire framework, filigree or fretwork are filled with transparent or nearly transparent enamels, for a jewel or stained-glass effect. This technique is used for jewellery and precious decorative objects.

plumbago an obsolete name for GRAPHITE.

plumbate ware a pre-Columbian ceramic ware from Central America. Its lustred slip, containing iron and aluminium, was heat-treated in a poorly controlled reducing fire. Technically and in appearance plumbate ware resembles Etruscan BUCCHERO WARE.

plumbic ochre an archaic name for MASSICOT.

plum gum see CHERRY GUM.

plum wood see FRUITWOOD.

plywood wood laminated in layers called plies or veneers, which are glued together under pressure with the grain of each layer running perpendicular to that of the adjacent layer. Artists' panels for painting may be made of thick 5-ply maple or birch. The common fir and other softwood plywoods are not acceptable as supports for permanent painting. See MAPLE DIE BOARD.

pochade a rapidly executed COLOUR SKETCH in oils. This term often refers to a small, rough landscape sketch done out of doors, to be used later in the studio as a reference for the final painting.

pochade box see SKETCHING BOX.

pochoir (*Fr.* stencil), **hand colouring** or **hand illustration** a stencil and stencil-brush process for making multicolour prints, for tinting black-and-white prints, and for colouring reproductions and book illustrations, especially fine and limited editions. Pochoir, as distinguished from ordinary stencil work, is a highly refined technique, skillfully executed in a specialized workshop.

point 1. a sturdy, hardened-steel rod, usually hexagonal and from 4 to 8 inches in length, with one pointed end. It is used for carving stone and is struck with a mallet. A bull point is a thick, stubby version. See illustration at CHISEL.

    2. see NEEDLE.

pointillism, pointillisme or **divisionism** a branch of French IMPRESSIONISM in which the principle of OPTICAL MIXTURE, or *broken colour*, was carried to the extreme of applying colours in tiny dots or small, isolated strokes. Forms are visible in a pointillist painting only from a distance, when the viewer's eye blends the points of colour to create visual masses and outlines. The inventor and chief exponent of pointillism was Georges Seurat (1859–1891). Its other leading figure was Paul Signac (1863–1935).

pointing 1. *(sculpture and stone carving)* a technique of reproducing a clay or plaster model or of copying a finished work through measurements. From many points on a series of planes about the model, measurements are made to the precise depths of the model's form. At corresponding points on the block of stone (or other medium), holes are drilled to the correct depths, and the surrounding stone is then cut away. Pointing may be done in stages: the first step, with relatively few measurements, produces a very rough form of the model in stone; at each succeeding step the measurements become more numerous, the carving more precise. Primitive pointing devices were used by the ancient Greeks; in the 19th century an adjustable pointing machine was developed that greatly facilitated transfer of measurements. The technique is now considered a craft rather than an art; most modern sculptors prefer DIRECT CARVING.
2. *(construction)* filling the spaces between stones or bricks with mortar or cement.

pointing trowel a small tool with a flat, finely tapered blade, used by masons and plasterers. The pointing trowel is used in filling the spaces between stones and bricks with mortar (pointing), in stopping small irregularities, and for work in corners and other difficult spots. In fresco plastering it is used to cut away the excess plaster of the intonaco and to create the joins between areas of the intonaco.

point of station *(perspective)* the point in space that represents the eye of the observer. In any perspective projection, the observer is thought of as having only one eye, which is on a level with the horizon depicted or implied on the PICTURE PLANE. Sometimes, as in a BIRD'S-EYE VIEW or WORM'S-EYE VIEW, the HORIZON LINE is located above or below the picture plane, respectively. See illustration at PERSPECTIVE.

poliment see BOLE.

polishing rouge see ROUGE.

polychrome or **polychromatic** decorated in several colours; multi-coloured. In art, the term is most frequently used to describe the decoration of wood and stone carving in full colour and gold. Much Egyptian, Greek, and other ancient sculpture was originally polychrome, as were such ancient buildings as the Parthenon. Polychrome decoration was extensively practised in mediaeval and Renaissance art.

Polyclitan school an ancient Greek school of sculpture. The name comes from the sculptor Polyclitus (Polykleitos) of Argos or Sicyon, who worked from 450 to 420 BC and who, next to Phidias, was the most admired sculptor of his era. He worked out a system of proportions for the human figure that were illustrated in his famous statue of an athlete called the *Doryphorus*, which was considered to be the canon. Unfortunately, the statue is known only in somewhat stilted Roman copies.

polyester resin any of a series of synthetic resins of the glyceryl phthalate group. Polyester resin is used industrially in the manufacture of paints and synthetic fibre, and it has been used as a moulding material for sculpture, for which it is well suited. It is THERMOSETTING, but before heat is applied the resin must be mixed with chemical additives, a catalyst and an accelerator. The transparent or translucent plastic is made opaque by the addition of fillers, such as inert pigments or metallic powders, and is given colour by adding permanent pigments. Like all synthetic resins, polyester is produced as a raw material for industrial use. Although it is entirely possible for sculptors to prepare and cast it, most works are cast from the sculptor's original model in an industrial workshop, where safeguards are maintained against the dangerously toxic effects of its solvents (notably methyl ethyl ketone) and other ingredients. Severe disabilities have resulted from haphazard use of polyester resin by artists. It may, however, be handled safely by employing forced ventilation and by wearing compressed air masks and protective gloves and clothing. The polyesters belong to the same group as the ALKYD RESINS, the difference being that the oil-modified alkyds are fluid coating materials soluble in artists' safe solvents.

polymer a synthetic or natural substance whose structural unit is a number of identical molecules linked together. The polymer form of a particular type of molecule has a higher molecular weight than the *monomer*, which is composed of single molecules. It also has a different set of physical properties. An example of a polymer is polyvinyl acetate, which is made from the monomer vinyl acetate by subjecting it to POLYMERIZATION. Another polymer, linseed oil, contains triglycerides, that is, molecules of glycerides of linolenic acid linked together in threes. Virtually every film-former is a polymer.

polymer colours water-miscible artists' colours in which the pigment is dispersed in an acrylic polymer resin or acrylic-vinyl copolymer vehicle. The resin is present in the form of myriads of tiny globules dispersed in the water, forming a milky-white, viscous fluid or LATEX. The mixture dries very rapidly, and the particles of resin coalesce, producing a continuous, adherent film. The colour then becomes impervious to water; it can only be removed with a strong solvent, and the brushes must be kept in water while they are in use. Polymer paints have a high degree of toughness, resistance to ageing, and more brilliance of colour and greater flexibility than oil colours. They are remarkably versatile and may be used to create effects that range from an approximation of the water media to an effect like that of heavy, impasto oil paint. They are, however, more suitable for a broad style and FLAT COLOUR than for the kinds of painting that require delicacy of control and BLENDING. Polymer colours should not be used on an oil-primed canvas or as an underpainting for oil colours – because the polymer colours retain elasticity longer than oil paints, it is doubtful that the two types of paint will adhere to each other permanently. Easel painting with polymer colours should be done on the ACRYLIC CANVAS specially primed for this purpose. There are several brands of polymer colours on the market. Although their handling is

POLYMERIZATION

substantially the same and their basic resins are identical, each make is sufficiently different from the others in choice of PLASTICIZER, WETTING AGENT, thickener or method of compounding, for individual artists to prefer one brand or another. Because of these differences, not all brands can be mixed with others; some such mixtures may curdle. Each brand is accompanied by several adjunct products such as POLYMER PRIMER (polymer gesso); MODELLING PASTE; POLYMER MEDIUM and a RETARDANT medium for slowing the drying of the colours in outdoor use.

Following the success of polymer paints in the industrial paint field, they were introduced in the mid-20th century to serve those contemporary art movements and trends in which high brilliance, application to a wide range of textural effects and, above all, the rapid completion of a painting of full-bodied PAINT QUALITY outweigh the superior manipulative properties offered by oil colours. Although polymer colours are necessarily unproved by the test of time and little or no data have been accumulated on optimum painting rules for enhancing longevity, technicians can foresee no faults. The new colours offer excellent promise to the experimentally minded painter. Special brushes (see BRUSH, ACRYLIC) have also been developed for use with the polymer colours.

polymerization a chemical change in which the molecules of a compound (the monomer) are rearranged to produce a new compound (the polymer) with a higher molecular weight, more complex structure, and new physical and chemical properties. Polymerization is employed in the manufacture of synthetic resins and stand oil, and plays a part, along with oxidation, in the solidification of DRYING OILS.

polymerized oil see STAND OIL.

polymer medium a milky liquid, or LATEX, sold with POLYMER COLOURS and ordinarily employed as a DILUENT. It is the same material as the polymer-colour vehicle in which the pigments are dispersed. A mat medium (the ordinary medium containing a flatting agent, usually a colloidal inert pigment) is also available in most brands of acrylic polymer products. Polymer mediums are also used as adhesives in collage techniques, as GOLD SIZES, as protective varnishes for polymer paintings, and as mat varnishes for paper collages and works on paper.

polymer primer a white paste composed of titanium white and other white or inert pigments ground in POLYMER MEDIUM, and used to prepare grounds for painting with POLYMER COLOURS. It is sold in flat, round tins with replaceable caps. Although most brands are labelled gesso, polymer primer has no significant properties in common with real GESSO and cannot be used as its substitute.

Polymer Tempera *(US)* a trade name for the original POLYMER COLOURS available to artists, developed by Alfred Duca of Boston in the late 1940s and based on POLYVINYL ACETATE. These colours were superseded in the 1950s by paints based on ACRYLIC RESIN polymers and acrylic-vinyl COPOLYMERS, which have superior characteristics.

polymethyl methacrylate see ACRYLIC RESIN.

polyptych 1. a set of paintings or bas reliefs on hinged panels, more than three, but usually five. See also TRIPTYCH; PREDELLA.

2. any painting done in more than three sections.

polyvinyl acetate (PVA) a VINYL RESIN, one of the clear, water-white, thermoplastic synthetic resins widely used in industrial coating materials. Polyvinyl acetate has been used since 1935 by museum conservators, who have employed it to coat and impregnate various artifacts for their preservation. Like the majority of the resins used in the coating materials industries, it can only be put into solution by powerful volatile solvents. It is completely insoluble in the mild and slowly evaporating liquids (turpentine and mineral spirits) that are required for use in artists' paints. However, this same property makes it valuable as an isolating varnish. In experimental sculpture, PVA has been used in a hot-melt moulding compound, and it is an excellent PARTING AGENT for polyester resin.

polyvinyl chloride (PVC) a colourless VINYL RESIN. It has been used as a component of industrial paints and as a base for silkscreen inks, but it is not stable enough for use in artists' colours. It is produced as a powder for moulding, in solution, in flexible and rigid sheets, and in solid blocks. In solid blocks it has been used to carve relief or intaglio printing blocks.

Pompeian blue 1. another name for EGYPTIAN BLUE.

2. a label for certain impermanent synthetic lakes that resemble the genuine Egyptian blue in hue. The real pigment is extremely scarce and would be unmistakably identified on its container.

Pompeian painting paintings uncovered in the ruined city of Pompeii, on the slopes of Mount Vesuvius. The city had been buried in an eruption of the volcano in AD 79. Although the paintings depart from the Greek two-dimensional painting without backgrounds and strive toward illusionism and atmospheric effects, they still shed much light on the Greek painting techniques from which Roman techniques were developed, and of which virtually no examples have survived.

Pompeian red a variant of TUSCAN RED.

pompier (*Fr.* pump maker or fireman) *(of a work of art)* pretentious or garish, usually in a trite, stereotyped way.

poncif 1. a French term for a drawing made by POUNCING.

2. any work that is dull and spiritless.

Pont Aven, school of the group of artists who were centred in the town of Pont Aven, in Brittany, when Paul Gauguin was in residence there from 1886–1891, and who were greatly influenced by Gauguin's antinaturalistic style.

pontata see GIORNATA.

pop art, new dada or **new realism** a style derived in the main from commercial art forms and characterized by outsized replicas of items of mass culture such as comic-strip panels, popular foods and brand-name packages. Pop art developed in New York in the late 1950s concurrently with the last major accomplishments in abstract expressionism, which it reacted against and, in the mid-1960s, superseded as the dominant avant garde form in the United States. Late in the decade pop art began to lose ground to MINIMAL ART and HARD-EDGE PAINTING. Among its leading exponents were Jasper Johns (1930–), Robert Rauschenberg (1925–), Andy Warhol (?1931–1987), Claes Oldenburg (1929–), Roy Lichtenstein (1923–), George Segal (1924–) and Robert Indiana (1928–).

popping the appearance in set plaster of small, conical holes, called *pops*. This defect, caused by particles of active or improperly slaked lime, may occur from three months to a year after setting. See LIME PUTTY.

poppyseed oil or **poppy oil** a DRYING OIL extracted from seeds of the opium poppy. It is odourless and very pale, and it gives oil colours an excellent buttery consistency, but in every other respect it is inferior to linseed oil: it yellows more with age, and its dry film is weaker and more prone to cracking. Poppy oil has been used to some extent in hand-ground colours but it is now little used except as an additive to some linseed-oil colours, to improve their consistency, and in some manufacturers' whites.

porcelain, hard paste or **hard-paste porcelain** the finest ceramic ware, usually made of clay, feldspar and flint, fired at high temperatures. True porcelain, called *shing yao* by the Chinese, was first produced during the T'ang Dynasty. It is characterized by a white or very light grey, translucent body that rings when struck. It was first made in Europe in the early 18th century. Because of its durability and resistance to attack, porcelain is also used for heavy-duty utilitarian products such as laboratory ware and electrical insulators. Compare EARTHENWARE and STONEWARE.

Early Oriental porcelain owed its distinctive qualities to kaolin and petuntse. European potters, in their attempts to duplicate this hard porcelain, first achieved serviceable but somewhat softer imitations of it with mixtures of clay and previously fired materials such as ground glass. Porcelain of this type, which is fired at lower temperatures than true porcelain, is now called SOFT PASTE. Johann Friedrich Böttger discovered the secret of its manufacture in 1709.

porcelain colours or *(US)* **ceramic colours** powdered metallic oxides and other compounds used in ceramic glazes, for decorating porcelain, china and terra cotta, and for porcelain enamelling on metals. Most porcelain colours are pale in powder form; their full, deep colour appears when the work is fired in a furnace or kiln. Ceramic colours usually contain flux and other ingredients that make them unsuitable for use in paints. see CERAMIC COLOURS.

porcelain enamel see VITREOUS ENAMEL.

porphyry a dark purplish-red igneous rock. It is one of the hardest of rocks, and was traditionally the best material for the MULLER and slab used for grinding artists' colours. It is capable of taking a high polish and is valued as a durable sculptor's material. Porphyry was first quarried in ancient Egypt.

porporino see MOSAIC GOLD.

portcrayon or **porte-crayon** a handle for holding chalk, crayons or charcoal, consisting of a split metal tube, usually double-ended, in which the crayon is secured by a ring that slides over the split end.

portcrayon

portfolio 1. a carrier or storage container for drawings or prints. It is made of two pieces of strong cardboard hinged together and held closed by a pair of tapes at the middle of each free edge. The conventional portfolio is covered with black paper embossed in a leather grain. **2.** an artist's stock or collection of works on paper offered for exhibition or sale. **3.** an assemblage of an artist's work, especially in commercial art, to be shown to clients as a representative sample, usually for the purpose of securing a commission.

Portland cement a popular building material, made by calcining or roasting limestone and clay in a kiln or furnace. Its main chemical ingredients are lime, silica and alumina. It is so named because of its resemblance to Portland stone, a pale-coloured building stone quarried in Dorset. Portland cement has hydraulic properties; that is, it will set under water, and it sets most strongly in the presence of moisture. The process of covering a concrete surface or object with wet cloths while it is setting is known as *curing*. A white variety of Portland cement can be used as a ground for murals, or coloured with pigments and used in works of art – such as creative or decorative reliefs and castings – that are exposed to severe outdoor conditions. Portland cement is an important ingredient in concrete, mortar and other building materials.

Porto marble or **Portor marble** see BLACK-AND-GOLD MARBLE.

portrait 1. a painting, sculpture, drawing, photograph or other representation, especially of the face, of an actual person; a likeness. Portraiture, the art of executing portraits, is part of most artists' training. Many painters execute self-portraits and portraits of families and friends as a discipline rather than as commissions. A portrait may be full length, head and torso, or head only. A sitter may be drawn or painted face-on (see FRONTAL DEPICTION) but is more frequently portrayed in half profile, less frequently in full profile, or, rarely, in PROFIL PERDU. The SILHOUETTE is also a kind of portrait. In sculpture, a portrait takes the form of a BUST or a HERM, a seated figure (such as the portraits of Egyptian pharaohs and gods), an equestrian figure, a freestanding one, or a reclining effigy intended for a tomb. Some portraits have been executed in relief or intaglio as well, most notably busts on coins and medals and full-length memorial-brass images. Many sculptured portraits are life-size or larger. Painted portraits range from life-size or somewhat larger to the tiny MINIATURES especially popular in the 17th and 18th centuries.

POSTER COLOURS

The portraitist's technique varies widely, depending to a great extent on the artist's attitude toward his or her subject and art, that is, whether the artist reveres truth or beauty more. The key factor in a review of the history of portraiture is that artists have always worked for patrons who wanted to perpetuate their own memories. Most early portraits of rulers and dignitaries are completely idealized. This was especially true in Classical Greece, where carved portraits represented ideal beauty at the expense of individual characteristics, and in ancient Egypt, where portraits were executed as a monument to the sitter's greatness rather than as a commemoration of the sitter's physical appearance. On the other hand, Etruscan and Republican Roman portraiture was by and large very realistic; it included every detail of the sitter's physiognomy and figure, beautiful or ugly. Many portraits were made from DEATH MASKS. Portraiture became a lost art during the Middle Ages, when artists took divine rather than human figures as their subjects. It was revived during the Renaissance, when it flourished as people became more than ever the chief subject of art. Portraiture even entered somewhat into Renaissance religious art, with the donor portraits found on many altarpieces and devotional paintings. Many of the portraits of the 17th and 18th centuries flatter their subjects by depicting them as mythological figures or by placing them in allegorical settings. Rubens' cycle of paintings in the Luxembourg Palace chronicles the life of Maria de' Medici with allegorical imagery; François Boucher painted his patroness Mme. de Pompadour in mythological garb; and Antonio Canova sculptured Pauline Borghese as Venus. Van Dyck, who was perhaps above all a portraitist, captured a likeness while at the same time flattering the sitter. Notable examples are his portraits of Charles I, whom he usually painted on horseback or in a landscape with a low horizon line, in order to make the short English king, who was very sensitive about his height, appear taller and more stately.

Some portraits appear almost to be genre paintings. This is true of Frans Hals's rosy-cheeked young men and Chardin's honest bourgeois women. It is true also of Goya's portraits, in some of which are elements of caricature. Several of the Romantic painters, most of the Impressionists, and all of the Expressionists sought to give sensitive insight into the character of their sitters rather than to express only their physical appearance. Delacroix's portrait of Chopin and Rodin's monumental sculpture of Balzac are prime examples of this.

2. a range of canvas sizes sold in France, in proportions at one time considered appropriate to portrait and figure painting. See table at CANVAS SIZES, FRENCH; see also CANVAS SIZES, PORTRAIT.

poster colours or *(US)* **show card colours** inexpensive opaque colours made with a simple water-soluble binder such as gum or glue-size, sold in jars and intended for work in which no sensitive manipulations or delicate effects are required, such as posters, flat designs, and children's work. The pigments in poster colours are not selected to conform to the standards for permanent painting.

postiche *(Fr.)* a fake, a spurious addition. The word comes from the Spanish *postizo*, short for *apostizo*, 'false' or 'imitation'.

Postimpressionist painting general term for the trends in art, from the mid-1880s to the early 1900s, in reaction to IMPRESSIONISM. Where the Impressionists had presented an objective, analytical portrayal of nature in terms of light, the Postimpressionists Paul Gauguin (1848–1903) and Vincent van Gogh (1853–1890) were concerned with the subjective or emotional content of what they observed, as well as the formal qualities. Paul Cézanne (1839–1906), who had exhibited with the Impressionists, worked with new ways of controlling form and space, and Seurat (see POINTILLISM) created severely formal compositions while further refining the Impressionist breakdown of light. The paintings of this period were received with hostility and derision by press and public.

post-painterly abstraction *(US)* the ultimate rejection of the painterly self-involvement of Expressionism. The term was used for the work of those American artists such as Frank Stella (1936–) who broke from ABSTRACT IMPRESSIONISM without returning to representational painting.

potassium silicate or **potassium water glass** see LIQUID SILICATE.

potboiler a work turned out primarily for monetary gain. Its second-rate character is usually obvious, especially when the artist is known for finer efforts.

pot-cheese paint see CASEIN.

potent cross or **Jerusalem cross** a cross with short crossbars at the ends of the four arms, each arm forming the letter 'T'. The potent cross is similar to the cross-crosslet, but the latter has crossbars near, not at, the ends of the arms. Both forms are common in heraldry. The term *potent* derives from an old French word for 'crutch'. See CROSS for illustration.

potstone an inferior grade of SOAPSTONE, used in China since ancient times for making hollow vessels because of the ease with which it may be carved.

potter's clay native CLAY selected for its fineness, plasticity, absorbency and other qualities that make it suitable for various ceramic uses. Clay is seldom used alone but is mixed with other minerals and chemicals to obtain required performance properties. The principal types of ceramic clay are pure clay, earthenware clay, BALL CLAY, FIRECLAY, Bentonite slip clay, and stone-ware clay. See CLAY BODY.

potter's knife or **fettling knife** a kind of spatula with a narrow blade that tapers from the handle. See FETTLE.

potter's palette any of several thin, flat, flexible steel tools, used to scrape, smooth, finish, or decorate plaster or clay forms. A potter's palette may be an oval, a rectangle, or a parabola with a flat side, and measures about 2 by 4 inches. It has either smooth or serrated working edges.

potter's pink or **mineral lake** a pure, not very intense pink pigment made by roasting chromium and tin oxides in a furnace. It is used in ceramics, and is similar to PINK COLOUR. Potter's pink is said to have been discovered *c.*1790–1800 by an unknown Staffordshire potter. Despite its

potter's palette Examples.

permanence, it has found little acceptance among painters because of its weak colour and high cost. Potter's pink has been recommended as an addition to the limited fresco palette, but it is not always available.

potter's wheel a turntable on which clay pots and other vessels are thrown, or shaped. The simplest form of wheel is the kickwheel. To operate it, the potter kicks at some form of disc or crank with a steady motion of the foot in order to keep the turntable rotating. Power-driven wheels, whose speed can be regulated by the potter as he or she works, are usually used. The potter's wheel has been in existence from the times of the ancient Egyptians and Chinese up to the present day. It is no longer used in commercial ceramic manufacture, except for making large stoneware jars, but is part of the basic equipment of the artist-potter.

pottery 1. ceramic ware; more specifically, coarse vessels fired at relatively low temperatures, classified as EARTHENWARE as opposed to porcelain.

2. a workshop in which ceramic ware is made.

pottery, Greek see GREEK POTTERY; VASE SHAPES.

pounce 1. a fine powder of charcoal, chalk or pipe clay used in POUNCING to transfer a drawing to another surface. If chalk or clay is used, it is usually mixed with a pigment in order to make the transferred lines more visible. A pigment such as umber is sometimes used alone as pounce.

2. a fine resinous powder, usually a mixture of sandarac and pumice or cuttlefish bone, with which parchment or unsized paper is dusted to prepare it for drawing or writing with ink. Similarly, pounce may be sprinkled over an erasure to keep reapplied ink from spreading. It was formerly used instead of a blotter to dry ink after writing and was kept in a pounce box, a special container with a perforated lid for sprinkling the powder.

pouncing a process for transferring a drawing or design to paper, a wall, a canvas, or other surface. The lines of the original drawing or CARTOON are pricked with a needle or a PERFORATING WHEEL, and then a pounce bag, a square of wide-mesh cloth in which a quantity of POUNCE has been wrapped and tied, is gently tapped along the perforations. The powder passes through these tiny punctures, duplicating their pattern on the surface to receive the drawing. When the original work must be preserved intact, as is usually the case with a cartoon for fresco, it is traced on to a sheet of tracing paper that is pounced instead of the original. Both the pounce powder and the auxiliary cartoon are designated by the Italian word *spolvero*.

pourpre français see FRENCH PURPLE.

Poussinisme see RUBÉNISME.

Pozzolana a volcanic clay used with lime as an aggregate in stucco, or combined with Portland cement to form Puzzolan cement. Its name comes from a deposit of the substance in Pozzuoli, near Naples, where it was used in ancient times by the Romans.

Pozzuoli blue another name for EGYPTIAN BLUE.

Pozzuoli red a native red earth-pigment mined at Pozzuoli, near Naples. It is the traditional fresco red used by painters since the Italian Renaissance, and is esteemed for its bright, rosy hue and its unique property of setting like cement.

précieux overrefined, extremely precious in treatment, to the detriment of the work as a whole.

precipitated chalk pure artificial calcium carbonate, frequently a by-product of drug and chemical manufacturing. It is one of the whitest of powders. It is used industrially as an INERT PIGMENT (and in many other products), and is employed by artists in making GESSO grounds and pastel crayons. Native calcium carbonate, or WHITING, serves similar purposes, but is neither as white nor as uniformly fine in texture.

precision drawing see MECHANICAL DRAWING.

precisionism a style of art, exemplified best in the paintings of the 20th-century American artists Charles Sheeler (1883–1965) and Charles Demuth (1883–1935). Precisionism is characterized by its industrial subject matter, clean precise lines and geometric forms, and the bright clear use of light.

pre-Columbian art art of the early civilizations on the American continents prior to their discovery by Columbus.

predella 1. a platform on which an altar stands.

2. a steplike platform at the back of an altar top on which candlesticks, flowers, or an ALTARPIECE may be set.

3. a painting or relief carving decorating the faces of either of these.

4. a long, narrow panel running horizontally along the lower edge of the altarpiece itself. In Renaissance altarpieces, particularly those in the form of triptychs or polyptychs, the predella is often an integral part of the structure, and its face usually contains a series of small paintings or carvings (*predelle*) related in subject matter to that of the main panels. Many altarpieces have been disassembled and their parts scattered. Among the extant works with *predelle* are Fra Angelico's *Annunciation* at Cortona and Gentile da Fabriano's *Adoration of the Magi* in the Uffizi Gallery.

prehistoric art art that antedates recorded history. Notable among surviving examples are the cave paintings of Altamira, in Spain, and Lascaux, in France.

Pre-Raphaelite Brotherhood the name chosen by a group of young mid-19th century English artists – of whom Dante Gabriel Rossetti (1828–1882) and John Everett Millais (1829–1896) are perhaps the best known – who sought a return to the joy and simplicity that in their view was characteristic of early Italian art, that is, before the advent of Raphael (1483–1520). Their collective style was distinguished by their choice of uplifting, morally serious subject matter, their fidelity to nature down to the most minute detail, their love of the mediaeval, and a sharp, clear technique. The brotherhood lasted only five years before dissolving, with the artist-members going their own ways.

Presdwood see MASONITE.

preservative any substance added to paints made with water binders to prevent fermentation and MOULD infestation. A disinfectant preservative (such as phenol) or a mould preventative (such as sodium orthophenylphenate) is added to the vehicle during manufacture. Such chemicals are effective in very small amounts so that the paint is in no way harmed. Nonvolatile mould preventatives give permanent protection, but the volatile preservatives act only on the material in its wet stage.

pressure-sensitive tape a strip of paper, cloth, or plastic coated on one side with an adhesive that operates when pressure is applied. Cellophane tape, best known by the tradename of Sellotape, is made of transparent plastic. It has a pressure-sensitive adhesive on one side. Ordinary cellophane tape must not be used on paper that is to be permanently preserved because it turns brown and sticky after a relatively short period of time. The acetate type, or transparent mending tape, which has a mat surface and appears colourless in the roll, has a much higher degree of permanence and does not change colour. It is therefore suitable for most general mending and splicing of paper, although museum conservation specialists do not recommend any plastic tape for mounting or repairing works of art, but rely on simple flour or starch paste for most paper repairs.

Masking tape is a strong brown-paper tape of crinkly texture, made in rolls of various widths. Its pressure-sensitive adhesive holds the tape firmly to any dry, hard, nonfibrous surface, and it may be peeled away easily. It is widely used in decorative painting, especially when spray coatings are to be applied, to mask or protect areas that are to be left blank or have already been painted, and to control sharp edges or stripes. A variety known as *drafting tape* has a smooth texture and an adhesive that will peel away from paper without damaging the fibres as ordinary masking tape may do; this variety may be used to attach paper to a drawing board.

Cloth pressure-sensitive tapes in an assortment of widths and colours are useful for the temporary binding of a canvas that is exhibited without a frame, but are not permanent and should be removed after the occasion for their use is over. Pressure-sensitive tapes in general are not considered sufficiently durable to be used as permanent elements of works of art, mats, mounts, or frames.

press view a preview of an art exhibition to which newspaper and magazine critics are invited.

pricking 1. the puncturing of the cartoon or *spolvero* for POUNCING with a needle rather than with a PERFORATING WHEEL.

2. a test of the age of an old painting. When an impasto area, or thick spot, of an old oil painting is pricked with a needle, the old paint will resist the needle's penetration. On the other hand, the relatively newly applied paint of a recent copy of an old work will be penetrated by the needle, and the softer consistency of the paint will be divulged. This is not in itself a test of authenticity, since an old copy will not be penetrated by a needle either, and forgers have been known to bake their copies to harden the paint and sometimes to crack the paint surface in order to give the painting the appearance of age. Nevertheless, pricking has been widely used as one of a series of tests to confirm the date and authenticity of paintings.

primary colour one of the three chromatic colours from which all other hues, tones and shades may theoretically be obtained by mixture, with the assistance of black and white. Red, yellow, and blue are the three paint primary colours. In practice, it is necessary to use secondary and intermediate colours such as green and violet, as well as red, yellow and blue pigments of various shades to duplicate many hues, because an artist's pigment is not PURE COLOUR: the wavelengths of its minor components differ from the dominant wavelength, affecting the colour produced. For the same reason, a mixture of the three primary colours will produce blackish tones rather than pure black. Red, blue and green are the three beam-of-light primary colours. When mixed together according to the additive system (by projecting all three transparencies on the same spot on a white screen) they produce white light. See COLOUR.

primary structure see MINIMAL ART.

prima vera, **primavera** or **white mahogany** a pale yellowish wood from the tree *Cybistax donnellsmithii*, found throughout the tropical regions of the Western Hemisphere. Prima vera is used for veneer, which may be striped or mottled, depending on the grain of the wood.

primer a white GROUND or coating that is applied over a coat of size to a surface before painting. It provides a base that is a brilliant white and gives uniformity of texture, absorbency and structural stability. A coat of white lead in oil or a mixture of zinc white and titanium white in oil is the usual primer for oil painting. A prepared canvas is sold as either a single primed or a double primed canvas; the former is relatively supple, the latter more rigid. Although this process may be referred to as priming, and the prepared canvas is said to be primed, the material used in oil painting as a primer is invariably called a GROUND. Metals requiring a primer are usually roughened with an abrasive and covered with two coats of white lead in oil. Plaster walls, prior to receiving paint, are covered with a ready-made plaster primer, which adheres well without excessive penetration. It dries to a mat finish and provides a good surface for receiving and holding the final painted coat.

primitive 1. *(art)* naive or self-taught, that is, not subject to the influence of previous or contemporary work. The best-known French primitive painter was Henri Rousseau (1844–1910). Notable American primitives were Edward Hicks (1780–1849) and Grandma Moses (1860–1961).
2. pertaining to the art of peoples who adhere to a traditional pattern of

life, without evolving socially or artistically over the generations. Most primitive art – in wood, stone, metal, or clay – is created for some religious or practical purpose. African masks and statues had a substantial influence on such 20th-century European artists as Derain and Picasso. Fine work has also been found in such places as New Guinea and other parts of Oceania, in Alaska, and in the southwestern United States, among such peoples as the Navaho.

primitives, Italian an outmoded term for the Italian tempera painters of the 13th and 14th centuries, as distinguished from the later artists of the RENAISSANCE. By gradually breaking away from the conventions of BYZANTINE art, they ushered in the Renaissance. Among them were Cimabue (1240–1301) and Giotto (?1267–1337) in Florence, and Duccio and the Lorenzetti brothers in Siena (see SIENESE SCHOOL). Later painters such as Fra Angelico (1387–1455), Paolo Uccello (*c.*1396–1475), Piero della Francesca (*c.*1420–1492) and Sandro Botticelli (*c.*1445–1510), working when tempera technique had become a more controlled and expressive medium, were still considered primitives by the Victorians.

primrose yellow 1. *(US)* an unstandardized term applied in industry to the lightest shade of chrome yellow.
2. a hue designation (palest yellow) rather than the name of a specific artists' pigment. Like lemon yellow, primrose yellow is a fancy name that contributed to confusion in pigment nomenclature. Such hue words may now be used descriptively, provided that the accepted pigment name accompanies it.

print any one of multiple impressions made on paper from the same plate, block, stone, screen, transfer paper or film negative. In the fine arts, the various processes by which ORIGINAL PRINTS are made are called the GRAPHIC ARTS and the individual prints are called PROOFS.

printing ink any ink used in printing. Printing inks are made by dispersing a pigment in a drying-oil vehicle in a roller mill. Thus, they resemble artists' oil colours more than they do writing and drawing inks. The composition of an ink varies according to whether it is to be used for letterpress (relief), lithographic (planographic) or gravure (intaglio) printing. Lampblack is the pigment usually used for black inks in letterpress and lithography. In these two processes most coloured inks are thinly deposited for a transparent effect, so that most of the pigments used are chosen for clarity and brilliance. Transparency is sometimes increased by addition of an extender such as aluminium hydrate. Heavy or opaquely pigmented inks are used chiefly for special purposes, especially on dark-coloured paper. In gravure, the ink is deposited on a plate in depressions of varying depth rather than being thinly spread on an even surface, and different properties are required accordingly. Ivory black or Frankfort black is usually used instead of lampblack, and sometimes the tone of a black ink for etching is warmed by adding burnt umber. The usual vehicle in a printing ink is a specially prepared linseed oil known as a BURNT-OIL VARNISH.

prismatic colour see DIFFRACTION COLOUR.

problem picture a painting of obscure meaning depicting people involved in a situation or event of a mysterious or anomalous nature.

process colours commercial silkscreen colours, either oil or tempera. They are called *process* to indicate that they are specially formulated with ingredients that give the paint the proper consistency, flexibility and drying time for silkscreen use. These colours contain unidentified vehicles and only a few have the names of artists' permanent pigments. While the process colours are widely used by serigraphers, the printmaker who is concerned with the permanence of his or her works will use standard artists' oil colours, which, like the process colours, may be mixed with a clear TRANSPARENT BASE.

production art see CONSTRUCTIVISM.

profile 1. an outline, especially the contour of a face viewed from the side. See also PROFIL PERDU; SILHOUETTE.

2. *(ceramics)* a tool with which clay is shaped on a revolving potter's wheel. The profile is a metallic plate, the working edge of which is the negative of the exterior contour of the object to be shaped.

profil perdu (*Fr.* lost profile) **1.** a profile that is seen not directly side-on but more from the back of the head; thus, a turned-away face, showing chiefly the contour of the cheek and the jaw. The *profil perdu* was used especially by the Impressionist painters.

2. the view of any object when turned so that its front is barely visible.

progressive proofs sets of PROOFS of all the stages in the creation of a COLOUR PRINT, compiled by the artist as a record or for demonstration purposes. The progressive-proof set contains a proof held out from each colour run, showing the multicolour print at each stage. A set of *successive proofs* is made up of a proof of each single colour impression.

projection a kind of construction used in mechanical drawing; a system of perspective that is nonlinear, that is, it has no VANISHING POINTS. Like linear perspective, however, projections are used to represent three-dimensional objects on two-dimensional surfaces. Unlike linear perspective, which aims chiefly to create the illusion of actuality, systems of projection are used, particularly in mechanical drawing, to communicate more specific dimensional and geometric information. In order to do this, a projection of an object may distort its appearance to some extent. The principal types of projection are either axonometric or oblique. ISOMETRIC PROJECTION, DIMETRIC PROJECTION and TRIMETRIC PROJECTION are considered axonometric; that is, they differ with respect to the angles formed by the three axes and, more significantly, according to the corresponding amount of FORESHORTENING of each axis. In oblique projection, an object is represented with two of its axes parallel with those of the PICTURE PLANE, causing the face of a cube, for example, to be shown unaltered, that is, with four 90° angles. Depending on the angle at which the third axis is drawn and the corresponding amount of foreshortening, the construction is called either simply an OBLIQUE PROJECTION or a *cavalier projection*. See figure overleaf.

projection Axonometric projections: (A) isometric,
(B) dimetric, (C) trimetric. Oblique projections: (D) oblique;
(E) cavalier.

Proletcult in Russia, the Organization for Proletarian Culture, founded in 1906, although it did not become active until after the Revolution of 1917. Its aim was to create a proletarian art and culture, working with industry in order to unite industry and art. Its leaders believed that Proletcult should be autonomous, not a branch of Party or government. Its chance came in 1922, when Lenin's New Economic Policy forced the government to relinquish its exclusive patronage of the arts. The Constructivists and other progressive artists (see CONSTRUCTIVISM; SUPREMATISM), who had had great power in directing the country's artistic life since the Revolution, either allied themselves with Proletcult, which supported them economically, or left the USSR for exile in Paris, Munich or Berlin. Under Proletcult, artists became artist-engineers, creating strictly functional industrial design, for the rest of the 1920s. In 1932 the Party once more took over the supervision of Soviet art (see SOCIALIST REALISM).

proof 1. *(graphic arts)* any print.

2. *(commercial printing)* a trial impression, taken at some stage in the printing process in order that it may be examined and, if necessary, corrected.

Trial proofs are also pulled in graphics so that the printing surface from which they are made may be examined and corrected. An impression taken by the artist before the plate is completed or its inking routine is perfected is called a STATE or stage. (The special series of colourprint proofs known as PROGRESSIVE PROOFS and successive proofs are comparable in a way to a set of black-and-white prints compiled by taking one proof from each succeeding state.) In engraving, the final proof of state, which is without the artist's signature, a title, the publisher's mark, etc., is called an *unlettered proof* or a *proof before letter*. When these inscriptions and marks have been added, the impression is called a *proof after letter*. When the artist has added his or her signature and perhaps a title to the block or plate, the artist begins to print the edition, marking each proof in pencil in its lower left margin with a fraction that indicates the size of the edition and the number of each impression in the order of printing; the third proof of an edition of twenty-five, for example, would be marked $\frac{3}{25}$. The practice of numbering proofs in this way is a relatively modern one. Because the copper plate in ETCHING and DRYPOINT tends to wear down rather rapidly, the low-number proofs of an edition are considered more desirable than the higher-number proofs. Etchings and drypoints are often printed in LIMITED EDITIONS. In other printmaking techniques, the number of the proof has no significance in an edition of reasonable size.

Proofs, especially engravings, that are pulled by someone other than the creator of the original design may be inscribed with the names of all the people or firms involved in their production, each of whom is identified with a standard abbreviation as artist, engraver, printer, or publisher (see DEL). See also COUNTERPROOF; ORIGINAL PRINT; RESTRIKE.

proof after letter; proof before letter see PROOF.

proportion in any composition, the mathematical relationship of the parts to each other and to the whole (see also ASYMMETRY; DYNAMIC SYMMETRY). Specifically, the term refers to the mathematical and geometric relationships of the parts of the human body and the ratio of each part or unit of parts to the whole mass and form. The average human body is between 7 and $7\frac{1}{2}$ times as tall as the length of its head, and the arm spread is approximately equal to the height of the figure. A SCHEMA for drawing the ideal body, however, often divides the body into an evenly divisible number of parts (for example, the total height equals 8 heads). One theory of proportion, the GOLDEN MEAN, provides for a continuous halving of the body and of the fragments of the body resulting from each prior division.

What the proportions of the human figure are and what they should be have been debated throughout the history of art. The outstanding early treatise on the subject is Vitruvius's *De Architectura*, written in the 1st century BC. Other important studies were made during the Renaissance, notably by Leonardo da Vinci (1452–1519) and Albrecht Dürer (1471–1528).

proportional calipers sculptors' large calipers that have a pair of jaws at either end, one pair large and one small. A sliding setscrew permits adjustment so that proportional measurements can be made for enlarging or reducing an original work when making a copy. See illustration at CALIPERS.

Protogeometric period the earliest phase of HELLENIC ART (1100–900 BC). The principal art form during this period was pottery decorated with painted geometric designs. It was followed by the GEOMETRIC PERIOD.

proto-porcelain a primitive Chinese pottery ware made before the perfection of the porcelain process.

prototype an original creation as opposed to works that stem from it or are reproduced or copied from it. A copy or replica of an original model is called an ECTYPE.

provenance the record of ownership for a work of art, ideally from the time it left the artist's studio to its present location.

Prussian blue, Berlin blue, bronze blue, iron blue, Paris blue or **paste blue** ferric ferrocyanide. It is a deep cyan-blue pigment with a very greenish undertone and a full-strength, dark mass tone that has a bronzy sheen. Few other pigments equal it in COLOURING POWER. Prussian blue, discovered in 1704, is the earliest synthetic pigment of established date. It is also the first of three blue pigments (including ultramarine and phthalocyanine blue) discovered under similar accidental conditions. Diesbach, a Berlin colourmaker, stumbled on Prussian blue when he was given the wrong material during an experiment with a shade of red. His inadvertent use of a partially refined animal product rather than a pure chemical, together with the highly complex nature of the resulting reaction, almost certainly precludes the possibility that Prussian blue could have been invented independently elsewhere. Diesbach's method of production was kept secret until 1724, when it was published in England by John Woodward. First used by artists about 1770, Prussian blue won wide acceptance for 165 years, although its behaviour in oil and watercolour tends to be erratic; it will hold up well in full strength and fade in weaker tints, or the reverse, depending on its manufacture. Prussian blue and a COMPOSITE PIGMENT product, CHROME GREEN, are used in large quantities for industrial purposes. For permanent painting, Prussian blue was replaced in 1936 by the completely reliable PHTHALOCYANINE BLUE, which has identical colour and pigment properties.

Among the many names for varieties of Prussian blue are ANTWERP BLUE (also known as *Haarlem blue*); BLUE LAKE; BRUNSWICK BLUE; CELESTIAL BLUE; *Monthier blue* and SOLUBLE BLUE. Highest-quality Prussian blues are known as *Chinese blue*, *Milori blue* and *steel blue*. TURNBULL'S BLUE, produced as an intermediate stage in one process for the manufacture of Prussian blue, is not used as a pigment.

Prussian brown or **iron brown** precipitated iron (ferric) hydroxide. It is used as a drier in the manufacture of cooked oil varnishes. Its name derives from an obsolete method of preparation, which involved the calcining of rejected grades of Prussian blue. Occasionally used as a pigment during the 19th century, Prussian brown is no longer considered a useful addition to the permanent brown pigments because of its dull colour effect and indifferent pigment properties.

Prussian green see BRUNSWICK GREEN.

Prussian red an old name for LIGHT RED.

psychedelic art decorative and abstract art inspired by the stimulus colours and shapes said to be experienced by persons under hallucinatory drugs, especially LSD. It was introduced as a new style in the United States in 1966. Among the typical psychedelic designs are hard-edge areas of flat colour in swirls and swelling curves that closely resemble those of ART NOUVEAU; patterns resembling those of iridescent oil films on water; profuse melanges of rectangular and pointed shapes; and sometimes splotches of fireworks. The colour is typically soft and high in key with mauves and pale greens predominating, but sometimes brilliant and intense. The special calligraphy that accompanies such designs is in a swelling, curvilinear style evolved from art nouveau.

psykter a type of ancient Greek jar narrow at top and bottom, but with bulging shoulders. The shape was designed to keep liquids cool. See VASE SHAPES for illustration.

puddle the pool of molten metal that forms when the welding torch is used (see WELDING). A good weld is made by forming a small puddle at some point on a seam of metal, then distributing an equal amount along the seam, forming another puddle, and so on in a regular sequence. The puddle is made by melting a FILLER ROD and/or the edges of the metal to be joined.

pug *(ceramics)* to prepare clay for use by ridding it of air bubbles in a specially designed mixing machine called a pug mill. See also WEDGE.

pulling the making of prints. In the graphic arts and the printing trade one speaks of *pulling* a PROOF rather than of printing or making it.

pulling pliers or *(US)* **stretching pliers** heavy pliers with elongated jaws for grasping the edges of a piece of canvas in stretching it on a CHASSIS. A squarish extension at the middle of the lower jaw is called the hammer; its most important function is to supply leverage against the back of the STRETCHER bar. The usual procedure is to grasp the pliers with one hand, holding the edge of the canvas taut, while with the other hand, a tack or staple is driven. In the 19th century, this tool was called *straining pincers*.

pulling pliers

pumice or **pumice stone** a lightweight pale grey substance of volcanic origin. It is used in powdered form as a mild abrasive in several degrees of fineness, and is also available in lump form. In painting, powdered pumice is used to make grained-surface pastel paper; it may be added to a ground to give tooth to the painting surface and is sometimes mixed with paints to coarsen their textures.

pumping another name for retroussage (see WIPING).

punch a tool used in decorative work to stamp designs or elements of designs on such surfaces as gilded gesso panels and leather articles. The usual punch is a slender, tapering 3-inch rod of steel or brass with a design cut into its point; the design is stamped into the surface by holding the point against it while the butt end is struck or tapped with a light mallet.

punch'ong a Korean method of decorating ceramics. The entire ware is covered with an ENGOBE whose colour contrasts with that of the CLAY BODY. The engobe is worked on by SGRAFFITO or loosely applied iron or cooper oxides.

Punic wax a term used by Pliny and others for the treated or processed beeswax used in ancient ENCAUSTIC painting. Neither Greek nor Roman sources identify this material with certainty, and scholars have presented varying opinions about the nature of its composition. The modern consensus is that Punic wax was not markedly different from white refined beeswax.

Purbeck marble a fossil-rich limestone, quarried in Dorset. It takes a high polish.

pure colour 1. a colour or hue that is unmixed with other hues. Beam-of-light or spectrum colours are pure colours, but no paint or pigment colour is free from some elements of another hue.

2. *(painting)* an unmixed colour straight from the tube, lightened only with white and deepened only with more of the same paint when necessary, without the use of other pigments.

purity of colour the clarity of a colour according to its type. For example, alizarin has a clear, clean undertone, while it is natural for Indian red to be comparatively muddy in undertone.

purity of pigment freedom from adulteration or impurities.

puree see PIURI.

pure scarlet see IODINE SCARLET.

Purism an art movement that began with the publication of a manifesto, *After Cubism*, (1918) by the painter Amédée Ozenfant (1886–1966) and the architect Le Corbusier (Charles Edouard Jeanneret, 1888–1962). The Purists felt that Cubism had become too decorative and fantastic; they wished to retain some of the Cubist principles but to return to simplicity and pure function. They sometimes used the machine as the symbol of these desirable qualities. Their subjects were mainly still lifes, painted in pure colours with sharply delineated, geometrically simplified forms. The sculptor Constantin Brancusi (1876–1957) was also associated with Purism.

purpleheart see AMARANTH.

purple of Cassius a permanent pigment made by precipitating gold and tin chlorides. It was discovered by Andreas Cassius in Germany (mid-17th century). Since purple of Cassius resists high temperatures, it has been used in ceramics and in colouring ruby glass. Artists have used it in enamelling, painting on procelain, and miniature painting; it has also been suggested as a fresco pigment. Purple of Cassius was replaced by cobalt violet in the mid-19th century.

purple of the ancients see TYRIAN PURPLE.

purple pigments see VIOLET PIGMENTS.

purpurin one of the two colouring principles of the madder root. The other is ALIZARIN. Synthetic purpurin became available in the 1920s and provided a purple lake (alizarin violet) that was expected to surpass alizarin crimson in colour stability by dint of an additional hydroxy group in its formula. However, it proved insufficiently permanent for artists' use.

purpurino see MOSAIC GOLD.

purpurissum a Latin name for the pigment made from TYRIAN PURPLE dye.

putto *(pl.* **putti)** or **amorino** a chubby nude infant, often depicted in art from the 15th century on, especially in Italy. When a child angel is represented, it may also be called a *cherub*; a *cupid* is a similar figure representing the pagan god of love.

putty see PICTURE PUTTY.

Puzzolan cement POZZOLANA combined with PORTLAND CEMENT.

PVA see POLYVINYL ACETATE.

PVC see POLYVINYL CHLORIDE.

pwree see PIURI.

pyrometer a device for measuring temperatures above the range of a mercury thermometer, as in a furnace or kiln. The standard pyrometer operates by measuring the electrical resistance in a thermocouple, of which one end (the hot junction) is inside the kiln while the other (the cold junction) is connected to a dial that records the temperature. Another type is the optical pyrometer, which is focused on the heated area from a convenient distance and angle and which measures the intensity of the light emitted. A third type, also focused from a distance, is the radiation pyrometer. The automatic, built-in pyrometer in an electric kiln may be set at a desired temperature. Like its standard, nonautomatic counterpart, it measures heat by means of changes in electrical resistance.

pyrometric cone a clay cone used to determine the approximate temperature of an oven or KILN that does not have a PYROMETER. Each numbered cone has a known melting point, and arches over when this temperature is reached. Several cones with successively higher melting points may be used at once, to indicate the rising temperature in the kiln as it heats up.

pyrometric cones (left to right) The cones before firing, at the desired temperature, and at excessive heat. The cones are set at slight angles; the maturing temperature is indicated when the cone for that temperature (here, the left-hand one in the centre) is half down. The other cone (several may be used) melts at a lower heat, and serves as a warning.

pyroxylin a general term for all cellulosic plastics and solutions such as lacquers made from CELLULOSE NITRATE, CELLULOSE ACETATE, or photographic film scrap. The term *pyroxylin* is now less frequently used than it was in the past.

pyxis a small box used by the ancient Greeks for storing ointments. It was generally cylindrical, and the lid had a knob or finial in its centre. The anglicized term *pyx* is used today in the church for a box for holding and carrying the sacrament. See VASE SHAPES for illustration.

Q

quadra **1.** a square frame or border, such as that enclosing a bas-relief. **2.** FILLET.

quadrate cross a cross with a square superimposed over the intersection of the arms so that its corners project from the angles between the arms. See CROSS for illustration.

quadratura a fanciful form of decoration, first employed by the Romans, then later by the artists of Baroque Italy, in which architectural forms are painted on the walls or ceiling of a room in order to give the illusion that they are an extension of the real architecture of the room into an imaginary space.

quadrille paper **1.** paper faintly ruled with small squares. **2.** paper so patterned with a watermark or a plate finish. See CROSS-SECTION PAPER.

quadro riportato a ceiling picture that is painted without the illusionistic foreshortening characteristic of the BAROQUE, that is, as if the scene were to be viewed at normal eye level. It was mainly a NEOCLASSICAL technique, whose progenitor is generally regarded as being the 18th-century German artist Anton Mengs (1728–1779).

quadruple plate see BRITANNIA METAL.

quarry water the moisture held within certain limestones and sandstones when freshly quarried. Such stones are soft at first but become hard on ageing, as the moisture disappears.

quarter round any convex strip or moulding, the profile or projected profile of which is a quarter circle.

quartz **1.** the crystalline mineral silicon dioxide. **2.** (in powdered form) the inert pigment SILICA.

quartz inversion *(ceramics)* the series of changes in the crystalline structure of clay that occur during firing. This phenomenon helps account for the necessity of firing and cooling ceramic ware at a slow rate.

quatrefoil see FOIL.

quattrocento *(It.)* the 15th century. The term is commonly used to designate Italian art of that period.

queensware **1.** the creamy white earthenware first produced in 1763 by Josiah Wedgwood and named after Queen Charlotte, wife of George III. **2.** any cream-coloured English earthenware.

quenching the process of plunging a hot metal into liquid, usually water, in order to cool or harden it. It may be part of the processes of ANNEALING and tempering (see TEMPER).

quercitron lake an obsolete yellow LAKE pigment made from quercitron, a NATURAL DYESTUFF obtained from the powdered bark of the black quercitron oak. Many old lakes were made from quercitron, including flavine lake and gallstone.

quick-drying size see GOLD SIZE.

quicklime see LIME.

quill see BRUSH, QUILL; PEN.

quinacridone deep gold an excellent SYNTHETIC ORGANIC PIGMENT of high performance with strong molecular bonding. It is probably the most lightfast organic pigment of this shade. However, it appears slightly dull in tints and is difficult to disperse.

quinacridone red a brilliant bluish or rose-red SYNTHETIC ORGANIC PIGMENT. Besides this relatively yellowish or scarlet shade, bluish, magenta and violet shades are also made from the same dyestuff (linear quinacridone) that yields quinacridone red.

quinophthalone yellow a transparent SYNTHETIC ORGANIC PIGMENT with high colouring power and excellent lightfastness.

R

R *abbrev. for* rough. See WATERCOLOUR PAPER.

RA Royal Academician. Members of the ROYAL ACADEMY OF ARTS are entitled to use these letters after their names.

rabbitskin glue see GLUE.

raffia a strong fibre obtained from leafstalks of the raffia palm (*Raphia rufia*) native to Madagascar. Raffia, dyed in bright colours, was a popular material for weaving, basketry and other craft work but has now been largely superseded by synthetic materials.

rag-wiped see WIPING.

raku ware an earthenware developed by Japanese potters in the 16th century. It is usually thick, resistant to thermal shock, and quite irregular in form and colours. Raku ware is often used in the traditional tea ceremony.

ramiform having a branched structure or a twiglike linear pattern.

rance or **Belgian marble** a dull-red MARBLE with blue and red streaks and veins.

Rapidograph *(US)* a tradename for a STYLOGRAPH.

rasp any of a number of file-like steel tools with sharp raised points rather than the ridges found on the surface of the usual file. Rasps are used in sculpture and ceramics for rough-shaping, abrading and striating stone, wood, plaster and clay. Double-ended, all-purpose rasps are sold in a variety of lengths and blade shapes. *Rifflers*, used for working in depressions, are small double-ended tools with fine, thin blades, variously curved or shaped. A special rasp made specifically for use on plaster (sometimes called a *grater*) is also double-ended, with rectangular abrading surfaces like those on a kitchen grater. Single-ended rasps especially made for use in wood carving are available in several sizes and with either a fine or a coarse tooth. There is also an open, double-sided wood-carving rasp with one side fine, the other coarse.

rasp (A) Plaster rasp; (B) all-purpose rasps; (C) riffler;
(D) common woodcarving rasp; (E) double-sided
woodcarving rasp with fine and coarse teeth.

raw glaze a glaze containing no fritted ingredients (see FRIT).

raw sienna a brownish-yellow EARTH COLOUR obtained from a natural clay containing iron and manganese. It is one of the basic permanent artists' pigments. Since raw sienna is semiopaque and has more subtlety of colour than yellow ochre in tints with white, it is usually preferred to yellow ochre for creating flesh tones. As an oil colour, raw sienna requires little or no stabilizer in its manufacture, since it tends to have a short consistency that handles well under the brush. Raw sienna was originally found near the Tuscan city of Siena, as its Italian name, *terra di Siena*, indicates; the best grades are still imported from Italy. It is called 'raw' to distinguish it from BURNT SIENNA. *Italian earth* is an old name for both raw and burnt sienna.

raw umber see UMBER.

Rayonnism or **Lutschism** a theory and technique of painting devised by the Russian painter Michel Larianov (1881–1964) and also practised by Natalia Goncharova (1881–1962). Larianov's manifesto on the subject, published in 1913, dealt with the dispersion of colour as light rays emanating from objects, as demonstrated in his work with parallel or intersecting beams of light. Rayonnism (called Lutschism in Russia) was based on Impressionist ideas, and was probably influenced by the contemporary Cubist and Futurist movements. It was only one of the styles in which Larianov and Goncharova painted between 1911 and 1914. Certain of their works are considered by some to be among the earliest examples of nonobjective painting.

ready-made a man-made object, usually mass-produced, that was not made with any artistic consideration in mind but is mounted or displayed as an aesthetically significant structure; a form of FOUND OBJECT. Among the earliest ready-mades was a porcelain urinal exhibited in New York in 1917 by Marcel Duchamp, a founder of the Dada movement.

realgar, arsenic orange or **red orpiment** native arsenic disulphide; a poisonous, bright reddish-orange pigment. Although realgar does not fade, it is likely to react with other pigments. Used in most early civilizations, it was replaced in the late 19th century by cadmium orange. In the late 18th and early 19th centuries, an artificial variety of realgar, similar to King's yellow, was made, but only in insignificant amounts, since it was far costlier than the native product. Early names for realgar are roseaker and SANDARACA.

realism 1. (also called **naturalism**) in general, the depiction of human figures, real objects, or scenes as they appear in nature, without distortion or stylization.

2. representational or objective painting as distinguished from abstract painting, although it is less confusing to use the word *reality* than *realism* in this case. In MAGIC REALISM and TROMPE L'OEIL painting, additional elements are involved.

3. an art movement in France from about 1850 to 1875. The first Realist exhibition was organized in 1855 by Gustave Courbet (1819–1877) in protest against the rejection of his works by the Academy. Nineteenth-century Realism sought to counter the idealized subject matter of Romantic and Neoclassical painting with a frank or even harsh picture of everyday life.

4. see SOCIALIST REALISM.

realization see PERFORMANCE ART.

rectified turpentine turpentine that has been purified, especially through distillation. Since all turpentine is distilled or double-distilled, the term has no significance as an indicator of quality.

red chalk see SANGUINE.

reddle see RUDDLE.

red-figured pottery ancient Greek pottery decorated in red on a black background. Made as early as the last quarter of the 6th century BC in Athens, this type of pottery superseded the earlier and less highly developed BLACK-FIGURED POTTERY toward the middle of the 5th century. White backgrounds and occasional supplementary colours also came into limited use during the late 5th and the 4th centuries BC.

red indigo another name for ORCHIL.

red iron oxides native red earths that contain various amounts of iron oxide and occur the world over. They are known by the names of their places of origin, for example, PERSIAN GULF OXIDE, VENETIAN RED, SPANISH RED. They were the basic reds of the palette from the time of the prehistoric cave painters to the mid-19th century, but gradually they were almost entirely replaced by their artificial counterparts INDIAN RED, LIGHT RED, and Mars red (see MARS PIGMENTS) – pure iron oxides that are finer, brighter, more uniform in texture, and of higher colouring power. In 1942 the United States PAINT STANDARD eliminated the native red earths from its list. The old Latin name for red-earth pigment is SINOPIA. See also ROUGE.

red khaya see MAHOGANY.

red lead lead monoxide and lead peroxide; a heavy, opaque, orange-red pigment. Red lead is no longer used as an artists' colour, since it has poor brushing qualities and will darken on exposure to light. One of the early artificial or man-made pigments, red lead was used by the ancient Greeks and by the Romans. Pliny called red lead *secondarium minium*. When he and other writers of the classical era wrote of *minium*, they meant cinnabar (native mercuric sulphide), but by the Middle Ages, the name *minium* came to be applied exclusively to red lead. It was then rather extensively employed in illuminated manuscripts, and its use, through the Latin verb *miniare* ('to colour with red lead'), gave rise to the word MINIATURE. Today, red lead is chiefly used in industry as a primer for structural steel. Another of its obsolete names is saturnine red.

red ochre an earth colour made from red earth or clay, less intense in colour and weaker in colouring power than the red oxides. Red ochre is also made by calcining selected grades of yellow ochre; this type is sometimes called *burnt ochre*.

red oil crude oleic acid called for in some of the older recipes, especially as an ingredient of metal cleaners and polishes.

red orpiment see REALGAR.

red oxides see RED IRON OXIDES.

red pigments the following pigments that approved in the United States for use in oil paints by ASTM and are generally acceptable in all other easel-painting techniques: LIGHT RED; INDIAN RED; VENETIAN REDS; Mars red and Mars violet (see MARS PIGMENTS; CADMIUM RED; QUINACRIDONE RED; NAPHTHOL RED; NATURAL ROSE MADDER; THIOINDIGOID; VERMILION; PEREYLENE RED; ANTHRATHONE RED and perinone red.

red sable see BRUSH, RED SABLE.

reduced pigments or **let-down pigments** dry pigments that are combined with INERT PIGMENTS in order to reduce their colouring power. Sometimes, reduction improves the performance of a pigment, as in the case of phthalocyanine blue, which is usually too powerful at full strength. In many cases, however, the aim is adulteration. Although reduced colours are unchanged in general hue, they are inclined to be less clear or a degree muddier than full-strength CP pigments.

reducing see ENLARGING.

reducing glass see DIMINISHING GLASS.

reduction firing a FIRING during which, by limiting the entry of oxygen, a scarcity of oxygen is maintained in the atmosphere of the KILN. Reduction firing enables the ceramist to produce special effects, such as the celadons from iron glazes, or purples and oxblood reds (*sang de boeuf*) from copper glazes. Since it is difficult to achieve consistent results with a reduction fire, commercial potters favour an oxidizing fire. The same variability, however, makes reduction firing popular with artist-potters.

reeding closely spaced parallel or nearly parallel convex ribs forming a moulding or embellishing a surface. Reeding is widely used to decorate the legs of furniture and the rims and bases of hollow ware (see GADROON). It is distinguished from fluting, in which the pattern of raised and lowered areas is essentially reversed. See illustration at FLUTING.

reed pen see PEN.

reflected colour the light that is reflected from a coloured surface and is tinged with that colour. On striking an object, it alters the colour of the object. In planning or selecting a studio, artists try to avoid the effect of light reflected through windows from trees, brick buildings, or other coloured areas.

reflected light the portion of light that is deflected from a surface, as distinguished from transmitted or absorbed light. White light, when reflected from a coloured surface, is tinged with the colour of that surface.

refraction *(of light)* the bending or deflection of a ray of light from a straight course as it passes obliquely from one medium to another (for example, from air to a transparent pigment). The amount of deflection is related to the speed of light in the two mediums, and the REFRACTIVE INDEX.

refractive index (RI) or **index of refraction** the ratio between the speed of light in air and its speed in the substance. The refractive index of a pigment and its vehicle is an important factor in both the colour value and the hiding power of a paint. The greater the difference between the refractive index of a substance and that of its surrounding medium, the more light will be reflected and the less absorbed; the smaller the difference, the less light will be reflected and the more absorbed. Hence, when dry cobalt blue (RI 1.75) is surrounded by air (RI 1.00), much light is reflected, and the dry pigment has a rather pale hue. When the same pigment is ground in linseed oil (RI 1.484), less light is reflected, more is absorbed, and the pigment appears as a deep navy blue. The change in the colour of pastels when they are sprayed with fixative, and the differences between a varnished and an unvarnished picture, may be explained in the same way.

refractory *(ceramics)* **1.** *adj.* having a point of fusion higher than the temperatures used in firing pottery and porcelain. Firebrick and kiln linings are made of refractory material.

2. one of a class of mineral substances that are infusible at these temperatures. A refractory such as flint is sometimes added to ceramic clays, slips, and glazes so that its properties balance those of the flux.

regionalism a strictly American style of painting that evolved in the 1930s and 1940s and derived to a large extent from patriotic impulses, in which the painter strived to depict on canvas the peculiar characteristics of a region or locale. Thomas Hart Benton (1889–1975) and Grant Wood (1892–1942) are viewed as the leading exponents of regionalism.

register *(multicolour printmaking)* the precise alignment (usually by means of register marks) of the blocks, stones, plates or silkscreen stencils for all the colour runs needed to pull a single multicolour proof (each major colour requires a separate printing surface), so that the separate impression created on the paper by each successive colour will be perfectly coordinated with all other colours in the final print (see COLOUR PRINT). When the printing surfaces and the impressions made from them are aligned, they are said to be in register. The paper must always be kept in the same position throughout the series of colour runs required to pull the composite multicolour proof. This is accomplished with the use of register guides.

register guides small contrivances set on the bed of the press to guide or hold the paper in position so that each impression will be in exact alignment with the others. In lithography, colour registration is achieved through the use of cross marks on the paper and on the stone or plate for each colour impression. A proof is positioned through the use of needles that pierce the paper at the centre of each cross mark and are set into slight indentations made at the centres of the cross marks on the stone.

register mark *(multicolour printmaking)* small dots, circles, crosses or other characters placed on the edge or margin of the KEY BLOCK, key plate, or keystone, and traced on precisely the same point of each block, plate, or stone that is made from the key. These marks are made to enable the printer to align the printing surfaces, so that each colour impression will be in register with all the other impressions. Such marks are also often placed on silkscreen stencils to register them for multicolour printing.

reglet see FILLET.

reinforced concrete concrete that has metal bars running through its mass to increase its tensile strength and strengthen its resistance to damage by external forces.

release agent see PARTING AGENT.

relief *(sculpture)* any work in which the figures project from a background. Reliefs are classified by the degree of projection. In high relief (deep relief, sometimes known by the Italian term *alto-rilievo*) the figures project at least half of their natural circumference from the background. In low relief (bas-relief or *basso-rilievo*) the figures project only slightly and no part is entirely detached from the background (as in medals and coins, in which the chief effect is produced by the play of light and shadow). Between these two types is middle relief (demirelief, half-relief or *mezzo-rilievo*). The lowest degree of relief, in which the projection scarcely exceeds the thickness of a sheet of paper, is called crushed relief (*rilievo stiacciato* or *rilievo schiacciato*). There is also a relief in reverse, called hollow relief, in which all the carving lies within a hollowed-out area below the surface plane, and which, through an illusion of depth and roundness, looks like raised relief. Hollow relief, also called sunk or concave relief (*cavo-rilievo*), incised relief (*intaglio rilievato*), and coelanaglyphic sculpture, is the kind of carving done on gems by the Greeks and Romans. Relief sculpture must be distinguished from SCULPTURE IN THE ROUND. See REPOUSSÉ; INTAGLIO.

relief block printing a general term for any contemporary relief printmaking method (see RELIEF PRINTING) in which shaped or textured printing elements – natural, manufactured, moulded, built-up, or carved – are adhered to a board, inked, and then handprinted in the manner of a WOODCUT. Sometimes, the printing surface is coated with a plastic spray to make substances such as cloth, cardboard or gesso impervious to the printing fluid or to permit cleaning of the block after printing.

The term relief block printing is also used to designate direct printing from a textured surface such as a wire-brushed wood block or a small portion of a weathered log. A print made from a built-up relief block, but inked and printed as an intaglio surface, is known as a COLLAGRAPH.

Such printing methods, however ingenious, are not very highly rated by traditional standards. Nevertheless, because they can be used to create interesting effects with tonal areas and textures, the relief block and the collagraph have been quite widely used for serious works by present-day printmakers.

relief printing one of the three major categories of printmaking techniques (the others being INTAGLIO and PLANOGRAPHIC PRINTING). It includes all those printing processes in which all nonprinting areas of the block or plate are carved, engraved, or etched away, leaving on the original plane surface only the lines and areas to be printed. A relief block or plate is inked with a BRAYER or a DABBER, and the impression is made by these relief areas as the ink is transferred to paper, either by hand or

in a press. WOODCUT, WOOD ENGRAVING, line and halftone PHOTOEN-
GRAVING, MEZZOTINT, ANASTATIC PRINTING, STIPPLE ENGRAVING, and
LINOCUT are the most common relief printing processes. The intaglio
plates used for ETCHINGS and ENGRAVINGS are also sometimes inked and
printed as relief plates, in which case the engraved or etched lines and
areas appear in the proofs as whites on a solid-ink ground (see WHITE-LINE
CUT). See also RELIEF BLOCK PRINTING.

relining see LINING.

reliquary a casket, chest, shrine or other repository for keeping or displaying sacred relics, especially in churches. During the mediaeval era,
in accordance with the veneration in which relics were held, reliquaries
were made with the utmost skill and artistry, and were often adorned
with gold, precious jewels, exquisite painting, enamelling or carving.
Many were in the form of miniature buildings. Some were made of
precious metals in the shape of the relic they contained, usually the
remains (for example, an arm or a finger) of a saint or martyr.

remarque a small sketch in the margin of the proof of an ETCHING. A
print with a remarque is known as a *remarque proof*. The artist makes
remarques on an edge of the plate while etching the large drawing, either
to aid in making corrections in the large etching from one STATE to the
next or to test the degree of BITING of the mordant before immersing the
entire plate in the acid bath. Although such remarques are supposed to
be removed with a scraper and burnisher before the final edition of the
plate is printed, they are often seen on proofs of advanced states and are
sometimes even left in the final edition. During the 19th century, remarques of small details related to the subject of the large etching were often
intentionally etched and left on the plate, especially in prints of landscapes
and seascapes. A seascape might, for example, have an elegant little sketch
of a beached boat in a lower corner.

Rembrandt's ground an ETCHING GROUND composed of beeswax and
one or more resins (usually pitch, mastic and/or asphaltum) in various
proportions. Several recipes for Rembrandt's ground have been published. There is no evidence concerning the origin of these grounds –
Rembrandt left no records of any kind. In fact, the grounds known as
Rembrandt's ground were probably not used before the 18th century.
Recipes for Rembrandt's ground are still used today by etchers who
prepare their own grounds.

Renaissance (*Fr.* rebirth) a comparatively brief but tremendously important period in Western European history and culture that followed the
mediaeval era and produced the beginnings of modern thought. The term
Renaissance does not imply that art was dead during the centuries that
preceded it, but that the period was marked by a revival of the spirit of
Greece and Rome. The renewal of the ancients' concern with people,
embodied in the philosophy called Humanism, meant an increasing pre-
occupation with the importance of the individual and with secular life.

Although scholars, including art historians, disagree on the dates of
the Renaissance period, the Italian Renaissance in art may be considered

to have begun in Florence about 1400, and to have continued until the death of Michelangelo Buonarroti (1475–1564) or, in Venice, until the death of Tintoretto (Jacopo Robusti, 1518–1594). Sometimes, however, the period is said to have begun with Giotto di Bondone (?1267–1337). The years from about 1500 to about 1530, when painting and sculpture reached a peak of technical mastery and artistic perfection, are often called the High Renaissance.

In Northern Europe mediaeval traditions in painting persisted longer. In Flanders and Holland, the Renaissance may be said to have started with the brothers Jan (1385–1441) and Hubert van Eyck (?1370–?1426) and ended with Pieter Breughel the Elder (1525–1569), but 15th-century Low Countries painting has also been called 'the flowering of the Middle Ages.' The Renaissance in Germany began with Albrecht Dürer (1471–1528) and continued, especially in architecture, until the middle of the 17th century. The influence of Renaissance painting was carried to Britain by the German painter Hans Holbein the Younger (1498–1543), but an English Renaissance style of architecture did not develop until about 1600, and its influence continued into the 18th century.

The Renaissance produced great technical advances in painting and a number of innovations in the other arts, as well as the advances in the mechanical arts, manufacturing, and international trade and communications that led to a new availability of materials and processes. In Italy, linear perspective was invented and developed by a number of painters and architects, beginning with Filippo Brunelleschi (c.1377–1446) and including Leone Battista Alberti (1404–1472), Paolo Uccello (1396 or 1397–1475) and Piero della Francesca (c.1420–1492). A turning point in the history of painting techniques came in the 15th century, when oil painting was perfected in Venice (see OIL PAINTING, DEVELOPMENT OF). Leonardo da Vinci (1452–1519) first employed the technique of chiaroscuro. Among the many other outstanding painters of the period were Sandro Botticelli (c.1445–1510) and Raphael Sanzio (1483–1520). Other developments in painting included secular portraiture, unknown since Roman times, and landscape painting. Printmaking, in the form of woodcuts, engraving and etching, began as a major art form with the increased availability of paper in the early 1400s.

In sculpture, the revival of the classical attitude towards human physical beauty led to remarkable achievements, starting with the work of Donatello (c.1386–1466), which had a profound influence on his contemporaries, and culminating in the monumental marble statues of Michelangelo.

rendering an architect's accurate, detailed drawing, usually made in order to present plans for a building or other project to a client. The architect executes the rendering in an attractive manner by using watercolour washes and by drawing the building or buildings in an attractively landscaped setting.

repaint an area of a damaged painting that has been restored by INPAINTING.

repeat glass a square frame in which four rectangular lenses are set closely together. When a design is viewed through the glass, it is seen as a quadruple image. It is used by designers of textiles and other products to visualize repeat patterns. The usual model is about 7 × 7 inches.

replica an exact copy or duplicate of a work, in the same size and in the same medium as the original and done by the artist who created the original (or, sometimes, done under the artist's direct supervision). A replica is considered in all important respects to be the equal of the original and of other replicas of the same work. The word is sometimes loosely used for any copy of a work done in the same medium by someone other than the creator of the original. See also COPY; ORIGINAL; REPRODUCTION.

repoussage (*Fr.* a pushing or pounding back) a technique by which the surface of a copper plate used in etching or engraving is smoothed out and made level after it has been altered or repaired. (When a plate is corrected or repaired by rubbing the surface with a scraper or a burnisher, a depressed spot is usually left that would smudge if printed.) In repoussage, the plate is laid facedown on a hard flat surface, and the back of the spot to be levelled is tapped with a broad, flat-headed hammer.

repoussé (*metalwork*) a technique for decorating a surface by hammering the REVERSE of the object, sometimes into a mould of wood that has been carved in intaglio, to create designs in relief. Repoussé work is often refined by CHASING the decorated surface. Repoussé is used widely to ornament fine metal wares, especially silver hollow ware. It is also used by sculptors to create relief panels and plaques from sheet metal, especially copper.

representational art art in which recognizable objects, figures or elements in nature are depicted, as distinguished from NONOBJECTIVE or ABSTRACT ART.

reproduction any copy, likeness or counterpart of an original work of art or of a photograph, in the same medium as the original or in another, and done by someone other than the creator of the original. Compare REPLICA; see also COPY; ORIGINAL; ORIGINAL PRINT.

reredos see ALTARPIECE.

reserve 1. (*decorative arts*) an area that retains the original colour of the surface or ground. When colour glazes are applied to a piece of pottery, for example, those areas that are left undecorated, thus retaining the natural colour of the clay, are called the reserve.
2. a line that circumscribes a monogram, a cachet, a cipher or initials. See also CARTOUCHE.

resin an amorphous, transparent or translucent solid organic material, soluble in a VOLATILE SOLVENT either cold or when melted by heating. The resulting solution is used in varnishes and other coating materials. Resins may also be added to solid compounds by fusion. The various resins differ widely in such properties as colour, odour, solubility and hardness. Resins may be classified according to origin as natural, synthetic or artificial.

Natural resins are the hardened exudations of certain trees. Those obtained from living trees are called *recent resins*; those dug from the ground (or from the beds of streams), where they have been deposited by the vegetation of former times, are called *fossil resins*. The more familiar natural resins are ACCROIDES; AMBER; COPAL; DAMAR; ELEMI; ESTER GUM; KAURI; MANILA COPAL; MASTIC; ROSIN; SANDARAC; and SHELLAC (an insect resin).

Synthetic resins are the products of modern chemistry. They are synthetic organic compounds with resinous properties – that is, they resemble the tree resins in appearance and performance characteristics. They are, however, more uniform and have greater clarity, durability, flexibility and resistance to chemical attack. Although they have replaced the natural resins successfully in industrial products, only a few are suitable for use in artists' materials. Most of them are insoluble in the mild solvents that artists must use; they require strong solvents that evaporate too rapidly and give off obnoxious or toxic vapours. Among the groups or families of synthetic resins from which materials for painting and sculpture have been made are methacrylate or ACRYLIC RESIN; ALKYD RESIN; POLYESTER RESIN; VINYL RESIN; melanine resin; PHENOLIC RESIN; polystyrene and urea-formaldehyde resin. When a synthetic resin is used in its solid state to mould or fashion various articles, it is known as a PLASTIC. Synthetic resins, according to how they react to heat and pressure, are broadly classified as either THERMOPLASTIC or THERMOSETTING. Although the cellulose polymers – cellulose acetate, cellulose nitrate, and ethyl cellulose – are processed from a natural material and so do not conform to the definition of a synthetic resin, they are always classified and studied with the synthetic resins.

An artificial resin is a product that does not have individually unique properties but is made or compounded of various substances to imitate the properties of another resin. It may contain natural or synthetic resins and various chemical substances. An example is a mixture of Manila copal, carnauba wax and castor oil, which in an alcohol solution is a cheap varnish used as a substitute for shellac.

In the varnish industry, the word *gum* is frequently used for the more correct term, resin. A true gum is water soluble, and when ignited chars to a black mass as sugar does. A resin is insoluble in water and burns with a smoky flame.

resist 1. any substance that is used to block out or mask temporarily a surface area, in order to prevent or impede an action (as of a chemical) on the masked area. In any process in which lines or surface areas are to be incised with acid – as in glass etching and the metal-plate printing techniques of etching, aquatint, photoengraving and gravure – a resist (sometimes called acid resist) is used to mask areas that are not to be bitten by the mordant and to protect the back and edges of the plate. In the graphic-arts processes of etching and aquatint, a resist known as stopping-out varnish is used in the STOPPING-OUT process, and the ETCHING GROUND itself is a form of resist. In ceramics, a resist is applied to portions of a ceramic ware to prevent a glaze, engobe or colouring oxide from taking on those portions. This may be a ready-made wax emulsion that is applied to the ceramic surface cold, or it may be a homemade resist of a resin in molten beeswax. A resist is used in dry-foot firing and for decorative purposes. In electroplating, the deposition of a metal on a selected area is blocked with the use of a nonconducting resist. Resists used in fabric dyeing may be either mechanical shields or chemicals that prevent the fixing of a colour. In industrial textile printing, a pastelike resist is printed on the cloth with engraved metal rollers before the fabric is dyed; in batik printing, this resist is molten beeswax.

2. a liquid FRISKET or rubber cement used with watercolour mediums.

restoration the repair or reconditioning of works of art by replacing missing parts and filling in missing areas. See also CONSERVATION.

restorer see CONSERVATION.

restrainer a fluid used along with a solvent such as alcohol in cleaning or stripping oil paintings to reduce the strength and slow down the activity of the solvent and thereby lessen the danger of skinning (see SKIN). The restrainer may either be mixed with the solvent before use or applied alternately with the solvent so that it acts as a sudden, intermittent brake on the solvent action. Turpentine is the substance most frequently used as a restrainer.

restricted palette or **limited palette** a selected, relatively small number of artists' colours, sometimes including the primaries and sometimes from a limited part of the spectrum. An artist may be said to use a restricted palette in a single painting or as a regular practice. The artist may do so for several reasons: for convenience when using a small, portable outdoor sketching box; as a point of discipline, in the case of a student; to conform to some aesthetic belief or preference (see BROWN SAUCE); or because a wider range of colours is unavailable. A palette of less than a dozen pigments may be called restricted; from 12 to 15, complete; and over 15, elaborate.

restrike 1. an impression made from a plate, block, lithograph stone, silkscreen stencil, mould or die of any multiple-replica process after the original edition has been exhausted.

2. an impression made after the first edition has been out of circulation for an appreciable length of time. See also ORIGINAL PRINT.

rest-stick see MAHLSTICK.

retable see ALTARPIECE.

retardant an ANTOXIDANT fluid added to paints in order to delay their initial setting or drying. It is used especially by the portraitist or other artist who works on an oil painting two or more days in succession. The most highly recommended retardant is OIL OF CLOVES, which is quite effective when a few drops are mixed into the colours. Other retardants are oil of rosemary, oil of lavender and pine oil. Butyl lactate, which has a very slow rate of evaporation, is used to retard the drying of industrial lacquers.

reticulation a network of cracks. See CRACKLE; CRAZING.

reticule see DRAWING FRAME.

retouch or **retouch varnish** a very thin solution of dammar or other nonyellowing resin that an artist sprays or brushes over a dry, unfinished oil painting before resumption of painting with fresh colours. The retouch temporarily brings dry or sunken-in areas up to the depth and intensity of wet paint, so they can be accurately matched with the new paint. Retouch is meant to be used sparingly and very thinly to avoid complicating the paint structure with an additional varnish film.

retouching the making of changes on a finished picture by going over it with fresh paint. The term is usually confined to work done on a picture by the artist who originally painted it. See also INPAINTING.

retreating colours see ADVANCING AND RETREATING COLOURS.

retroussage see WIPING.

Reubens madder see RUBENS MADDER.

reverse the less significant face of a two-sided object, such as a coin, a medal, a seal or a panel with a painting on each side. The more significant side is known as the *obverse*.

Rhenish school a group of German artists of the late Romanesque period working in and around Cologne. The outstanding figure of this group was Nicholas of Verdun, whose goldwork was at once more monumental and more expressive than most sculpture of the period. His greatest work is the *Three Kings' Shrine* (*c*.1200) in Cologne cathedral. The Rhenish school also did remarkable work in enamel, notably the *Victor Shrine* in Xanten (1129).

rheology see CONSISTENCY.

rhyton a type of painted vase made by the ancient Greeks for use as a drinking vessel. A development of the ancient drinking horn, it was made to resemble the head of a ram, donkey, goat, griffin, deer, or other animal. Frequently Dionysiac or erotic subject matter was employed in its decoration. The rhyton came to Greece from the east in the 5th century BC. See illustration at VASE SHAPES.

rib (*ceramics*) a tool, usually of hardwood, used in throwing pots. The ancient potters used the rib of an animal.

rice paper see DRAWING FRAME. **rich lime** LIME of the highest quality, containing no gypsum and a minimum of impurities. It is the grade required for fresco plastering.

ridge see BURR.

riffler see RASP.

rigger a LETTERING BRUSH, half the width of the standard lettering brush of the same numbered size and made with short, medium, and long hairs. The term originated from a pointed brush used in the days when sailing vessels with their rigging accurately depicted were popular subjects for painters.

rilievo schiacciato see RELIEF.

rilievo stiacciato see RELIEF.

Rinman's green see COBALT GREEN.

Ripolin a European trade or brand name for household ENAMELS. The name was widely publicized because the product was used by Picasso.

riser see VENT.

ritoccata *(It.)* a retouched area on a painting.

river marble *(US)* a kind of LIMESTONE whose surface, when polished, has markings that resemble winding rivers. See also FOREST MARBLE.

Roberson's medium a proprietary painting medium made by the English firm of that name during the 19th century, and probably consisting of copal varnish, poppy oil and white wax.

rocaille an ornamental style based on the forms of shells and water-worn rocks, and characterized by elaborate scrolls. It was popular in 18th-century France, especially during the reign of Louis XV. The term ROCOCO was probably derived from rocaille.

rock concreted earthy material. Igneous rock, such as granite and basalt, is formed by the cooling of molten masses deep in the earth and their subsequent hardening as geological changes bring them closer to the surface. Sedimentary rock, such as limestone and sandstone, occurs where water has flowed, depositing layers of sediment that are slowly mixed with organic and other particles by erosion. Metamorphic rock is igneous or sedimentary rock that has been radically changed by natural forces such as pressure, heat and chemical reaction. Marble is a metamorphic form of limestone. Cut rock is called STONE.

rocker or **cradle** a special steel tool with a slightly curved, serrated front edge, used in MEZZOTINT to prepare the surface of the plate. The tool is moved with an undulating or rocking motion across the plate. Six movements of the rocker (up, down, side-to-side and across at angles) constitute a single stroke, and many such strokes are needed to abrade the surface of a mezzotint plate completely.

rocker

Rockingham Royal Black *(US)* a Virginia MARBLE, considered the best American black marble. It is jet black and is veined irregularly with white lines.

rock soap see MOUNTAIN SOAP.

Rocky Mountain school *(US)* a group of 19th-century American painters, of whom Albert Bierstadt (1830–1902) is the best known. These painters sought to capture the scenic glory of the newly emerging western territories.

rococo a style of art and interior decoration in the 18th century, especially in France during the reign of Louis XV. It was a gay, delicate refinement of the elaborate, curvilinear forms of the High Baroque in Italy, reduced to a smaller scale. Rococo represented a reaction against the heavy, ornate classicism of the arts under Louis XIV, exemplified in the palace of Versailles. Rococo painting was devoted to light, intimate scenes of the more frivolous aspects of courtly life, sometimes in a pastoral setting. It was characterized by charm and artificiality. Its chief exponents included Jean Antoine Watteau (1684–1721), François Boucher (1703–1770), and Jean Honoré Fragonard (1732–1806). Sculpture tended to be delicate and small in scale; the work of Clodion (1738–1814) is typical. The work of Giovanni Battista Tiepolo (1696–1770), which was vast and airy, flamboyant and theatrical, is considered the greatest manifestation of the rococo style in Italy.

rod see FILLER ROD.

roller 1. *(relief printing)* see BRAYER.

2. *(lithography)* a cylinder like a rolling pin, about 4 inches in diameter, with a hand grip at either end, used for ROLLING UP the lithograph stone. It is made of a single piece of hardwood, covered with felt, over which a soft, fine calfskin cover has been sewn. A new roller or an old one that has been put away for a while cannot be used until it has been conditioned by impregnating it thoroughly with BURNT-OIL VARNISH.

roller mill a machine that disperses pigments in a vehicle for artists' oil colours. The most modern type of roller mill has five steel rollers mounted vertically. Water runs through each roller to cool it. The first roller revolves most slowly of all, and each successive roller moves more rapidly than the one preceding it. Pigment that has been mixed with oil to a dry paste consistency is run between the first and second rollers, then between the second and third, and so forth, until it is removed from the fifth roller by an attached scraper or doctor blade. The most common mill in use, however, is a horizontal three-roller mill. Another type of mill for grinding fluid colours is the BALL MILL. Colours may be ground manually with a MULLER.

rolling up the process in LITHOGRAPHY by which the stone is inked. After the LITHOGRAPHIC ETCH, GUMMING UP, and washing away the surplus gum, the drawing on the stone is washed away with turpentine. Although the drawing seems to disappear, the adsorbed fatty acid layer remains in the surface of the stone and will attract the ink when it is applied. The stone is then dampened with a sponge and water, and printing ink is carefully applied with a ROLLER (whence the expression *rolling up*). The wet, desensitized areas repel the ink, while the areas that were drawn on receive it. The pressure of the roller enhances adsorption by the stone of the ink's fatty acids (pressure is one of the ways in which adsorption of a material by a surface is induced), ensuring precise retention of ink in subsequent inkings.

roman 1. a calligraphic hand that developed during the 15th century as a result of the Humanist reaction against the mediaeval GOTHIC hand. Originally the roman hand was called the *antiqua*, a name reflecting the fact that it was modelled on the neat Carolingian minuscule of the 9th century, which had in turn been developed from Latin cursive scripts. The *antiqua* was a very legible, rounded hand that was used for books.

It was extremely well suited to printing and, with the advent of the printing press at the end of the 15th century, it was adopted as type and thus standardized (see below).

2. the most common style of ordinary lettering used today (which school children learn when they are taught to 'print'). It is a style founded on the classic Roman alphabet, the ideal model of which is the inscription on the Column of Trajan (AD 106–113) in Rome.

3. *(typography)* a serif typeface; that is, one characterized by serifs and a noticeable contrast between thick and thin lines within each letter. Among roman typefaces a distinction is made between old style and modern. Old-style roman type, such as Caslon and Garamond, is modelled after the type of early printers; modern roman typefaces, such as Bodoni, are more stylized, with flattened serifs and a greater contrast between thick and thin lines. The wide use of roman fonts in printing has fixed that script, rather than Gothic, in handwriting as well.

4. *(printing)* an upright alphabet of any typeface, sans serif as well as serif, as distinguished from an ITALIC or slanting alphabet. See illustration at TYPOGRAPHY.

Roman art the art of Rome and its colonies from the late 2nd century BC to the close of the 4th century AD. Like Roman civilization as a whole, Roman art was heterogeneous in its origins, owing much to the Greeks, Etruscans and Egyptians. While much of it was influenced by or merely imitative of HELLENIC ART, a distinctive Roman style existed, especially in portrait and relief sculpture. Portrait busts and figures were highly individual, realistic and expressive, although, with the establishment of the Empire in the late 1st century BC, the concept of the divine ruler led to a certain idealization and stylization in the portrayal of various emperors. Roman relief sculpture was innovative in its depiction of specific historical events; narrative reliefs appeared on triumphal arches, columns and monumental altars. These reliefs displayed a high degree of spatial contrast in the various figures; on the other hand, certain relief panels were treated pictorially, with a realistic landscape or other background as carefully detailed as the foreground. Roman wall painting evolved from a rather flat style to one in which architectural perspectives and forms were used to create an illusion of depth (see ILLUSIONISM). Light was also used to create this illusion, but it does not seem to have been studied or used systematically, even in a single painting. Panel paintings also existed. Like much of Roman sculpture, many of the Roman paintings may have been copies of Greek works.

Romanesque pertaining to European art of the period immediately preceding development of the Gothic style. Some authorities give the designation *Romanesque* to art produced as early as the 7th century, although others give the 11th century as the starting point. The Romanesque style was superseded by the Gothic about AD 1200. Romanesque art was primarily of and for the Church, and it existed in a variety of regional styles.

Painting, which survives today mainly in illuminated manuscripts, had a decorative linear quality and showed some Byzantine influence. Fresco and mosaic work were also popular.

The period was marked by revival of monumental stone sculpture, which was created in great profusion as architectural ornament and relief, although large figures were seldom found outside niches. Freestanding statues were usually small products of the metalworker's art.

The Romanesque church was characterized by rounded arches and vaults, piers rather than columns, and an abundance of arcades. The ribbed groined vault, developed during this period, was to be extremely important in Gothic architecture.

Romanists 1. (also called **Italianizers**) non-Italian artists who were attracted to the arts and antiquities of Rome. The terms were applied particularly to Flemish artists of the early 16th century who visited Rome and later influenced the art of their homeland by painting in the manner of the Italian Renaissance. Notable among the Romanists were Jan Gossaert (also called Mabuse), Frans Floris de Vriendt, and Bartholomaeus Spranger.

2. to the many artists who have expressed their admiration for the city of Rome by painting pictures of it, particularly of its ruined monuments of classical times.

Roman linen handwoven Italian linen of the 17th and 18th centuries.

Roman ochre 1. a variety of YELLOW OCHRE with a relatively warm or golden tone.

2. an ochre produced in Italy *(Italian ochre)*.

3. the ochre used in ancient Rome.

Roman sepia SEPIA blended with burnt sienna or alizarin crimson to produce a warmer or more reddish tone.

romanticism an approach to art that emphasizes the personal, the emotional and the dramatic, which it often expresses through the use of exotic, literary or historically remote subject matter. In the 19th century, the Romantic movement arose as a reaction to the austerity of Neoclassicism and as an expression of the spirit of revolution that characterized the age. In painting, Eugène Delacroix (1798–1863) and Theodore Géricault (1791–1824) in France and J.M.W. Turner (1775–1851) in England were leading Romantics. In sculpture, François Rude (1784–1855) and Antoine-Louis Barye (1795–1875) are notable. Art historians use the words *classicism* and *romanticism* in a general sense for basic and opposing attitudes in art and architecture. Both classical and romantic influences are sometimes seen in the work of a single artist or school.

Roman white an obsolete name for WHITE LEAD.

rondel or **rondelle 1.** any circular work of art or other object or circular element of such a work.

2. a disc of glass in stained-glass work.

rondo see TONDO.

roseaker an ancient name for REALGAR.

rose carthame a French name for SAFFLOWER PIGMENT.

rose madder see NATURAL ROSE MADDER.

rosemary, oil of an ESSENTIAL OIL sometimes recommended as a RETARDANT in oil painting.

Rosenstiehl's green see MANGANESE GREEN.

rose pink a reduced grade of BRAZILWOOD LAKE, weak and fugitive.

rosette a painted, carved or sculpted ornament having a circular arrangement of parts resembling the petal of a rose.

rosewood any of several woods obtained from trees of the genus *Dalbergia*, and valued for their rich red colour, fine grain, smooth texture and ability to take a high polish. Rosewood is so named on account of the roselike fragrance it emits when sawn. It is used in cabinetwork and for veneer.

Brazilian rosewood (from *Dalbergia nigra*), or palisander, is one of several unrelated woods sometimes called JACARANDA. A hard, close-textured wood of purple or red to tawny colour, it is the finest of the rosewoods. *Honduras rosewood* is paler. *East Indian rosewood* (from *Dalbergia latifolia*) has a striped grain and considerable variation in colour, from yellow to red or deep purple.

AFRICAN BLACKWOOD is related to the rosewoods, although African rosewood (see BUBINGA) belongs to a different genus, as does Australian rosewood (*Dysoxylum fraseranum*). See also KINGWOOD.

rosin a resin obtained from several species of pine trees in various parts of the world. The trees are tapped, and the exudation, a thick, viscous material (known as GUM THUS), is distilled. The volatile distillate is turpentine; the solid resin that remains is rosin. Rosin is also produced by distilling the tree stumps and wood scraps. Rosin has too many undesirable properties to be used as an ingredient of varnishes and paints for any purpose, but because it is one of the cheapest of raw materials, it has been used in them as an adulterant. However, it has many other uses in the arts for various adhesive, sealing, and other mechanical purposes. Rosin was once also known as COLOPHONY and Greek pitch.

Ross board *(US)* a tradename for a large and varied range of textured boards that are similar to COQUILLE BOARDS.

rosso antico *(It.* antique red) **1.** a deep, brick-red MARBLE, sometimes purplish, with thin black veins and white splotches, from Cape Matapan in Greece. It was popular with ancient Greek, Roman and Etruscan sculptors. The Romans called it *marmor Taenarium*.

2. a red quartz and feldspar rock used by ancient Egyptian and Roman sculptors.

3. a red ceramic ware with a mat finish.

rouge or **polishing rouge** any of the smooth, finely powdered grades of RED IRON OXIDE pigments used for polishing metals. Cosmetic rouge is made from the more brilliant and varied dyestuffs. *Green rouge*, a similar polishing agent, is CHROMIUM OXIDE GREEN.

rouge flambé 1. a hue designation for a deep mottled red of a pronounced bluish shade.

2. see SANG DE BŒUF.

rouge végétal a French name for SAFFLOWER PIGMENT.

roughcast 1. *n.* coarsely textured or pebbled stucco or plaster; thrown or unsmoothed plasterwork.

2. *n. (ceramics)* pottery that has been given a rough surface texture prior to firing.

3. *vb (sculpture)* to fashion roughly, without finish or correction.

roughhew *(sculpture)* to carve or shape roughly all over either as a first stage prior to further refinement or as a complete technique.

rough see WATERCOLOUR PAPER.

roulette an instrument with a small, sharply ridged, revolving cylinder at the end of its handle, used in INTAGLIO printmaking for making dotted lines and areas on a copper plate. It was in general use in the days when MEZZOTINTS and ENGRAVINGS were widely used for reproducing portraits and other pictures in which HALFTONES were desired. The roulette may be used in DRYPOINT, AQUATINT, and other techniques, but while some graphic artists have achieved interesting effects with it, most dislike the measured, mechanical quality of the dotted patterns it produces on the plate.

The roulette and two variants, the chalk roll and the matting wheel, are used in CRAYON MANNER to create densely dotted lines and areas on the plate. The cylinders of the chalk roll and the matting wheel are thicker than the wheel of the roulette and have several rows of teeth.

roulette (top to bottom) A roulette, a chalk roll, and a matting wheel.

Royal Academy of Arts a society founded in London in 1768 to advance the fine arts in England. For a century it was the only significant English art school. Members are entitled to use the letters RA after their names. By the middle of the nineteenth century it had become associated with artistic conservatism.

royal blue 1. a hue designation for a rich mid-blue rather than a specific pigment.

2. an unstandardized name for smalt, ultramarine blue, and various synthetic organic pigments.

royal green see CHROME GREEN.

royal red a pigment made from eosin dye. This SYNTHETIC ORGANIC PIGMENT fades rapidly on exposure to daylight.

royal scarlet 1. a brilliant, but fugitive red lake pigment made from a synthetic dye.

RUBBER CEMENT

2. see IODINE SCARLET.

rubber cement a thick, viscous solution of gum rubber in benzol and other solvents. It is very useful as an adhesive, but only for temporary purposes, since it soon turns dark brown and loses adhesion. Rubber cement serves as the adhesive base for a FRISKET and is also widely employed as a RESIST in engraving, watercolour painting, fabric printing, etc. to mask areas the artist wishes to leave untouched. It is easily applied, produces little or no wrinkling, curling or shrinking of the paper, and can be quickly and safely removed by rippling it away with a finger.

rubber mould a widely used substitute for, and often an improvement on, the plaster MOULD for casting sculpture in plaster, composition, imitation stone, plastics and low-temperature metals. Modern rubber moulds are made of cold rubber, a special compound based on synthetic rubber, which may be painted or sprayed on the model. Its advantage over plaster is its flexibility, which enables it to be used on complex and UNDERCUT models from which it can be pulled away and reused indefinitely.

rubbing a handmade replica of an incised or carved surface, taken by holding a piece of paper tautly on the work and rubbing the paper with a black or coloured material. The traditional materials for rubbing are Japanese paper and a lump of black material called HEELBALL. Powdered graphite mixed with oil to a stiff, dryish consistency and applied to the paper with a dabber is sometimes preferred to heelball, especially to rub fine or weak lines. Rubbings have been made of relief work of all kinds and from every cultural epoch: of designs incised on stone, especially of ancient Chinese and other Asiatic cultures; of memorial brasses in mediaeval churches and cathedrals; of tombstones of the colonial period in America; even of fish, in Japan. Artists have also used the rubbing technique as a creative process, using colours and making additions to, and variations of, the lines of the original. See also FROTTAGE.

rubbing block or **rubbing brick** a brick-shaped block of coarsely textured stone or a composite abrasive material, used in smoothing marble.

Rubénisme a French art movement of the late 17th century that propounded the supremacy in painting of colour over design. It was in conflict – sometimes violently – with the Poussinistes, who insisted that design was the principal element in painting and colour was mere decoration. This argument antedated not only Rubénisme and Poussinisme but also the two artists, Rubens and Poussin, whose names were attached to it after their deaths by their followers. The leading painter in the Rubéniste style was Watteau. See also DISEGNO; LINEAR; PAINTERLY.

Rubens brown see VAN DYKE BROWN.

Rubens madder, Reubens madder or **madder brown** a permanent, transparent lake with a brownish-orange undertone. Rubens madder is now made from synthetic alizarin, but some lots are known to have been off-shade, faulty batches of alizarin crimson and of MADDER LAKE.

rub-out a test by which the colour and quality of pigments are compared. It is made by using a muller to rub the dry pigments to a stiff paste with a little linseed oil and placing a dab of each side by side on a piece of thin, clear glass or a microscope slide with a palette knife. When the glass is turned over and the rub-outs are examined in a good light, minute differences in colour quality may be discerned, especially at the point where the two dabs touch each other, the line of demarcation. In the laboratory, precise methods are used for making rub-outs: the pigment is weighed on an accurate balance, the same number of drops of oil are added to each regardless of consistency, and each is given the same number of rubs with a muller to spread it on the slide.

rubrication the process of highlighting the heading of a chapter, initial letters, or section titles of a book by colouring them differently from the rest of the text. Rubrication is found throughout mediaeval and Renaissance literature.

ruddle or **reddle** any red earth-pigment, such as red ochre or red iron oxide, used in its native state, that is, without processing. The *ruddleman* or *reddleman* was a miner of or dealer in ruddle, who went about covered with red dust, marketing wares from town to town. Lemnian ruddle is a red earth mined on Lemnos.

ruling pen a basic drafting implement used to inscribe lines of uniform thickness and usually guided by a straight edge, French curve, template, etc. The standard ruling pen has a short, slender handle and a point made of two parallel blades between which a drop of ink is placed with a dropper; the ink supply is limited to control the flow. The gap between the blades can be widened or narrowed with a screw to produce thicker or thinner lines. The pen comes in a variety of sizes. A special type of ruling pen has one curved blade and is used for drawing curved lines; it may be attached to the marking arm of a compass for the drawing of arcs and circles. The ruling pen is sometimes classified as a drawing pen.

ruling pen

runner **1.** any device that has a grinding surface, as a muller for grinding oil colours, or the revolving part of a mill.
2. *(casting)* see GATE.

runs the effects of applying wet paint to a surface held in a vertical position so that the paint flows down towards the bottom of the support. See also CURTAINS; FRILLING; STREAMLINES; TEARDROPS.

Russian Futurists twentieth-century Russian artists, such as Mikhail Larionov (1881–1935) and Kasimir Malevich (1878–1935), who were greatly influenced by the modern movements of Expressionism and Cubism, which were developing in Western Europe.

Russian sable hair from the tail of the Russian fitch, occasionally used for artists' brushes. Russian sable is somewhat inferior in quality to red sable.

rust **1.** hydrated ferric oxide; it is a brittle, porous, reddish-brown coating formed on the surface of iron or steel when it is exposed to moisture or

RUTILE

otherwise chemically attacked. Rust has traditionally been considered undesirable corrosion; however, a type of steel called *weathering steel* that forms a handsome, self-protecting surface of rust has been developed and is often used in sculpture and architecture. The term *rust* is sometimes used for corrosion on metals other than iron and steel.

2. a hue designation for a reddish-brown colour typical of iron rust.

rutile one of the two titanium ores suitable for making the pigment titanium white; the other is ILMENITE. Rutile is also used as a yellow or ivory colorant in ceramic glazes.

RWS the standard abbreviation used after their names by members of the Royal Society of Painters in Water Colours.

S

sable brush see BRUSH, RED SABLE.

saccharoidal *(of stone)* characterized by a crystalline or granular texture resembling that of a lump of sugar.

sacra conversazione *(It.* holy conversation) a painting of the Madonna and Child with saints, in which the characters are depicted in realistic association with one another. Prior to the mid-15th century, each sacred personage was painted on a separate panel of a polyptych.

safflor another name for SAFFLOWER PIGMENT.

safflower oil a pale, nonyellowing DRYING OIL of good film-forming properties and excellent colour retention. Safflower oil has long been used in India, and has been cultivated and used industrially in the United States on a large scale during the 20th century. Safflower oil has been used as a substitute for linseed oil in artists' oil colours to some extent; however, little has yet been published on its efficacy from either a scientific or a practical viewpoint.

safflower pigment an obsolete, fugitive, red LAKE made from safflower dye. It is a natural dyestuff made from the dried petals of the safflower plant *(Carthamus tinctorius).* Safflower was used even in ancient times for making pigments and for dyeing textiles. Safflower pigment is also called *safflor* and, in French, *rose carthame* and *rouge végétal.* Safflower is also a distortion of the term ZAFFER.

saffron a fugitive yellow NATURAL DYESTUFF prepared from the dried flowers of *Crocus sativus.* It was used in Roman and mediaeval times, but has long been obsolete as a pigment colour.

sagger or **saggar** *(ceramics)* a thin-walled box made of FIRECLAY. It is used in a simple kiln as a container for delicate articles, protecting them against direct contact with the flame. Some saggers have provisions for holding pins to support the ware and prevent pieces from touching each other. BITSTONE is spread over the bottom of a sagger to support the ware.

sagging see FRILLING.

Saint Andrew's cross or **saltire** a cross in the form of the letter 'X'. This form, the crux decussata, was one of several types of crosses used by the Romans in crucifixions. The name saltire is particularly used in heraldry. See CROSS for illustration.

Saint Anne marble a deep, blue-black MARBLE with short, white veins, from Saint Anne, Belgium.

Saint Anthony's cross see TAU CROSS.

Saint Lazarus, cross of see TREFLED CROSS.

Salian art a style of German art that flourished between the early 11th and early 12th centuries. The Salian style seems to have been a reaction against the expressiveness and sometimes extreme intensity of Ottonian art and a return to the static and symmetrical canons of Byzantine models. The principal centres of this style in sculpture and painting were Regensburg and Salzburg.

salon the official exhibition of the French Royal Academy of Painting and Sculpture, later known as the *Académie des Beaux-Arts*. The conservative policies of the Salon in the 19th century drove many artists – most notably the Impressionists – to create rival salons in order to exhibit their work. (See below.)

salon d'automne a Parisian exhibition that has been held every year since its inception in 1903 as a reaction to the conservative policies of the official SALON. The Salon d'Automne exhibited the paintings of Matisse and Cézanne in its early days, gaining acceptance for their work.

Salon des Indépendants an annual art exhibition in Paris. It was first held in 1884 by a group of painters, including Seurat and Redon, whose work had been rejected by the official salon (see ACADÉMIE DES BEAUX-ARTS).

Salon des Refusés an art exhibition held in Paris in 1863, considered a landmark in the history of modern painting. It was set up by Emperor Napoleon III, at the instigation of the artists involved, in order to exhibit paintings that had been refused for the official annual salon of the Academy (see ACADÉMIE DES BEAUX-ARTS). The show's major sensation was Manet's *Déjeuner sur l'herbe*, which caused a scandal by portraying nude and clothed figures together in a scene of everyday life. Other exhibitors were Monet, Pissarro and Whistler.

salt glaze a transparent ceramic glaze applied by adding common salt to the flame of a kiln while it is at its top heat. The salt vaporizes and combines with the surface of the body, forming a glassy film of sodium silicate. The surface of salt-glazed pottery has a pleasing semigloss finish of a pebbled or orange-peel texture, which is particularly effective on modelled or raised designs and on underglaze decorations. Salt glazing was first employed in Germany and Holland as early as the 12th century. With the development of English pottery in the 18th century, very fine salt-glazed wares were produced; these are now sought by collectors.

saltire see ST. ANDREW'S CROSS.

samba see AYOUS.

Samian pottery see TERRA SIGILLATA.

sandarac a North African resin obtained from the alerce tree (*Calitris quadrivalis*) in the form of yellowish, opaque tears and broken cylindrical pieces. It can be dissolved in alcohol to make spirit varnishes and also in oil to make cooked varnishes. Sandarac was known to the Romans and to mediaeval painters and was employed in the early days of oil painting. Some investigators believe it may have been the *amber* of old varnish recipes. Its outstanding property is hardness, and it was once widely used, with softer resins, to make spirit and oil varnishes with balanced properties. It is little used now, DAMMAR and ACRYLIC RESIN having replaced it in artists' varnishes, the synthetic resins in industrial varnishes.

sandaraca 1. a word used by the Romans for the red pigment REALGAR. **2.** the name for SANDARAC resin in mediaeval times.

In some ancient writings the precise meaning of the term sandaraca must be deduced from the context. It is probable that some Latin writers considered its meaning to be red pigment, for the term was variously applied to red earths, a reddish-yellow lead oxide and cinnabar.

sand box a box containing sand, which serves as a cushion for sheet metal being shaped by hammering. It is also used in the repair of china and glassware to assist in holding the broken pieces in place while the cement sets.

sand casting the process of casting metal sculpture, especially hollow bronzes, in a mould made of FOUNDRY SAND. The sand is packed carefully around a plaster cast of the original piece of sculpture in easily separated units to form a sand PIECE MOULD that is a negative of the original. The pieces are held together by a surrounding steel frame called a *flask* until it is time to remove the finished bronze cast. When the sand mould is enclosed in the flask, the plaster model is removed and a CORE made of sand on an armature is fitted into part of the empty space. After the sand mould has been dried out in an oven, molten metal is poured into the space left between the core and the inside of the negative. The sand is permeable enough to allow gases and steam to escape. When the bronze has cooled and hardened, it must be smoothed and finished, as must metal cast by the alternative LOST-WAX PROCESS. Sculptors almost always send their work to a foundry to be cast in metal, although they may either finish the completed cast themselves or supervise the expert workmen who do the work.

sand coat, sand finish or *(It.)* **arenato** the third layer of plaster that makes up the support of a FRESCO, and which typically consists of one part lime putty and two-and-a-half to three parts sand or marble dust. Finely crushed pottery is sometimes used to replace as much as a third of the sand. The sand coat is laid when the BROWN COAT is firmly set but still moist; it is applied and smoothed with a FLOAT. See also INTONACO; SCRATCH COAT.

sanders blue or **saunders blue** an old anglicization of *bleu cendres*, the French term for ULTRAMARINE ASH.

sand-grain ground an AQUATINT ground prepared by placing a sheet of sandpaper face down on a plate that has been completely coated with a resist and running the sandwich of plate, ground and sandpaper through an etching press to produce fine, uniformly spaced pits in the ground, through which the MORDANT will bite. The American artist Joseph Pennell (1857–1926) was a master of sandgrain aquatint.

sandstone a porous stone made up of fine grains of sand bound together with silica or another substance, such as iron oxide, clay or calcite. The varieties of sandstone differ greatly in durability, hardness, ease of carving and ability to take a polish. Much sandstone is most easily worked when it has just been quarried. Newly cut stone often contains quarry water that carries dissolved minerals. Upon exposure of the stone to air, the moisture gradually evaporates and the remaining minerals harden the stone.

sang de bœuf or **rouge flambé** a dark, mottled, ox-blood red porcelain of the most exquisite quality, made in China during the Ming Dynasty (1368–1644). The colour is obtained by reduction firing of a copper glaze.

sanggam a Korean method of decorating pottery. It resembles MISHIMA, except that depressions are incised into the clay, rather than pressed or stamped, before being filled with a contrasting engobe.

sanguine 1. a hue designation for a red that is close to BURNT SIENNA. **2.** a pencil or crayon of that colour made with clay or chalk containing red iron oxide. Sanguine is the principal colour in which CONTÉ CRAYONS are manufactured and is the usual red in drawings done À TROIS CRAYONS. The common designation *red chalk* usually refers to a chalk of this colour. **3.** a drawing done with sanguine crayon.

sans serif see SERIF; GOTHIC.

santa conversazione a CONVERSATION PIECE of a devout character.

sap green, bladder green, iris green or **verd vessie** an outmoded LAKE pigment of a rather dark yellowish green, made from unripe BUCKTHORN BERRIES. The original sap green faded quite rapidly on exposure to daylight. Some modern pigments of this name are more permanent, but the term *sap green* is unstandardized and has become unreliable.

saponify to make into soap. An oil, fat or wax can be saponified by boiling it with an alkali. An example is the saponified wax paste made by adding ammonia to molten beeswax and used in wax-tempera EMULSIONS.

saponin the powdered bark of the soapbark tree (*Quillaja saponaria*). Saponin has a foamy, soaplike character when mixed with water. It is used for cleaning delicate materials that would be injured by ordinary soap, and has been recommended as a mild detergent in picture cleaning.

sapwood the wood beneath the bark of a tree and surrounding the HEARTWOOD. It is softer than the heartwood and, in some trees, differs from it in colour, grain or texture.

sarcocolla a GUM obtained from a plant native to Iran; it is frequently encountered in recipes from very early times up to the 19th century, but has been little used in modern times. GUM ARABIC is usually used in its place, although the two gums differ in composition.

Sarrancolin marble a variegated French breccia marble, usually with grey, red or yellow predominating, quarried near Sarrancolin, in the Pyrenees. See MARBLE; BRECCIA.

satinwood any of several golden-toned hardwoods of mottled grain and excellent working qualities. Satinwood has long been valued as a furniture wood and for inlays in mahogany and rosewood. *East Indian satinwood* or *Ceylon satinwood* (from *Chloroxylon swietenia*), a pale-gold wood, is generally considered the true satinwood, although *West Indian satinwood* (from *Zanthoxylum flavum*), which is bright gold, is equally popular. *Brazilian satinwood* (from *Euxylophora paraensis*) is also used, chiefly for veneer.

saturation *(colour terminology)* vividness or intensity of colour; the degree of freedom from white or dulling elements.

saturnine red an old name for RED LEAD.

sauce see CRAYON SAUCE.

saunders blue see SANDERS BLUE.

Saxon blue see SMALT.

scagliola plaster of Paris or cement mixed with pigments, marble dust and other inert fragments, and sometimes glue. It is applied to surfaces to simulate the decorative effect of variegated marble and other stones.

scale 1. a ratio of the proportions or dimensions of a drawn object or scene to those of the original. When, for example, a drawing of a building is in the scale of one inch to ten feet, one inch in the drawing stands for ten feet of the actual size of the building. See SCALE DRAWING.
2. a ruler used in mechanical drawing. See SCALE, ARCHITECTS'; SCALE, ENGINEERS'.
3. the relative size or extent of a work of art, as in a painting that is executed 'on a grand scale'.

scale, architects' a ruler with two or more faces, marked off in various scales proportional to a foot, and subdivided into inches. It was used by architects in making scale drawings. Common scales were $1'' = 1'$, $\frac{1}{2}'' = 1'$, $\frac{1}{4}'' = 1'$, $\frac{1}{8}'' = 1'$, $\frac{3}{8}'' = 1'$, $1\frac{1}{2}'' = 1'$, $3'' = 1'$, $\frac{3}{32}'' = 1'$, and $\frac{3}{16}'' = 1'$. Thus, where $\frac{3}{8}'' = 1'$, for example, each $\frac{3}{8}''$ would be subdivided into twelfths, representing inches. Architects' scales were often made of boxwood but came in a variety of woods, sometimes with plastic facing, or might be made entirely of plastic or aluminium. Both edges of a face were used, and each edge might have a scale reading in either direction, so that there might be four different scales to a face. Multiple-faced scales might be triangular or trefoil shape in cross section, or any of a variety of other shapes. A common variety had 6 faces bearing a foot rule and 11 scales.

scale, architects'

scale, engineers' a scale that differs from an architects' scale in that it is based on the decimal system rather than inches, so that a scale foot is divided into tenths instead of twelfths. Common scales range from $1'' = 10'$ to $1'' = 60'$. Engineers' scales are read in only one direction, so that there may be only two scales to a face, or a total of 6 in the trefoil model. Artists have found both architects' and engineers' scales useful for such purposes as enlarging and reducing sketches and drawings.

scale drawing a representational drawing, plan, map or chart whose dimensions or distances are in the same ratio to each other as are those of the actual thing drawn.

scarab 1. a representation of a beetle, which was much used by the ancient Egyptians as a symbol, seal, amulet, and the like.
2. a gemstone cut into the shape of a beetle.

scarlet lake 1. *(obsolete)* a semitransparent LAKE pigment made from cochineal, sometimes with the addition of vermilion.
2. bright scarlet colours made, since the late 19th century, from synthetic dyestuffs.

Scarlet lake is no longer used as an artists' pigment, since it is impermanent and some varieties bleed in oil. The synthetic scarlet lakes are much more lightfast than cochineal scarlet but are not sufficiently permanent for use in artists' colours.

scarlet vermilion the bluish, or least yellowish, variety of VERMILION. Variants of true vermilion do not differ greatly.

scauper see SCORPER.

scenic colour see SIZE COLOUR.

Scheele's green copper arsenite, a bright-green, poisonous pigment discovered in Sweden (1778) by C.W. Scheele, a German chemist. Although it may be produced in a wide range of green shades, Scheele's green is inferior in properties to EMERALD GREEN, which has always been preferred. Scheele's green is not suitable for use as an artists' pigment, since it has the same defects and hazards as emerald green.

schema (*pl.* **schemata**) a simple, generalized depiction or diagram employed as a guide to correct composition and proportion. Geometric schemata are often used to instruct students in figure drawing, indicating by means of spheres, cubes and lines the relative shapes and proportions of the head, torso and limbs. A head is often schematized as an ovoid; a vertical line shows the location of the centres of the nose, mouth, and chin, while transverse curves indicate the placement of eyes, tip of the nose, and lips.

schizzo see ESQUISSE.

Schnitzer's green an early variety of CHROMIUM OXIDE GREEN made by a special process.

school a term used in art to identify the group to which an artist may belong. It may be a broad identification, such as national origin (for example, Flemish school), but may also indicate the artistic tendency (for example, naturalist school), or the adherence to a movement (for example, Impressionist school) of an artist or an artist's work. It may also classify a work whose artist is unknown, indicating the master (for example, school of Giotto) or locality and period (for example, Sienese school), whose influence is most apparent.

School of Cologne a group of painters working in Cologne from the late 14th century to the mid-16th century. The majority of these artists are unknown by name. Their work was done chiefly in the decoration of churches and maintained its preference for idealized and refined representations of the subject matter long after the Flemish and Dutch schools had devoted themselves to a more realistic approach. The influence of Dirk Bouts did, however, make itself felt in the late 15th century.

The best-known painter of the Cologne school was Stefan Lochner, who worked there in the mid-15th century. The last significant painter of the school, Bartholomaeus Bruyn, died there in 1555.

School of Paris a term used broadly to designate all the painters working in Paris in the 20th century up to the Second World War, with the possible exception of abstract and Surrealist painters. The so-called school reached its peak in the 1920s and 1930s, when artists from all over the world seemed to feel that Paris was the only possible place to be. The term does not denote a particular style, but is applied to the Fauves, the Cubists (one of whom, Picasso, is often considered the outstanding figure of the school), and a host of other artists, including Amedeo Modigliani (1884–1920), Jules Pascin (1885–1930), Chaim Soutine (1894–1943), Marc Chagall (1887–1985), Maurice Utrillo (1883–1955), and Moïse Kisling (1891–1953).

Schweinfurt green see EMERALD GREEN.

scooper see SCORPER.

scorper, scauper or **scooper** in WOOD ENGRAVING, a solid metal tool with a bevelled, rounded point used to scoop out wood from the block so as to create nonprinting spaces, leaving on the level of the original plane only the lines and areas that will print.

scotia a concave moulding with a wide, flaring curve whose profile resembles a parabola. The scotia is used especially in bases of classical columns.

scotia

scrambled colours oil colours lightly mixed on the palette with the brush so that the original hues can still be seen in streaks or swirls, as distinguished from colours thoroughly mixed to a homogeneous tint. Loosely mixed colours tend to produce a livelier or more vibrant effect than those whose ingredients are fully and carefully blended, although smoothly mixed colours are more appropriate to certain styles and techniques.

scraper 1. an implement used in ENGRAVING and other metal-plate techniques in which the plate is incised, to remove the burr or other unwanted roughness, to reduce the darkness of the printing of an area, and to create light spots or highlights on the plate. It consists of a triangular steel blade with three concave sides that form three sharp edges along the length of the blade and taper to a point at its tip. The blade is fitted into a knife handle.

2. the leather-covered wooden bar in a LITHOPRESS, under which the

scraper A triangular steel scraper used in engraving and other
metal-plate print-making techniques.

lithograph stone passes. The scraper applies the pressure that effects a
transfer of ink from the stone to the paper that lies on it.

scraperboard or *(US)* **scratchboard** a specially coated cardboard used to
create white-line-on-black drawings that, when reproduced, resemble
wood engravings. The board usually has a smooth GESSO coating that
the artist coats with drawing ink. A white-line drawing is executed by
scraping away lines and areas of the ink, exposing the white board underneath. Special scraperboard tools are used for this purpose. These are
either separate tools or interchangeable blades, some made to fit in a
standard penholder, others sold in sets with a special metal handle. The
standard blade is triangular. With a curved-edge blade, fine lines can be
scratched with the point and broad lines drawn with the edge, while a
razor-sharp straight-edge blade may be used not only as a scraperboard
tool but also as a cutter and an eraser for other kinds of work. A MULTIL-
INER TOOL, with which several parallel lines can be drawn with one
stroke, is frequently used for hatching and cross-hatching. Scratched
areas can be reinked and drawn on again if the artist wants to change or
correct a drawing. Large areas of ink can be scraped away to create what
is essentially a black-line drawing on white, resembling a WOODCUT
rather than a wood engraving. Scraperboard tools may also be used to
create highlights on textured drawing boards.

Scraperboard drawing, which was introduced in the 19th century, has
been widely used in the commercial arts. Because the technique produces
excellent originals for reproduction, it is used for nearly every published
illustration or commercial art design done in the manner of wood engraving. Scraperboard is not often used as a medium for unique works of art,
because the original has an irregular, scratchy appearance. This irregularity does not appear, however, in reproductions.

scratchboard see SCRAPERBOARD.

scratch coat or *(It.)* **trullisatio** the first rough coat of wall plaster. A
typical recipe for use in fresco is one part lime putty to one and a half parts
coarse sand. If the plaster is to be applied to lath rather than masonry, goat
hairs or fibres are added to prevent curls of plaster from dropping away
at the rear. See also BROWN COAT; INTONACO; SAND COAT.

scrim 1. a piece of heavy fabric used for reinforcing cast sculpture. **2.** any
strong, coarse cloth used for reinforcement, such as one glued to a surface
to prevent warping or shrinking. A scrim for plaster may be made of a
coarse cotton or linen canvas.

scrimshaw whale ivory or whalebone, carved or engraved and sometimes tinted, and made into various decorative and useful objects. This folk art form was practised by sailors especially during 19th-century whaling days.

scroll 1. a decorative motif consisting of any of several spiral or convoluted forms, resembling the cross section of a loosely rolled strip of paper.
2. a curved ornamental moulding common in mediaeval work.

scuffing see DRAGGING STROKE.

sculp. an abbreviation of the Latin word *sculpsit*, meaning 'he (or she) carved it' or 'he (or she) engraved it'. Sometimes it is inscribed after the artist's signature on a piece of sculpture to indicate that it is an original direct carving rather than a cast or copy. When it appears preceded by a name in a lower corner of the margin of a print, *sculp.* identifies the engraver or etcher; it has the same meaning as *inc.*, an abbreviation for the Latin *incidit*, 'he (or she) cut it'. For an explanation of other terms used for marking proofs, see DEL.

sculpture the creation of three-dimensional forms by CARVING, MODELLING or assembly. In carving, the sculptor removes unwanted material and, as Michelangelo expressed it, reveals the form imprisoned in the mass; wood, stone and other hard materials are used. In modelling, on the other hand, the sculptor creates a form by building it up from an amorphous lump of plastic material. Modelling in clay is often a preliminary step to casting in a more durable material such as metal or plaster. Assembly is the joining of prefabricated elements, as in welded metal constructions. A sculptor's work may take the form of SCULPTURE IN THE ROUND or RELIEF. See LOST-WAX PROCESS; SAND CASTING; WELDING.

sculpture in the round freestanding, three-dimensional sculpture, as opposed to RELIEF. Sculpture in the round has form on all sides and may be viewed from any angle.

sculpture painting an obscure term for low RELIEF.

scumble 1. a thin layer of opaque or semiopaque colour applied over an area of an oil painting without completely obscuring the underpainting. It results in a toning, haziness or dulling of the total colour effect. See OVERPAINTING.
2. a casual rubbing or smearing-over of a dried oil painting with a thin, transparent application of paint – using a brush, rag or the ball of the thumb, as distinguished from the controlled placing of a GLAZE.
3. a light coating of charcoal or chalk, rubbed or smeared over the surface of a drawing to make it softer and less linear.

sealant an industrial paint makers' term for a material used as a sizing to prepare plaster or wood for painting by reducing its absorbency. A wood sealant is a fluid or paste material used to prepare wood for the application of stain, varnish, lacquer or paint.

sealing wax a thermoplastic compound used to seal letters and documents. It retains a sharp impression of any embossed object and is also useful as a sealer for general workshop and studio purposes. A traditional recipe is shellac, Venice turpentine and rosin melted together in proportions of about 4, 3, and 1 and mixed with vermilion or another pigment. Sometimes, inert pigments and small amounts of tallow or wax are also called for.

seam line a line or fold found where two pieces of something have been joined together. In cast sculpture, seam lines indicate where parts of the mould were fitted together. They are carefully polished and removed by the sculptor.

seascape a painting, drawing, print or photograph in which the sea is the most prominent feature. When a seascape includes boats and other nautical features, it is usually called a *marine*.

season to cure or treat wood to increase its stability and its resistance to warping, splitting and shrinking. The usual process is ageing under controlled temperature and humidity with free access to air. Properly seasoned wood can be used to make panels and for carving, etc.

secco (*It.* dry) **1.** the art or technique of painting a mural on dried lime plaster.

The technique sometimes goes by the rather contradictory name of *fresco* ('fresh') *secco*. It is executed with colours ground in a BINDER (as a casein solution or a tempera emulsion) and applied to set plaster. The result is a pleasing mat surface of moderately bright colour that resembles the effects of FRESCO but lacks its brilliance and purity. Secco, furthermore, is a surface coating, and therefore much less permanent than fresco, in which the colours are absorbed into wet, freshly laid plaster and become an integral part of the wall. Although secco is a technique of great antiquity, it is frequently regarded as a substitute or second-best process, for use when limitations of time, working space and money or other circumstances preclude use of true fresco. (See also MEZZO FRESCO.)

In a widely employed version of the secco technique – described in accounts recorded as early as the 11th century – a finished, dry wall of pure lime plaster is drenched with LIMEWATER or BARYTA WATER the night before work is to start, and again in the morning. Painting is done with CASEIN COLOURS, which combine with the lime in a strong, permanent bond. This method is also called *limewash painting*.

In another secco technique, waterground colours are mixed with milk of lime and, for those pigments (especially blacks and blues) that are apt to powder away, a small amount of weak casein solution. Most painters find it difficult to work on a brilliant white surface and prefer to tint the limewash to a pale tone. The painting itself is usually executed in two coats, the underpainting in lighter values than the final colours.

The word *secco* (as in the phrase *a secco*) is frequently used by Cennino Cennini (*c.*1370–*c.*1440) and other Italian writers to denote touching up a dry fresco painting with tempera colours, or applying certain colours that require the protection of a binder (such as genuine ultramarine) to the dried fresco.

2. a mural painted by the secco technique.

secondary colour any of the three colours that are the result of mixing the three pairs of PRIMARY COLOURS. In subtractive colouring, the secondaries are green (blue and yellow), orange (red and yellow) and violet (red and blue). See COLOUR and illustration at COLOUR CIRCLE.

Section d'Or see GOLDEN MEAN.

section lines *(mechanical drawing)* closely parallel, diagonal lines that conventionally indicate an area shown in cross section. See illustration at CROSS SECTION.

sedimentary rock see ROCK.

seed lac see LAC.

seicento *(It.)* the 17th century. The term is commonly used to designate Italian art of that period.

selenium red an unstandardized name for CADMIUM REDS, relating to their selenium content.

self-hardening clay a prepared mixture of synthetic resin and inert pigments or fillers that dries – by low-temperature baking in a kitchen oven and without kiln firing – to a strong, cohesive hardness superficially resembling that of fired ceramic ware. Sold under various tradenames and intended for amateur craft use, this type of mixture is used for decorative items that do not approach the durability or usefulness of kiln-fired pottery. All clay-and-water mixtures harden on evaporation of the water, but the term *self-hardening clay* refers only to the specific type of preparation described.

semiabstract see ABSTRACT ART.

semidrying oil a vegetable oil that can be made to dry or form a solid film by chemical treatment, but does not do so on simple exposure to air, as does a drying oil. Among the semidrying oils are corn oil and SOYA BEAN OIL. They are not used in artists' oil paints.

semigloss finish see GLOSS.

semimat see MAT.

semiopaque see OPAQUE.

semitransparent see TRANSLUCENT.

Senegal gum see GUM ARABIC.

sepia a semitransparent brown pigment obtained from the ink sac of the octopus and other cephalopods. Since sepia, although fairly permanent in dull light, fades rapidly in bright daylight, it is not generally approved for modern use as a watercolour and drawing ink. Sepia does not work well in oil; any oil paints so labelled would contain a mixture of other pigments. Although sepia was one of the inks used by the Romans, it enjoyed its greatest popularity during the century after about 1780, when it largely replaced the older BISTRE for wash drawings, chiefly because of the greater variety of pleasing tones it yields on dilution. Sepia is a rather warm reddish brown, easily distinguishable from bistre, which is comparatively cool and greenish; the difference is roughly comparable to that between the warm brown of umber and the cooler tone of raw umber. A mixture of sepia and BURNT SIENNA or alizarin crimson is known as ROMAN SEPIA.

seraya Philippine MAHOGANY.

serial art an offshoot of SYSTEMIC ART, in which identical geometric forms, usually ready-made commercial objects (for example, cement blocks) are assembled into a single modular unit.

serif *(calligraphy and typography)* **1.** a small line or embellishment that finishes off a stroke in a letter.

2. (also called **roman type**) a kind of typeface that has serifs. See also ROMAN. Those fonts known as GOTHIC type are also called *sans serif*, i.e. 'without serifs'.

serigraphy *(US)* creative SILKSCREEN printmaking, in which the artist designs, makes, and prints his or her own stencils. All the standard techniques for preparing silkscreen stencils are used in making serigraphs, but the TUSCHE-WASHOUT METHOD, the most popular by far, and the FILM-STENCIL METHOD are especially used.

A serigraph differs from most other graphic-arts proofs in that its colour areas are paint films rather than printing-ink stains. It is, in addition, a direct, extremely versatile technique that can simulate, in an unlimited range of colours, the impasto of oil colours, the transparent washes of watercolours, and the effects of gouache and pastel – which justifies the widely held opinion that serigraphy is as much a painter's as a printmaker's medium. When the artist uses the best rag paper, permanent pigments and a nonyellowing acrylic or alkyd transparent base, the prints are probably as permanent as any other.

It has been said that a commercial silkscreen print is a sterile, literal translation of an artist's sketch, and therefore, a product rather than a creation, while a serigraph is a lively, free translation of the artist's concept and, therefore, a meaningful work of art.

In serigraphy, following standards established for the production of ORIGINAL PRINTS, the artist is expected to execute the entire process without assistance. If the artist prints a numbered LIMITED EDITION, he or she destroys the stencils after completing the run or clearly identifies a RESTRIKE edition. Restrikes, however, are seldom a consideration in serigraphy because, for any edition of a print, most serigraphers use no more than one or two screens, cleaning and restencilling them after each colour run. Many serigraphers preserve complete sets of successive and PROGRESSIVE PROOFS.

The use of silkscreen as an artist's medium began in 1938, when a group of New York artists under the auspices of the Federal Art Project experimented with silkscreening, and developed all its artistic potentials. This group gave the technique the new name 'serigraphy' and later formed the nucleus of the National Serigraph Society, which actively promoted the new print form for twenty years. **serpentine** a decorative green stone, consisting of a hydrous magnesium silicate. Common serpentine is usually dull green and mottled like a serpent's skin. Precious serpentine is a rich, translucent green. One compact type of serpentine, used for carving, is often called *verd antique* or *green marble*, and is commercially classed as a MARBLE. Another type of serpentine is called MARMOLITE.

set 1. *(painting)* to prepare a palette with colours.

2. *(ceramics)* to load a kiln for firing.

severe style the name given to the period of transition in Greek sculpture (480–450 BC) that occurred between the Archaic and Classical periods. It is distinguished by an emphasis on characterization, simplicity or severity of style, and elements of majesty and grandeur.

Sezession see ART NOUVEAU.

sfregazzi *(painting)* a fine, delicate glaze of shadows over flesh tones, spread by tapping with the fingertips.

sfumato *(oil painting)* the creation of soft, delicately blended effects by the fusion of one tone into another, particularly in glazes. This Italian term is frequently used in reference to the paintings of Leonardo da Vinci, who was the first of the great masters to employ the procedure to secure airy or atmospheric effects.

sgraffito 1. a method of decorating (known also in the past as GRAFFITO) in which a design is created by incising or cutting lines through one layer of plaster or STUCCO to reveal the contrasting colour of an underlayer. Mural decoration by sgraffito was developed during the Italian Renaissance, when it became a common practice to decorate stuccoed facades of buildings with cameolike designs and to incise arabesques over doorways. The usual colour of the underlayer was a blackish-brown, produced by mixing burned straw with the plaster. Sgraffito executed with pigmented cement has been used in modern revivals of the technique. **2.** pottery objects similarly decorated, by incising the slip before firing. Early pieces of majolica were often partly ornamented by this technique, which was also employed by English potters of the 18th and 19th centuries. **3.** a method of drawing on STAINED GLASS by scratching through a thin film of coloured glass and revealing the clear glass to which it was fused by FLASHING. This technique was widely used before the methods of painting on glass with grisaille, silver stain and other materials were fully developed.

shade 1. a full or definite degree of difference between two colours, analogous to the difference between notes in a musical scale. One blue may be a shade darker, lighter, deeper, redder, greener, etc., than another. **2.** a chromatic colour that has been darkened by the addition of black. **3.** the dark or relatively dark parts of a figure, object, or scene in a painting, drawing, etc.

shading 1. gradation of tone, or the merging of one shade or value into another. **2.** the toning or filling in of areas of a picture (as by cross-hatching and by lightening or darkening a colour) by means of which shadows, three-dimensional form, and the absence of full illumination are depicted.

shading film a film or screen in any of a variety of patterns or dots, used for shading areas in drawings, maps or charts. A piece of adhesive-backed film cut to the shape of the area to be shaded is either adhered directly to the drawing by rubbing it into place or transferred to a transparent overlay. The use of dots gives the shading a HALFTONE effect.

shadow edge a fine contour line of brightness on the edge of drawn or painted figures and objects. It is a subtle effect, used to create a natural edge where solid colour would give a sharp two-dimensional or papery effect. It is especially used by portrait painters to create a suggestion of back lighting, some small degree of which can be seen on the edges of figures in most light conditions.

shale black see SLATE PIGMENTS.

shard or **sherd** a fragment of broken pottery.

sheen a dull satiny gleam on a surface, which reflects light but is not bright enough to be called a gloss. Sheen is a more subdued or surface effect than lustre, which is generally thought of as a finish that gives the impression of depth.

Sheffield plate metalware produced by coating copper with silver by fusing the two metals with heat. The process of making Sheffield plate was discovered in 1741 by Thomas Boulsover of Sheffield, and developed during the 18th century in that town, where the finest wares continued to be produced even after the manufacture of Sheffield plate spread in the 19th century to the rest of Europe, to Russia and, to a lesser extent, to the United States. Essentially, Sheffield plate was made by fusing a sheet of silver to an ingot of copper in a coke furnace, after which the fused metal was cooled, cleaned in an acid bath, and then rolled into thin plate that could be worked in the same way as sheets of solid silver. After the object had been fashioned, it was cleaned again and then burnished with agate, haematite, or some other hard substance. Silver-plated wire was also produced by this process.

To protect buyers from the fraudulent representation of Sheffield plate as solid silver, the use of hallmarks on this plate was forbidden until 1784, when an officially regulated system of marks was established. Although Sheffield plate did not have the inherent value of pure silver, the generally fine workmanship with which it was crafted and its softer, richer colour made it highly valued. Nearly a century after it began, the manufacture of Sheffield plate was almost entirely superseded by the cheaper ELECTRO-PLATING process, so that most genuine Sheffield plate now has antique status.

shellac 1. an alcohol-soluble resin, the most highly refined form of LAC. **2.** the varnish made by dissolving shellac in alcohol. Two grades are made, orange shellac and bleached or white shellac. Fluid shellac varnish has a characteristic cloudiness, which is due to waxes that are imperfectly soluble. It dries, however, to a clear finish that is hard and glossy, with a characteristic ORANGE-PEEL EFFECT. Shellac is used mostly for varnishing floors and furniture. It is also used on a mould in plaster casting to separate the plaster mould from the plaster cast. Because of its tendency to darken on ageing, shellac is not used on surface layers in permanent painting, but it is valuable for some purposes where it is covered by paint. For example, white shellac diluted with several parts of alcohol is used as a SIZE for gesso.

shell gold; shell silver a tiny drop or *button* of dried watercolour made of GOLD POWDER or SILVER POWDER ground in a gum-arabic medium and sold in small natural shells. These precious materials are also sold in the form of tablets (more than ten times the size of the drop in a shell).

shell marble, fire marble or **lumachelle** a dark grey-brown MARBLE, closely packed with fossil shells, the nacreous coating of which gives the polished stone a brilliant fire or CHATOYANT gleam. Traditionally, the choicest varieties of shell marble come from the Tyrol.

shield of David see SOLOMON'S SEAL.

shim any bit of material used in sculpture, construction, machine work, or cabinetwork to separate one surface from another, as a levelling device, or to create a snug fit. In sculpture, shims are pieces cut from thin sheet metal (usually brass) and set about a quarter of an inch into a soft model to make a FENCE along the lines of separation of a plaster piece mould. Shims so used are often called *dividing brass*.

shing yao the Chinese term for pure PORCELAIN.

ship curve see FRENCH CURVE.

shivering a defect of ceramic glazes caused by high compression. The effect is similar to CRAZING but is accompanied by a raising or cleavage of the glaze along the cracks. See SPALL.

short 1. *(of artists' oil colours)* having a thick, smooth consistency as distinguished from a sticky, stringy, or fluid consistency.

2. *(of a clay or body)* lacking workability. Short clay may be made more plastic by adding a FAT clay such as BALL CLAY or BENTONITE.

short-oil varnish see OIL LENGTH.

shot *(of textiles)* woven to give changeable or iridescent colour, so that the material appears to have two colours. The effect is achieved by weaving threads of two different colours or undyed threads of two different materials that take dyes differently.

show card brush see LETTERING BRUSH.

show card colours see POSTER COLOURS.

shuttering wooden moulds, constructed in situ, for shaping or casting concrete forms.

siccative 1. a material added to oil colours to speed their drying (see DRIER).

2. pertaining to the effect produced by such a material. In ceramics, a siccative is used to help dry the oils used in underglaze colours.

Sicilian brown an old name for raw UMBER.

Sienese school the painters of Siena, in Italy, especially during the late 13th century and the 14th century. Sienese tempera painting represented a departure from the mediaeval tradition of Byzantine art and was notable for its decorative linear element. The *fonda d'oro*, or solid gold background, is an outstanding characteristic of many Sienese paintings. Important among Sienese artists were Duccio di Buoninsegna (c.1255–1319), Simone Martini (c.1284–1344), and the brothers Ambrogio Lorenzetti (active 1319–1348) and Pietro Lorenzetti (active 1305–1348).

sienna the native earth colours RAW SIENNA and BURNT SIENNA.

Sierra Leone copal see COPAL.

signal red a variety of PARA RED used in the early 20th century for railway signals. It was preceded in use for this purpose by antimony vermilion and realgar, and replaced after 1919 by the more permanent cadmiums.

significant form the term introduced by the critic Clive Bell (1881–1964), in *Art* (1914) to describe a formal attribute possessed by every work of art that evokes a particular aesthetic emotion through its arrangement of line and colour. Bell contended that no matter how successful a work may be from a purely technical point of view, if it does not evoke an emotional response based on the aesthetic significance of its FORM, it should not be called art.

sign paper or **banner paper** an inexpensive, smooth white paper available in 50-foot rolls, 36 and 42 inches wide. In addition to its use for commercial sign-writing, it is frequently employed by painters for temporary, full-size preliminary drawings or cartoons. Made from wood pulp, it is not suitable for permanent work. Coloured sign paper, in a variety of pale and deep colours, available in rolls up to 107 inches wide, is also known as *background paper*.

sign-writer's cutter a flat, white bristle brush of top quality, with a chiselled end (see CHISEL BRUSH) and a short handle made in 1- to 3-inch widths; it is sometimes simply called a *cutter*. In addition to its use by sign writers, it is an ideal brush for varnishing paintings, as it deposits a thinner, more controlled layer than the ordinary house painter's varnish brush.

sign-writer's cutter

sil a Roman name for YELLOW OCHRE. The Romans had many kinds to choose from, but the most esteemed and most expensive was the Attic sil, from Greece.

silex see SILICA.

silhouette 1. any portrait, design or image in profile in a single hue. Silhouettes were originally profile portraits in black or some other uniform tint, usually taken from a shadow cast by a candle on a sheet of paper. The hair or hairline was sometimes differentiated from the rest by a slightly lighter shade. The French nobility derisively named the technique after Etienne de Silhouette, the unpopular minister of finance in 1759; his detractors claimed that the mere outline portrait was symbolic of his shallow and empty-headed nature. Silhouette portraits were common during the 18th and 19th centuries, when they were most often freehand cutouts of black paper pasted on a white cardboard mount; sometimes a contrivance called a *physionotrace* was used to trace the sitter's profile. **2.** the outline of a person or thing.

silica or **silex** powdered quartz, an INERT PIGMENT sold in several degrees of fineness. Silica has a sharp grain and is useful for imparting TOOTH to coating materials and GROUNDS.

silica gel a colloidal form of silica, used by, for example, conservators as a dehumidifier. It is available for this purpose in the form of pale, amber-coloured, highly absorbent granules, which are kept in little cloth bags near objects that are prone to injury by dampness when put away in storage or kept in exhibition cases. By absorbing moisture from the atmosphere, silica gel helps prevent formation of mould, warping of materials and softening of water-soluble coatings.

silicones a series of synthetic RESINS that contain silica, useful in industrial coating materials and numerous other products. They belong to a different class of materials from LIQUID SILICATE, the end product of which is inorganic silica or silicate. The silicones should not be used in permanent creative art.

silicon ester any of several organic salts of silicic acid, including ETHYL SILICATE, methyl silicate and amyl silicate. They have similar properties, but only ethyl silicate has been made available to artists. See also LIQUID SILICATE.

silkscreen a colour stencil printing process in which the colouring matter is forced with a SQUEEGEE through a fine screen, on which nonprinting areas have been blocked out, onto the printing surface below. Silkscreen is widely used commercially for printing posters and show cards; for creating designs on cloth, wallpaper, furniture, glass and ceramic wares; for printing electronic circuits; and for printing instructions on a great variety of manufactured objects. The creation of artists' ORIGINAL PRINTS by the silkscreen method is discussed under SERIGRAPHY.

The screen most commonly used in the process is a fine nylon cloth BOLTING CLOTH (or, less frequently, organdy or wire-mesh cloth), stretched on and attached to a wooden frame. In a serigrapher's studio, the frame is commonly hinged to a flat bed or table, on which the paper or other printing surface is placed. A simple prop bar, called a *butterfly*, keeps the screen raised above the bed while a printed proof is removed and fresh paper is inserted; the prop bar drops by its own weight when the screen is lifted and is flicked aside when the operator is ready to pull another proof. The screen may also be held with a spring that has just enough tension to raise and suspend it and permits it to be lowered with a slight pressure. In commercial workshops the screen may be raised and lowered with counterbalances or pulleys.

In preparing the screen for printing, all the nonprinting areas are blocked out by any of the processes referred to below. The margins of the screen are also blocked out to allow free manipulation of the squeegee and to provide space to hold the charge of paint. The printing surface, such as a poster board or a sheet of paper, is inserted on the bed beneath the screen. A special paint is poured along the margin of the screen and is pushed from one side to the other with a squeegee, which presses it through any area that is not stopped out. Each pass of the squeegee produces on the printing surface an unreversed duplicate of the original

SILKSCREEN

silkscreen Apparatus.

design. In multicolour prints (see COLOUR PRINT) a separate stencil is needed for each colour run.

A number of different techniques are used to prepare the screen stencil, and two or more processes may be combined in making a single print. The TUSCHE-WASHOUT METHOD, which is the most spontaneous and admits of the greatest variety of creative effects, is the principal technique used in serigraphy. The BLOCK-OUT STENCIL METHOD and the FILM-STENCIL METHOD are also used by serigraphers for simple designs. The PAPER-STENCIL METHOD and especially the film-stencil method (less sensitive processes than the tusche-washout) are most often used for commercial work, such as posters and advertisements. The PHOTO-GRAPHIC-STENCIL METHOD is a process for reproducing photographs or works of art in any other medium.

A great variety of printing mediums are suitable for silkscreen work: inks, oil and tempera colours, dyes and lacquers can all be used, provided they have the proper viscosity, plasticity and drying time (if the paint dries too quickly it will clog the screen) to pass through the screen with facility. Silkscreen printing mediums are bought ready-made and contain the proper varnishes, vehicles, driers, etc. in amounts that give the paint the correct consistency. PROCESS OIL COLOURS (so called to differentiate them from paints and artists' colours) are by far the most popular medium used for silkscreening on paper, although process tempera colours are also becoming popular. Dyes and lacquers are usually reserved for printing on cloth. Silkscreen paints are sold in a wide range of colours but can also be mixed to produce other tones or hues. The colour sensitivity of commercial silkscreen work is usually decidedly inferior to that of serigraphs printed by artists who mix their own colours.

Artists' oil colours are mixed with a transparent base to give them the correct degree of plasticity and to achieve transparent printing effects. All the standard water-based paints are rather difficult to use, because they dry too quickly and clog the screen. They also share with the process tempera colours several other drawbacks: they cannot be used on screens blocked out with either glue or paper, since they will dissolve glue and cause paper stencils to warp, making sharp impressions impossible; they make an organdy screen limp and unusable; and they cannot be printed on thin paper, for while drying they will cause the paper to buckle.

Although silkscreening has its roots in ancient Oriental stencil printing, its invention is sometimes credited to Samuel Simon, of Manchester, who patented a silkscreen process in 1907. In the period between the World Wars, its commercial application was perfected, and the medium has since achieved the status of a major industry.

silky oak SEE LACEWOOD.

silver-gilt silver that has been coated with a thin layer of gold.

silver leaf silver beaten into thin leaf for use in GILDING. Because silver is somewhat less malleable than gold, silver leaf is usually about three times as thick as GOLD LEAF and thus is easier to handle. Unlike gold it requires lacquering or varnishing to prevent tarnishing and is therefore often replaced by PALLADIUM LEAF. ALUMINIUM LEAF, an inexpensive imitation of silver and palladium leaf, is used chiefly in the commercial arts. The use of silver for gilding has not been as extensive as the use of gold. Silver was sometimes used in mediaeval and Renaissance painting for the armour of figures, and although it was used in 13th- and 14th-century northern European painting for backgrounds and details, it was probably originally coated with a gold-coloured varnish.

silver paint SEE ALUMINIUM POWDER.

silver point 1. a pointed rod of silver which, when drawn across paper that has been specially coated with white pigment, leaves minute particles of the metal embedded in the surface, producing a greyish line that darkens in time as the silver tarnishes.

The traditional point is a silver rod about $\frac{1}{4}$ inch in diameter and 3 to 4 inches long; it frequently has a twisted shaft to give the artist a better grip. A silver point may either be pointed at both ends or have a flat chisel edge at one end for making broader strokes. It can easily be made by a silversmith when it cannot be found in an art-supply shop, but most artists use a bit of silver wire instead, inserting it in a mechanical pencil or an etching-needle holder and bringing the wire to a point by rubbing it on fine sandpaper.

2. a drawing so made. The colour and delicacy of the lines in silver-point drawings have always been admired.

In mediaeval and Renaissance silver point, the paper, parchment, or board was coated with calcined bone in a glue medium. Modern silver-point paper is made by coating rag paper with zinc white in a watercolour or casein binder; a pigment may be added to the coating if tinted paper is desired. Any soft metal, such as copper, lead, platinum or gold, can be used to draw lines on silver-point paper. Platinum and gold have been used to a small extent, but since these metals do not tarnish, the lines they make remain quite pale.

Silver point was used extensively during the Renaissance both for the underdrawing in panel painting and as a medium for fine drawings. The latter were done on white or tinted grounds and were commonly highlighted with white watercolour applied with a brush. Silver point remains a standard artist's technique for fine drawings.

SILVER POWDER

silver powder pulverized silver, which when ground in a watercolour vehicle is sometimes used in GILDING as silver paint. Unless coated with shellac or varnish after it is applied to a surface, silver paint will tarnish rapidly. Its principal use is in painting, where it is used to draw fine lines and create delicate silver highlights. Silver powder is sold in the form of tablets and in shells (see SHELL GOLD).

silver stain a solution of silver salts formerly used to alter the colour of local areas of STAINED GLASS. Painted on the glass and then fired, silver stain imparted a strong yellow or orange tinge to clear glass and could be used on coloured glass to produce other colours, for example, on blue to make a brilliant green. Developed in the Near East in mediaeval times, silver stain came into common use in Europe in the 14th century. Together with JEAN COUSIN, a red stain, it considerably widened the variety of effects that glaziers could achieve with GRISAILLE, the only other form of glass paint known at the time. It was extensively used until the development in the 16th century of painting on glass with vitreous ENAMELS.

silver white a translation of *blanc d'argent*, the French term for FLAKE WHITE. In English, silver white is not a reliably specific term, since it has been applied to both flake white and ZINC WHITE.

simple-solution varnish a VARNISH made by dissolving a resin directly in a VOLATILE SOLVENT, as distinguished from the more complex oil varnish, which is made by cooking the resin with a drying oil and a drier. In industrial practice, simple-solution varnishes are usually called SPIRIT VARNISHES and are sometimes referred to as *cold cuts*.

Simultaneism see ORPHISM.

simultaneity one of the elements or essential principles of the movement known as FUTURISM. It postulates a joining or association into one creative act of all the emotions, memories, associations, ideas and intentions that are in the mind of the artist during the creation of a work. Before the Futurists used the word, Apollinaire had applied it to a Cubist principle. It is sometimes used for the technique that is better called SIMULTANEOUS REPRESENTATION.

simultaneous representation the depiction in a picture of more than one view of the same person or object. A face, for example, may be shown essentially in profile but contain elements of a front view. This technique was first widely exploited by the Cubists, although painters from the Renaissance to the Postimpressionists often used mirror reflections as an excuse to show more of an object than could normally be seen from a single viewpoint. Simultaneous representation has also been called *simultaneity*, a word used by Apollinaire in writing of the Cubist principle. It should not be confused, however, with the principles of Orphism, a movement that some of its proponents called Simultaneism.

Singapore dammar one of the two principal varieties of DAMMAR imported in commercial quantities; the other is Batavia dammar. Singapore dammar is considered better for artists' varnishes because it is paler and has less tendency to BLOOM. It is sorted into several numbered grades, of which the purest, Number One, consists of pale, sometimes colourless, rounded pebbles, drops and stalactitic pieces. It appears dull because of resin dust, but actually is perfectly clear, as is apparent if it is broken into facets. It is held to contain no colouring matter that will darken – its yellowish tinge is from such natural impurities as leaves and bark. It has a characteristic mild odour. See MATA KUCHING DAMMAR.

singerie a depiction of monkeys engaged in apish tricks or acting out various human roles.

single-fired *(of ceramic wares)* fired only once, after the application of glaze to the unfired clay body.

single-stroke brush or **one-stroke brush** a broad, flat red-sable brush made in sizes varying from one-eighth of an inch to an inch in width. Originally designed for lettering and sign writing, it is an increasingly popular watercolour brush, used for putting in broad washes and as a versatile flat-and-edge stroking brush that is capable of making very thin lines as well. Some artists prefer the cheaper grades of single-stroke brush, in which red sable is mixed with the firmer, more resilient ox hair.

single-stroke brush

sinking in the unequal penetration of oil paint into the ground in areas of different degrees of absorption, producing the appearance of dull, lustreless spots on the painting after it has dried. The defect is usually remedied by applying a coat of picture varnish. Few oil paintings will dry without sunken-in spots, and one of the purposes of a picture varnish is to rectify this condition. Sinking in that does not respond to varnishing but requires more extensive conservation measures is commonly due to improper materials or methods of application. A sunken-in spot is occasionally identified by its French term, *embu*.

sinopia, sinope, sinaper or **sinopis 1.** an obsolete name for native RED IRON OXIDE pigment, deriving from the city of Sinope in Asia Minor, an important classical source of red earth. The name is found in early Latin writings and was used in Italy until the Renaissance (Cennino Cennini speaks in *Il Libro dell'arte* of its suitability for fresco, tempera, and secco), after which it began to be replaced by other names such as red ochre, Venetian red, Spanish red, rouge, terra rosa and ruddle. During the Renaissance, chalk pigmented with sinopia was frequently used for a full-scale sketch on plaster made as the artist's preliminary guide for the FRESCO that was to cover it.
2. by extension, the fresco underdrawing itself. Many *sinopie* for Renaissance frescoes have been uncovered in recent years, thanks to modern methods of art conservation. They often show a far greater spontaneity and freedom from the stylistic conventions of the time then the fresco itself.

sinter 1. *n.* the natural binder in OOLITIC ROCKS. Sinters are usually lime or silica precipitated by the evaporation of lake and river water when the rocks were formed.

2. *vb (ceramics)* to fire a ware above the point at which it can be reconstituted with water to the plastic state, but below the point of fusion.

size 1. an extremely dilute solution of a gluey or resinous substance applied to a surface in order to reduce its absorbency or porosity and make it more receptive to application of paint or another coating material. In oil grounds on canvas, *sizing* (the application of size) is expecially important, since direct contact with oils causes the canvas fibres to become brittle and to decay. Hide glue is commonly used for sizing; on rigid surfaces, such as panels and walls, weak shellac is also used. Size serves to fill pores and to isolate coatings or prepare surfaces to receive them. Sizes are always kept very dilute so as not to complicate the paint structure by forming an appreciable surface layer (as varnish does) and because in most kinds of painting it is not desirable to eliminate completely the absorbency of a surface.

2. an ordinary glue solution of any strength that may be used as a paint BINDER, a RETARDANT for plaster, and other purposes.

size colour or **scenic colour** paint made by mixing dry, opaque pigment with a hot glue solution, and with oil or casein to make it dry to a film insoluble in water; used to paint stage scenery. It is similar to DISTEMPER and POSTER COLOURS. Size colour is easily applied to large areas, can be used on cheap paper or on canvas requiring little or no preparation, and, since it is opaque, can be altered or painted over easily when dry.

sketch 1. a preliminary drawing, painting or model, often rough and sometimes rapidly executed, that presents the characteristic lines and feeling of the thing drawn, while it necessarily neglects some of the details. In this respect it differs from a STUDY, which tends to be detailed and in no way spontaneous. The sketch may be a CROQUIS, or it may be a rapid NOTE made to capture an ephemeral effect such as the expression of a face or the action of a figure; when such a note catches an atmospheric effect on a landscape, it may be called a POCHADE. A sketch may also be a more carefully worked out embodiment of the artist's ideas, such as an ESQUISSE, that is closely linked to the ultimate work of art and may be used as a guide for assistants working on the final project; Rubens, who had a large workshop in order to fill his many commissions, often made such sketches for his apprentices.

2. an early stage in the execution of the ultimate work itself, such as a block of stone that has been reduced to a rough approximation of its intended form or a canvas or wall that has been prepared with an underdrawing or underpainting (see ABBOZZO; ÉBAUCHE; MACCHIA; SINOPIA). See also COLOUR SKETCH.

sketching box a small, compact wood or metal box fitted with a handle, used for carrying oil-painting equipment on field trips. It is fitted with compartments and/or trays for carrying brushes, tubes of paint and bottles of turpentine and linseed oil. Many commercially sold sketching boxes are equipped with a palette, and some have space in the lid for carrying one or more small canvas panels. A small sketching box is also known as a *pochade box*.

sketching easel see EASEL.

skew chisel or **straight skew** a chisel whose cutting edge is at an acute angle to its shank, as distinguished from a standard chisel (or *straight*, as it is sometimes called), whose edge is at right angles to its shank. The skew chisel is sometimes called simply a *skew*. See illustration at WOOD-CARVING TOOLS.

skim coat see BROWN COAT.

skin to overclean an oil painting. When every vestige of the varnish is removed, the colours have a frosted appearance. Skinning may also imply the actual removal of colour, especially the surface glaze. Use of a RESTRAINER may help prevent skinning during cleaning, but the conservator's skill is of the utmost importance.

sky blue a hue designation for any azure colour. In the past the term was also applied to artists' colours made by combining zinc white and ultra-marine blue.

skyphos ancient Greek pottery drinking cup with a deeper bowl than that of the kylix and generally made in smaller sizes. The typical skyphos had two short handles attached horizontally to its edge; looped handles were often used. See VASE SHAPES for illustration.

slab the stone or glass surface on which artists' colours are ground with a MULLER.

slab method a technique of forming pottery by hand. A mass of wet clay is flattened to a slab with a rolling pin, its thickness determined by the size of the article to be produced. The slab may be bent into various shapes, joined to other slabs with slip, or PADDLED over a wood form. Another manual technique is the COIL METHOD.

slaked lime see LIME.

slaked plaster of Paris inert calcium sulphate, produced by soaking PLAS-TER OF PARIS overnight in a relatively large amount of water so that it loses its setting power. In mediaeval times it was used to make gesso, although whiting or chalk had replaced it in most localities by the end of the 15th century.

slant a slab with one or more wedge-shaped depressions, used to hold ink and watercolours in various dilutions; a palette for wash drawings. A slant with both sloping and circular wells is commonly called a *well slant*, and a small slant of either type with shallow depressions is sometimes called a *tile*. All slants were formerly made of porcelain but they are now frequently made of plastic and, occasionally, aluminium. The cover of a typical watercolour box is usually designed to perform the function of a slant. A large, circular slant containing six or eight depressions and with a cup or basin in the centre is known as a *basin slant*. See figure.

slate pigments powdered slate in greyish-black, dull-red, ochre-yellow, and dull-green hues, that are sometimes used as cheap pigments in industrial products. Although *slate black*, also called *shale black*, was one of the earliest pigments used in water mediums, it is not in general use

slant Well slant.

by artists. Slate black is gritty and has very low tinctorial and hiding power. Since its hardness is destructive to grinding mills, slate black is never very finely pulverized.

slice any spatulate instrument with a wide or flaring blade, such as the WALL SCRAPER and the broad putty knife.

slicker a 1-inch CHISEL BRUSH with a short handle, made of bristle and designed as a pick-up brush, that is, for taking the excess varnish out of corners in finishing furniture and in similar operations. Some artists have found it useful for applying varnish.

slip 1. *(ceramics)* a very fluid mixture of clay and water, sometimes with colour oxides added. It is used for decorating pottery by pouring or dripping, for SLIP CASTING, and as an adhesive for luting sections of a body (see LUTE) – for example, attaching the handle of a teacup.
2. a small, shaped piece of very hard fine-grained OILSTONE, used for sharpening woodcarving and woodcut tools. A number of rounded, wedge-shaped and conical carving-tool slips are made, their contours designed to align with the edges of gouges and parting tools.

slip casting the production of ceramic ware by pouring SLIP into a mould made of absorbent plaster. After the mould has absorbed water from the slip for a few minutes, a wall of clay builds up, the still fluid portion of the slip is poured out, and upon drying, the piece shrinks away from the mould. See also SLUSH MOULDING.

slip clay a clay that in its natural state contains sufficient flux to be used for glazing.

slip decoration or **slip trailing** the application of SLIP to a piece of pottery with a syringe device so as to create slightly raised, linear decorations.

slow-drying size see GOLD SIZE.

slush moulding the technique of producing a hollow plastic cast by pouring a prepared liquid, such as a PHENOLIC RESIN, into a MOULD and stirring until the liquid sets slightly on the inner surfaces, then pouring out the liquid. The coating left in the mould is permitted to solidify. This type of casting is somewhat limited in its range of available materials and colours, and the quality of results is below that of other casting techniques. However, it is an efficient and economical method of creating thin-walled or shell casts, especially in amateur or craft work. See also SLIP CASTING.

smalt an obsolete blue pigment, differing from the usual inorganic colouring material in that it is composed of glass coloured with cobalt oxide rather than being a chemical compound. The special cobalt oxide (or *zaffer*) obtained by roasting cobalt ores is mixed with molten glass to produce smalt, which appears black in lump or coarse form. As a pigment, smalt was a very difficult material to handle. Developed during the 16th century, it became a standard product during the 17th and 18th centuries, but went out of use in the early 19th century after the introduction of cobalt and ultramarine blues. A cobalt-blue glass paint and ceramic pigment was made in Persia and is believed to have been exported to China and other eastern lands some centuries before its invention in Europe. In the 20th century, smalt, some of which is said to be still made in the original 300-year-old factories in Saxony, is used as a ceramic colour and is also employed to make a type of old-fashioned sign that has a sparkling black crystalline background and gilded wooden letters. Obsolete names for smalt are AZURE BLUE, Dumont blue, HUNGARY BLUE, and Saxon blue. ESCHEL is considered a grade of smalt.

smalto a glass or glazed ceramic TESSERA.

smaragd green an alternative name for VIRIDIAN, taken from the Greek word *smaragdos*, meaning 'emerald'.

Smillie's bath a solution of hydrochloric acid and potassium chlorate that is used as a MORDANT in AQUATINT. Although it has the same ingredients as DUTCH MORDANT, Smillie's bath is much more concentrated, containing only five parts water to each part hydrochloric acid.

smoking the process in ETCHING and DRYPOINT by which a coating of transparent or translucent ETCHING GROUND on the plate is blackened as the final preparation for drawing on the surface with a NEEDLE. The plate is usually smoked by holding it, with a hand vice, face down over the flame of a bunch of thin wax tapers that have been twisted together, producing a coating of soot on the etching ground. Smoking increases the visibility of the design when it is drawn with the needle; lines cut through a light etching ground would be difficult to see. Some etching grounds are already dark in colour and do not require smoking.

smooch a smudged or smeared area in a drawing done with a soft medium such as soft pencil, pastel or lithographic crayon. When deftly executed with the fingers or the whole hand, smooching is an effective way of shading in a casual or spontaneous manner.

snakestone see AYR STONE.

snakewood or **letterwood** a reddish-brown hardwood with dark spots that resemble snake markings. Snakewood is obtained from the tree *Piratinera guianensis*, native especially to Surinam, French Guiana, and Guyana. It is very durable and heavy, and is used for modelling tools and walking sticks. Several other woods, unrelated to the above are also known as snakewood because of their distinctive markings or shape.

snap a tacky or adhesive quality in printing inks, as opposed to a smooth or buttery consistency.

soak *(ceramics)* to maintain a certain temperature in a kiln during the glaze-firing cycle. This practice enables the melted glaze bubbles to flatten before the temperature is lowered.

soapstone a metamorphic stone formed from igneous rocks with a high magnesium content; a dark, compact variety of TALC. It is called soapstone because it is smooth and slightly greasy, or soapy, to the touch. It is easily carved and takes a relatively good polish. Types of soapstone used for carving include POTSTONE and STEATITE.

Socialist Realism the official artistic style in the former Soviet Union. Its dominant position was established in 1932 when the Communist Party took over the function of patronage and control of the arts, which it had relinquished to the PROLETCULT ten years earlier. Socialist Realism confirmed the end of experimentation and abstraction in Russian art. It called for a conservative, academic art, literary and heroic, devoted to glorifying the State and the People in painting and sculpture, and to functional design within a traditional context in architecture. The opposition of the Communist Party to abstract and experimental art became much modified in later years.

sodium silicate see WATER GLASS.

softener see BLENDER.

soft art any sculpture made from flexible, pliable material which differs from the traditional rigid substances such as marble or stone. One of the best-known examples of soft art is *Dual Hamburger*, by the Swedish-born American artist Claes Oldenberg (1929–), who is generally considered the progenitor of the soft art movement.

soft-ground etching or *(Fr.)* **vernis mou** a method of ETCHING that produces prints that have a softness of line and a grainy character suggestive of crayon strokes or of the grainy lines characteristic of a lithograph or a crayon-manner print. The plate is coated with an ETCHING GROUND that differs from the ground used in normal etching in that it is at least half tallow, which imparts a greasy, tacky quality to the ground. When a sheet of paper is laid on a soft-ground plate and firmly drawn on with a pencil, the ground under these strokes adheres to the paper and is lifted away when the paper is pulled off. The plate is then bitten rather slowly, usually in a bath of DUTCH MORDANT. In addition to the crayon effect, the soft-ground line differs from that made with a needle in that it can be made to vary in printing strength through width of biting instead of depth. Less STOPPING OUT and fewer time-consuming operations of other types are required. Different effects can be achieved by using various types of paper and pencil. Various textiles can also be used instead of paper to create special textures in the print. The technique was invented in the middle of the 18th century. Although it was at one time rather overshadowed by lithography, it has been somewhat revived in recent years. The soft-ground method is used both alone, as an expeditious yet effective technique, and with other intaglio methods, especially AQUA-TINT for which it is an excellent linear preparation.

soft paste the clay mixture used to make a softer porcelain. It usually contains ground glass or ingredients used in making glass. See also HARD PASTE.

soft-paste porcelain or **artificial porcelain** any of a number of porcelains, somewhat softer and fired at lower temperatures than so-called true porcelain. Soft-paste porcelain is also called 'artifical porcelain' because it was first made in imitation of Chinese porcelain.

soft soap a liquid soap, usually tincture of green soap, used in sculpture as a PARTING AGENT, especially to separate a plaster cast from a plaster mould.

soft solder a SOLDER that melts readily. It either requires less than the red heat needed to fuse a HARD SOLDER, or acts as an adhesive without heat, like a glue.

soft steel see MILD STEEL.

softwood the wood of conifers such as the pines and firs and of a few deciduous trees such as poplar. It is softer and less durable than the hardwood of such trees as the maple, birch and walnut.

solder 1. *n.* a metallic alloy, usually of lead and tin, used to join two metal surfaces together.

2. *vb* to join two metal surfaces by means of such an alloy. First the surfaces to be joined are cleaned with a FLUX, then a soldering iron or blowpipe is used to melt the solder. Soldering is done at a much lower temperature than WELDING, although red heat is needed to fuse a hard solder. A soft solder joins with little or no heat. There are many special solders, such as silver solder, which contains silver and is used for joining that metal. The solder adheres to both surfaces to be joined, holding them together when it hardens again, like a cement. Soldering does not produce as strong and durable a joint as welding.

solferino a reddish-violet pigment made from fuchsine (magenta). It was a fugitive lake sold to artists in the 19th century.

Solnhofen stone a blue-grey Bavarian LIMESTONE, mined in Solnhofen, in Germany, and used in lithography (see LITHOGRAPH STONE).

Solomon's seal, Magen David, Mogen David, shield of David or **Star of David** two equilateral triangles interlaced to form a six-pointed star. This symbol has been used for centuries as an emblem of Judaism and as a talisman. The two triangles are often shown with one dark, the other light, to represent the union of body and soul. One source of the

solomon's seal

figure's magical attributes may be the fact that it can be drawn in a continuous line, as can the PENTACLE.

soluble blue a variety of PRUSSIAN BLUE processed so that it is soluble in water. It is not suitable for artists' colours, but is used in printing the lines on ruled paper.

solvent see VOLATILE SOLVENT.

solvent naphtha see COAL-TAR SOLVENT.

solvent retention a defect or shortcoming of some varnishes that dry too slowly or remain soft and tacky for a long time because remnants of their volatile solvents are entrapped within the lattice-like molecular structures of their films. In general, resins that are less readily soluble have better solvent release, and sometimes the addition of one of these resins will improve a varnish that dries too slowly. Solvent retention is more frequently encountered in lacquers and complex industrial finishes than in artists' varnishes.

soot brown an obscure name for BISTRE.

Sorel cement see OXYCHLORIDE CEMENT.

sotto in sù (*It.* from below upwards) extreme FORESHORTENING of figures and scenes in a ceiling painting, so that, from directly beneath it, they appear to be suspended in space rather than contained within a PICTURE PLANE. This form of perspective is perhaps most familiar from the frescoes of Giovanni Battista Tiepolo (1696–1770).

South American grenadilla see COFFEEWOOD.

soya bean oil a SEMIDRYING OIL, used in industrial paints and varnishes because of its low cost and its resistance to yellowing, especially in combination with alkyd resins. It is not used in artists' colours.

spackle 1. *vb* to fill in or STOP holes in plaster or other coarse surfaces with stiff plaster, plaster of Paris, putty or proprietary materials such as crack-filler and patching plaster.
2. the material used. Spackle is smoothed with a broad putty knife while it is still wet. The term *spackle* is derived from the German *spachteln*, 'to spread or fill with a spatula'.

spall 1. *n.* a chip, splint, sliver or small fragment with at least one ragged edge broken away from a stone carving, either in process of creation or from a finished work. The term can also be used of chips of ceramics, glass, and other objects prone to chipping.
2. *vb* to break off by chipping, splintering, etc.

Spanish black or **cork black** a variety of VINE BLACK made from charcoal produced by burning cork.

Spanish red a relatively dull, coarse RED IRON OXIDE pigment from Spain, or a similar grade produced elsewhere. It is more suitable for the cheaper kinds of industrial paints than for artists' colours.

Spanish white a superfine grade of WHITING.

spar varnish a waterproof, tough, durable industrial coating designed to resist severe conditions of wear and exposure on boats, floors, etc. The older spar varnishes were made by cooking one of the harder resins such as copal or kauri with linseed or tung oil and driers. The modern ones contain synthetic resins such as phenolic resin. Spar varnishes cannot be used in permanent painting because they turn dark and become brittle with age.

spatter paint or ink applied so as to cover a surface with an irregular, usually sparse pattern of fine dots or specks. It may be produced by drawing a stiff brush loaded with paint across the teeth of a comb and allowing the tiny drops to fall on the surface, or by spraying with an AIRBRUSH or SPRAYER adjusted to emit relatively coarse drops rather than the fine mist that produces a homogeneous coating.

spatula *(painting)* a large, flexible, very finely tempered steel blade. It is used for mixing, grinding, stirring and other heavy-duty operations in the studio. The spatula has straight sides, bluntly rounded ends, and, typically, a 6-inch blade. See also AMASETTE.

spectrophotometer a laboratory device for the measurement of surface colour in terms of wavelength, TRISTIMULUS VALUES and CHROMATICITY coordinates. In a typical model, a beam of light is converted into a spectrum band by being passed through a prism. The spectrum is blocked off by a plate with a narrow slit of adjustable width, and can be moved so that any desired portion is transmitted through the slit and onto the sample. The sample absorbs some of the rays and transmits the rest. The transmitted rays impinge on a sensitive phototube and are changed to an electrical signal, which is amplified and read on a meter. When measurements are made in the ultraviolet and infrared sections of the spectrum, special light sources are used.

spectrum the band of rainbow colours seen when sunlight (white light) is passed through a prism. It represents the visible wavelengths of radiant energy, having violet at the left end and red at the right end. The invisible wavelengths beyond violet on the low-energy side of the spectrum band are called *ultraviolet*, and those beyond the red or high-energy side are called *infrared*. See COLOUR; COLOUR CIRCLE.

speed of dry see DRYING TIME.

spermaceti a clean, white, translucent wax obtained from the head cavity of the sperm whale. It is rather brittle and has a melting range of 41–44 °C. Spermaceti was formerly an important material in the arts but has been superseded by other waxes or combinations of waxes.

sphinx a carved image of a recumbent lion with a human or animal head fixed in an inscrutable frontal gaze. It was a popular motif in ancient Egyptian art. The *androsphinx*, or human-headed sphinx, was the most common; other forms were the *criosphinx*, with a ram's head, and the *hieracosphinx*, with the head of a hawk. The most notable sphinx is the huge example near the pyramids of Gizeh. In Greek mythology the sphinx was a monster with the body of a winged lion and the head and breasts of a woman; it appears in the story of Oedipus.

spider wheel the large outer wheel by which an etching press is operated. The four long protruding spokes of the wheel act as a handle that turns the gears shunting the bed through the rollers of the press. The spokes offer the printer great leverage in operating the press.

spike lavender see SPIKE OIL.

spike oil or **oil of spike lavender** a VOLATILE SOLVENT distilled from a broadleafed variety of lavender, *Lavandula spica;* it should not be confused with the fragrant OIL OF LAVENDER used in perfumery. Spike oil was first produced and used as a thinner for oil paints in the 16th century, and for about two centuries was at least as widely used as turpentine, because of its greater availability. The plant from which it is extracted grows wild in Europe and has been extensively cultivated in Spain. As a paint thinner, its action closely resembles that of turpentine, although it tends to oxidize and become gummy more rapidly and evaporate more slowly. Because of the latter property it has been suggested for use in varnishes to improve their flow and LEVELLING.

spinning the shaping of a sheet of metal against a wooden form on a lathe. After about 1825, most silver and pewter hollowware was made this way rather than by the earlier method of hammering the metal into the shape desired.

spirit 1. alcohol.

2. other products of distillation, such as beverage liquors and the petroleum solvent white spirit. See also SPIRIT VARNISH.

3. *(US)* (usually *pl.*) a few volatile liquids, such as spirits of turpentine and mineral spirits.

spirit fresco or **Gambier-Parry spirit fresco** mural painting with colours made by grinding pigments in varnish, a process developed about 1880 in England by T. Gambier-Parry. Spirit fresco was devised in an attempt to find a reasonably simple technique for producing paintings with the visual effects of true fresco that could survive rigorous British climatic conditions. The process proved to be unsatisfactory and was soon abandoned, but its recipes are still in circulation.

spirits of turpentine see TURPENTINE.

spirit varnish any SIMPLE-SOLUTION VARNISH. The term originally meant a varnish in which alcohol was the solvent, but in the industrial coating-material field it has come to include all such varnishes, whatever the volatile solvent.

spit a fragment of the firebrick lining of a ceramic kiln, which may fall on the ware, causing a blemish.

spit-out *(ceramics)* the blistering of a glaze on firing, a defect caused by air or gas bubbles. See also BLISTER GLAZE.

spitsticks the three smallest sizes of TINT TOOL that are used for fine lines and delicate work in WOOD ENGRAVING.

spline a narrow strip of flexible transparent plastic that is used in mechanical drawing as a ruler for curved lines. The spline can be bent in any curve desired but, unlike the ADJUSTABLE CURVE RULER, will not hold its shape unless specially designed lead spline weights are hooked into the groove that runs the length of the strip; these weights prevent the spline from shifting its position on the paper. The spline is available in

spline

lengths up to 10 feet and replaces the adjustable curve ruler when especially long curves need to be drawn.

spolvero (*It.* fine dust) **1.** a secondary CARTOON that has been traced in outline from the original. The spolvero is pricked for POUNCING in order that the original cartoon may be preserved.
2. the dotted outline produced on the wall or canvas by the POUNCE that has been dusted through the cartoon or preparatory sketch.
3. a pounce bag.
4. *(rare)* the pounce itself.

spoon gouge see BENT GOUGE.

sprayer any device used by artists to deposit a very thin, uniform coating of a fluid material in a spray or mist on a surface. Sprayers are used to apply retouch varnish to oil paintings, fixative to pastels and drawings, and size to an absorbent surface. The simplest kind of sprayer is the mouth blower, a straight, slender tube joined to a wider tube, collapsible for transport and compact storage; the end of the thin tube is placed in the liquid, and the wider tube is blown through with a steady breath. The air stream blows across the top of the thin tube, lifts the liquid and then disperses it in a fine spray. The blower is used only on materials that are not adversely affected by the condensation of moisture from the breath. Another type of sprayer is the ordinary atomizer with a rubber bulb and glass container. The best modern, inexpensive sprayer in art-supply shops is a plastic device that holds a replaceable pressure can of propellant and a 4-ounce glass jar to hold the fluid to be sprayed. See also AIRBRUSH; SPRAY GUN. See figure overleaf.

spray gun a heavy-duty spraying device for large-scale painting on a flat surface. Artists sometimes use this industrial equipment for preparing walls for painting and for varnishing murals. For varnishing, a power gun with a moisture trap is best, as moisture produced by condensation will spoil the varnish, and a powerful spray is necessary to obtain a smooth coating.

sprezzatura studied carelessness. In art the term is applied to the effect given by some works of having been done without apparent effort.

sprigging applied, raised decoration of pottery. Plastic clay is formed in a press mould and applied to the pot by luting, that is, using slip as an adhesive. The moulded form becomes an embossed element of the ware.

sprayer (left) A sprayer with a can of propellant under pressure and a jar holding the liquid to be sprayed. (right) A simple mouth blower, folded.

spruce ochre a variety of YELLOW OCHRE with a reddish cast.

sprue *(casting)* **1.** the entrance hole and main channel in the wall of a MOULD through which the liquid material is poured; it is joined to the model by smaller channels, called GATES.

2. the waste piece of material formed by the channel.

spur see STILTS.

squaring, squaring off or **graticulation** a method for transferring a drawing to another surface on a different scale, especially to a larger surface that is to be painted, such as a canvas or a wall. In this method, the drawing is ruled off into squares, and the same number of squares are then ruled on the surface to which the drawing is to be transferred. Each square of the drawing is then copied freehand on to the corresponding square of the other surface. When a drawing is to be transferred to a wall, the wall can easily be squared with lines created by dipping a length of twine or cord into powdered charcoal or another dry pigment such as burnt umber, stretching it tightly on the wall between points that have been marked off, and snapping the cord smartly. Squaring was used in ancient Egyptian wall painting and may have been used even earlier.

squeegee the tool used in SILKSCREEN and SERIGRAPHY to force paint through the screen on to the printing surface. The squeegee is a thick blade of firm but flexible synthetic rubber, set into and protruding from a hardwood bar. The blade has square corners and must be square-cut along its edges to create clear, sharp impressions. When the edges become dull, they are sharpened by stroking the flat surface of the blade over sandpaper or garnet cloth.

The size of the squeegee (and of the frame) depends on the size of the design or print being made. The squeegee must be at least an inch longer than the width of the design to be printed. The squeegee customarily used by serigraphers has a short, thick handle centred on the back of the tool, but some prefer a handleless type with the back shaped to fit the artist's grip. A long squeegee must be held with both hands; an extremely long squeegee (they are sold in lengths up to eight feet), such as that used in textile or wallpaper printing, is operated by two people. To make a serigraph impression, the squeegee, with its handle inclined forward, is pushed across the screen from one side to the other with a firm, unfaltering stroke; the blade pushes paint before it, and its edge forces the paint through the screen. As soon as the first area has been covered, the pass must be ended by raising the squeegee abruptly. Each pass creates an impression on the printing surface beneath the screen. If several proofs are to be pulled, the passes are made alternately from the left and right sides; the paper is replaced between strokes, and the artist changes hands for each pass. Mastery of this operation comes only with experience, but once the skill is acquired the application of paint with the squeegee can be controlled with great sensitivity.

squeeze an impression taken from any carved or incised object by pressing a plastic material into its depressions. A positive replica may be made from the negative squeeze.

stabile see MOBILE.

stabilizer the additive used in artists' oil colours to help keep the pigment and oil in suspension so that the separation of pure oil from the colour is minimized. The term has been borrowed from emulsion chemistry. White refined beeswax is used as a stabilizer by artists who make their own oil colours, but commercial manufacturers use aluminium stearate, a waxlike substance. It is believed that if the volume of such an additive is kept to a small percentage (2% or less), it will not harm the longevity and colour stability of the resulting paint films. When wax is used as a stabilizer, it serves a dual purpose, for it also acts as a PLASTICIZER.

stacco a method of transferring a FRESCO painting from its original wall. In the stacco technique, the colour is removed together with the INTONACO layer of plaster. Layers of cloth are glued with animal glue to the face of the painting, then carefully pulled. The intonaco adheres to the cloth, since it is already loosened from its undercoat of plaster by the conditions that have made the transfer necessary, generally seepage of water and destructive chemicals through the wall. More cloth is attached to the back of the intonaco, and the cloth is removed from the face of the painting, which can then be attached to a new support. See STRAPPO for a different method of transfer.

staffage the addition of human figures and animals to any picture intended primarily to represent a landscape, town view, architectural depiction, or other such general scene. The figures are secondary and are added primarily to enliven the composition. Although most landscape artists people their own landscapes, some, particularly the 17th-century Dutch painters, often employed other artists to perform this function.

stage see STATE.

stain 1. to colour wood by applying a dye or transparent pigment in such a way that the grain and texture remain visible.

2. a dye solution or pigmented fluid or paste so used. A wood stain may be made with an oil, alcohol, or water base. An oil stain does not affect the smoothness of the wood surface, whereas a solvent or water stain is apt to raise the grain. Wood may also be stained by immersion in a hot solution of certain chemicals, such as potassium permanganate or one of the bichromates.

3. a potters' term for the ceramic colour ingredient added to a clay, slip, or glaze.

stained glass coloured glass used in windows. The designs of stained-glass windows are produced by two distinct methods: (a) juxtaposing differently coloured pieces of glass to form patterns, and (b) painting on clear or coloured glass. Since the invention of GRISAILLE in the 9th century, the two methods have been used side by side. After the development of other colouring materials, such as SILVER STAIN and JEAN COUSIN, and the invention in the 16th century of an entire palette of colours in vitreous ENAMELS, the older method – a form of the art of mosaic – gave way to the newer, and the making of stained glass became, in effect, a branch of the art of painting.

Schedula Diversarum Artium, by Theophilus Presbyter, gives considerable information about the process of making stained-glass windows in the 12th century. The glass was coloured by adding various metallic oxides – such as iron, copper, manganese, and cobalt – to the molten glass. Darker shades tending toward opacity were fused in very thin films with sheets of clear glass by a process called FLASHING. Using a technique of SGRAFFITO, glaziers could scratch or abrade designs through the films to reveal the clear glass.

The glass was carefully cut with a point of hot iron (or, in a later period, of diamond) into shapes previously drawn on a board whitened with chalk. The pieces were then set into a temporary framework to be painted with grisaille and fired again. Next, the pieces were fastened together by inserting their edges into deep grooves on either side of precast strips of lead. The leading of windows during the great centuries of the art formed an important part of their composition – a function that artists often emphasized by darkening with grisaille the areas bordering the strips. The leaded window was then fitted into an iron frame, or armature, which was fastened into place in the window aperture. In later centuries, various inventions refined these techniques and made them more flexible, but did not radically alter them.

Coloured glass was used in windows as early as the Roman era. Entire windows, dating from this time, were recently unearthed in the ancient harbour of Corinth. Stained glass was found in Christian churches in the 4th century and was well known in western Europe in the 6th century. Elaborate windows of stucco and coloured glass were popular in the Muslim world a century or two later and reached their high point in Egypt in the 12th and 13th centuries. (Silver stain was also widely used in the East, at least by the 8th century.) In the western world, many famous artists, from Donatello and Dürer during the Renaissance, to Rouault and Matisse in the 20th century, have designed stained-glass windows. The greatest single period in the history of the art is generally considered to be the 13th century, when such masterpieces as the windows of the cathedrals of Bourges and Chartres were produced.

staining power see COLOURING POWER.

stamnos a type of ancient Greek pot – a large storage urn with a relatively small, covered mouth. See VASE SHAPES for illustration.

stand oil a BODIED LINSEED OIL of high viscosity, used as an ingredient of oil-painting mediums, tempera emulsions, and varnishes. Modern pale stand oil is made by heating linseed oil at a temperature of about 550° F in aluminium or glass-lined kettles for 15 hours or more. During this time it undergoes the chemical reaction of polymerization and becomes as thick as honey. In order to minimize oxidation so that the product is a true polymerized oil, air is excluded by cooking the oil in a vacuum or in an atmosphere of carbon dioxide. Stand oil is the least prone to yellowing of any type of linseed oil; it produces a tough, flexible film and tends to level out smoothly. Heavy-bodied oils of all types have been used since mediaeval times, but the term 'stand oil' does not appear before the 19th century. The Dutch are generally given credit for its introduction.

stanniferous glaze a ceramic GLAZE opacified with tin oxide.

Stapart's ground an ETCHING GROUND used in AQUATINT. It is prepared by covering the surface of the plate with a white wax ground on which salt is dusted. When the plate is heated, the salt grains penetrate the wax. The plate is then immersed in cold water, which cools it and washes the salt out of the ground, leaving tiny flowerlike pits in the ground and exposing the plate underneath to the action of the mordant. Stapart's ground was invented in Paris in 1773.

staple gun, stapler or *(US)* **tacker** a hand-held device that drives steel staples into wood, wallboard and other materials by compression and release of a strong spring activated by pulling a trigger. It is widely used by artists and suppliers of stretched canvas as it can replace the more laborious operation of stretching with hammer and carpet tacks. However, art technicians and conservators disapprove of the use of lightweight staples, especially the common variety with points of five-sixteenths of an inch. They do not hold the wood nearly as well as carpet tacks, and their tendency to weaken when rusted is a serious hazard. Heavier staple guns with sturdier and longer staples give better results.

star see PENTACLE; SOLOMON'S SEAL.

star drill a chisel-like steel rod whose point is channelled with radiating lines in a star design. It is used to drill holes in stone, concrete, and plaster by striking with a hammer, rotating the drill before each blow. See illustration at CHISEL.

Star of David see SOLOMON'S SEAL.

state or **stage** *(graphic arts)* **1.** a plate or block in any condition of preparation preliminary to its use in the printing of the regular edition.

2. an impression taken from such a plate or block as a guide for further work to be done. When such trial proofs, especially common in intaglio printmaking, are exhibited or leave the artist's possession, the artist marks them, according to the order of their execution, first state, second state, etc., to distinguish them from the definitive edition made from the finished plate. See PROOF.

statuary marble any white, crystalline, saccharoidal marble suitable for sculpture, such as Parian marble or Carrara marble.

statue any carved or modelled figure, especially of a person or animal.

statuette 1. any carved or modelled figure that is half or less than half life-size.

2. a FIGURINE.

steady or **steady rest** a block, projecting arm, or other simple device used to hold or assist in holding an object firmly in position while it is being worked on, as in carving or in the application of a tool to a piece on a potter's wheel, banding wheel, or other revolving device. See also HOLD-DOWN.

steatite or **lard-stone** a kind of greyish-green, tan or brown SOAPSTONE. It is soft and easily cut, and has been used for carving, especially by primitive peoples.

stecca (*It.* stick) **1.** (*Fr.* **amasette**) a mediaeval wood, horn, or metal-edged SLICE used in artists' studios in grinding colours and coating gesso panels, among other purposes.

2. a pointed implement used to inscribe a surface. A pottery slip that has been incised or inscribed with such an implement is described as *alla stecca*.

steel iron containing a small percentage of carbon and often small amounts of other metals. It is an atypical ALLOY, since carbon is a nonmetallic element. Different kinds of steel are produced by different refining treatments in the molten state. Their properties also vary according to the kinds and amounts of metals alloyed with them. The most malleable steel, called MILD STEEL or soft steel, has a low carbon content. Carbon steel contains only iron and carbon; alloy steel contains one or more additional metals. Stainless steel is made stain- or rust-resistant by the addition of chromium. In general, steels are harder and have much greater structural strength and resistance to corrosion than iron.

steel blue see PRUSSIAN BLUE.

steel engraving the impression produced on an engraved steel plate. The development of steel engraving (*c*.1823) is considered a significant advance in the INTAGLIO printing process, since a steel plate is less subject to wear and therefore can produce many more prints than the copper and zinc plates traditionally used.

steel facing a nickel or chromium coating that is electroplated on the etched or engraved copper plates used in INTAGLIO printing. Copper plates are so treated in order that they may be used to print larger editions instead of being limited to the relatively few fine proofs that can be pulled before the surface of the plate begins to wear down. Contrary to what is implied by the term 'steel facing', nickel or chromium, not steel, are used for this purpose. Steel facing has enabled the use of etchings and drypoints as book illustrations and has made possible the large-scale production and sale of popular intaglio prints. The propriety of giving a copper plate a steel facing has been questioned, since treating a plate in this way lowers the value that etching or drypoint proofs would have if printed in a small edition and because steel-faced drypoint plates formerly produced prints inferior to the early proofs pulled from an untreated plate. Now, however, steel facing is considered an acceptable process in the graphic arts. The process itself has been greatly improved to produce delicate effects, and the prevailing view is that prints should be made available to the greatest possible number of collectors.

stellate star-shaped or radiating like a star.

stencil cutter or **stencil knife** a small tempered-steel knife with a slim handle and an oblique cutting edge, like the standard hatchet-type blade. The stencil knife, used to cut friskets and stencils, is especially designed for cutting silkscreen stencil film (see FILM-STENCIL METHOD), a sensitive operation that requires a delicate, sharp, easily controlled blade. Several types are available, including double-blade cutters for parallel lines, *swivel knives* with ball-bearing action for irregular curves, and COMPASS CUTTERS for circles and arcs.

stencil cutter (top) A standard knife. (centre) A swivel knife. (bottom) A double-blade cutter.

stencilling any method of creating multiple copies of a design by cutting the design out of a thin yet durable sheet (for example, thin brass, plastic, oilproof and waterproof cardboard) and dabbing, pouncing, spraying or rubbing a colour substance through the openings. The small uncut areas left to join islands in the design are called *ties*. One artists' technique that employs stencils is POCHOIR, a method of colouring prints. Serigraphy and silkscreen are correctly described as stencil processes, and the draftsman's use of TEMPLATES is similar to stencilling.

stereochromy see MINERAL PAINTING.

sterling silver 1. silver of a legally fixed standard of purity, that is, 92.5% pure silver and 7.5% copper.

2. silverware of such a standard.

stick lac see LAC.

stil-de-grain the French name for BROWN PINK.

stile Liberty the name by which the ART NOUVEAU movement is known in Italy, from the name of the London firm that supplied textiles decorated in that style.

still the apparatus used in DISTILLATION. The basic still is a closed metal pot, usually copper, from which a long tapered tube extends at a downward angle, sometimes terminating in a tubular coil. Its laboratory version, made of glass, has a water-cooled delivery tube.

still life a painting or drawing of a group of inanimate objects contrived by the artist according to some theme, either symbolic or merely aesthetic. The still life is usually set indoors and contains at least one man-made object, perhaps the table on which the group is arranged or, in a floral still life, the vase that contains a bunch of flowers, thus differing from a drawing from nature, which portrays such objects as rocks and flowers in their natural setting. Although the still life was painted from ancient Roman times on, it was almost always incorporated into a larger composition until the 16th century, when Dutch and Flemish painters adopted it as an independent form. The still life was brought into its own in the 18th century by the French painter J.B.S. Chardin. It was a favourite form of the Impressionists and such post-Impressionists as Van Gogh and Cézanne.

stilts *(ceramics)* small three-pronged supports made of hard-fired clay on which wares are set for firing in a kiln. Smaller supports, called *spurs*, each with a single point, serve the same purpose. Both are inexpensive items intended to be discarded after a single use.

stimulus colours colour effects perceived when the retina of the eye is excited by means other than looking at a coloured object, for example, a blow or pressure on the eyeball, hallucinatory drugs, or shutting one's eyes in a dark room. The memory of stimulus colours inspires much of PSYCHEDELIC ART.

stipple *(painting)* **1.** to apply small dots of colour with the point of the brush.

2. to apply paint in a uniform layer by tapping or pouncing a vertically held brush on the surface in repeated staccato touches.

stipple engraving ENGRAVING, ETCHING, or wood engraving in which the design areas are made up of small dots or flecks, sometimes in conjunction with engraved or etched lines. The GRAVER, NEEDLE and ROULETTE can all be manipulated to create stippling on the plate or block or in the etching ground. In a stipple wood engraving, the dots may actually be very short incised lines. The stipple engraving is usually inked and printed as a relief plate (see RELIEF PRINTING), the incised dots showing as whites in the proofs. See also CRAYON MANNER; DOTTED MANNER.

stomp see STUMP.

stone 1. cut ROCK, suitable for carving and building. It is one of the traditional materials of the sculptor, and has been carved, drilled and polished since prehistoric times. The most commonly used stones are SANDSTONE, MARBLE, and LIMESTONE, as well as GRANITE and related types of igneous rock.

2. *(commercial usage)* any type of stone except marble.

stone green see GREEN EARTH.

stone ochre see OXFORD OCHRE.

stone rubbing see RUBBING.

stoneware a dense, opaque, durable, nonabsorbent, hard-paste ceramic ware. Heavy-duty items such as crocks, mortars and utensils for chemical and factory use are made of stoneware. Familiar examples are the salt-glazed jugs and crocks made by 19th-century potteries.

stone yellow see OXFORD OCHRE.

stop to make a small or delicate repair by filling in or plugging a hole or depression in a damaged work of art, so that the restored area is on the same level and has the same texture as the surrounding area. Some of the materials used for this purpose by conservators are gesso, picture putty and, on stone or concrete, tinted cement. For coarser repairs on plaster walls, see SPACKLE.

stopping out 1. the application of stopping-out varnish (a thin and manageable acid-proof RESIST made for the purpose) to certain lines and areas of an etched plate to protect them from deeper BITING when the plate is reimmersed in the MORDANT in order to deepen or strengthen other lines and areas. See ETCHING and AQUATINT. Because the darkness of the printing of an etching is governed by the depth of the biting, an artist who wants several different intensities of ink in prints must repeat the stopping-out process several times in order to achieve the tonal gradation that results from successively deeper etches.

2. the mechanical blocking out of areas of the screen in SILK SCREEN and SERIGRAPHY so that paint will not pass through the mesh and print those areas. All the nonprinting areas of the screen not blocked out by the stencil must be stopped out with paper, lacquer or glue. A pinhole in the stencil or other defect in the stencil or screen can be repaired by stopping it out with a touch of glue. A fault in a nonprinting area that is discovered while a stencil is being printed may be repaired without halting the run by placing a bit of newspaper under the spot on the underside of the screen. It is held in place by the sticky paint on the screen long enough to finish printing the edition.

storytelling art see LITERARY.

stove enamel or *(US)* **baked enamel** any industrial, pigmented, synthetic-resin coating designed to resist hard wear. After a coating is applied, the treated item is baked in an oven at 250° to 350° F. These coatings surpass the air-dried industrial ENAMELS in every respect. The term is sometimes erroneously applied to genuine PORCELAIN ENAMEL, which is fired in a kiln at high temperatures.

straight see CHISEL.

straightedge any flat, heavy bar used for ruling and cutting mats, paper, leather, glass and other materials in a straight line. An ordinary ruler may be used as a straightedge.

straight skew see SKEW CHISEL.

strainer a framework or chassis for mounting canvas, that has rigidly joined corners and therefore cannot expand. Its opposite, the expansible chassis, is called a STRETCHER. Lightweight strainers on which muslin or thin linen is stretched have been widely used for mounting prints and other works on paper. Museum conservators condemn the use of the strainer or nonexpansible chassis for oil paintings on canvas because of the frequency with which canvases require tightening by expanding the corners of their stretchers. Canvases become loose for a variety of reasons, and if this condition is ignored or neglected, wrinkles or other irregularities tend to become permanently set and rigid.

straining pincers see PULLING PLIERS.

strappo a method of transferring a FRESCO painting from its original wall. In the strappo technique, layers of cloth are attached to the face of the painting with a very strong animal glue. When the cloth is pulled away, the paint layer comes with it and is given a new backing of cloth. This technique is used in preference to the STACCO method when the INTONACO layer of plaster has deteriorated badly.

Strasbourg turpentine an oleoresin or BALSAM obtained from Central European fir trees, especially *Abies excelsa* and *Abies pectinata*. It is a product very similar in its properties to VENICE TURPENTINE and, similarly, used by artists for centuries as an ingredient of mediums and mastics and other varnishes. It is the *olio d'Abezzo* mentioned by Italian writers. During the 17th century, it was an important item of commerce, and most artists seem to have preferred it to Venice turpentine, which is now in wider use. Both Strasbourg turpentine and Venice turpentine are universally approved for use in permanent painting. They are not to be confused with TURPENTINE.

streamlines a defect that may appear in paint or picture varnish that is applied to a painting while it is in a vertical position. It consists of fine, close, parallel vertical lines or striations. Other such defects are CURTAINS, FRILLING and TEARDROPS.

stretcher the chassis, or wooden framework, on which an artist's canvas is stretched by pulling it tight and tacking it to the edges of the rectangular framework all around. The usual stretcher is made of strips of wood one-and-three-quarter inches wide, with raised or flanged edges, and mitred and tongue-and-groove corners made by automatic machinery and universally interchangeable. These strips are available commercially in lengths from 8 to 60 inches and are assembled by the artist. After stretching a canvas, the artist hammers flat, triangular KEYS or wedges into slots in the inner corners of the chassis to make the canvas more taut. If the canvas subsequently slackens, these keys may be used to tighten it further. Nineteenth-century stretchers were heavier, measured $2\frac{1}{2}$ inches in width, and had crossbars in the larger sizes for greater rigidity and protection against warping. Such stretchers are still available from art-supply shops on special order, and are preferred by some painters. Some museum technicians and conservators require still better equipment: they use custom-made stretchers whose corners are fitted with mechanical tighteners in place of the wooden keys.

The common lightweight stretcher was a turn-of-the-century develop-

stretcher Strips and keys.

ment. It is notable for its economy and convenience, but is intended to be used only for paintings that are to be well braced in substantial frames; paintings left unframed or with simple stripping should be stretched on 2½-inch stretchers to prevent warping. A chassis in which no room is allowed for expansion is called a *strainer* rather than a stretcher, and is never recommended for use in permanent painting.

stretching frame a device for holding a sheet of lightweight watercolour paper taut, as an alternative to mounting it on a board. The paper is held between two rectangular frames of wood or aluminium, the smaller of which fits tightly inside the larger. The stretching frame, employed mostly for outdoor sketching, is used far less frequently than it was in the 19th and early 20th centuries.

stretching pliers see PULLING PLIERS.

stria the vertical rib between two adjacent grooves in FLUTING; an arris.

striation a surface marking consisting of closely parallel lines or grooves, either occurring naturally or applied. The term correctly refers to straight, narrow lines, but is also applied to broader stripes, such as the linear patterns on stone, especially marble. A stone showing such markings is said to be *striated*.

strike through the manifestation of a paint layer through a subsequent layer of paint. The colour or texture of some previous painting may become visible or partially visible through an overpainting that is intended to hide it. PENTIMENTO is one form of strike through.

striking see EMBOSSING.

strip 1. to remove the varnish from an oil painting with solvents. See also RESTRAINER; SKIN.

2. to frame a canvas by nailing lattice strips to its edges, usually running the horizontals full width and fitting the verticals between them. When used on the common lightweight chassis, stripping is a temporary expedient. It is quick, inexpensive and economizes on space in a group exhibition, but as a permanent method it does not brace the canvas at all.

striper see LINERS AND STRIPERS; DAGGER STRIPER.

strong drying oil see BLACK OIL.

strontium white strontium sulphate, native or artificial. Similar in its properties to BARYTES and BLANC FIXE, it was occasionally used as an INERT PIGMENT in Britain during the early 19th century. The white strontium pigments have long since been superseded by the barium sulphates, which are much cheaper.

strontium yellow strontium chromate, a permanent, semiopaque, pale citron-yellow pigment. Strontium yellow was useful to painters for obtaining a pale yellow with a more greenish cast than cadmium yellow, and for securing a different kind of green from those produced by mixing cadmium yellows with blues and greens. Strontium, barium and zinc yellows have the same hue; the cheaper barium yellow is much paler, or less intense, than strontium yellow. Strontium yellow is no longer available. Zinc yellow, which has colour properties identical with those of strontium yellow, is not approved for permanent painting.

stucco a plaster used as a finishing and protective coating on walls. The term almost always refers to a ROUGHCAST finish on outdoor walls, but stucco can also be smooth. Its usual composition is Portland cement, lime PLASTER or gypsum plaster, sand and, for the roughcast finish, pebbles or other aggregate. Limeproof pigments are added if colour is desired. In ancient Greece and Rome, a smooth, highly finished and polished surface was most admired. Throughout the Renaissance, a mixture of lime made from travertine and crushed or powdered marble was used. By careful craftsmanship and selection of the best materials, a fine surface and a stonelike durability were obtained, both on flat areas and in decorations that were modelled or pressed into the surface with hollow-carved wooden moulds dusted with powdered marble. Renaissance stuccoed facades were also frequently decorated by SGRAFFITO.

studio easel see EASEL.

study *(drawing, painting and sculpture)* a preliminary rendition of a projected work or, more often, a detail of that work, such as a head, figure, or flower. The artist makes a study to explore an idea for future development, if not for immediate use, and to become familiar with the problems involved in its depiction. The artist may also use a study to explore a technique or material, either in a purely experimental way or to evaluate its suitability for a projected composition. Because a study is the artist's vehicle for working out themes and techniques, it is a more carefully detailed representation than a sketch. The French word *étude*, meaning 'study,' is sometimes used as a title for a picture.

stump or **stomp** a cigar-shaped implement used in drawing to blend or smudge charcoal, soft pencil, pastel, chalk or crayon. It is made of tightly rolled paper, leather, or felt and is pointed at both ends. Stumps are usually 4 to 6 inches long. See also TORTILLON.

stumping chalk see CRAYON SAUCE.

stun *(sculpture)* 1. *vb* to bruise, discolour or cause a SPALL or chip in stone by striking with a blunt instrument.

2. *n.* a flaw so produced. See TERRACE.

S-twist see TWIST DIRECTION.

style 1. the singular mode of expression employed in the representation

stump (left) Stump. (right) Tortillon.

of FORM. Styles are classified according to such categories as historical period, school, nation or locality, or group of artists. Style also refers to the TECHNIQUE and particular characteristics of an individual artist.
2. see STYLUS.

style mécanique, le an early phase of PURISM. Its best-known exponent was Fernand Léger (1881–1955).

stylization the representation of natural forms more in accordance with artistic ideals or conventions than with observation of individual examples of those forms. Classical Greek sculpture, for example, showed human bodies as the artists believed they should look ideally, rather than as they really looked. Suppression of individual differences often involves intentional distortion of natural forms when universal characteristics are emphasized through exaggeration. Familiar examples are the sleek, elongated cats sculptured in ancient Egypt; the artists deliberately overstated certain characteristics, apparently in pursuit of the essence of catness. Stylization has been used for one purpose or another in every age from the prehistoric to the present.

stylograph, needle-point pen or **stylographic pen** a fountain pen used for drawing that has a tubular, needlelike point, rather than a nib. The ink supply is controlled by a check valve and released only when pressure is placed on the point. The flow of ink is measured and regular, enabling precise, neat lines to be drawn. The stylograph is available in a variety of point sizes, all relatively fine.

stylus or **style** any small, pencil-shaped instrument with a hard point, usually metal, used by artists for incising lines on a soft surface (for example, clay, wet plaster, gold) or for transferring a drawing with TRACING PAPER or GRAPHITE PAPER. The stylus is the oldest of artists' implements. Those used in ancient Greece and Rome to inscribe wax tablets had a sharp point for writing and a blunt end for eradicating mistakes and smoothing the wax surface.

styrene resin one of the groups or families of synthetic RESINS, whose properties are similar to those of the ACRYLIC RESINS. Styrene is not used in artists' paints or varnishes because it is not soluble in mild solvents, but it finds uses in sculpture casting materials. See FOAM PLASTIC.

sublime an 18th-century term denoting elements of grandeur and the awe-inspiring in works of art, most notably in landscape painting.

substrate or **substratum** *(painting)* **1.** a GROUND or underlayer.
2. the base or inert pigment used to make a LAKE.
   It is a rather outmoded term in art, but is still used in scientific and technical writings.

subtractive colour see COLOUR.

successive proofs see PROGRESSIVE PROOFS.

suction table a specially constructed, electrically heated table used in the conservation of paintings as the working surface in the lining of a canvas. The warmth of the table bed is regulated for the optimum working temperature of the lining adhesive. A cover of rubber sheeting is stretched over the table, and a pump mounted below causes the formation of a vacuum that flattens the rubber membrane over the canvas and causes its impregnation with the adhesive. The suction table was developed by museum technicians in the 1950s.

suede effect the permanent differences between the colour or gloss effects displayed by adjacent horizontal and vertical brushstrokes of the same oil colour. Many painters, notably in England, are of the opinion that the suede effect is peculiar to modern oil colours, and that it was not produced, or at least not to such an annoying extent, by colours made before the mid-1930s, which were always made with cold-pressed linseed oil. This problem is the subject of intensive laboratory research. The suede effect is an example of DICHROISM.

sugar lift an etching process in which a mixture of equal parts of sugar, water and INDIAN INK is brushed on to an etching plate, allowed to dry, then covered with a very thin coat of acid resist. The plate is left to soak in a bath of lukewarm water until the lift dissolves and exposes the plate. The sugar lift method is the most effective means of producing brushstrokes in an etching. Sugar lift should always be used in conjunction with aquatint in order to be effective. If an aquatint is not used prior to application of the sugar lift, the acid will not provide enough tooth to hold the ink. See AQUATINT.

sumac wax see JAPAN WAX.

sumi or **black watercolour** Japanese ink. See INK.

Sunday painter a person who paints as a hobby; a dilettante. The term implies that the painter pursues painting only on a day or days free from a regular occupation, or in the painter's spare time.

sunflower yellow a brilliant medium-yellow pigment used in Chinese painting, made from ORPIMENT.

sunk relief hollow RELIEF.

sun-refined oil a type of BODIED LINSEED OIL. It is obtained by placing linseed oil in a bottle with water, exposing it to the direct rays of the sun for several weeks, and shaking it occasionally. By this means, its viscosity is increased, the oil is bleached, and impurities settle out in the water layer. If it is also exposed to air, as in a flat tray, it oxidizes, becoming as viscous as honey; it is then called *sun-thickened oil*. The practice of refining a DRYING OIL by exposure to the sun is as old as the use of oils in paints; many of the older manuscripts and treatises describe it. Sun-refined oil is a traditional ingredient of painting mediums, but modern opinion rates it below stand oil in nonyellowing properties. It dries much more rapidly than stand oil. Colours containing sun-thickened oil tend to hold brushstroke textures rather than level out as stand-oil colours do. Sun-thickened oil is sold in bottles, although, like sun-refined oil, it can be made at home. These are the only processes of oil refinement feasible for artists to attempt.

superoxol a concentrated solution (30%) of hydrogen peroxide. (The ordinary pharmaceutical grade of hydrogen peroxide contains no more than 3 or 4%.) Superoxol may be used in the conservation of art works as a powerful bleach or oxidizing agent.

superrealism, photographic realism or **photorealism** a style of 20th-century art, including painting and sculpture, that evolved in the 1960s and is characterized by emphasis on the most minute realistic detail. Painters working in this style often paint from photographs, replicating on canvas every precise detail of a scene. Sculptors often use real objects, for example, clothing and furniture, to achieve the desired effect in a work.

support the structure on which the ground or the paint layer of a painting is laid. The usual support of oil painting is stretched linen canvas. Wooden or hardboard panels are used for tempera and casein painting, and sometimes for oil painting. Watercolour, gouache and pastel paintings are done on paper.

supra porta see DESSUS DE PORTE.

Suprematism or **Nonobjectivism** an art movement founded in Russia in 1913 by Kazimir Malevich (1878–1935); its manifesto was published in 1915. Suprematist art, derived from Cubism, was completely NONOBJECTIVE; it consisted of basic geometric forms and simple colours, conceived in terms of so-called pure feeling. Besides Malevich, who achieved the ultimate expression of his theory in *White on White*, exponents of the movement included Alexander Rodchenko (1891–1956), painter of *Black on Black*, who called the movement *Nonobjectivism*, and many of the artists associated with CONSTRUCTIVISM. They continued to contribute to the development of GEOMETRIC ABSTRACTION in Paris after 1922, when the Soviet government proscribed abstract and experimental art, and the majority of its practitioners left Russia. See ABSTRACT ART.

surface colour 1. the colour of a coating or top layer, as distinguished from that of a substance that is integrally coloured throughout its mass, especially in ceramics.
2. the colour effect of a surface viewed by reflected light, especially when associated with metals, as the yellow of gold, the red of copper.

surface tension the tendency of a liquid to form separate drops rather than flow and wet a surface evenly. Water has a high surface tension, alcohol a low one; alcohol added to water, therefore, will improve its wetting power. Watercolour paints contain a special WETTING AGENT so that the colours will take evenly on the paper without CISSING.

surfactant or **surface-active agent** any of a group of substances used for cleaning, wetting or dispersing. These substances operate by reducing surface tension in a fluid or the interfacial tension between two immiscible fluids, such as oil and water. They are especially useful for accomplishing the wetting or penetration of solids by aqueous liquids and serve in this way as detergent, emulsifying, or dispersing agents. They are more effective than soap in certain situations and are used by professional conservators for such purposes as picture cleaning. See PENETRANT; WETTING AGENT.

Surrealism an art movement of the 1920s and later. Surrealist artists attempt to give free rein to the subconscious as a source of creativity and to liberate pictorial ideas from their traditional associations. As a successor to DADA, Surrealism is characterized by use of some of its techniques, such as employment of the FOUND OBJECT. Artists who participated in both these movements included Ernst, Arp, and Picabia. An abstract Surrealism was practised by the painter Joan Miró (1893–1983). Other aspects of Surrealist art are the juxtaposition of unexpected objects or themes in an atmosphere of fantasy, and a pervasive dreamlike quality. Salvador Dali (1904–1989) and Giorgio de Chirico (1888–1978) are among the most important creators of the haunting, irrational, occasionally repellent dream world of Surrealist art. See also AUTOMATISM.

Sussex marble or **Petworth marble** a type of SHELL MARBLE from Sussex. The episcopal chair and altar stones in Canterbury Cathedral are made of Sussex marble.

swag see FESTOON.

swastika see GAMMADION.

Swedish green see COBALT GREEN.

sweetener see BLENDER.

swivel knife see STENCIL CUTTER.

sword liner see LINERS AND STRIPERS.

sycamore or *(US)* **harewood** a variety of MAPLE (*Acer pseudoplatanus*); it is a light-coloured wood with a delicate, figured grain, available weathered and in pink and silver-grey – all artificially coloured.

symbolism a style of art closely tied to the French literary Symbolism movement of the late 19th century, which is characterized by its rejection of art as the mere explicit representation of the real and concrete, in favour of the depiction of symbols and ideas – ideas that were usually spiritual or mystical in nature, representing the inner life of people.

symmetry an exact, regular, balanced arrangement of forms on either side of a central axis, one side of which mirrors the other. While pleasing to the eye in architecture, the use of symmetry in the pictorial arts may tend to appear static.

Synchromism a style of abstract painting developed by American artists Morgan Russell (1886–1953) and Stanton MacDonald-Wright (1890–1973) in the second decade of the 20th century that is characterized by its emphasis on colour – usually in large geometric patterns – as a means of artistic expression.

synthetic Cubism see CUBISM.

synthetic organic pigments pigments made from intermediates, which are in turn made from raw materials that are products of the distillation of coal tar. These processes are the out-growths of the intensive development of organic chemistry in the second half of the 19th century, followed by improvements and further discoveries in the 20th century. The synthetic dyes are superior to the older, natural dye-stuffs for industrial purposes, and have virtually replaced them, but relatively few have the light-resistance or pigment properties to be suitable for use in pigments for permanent painting. The discovery of the first coal-tar dye-stuff, PERKIN'S VIOLET (1856), was followed by the development of several groups or families of dyes. By the 1950s only three of such organic pigments were generally approved for permanent painting: alizarin crimson, phthalocyanine blue, and phthalocyanine green. The terms coal-tar colour and aniline colour were frequently used contemptuously. Since the 1950s, many more synthetic pigments have been adopted for use in permanent painting. See COAL-TAR COLOURS.

synthetic resin see RESIN.

synthetism the name given to a style of painting developed in the 1890s by French artists Paul Gauguin (1848–1903) and Emile Bernard (1868–1941) and the PONT AVEN SCHOOL that is characterized by the use of pure colour and of large patterns of simple forms.

systemic art a style of abstract art distinguished by the use of an organized system in depicting simple geometric forms.

T

table easel any of variously constructed small easels that are designed for use on top of a table, desk, or workbench. Table easels have a rectangular or, more commonly, a triangular framework of either wood or metal, and a centre post with an adjustable backrest by means of which the easel is given the desired tilt. The simplest models have a narrow tray at the base of the frame to hold a canvas or a board; others have, in addition, a sliding bracket on the centre post, to secure the supports at the top. Table easels can be folded flat for carrying and storage; some double as reading stands.

table easel Two designs.

taboret a small cabinet kept near an artist's drawing table or easel. Its top surface holds a palette or other implements, and it has drawers for brushes, colours and other equipment, a storage cupboard, and a rear compartment for pads and boards.

Tachisme or **art autre** French terms that correspond to ACTION PAINTING. European work of this type is perhaps somewhat more restrained than that of the New York school.

tacker see STAPLER.

tacking iron an electrically heated, straight-handled iron of very small dimensions, made to be used in DRY MOUNTING. It is touched briefly to the arranged layers of paper, DRY MOUNTING TISSUE, and cardboard in order to hold them in place until they are put in the dry-mounting press, where they are thoroughly bound. The tacking iron is a useful instrument for many other purposes where heat is applied in spots, such as in the relining of paintings with wax adhesives.

tacky sticky or adhesive to the touch, characteristic of a coat of varnish that is not completely dry. The quality of tack or tackiness is the opposite of oiliness, and in this respect it is a significant property of a printing or lithographic ink.

tactile values a term introduced by Bernard Berenson in *Italian Painters* *of the Renaissance* (written 1894–1907) to describe the illusion of three-dimensional form, which he postulates as the *sine qua non* of figure-painting as an art.

taille directe see DIRECT CARVING.

talc or **French chalk** a native magnesium silicate of common occurrence. Pulverized, it is used as a FILLER, or to impart a slippery or soapy quality to dry mixtures. In ceramics, it is a major flux in clay bodies fired at moderate temperatures. ASBESTINE and SOAPSTONE are varieties of talc.

tamp in casting plaster, to press a very heavy plaster mixture into a mould. It is done in order to obtain a dense, hard positive, although casts made in this way tend to be less uniform in quality than poured and vibrated casts.

Tanagra figurine a small painted terracotta statuette from ancient Greece, sometimes representing a person engaged in some daily activity. The name comes from a small town in Boeotia that was an important site of their production in the latter part of the 4th and during the 3rd centuries BC; these figurines were, however, made throughout the Greek lands. They have been admired for their grace and subtlety as well as for their depiction of the life of their time.

tape see PRESSURE-SENSITIVE TAPE.

tapping *(painting)* a dabbing, pouncing or stippling stroke of a brush or dabber.

tar any of the dark-coloured, viscous, residual products obtained by the distillation of organic materials such as petroleum, coal and resinous woods.

tarnish to dull or discolour the surface of a mineral or a metal either by chemical reaction, such as the tarnishing of silver by oxidation by the sulphur in the atmosphere, or by the deposition of a thin film of grime. See also PATINA.

tarsia see INTARSIA.

Tatlinism see CONSTRUCTIVISM.

tau cross or **Saint Anthony's cross** a cross in the shape of the letter tau, the Greek *T*. This cross, the *crux commissa*, was one type commonly used by Romans in crucifixions. See CROSS for illustration.

t-chisel a chisel with a bar at right angles to the shaft, forming the letter *T*, at its tip; it is used as a boring drill. See illustration at CHISEL.

teardrops or **tears** one of the defects that may appear in picture varnish or thin paint that is applied while the painting is in a vertical position. The varnish, flowing down, accumulates in drops, and dries to resemble raindrops on a window. Similar defects are STREAMLINES, CURTAINS and FRILLING.

tecali Mexican onyx. See ONYX MARBLE.

technical sketching see MECHANICAL DRAWING.

technique 1. the manipulative skill an artist employs in use of medium and mastery of material as well as general knowledge of the mechanical details of the artist's art. The manner in which an artist applies paint or mixes colours is the means by which he or she achieves a desired aesthetic intention. Therefore, the mastery of technique, although usually associated with apprenticeship or craft, can never be completely separated from the achievement of inventive artistic expression.

2. the entire process of employment of a specific method of painting, sculpture, etc., such as the technique of tempera painting or the technique of glazing.

tectiform in the shape of a house.

teinte French for TINT; at one time the word was common in English usage.

telamon (*pl.* **telamones**) (*Lat.* bearer or supporter) a column of a building carved in the form of a man, as a *caryatid* is in the form of a woman. The Greeks called such columns ATLANTES. See illustration at CARYATID.

temmoku, tenmoku or **hare's fur** a Japanese slip-glazed black or dark brown pottery originally developed during the Sung Dynasty in China. It is also called 'hare's fur' because it has streaks of tan and brown. The main colouring agent in temmoku is iron oxide.

temper 1. to prepare (especially) artists' pigments of the Renaissance era for use, by mixing with TEMPERA. Tempered, or tempera, colours were distinguished from fresco, in which no tempera is used.

2. to regulate the hardness and strength of a metal. A metal tool is tempered after it is made by reheating it and quenching it, that is, plunging it into water at a moment determined by the appearance of the metal. Tempering results in a tougher, less brittle tool, although tempered metal is softer than untempered metal.

tempera 1. (*originally*) a liquid binder or vehicle for powdered colours.

2. (*subsequently*) paint in which the vehicle is egg yolk and water, or another emulsion.

3. a technique of painting that employs colours made by dispersing pigments in a water-miscible emulsion vehicle, especially one in which the EMULSION is egg yolk and water. Egg tempera originated in mediaeval Europe and was the principal process used for easel painting until the development of oil painting during the 15th century.

The pigments used in egg tempera are ground in water to paste consistency and kept covered with a little water in screw-top jars. Just prior to use, the painter mixes equal parts of colour paste and egg yolk to make enough paint for the day's work. Some painters prefer to use artificial emulsions, such as GUM TEMPERA or egg-and-oil tempera, for the particular qualities and effects that they can produce. The painting is executed on a fully absorbent gesso panel with red sable brushes; the stroking is almost always done with the point of the brush. The point is also used for hatching to make gradations, since tempera colours do not blend. The tempera technique is particularly suited to linear styles of painting, and its soft glowing colour quality is not easily duplicated by any other means of painting. The colours dry at once and the paint layer becomes quite water-resistant. After about eight months' ageing, the film becomes extraordinarily tough and durable – so much so that defects do not develop in a properly mixed colour during centuries of ageing. A tempera film does not require varnishing; it can be polished to a pleasing satiny finish by rubbing it with absorbent cotton.

The materials of tempera paints were known to the Romans and Egyptians, who used them as paint binders. It is supposed, in the absence of any evidence, that the Greeks were also acquainted with water paints in which egg, milk, gums and glues served as binders, but tempera in the forms we know today had its crude beginnings, with relatively intractable materials, in Byzantine painting. It developed, in 14th- and 15th-century Italy, into a refined and standardized technique that served the needs of early Renaissance painters such as Giotto, Cimabue, Duccio and the Lorenzetti brothers, and reached a culmination of technical mastery with Fra Angelico and Botticelli. The developments in art during the 15th century embraced new requirements that pure egg tempera could not satisfy, and artists began to use oil glazes and more unctuous paints in intermediate processes that led eventually to oil painting.

The modern revival of tempera began at the end of the 19th century and the beginning of the 20th century in Britain, Germany, and the United States, when many painters found it most sympathetic to their pictorial aims, especially for BLOND PAINTING. Most recipes for artificial emulsions date from that period. Although a limited supply of ready-made materials is available, most artists who specialize in tempera prefer to make their own from egg yolk or other emulsions. They study written accounts of the traditional techniques that have come down to us, especially the most complete source for Italian tempera practice, *Il Libro dell'arte* by Cennino Cennini. The knowledge and training of this 14th- and 15th-century painter stemmed directly from Giotto's studio.

The word tempera is sometimes used incorrectly. Illustrators and commercial artists are prone to use tempera in referring to gouache or other opaque aqueous colours to distinguish those colours from oils, and the better poster colours sold in jars are sometimes labelled 'tempera'. True tempera colours, however, are sold only in tubes. Translators of French books have frequently confused tempera with distemper, since the word *détrempe* is used for both. See also MIXED TECHNIQUE; OIL TEMPERA.

template a draughtsman's pattern or guide for drawing certain standard shapes and symbols. A template is essentially a flat sheet, usually made of heavy clear plastic, in which holes of the shape or shapes desired have been cut in different sizes. The draughtsman uses the template like a stencil, tracing the selected pattern onto a surface by following the inside contour of the perforated shape with a writing instrument. Commonly, all the cutouts of a single template will be of the same geometric shape in a range of sizes. Circle templates and ellipse guides are widely available and much used by draughtsmen. Also available are specialized templates of architects' and engineers' symbols and combination templates of a variety of geometric shapes in a range of sizes. A template with circular, triangular, square and hexagonal cutouts, for example, is sold in art-supply shops. Templates are also made with musical and mathematical symbols and in a variety of lettering styles and foreign alphabets.

template

Ten, the 1. a group of 20th-century American artists (1900–1920) that was Paris-influenced and painted in the Impressionist style.
2. a group of American Abstract Expressionists who exhibited together in the late 1930s. Among its members were Mark Rothko (1903–1970) and Adolph Gottlieb (1903–1974).

tenebrism the practice or technique of painting in a dark, low key; the figures in such a painting are engulfed in shadow, but the scene is frequently relieved and partially illuminated by a dramatic beam of light. The name, derived from the Italian *tenebroso*, meaning 'dark' or 'gloomy,' was coined by later critics to characterize the work of Michelangelo Marisi da Caravaggio (1573–1610) and his followers in the early 17th century. Among these painters were Georges de La Tour (1593–1652), Jusepe de Ribera (1588–1652), and Francisco Zurbarán (1598–1664). See BAROQUE.

Tenebrosi or **Caravaggisti** the name commonly given to a school of 16th-century Italian painters of whom the best-known is Michelangelo Caravaggio (1573–1610). The style of these painters is characterized by contrasting use of light and shade. See CHIAROSCURO, TENEBRISM.

tenmoku see TEMMOKU.

Tennessee Pink a fine American MARBLE, suitable for sculpture. While a pinkish colour is characteristic of Tennessee marble, black, reddish, green, and buff varieties are also available. Tennessee marbles are harder and more compact than most other American marbles, and are often chosen for outdoor use. They are more difficult to carve and polish than many other marbles.

tepesuchil see LAUREL, sense 3.

term or **terminal figure** a quadrangular pillar tapering downward, surmounted by a sculptured head or upper part of a figure. Compare HERM, where only the head or bust is fully carved.

terpentinegeist see TURPENTINE.

terpentinöl see TURPENTINE.

terra alba another name for GYPSUM. It is not the same material as the inert pigment WHITE EARTH.

terrace or **terrasse** any flaw in marble, including a STUN, that can be rectified by excavating and filling in with cement.

terracotta (*It.* baked earth) a baked or fired CLAY, usually brownish red.

It is widely used by ceramic sculptors and potters, as well as by manufacturers of roof tiles. The term *terracotta clay*, or simply *terracotta*, is often used for any clay suitable for shaping and firing, except for the finest porcelain clays.

terra merita an obsolete yellow LAKE made from SAFFRON or curcuma root. See TURMERIC.

terra orellana see ANNATTO.

terra ponderosa an archaic Latin name for BARYTES.

terra sigillata (*Lat.* stamped earth) or **Samian ware** a Mediterranean ceramic ware decorated with relief figures, first made about 300 BC. This ware evolved from BUCCHERO WARE fired in an oxidizing atmosphere. The finest terra sigillata, known as *Arretine ware*, was produced at what is now Arezzo, in Italy.

terrasse see TERRACE.

terre verte French for GREEN EARTH.

tertiary colour any hue produced by a mixture of secondary colours. In pigment mixtures, such colours tend to be very dull or blackish. They are usually chromatic variations of greys and browns. They are frequently as useful to the painter as the more brilliant colours.

tessella a small or miniature TESSERA.

tessellated done in the manner of MOSAIC; composed of tesserae. See TESSERA.

tessera a small cuboid of hard, durable material used in making a mosaic. The traditional Venetian tesserae (called *smalti tipo antico*) in use since the Middle Ages are made of opaque glass in an almost limitless variety of colours. They are cubes measuring from three-eighths to three-quarters of an inch, cut from flat slabs with chisel blows or broken off with a tile cutter. They are usually set with their fractured sides exposed, to give the mosaic surface a sparkle or luster from the reflected light. Flat-surfaced tesserae may be set at slight angles to achieve this effect.

The mosaics of Greece, Rome and other ancient civilizations were composed of larger tesserae. The earliest ones were naturally coloured pebbles, the later ones, cut marble of many colours and pottery and ceramic shards. Gold tesserae, made by annealing gold leaf between two layers of clear glass, as well as discs of mother-of-pearl, were used in Byzantine mosaics. Modern mosaicists use, in addition to the antique Venetian tesserae, bits of cut stone, pressed glass or ceramics, and a variety of pebbles.

A miniature tessera may be called a *tessella* (plural *tessellae*), and any glass tessera is sometimes called a *smalto* (plural *smalti* or *smaltos*). Another, but infrequently used, term for tessera is the Latin *abaculus* (plural *abaculi*). A TILE, used especially in pavement and floor mosaics, is thin and flat, with a greater surface area than a tessera.

test panel a panel or plate of convenient size (often 3 × 5 inches) used in testing a paint or other coating material. The coating is applied in a layer of controlled thickness, in accordance with the specifications of the test. In the United States, cold-rolled 20-gauge sheet steel, 30–31-gauge tin plate, and .020-inch clad aluminium alloy are among the standard metal plates specified by the ASTM. When appropriate, paper, board, glass or canvas may be used.

Texas limestone an oolitic LIMESTONE quarried in Williamson County, Texas, USA. It ranges in colour from light buff to cream, and has been used for sculpture.

texture the tactile quality of the surface. In a work of art, the artist determines, by choice of technique and method of using it, whether a painted or carved surface is to be rough or smooth, regular or irregular. Norms have been established over the centuries to exploit the most desirable characteristics of each technique to best advantage. For example, the unflawed smoothness of a gesso panel contributes to the successful creation of effects in tempera painting. The rough texture of watercolour paper is needed to perfect the sparkle and brilliance of transparent watercolour. The artist chooses a finely woven portrait linen or a rough, irregular weave depending on whether the paints used are smooth and thin or ruggedly impasto; sculpture may have a flawlessly smooth surface or a rough-hewn texture. In oil painting, the artist may choose from a great variety of canvas weaves the one that will best serve the artist's style and technique. In addition to purely technical considerations, the artist also takes into account the appropriateness of textures to the content of the work. Abstract and experimental painters have frequently sought new textures to complement new ideas, and to enhance and reinforce the expression of developments that they have felt were not sufficiently well served by traditional materials. Other painters, despite the unconventionality of their work, have adhered to time-tested methods.

The painter may create special textures by adding foreign material, such as sand, marble dust, or small gravel, to standard oil colours. Sometimes cement is added to the paint. Sometimes the texture is built up with a ready-made UNDERPAINTING WHITE. The admixture of clean sand should have no ill effect on the longevity of a paint, as its relatively large particles remain outside the physical system of pigment particles dispersed in linseed oil, but the use of organic matter, such as sawdust, coffee grounds, and other substances that change on ageing, negates the whole concept of permanent painting by means of permanent materials. Even sand, if more than a moderate amount is used, may be undesirable, as it may produce a dry quality not conducive to permanent adherence to the ground. So far as is known, polymer colours and modelling paste may be built up to any degree of impasto or texture without ill effects.

Thénard's blue an early name for COBALT BLUE.

thermocouple see PYROMETER.

thermoplastic capable of being softened by heat and of becoming hard again when cooled. When used as PLASTICS, synthetic resins are broadly classified as either thermoplastic or THERMOSETTING. Examples of thermoplastics are the acrylic and vinyl resins. Such resins, when heated, can be shaped by pressure into forms that are retained after cooling. Fluid coating materials, or *film-formers*, are classified as thermoplastic (solidifying by evaporation of volatile solvents) or convertible (solidifying by undergoing some internal, irreversible chemical reaction after most of the solvent has evaporated).

thermosetting capable of being hardened, or fused and hardened, by heat. Materials that have this property are called *thermosets*; once so hardened they cannot be softened by reheating. The synthetic resins, according to the way they react to heat, are classified as either thermosetting or THERMOPLASTIC. Thermosetting resins, such as the phenolic resins, are usually produced in the form of fusible powders.

thimble a small porcelain support for ceramic wares during firing. It consists of a hook or arm attached either to a tapering cup or to a sleeve that slides over a vertical rod. Several thimbles are stacked vertically so that a number of flat, glazed objects, such as plates, may be placed in the kiln in a vertical pile without touching each other.

thinner any volatile liquid used for thinning or diluting paints and varnishes. The two thinners used by artists for diluting oil paints are TURPENTINE and WHITE SPIRIT.

thioindigoid red a SYNTHETIC ORGANIC PIGMENT with relatively clean colour and excellent lightfastness properties. Slight bronzing may occur in the mass tone if exposed out-of-doors. This pigment may also exhibit some solubility in some organic solvents.

thioindigo violet thioindigo red-violet B: a brilliant, intense, violet SYNTHETIC ORGANIC PIGMENT that was adopted in the 1960s as suitable for use in artists' colours for permanent painting. It is sold under various tradenames, but the label should carry its identification. It ranks among the most lightfast of organic pigments.

thixotropy the property possessed by some viscous or gel materials of changing consistency when rubbed, stirred, shaken, or otherwise subjected to shear; the word itself is from Greek roots meaning 'change by touch'. One example of a thixotropic material is a GEL MEDIUM for painting, which becomes fluid under the stroking of a brush; another is the modern dripless house paint, which behaves in the same way. Ultramarine oil colour displays thixotropic behaviour when its consistency varies between the acceptably smooth and the sticky or stringy, according to the rubbing or grinding it receives during preparation.

threading tool see MULTIPLE TINT TOOL.

three-point perspective see OBLIQUE PERSPECTIVE.

throw to shape on the POTTER'S WHEEL.

thumbnail sketch a rough sketch of very small proportions.

thumbtack see DRAWING PIN.

ties see STENCILLING.

tigerwood or **African walnut** a golden-brown African hardwood obtained from the tree *Lavoa klaineana*, which has a variable bold-figured grain. It has a glossy surface even without polishing. Tigerwood is used for furniture, veneer, gunstocks and inlaying.

tile 1. *(ceramics)* a thin, flat piece of earthenware or terracotta, usually square and frequently decorated with a ceramic glaze in either flat colour or a multicolour design. The tile is essentially a unit intended for covering walls, floors, etc., but the hand-decorated tile made by an individual potter is a ceramic speciality.

2. see SLANT.

Timonox a tradename for ANTIMONY WHITE, first introduced in Britain in 1920.

tinctorial power see COLOURING POWER.

tincture in art, an archaic term for a faint but effective strain of colour. See TINGE, sense 2.

tinge 1. a staining or permeation by a colour.

2. a small degree of modification of a colour. Two light blues may be close to the same SHADE except that one has a violet tinge. See also CAST.

tins *(sculpture)* the thin pieces of sheet metal used as mould dividers. See SHIM.

tint 1. a colour or hue modified by adding a relatively small amount of another colour. White paint is tinted pink by adding a small amount of red oil colour. Light blue paint may be made into lavender by tinting it with red, and different amounts of red will produce various tints.

2. *(graphic arts)* an area of uniform shade, considerably paler than a solid impression, produced by engraving the surface uniformly with dots, lines, or other repeated marks.

tint block *(printmaking)* a block or plate that has a uniform, overall engraved pattern of close hatching or dots so that it will print in a lighter tone than would a solid block or plate. See also TINT, sense 2; TINT TOOL.

tinting strength see COLOURING POWER.

tint tool a fine-pointed GRAVER, used in creating a so-called tint of very fine HATCHING or crosshatching in line ENGRAVING and WOOD ENGRAVING. Tint tools are available in six different point widths and are the principal gravers used in wood engraving. The three smallest sizes have rounded sides and are known in wood engraving as SPITSTICKS.

tinware, painted see PAINTED TINWARE.

tin white stannic oxide, used to produce an opaque white in ceramics. It is not a paint pigment.

tip, gilder's see GILDER'S TIP.

titanium green a dark green pigment, analogous to Prussian blue, that can be made by using titanium, or iron and titanium compounds, instead of the straight iron salts used for making Prussian blue. Titanium green is not in use, and was probably never made commercially.

titanium pigment the type of TITANIUM WHITE made with barium sulphate or some other inert component, as distinguished from pure titanium dioxide.

titanium white titanium dioxide; a dense, opaque, white pigment, highly inert chemically and therefore of the greatest permanence in all artists' paints. With the advent of economical hydroelectric power, large-scale production of titanium white became feasible, and it was introduced to artists about 1920. Some titanium whites are pure titanium dioxide; others (such as the type called *titanium pigment*) are coprecipitated with inert compounds such as barium sulphate, by a method similar to that used for making the cadmium-barium pigments. Although both types are acceptable for artists' use, the pure oxide has far greater COLOURING POWER, which is sometimes desirable, but frequently troublesome in mixtures. At one time, titanium whites were subject to yellowing in oil. Since titanium white is so inert, it does not combine intimately with oil (as flake white and zinc white do), and may settle out a bit in the wet paint layer, leaving a microscopic surface layer of oil or underpigmented oil, which would be prone to yellowing. Manufacturers claim that modern titaniums do not have this defect. In aqueous paints, titanium white has no faults. House-paint industry research has determined that a mixture of titanium and zinc (40 to 60% of either) dries to a paint film with better all-around qualities than either one alone; hence, this mixture is used as a PRIMER by many manufacturers of artists' canvases. This mixed white in oil, or COMPOSITE WHITE, is also sold in tubes under various tradenames.

tobacco-seed oil (TSO) a valuable drying oil, less susceptible to yellowing than linseed oil. Since the tobacco grown for the tobacco industry is harvested before it goes to seed, tobacco-seed oil (TSO) is obtained from wild plants in India. Work has been done in Britain on its development and application to coating-material purposes, especially as a non-yellowing constituent of alkyd resins and other products. There is little published information as to its applicability to artists' paints.

tole or **toleware** see PAINTED TINWARE.

toluidine red a brilliant, fiery red-yellow SYNTHETIC ORGANIC PIGMENT. It is used in industrial paints and printing inks but not in artists' colours for permanent painting.

toluol see COAL-TAR SOLVENT.

tonalism *(US)* a style of painting in which the artist strives to capture the effects of sunlight on the subject of the painting. Such American artists as the landscape painters George Inness (1825–1894) and Henry Ranger (1858–1916), both of whom influenced by the BARBIZON SCHOOL, were exponents of tonalism.

tondo or **rondo** a round or circular painting.

tone the quality of a colour. The term is used broadly in reference to a quality of CHROMA (for example, reddish tone, prevailing yellow tone), VALUE (for example, light tone, dark tone), SATURATION (for example, deep tone, pale tone), or brightness (for example, bright tone, dull tone). Tonal masses are colour areas, as distinguished from the linear elements of a painting. See also UNDERTONE; MASS TONE.

toned ground see VEIL.

toner 1. the most concentrated form of a SYNTHETIC ORGANIC PIGMENT, precipitated with little or no BASE.
2. a naturally insoluble compound that can be used as a pigment directly.

tongue lac see LAC.

toning or **toning down** *(oil painting)* the altering of the pervading colour of a surface by an all-over GLAZE or SCUMBLE.

tooth *(painting)* microscopic roughness or granularity in a ground. It is a desirable quality because it facilitates brush manipulation and increases the permanence of the paint's adhesion to the ground.

topia the Roman term for a large painting of a landscape or formal garden.

topographic landscape a landscape in which the terrain and features of a specific scene are accurately depicted.

top tone see MASS TONE.

torchon board a cardboard with a facing of TORCHON PAPER.

torchon paper a coarse-grained paper used for watercolour and gouache painting.

toreutics the art or technique of working in relief or intaglio, especially on metal. It includes embossing, chasing, engraving and fine carving.

tormented colour *(oil painting)* colour that has been manipulated excessively. Such treatment has no significance in some kinds of work, but in many styles of painting, overworking of the paint detracts from such important qualities as freshness, spontaneity, brilliance and general effectiveness.

torso a sculptured form representing the trunk of a nude male or nude female figure without head or limbs. The creation of the sculpted torso has progressed from the time of the RENAISSANCE, when sculptors reconstructed antique torsos and then proceeded to attach missing limbs to them, to more current times, when sculptors such as Rodin and Maillot have viewed the torso as beautiful in itself.

tortillon a small stump of tightly rolled grey or white paper, usually pointed at one end only, used to blend charcoal and pastel. Tortillons come in varying sizes; the most commonly used one is about two-and-a-half inches long and one-eighth of an inch in diameter. See illustration at STUMP.

totem another name for Mars red, one of the MARS PIGMENTS.

touch 1. any stamp or mark on an object that identifies its maker; especially, a maker's or assayer's mark, or both, stamped on PEWTER. Most frequently, a pewter touch was merely the maker's name, initials, or cachet; sometimes a town mark was used instead. The touch on a piece of British pewter has, in addition to the maker's name or initials, a symbol identifying the sovereign in whose reign the piece was executed and, on a vessel, a number indicating the capacity of the piece. In early American pewter, the letters or design of the touch were in relief against a depressed background that was stamped into the metal. After 1825, the mark itself was stamped into the surface. Although it was required in England that every article of pewter be so marked, it was not obligatory in America and elsewhere in Europe, and much pewter is therefore unmarked. See also HALLMARK.
2. a single application of paint to a painting surface. For example, a brushstroke is a touch, as is one mark made with a pastel crayon or a palette knife. Colour may be built up in a series of touches. In the expression 'the finishing touch' the word is used in a loosely figurative sense.

tracery 1. curved or foliated stonework in windows and arched openings, common in Gothic architecture.

2. any ornamental work in interlaced foliation or curving lines that is patterned after tracery. See illustration at FOIL.

tracing, caulking, cocking or **cogging 1.** a drawing copied from an original with a pencil or other pointed implement, using the original as a guide. A picture or a design is most easily traced on a piece of thin TRACING PAPER held over it, but heavier paper may also be used if it is placed over the original on a TRACING BOX. A drawing can also be transferred directly to another surface by rubbing the back of the original with charcoal or a dry pigment, placing the coated side down on the surface to receive the drawing, and lightly going over the lines to be traced with a pencil or stylus, thus transferring the charcoal or pigment to the new surface. Rather than coating the back of the original, the artist may instead sandwich a piece of carbon paper or GRAPHITE PAPER between it and the receiving surface. In either case, however, the pressure of the pointed implement may somewhat mar the original, and if the artist does not want to risk this, a thin sheet of transparent acetate should be placed over the original, or tracing paper should be used. Such reproducing-enlarging-reducing devices as the CAMERA LUCIDA, the CAMERA OBSCURA, and the PANTOGRAPH employ tracing techniques.

2. a drawing of the outline of a three-dimensional object made by moving a pencil along its contours so that the pencil point marks the surface against which the object is placed. In this sense, drawing with templates might be considered a form of tracing.

tracing box an apparatus that makes it possible to trace a drawing through paper that is heavier and more nearly opaque than ordinary tracing paper. It works on the same principle as placing paper over the drawing to be traced and holding the two against a windowpane. The light coming through the glass causes the lines of the drawing to appear more clearly through the top sheet of paper. The box is low and either slanted or flat, with a frosted-glass top under which a mirror is positioned to throw the light from an artificial source through the glass. The apparatus enables the artist to trace on a flat, level surface.

tracing cloth or **tracing linen** a thin, heavily sized muslin that is semi-transparent and may be used in place of tracing paper for tracing finished ink drawings, such as architects' plans and the work of technical illustrators, engineers, and draughtsmen. The sizing, which is a starch solution, gives the cloth stiffness and an even, consistent surface that readily accepts ink. Such cloth will resist a considerable amount of handling without damage, and tracings made on it can be blueprinted. Sold in rolls, tracing cloth may be blue or white and is glossy on one side, dull on the other. Although it is made of cotton, it is customarily called 'tracing linen'. Nowadays, sheets of Mylar or other synthetic materials are sometimes used instead.

tracing paper a thin, transparent or semitransparent paper used for tracing. It is sufficiently opaque for pencil drawing and transparent enough to enable one to follow the lines of the original. Tracing papers in many degrees of transparency are usually sold by the roll, but pads are also available. It is useful in developing, refining or improving a drawing or sketch. In drafting, prints may be made from a drawing on tracing paper. It is also used in transfer lithography. Acetate and other plastic sheets, slightly mat on one side, are sold under various tradenames for use when a high degree of transparency is needed.

tracing wheel see PERFORATING WHEEL.

traction fissure a type of crack in the paint film or varnish of old oil paintings. It appears when the film cracks and the edges of the crack recede to form wide gaps with ragged edges, through which the underlying paint layer or ground can be seen. It is sometimes erroneously called *creeping* or *crawling*, terms that refer to *cissing*, a defect of water paints.

tragacanth, gum see GUM TRAGACANTH.

trail, traile, trayle or **vignette** in Gothic decoration, a running design of grapes, leaves, and tendrils carved on wood or stone.

trail

trailing see SLIP DECORATION.

transfer *(conservation of paintings)* to separate the paint film and its ground from an unsound support and remount the picture on a new support. An extraordinarily tedious process, transferring has been practised since the 18th century and has been executed successfully on paintings supported by linen, canvas, wood and even plaster walls. Oil paintings on decomposed canvas are most commonly reconditioned by LINING, but occasionally a severe defect in the support makes transfer necessary. Fresco paintings are transferred by either the STACCO or STRAPPO techniques.

transfer lithography LITHOGRAPHY in which the drawing is not made directly on the stone or plate but is done on paper, after which it is transferred by a rather simple process to the stone or plate by a professional lithographer-printer or, less frequently, by the artist. After the stone is prepared for printing in the usual way, the proofs are pulled. Any paper with a grain that takes litho crayon well can be used as the transfer paper. Ordinary tracing paper and charcoal paper are popular. Industrial transfer paper is made for special factory purposes and is not well liked by artists. Transfer lithography is a boon to those who desire the advantage of spontaneous drawing and the convenience of using a portable medium. The artist is also saved the trouble of working on the stone in reverse, since the positive drawing is automatically reversed when transferred from the paper to the stone. Transfer lithography is also used by artists who through choice or inexperience have not mastered the technical processes of preparing and printing the stone but nevertheless want to exploit lithographic effects. Transfer lithography is more suitable for linear work and sketchy techniques than for creation of subtle gradations and a full range of tones. The quality of the printed areas is far below that produced by direct work on stone, and some manipulations, such as scraping the crayon drawing with blades and lithographic points, must be foregone. The proofs pulled by transfer lithography are entirely acceptable as ORIGINAL PRINTS, since the impressions are taken indirectly from the artist's actual crayon strokes. Tusche is sometimes used with a pen or brush in transfer lithography, but its manipulation on paper is tricky, and great care is required to use it well. Transfer lithography, which was employed by Toulouse-Lautrec and Daumier, has been in use since 1887.

transfer paper a paper coated with a substance that may be imprinted on a surface by the application of pressure, moisture or heat and pressure. Carbon paper and GRAPHITE PAPER are examples of transfer paper used by applying pressure, that is, drawing on the uncoated or reverse side with a firm pencil or stylus. Artists usually prefer graphite paper, whose marks are erasable, to the greasier carbon paper. They may make improvised transfer paper by rubbing tracing paper or another thin sheet with a soft pencil or chalk or by dusting it with pigment, depending on the nature of the surface to be imprinted. Transfer paper that works by moisture includes decalcomania paper, whose slip film may be applied to china, glass or marble. Heat and pressure are applied to a transfer paper coated with gold leaf or a bronze or pigment powder in hot die stamping of paper, cloth, plastics, leather and other materials. The paper backing of transfer paper is often GLASSINE PAPER. The special paper for transfer lithography is also called transfer paper.

transferred gold see GOLD LEAF.

Transite *(US)* a tradename for a thin ASBESTOS BOARD, sometimes used as a support for painting.

transitional pertaining to a style or a set of techniques characteristic of a period when the prevailing styles and methods are gradually giving way to and developing into something new. The term would apply, for example, to the methods that were used while egg-tempera was beginning to be modified with oily materials, eventually to be superseded by oil painting. In general, a transitional style can best be conceived of as the earlier of two consecutive styles, with its character significantly altered by elements of the succeeding style.

translucent or **semitransparent** *(of a pigment)* capable of transmitting light without affording clear visibility. A semitransparent paint transmits much light, but is not clear; a semitransparent glaze, when placed over another colour, will produce a pale or cloudy effect because of the reflection of light from the surface. See OPAQUE; compare TRANSPARENT.

transmitted light 1. light that passes through a substance.

2. the effect perceived when a transparent or translucent object is held up to a light source. See also REFLECTED LIGHT.

transparent capable of transmitting light freely; clear and glasslike without any opacity or cloudiness. When a transparent glaze of oil colour, for example, is placed over another colour, it produces a clean mixture of the two hues without much loss of clarity. Compare OPAQUE; TRANSLUCENT.

transparent base a medium or colour extender used in SILKSCREEN and SERIGRAPHY to reduce the normally opaque artists' colours and PROCESS OIL COLOURS to any desired degree of transparency, and to enhance their workability under the squeegee. Two kinds of transparent base are available. The superior, more permanent variety has the consistency and transparent appearance of petroleum jelly; it is made by combining aluminium stearate with a solution of nonyellowing alkyd or acrylic resin and mineral spirits. It can be added to colours in fairly large amounts without altering colour effects. A less expensive variety, which looks and feels rather like putty, does impair the brilliance of the colours to which it is added and is used chiefly as an extender in large-scale commercial silkscreening. Transparent base makes possible many interesting effects. A transparent colour printed over another colour will reveal the undercolour, creating new colour effects not otherwise possible with many pigments because of their opacity.

transparent brown, burnt green earth or **Verona brown** a fine, clear, deep, transparent brown pigment made by calcining GREEN EARTH. It is permanent for all painting techniques and especially useful for glazing.

transparent copper green a green resinate, made by fusing rosin with a copper compound. It was identified by A.P. Laurie (*The Pigments and Mediums of the Old Masters*, London, 1914) in several illuminated manuscripts from the 8th to the 15th centuries, where it was used as a transparent green colour. There is no other documentation of its use in mediaeval times.

transparent gold ochre 1. a rather rare native YELLOW OCHRE with a dull mass tone and a bright, transparent undertone.
2. a tube colour made by mixing alumina hydrate with regular opaque ochre.

A permanent and useful pigment, transparent gold ochre is not the same as the traditional industrial pigment golden ochre, which is unsuitable for permanent painting.

transparentizer 1. an ingredient added to a paint either during or after its manufacture to render it transparent. Examples are GEL MEDIUM and ALUMINA HYDRATE.
2. a commercially prepared liquid that, when applied to ink drawings on heavy drawing paper, will render the paper sufficiently transparent for use in making blueprints. Transparentizer is also used to revive old or soiled tracings and drawings for the same purpose.

travertine a form of limestone composed of calcium carbonate that is found near hot springs in Italy and is most often used for building purposes and outdoor sculpture.

trayle see TRAIL.

trecento the 14th century. The term is commonly used to designate Italian art of that period.

trefled cross a cross with three lobes (called *buttons*) at the end of each arm. This form suggests the trefoil, long a symbol of the Trinity. It is also known as the *cross of Saint Lazarus*, the *cross fleuronée* or the *cross botonée*. See CROSS for illustration.

trefoil see FOIL.

trial proof a proof of STATE, pulled from an intaglio plate while the plate is still being etched or engraved or while its inking routine is still being perfected.

triangle a drafting implement of flat plastic, wood, or other material, made in a great number of triangular shapes and sizes as guides for drawing lines at various angles. Two right-angled triangles, one with two 45° angles and one with an angle of 30° and an angle of 60°, are the most basic shapes. When these two triangles are used in combination with each other and with a T SQUARE, which serves as a base against which they are placed, angles of 15° and 75° can be drawn as well. Pairs of triangles are also used to rule parallel lines by sliding one triangle's edge along an edge of the other. An ADJUSTABLE TRIANGLE obviates the need for many differently shaped triangles.

trichlorethylene a nonflammable solvent that boils at a very high temperature (147 °C) and is used as a cleaner in industry. It has been suggested as a solvent for copal resin, but cannot be recommended as its fumes are injurious to health.

trickling a literal translation of the German term for CISSING; it is incorrect in technical usage.

trimetric projection a projection used in mechanical drawing in which all three axes have different degrees of foreshortening in relation to their lengths, causing all three dimensions to be drawn to a different scale. All three angles made where the axes meet will be different. See illustration at PROJECTION.

Trinidad asphalt a soft natural pitch from Trinidad. It is a constituent of some asphalt compounds, such as those used in paving. It can also be used as an ingredient in ETCHING GROUNDS and acid-proof resists.

triptych a set of three paintings or bas reliefs related in subject matter, connected side by side, and usually designed as a movable ALTARPIECE; especially, a work on three panels, hinged so that two half-sized flanking panels (called *wings* or *volets*) may close over the central panel. Counterparts of the triptych are the DIPTYCH, a two-panel work that may be closed like a book, and the POLYPTYCH, a work of more than three (usually five) parts. Typically, the principal subject is depicted on the central panel, related subjects on one or both sides of the wings. In addition, the entire work or its principal section is often set on a base or platform called the PREDELLA, which may also be painted or carved. Altarpieces in these forms were executed in painting, enamel, wood, ivory and metal for both Byzantine and Western churches throughout the mediaeval and Renaissance periods. Often their frames were elaborately carved, gilded or polychromed. Among the many important works in triptych form are Andrea Mantegna's *San Zeno Altarpiece* (1459) and Giovanni Bellini's *Frari Madonna* (1488). A modern triptych is Max Beckmann's *Departure* (1937).

tristimulus values *(colour measurement)* the chromatic components of a coloured surface expressed in terms of three spectrum colour stimuli, for example, red, green and blue. The CHROMATICITY of a colour, when measured with a COLOURIMETER or a SPECTROPHOTOMETER, may be recorded by means of a diagram showing the ratios of its tristimulus values expressed as chromaticity coordinates X, Y and Z.

trompe l'œil (*Fr.* deception of the eye) painting so realistic that it may fool the viewer into thinking that the objects or scene represented are real rather than painted. Trompe l'œil is used in ILLUSIONISM, and is characteristic of the 20th-century movement known as MAGIC REALISM. It is often an element in SURREALISM, as witness some of the meticulously depicted details in painting by Salvador Dali, for example.

One of the more familiar forms of trompe l'œil is the painted simulation (especially in Baroque buildings) of interior architectural elements such as pilasters, engaged columns, mouldings and even cupolas, executed in extremely realistic perspective. Large murals, such as Raphael's *The School of Athens* and the *Disputà* in the Vatican (1509–1511), have also been framed in painted-on architectural settings. Any convincingly real painting on a ceiling or high on a wall that is done in SOTTO IN SÙ perspective is also a kind of trompe l'œil. Michelangelo's classical nudes and figures of the prophets and sibyls on the ceiling of the Sistine Chapel (begun 1508) are good examples of trompe l'œil achieved through a mastery of perspective.

trophy the art term for the painted or carved representation of objects associated with or symbolic of victory or achievement. Trophies are often found in HISTORY PAINTING.

trucage *(Fr.)* fakery. A forger of works of art is a *truqueur*.

true blue see ULTRAMARINE BLUE.

trullisatio see SCRATCH COAT.

TSO see TOBACCO-SEED OIL.

T square or **tee square** a long flat ruler of wood or plastic, at one end of which is a crosspiece at a right angle, making the T-shape that gives the implement its name. The crosspiece is held against an edge of the drawing board to position the ruler for the drawing of true horizontal or vertical lines or to place it as a base for triangles with which angles are drawn. The T square is one of the draughtsman's basic tools.

tube a collapsible metal container for artists' colours in paste form. Tubes have been in use since the 1840s, and are highly effective in preserving colours, protecting them from oxidation, preventing the formation of skins, and delaying evaporation, as other types of container cannot do once they have been opened. Tubes are best when made of pure tin, and prior to the Second World War this metal was always used for containers of high-quality colours. Since then, however, tin has been in short supply, and most governments prohibit its use for this purpose. Lead, aluminium, alloy, and coated tubes are now in use, although all are inferior to tin on several technical grounds. Polyethylene tubes and squeeze bottles have not proved very successful. Well-prepared oil colours keep indefinitely in tubes, but aqueous paints and paints containing volatile solvents will eventually become hard or dry out completely, especially after the tubes have been opened. The standard or studio-size tube for artists' oil colours measures 1 × 4 inches, and should contain not less than 37 cc of paint; the so-called pound tube in which whites are packed measures $1\frac{1}{2}$ × 6 inches and should contain 150 cc of paint. The collapsible tin tube first appeared in dealers' catalogues about 1840 and soon supplanted the BLADDER, in which oil colours had previously been packaged. Its introduction is historically important, for it relieved the painter of the task of grinding fresh colours for each painting, and it made possible both the portable paint box and outdoor, or *plein air*, painting. The Barbizon school of landscape painters was active at that time.

tufa or **calcareous tufa** a porous, microcrystalline LIMESTONE, composed almost entirely of calcium carbonate. The ancients occasionally used it for sculpture.

tula NIELLO work done during the 18th and 19th centuries, named after the region in central Russia where it was produced.

tung oil a semidrying oil expressed from the nuts of *Aleurites fordii*, a tree indigenous to China, and formerly imported under the name *China wood oil*; since the 1920s it has been extensively cultivated in Florida. Tung oil is an important industrial material in the manufacture of hard-wearing varnishes and enamels. The thermal treatment with resins and driers necessary for its employment as a paint oil disqualifies it for use in artists' materials, especially with regard to colour retention. It differs from all other drying and semidrying oils (except oiticica oil) in that its fatty acids are oleic and elaeomargaric instead of linolenic and linolic.

turbith see TURPETH MINERAL.

Turkey brown see CYPRUS UMBER.

Turkey red or **Adrianople red** a hue designation for a deep, rich red, almost a maroon; it is not well standardized as a pigment name. Better grades are made with alizarin crimson, less permanent ones are other organic lakes. Turkey red was more widely used in the recent past as the name of a textile colour than as the name of a pigment. The term is less frequently used today.

Turkey umber see CYPRUS UMBER.

turmeric or **curcuma** a yellow NATURAL DYESTUFF prepared from the roots of certain Asiatic plants, especially *Curcuma longa*. It was formerly used to make coloured varnishes and lake pigments, but has been supplanted by modern dyes. It is now used only as a condiment.

Turnbull's blue a complex ferric ferricyanide; an azure-blue compound produced as an intermediate stage in one process in the manufacture of PRUSSIAN BLUE. Turnbull's blue is not used as a pigment.

Turner's yellow, Kassler yellow, mineral yellow, Montpellier yel-

low, Verona yellow, patent yellow or **Cassel yellow** lead oxychloride, an obsolete pigment produced in a variety of shades from bright yellow to orange. Patented in England by James Turner, it was widely used in the early 19th century. Turner's yellow has long been discarded, since it is impermanent and frequently turns black.

turning tool any of several similar tools with which clay or plaster is shaped on a revolving potter's wheel. Typically, a turning tool has a shaped wooden handle and a steel shank to which is attached, at a right angle, a flat steel plate. The three most common turning tools have plates shaped like a teardrop, a triangle and a parabola with a flat side.

turning tools

turnsole a violet NATURAL DYESTUFF obtained from the seeds of the European turnsole plant (*Chrozophora tinctoria*). It was used in pigment form by mediaeval and Renaissance artists, especially in illuminated manuscripts. Turnsole behaves like litmus and orchil – it is normally red, but turns blue or violet upon treatment with alkali. It was used to alter the colour of azurite.

turntable see MODELLING STAND.

turpentine or **spirits of turpentine** a colourless VOLATILE SOLVENT used by artists as a thinner in oil painting. It has an agreeable odour and a rate of evaporation that is highly suitable for the majority of painting manipulations. It is not dangerously flammable or injurious to health in normal use, although some individuals may be allergic to it and suffer skin irritation. In industrial paints it has been almost entirely replaced by WHITE SPIRIT, and many artists also prefer this petroleum substitute. The best grade of turpentine is sold under the name *pure gum spirits of turpentine*, which distinguishes it from a less desirable kind called WOOD TURPENTINE. Turpentine is produced by distilling the heavy, viscous oleoresin or BALSAM obtained by tapping pine trees. Originally, all heavy oleoresins from conifer trees were called turpentines, and this terminology still survives in a few cases, for example, Venice turpentine and Strasbourg turpentine. The distillate was called *oil of turpentine* (French: *huile de térébenthine*, German: *Terpentinöl*. Nowadays the term *Terpentingeist* – spirit of turpentine – is used).

The ancient Greeks and Romans found they could obtain a volatile liquid by boiling pine pitch with a sheepskin covering the kettle, fleece side down, then wringing the condensed liquid out of the fleece. But turpentine, alcohol, or any of the other volatile solvents were not available to artists until the general practice of distillation began about the year 1400.

turpeth mineral, turbith, mineral turbith or **mercury yellow** basic mercuric sulphate, a highly poisonous, bright-yellow pigment. Turpeth mineral was valued at one time for the fine semipermanent greens made by mixing it with Prussian blue, but has been discarded because it decomposed and turned black in some mixtures.

turquoise blue a hue designation for a light, greenish blue; it is not a specific pigment name.

turquoise green a scarce, clear bluish-green permanent pigment of medium saturation; a FURNACE PRODUCT made by roasting aluminium, chromium, and cobalt oxides. Sometimes used in ceramics, turquoise green is not ordinarily available as a paint pigment because the same hue can easily be made by mixing other greens. Common products sold under this name are synthetic organic lakes of little permanence.

Tuscan red a rich, maroon LAKE pigment made for industrial use by precipitating a dyestuff on an Indian red base. Tuscan red is permanent only when specifically stated to contain alizarin; otherwise, it may contain any impermanent red dye.

tusche a water-miscible black fluid that contains the greasy ingredients of LITHOGRAPHIC CRAYON, used in LITHOGRAPHY for drawing the design on the stone or plate with a brush or pen. Tusche is used to create effects that are less readily accomplished with crayon. Lines and areas applied with a brush or pen tend to print solid black and lack the grainy crayon effect. Tusche is also used in the TUSCHE-WASHOUT METHOD of preparing a SILKSCREEN stencil, the principal way in which screens are prepared in SERIGRAPHY. Tusche should never be called *ink*; the latter term is reserved for the printing ink with which the proofs are made (see LITHOGRAPH INK).

tusche-washout method a SILKSCREEN and SERIGRAPHY technique in which areas to be printed are painted directly on the screen with TUSCHE, and the nonprinting areas are stopped out with a layer of water-soluble glue, spread over the entire screen with a SQUEEGEE. The glue covers, but does not adhere to, the tusche, which is greasy. In the next step, the screen is washed with white spirit; this dissolves the tusche (carrying it away, with its loose covering of glue), but it does not affect the nonprinting areas stopped out with glue. Thus, only the design areas are left open and pervious to the paint that is to be driven through the mesh with a squeegee. As with the glue-cutout method, a tusche-washout stencil cannot be printed with water paints, because these would dissolve the glue. The printing areas may also be created partially or entirely with a LITHOGRAPHIC CRAYON, but crayon work is rather difficult to control on silk.

The tusche-washout method, the most popular among serigraphers of all the methods for making silkscreen stencils, affords great variety in technique and effect. It is a direct, spontaneous process that can reproduce free, loose painting; every brush stroke of tusche, every sketchy stroke of the litho crayon, will be recreated in paint in the prints. Textured surfaces may be reproduced on the silk by laying the screen on a rough surface such as Ross board, canvas or sandpaper, and drawing on it with a litho crayon. Tusche may be manipulated with a toothbrush, a comb, or any number of different tools; it can be stippled or spattered on, and if the screen is first sized with diluted starch paste, it can be applied with a thin brush or a pen, to create fine lines and crosshatching.

twill canvas canvas that has a diagonal weave rather than a square one. Twill weaves were popular in North America during the 18th and 19th centuries and were used by many early American portrait painters.

twist direction the direction in which strands of linen or any other textile fibre are twisted when spun. In an S-twist, the strands follow the curve of the letter S; in a Z-twist, they conform to the direction of the curve in the letter Z. The S-twist is also known as a lefthand or crossband twist, the Z-twist is known as a righthand or openband twist. In the preparation of artists' canvas, if a piece of tightly stretched linen of the S-twist type is wetted with water or size, it will lose tautness, and on drying it will sag and need to be retightened before the ground may be applied. With the Z-twist type, the linen remains taut or becomes even tighter on drying. Much of the linen available to artists is S-twist.

two-point perspective see ANGULAR PERSPECTIVE.

tympan see LITHOPRESS.

type-high *(printing block or plate)* having a thickness of .9186-inch thick, the height of type used in commercial letterpress printing. Printmaking blocks of this thickness can be printed in a standard flatbed printing press. Linocut and woodcut blocks are usually made type-high.

typography the art of printing with movable type, especially with regard to design and skill in *composition*, as the typesetting process is called. An important aspect of design is the selection of the typeface – the font, size and spacing to be used – as well as the particular alphabet or alphabets, that is, ROMAN, ITALIC, boldface, small capitals, etc. Design is concerned not only with the configuration of the individual letters, but also with such considerations as the proportions of height and width of the text to be set, the relationship of margins to the text and to each other, and the division of the page into one or more columns. Closely related to these aspects of type design are the use of illustration in a text, its placement, etc. The elaborate initial letters that sometimes begin a body of text are a good example of integrated text illustration.

Type is divided roughly into two categories according to its use: *text faces*, which are used for the main body of a manuscript; and *display faces*, which are used extensively in the commercial arts for headlines, advertising slogans, and the like, and in books for the title pages and chapter headings. As a rule, display faces are bolder than text faces and more stylized, sometimes derived from or patterned after some calligraphic hand. To serve its purpose of attracting attention, display type is usually set in large sizes and is leaded, or spaced, so that there is more

Garamond: old-style roman **Futura: gothic**

Bodoni: modern roman *Futura: italic gothic*

Bodoni: italic roman **Old English: black letter**

typography Serif and sans-serif faces.

room between lines of type. It is often letterspaced as well, so that the space between the individual characters is widened.

Most typefaces fall into one of two main categories: SERIF or roman type, and sans-serif or GOTHIC type. Both serif and sans-serif fonts have a slanting italic alphabet as well as an upright roman one. A third group of typefaces is known as black-letter type; although it might better be designated as authentic gothic, since the elaborate fonts of the black-letter variety are directly derived from the Gothic calligraphic hand. Black-letter faces do not have an italic alphabet.

The technique of printing with movable type was invented in the 15th century by Johann Gutenberg and almost entirely superseded copying by hand (see CALLIGRAPHY) and printing by wood engraving (see BLOCK BOOK), the common methods of duplicating a manuscript prior to that time. Probably the most notable improvement in typography since the invention of movable type has been the invention of machines to set type. The monotype and linotype machines, perfected at the beginning of the 20th century, and the more recently developed computer typesetters are both faster and more economical than setting type by hand. For this reason the standard smaller sizes of type are set today almost entirely by machine.

Tyrian purple, Grecian purple, murex purple, purple of the ancients or **whelk red** the celebrated purple dye of the Roman period and later. It is a natural dyestuff made from several varieties of murex shellfish, principally *Murex brandaris*. Tyrian purple was used in ancient Rome to dye emperors' togas, and came in many shades, the most desirable of which varied from reddish or pinkish to bluish (known as Byzantium purple) or violet, depending on the fashion of the times. In 1908 the colouring matter of Tyrian purple was discovered to be identical to that of a synthetic dye invented in 1904; both have been superseded by more satisfactory dyes. The Romans called Tyrian purple *ostrum*, and the lake pigment made from it *purpurissum*.

Tyrolean green earth one of the best commercial grades of GREEN EARTH.

Tyrrhenian Etruscan. The term was used in Classical times for the Etruscans or the unknown people from whom their civilization developed. It is still the name of the sea that borders the western coast of ancient Etruria.

U

U-gouge see GOUGE.

uintaite see GILSONITE.

ultraism a term that lumps together all the radical concepts of 20th-century art movements, as opposed to the traditional or academic principles preceding them. The word is usually used pejoratively by traditionalists rather than as a meaningful classification.

ultramarine ash or **bleu cendres** a by-product of the refining of natural ULTRAMARINE BLUE consisting of a remnant of lapis lazuli mixed with the greyish rock with which it is associated; it is a weak, neutral greyish-blue pigment, in limited use as a permanent watercolour pigment. Old names for ultramarine ash are *mineral grey*, *sanders blue* (or *saunders blue*), and *vein stone*.

ultramarine blue, artificial ultramarine, French blue, French ultramarine, Gmelin's blue or **Royal blue** a brilliant blue pigment, whose mass tone is a bright middle blue (sometimes called *true blue*) that is neither notably greenish nor purplish, but whose undertone is the most purplish, or least greenish, of all the permanent blues. Ultramarine blue is a FURNACE PRODUCT; it is permanent for all easel-painting techniques but is not used in FRESCO, since it is susceptible to acid impurities in the atmosphere when not protected by a film or binder.

The original ultramarine was made from the semiprecious stone lapis lazuli. Processes for making the pigment in the West date from the 12th century, but it was being made six centuries earlier in Eastern countries. Its name is from the Italian *azzurro oltremarino* ('blue from beyond the sea'), so called because lapis came from Afghanistan and other parts of the Orient. It was manufactured by a complex and arduous flotation process that separated the lapis from the grey gangue rock with which it is associated in nature. Genuine ultramarine was the costliest of all painting materials, worth more than twice its weight in gold. Princes handed it out to their painters, who are said to have continually washed their brushes in water in order to recover a pinch of the precious pigment for themselves. Inferior blues were used for ordinary paintings.

Several accidental observations led to the discovery of artificial ultramarine blue. The first of these was recorded in 1787 by Goethe, who reported from Sicily that a blue crust formed in lime kilns was used locally as a pigment. During the last years of the 18th century and the first two decades of the 19th, bright blue crusts resembling ultramarine were observed in furnaces where the Leblanc process for making soda (introduced in 1791) was being carried out. Making these observations a starting point in an earnest search for a way to synthesize ultramarine, chemists and colourmakers in France and Germany were at first misled by the prevalent conception that its colouring principle was iron. In 1806 Desormes and Clement established the composition of native ultramarine to be sulphur, sodium, silica and alumina. In 1814, N.L. Vauquelin published a very similar analysis of blue material supplied by M. Tessaert from a disused soda furnace at St Gobain.

All colourmakers were then convinced that a process for making artificial ultramarine was imminent; and in November 1824 the *Société d'Encouragement pour l'Industrie Nationale* posted a prize of 6,000 francs for the first practical method of producing it at a cost of under 300 francs per kilogram. In December 1828, the prize was awarded to J.B. Guimet, who had made ultramarine in 1826 but had withheld its introduction pending the perfection of details and the results of trials by artists in Paris to whom he had supplied the new blue. Among these painters were J.A.D. Ingres (1780–1867), who had used the pigment in a ceiling painting (*The Apotheosis of Homer*), and Horace Vernet (1789–1863), who had used it throughout the large *Battle of Fontenoy*. The Guimet process remained unpublished for decades after the award. Immediately afterwards, however, and entirely independently, Christian Gmelin of Tübingen, in Germany, published a process, which was closely followed by others. By the 1830s, factories were established throughout Europe and North America, and ultramarine came to be the common blue of industry and the arts. Curiously, two other blue pigments, Prussian blue and phthalocyanine blue, were discovered through similar accidental observations.

NEW BLUE is an unstandardized name applied to special shades of ultramarine. *Armenian blue* and *lazuline blue* are old names for genuine lapis ultramarine. See also ULTRAMARINE GREEN; ULTRAMARINE VIOLET.

ultramarine green a pale green similar in composition and manufacture to ULTRAMARINE BLUE. It was introduced in Germany in 1828, but never became popular, although it is still used in some low-cost watercolours and oil colours. In oil it is a dull moss-green and has extremely weak colouring power.

ultramarine violet or **violet ultramarine** an extremely weak pigment, pale lavender in the dry state, dark and rather dull in oil. It is identical in pigment properties to ULTRAMARINE BLUE, of which it is a variant. *Mineral violet* is a name formerly shared with manganese violet.

ultraviolet light the part of light that lies beyond the visible SPECTRUM at its violet end, and whose wavelengths are shorter than those of visible light. Light that contains ultraviolet radiations is actinic; that is, it produces photochemical reactions such as those involved in the fading of pigments and dyes, the embrittlement of paints, and the formation of an image on photographic film or paper. Concentrated ultraviolet light sources are used in the laboratory in ACCELERATED TEST procedures. The ultraviolet component of direct sunlight has a powerfully destructive effect on all organic painting materials. The standard of permanence in normal artists' materials is predicated on the assumption that the work of art in which they are used will be preserved under indoor conditions of diffuse daylight or artificial light.

umber (*Lat.* umbra: shade or shadow) the artist's two principal brown pigments, raw umber and burnt umber; they are EARTH COLOURS containing manganese as well as iron oxides. *Raw umber* is a cool greenish brown; *burnt umber*, made by calcining raw umber, is a darker reddish brown. Both have good HIDING POWER, although burnt umber is somewhat more transparent than raw umber. Both are permanent, have excellent colour properties, and yield a variety of subtle, clear tints with white. In oil, they tend toward chalkiness in mixtures of dark tones. Since they are among the most rapid driers in oil and produce tough, flexible, leathery films, painters avoid using them full-strength in underpaintings, where a less flexible overpainting would be dangerous (see FAT OVER LEAN).

Although umber was undoubtedly employed as a pigment in very early times, the name does not appear to have been in use prior to the late Renaissance. The best umber, mined on the island of Cyprus, is known as Cyprus umber, Turkey umber, or Turkey brown. Old names for burnt umber are *chestnut brown, jacaranta brown* and *euchrome. Sicilian brown* is an old name for raw umber. *Vandyke umber* is a variety of burnt umber resembling Vandyke brown.

Umbrian school a group of 15th-century Italian painters, centred in the province of Umbria, in central Italy, during the High Renaissance. The greatest of these were Raphael (1483–1520) and Perugino (1446–1523).

uncial one of the earliest Greek book hands, characterized by rounded capital, or majuscule, letters. It was later adopted in the West and used for the finest Biblical codices. As a Latin book hand, it flourished until the 10th century, and a number of manuscripts copied in this beautiful hand are still extant. It was usually written with a reed pen on soft paper or parchment, to which the rounded letters were well suited; angular letters would have torn the surface of the parchment. Some Latin codices of the same period were written in a HALF-UNCIAL hand – a smaller, more cursive form of the uncial.

undercut 1. a part of a piece of sculpture that protrudes and curves under. **2.** the corresponding part of the MOULD in which the cast metal is encased. A piece with complex undercuts is difficult to remove from a plaster mould. Although it can be handled in a well-sectioned PIECE MOULD, a rubber mould is recommended for casting such a piece.

underglaze *(ceramics)* colour applied to the surface of the clay body before the application of a transparent GLAZE.

underpainting or **first coat** the preliminary layer or layers of colour on a painting surface, beneath the OVERPAINTING, or final coat. Many types of underpainting exist, from the VEIL used to tint a white ground to the multilayered surface that is finally covered by a transparent GLAZE. The first layer of colour may be blocked out in dilute oil colours as a guide for the artist when building up the composition and colour effects. See ABBOZZO; SINOPIA; MACCHIA; ÉBAUCHÉ; GRISAILLE; DEAD COLOURING.

underpainting white or **textural white** a specially prepared oil paint used for building up textures and for adding crisp impasto touches to a picture. It was developed in the United States in the 1950s and is sold in pound tubes. The ingredients used in the various brands of underpainting white are known only to the manufacturers, and there is no information on their permanence and ultimate behaviour either alone or in combination with oil colours. A traditional white for crisp touches is made by mixing three parts of flake white in oil with one part of zinc or titanium egg-tempera white.

undertint a thin, transparent first coating over a white ground; a VEIL or IMPRIMATURA.

undertone 1. the colour effect of a pigment when viewed by TRANS-MITTED LIGHT.

2. the colour characteristics of a paint or pigment when it is diluted with white. The undertone of a pigment may have different colour characteristics from its MASS TONE. For example, alizarin crimson has a bluish undertone; cobalt yellow oil colour has a dull tan mass tone, and is a bright, transparent golden yellow when spread out thinly. Burnt sienna exhibits three colour effects: a mahogany mass tone; a fiery orange undertone by transmitted light; and a salmon pink undertone when mixed with white. In other pigments, such as the cadmiums, the undertone as seen when mixed with white has the same colour characteristics as the mass tone.

United States Pharmacopeia see USP.

Unit One a short-lived group (1933–1935) composed of avant-garde British artists, of whom the best-known is the sculptor Henry Moore (1898–1986). The group shared a sympathetic artistic philosophy rather than a specific doctrine and had a substantial impact on British art in the decade after the group's disbandment.

unlettered proof see PROOF.

Upson board see WALLBOARD.

uranium yellow uranium oxide, a permanent bright yellow that is too expensive for practical use as a pigment. Uranium compounds, prior to their employment in atomic fission, were used to some extent in ceramics and glass, where they typically imparted a bright transparent yellow with a green fluorescence.

USP United States Pharmacopeia. When the initials USP accompany the name of a chemical or drug, they indicate that the material meets the standards of purity and potency of the United States Pharmacopeia and is suitable for pharmaceutical use. USP grades are not necessarily chemically pure (see CP). See also BRITISH PHARMACOPOEIA.

Utrecht school a group of early 17th-century Dutch artists, working in and around Utrecht, Holland, who were particularly influenced by the Italian master Caravaggio (1571–1610). The group included Dirck van Baburen (1595–1624) and Gerrit van Honthorst (1590–1656). Though the group produced no masterpieces, it did influence Rembrandt, Frans Hals and Jan Vermeer.

V

value an artists' term for the degree of lightness on a scale of greys running from black to white. Chromatic colours can be similarly evaluated; the darker ones are said to be lower in value or in a lower KEY. The scientists' term for value is *lightness*.

Vandyke brown a brown earth colour popular in the 18th and 19th centuries but no longer used by artists concerned with permanence. In addition to the inorganic oxides or silicates of the usual earth colour, Vandyke brown contains a percentage of humus (partially decomposed vegetable matter from leaves, roots, etc.), which renders it unstable in paints, causing oil paintings to crack and watercolours to fade. Vandyke brown was originally valued for its extraordinarily clear, nonchalky character, especially in mixtures, but has been replaced by transparent brown and burnt sienna in mixtures. A once-popular mixture of Vandyke brown and emerald green has been replaced by phthalocyanine blue and burnt sienna. Cassel earth, also known as Cologne earth, is a variant that closely resembles Vandyke brown; *Rubens brown* is a variety of Vandyke brown.

Vandyke red copper (cupric) ferrocyanide; a bright brownish-red to reddish-brown pigment. Vandyke red is not widely used, because it is poisonous and of doubtful stability in contact with polluted air. Brown shades have been called *Hatchett's brown* or *Florentine brown*.

Vandyke umber a variety of burnt UMBER, the hue somewhat resembling that of the impermanent Vandyke brown.

vanishing point *(linear perspective)* a point at an infinite distance on the HORIZON LINE at which any two or more lines that represent parallel lines will converge. The principle of convergence to a vanishing point is based on the observable phenomenon that receding parallel lines, such as the rails of a railroad track, do appear to come together on the horizon. Depending on the number and the orientation of axes in the composition of a picture, a drawing in perspective may have one or more vanishing points, all on the horizon line or on the extensions of that line beyond the PICTURE PLANE. A rectangular solid drawn in OBLIQUE PERSPECTIVE, as in a BIRD'S-EYE VIEW or a WORM'S-EYE VIEW, will have three vanishing points, one of which will not be on the horizon line but rather below or above it, respectively. See illustrations at LINEAR PERSPECTIVE and PERSPECTIVE.

vaporization casting see LOST PATTERN CASTING.

varnish 1. a solution of a resin in a volatile solvent that, brushed or sprayed on a surface, dries to a hard, glossy, and usually transparent

436

film, which serves as a protective or decorative coating. **2.** the coating itself.

There are two basic types of varnish: SIMPLE-SOLUTION VARNISH, in which the resin is dissolved directly in the solvent, and OIL VARNISH, in which the resin is cooked or melted with a drying oil and a drier, then thinned with the solvent. Industrial varnishes such as COACH VARNISH and SPAR VARNISH were once made by this cooking process, as was COPAL varnish, once widely used as a picture varnish and in painting mediums. Most modern industrial varnishes are made with synthetic resins. Modern varnishes for use by artists are all of the simple-solution type, such as DAMMAR varnish, MASTIC varnish and acrylic varnish. In industrial practice a simple-solution varnish is also called a *cold cut*, even though steam or mild heat may be used to expedite the solution. Many types of simple-solution varnish are called *spirit varnish* – an imprecise term, since the solvent used may be spirit (alcohol) or another substance, such as spirits of turpentine or amyl acetate.

During manufacture, varnishes may be coloured red, yellow or orange with moderately permanent resinous dyestuffs, such as accroides, gamboge or dragon's blood, and a whole range of brilliantly coloured varnishes may be created by the use of oil- or alcohol-soluble synthetic dyes. While such varnishes are sufficiently lightfast and permanent for use on industrial products and in decorative work, they cannot be recommended for the artist. They have been used to make transparent glazes, but more permanent results are obtained by glazing with such permanent pigments as cobalt yellow, Hansa yellow and alizarin crimson. Specific uses of varnishes in the arts are discussed at PICTURE VARNISH; ISOLATING VARNISH; and MIXING VARNISH. See also INTERMEDIATE VARNISH; MAT VARNISH; RETOUCH; FIXATIVE.

varnishing day or *(Fr.)* **vernissage** a private viewing of an exhibition by a group or society of artists, or in a museum or comparable institution. It is usually held on the afternoon or evening preceding the public opening. Admission is by invitation, and the occasion is usually in the nature of a reception. The term 'varnishing day' has been virtually replaced in modern times with *opening*, which applies also to a corresponding private viewing of a one-person show.

Originally varnishing day was granted to artists to apply finishing touches and the final coat of varnish to their paintings, after they were hung in place for the exhibition. Critics were often invited, and the word gradually took on its present meaning.

varnish size see GOLD SIZE.

vase shapes ancient Greek pottery was made in a large number of conventional shapes, more or less standardized in general form but with wide variations in different periods and localities. Each was designed for a specific use or function. See ALABASTRON; AMPHORA; ASKOS; BLACK-FIGURED POTTERY; CANTHARUS; HYDRIA; KIATHOS; KRATER; KYLIX; LAGYNOS; LECYTHUS; LOUTROPHOROS; OINOCHOE; OLPE; PITHOS; PSYKTER; PYXIS; RED-FIGURED POTTERY; RHYTON; SKYPHOS; STAMNOS.

VASE SHAPES

hydria

amphorae

kylix

kelebe

loutrophoros

volute krater

column krater

bell krater

calyx krater

oenochoe

lagynos

psykter

stamnos

lecythus

askos

pyxis

alabastron

skyphos

pithos

cantharus

kiathos

rhyton

olpe

vase shapes

veduta a painting, drawing or print of the whole or a considerable portion of a town or city. Piranesi's engraved series on Rome is an outstanding example. A *veduta ideata* is a scene that is realistically conceived but whose elements are completely imaginary.

vegetable black see LAMPBLACK, VINE BLACK and CHARCOAL BLACK.

vegetable oil or **vegetal oil** any oil extracted from nuts and seeds. The vegetable oils are obtained in various parts of the world and may be classified as DRYING OILS, SEMIDRYING OILS and NONDRYING OILS. They are chemically close to the fats and waxes and undergo comparable reactions. They are to be distinguished from the chemically inert mineral oils and waxes, with which they have nothing in common except what could be broadly called an oiliness or waxiness.

vegetable violet a highly fugitive, bright violet lake made from LOGWOOD.

vegetable wax see JAPAN WAX.

vehicle the liquid in which pigments are dispersed to make paint, so called because it carries the colour. Paint vehicles have an *executive* function: they put the colour in liquid or plastic form so that it can be spread out and manipulated; a *binding* function: they lock the pigments together in a cohesive mass or film; an *adhesive* function: they act as a glue or cement as they dry, attaching the colours to the ground; and, sometimes, an *optical* function: they may bring out the depth and intensity of the pigment colours, giving them a different colour quality from that of the dry state. The vehicles used in oil colours, polymer colours and encaustic have this last property to a marked degree, while the vehicles of gouache and casein paints have little or no visual effect on the pigment colours. See also FILM-FORMER.

veil 1. (also called **undertint** or **imprimatura**) a thin, transparent layer or glaze of oil colour applied over a white GROUND. It adds colour to the ground while enabling it to retain its brilliant reflective power, a result that is not obtained when the ground is tinted by mixing colour with it. A ground coloured by a veil is known as a *toned ground*.

2. *(graphic arts)* see WIPING.

vein stone an old name for ULTRAMARINE ASH.

velatura in painting, a VEIL or very thin GLAZE of colour over a dried underpainting; the word usually implies an extremely attenuated layer, such as may be applied by lightly tapping a trace of oil colour over the surface with the fingertips.

vellum a fine PARCHMENT, traditionally made from the skins of newborn calves, but also from skins of newborn kids or lambs and occasionally of stillborn animals *(uterine vellum)*. Parchment and vellum have been almost entirely superseded by heavy papers with the same names.

vellum paper 1. a heavy, high-grade paper, natural or cream-coloured, used for certificates and diplomas.

2. any paper with a finish resembling that of VELLUM. It is smoother than PARCHMENT PAPER, with excellent surface and writing qualities, and is widely used for stationery.

VELVET BROWN

velvet brown or **fawn brown** a COMPOSITE PIGMENT composed of ochre (preferably dark) and either burnt umber or burnt sienna.

veneda a greyish-black colour made by mixing black pigment with lime for fresco, and with white lead for tempera on gesso panels or parchment. It was recommended by early writers for underpainting greens, especially foliage, in fresco and tempera painting. Veneda is mentioned in the manuscripts of Theophilus Presbyter (*An Essay Upon Various Arts*, 11th century) and of Jehan le Begue (15th century). In *Il Libro dell'arte* (15th century), Cennino Cennini also instructs the artist to underpaint greens with black or blackish mixtures, but gives no specific name to these mixtures.

veneer a sheet of wood of attractive colour and grain, sliced or cut from the log as thinly as is practical. It is used for furniture or to face thicker wood that is less costly and less attractive. Most veneer is sliced from the log in a continuous spiral cut and must be flattened. On the theory that such veneer tends to resume its original curves and so may pull away from the adhesive that attaches it to the base wood, veneer sawn from the log has been recommended as more stable for fine work than sliced veneer. Sawn veneer, however, is much more costly because the saw produces as much sawdust as veneer.

Venetian blue see ITALIAN BLUE.

Venetian red formerly, a native earth pigment mined in various localities; now, light red of which about 25% is added gypsum, making it inferior to pure light red and not satisfactory as a permanent pigment for oil painting.

Venetian school the painters who pioneered in the development of oil painting in Venice during the 16th century. Paintings of this school were characterized by a rich, glowing tone that was created by building up colours of varying warmth and solidity layer by layer. This pervasive golden glow, and the Venetians' structural use of colour in general, departed from the earlier attitude toward colour as merely a decorative element of the design. It marked, as well, a revolutionary change from the linear or dry quality of 15th-century painting to the more opulent and billowing forms for which artists turned to oil painting. The Venetian painters were also pioneers in the painting of secular subjects, and in the use of the landscape background as an integral part of the subject matter. Among the leading figures of this school were Giorgione (1478–1510), Giovanni Bellini (1430–1516), Titian (*c.*1490–1576), and Tintoretto (1518–1594).

Venice turpentine the thick, very viscous exudation from the Austrian larch (*Larix decidua*); a traditional ingredient of oil painting and glazing mediums. It is permanent and acceptably nonyellowing. Venice turpentine is very similar to STRASBOURG TURPENTINE.

vent, air drain, air jet or **riser** an opening or channel in a MOULD, made to permit air and gases to escape easily when the mould is filled with molten metal or another liquid substance.

ventilago a red NATURAL DYESTUFF obtained from the East Indian plant

Ventilago maderaspatana. Ventilago fades badly on rather short exposure to daylight.

verdaccio a mixture of burnt sienna, ochre, lampblack and chalk with a neutral or greenish-brown colour resembling raw umber. As described by Cennino Cennini (*Il Libro dell'arte*), verdaccio was used by early Italian fresco and tempera painters for outlining, shading and underpainting.

verd antique see SERPENTINE.

verde ceniza see EMERALD GREEN.

verderame see VERDIGRIS.

verdet copper acetate crystals; a brilliant, dark-green, poisonous pigment of doubtful permanence, soluble in water, and formerly used in watercolour.

verdigris 1. (also called **Montpellier green**, *(It.)* **verderame** or *(Lat.)* **viride aeris**) hydrated copper acetate; a light bluish-green pigment, permanent to light but unreliable in paints because it reacts with some pigments and is affected by the atmosphere. One of the earliest artificial pigments, verdigris was made by the Greeks and Romans; it became obsolete during the 19th century. Verdigris was also used as a drier for linseed oil in the 17th and 18th centuries, especially in Spain.
2. (also called **aerugo**) the green PATINA formed on copper and bronze by oxidation.

verditer, blue see BREMEN BLUE.

verditer, green see BREMEN GREEN.

verd vessie see SAP GREEN.

verism 1. the 20th-century concept that the subject matter of art need not be confined to previously accepted standards of beauty, nobility or heroism, but that everyday, even vulgar or repugnant, subjects can have aesthetic value.
2. the clinically objective type of painting associated with the NEUE SACH-LICHKEIT school.

vermeil 1. a golden finish on a base metal or a surface that has been silvered, produced by coating that surface with a transparent red or orange-red lacquer.
2. the lacquer used for this purpose. The application of vermeil is essentially a 19th-century gilding process, which is little used today.
3. in the 17th and 18th centuries, a term for FIRE GILDING.
4. a red colour, somewhat paler than vermilion.
5. *(poetic)* any vermilion-like colour.

vermilion manufactured mercuric sulphide; a brilliant, pure light-red pigment, very opaque and very heavy, which brushes out well in oil. Vermilion (called *chu sha*) was made and used in China at an early date; the earliest European use dates from about the 8th century. Vermilion replaced the inferior CINNABAR (native mercuric sulphide ore). An important, widely used artists' colour from mediaeval times to the 20th century, vermilion was unreliably permanent, especially when not protected by varnish, wax or glazes. Although it has survived for centuries on many paintings, vermilion has occasionally turned dark in spots on other paintings, reverting to the black form of mercuric sulphide for reasons still unknown to science. Vermilion was replaced in the 1920s by the completely reliable light cadmium red. Varieties of vermilion include CHINESE VERMILION, English vermilion, SCARLET VERMILION and ORANGE VERMILION. The term *ethiop* refers to amorphous black mercuric sulphide, an intermediate stage in one method of making vermilion.

vermilionette another name for AMERICAN VERMILION.

vermilion wood see PADOUK.

Vermont White Statuary a fine-grained American white MARBLE, prized by sculptors. Vermont marbles often have bluish-grey clouds and veins, and are also available in a large number of richly coloured varieties.

vernalis the name given by the Society of Tempera Painters to the ceramic colour VICTORIA GREEN when used as a fresco pigment. Made by heating chalk and viridian, vernalis is permanent, but not ordinarily available.

Vernet green or **Horace Vernet green** a variety of BREMEN GREEN named after Horace Vernet, the French 19th-century painter.

vernice liquida a dark, viscous, cooked oil and resin compound used as a picture varnish by mediaeval and early Renaissance tempera painters; the earliest such material mentioned in Italian writings. Warmed vernice liquida was rubbed on the picture surface with the palm of the hand. Its use as a protective coating ceased during the 15th century after the introduction of volatile solvents made possible the mixing of thin, flowing varnishes comparable to those we know today. It is believed probable that the so-called transitional tempera painters of the 15th and 16th centuries used vernice liquida as one of the oily ingredients in their paints.

vernis martin a warm-toned or reddish shade of BRONZE POWDER, that is widely available. It is named after an 18th-century French varnish that was mixed with bronze powder or applied over gold leaf on fine furniture, decorative panels, and objets d'art of the period.

vernis mou (*Fr.* soft varnish) another name for SOFT-GROUND ETCHING.

vernissage see VARNISHING DAY.

Verona brown see TRANSPARENT BROWN.

Verona green one of the best commercial grades of GREEN EARTH.

Verona yellow see TURNER'S YELLOW.

Veronese green or **Paolo Veronese green** an unstandardized name given to a wide variety of green pigments, after the 16th-century Venetian painter, Paolo Veronese, whose greens were probably palette mixtures of blue and yellow.

vert antique a finish used for BRONZING plaster casts and other surfaces to simulate the natural green PATINA of old bronze or copper. A vert-antique finish is usually produced by applying to the surface a ground coat of casein paint the colour of an old penny and then stippling on a coat of semiopaque green copper carbonate. Vert antique is also used commercially; for example, in the United States the roof of a house might be given a vert-antique finish to simulate patinated copper.

vert émeraude see VIRIDIAN.

vesica piscis see AUREOLE.

Vesperbild the German term for PIETÀ.

Vestorian blue see EGYPTIAN BLUE.

V-gouge see PARTING TOOL.

vibrate *(sculpture)* to shake a mould and its fluid contents rhythmically in order to distribute the cast materials evenly in the mould, thus ensuring maximum definition of detail in the positive cast.

Victoria green 1. a COMPOSITE PIGMENT supposed to contain 80 parts viridian, 40 parts zinc yellow, and 10 parts zinc white, although inferior grades may also contain inert pigment. The label is not a reliable index. **2.** the ceramic colour VERNALIS.

Victoria red one of several tradenames for chrome red. See CHROME YELLOW.

Vienna blue see COBALT BLUE.

Vienna green see MITTIS GREEN.

Vienna lake see CARMINE.

Vienna red a variety of chrome red. See CHROME YELLOW.

Vienna ultramarine see COBALT BLUE.

Vienna white a chalk made by air-slaking lime putty, as in the production of BIANCO SANGIOVANNI. It was once used as a polishing powder for metals, not as a pigment.

Vierge de Pitié the French term for PIETÀ.

vignette 1. *(painting and photography)* a picture without defined borders, whose edges shade off or merge into a background.
2. in architecture, a TRAIL, or design of grapes, vine leaves, and tendrils used on the capitals of columns.
3. in book printing, the vine-grape-tendril design used as a decoration on the title page or as a tailpiece.

vine black, grape black, marc black or **yeast black** an impure CARBON PIGMENT with a bluish undertone, made by burning selected vegetable materials, such as grapevines and other substances. Vine black is greatly inferior in intensity, colouring power and chemical purity to lampblack, ivory black, and Mars black. Although vine black was offered to artists during the 19th century, it is seldom encountered today. Good grades of vine black are sometimes known by the unstandardized term vegetable black. Varieties of vine black include KERNEL BLACK and Spanish or cork black. DROP BLACK, also known as Frankfort or German black, is an industrial grade of vine black.

vinyl resin any of a family of thermoplastic synthetic resins derived by polymerization or copolymerization of various vinyl compounds, chiefly vinyl acetate, vinyl chloride and vinylidene chloride. Vinyl resins are clear, water-white, nonyellowing products, some of which are used to make coating materials. Few of the vinyl products are practicable for use in artists' materials, because they can be put into solution only with powerful solvents that emit obnoxious and toxic fumes. Two exceptions are a polyvinyl isolating varnish containing isopropyl alcohol that thins with alcohol and *Flashe*. Flashe is a tradename for a paint made by dispersing in a vinyl emulsion that thins with water. Vinyl acetate is sometimes used as a copolymer with acrylic resins in the water-dispersed polymer colours. See POLYVINYL ACETATE; POLYVINYL CHLORIDE.

violet carmine a COMPOSITE PIGMENT, formerly made from various natural-dyestuff lakes. A modern permanent variety, made from alizarin crimson and cobalt blue, is not widely sold. Violet carmine has been replaced in permanent painting by light cobalt violet and several SYNTHETIC ORGANIC PIGMENTS.

violet madder-lake see ALIZARIN VIOLET.

violet pigments the following pigments, approved by ASTM for use in the United States in oil paints, and generally acceptable in all other easel-painting techniques: MARS VIOLET, ULTRAMARINE RED, ULTRAMARINE VIOLET, QUINACRIDONE VIOLET, DIOXAZINE PURPLE, ISOVIOLANTHRONE VIOLET and MANGANESE VIOLET.

violet ultramarine see ULTRAMARINE VIOLET.

viride aeris see VERDIGRIS.

viridian or **smaragd green** hydrated chromium hydroxide; a bright-green pigment with a transparent, cool, emerald-green undertone and a dark mass tone that tends to be blackish at full strength. Viridian is absolutely permanent in all artists' colours and for all industrial uses except high-temperature work, since it is a furnace product that reverts to chromium oxide green when roasted above a dull red heat. Viridian was discovered in Paris in 1838 by Pannetier and his protégé, Binet, who kept their method secret until a process was published by Guignet in 1859; it is said to have been introduced in England by the firm of Winsor and Newton in 1862. In the United States, prior to the standardization of pigment nomenclature in 1957, viridian was sometimes called by its French name, *vert émeraude*, of which the literal English translation is 'emerald green', an entirely different pigment. Similarly confusing names for viridian are *emeraude green* and *emerald chromium oxide*. Some obsolete names are *Pannetier's green*, FRENCH VERONESE GREEN, and *transparent oxide of chromium*. *Casali's green* and *Mittler's green* are varieties named after early workers on viridian. *Guignet's green*, another of its names, identifies the pigment made by the standard process.

viscosity the resistance of a liquid to flow, the opposite of *mobility*. Thick, heavy-bodied liquids like stand oil have high viscosity. See CONSISTENCY.

vitreous 1. of or pertaining to glass.

2. glasslike; having the external properties of glass, such as hardness, high gloss, and resistance to chemical attack. Hard-glazed porcelain and porcelain enamel are vitreous substances. All pottery that has been fired in a kiln may be said to be *vitrified*.

vitreous enamel or **porcelain enamel** an opaque or glassy coating of, for example, powdered frit, fused to a metal panel (usually iron or steel; occasionally aluminium, copper, or some other metal) by firing at about 1500° F. Vitreous enamelling, the standard industrial process used for such items as cookers and, formerly, outdoor signs and panels for building fronts, has been adapted to artists' use for mural painting and decoration in exposed locations where weathering and environmental conditions are more severe than any paints can withstand. In 1937, a group of thirty painters in the United States launched a project to decorate part of the New York subway system with murals painted on vitreous enamel, using CERAMIC COLOURS ground in a suitable vehicle; the panels would then be returned to the enamel factory for firing. They held an exhibition at the Museum of Modern Art in February 1938, but circumstances prevented them from putting the plan of subway decoration into effect. See also ENAMEL.

Vitruvian scroll or **wave scroll** a decorative motif found especially in Roman friezes, consisting of a series of convoluted forms resembling a succession of waves. See SCROLL.

Vitruvian scroll

volatile solvent any of a group of organic liquids that evaporate readily at normally low temperatures and are used, depending on their individual properties, as solvents for resins and as thinners or diluents for oil paints, varnishes, mediums and lacquers. Most of them are immiscible with water; most are flammable to various degrees. In order for a solvent to qualify as a thinner for artists' materials, its odour must not be obnoxious, its fumes must not be toxic, its rate of evaporation must meet the requirements of the technique or process in which it is to be used, it must be miscible with the other ingredients in every proportion, and it must not react chemically with them or have a destructive effect on their dry films when applied over them. The volatile solvents widely used in artists' paints and varnishes are TURPENTINE and WHITE SPIRIT. Among the other solvents used in industry and sometimes by artists or manufacturers of artists' materials are ACETONE, BANANA OIL, BENZINE, BUTYL LACTATE, CARBON BISULPHIDE, CARBON TETRACHLORIDE, COAL-TAR SOLVENT, DIACETONE ALCOHOL, ETHYL ACETATE, ETHYL ALCOHOL, KEROSENE, NAPHTHA and SPIKE OIL. See also DISTILLATION; MUTUAL SOLVENT.

volet one of the wings or folding panels of a TRIPTYCH or polyptych.

Vorticism a British art movement founded by the painter-writer Wyndham Lewis (1882–1957) in 1912 and ended by the First World War in 1915. Its art was abstract and sometimes entirely nonobjective. Although short-lived and confined to the activities of Lewis and his intimate circle of painters, sculptors, and writers, Vorticism was important in that it embraced French Cubist and Italian Futurist concepts and exposed British painters to their influence. Two issues of a publication called *Blast* contained its manifestos and other statements. Among artists actively associated with the movement were the sculptors Jacob Epstein (1880–1959) and Henri Gaudier-Brzeska (1891–1915) and the painters William Roberts, Edward Wadsworth (1889–1949), and C.R. Nevinson.

V-tool see PARTING TOOL.

Vitruvian scroll

W

wad clay or **wadding clay** a low grade of FIRECLAY. It is usually used to level the setter shelves or bungs of SAGGERS in a KILN. Wads may also be used to lute, or seal, the lids of saggers.

wallboard various rigid boards made of composition materials and used primarily in the construction of interior walls, ceilings and partitions. Since the introduction of wallboards in the last century, artists have attempted to use them as supports for painting. The term *wallboard* was first applied specifically to a soft, laminated pasteboard made of wood pulp and/or waste paper. It is still being made in such well-known brands as Beaverboard; the term *beaver board* is sometimes used as a general synonym for this type of board. It is used in art classes and for temporary purposes but is not durable or stable enough for permanent painting. Other boards that lack the structural stability and durability for use as permanent supports are the loose-textured insulating boards, compo board and plasterboard. The successful adaptation of wallboard to artists' purposes occurred with the introduction in the late 1920s of the MASON-ITE process, a patented method of creating a dense board from exploded and compressed wood fibres. Wallboards of this dense, hard quality are called *hardboards*. Many are now on the market. Hardboards made by certain processes may contain added binders that make them prone to warping, especially when gesso is applied to them. Large hardboard panels are usually braced at the rear by a framework of wooden strips, glued on to prevent the support from bending or becoming curved by its own weight.

walling wax or **bordering wax** beeswax, which when warmed to plastic consistency, is used to build a raised border or wall around the edges of an ETCHING plate, thus making it possible to apply the MORDANT directly to the surface of the plate. Use of walling wax eliminates the need to immerse the entire plate in an ACID BATH, which would be both awkward and expensive to do, for example, when etching an extra-large plate.

wall of Troy pattern see GREEK KEY PATTERN.

wall painting see MURAL.

wall primer see PLASTER PRIMER.

wall scraper a well-tempered, flexible steel SLICE, about 3 inches wide at its edge. It somewhat resembles the spatula or AMASETTE originally used to gather oil colour during grinding of the colour, and is a generally useful studio implement. One of its special uses is in the DRAW-OUT.

walnut any of the common hardwoods obtained from trees of the genus *Juglans*. *Circassian walnut* or *French walnut* (*Juglans regia*), which has a tawny wood with dark streaks, is used chiefly for furniture and veneer.

wall scraper

American walnut or *black walnut* (from *Juglans nigra*) is a dark- or medium-brown hardwood of very desirable texture, grain, durability, uniformity, and working properties; variations in colouring, or in straightness or curliness of grain, are never very far from an average. *Butternut* (from *Juglans cinerea*), sometimes called *white walnut*, is a yellowish-grey wood that is also much used by wood carvers. For African walnut, see TIGERWOOD.

walnut oil a vegetable DRYING OIL, expressed from the common, or English, walnut. It has been known as a paint oil since mediaeval times but, although used from time to time in artists' colours, it never achieved the popularity of linseed oil. Leonardo da Vinci valued it, and 18th-century writers recommended it for use with some pigments. Modern scientific opinion rates it less desirable than linseed oil. Although it is produced in quantity for commercial and culinary use, few specialists in our time have investigated its possibilities for oil colours. Like other nut oils, it becomes rancid on ageing.

Wanderers, The a Russian art movement organized by Nicholas Kramskoy in 1872. The realistic paintings of the Wanderers were social and propagandistic in purpose, expressing growing dissatisfaction with the absolute regime of the czars. The group implemented its desire to enlighten and educate the people through art by sending exhibitions to many provincial cities. It included V.V. Vereshagin, Ilya Repin, Vladimir Makovsky, W. Polenov, and Lebediew.

warm colours those colours in which red and yellow are dominant. Yellowish or brownish greys are called *warm greys*. All warm colours lie in the red-yellow half of the COLOUR CIRCLE. See also COOL COLOURS.

warning coat a coloured layer of plaster included in a WASTE MOULD to indicate how close the cast is when the mould is being destroyed by chipping out, in order to avoid damaging the cast.

warping the bending or arching of a support that should be flat, as a result of unequal contraction due to moisture, heat or drying. Expert framing in sturdy frames helps prevent warping of panels. Museums find that the best environment for survival of wood panels includes a constant atmospheric humidity of about 55%. Professional conservation treatments are required for the restoration of warped panels to a flat condition. (See CRADLING, PARQUETAGE.) Paintings on canvas mounted on ordinary, lightweight stretchers are likely to warp if they are hung unframed; such paintings will not warp if they are braced in substantial picture frames. Canvases mounted on heavy $2\frac{1}{2}$-inch stretchers do not warp.

wash an application of dilute watercolour to paper. Although any transparent touch of thinned-out watercolour, as distinguished from full-strength or concentrated colours, can be called a *wash*, the term usually refers to a uniform broad area such as a sky, applied quickly with a large, full brush. Sometimes, dilute watercolour, applied very wet, is allowed to run down to one end of the paper by tilting the board to a vertical position. This creates a gradated tone, as the paper dries sooner at the upper part, and the colour, flowing down, becomes more concentrated at the bottom. See also WASH DRAWING.

wash drawing a brush drawing done on paper with multiple dilutions or washes of India ink or MONOCHROME watercolour. Most wash drawings include linear elements, and are then called *pen-and-wash drawings*.

wash gilding see FIRE GILDING.

waste mould *(casting)* a plaster MOULD that can be used only once, because it must be broken up in order to remove the cast from it.

watercolour 1. the technique of painting with pigments dispersed in a GUM ARABIC solution.

2. a work of art so produced.

3. the paint used in this technique. Besides the gum, which acts as a BINDER, the ingredients in watercolour paint include a PLASTICIZER such as HYDROMEL or sugar water, GLYCERIN to keep the paint moist, a WETTING AGENT to obtain a uniform flow of paint on surfaces, and a PRESERVATIVE such as phenol. Watercolours are applied to special handmade WATERCOLOUR PAPER with hair brushes, the finest of which are made of red sable (see BRUSH, RED SABLE).

Watercolours are characterized by a luminous transparency, although GOUACHE is sometimes considered an opaque watercolour technique. True watercolours are most often applied with free, loose strokes and broad WASHES; the grain and whiteness of the paper add to the brilliance and sparkle of the finished work.

Water paints were used throughout the Middle Ages in the decoration of parchment manuscripts (see ILLUMINATION). During the 16th, 17th and 18th centuries, they were little used except in MINIATURE painting, which was commonly done on card or ivory, although parchment and porcelain were also used. Chinese and Japanese painters have made extensive use of watercolour on fine textiles such as silk, as well as on paper made of bark or rice.

The modern technique of transparent watercolour painting was developed in England during the late 18th and early 19th centuries. At the beginning of this period, watercolour drawing, in which sepia or blue tints were superimposed on pen-and-ink designs, gave way to monochrome. This in turn was superseded by a more versatile technique in which colour was applied with ever-greater freedom and imagination. Today, a broad, fluid handling of masses of colour characterizes watercolour technique.

Watercolour paints were being made commercially by the late 1700s. They were at first hard, dry cakes about $\frac{3}{4}'' \times 1\frac{1}{4}'' \times \frac{1}{4}''$, or half-cakes, embossed with the maker's trademark. Moist watercolours, obtained by adding glycerin and sold in pans, were introduced about 1835; they are still used by many painters. The glycerin prevents the paint from caking in the pan and, by slightly delaying the setting of the colours, facilitates their application. Watercolours in paste form, sold in collapsible tubes, appeared about 1900; they are easy to handle and are the most popular kind.

Many of the finest watercolourists of modern times have been British and American. Among the British painters who contributed to the flowering of the art in the late 18th and 19th centuries were John Robert Cozens (1752–1797), William Blake (1757–1827), Thomas Girtin (1775–1802), J.M.W. Turner (1775–1851), and John Sell Cotman (1782–1842). The Americans who followed them include Winslow Homer (1836–1910), John Marin (1872–1953), Edward Hopper (1882–1967), Charles Demuth (1883–1935), and Charles Burchfield (1893–1967).

watercolour paper paper used as both ground and support for watercolour painting. For permanence and best performance, artists select a handmade paper, especially prepared from cotton rag, sometimes with a small percentage of linen, and containing no residual bleach or other added material except a little glue size to reduce absorbency. Watercolour paper is available in several weights designated by numbers that indicate the weight of a ream (500 sheets) of imperial size (see PAPER DIMENSIONS). The lightest-weight paper is 72 pounds; 140-pound paper is twice as costly. Papers of both these common weights are stretched on a drawing board for use in serious work. The heavier grades, from 280 to 400 pounds, may be used without stretching; their bold textures, sparkling effects, and ability to withstand vigorous treatment, such as scraping with a knife and repeated scrubbing, make them highly esteemed by watercolourists.

Handmade papers are available in several textures. *Cold pressed* (CP) is the usual moderately coarse grade. *Rough* (R) or *not pressed* (NP) papers (sometimes called, simply, *not*) have decidedly rough textures and are more frequently available in heavy rather than lightweight varieties. *Hot pressed* (HP) is rather dense and smooth; it is not generally used for transparent watercolour painting, but is useful for gouache and for many drawing purposes. Fine, handmade watercolour paper is also sold in blocks or pads of various sizes.

Because the working qualities of watercolour paper improve with age, artists have traditionally sought out old stocks, especially those that are watermarked with the maker's name or trademark and the year of manufacture. Traditionally, in papers that are stamped or watermarked, the legible side is considered the *right* side, without flaws and even in texture; but top-quality watercolour paper seldom has any blemishes, and may therefore be used on either side.

water gilding the technique of adhering precious-metal leaf to a gesso or bole ground that is moistened with water immediately before each leaf is laid. Water gilding, which is an older method for laying leaf than MORDANT GILDING, is used chiefly for fine frames and decorative work and for small flat work such as illumination of manuscripts, decoration of book covers, gilding in tempera on gesso panels, and gilding the edges of book pages. If desired, water gilding can be burnished to a high mirror finish, whereas mordant gilding cannot. See also GOLD SIZE.

water glass sodium silicate, a thick, viscous LIQUID SILICATE with alkaline properties. It was tried, unsuccessfully, as a paint binder during the 19th century.

water-glass painting see MINERAL PAINTING.

water-in-oil emulsion see EMULSION.

watermark a design, pattern, or mark on paper, usually produced by a raised area in the roll on which the paper is made. The marked area is thinner than the rest of the sheet, so the watermark is easily seen when the paper is held up to the light. Watermarks on handmade papers are made by very low relief moulds or designs of fine wire set on the screen on which the moist pulp collects. See also LAID PAPER.

water-of-Ayr see AYR STONE.

water paints see AQUEOUS PAINT.

water-white *(of a material)* colourless or transparent. Examples of such materials are glycerin and window glass.

wave scroll see VITRUVIAN SCROLL.

wax 1. a plastic substance secreted by bees. See BEESWAX.
2. any of the many substances resembling it in physical properties. CHINESE INSECT WAX and beeswax are animal in origin; among the many vegetable waxes are CARNAUBA WAX, CANDELILLA WAX, and JAPAN WAX; PARAFFIN, CERESIN, MONTAN WAX, and OZOKERITE are examples of mineral waxes. Waxes are related to oils, but are not fluid at normal temperatures. Since they have a lower degree of permeability to moisture than resins or oils, they are useful as protective coatings wherever their relative softness is not a disadvantage. Animal and vegetable waxes behave much like animal and vegetable oils; they enter into the same reactions, including saponification and emulsification. Mineral waxes are chemically inert, as are mineral oils. A wax does not have a precise melting point; its melting range is usually expressed in maximum and minimum figures stated in degrees Centigrade. All waxes melt at less than 100 °C, the boiling point of water, and can therefore be liquefied in boiling water. Each wax used in the arts is chosen for a specific purpose according to its properties, the most significant of which are its melting range and its hardness when in a solid state. When a recipe for artists' materials calls for wax without specifying the variety, *white refined beeswax* is always meant.

wax painting see ENCAUSTIC.

Weather Ometer *(US)* the tradename for a laboratory accelerated testing device in which samples of coating materials are exposed to a carbon arc, as in the FADE OMETER, but with the addition of intermittent cycles of a water spray to simulate the conditions of outdoor weathering. Since few works of art are required to resist outdoor exposure, use of the device with artists' materials is limited to testing paints that might be used in outdoor murals. See also ACCELERATED TEST.

wedge 1. *vb (ceramics)* to prepare a lump of clay for use by alternately cutting it (usually on a taut wire) and pounding it vigorously (on a slab) until it is in a homogeneous, plastic condition, free from air bubbles. See also PUG.

2. *n.* the KEYS in a canvas stretcher.

weld, arzica or **gaude yellow** a bright-yellow NATURAL DYESTUFF made from dyer's rocket (*Reseda luteola*), a plant formerly cultivated extensively in Britain, France and Germany. Weld has been used since mediaeval times to dye fabrics and to make lake pigments. It became commercially important during the 15th century but was replaced in the 19th by synthetic dyes of superior properties. Weld is one of the more permanent of the natural dyestuffs, and a small quantity is still grown in Normandy for use in dyeing silk. The colouring principle of weld (luteolin) has been made synthetically.

welding the process of joining together two pieces of metal by fusion. Intense heat is supplied by an oxyacetylene torch in gas or OXYACETYLENE WELDING and by electrical means in ARC WELDING. Sometimes a FILLER ROD is melted along the joint, in the process known as BRAZING. The direct welding of two pieces by combining the molten edges is called *fusion welding*. Welding is done at much higher temperatures than soldering (see SOLDER) and results in stronger, more durable joints. It is used in making DIRECT METAL SCULPTURE.

well slant see SLANT.

West Indian satinwood see SATINWOOD.

wet clay sculptor's CLAY that is mixed with water before use, as distinguished from MODELLING CLAY.

wet-into-wet the application of paint to a surface that already has a wet coating on it. One form of wet-into-wet consists of painting tempera paint into wet oil paint or vice versa. See MIXED TECHNIQUE.

wetting agent, noncrawl solution or **noncreep solution** a liquid added in very small amounts to watercolour or another water paint in order to reduce the surface tension of the water in it, so that the paint will flow freely and take evenly on the paper. Water has a tendency to form drops, which is further encouraged by the tendency of some surfaces to repel water. A good wetting agent breaks down the surface tension of the water and eliminates the resistance of the paper. The standard wetting agent formerly used in the manufacture of watercolours was *oxgall*, a by-product of the meat trade. The modern wetting agent is a clear, colourless synthetic product related to detergents. It is sold in small dropper bottles in art-supply shops, and also in larger bottles in photographic supply shops (it is used in developing film).

wetting down the flooding of a stone with water in order to discover veins and patterns, or to bring out the grain before carving or polishing.

whelk red see TYRIAN PURPLE.

whetstone a hard stone used for sharpening edged tools. Relatively coarse-grained whetstones are used dry for basic sharpening and are usually made of artificial abrasives such as CARBORUNDUM. Hard, fine-grained stones for finishing the edges of carving knives, gouges, etc., are usually oiled before use. See OILSTONE.

white earth a pure white variety of clay, whose major components and pigment properties are similar to those of GREEN EARTH. Because of the clarity and high absorbency of white earth, it is well suited for, and in limited use as, a BASE for certain LAKES. White earth is not the same material as *terra alba*.

white lampblack see FRENCH-PROCESS ZINC OXIDE.

white lead basic lead carbonate. The use of white lead, one of the oldest of the artificial or manufactured pigments, dates back to the earliest recorded civilizations in Europe and China. It is used in oil paints, and has the best pigment properties of any of the permanent pigments, since it is a good drier, has superior brushing qualities, and forms the toughest and most durable of paint films. Two defects, which have been greatly exaggerated by proponents of other white pigments, are its toxic nature and the fact that it will yellow or turn brownish on contact with sulphur. The latter defect is of slight consequence in oil paintings, where the pigment is locked in by the oil and protected from the action of sulphur gases in the atmosphere. In any case, artists' paintings are usually preserved under conditions that preclude exposure of white lead paint films to harmful concentrations of sulphur. White lead in oil will not react with any of the other approved permanent pigments, including the cadmiums and ultramarine blue, unless these are of low quality and contain free sulphur. Since lead is a cumulative poison – its toxic effects increase as small amounts build up in the body – white lead is not used in aqueous paints, pastels, or the types of paint used by children. However, mature artists do not readily contract lead poisoning if they obey the simple rules of cleanliness and do not swallow white lead paint or breathe in its dust.

White lead is manufactured in a variety of ways, but the grade most suitable for use in artists' oil paints is made largely by what is called the *Dutch process* (see DUTCH-PROCESS WHITE LEAD). The artists' pigment is called FLAKE WHITE. Also acceptable, but less frequently available, is another variety of white lead called CREMNITZ WHITE. White lead was the only opaque white pigment used in the entire history of artistic oil painting up to the 20th century; its good properties are responsible in part for the survival and success of the oil technique. ZINC WHITE and TITANIUM WHITE, which are nontoxic and nonyellowing, are entirely acceptable pigments for use in artists' colours, but they are inferior to flake white as oil colours in most respects.

Several names were used in Britain during the 19th century for different grades and variants of white lead, such as *Flemish white*, *London white*, *Nottingham white* and *Roman white*. The Latin term *cerussa* was applied to white lead rather than to flake white. French white and silver white are unstandardized terms that have been used for both flake and zinc whites.

In ceramics, white lead is a common flux for glazes fired at low temperatures.

white-line cut a relief print (see RELIEF PRINTING) in which the nonprinting engraved (or, in ANASTATIC PRINTING, etched) lines form the subject, producing a design in white lines and areas on a black ground. Most WOOD ENGRAVINGS are white-line cuts. The process of engraving or etching a white-line cut is known as working from black to white. Most prints are black design lines and areas on white paper and are developed on the plate, block or stone from white to black.

white mahogany see PRIMA VERA.

white pigments any of the following pigments approved in the United States for use in oil paints by ASTM and as being generally acceptable (except as noted) in all easel-painting techniques: FLAKE WHITE (except in water mediums and pastel), TITANIUM WHITE, and ZINC WHITE. White pigments that do not retain their whiteness and full opacity in oil are classified as INERT PIGMENTS. Some inert pigments serve as whites in some coatings, for example, BLANC FIXE in GOUACHE COLOURS.

white spirit or *(US)* **mineral spirits** a paint thinner, used as a substitute for turpentine and sold under the tradenames of the various oil companies. It may be odourless or smell faintly like benzine, and it has a low flash point. It is refined especially for use as a thinner for varnishes and oil paints and is preferred to turpentine by some artists because it costs less, is not sticky, and is free of turpentine's residual odour.

white walnut another name for butternut. See WALNUT.

whitewash an inexpensive white coating for rough work on walls or ceilings. It is neither permanent nor waterproof. The term usually means lime mixed with water, but CALCIMINE and other inexpensive water paints may also be called *whitewash*. Whitewash has been used in the past to impose artistic censorship by hiding mosaic and fresco mural decoration for religious or political reasons. Many such works have been reclaimed in modern times by washing away the coating.

white wax white refined BEESWAX.

whiting or *(US)* **English white** native calcium carbonate mined in various parts of the world, but notably from the chalk downs of southern England, and used as an INERT PIGMENT in such products as GESSO. It is also the major flux used in ceramic glazes that are fired at high temperatures. The standard grade of whiting, called *extra gilder's*, is greyish or creamy off-white in colour, uniformly fine, and free from impurities. A cheaper, more greyish variety, called *commercial*, is suitable only for less demanding uses, such as making window putty. A superfine, purified grade of whiting, known as *Spanish white* or *Paris white*, is not ordinarily obtainable from most retail paint shops. Artificially prepared calcium carbonate, known as PRECIPITATED CHALK, is much whiter than whiting.

whole length see FULL LENGTH; CANVAS SIZES, PORTRAIT.

wing see TRIPTYCH.

wiping the process of removing ink from the plane surface (the nonprinting areas) of INTAGLIO plates, so that the ink will remain only in the etched or engraved lines. The plate must be wiped to obtain distinct lines and clean white areas in the proofs. This is usually accomplished with the palm of the hand (hand-wiped) or with tarlatan or a similar open-weave fabric (rag-wiped). Some graphic artists prefer to leave a trace of ink on the surface of the plate to blur lines and soften contrasts, thus toning down the cold, bare appearance of a print pulled from a cleanly wiped plate. One method of doing this is to blot the plate with veils (balls of cotton gauze or muslin), a technique known as *retroussage*. The object of retroussage (or *dragging* or *pumping*, as the technique is also called) is to deposit a uniform trace of ink on the surface of the plate with a minimum disturbance of the full charge of ink in the intaglio lines. Veils may also be used on plates that have already been hand- or rag-wiped to draw a little ink from the incised lines and deposit it on the edge of the etch or furrow; when an engraved plate is so treated, the slightly smudged lines in the proofs resemble somewhat the lines produced by the BURR in DRYPOINT. Veils may also be used to create highlights by removing ink from certain areas. Because retroussage also tends to conceal in the prints slight defects that may be on the plate, such as those caused by FOUL BITING, some purists do not approve of the technique and insist on a perfectly clean black-on-white print.

wire-end tool see MODELLING TOOLS.

woad a blue NATURAL DYESTUFF made from the woad plant (*Isatis tinctoria*), which was extensively cultivated in Britain and other European countries from very early times. Woad was replaced by the more durable and efficient INDIGO after the latter was imported from India. The two products are so similar in chemical composition that indigo and woad pigments cannot be differentiated in old paintings.

wood alcohol see METHANOL.

woodcarving knife any of a number of steel knives with variously shaped blades used for chip carving in wood sculpture and as a supplement to chisels for cleaning up cutaway areas. The steel from which these knives are made is tough and durable but may be sharpened to a keen cutting edge. The blades are set in sturdy wooden handles. The knives used in woodcutting, known as *carvers*, are somewhat smaller than wood-carving knives. They have a short angular blade set in a cord-wrapped handle for a better grip. See illustration at WOODCARVING TOOLS.

woodcarving tools an assortment of sculptors' CHISELS, GOUGES, PARTING TOOLS and WOODCARVING KNIVES, set in wooden handles sturdy enough to be struck with a MALLET. The ADZE and the RASP are also used in wood carving. These cutting tools, extensively used in wood sculpture, average between 8 and 10 inches in length and are available in a wide range of blade sizes, so that lines from about $\frac{1}{16}$ of an inch to an inch in width may be incised. The different kinds of blades (straight, curved, U and V) incise lines and areas of different depths and shapes. Approximately half-size versions of these sculptors' cutting tools are used in the graphic arts for woodcutting. Woodcarving and WOODCUT TOOLS are sharpened by whetting them on a SLIP. See figure overleaf.

woodcut 1. a RELIEF PRINTING technique in which the printing surface is carved with special WOODCUT TOOLS from a block of wood. The art of making woodcuts is occasionally termed *xylography*.

WOODCUT

woodcarving tools (A) Straight chisel; (B) skew chisel;
(C) straight gouge; (D) short bent gouge; (E) long bent V-gouge;
(F) fishtail tool; (G) parting tool; (H) wood-carving knives;
(I) carver for woodcut.

2. an ORIGINAL PRINT made by this method.

The woodcut block is cut from a smoothed plank cut longitudinally from the tree trunk so that the grain runs in parallel lines in the block. This is the most significant way in which the woodcut differs from the WOOD ENGRAVING, in which end-grain blocks, cut transversely from a log, are used. The traditional woodcut block is seasoned hardwood, such as apple, pear, beech or sycamore. A mid-20th century trend toward large colour prints made from wood blocks has brought into use planks of inexpensive, more readily obtained softwoods, such as pine. Softwood blocks are not used in traditional woodcuts, because they cannot be carved in every direction with the same freedom as wood blocks of more compact grain and because the wood-grain pattern of the plank shows in the prints. .Contemporary printmakers exploit the latter feature, creating large prints in which the grained pattern is an integral part of the work. Heavily grained surfaces such as weathered or wire-brushed wood are also sometimes used today in direct RELIEF BLOCK PRINTING.

In many woodcuts a great deal of wood must be cut away; today, graphic artists often expedite this process by using a small electric drill with various routing attachments.

Woodcuts are inked with BRAYERS. Before the 19th century, they were inked with a leather dabber. If the block is TYPE-HIGH, it may be printed on an ordinary flatbed printing press. The hand method for printing wood blocks, still widely used in artists' studios, consists of placing the proof paper on the face-up inked block, covering it with another piece of paper or a thin card, and accomplishing the transfer of ink by rubbing the whole surface with some smoothly gliding implement, such as a BAREN or the bowl of a large wooden spoon.

Woodcut, which developed from the process of printing textile patterns with wood blocks, began to be used in Europe toward the end of the 14th century. The oldest extant woodcuts are playing cards. The BLOCK BOOKS of the 15th century were illustrated with simple linear designs, and most were hand-coloured. Although these early prints, which were chiefly of religious subjects, were technically and pictorially crude, by the early 16th century the art of woodcutting had been elevated in Germany to the highest degree of technical and aesthetic accomplishment by accomplished woodcarvers. These skilled artisans carried out the designs of such artists as Albrecht Dürer (1472–1528), Lucas Cranach (1472–1553), and Hans Holbein the Younger (1498–1543), whose *Dance of Death* was cut by a great master of the craft, Hans Lützelberger. So accomplished were these artisans that artists were content merely to supervise the actual cutting of the blocks. The woodcut developed simultaneously in Italy, where the Mannerist artist Francesco Parmigianino (1503–1540) did many drawings that were cut by Ugo da Carpi, and in the Netherlands, where Lucas van Leyden (1494–1533) – who was greatly influenced by Dürer – worked. Although woodcuts continued to be used in the 16th century to illustrate books, they also came into their own as original prints during this period. In the 17th century, the use of line engraving and etching for fine-arts prints relegated woodcut to the status of a reproductive technique. It was supplanted in turn in this reproductive function in the 18th century by wood engraving, but it began to be revived as an artistic medium in France in the last half of the 19th century, when it was used by Gauguin and Millet. Edvard Munch, who designed, cut and printed his own woodcuts, experimented extensively with the medium and did much to spur on its revival. See also CHIAROSCURO WOODCUT.

woodcut tools tools such as chisels, gouges, parting tools, knives (carvers), etc. that are used to incise a woodcut block. These shorter versions of sculptors' WOODCARVING TOOLS are between 5 and 6 inches in length and have proportionately smaller cutting edges than woodcarving tools. Since woodcut tools are not intended to be struck with a mallet, they have straight wooden handles that are easily grasped.

wood engraving 1. a RELIEF PRINTING technique in which a block of wood is incised with a GRAVER, TINT TOOL or SCORPER to create a printing surface. The technique is occasionally termed *xylography*.
2. an ORIGINAL PRINT pulled from such a surface.

The blocks used in wood engraving are transverse cuts, or the end grain, of the hardest hardwoods, differing in this way from the blocks used for WOODCUTS, which are longitudinal cuts and have a parallel grain. Boxwood is preferred for wood engraving, but red maple is also used. Since the trees from which boxwood is obtained are not very large in diameter, large blocks are made by bolting smaller ones together. Before the block is incised, the design is drawn with a pencil on the surface, which is first coated with very dilute Chinese-white watercolour; this serves as a background on which the pencil markings will be visible and as a surface that has enough tooth to take the drawing. The block may be held on a small sand-filled leather cushion while it is being engraved. Once the drawing has been cut in the surface, the watercolour ground is washed away, and the block is inked and printed the same way as a woodcut block, either in a press if it is TYPE-HIGH or by hand. Wood engraving is essentially a direct, WHITE-LINE technique; the design in the proofs is made by the nonprinting areas of the block.

Wood engraving was developed in Britain during the last half of the 18th century. Its first master was Thomas Bewick (1753–1828), whose book illustrations of nature subjects are widely admired. William Blake (1757–1827) also used the process, sometimes sketching directly on the block with the graver. By the mid-19th century, wood engraving had become a standard method for illustrating books and magazines, and a large number of engravers became highly skilled in reproducing drawings, paintings and photographs. The use of wood engraving for these purposes came to an end with the advent of photoengraving, but during the 20th century it has been revived as a fine-arts process for making original prints. SCRAPERBOARD work imitates the effects of wood engraving; virtually all commercial illustration that displays the white-line effect of wood engraving has been done on scratchboard.

wood turpentine a kind of TURPENTINE made by distilling the stumps and scraps of pine trees. It is sold as a less-expensive substitute for gum turpentine. Although wood turpentine is an excellent solvent and thinner, it is generally rejected for artists' use because of its pungent odour, which resembles that of pine sawdust, and because some individuals suffer headaches from its vapours under indoor conditions.

workable fixative see FIXATIVE.

World of Art or **Mir Iskusstva** a Russian art movement. Founded in 1890 in reaction to the didactic realism of the WANDERERS, it embraced the doctrine of 'art for art's sake' and was influenced by French Impressionism. After the revolution of 1905, the artists of this movement turned from interpretation of the natural world to a decorative, linear style that influenced mural painting, book illustration, graphics, and the art of the theatre, especially sets for the Russian ballet. The group was led by Alexander Benois, and included Leon Bakst, Golovin, Sudeikine, and Nicholas Roerich, among others, as well as Konstantin Somov, of the prerevolutionary Blue Rose group.

worm's-eye view a scene drawn or painted as if observed from a point below it. Any correctly drawn worm's-eye view will be in OBLIQUE PERSPECTIVE (see illustration at LINEAR PERSPECTIVE). The HORIZON LINE is placed or imagined close to the bottom of the picture or even below it, so that there is an upward convergence of all vertical lines parallel to

the picture plane. The lowered horizon line, corresponding to a low
POINT OF STATION, causes most or all of the composition to lie above the
horizon line. The worm's-eye view is useful for accurately depicting
things that are typically seen by looking up. See also BIRD'S-EYE VIEW.

wove see LAID PAPER.

wrinkles a defect of oil colours, polymer colours, varnishes and lacquers,
consisting of irregular ridges and furrows that form in the paint or surface
film after a certain amount of ageing when faulty materials or improper
methods of application have been employed. Induced by shrinkage and
compression, wrinkling occurs most frequently in underpigmented
paints and lacquers in which the films are insufficiently reinforced by
masses of pigment particles. Underpigmented glazes, however, do not
wrinkle, because of the thinness of their layers. Clear coatings may
develop wrinkles when applied so thickly that loss of volume through
evaporation is a greater factor than it would be in a thin coating. Compression caused by rolling a canvas with the painted face inward may
cause wrinkles in a flexible coating; the same action causes a brittle coating
to crack. On further ageing and loss of elasticity, wrinkles commonly
develop into cracks, and when there is less than normal adhesion between
film and ground, cleavage occurs. Some materials, such as asphaltum,
megilp and binders with an overabundance of drier, have an inherent
tendency to wrinkle. Blistering in long, thin lines may be mistaken for
wrinkles.

X

xanthorrhoea see ACCROIDES.
xylene see COAL-TAR SOLVENT.
xylography 1. see WOODCUT.
    2. see WOOD ENGRAVING.

Y

yachting style a term used in France as a synonym for ART NOUVEAU.
yeast black see VINE BLACK.
yellow berries see BUCKTHORN BERRIES.
yellow carmine a very fugitive yellow LAKE pigment of vegetable origin and transparent olive hue. It is similar to, and probably a variant of, BROWN PINK.
yellow earth see YELLOW OCHRE.
yellowing or **after-yellowing** the discoloration or tonal degradation of a painting. It may be caused by the use of oils and varnishes that are inherently prone to become yellowish or brownish on ageing; by the excessive use of linseed oil, the slight yellowing of which would be masked by pigment in a well-proportioned paint; or, most frequently, by the accumulation of grime, which encrusts the surface and becomes embedded in the varnish. Most badly yellowed oil paintings can be restored to their original colours by removing the old varnish and applying a fresh coat.
yellow lake a term that has been applied to transparent yellow lake colours of various kinds – formerly, those made from natural dyestuffs; today, those made from synthetic dyes. No artists' colour so labelled is permanent.
yellow ochre or **yellow earth** an opaque pigment, refined and processed from bright-yellow earths usually containing clay, and coloured by hydrous iron oxide (limonite). It is one of the artists' basic colours, employed in every culture and civilization since prehistoric times. Ochres are mined the world over; the highest grades come from those areas where the best ores occur and where the most efficient methods have been developed for producing a uniform and economical product. Most of the best kinds of ochre come from southern France in well-defined standard grades. Another fine grade, OXFORD OCHRE, is produced in

limited amounts in England. Like all iron-bearing earth colours, ochre becomes red when calcined; burnt ochres and RED OCHRES have been largely replaced by light red. Among the many varieties of yellow ochre are ROMAN OCHRE (also called Italian ochre); FLESH OCHRE; BROWN OCHRE; SPRUCE OCHRE and TRANSPARENT GOLD OCHRE. *Chamois* and *minette* are obsolete names for yellow ochre; *sil* was the name used by the ancient Romans. Yellow ochre is often simply called ochre.

yellow oxide of iron another name for Mars yellow, one of the MARS PIGMENTS.

yellow pigments any of the following pigments, approved for use in oil paints in the United States by ASTM and generally acceptable (except as noted) in all other easel-painting techniques: ARYLIDE YELLOW, cadmium yellow (see CADMIUM RED), COBALT YELLOW, NAPLES YELLOW (except in pastel and water mediums); Mars yellow (see MARS PIGMENTS), YELLOW OCHRE, NICKEL TITANITE YELLOW, DIARYLIDE YELLOW, ANTHRAPYRIMID-INE YELLOW, ISOINDOLINONE YELLOW, flavanthrone yellow, QUINOPH-THALONE YELLOW, nickel azo yellow and BENZIMIDAZOLONE YELLOW.

yellow ultramarine an obsolete name for BARIUM YELLOW.

yellow varnish a dammar resin dissolved in linseed oil with the aid of heat. The name was given to this product by Jacques Maroger, who in the 1940s introduced a painting medium that was a reverse, or water-in-oil, emulsion. The pigments were dispersed in yellow varnish, then mixed into the emulsion, a paste made by lightly whipping a gum-arabic solution into the same varnish. This medium was discarded, and the name was applied to another one (see MAROGER MEDIUM).

yellow weed dyer's rocket (*Reseda luteola*), the source of the yellow natural dyestuff WELD. In the United States, several other weeds are sometimes called yellow weed.

young fustic or **fustet** a yellow NATURAL DYESTUFF extracted from the wood of the Venetian sumac (*Rhus cotinus*), which grows in southern Europe and the Near East. The colouring extract, continin, was formerly used to dye textiles but is not sufficiently lightfast for use in pigments. Another yellow dyestuff called FUSTIC (or old fustic) is a different material.

Z

zaccab a white earth mixed with lime, used in Yucatán, in Mexico, as a building and plastering material, and for sculpture.

zaffer or **zaffre** cobalt oxide prepared for use in the manufacture of the blue pigment SMALT. Also considered to be partially processed smalt, zaffer was sometimes mixed with the finished product to produce another grade of smalt called *eschel*. The term *zaffer* was frequently distorted to *safflower* by workers in Britain and the United States.

Zapon a German tradename for cellulose LACQUERS.

zebrano see ZEBRAWOOD.

zebrawood 1. (also called **zebrano** or **zingana**) an African wood (from the tree *Brachystegia fleuryana*) with a grain of fairly evenly spaced parallel light straw-coloured and dark brown stripes. **2.** a striped, hard South American wood (from *Connarus guianensis*) used in cabinetwork.

zinc chromate or **zinc chrome** see ZINC YELLOW.

zinc etching see ANASTATIC PRINTING.

zinc green 1. see COBALT GREEN. **2.** an industrial COMPOSITE PIGMENT that is a mixture of zinc yellow, Prussian blue (steel or Milori) and barytes.

zinc oxide a white powder produced in many grades for various uses, such as ZINC WHITE pigments, pharmaceuticals and cosmetics. It is sometimes used as an ingredient of ceramic glazes. Although zinc ores were used in ancient times to make brass, zinc was not known as a metal until it was identified as an element by Margraaf in Germany in 1746.

zinc white the artists' term for a variety of ZINC OXIDE made by the so-called fume, or French, process (see FRENCH-PROCESS ZINC OXIDE.) Zinc white is a brilliant, snow-white pigment, without fault in watercolour and other aqueous paints. Although it excels in whiteness, zinc white is in other respects inferior in oil to FLAKE WHITE. It is only semiopaque, has poor drying qualities, and tends to produce weak films. On the other hand, unlike flake white, zinc white is not discoloured by the action of sulphur gases in the atmosphere, since the resulting zinc sulphide is also white. As early as 1782, chemists began their efforts to adapt zinc oxide for use as a pigment to replace white lead. Zinc white was first introduced to artists in 1834, when the English firm of Winsor & Newton put it out as a watercolour under the name *Chinese white*. Zinc white began to appear as an artists' oil colour in the second half of the 19th century. By the first quarter of the 20th century, it had become sufficiently improved for artists to find it a satisfactory alternative to flake white. Despite the all-round superiority of flake white, zinc white is widely used by painters, especially by those who fear the toxic properties of flake white. *Florence zinc oxide* is a United States tradename for pure zinc oxides made by the French process. Mixtures of zinc and titanium whites are sold under various names (see COMPOSITE WHITE). *French white* and *silver white* are unstandardized terms that have been used for both flake and zinc whites.

zinc yellow, zinc chromate or **zinc chrome** zinc chromate, a pale citron-yellow pigment not approved for use in permanent painting because of its partial solubility in water and the tendency of most samples to turn greenish on exposure to light.

zingana see ZEBRAWOOD.

zinnober green one of many synonyms for the industrial pigment CHROME GREEN.

zirconium drier a DRIER made from a zirconium compound. It is used to balance the drying action of cobalt drier by promoting drying from within; cobalt tends to dry more rapidly on the surface. The effect is a glossier surface, because rapid surface drying tends to make a paint duller than one that has dried evenly throughout.

zirconium oxide a white powder produced by treating zircon and used in ceramic and glass manufacture. Zirconium oxide was sometimes included in lists of paint pigments, although its indifferent pigment properties and high cost scarcely qualify it for artists' use.

Zircopax *(US)* a tradename for an opacifier used in ceramic glazes.

zones of recession the foreground, middle distance and background in any composition that attempts to represent spatial depth. In LEGITIMATE CONSTRUCTION, the area of a picture's surface is apportioned among the three zones according to strict rules of LINEAR PERSPECTIVE. Hazing the middle distance in order to differentiate better between foreground and background is a technique employed in AERIAL PERSPECTIVE, particularly for Chinese landscapes. The exaggerated foreground is a characteristic of Baroque painting, particularly with such Northern painters as Rubens and Vermeer. Perspective reduction in their works is often sudden, causing a striking contrast between the dimensions of the foreground and the background.

Z-twist see TWIST DIRECTION.

COLLINS DICTIONARY OF GEOLOGY

Dorothy Farris Lapidus

Consultant Editor: Isobel Winstanley

The *Collins Dictionary of Geology* is a new and authoritative guide to current terminology in this increasingly important field.

The Dictionary is primarily directed towards the requirements of first and second year undergraduates. Containing more than 3000 entries, it gives comprehensive coverage to the major areas of study, ranging from geophysics and geomorphology through stratigraphic terminology to palaeontology and igneous petrology. Practical applications, such as mineralogy and economic and engineering geology, are also covered, as are the principal methods of rock exploration and analysis.

Concise initial definitions for each term are supported by encyclopaedic detail where appropriate, and the extensive cross-referencing system together with the numerous illustrations facilitate access to the rich veins of information contained in the Dictionary.

The *Collins Dictionary of Geology* is thus an invaluable tool not only for students of the geological sciences but also for students and workers in related fields such as geography, surveying and environmental management.

Dorothy Farris Lapidus is a lecturer and writer from New York. Dr Isobel Winstanley tutors in Earth Sciences at the Open University.

ISBN 0 00 434148 1

COLLINS DICTIONARY OF BIOLOGY

W. G. Hale and J. P. Margham

The *Collins Dictionary of Biology* is a completely new, authoritative and comprehensive guide to the complex discipline of biology. The book is directed primarily to the needs of undergraduates and advanced school students, but will also prove an invaluable source book for anyone with an interest in this wide-ranging and fascinating subject.

The Dictionary has over 5,600 entries ranging from *abdomen* to *zymogen*. There are also 285 diagrams illustrating such features as the generalized structures of animals, genetic organization, parts of plants and animals, etc., plus numerous tables.

All the major fields within biology are covered, including anatomy, biochemistry, ecology, genetics, physiology, evolutionary theory and taxonomy. The entries have been structured to provide more than an isolated definition of the term in question. An entry such as *acquired characters* is thus set in the context of the development of evolutionary theory, while the series of genetic entries guides the reader through such concepts as the basis of *genetic code* and the industrial implications of *genetic engineering*. The Dictionary also includes brief biographies of major biologists.

Professor Hale is Dean of the Faculty of Science and Head of the Department of Biology at Liverpool Polytechnic. Dr Margham is Principal Lecturer and Course Leader for the B.Sc. Honours Applied Biology Degree at Liverpool Polytechnic.

'. . . exemplary in every respect . . . a data bank of diverse facts about the science of life.' – *Literary Review.*

ISBN 0 00 434351 4

COLLINS DICTIONARY OF ENVIRONMENTAL SCIENCE

Gareth Jones, Graham Hollier, Jean Forbes and Alan Robertson

The *Collins Dictionary of Environmental Science* is the most comprehensive paperback dictionary available on the subject of environmental science.

Awareness of the effects of human activity on our planet's resources has been growing constantly over the last 20 years, and environmental science has evolved to examine the interaction of people and the environments in which they work and live. The Dictionary is a completely new guide to this important multi-disciplinary field of study and its clear, helpful definitions make it an invaluable source book as the debate over environmental issues becomes increasingly technical.

Containing over 1,800 entries, many of which are extensively cross-referenced, and more than 80 diagrams, the Dictionary draws together topics from a wide range of related fields in the biological, physical and social sciences including geology, geomorphology, climatology, botany and zoology. The Dictionary describes many facets of the natural, built and agro-socio environments. Aspects of ecology and conservation are also covered in depth, as are items of topical importance such as biosphere pollution, the nuclear industry, inner-city renewal and government management of urban and rural environments.

Gareth Jones is a senior lecturer in geography and Graham Hollier is a lecturer in geography, both at Strathclyde University, Jean Forbes is a senior lecturer at the Centre for Planning at Strathclyde University, and Alan Robertson is a chartered town planner.

ISBN 0 00 434348 4

COLLINS DICTIONARY OF SOCIOLOGY

David Jary & Julia Jary

The *Collins Dictionary of Sociology* is an up–to–date resource for those concerned with the complex discipline of sociology. The book is primarily directed at the undergraduate market, but is sufficiently accessible in style and organization to be useful to the 'A' level student and the general reader. However, while its breadth recommends it to a wider readership, its depth of treatment of some of the more complex issues will make it a convenient reference book for academic sociologists.

The Dictionary explains a wide range of terms and concepts from every area of sociology, and a selection of those most likely to be met from associated disciplines such as psychology, economics, anthropology and political science. It also provides a useful coveage of methodological terms and research techniques.

The treatment and organization allows the reader to build comprehensive coverage of all sociological schools, or to compare perspectives. Its coverage extends from *Social Class* to *Sexuality,* from *Functionalism* to *Feyerabend,* and from *Lumpenproletariat* to *Likert Scale.* There are also biographical entries on key figures in the development of sociology.

The *Collins Dictionary of Sociology* is an essential reference work for all who require a clear, balanced and comprehensive guide to sociology, or for anyone with an interest in contemporary society.

David Jary is Professor of Sociology at Staffordshire Polytechnic. Julia Jary teaches psychology part-time at Staffordshire Polytechnic and for the Open University. The Dictionary has been compiled with the assistance of a skilled editorial team of specialists from the main sociological fields.

ISBN 0 00 434373 5 (hardback)
ISBN 0 00 434359 X (paperback)